AUSTRALIAN WAR STRATEGY 1939~1945

AUSTRALIAN WAR STRATEGY 1939-1945
A DOCUMENTARY HISTORY

John Robertson
&
John McCarthy

University of Queensland Press
ST LUCIA • LONDON • NEW YORK

First published 1985 by University of Queensland Press
Box 42, St Lucia, Queensland, Australia

© John Robertson and John McCarthy 1985

This book is copyright. Apart from any fair dealing for the purposes of private study, research, criticism or review, as permitted under the Copyright Act, no part may be reproduced by any process without written permission. Enquiries should be made to the publisher.

Typeset by Savage Type Pty Ltd, Brisbane
Printed in Australia by Dominion Press — Hedges & Bell, Melbourne.

Distributed in the UK and Europe by University of Queensland Press
Dunhams Lane, Letchworth, Herts. SG6 ILF England

Distributed in the USA and Canada by University of Queensland Press
5 South Union Street, Lawrence, Mass. 01843 USA

Cataloguing in Publication Data

National Library of Australia

Robertson, John, 1935 — .
   Australian war strategy 1939–1945.

   Bibliography.
   Includes index.

   1. World War, 1939–1945 — Australia.
   2. Strategy. I. McCarthy, J. (John),
   1933 — . II. Title.

940.54′0994

Library of Congress

Robertson, John, 1935 —
   Australian war strategy 1939–1945.

   Bibliography: p.
   Includes index.
   1. World War, 1939–1945 — Australia. 2. Australia —
History — 20th century. 3. Military art and science —
Australia — History — 20th century. 4. Strategy — History
— 20th century. I. McCarthy, John, 1933 — .
II. Title.
D767.8.R64   1985   940.53′94   84-11957
ISBN 0 7022 1924 X

for
R.M., L.M.,
J.B., W.R.,
and I.R.

CONTENTS

Preface   ix

Acknowledgements   xi

Explanatory Note   xii

Abbreviations   xiii

Chronology   xvii

List of Documents   xxi

Part I The Distant War, 1939–1945

1. The Navy and the War Against Germany and Italy, 1939–1941   4

2. The Decision to Raise and Despatch the Second AIF   25

3. Australian Policy and the Air Offensive in Europe   44

4. The Middle East: The 2nd AIF and the Prelude to Battle   73

5. Disaster in Greece and Crete   87

6. The Syrian Campaign   110

7. The Relief of Tobruk   123

Part II The Pacific War

8. The Singapore Strategy 1938–1941   140

9. The Dutch Alliance and Portuguese Timor   168

10. Australia and the Higher Direction of the War, December 1941–April 1942   178

Contents

11. ABDA Command   185

12. Malayan Fiasco   200

13. Rabaul, Ambon and Timor   216

14. The Destination of 1 Australian Corps   224

15. The Fate of the *Orcades* Party   240

16. Two AIF Brigades to Ceylon   247

17. The Defence of Mainland Australia   256

18. The Arrival of the Americans   277

19. The New Anglo–American Global Command Structure, March–April 1942   301

20. The Royal Navy's Retreat from the 'Malay Barrier'   307

21. Making the Southwest Pacific Area Secure   312

22. Crisis of Command: The RAAF in SWPA   339

23. Papua   357

24. New Guinea, January 1943–April 1944   381

25. What Future Role for the Australian Army?   390

26. The Mandate Campaigns   401

27. Borneo   417

Appendices

1. Select List of Australian Office Holders 1939–1945   431

2. Biographical Notes   434

Subject Index   449

Name Index   458

PREFACE

The *Official History of Australia in the War of 1939–1945* included no volume of documents. In contrast, the New Zealand official histories included three such volumes on the participation of that Dominion in the war. The need for an Australian counterpart was obvious, but the official history project never prepared one. Others could not attempt such a work because the archives, generally speaking, were not open to unofficial, independent scholars. Work on this present unofficial volume began when the replacement of the '50 year rule' by the '30 year rule' led to an earlier-than-expected opening of the federal government's archives for the years to 1945.

The machinery that ran the Australian war effort of course produced an enormous quantity of documents. The editors sometimes felt that the arguments over strategy produced a 'war of words' comparable in expenditure to the bullets fired at the 'sharp end'! The major task of searching through the files for documents that illustrated significant policy decisions was undertaken by the project's first research assistant, Mrs Wendy Way. This book is based on the five filing-cabinet drawers containing photocopies which represented the results of her skilled and tireless preliminary selection from the archival sources.

Because space was limited, the editors could not be comprehensive in covering all relevant issues. As we were obliged to restrict ourselves to choosing a small proportion from the original selection, our general rule was to try to give an adequate coverage of chosen topics rather than to spread ourselves more widely and, consequently, more thinly.

We decided, therefore, to concentrate primarily on the leadership's handling of the armed forces-in-being; on the planning for their future use, and on the campaigns in which they fought. The dealings with allied governments over war strategy could thus also be encompassed. It followed, however, that we could not give full attention to all issues involved in raising the forces and in organising the war economy. With reluctance we had to exclude our documents on equipping the forces; for example, on the manpower policy that resolved the competition among the armed services, and the munitions industry and the civilian economy for the scarce resource of labour. Among other things, this meant that the magnificent part played by women and other civilians in Australia's war effort could not be illustrated. There is, naturally, a need for at least another volume of documents devoted solely to the 'home front'.

We trust that by concentrating on the themes indicated we have been able to do some justice to the most significant issues and episodes relating to the use of Australia's armed forces during the war. Students and general readers will be able to supplement their reading of secondary authorities with these selections from the most important cables and memoranda of Australia's war leaders. To do this without the expense of a research visit and the often tedious work of searching through the archives, should be useful.

ACKNOWLEDGEMENTS

We are deeply indebted to Mrs Shirley Lithgow, Mrs Way's successor, whose meticulous and dedicated work ensured that the project did not lose momentum. We are most grateful for the help so obligingly given by the archivists and librarians of the following repositories: MacArthur Memorial Library, Norfolk, Virginia; the Public Record Office, London; the Australian War Memorial, Canberra; the Australian Archives, Canberra and Middle Brighton.

Extracts from official documents in the Public Record Office are Crown copyright and are quoted by permission of the Controller, H.M. Stationery Office. Crown copyright documents from the Australian Archives appear by permission of the Australian Archives.

We wish to thank Mrs Anne Chambers, Ms Rosalind Hall and Mrs Beverley Stuckey for their work in typing the book and for mastering the marvels of modern technology so that the assembled corpus was put on the appropriate magnetic tape. We also are grateful to Mr Malcolm Smith and the staff of the Computer Centre, Faculty of Military Studies, University of New South Wales at Duntroon, for help and advice in preparing the manuscript for the publisher.

The book would not have been possible without generous financial assistance from the Australian Research Grants Scheme. Publication was assisted by a grant from the Australian War Memorial. The index was prepared under a grant from the History Department, Faculty of Military Studies, University of New South Wales at Duntroon.

EXPLANATORY NOTE

An Australian infantry division contained between 14,000 and 20,000 troops organised into three brigades. In turn, each brigade contained three battalions. Each division was supported by 'non-divisional' troops.

Between 1939–45 a *battleship* was considered to be the largest and most heavily armoured class of ship. It carried in its main batteries guns of 12" or larger calibre. A *battlecruiser* was a class of ship designed to carry much the same firepower as a battleship but reduced armour protection gave the ship greater mobility. A cruiser was a large, fast, moderately armoured and gunned warship of between 6,000 and 12,000 tons. The Australian light cruisers had a main armament of 6" calibre guns and the heavy cruisers of 8" calibre guns.

The size of a squadron in the RAAF varied considerably with the type of aircraft employed. Generally it ranged from 12 to 18 aircraft with at least a fifty per cent reserve. In classic form, a squadron was divided into three flights.

ABBREVIATIONS

AA	Anti-Aircraft
AA	Australian Archives
AAF	Allied Air Forces
AASC	Australian Army Service Corps
ABDA	Australian-British-Dutch-American (Command)
AC	Army Co-operation
ACH	Area Combined Headquarters
ACM	Air Chief Marshal
ADB	American-Dutch-British
Adv.	Advance, Advanced
AFC	Australian Flying Corps
AFV's	Armoured Fighting Vehicles
AIF	Australian Imperial Force
ALF	Allied Land Forces
ALO	Air Liaison Officer
	Australian Liaison Officer
ALP	Australian Labor Party
AMC's	Armed Merchant Cruisers
AMF	Australian Military Forces
ANZAC	Australian and New Zealand Army Corps
AOC	Air Officer Commanding
AOC-in-C	Air Officer Commanding-in-Chief
ARP	Air Raid Precautions
A/S	Anti-Submarine
A/T	Anti-Tank
AVM	Air Vice Marshal
AWM	Australian War Memorial
BD	British-Dutch
Bde	Brigade
BGS	Brigadier, General Staff
BM	Brigade Major
Bn	Battalion
CAS	Chief of the Air Staff
CCC	Civil Construction Corps
CCS	Combined Chiefs of Staff
CG	Commanding General (US)
CGS	Chief of the General Staff
CID	Committee of Imperial Defence
CIGS	Chief of Imperial General Staff
C-in-C	Commander-in-Chief

Abbreviations

CMF	Citizen Military Forces
CNS	Chief of the Naval Staff
CO	Commanding Officer
COS	Chief(s) of Staff
CRA	Commander, Royal Artillery (of a division)
DCAS	Deputy Chief of the Air Staff
DCGS	Deputy Chief of the General Staff
DEMS	Defensively Equipped Merchant Ship
DO	Dominions Office
EATS	Empire Air Training Scheme
ETA	Estimated Time of Arrival
FCT	Federal Capital Territory
FF	Free French
GHQ	General Headquarters
GL	Anti-Aircraft Gun-Laying
GMT	Greenwich Mean Time
GOC	General Officer Commanding
gr.unde.	Group Undecipherable
GSO	General Staff Officer
GSO1	General Staff Officer, Grade 1
HMAS	His Majesty's Australian Ship
HMS	His Majesty's Ship
HQ	Headquarters
IG	Inspector-General
L and C	Lines and Communications
LHQ	Land Headquarters
L of C	Lines of Communications
MCO's	Movement Control Officers
ME	Middle East
MG	Machine Gun
MLC's	Motorised Landing Craft
MMBA	MacArthur Memorial Bureau of Archives, Norfolk, Virginia, USA
MT	Mechanical (Motor) Transport
NAAFI	Navy, Army and Air Force Institute
NCO's	Non-Commissioned Officers
NEI	Netherlands East Indies
NG	New Guinea
NGF	New Guinea Force
OR	Other Rank(s)
OTU	Operational Training Unit
PRO	Public Record Office, London
RAAF	Royal Australian Air Force
RAF	Royal Air Force
RAN	Royal Australian Navy
RDF	Radio Direction Finding (Radar)
Recce.	Reconnaissance

RFC	Royal Flying Corps
RG	Record Group
RN	Royal Navy
RNVR	Royal Navy Volunteer Reserve
SEAC	Southeast Asia Command
S. of S.	Secretary of State
SWPA	Southwest Pacific Area
SWPC	Southwest Pacific Command
UK	United Kingdom of Great Britain and Northern Ireland
USA	United States of America
USAAF	United States Army Air Forces
USN	United States Navy
VCNS	Vice-Chief of the Naval Staff
VDC	Volunteer Defence Corps
WAAAF	Women's Australian Auxiliary Air Force
W/T	Wireless Telegraphy

Conversion Factors
(to two decimal places)

1 inch = 2.54 centimetres
1 foot = 0.30 metre
1 square mile = 2.59 square kilometres (km^2)
1 lb = 0.45 kilogram
1 hundredweight (cwt) = 50.80 kilograms
1 yard = 0.91 metre
1 mile = 1.60 kilometres (km)
1 ton = 1.02 tonnes
1 gallon = 4.54 litres
£1 = $2, 1s = 10c, 1d = 0.83c

Except where otherwise indicated, we have reproduced in these documents grammatical and spelling mistakes in the originals. All source material from the Australian Archives in Canberra controlled by the series system is prefixed by *CRS* (Commonwealth Record Series). The series CRS A 5954 (Shedden Papers) was previously numbered MP 1217. All items cited from AWM 54 are held in the Australian War Memorial Official Written Records Collection: 'Written Records, 1939–1945 War'.

CHRONOLOGY

1939
1 September	Germans invade Poland
3 September	Menzies broadcasts that Australia is at war
31 October	Concept of despatching a self-contained air expeditionary force to Europe is abandoned. Five Australian destroyers are released for service in the Mediterranean
7 November	RAN ships placed under Admiralty strategic control
27 November	Negotiations completed in Ottawa covering Australia's participation in the Empire Air Training Scheme
22 December	Air Vice-Marshal Goble's resignation as Chief of the Air Staff accepted by War Cabinet

1940
9 January	First convoy of 2nd AIF (16th Brigade, 6th Division) sails for the Middle East
15 February	Air Chief Marshal Sir Charles Burnett assumes position of Chief of the Air Staff
10 May	German offensive against France and the 'low countries' begins
10 June	Italy declares war
17 June	Australian troops arrive in the United Kingdom
17 June	France asks for an armistice
19 July	HMAS *Sydney* sinks the Italian cruiser *Bartolomeo Colleoni*
5 September	First Empire Air Training Scheme draft leaves Australia for Canada
13 September	An Italian army invades Egypt
27 September	Tripartite Pact between Germany, Italy and Japan signed
October–Nov	7th Division, 2nd AIF sails for the Middle East
28 October	Italy invades Greece
15–17 November	Australian troops in the United Kingdom begin to leave for the Middle East
6–8 December	German raiders attack and sink five vessels near Nauru
27 December	The German raider *Komet* shells installations at Nauru

1941
3–5 January	Battle of Bardia
6 February	6th Division captures Benghazi
18 February	8th Division arrives in Singapore
22–23 February	Athens conferences on British aid to Greece

26 February	Australian government agrees to the British proposal to employ the 6th and 7th Divisions in Greece
16 March	First Australian troops arrive in Greece
31 March	General Rommel launches his counter-offensive in North Africa
6 April	German forces invade Greece and Yugoslavia
11 April	Siege of Tobruk begins
22 April	Start of evacuation of troops from Greece
2 May	Pro-Axis Iraqi revolt; British attacked at Habbaniya
20 May	German airborne troops attack Crete
1 June	Allied forces withdrawn from Crete
8 June	7th Division enters Syria
15 June	Allied offensive in Middle East code-named *Battleaxe* launched. Rommel's forces inflict heavy defeat
21 June	Allied forces enter Damascus
30 June	HMAS *Waterhen* sunk
12 July	Acre convention ends fighting in Syria
17 July	Retirement of Admiral Sir Ragnar Colvin as Chief of Naval Staff. Another British Admiral, Sir Guy Royle immediately assumes the position
24 July	Japanese forces land in southern Indo-China
21 August	Start of relief for Australian troops at Tobruk
7 October	John Curtin, leader of the Australian Labor Party, becomes Prime Minister
19 November	HMAS *Sydney* sunk in action with the German raider *Kormoran*
27 November	HMAS *Parramatta* torpedoed and sunk
7–8 December	Japanese begin landings in Thailand and Malaya. American naval forces attacked at Pearl Harbor
9 December	Siege of Tobruk lifted
10 December	The British battleship *Prince of Wales* and battlecruiser *Repulse* sunk by Japanese aircraft
12 December	An Australian battalion and an independent company reach Timor

1942

23 January	Japanese forces attack and capture Rabaul
26 January	Creation of the Anzac naval area. Advance party of 1st Australian Corps reaches Batavia
30 January	Japanese attack Ambon
4 February	Tol massacre of Australian prisoners of war by the Japanese
8 February	Japanese land on Singapore Island
15 February	Singapore Island and the naval base are surrendered to the Japanese
17 February	Australian troops on *Orcades* reach Batavia
19 February	First Japanese air attacks on Darwin

19–20 February	Japanese forces land on Timor
28 February	Japanese invade Java
1 March	HMAS *Perth* sunk by Japanese naval forces in the Java Sea
8 March	Lae and Salamaua occupied by Japanese. Australian forces in Java surrender. Japanese forces enter Rangoon
9 March	Leading bde of 7th Div. from Middle East arrives Adelaide
17 March	General MacArthur arrives at Darwin from Mindanao
25 March	Australian troops disembark in Ceylon
26 March	General Blamey appointed Commander-in-Chief Australian Military Forces
4 April	Sir Charles Burnett resigns as Chief of the Air Staff
6 April	41st United States Division arrives in Australia
9 April	Trincomalee suffers heavy air attack from Japanese carrier based aircraft. British aircraft carrier *Hermes* sunk. Luzon surrendered. HMAS *Vampire* sunk by the Japanese
18 April	General Blamey appointed to command Allied Land Forces in the Southwest Pacific Area. GHQ SWPA established in Melbourne and General MacArthur formally takes command of all Allied forces in the area
5 May	Air Vice-Marshal G. Jones appointed Chief of the Air Staff
5–8 May	Battle of the Coral Sea
4–6 June	Battle of Midway between Japanese and American carrier forces
21 July	Japanese land in Papua at Gona
9 August	HMAS *Canberra* sunk in a brilliant night action conducted by the Japanese in the Battle of Savo Island
25–26 August	Japanese land forces at Milne Bay
6 September	Japanese defeated at Milne Bay
17 September	Advance on Port Moresby by the Japanese over the Owen Stanley Ranges halted
2 November	Kokoda recaptured
9 December	Australian troops retake Gona

1943

2 January	American forces take Buna
23 January	End of organised Japanese resistance in Papua
19 February	Amendment of the Defence Act to allow militia forces to serve outside Australian territory
21 August	Australian Labor Party wins federal election
11 September	Australian troops enter Salamaua
16 September	Elements of 7th and 9th Divisions enter Lae
2 October	Finschhafen recaptured

1944

24 April	Australian troops enter Madang
6 June	Allied invasion of Normandy

15 September	6th Div. begins arriving at Aitape, NG
4 November	Leading troops of 5th Div. land on New Britain
17 December	Troops of 6th Div. cross the Danmap in the drive on Wewak
30 December	Bougainville offensive begins

1945

27 Mar–1 Apr	Japanese sustain heavy losses in mass infantry charges against Australians at Slater's Knoll, Bougainville
1 May	Australian forces land at Tarakan
7 May	Unconditional surrender of Germany
11 May	6th Division recaptures Wewak
1 July	Australian troops land at Balikpapan
5 July	Death of John Curtin
13 July	J.B. Chifley becomes Prime Minister
15 August	Japan surrenders
2 September	Surrender ceremony on USS *Missouri* in Tokyo Bay

LIST OF DOCUMENTS

Doc.	Place & Date	Document	Content	Page

1. The Navy and the War Against Germany and Italy, 1939–1941

Doc.	Place & Date	Document	Content	Page
1.	29.8.1939	Boucher to Street. Minute.	Recommends despatch of a cruiser to the Mediterranean.	4
2.	19.9.1939	Shedden to Boucher. Dominions Office Cablegram 191.	Proposals for employment of the RAN.	6
3.	26.9.1939	Macandie to Shedden. Minute.	Remarks by Naval Board on Dominions Office Cablegram 191.	7
4.	Sydney 31.10.1939	Cabinet Minute.	Five destroyers to proceed to Europe.	8
5.	15.12.1939	Colvin to Acting Minister for the Navy. Memorandum.	Escort for first Australian Troop Convoy.	8
6.	Melbourne 27.2.1940	War Cabinet Minute (174).	Exchange of HMAS *Australia* with a Royal Navy cruiser.	10
7.	17.5.1940	Macandie to Cameron. Minute.	Proposals for providing more trained seamen for the Royal Navy.	10
8.	12.6.1940	Colvin to War Cabinet. Report.	Naval dispositions following Italy's entry into the War.	11
9.	Not Dated [c.2.12.1940]	Colvin to Hughes. Memorandum.	Review of Empire's world-wide naval responsibilities and use of RAN ships.	13
10.	9.12.1940	Memorandum for Hughes.	German raider attacks British steamers off Nauru.	18
11.	10.12.1940	Colvin to Hughes. Memorandum.	Explanation for raider attack. Proposals for protecting shipping between Nauru and Australia and New Zealand.	19

Doc.	Place & Date	Document	Content	Page
12.	28.12.1940	Macandie to Strahan, Shedden, and Hodgson. Teleprinter Message D.1020.	Message from Nauru of German raider attack on 26 December 1940.	20
13.	Melbourne 9.1.1941	Advisory War Council Minute (83).	Further action to safeguard shipping between Nauru and Australia.	21
14.	Melbourne 10.7.1941	War Cabinet Minute (1194).	Valedictory to Colvin.	22
15.	30.11.1941	Teleprinter Message D.3265.	Report of air and surface search for *Sydney*.	23
16.	Melbourne 4.12.1941	War Cabinet Minute (1528).	A reconstructed account of the sinking of *Sydney*.	23

2. The Decision to Raise and Despatch the Second AIF

Doc.	Place & Date	Document	Content	Page
17.	November 1934	Report by Sir Maurice Hankey.	Raises possibility of Australian govt. sending troops abroad to protect Australian interests.	25
18.	London 8.9.1939	Eden to Whiskard. Cablegram 191.	Suggests raising an Australian Expeditionary Force.	26
19.	Melbourne 13.9.1939	Military Board Report.	Raising of a special force for continuous service either in Australia or overseas.	27
20.	15.9.1939	Prime Minister Menzies. National Broadcast.	Enlisting of a special force of 20,000 men.	29
21.	Melbourne 21.9.1939	Squires to Shedden. Memorandum.	Discusses recommendations for the Army in Dominions Office Cablegram 191.	30
22.	London 13.11.1939	Conclusions of discussions between Ministers from Dominions and a representative from India, held 3.11.1939.	Despatch overseas of Australian military forces.	33

Doc.	Place & Date	Document	Content	Page
23.	London 6.11.1939	Northcott to Squires [via Casey]. Cablegram C.7.	Recommends sending of 6th Division to Middle East.	34
24.	London 23.11.1939	Casey to Menzies. Cablegram C38.	Recommends sending a special division abroad at the earliest.	36
25.	Canberra 28.11.1939	Cabinet Decision (F.C. 10).	Despatch of 6th Division overseas.	38
26.	Broken Hill 22.9.1939	Housewives' Progressive Association to McKell, Leader of the NSW Labor Party. Letter.	Requests Labor leaders to organise resistance to recruiting men for overseas service.	38
27.	Brisbane 8.12.1939	Amalgamated Society of Carpenters and Joiners of Australia to Menzies. Letter.	Protesting against govt's decision to send Australian forces overseas.	39
28.	Leeton 18.12.1939	Willimbong Shire Council to Nock M.P. Letter.	Protesting against conscription and sending abroad of an Expeditionary Force.	40
29.	Speers Point 27.12.1939	Boolaroo — Speers Point Branch of the ALP to Menzies. Letter.	Protesting against sending forces overseas.	41
30.	17.1.1940	Statement of reasons for the Military Board's recommendations.	Recommends raising a second division for overseas.	42

3. Australian Policy and the Air Offensive in Europe

31.	London 8.9.1939	Eden to Whiskard. Cablegram 191.	Proposals for Australian Air Force.	44
32.	19–22.9.1939	Street to Cabinet, Submission.	Despatch overseas of an Air Expeditionary Force.	46
33.	22.9.1939	Goble to Shedden. Minute.	Recommends policy regarding air assistance overseas.	46
34.	London 22.9.1939	Captain Balfour's Note.	Bruce's proposals for Dominion co-operation in the air.	47

List of Documents

Doc.	Place & Date	Document	Content	Page
35.	Sydney 4.10.1939 and Melbourne 5.10.1939	War Cabinet Minutes (11) and (13).	Australian contribution to Empire Air Defence.	49
36.	London 17.10.1939	Note by Bruce on discussions with Air Ministry.	Doubts about proposed Air Expeditionary Force.	50
37.	Canberra 30.10.1939	Whiskard to Menzies. Letter.	Alternate proposal to Air Expeditionary Force.	50
38.	Sydney 31.10.1939	Cabinet Minute.	In lieu of proposed Air Expeditionary Force, Australia would man the nine Sunderlands and participate in Empire Air Training Scheme.	51
39.	Canberra 13.10.1939	Menzies to Bruce. Cablegram [not numbered].	Secondment of an RAF Officer as Chief of the Air Staff.	52
40.	Melbourne 4.1.1940	War Cabinet Minute (112).	Appointment of Sir Charles Burnett as Chief of the Air Staff.	52
41.	Frankston 1.1.1940	Whiskard to Eden. Letter.	Discussion with Menzies about Goble's resignation.	54
42.	Not Dated	Notes on A.C.M. Burnett while in Australia.	Biographical notes on Sir Charles Burnett.	55
43.	Not Dated [c. 30.11.1939]	War Cabinet Paper.	Summary of Empire Air Training Scheme.	57
44.	8.1.1941	McEwen to War Cabinet. Paper.	Empire Air Training Scheme — Formation of Squadrons manned by Australian aircrews and infiltration of ground staffs.	60
45.	4.7.1941	Menzies to Bruce. Cablegram 3495.	Establishment of an RAAF Overseas Headquarters in United Kingdom.	63
46.	[April 1943]	Statement requested by Shedden.	Relation of Australian defence to Empire Air Training Scheme.	65

List of Documents   xxv

Doc.	Place & Date	Document	Content	Page
47.	Canberra 11.12.1942	Drakeford to Curtin. Letter.	Availability of Australian aircrews with war experience.	68
48.	12.4.1943	Advisory War Council, Agendum No. 10/1943.	Relief of EATS personnel from overseas service, and concentration of RAAF personnel into Australian squadrons.	70
49.	February 1946	Jones to Drakeford. War Report ... RAAF, 3.9.1939-31.12.1945.	Casualties to RAAF personnel.	72

4. The Middle East: The 2nd AIF and the Prelude to Battle

Doc.	Place & Date	Document	Content	Page
50.	Melbourne 26.1.1940	Squires for Bruce. Draft Cablegram.	Requests appreciation military situation in Near and Middle East, particularly information on employment and equipping of Australian troops.	73
51.	London 13.2.1940	Bruce to Menzies. Cablegram 114.	Contains appreciation of military situation in Middle East, together with Bruce's comments.	74
52.	Canberra 9.3.1940	Commonwealth Government to [Eden]. Cablegram 91.	Principles governing control and administration of 2nd AIF while abroad.	75
53.	1.5.1940	Menzies to Eden. Cablegram [Not Numbered].	Requests appreciation on likely possibilities of prospective situation before deciding about Australian troop convoys.	76
54.	2.5.1940	Appreciation by Australian Chiefs of Staff. War Cabinet Paper.	Discusses likely strategical consequences of Italy's entry into war.	77

Doc.	Place & Date	Document	Content	Page
55.	8.5.1940	Menzies to Eden. Cablegram 208.	Concerned that Italy entering war may cause difficulties in equipping Australian troops.	79
56.	London 12.6.1940	Caldecote to Menzies. Cablegram 202.	Australian troops in UK for training would be used in defence of UK if necessary.	80
57.	London 23.6.1940	Churchill to Menzies [via Caldecote]. Cablegram [Not Numbered].	Comments on reconstituting and equipping AIF.	81
58.	Gaza 7.7.1940	Blamey to White. Cipher Message.	Appreciation of situation in Middle East, July 1940.	81
59.	London 30.8.1940	Note by Bruce.	Discussion with Dill on importance of having all AIF in Middle East and being fully equipped.	82
60.	7.9.1940	Menzies to Caldecote. Cablegram 471.	Stresses importance of maintaining control of Middle East and urges maximum effort there.	83
61.	London 24.9.1940	Bruce to Menzies. Cablegram 836.	Pressing for continuation of air reinforcements to Middle East, instead of being retained in UK.	84
62.	2.11.1940	Menzies to Bruce. Cablegram 949.	Contains message from Blamey. Bruce to exercise continuous pressure on UK to ensure AIF is fully equipped.	85

5. Disaster in Greece and Crete

Doc.	Place & Date	Document	Content	Page
63.	London 24.2.1941	British War Cabinet. Report by British Chiefs of Staff Comittee.	Policy in Middle East and Eastern Mediterranean.	87

Doc.	Place & Date	Document	Content	Page
64.	[London] 24.2.1941	British War Cabinet. Extract from WM(41) 20th Conclusions, Minute 4.	Menzies' comments on possible employment of 7th Division in Greece.	89
65.	London 25.2.1941	Menzies to Fadden. Cablegram 153.	Recommends Australian troops be employed in Greece.	90
66.	26.2.1941	Shedden to Menzies. Memorandum.	Comments on future employment of AIF.	91
67.	Sydney 26.2.1941	War Cabinet Minute (838).	Agrees to use of two Australian divisions in Greece.	92
68.	London 1.3.1941	Menzies to Fadden. Cablegram 165.	Reassures Fadden that no Dominion troops will be sent to Greece unless fully equipped and that withdrawal will be possible if necessary.	93
69.	Middle East 5.3.1941	Blamey to Menzies. Letter.	As Australian and New Zealand troops make up majority of Force to be used in Greece, Blamey feels he should be considered for command of operation.	94
70.	London 6.3.1941	British War Cabinet. W.M. (41) 25th Conclusions. Minute 1. Confidential Annex.	Menzies' comments on problems of proposed Greek campaign.	95
71.	London 8.3.1941	Menzies to Fadden. Cablegram M13.	Gives two reasons for proposed military commitment to Greece.	96
72.	Alexandria 10.3.1941	Blamey to Fadden [via Spender]. Cablegram [Not Numbered].	Greek military operation extremely hazardous in view of disparity of opposing forces in numbers and training.	97

Doc.	Place & Date	Document	Content	Page
73.	Canberra 10.3.1941	Fadden to Menzies. Cablegram 123.	Commonwealth govt endorses Greek operation if military advisers, having evaluated risks, decide to embark upon it.	98
74.	Middle East 12.3.1941	Blamey to Spender. Letter.	Proposed Greek operation is most hazardous, and strongly urges action to ensure adequate forces are provided quickly.	99
75.	Middle East 30.3.1941	Wavell to Churchill. Cablegram 0/52955.	Did not consult Blamey prior to UK agreement with Greece.	100
76.	London 30.3.1941	Cranborne to Whiskard. Cablegram 162.	Lustre decision justified.	101
77.	London 15.4.1941	Menzies to Fadden. Cablegram M59.	Wavell blamed for military reverses. Extending stay in London because of Middle East crisis.	101
78.	18.4.1941	Fadden to Cranborne. Cablegram 237.	Important that Australian troops be evacuated immediately from Greek mainland, and not be used to hold Crete, but reassembled in the Middle East as a complete Corps.	102
79.	London 19.4.1941	Dill to Wavell. Cablegram 62362.	Recommends the appointment of Blamey to high command.	103
80.	13.7.1941	Report by Brigadier G.A. Vasey.	Organisation problems and evacuation from Crete.	103
81.	Melbourne 4.6.1941	War Cabinet Minute (1113).	Casualties in Crete.	107
82.	Cairo 7.8.1941	Blamey to [Spender?]. Letter.	Reasons for failure of Greek campaign.	107

List of Documents   xxix

Doc.	Place & Date	Document	Content	Page

6. The Syrian Campaign

Doc.	Place & Date	Document	Content	Page
83.	London 30.6.1940	Caldecote to Menzies. Circular Cablegram D.299.	Proposed declaration on Syria and Lebanon.	110
84.	1.7.1940	Menzies to Caldecote. Cablegram 338.	Response to proposed declaration on Syria and Lebanon.	110
85.	London 16.5.1941	Bruce to Fadden. Cablegram 330.	Appreciation of possible action in Syria.	111
86.	Middle East 17.5.1941	Wavell to Dill. Cablegram O/65182.	7th Australian Division would be used in Syria.	112
87.	Cairo 19.5.1941	Lampson to Eden. Cablegram 1424.	Appreciation of possible action in Syria.	113
88.	London 24.5.1941	Bruce to Menzies. Cablegram 363.	Concerned about recent developments in Syria and suggests Menzies cable Churchill.	114
89.	Canberra 29.5.1941	War Cabinet Minute (1111).	Considered Bruce's cable of 24.5.1941.	115
90.	29.5.1941.	Menzies to Churchill [via Bruce]. Cablegram 2649.	Suggests occupation of Syria and importance of air strength.	116
91.	4.6.1941	Menzies to Churchill [via Cranborne]. Cablegram 344.	Concerned by delay in occupying Syria.	118
92.	Middle East 5.6.1941	Wavell to Dill. Cablegram O/70371.	7th Australian Division included in Force to occupy Syria.	118
93.	3.10.1941	Lavarack to War Cabinet. Report.	Report on Syrian campaign.	120

7. The Relief of Tobruk

Doc.	Place & Date	Document	Content	Page
94.	12.4.1941	Fadden to Menzies. Cablegram 222.	Contains text of cablegram sent to Blamey. Urges greater use of Canadian or British troops in Middle East.	123

List of Documents

Doc.	Place & Date	Document	Content	Page
95.	21.6.1941	Menzies to Blamey. Cablegram 13.	Asks for urgent assessment of Middle East situation.	124
96.	Cairo 18.7.1941	Blamey to Auchinleck. Minute.	Recommends immediate relief of Australian troops at Tobruk.	125
97.	20.7.1941	Commonwealth government to Churchill [via Cranborne]. Cablegram 456. [Also a note dated 25.7.1941 which was added to a copy of the cablegram the War Office sent to Auchinleck.]	Desires Australian troops at Tobruk be relieved and stresses importance of Australian troops in Middle East being aggregated into one force.	126
98.	6.8.1941	Menzies to Churchill [via Cranborne]. Draft Cablegram.	Pressing for relief of 9th Division and re-assembly of Australian corps.	127
99.	London 9.8.1941	Churchill to Menzies [via Cross]. Cablegram 556.	Military factors must be considered before garrison at Tobruk can be relieved.	127
100.	Middle East 10.9.1941	Auchinleck to Churchill. Cablegram 1558.	Difficulties in relieving troops in Tobruk. Abandons further large-scale relief of Australian personnel in Tobruk.	128
101.	Bundaberg 10.9.1941	Mansfield to Fadden. Letter.	Tobruk garrison must be relieved.	130
102.	15.9.1941	Commonwealth government to Churchill [via Cranborne]. Cablegram 590.	Requests withdrawal of 9th Division from Tobruk and concentration of AIF.	130
103.	London 18.9.1941	Churchill to Lyttelton. Cablegram [Not Numbered].	Astounded by Australian govt's decision.	131
104.	London 18.9.1941	Churchill to Auchinleck. Cablegram [Not Numbered].	Open dispute with Australian govt must be prevented.	132

Doc.	Place & Date	Document	Content	Page
105.	London 29.9.1941	Churchill to Fadden. Cablegram WINCH [Not Numbered].	Hopes Australian govt reconsiders decision.	132
106.	Melbourne 15.10.1941	War Cabinet Minute (1404).	Relief of 9th Division at Tobruk to be carried out.	133
107.	Cairo 22.12.1941	Lyttelton to Churchill [via Lampson]. Cablegram 4038.	Hopes Australian govt can be persuaded to replace Blamey.	134
108.	Not Dated [c. late December 1941]	Attlee to Churchill. Minute.	Suggests Churchill might persuade Curtin to employ Blamey in another sphere.	134
109.	London 7.1.1942	Churchill to Curtin. Draft Cablegram [Never sent].	Suggests transfer of Blamey — perhaps to Australia.	135

8. The Singapore Strategy 1939–1941

Doc.	Place & Date	Document	Content	Page
110.	London 4.3.1938	Committee of Imperial Defence, Minutes of Meeting.	Malaya — period before relief. Australian attitude to securing Singapore base.	140
111.	London 20.11.1939	Note by Bruce. Joint Meeting [between Ministers of the United Kingdom and of Dominions].	Feels Churchill's strategy would be to win war in Europe before dealing with war in Far East.	142
112.	London 21.11.1939	Churchill's memorandum.	Australian and New Zealand naval defence.	144
113.	London 28.6.1940	Caldecote to Commonwealth government. Cablegram 228.	Because of defeat of France, unable send a British fleet to Far East. Requests Australian ground and air forces be sent to Malaya.	146
114.	London 11.8.1940	Caldecote to Menzies. Circular Cablegram Z214.	British Chiefs of Staff's appreciation of situation in Far East.	147
115.	23.8.1940	Australian Chiefs of Staff, Report.	British Chiefs of Staff's appreciation of Far Eastern position.	148

Doc.	Place & Date	Document	Content	Page
116.	Melbourne 28.8.1940	War Cabinet Minute (459)	Agrees to 7th Division being employed in Malaya.	149
117.	Melbourne 23.9.1940	War Cabinet Minute (523)	UK recommendation that 7th Division be sent to Middle East rather than Malaya.	150
118.	Canberra 26.11.1940	War Cabinet Minute (632).	Review by Chiefs of Staff of Singapore Defence Conference.	151
119.	London 23.12.1940	Churchill to Menzies [via Cranborne]. Cablegram 510.	Grateful for promised troops and equipment for Singapore.	152
120.	London 28.1.1941	Cranborne to Whiskard. Cablegram 49.	UK military advisers' views on defence of Singapore.	152
121.	Melbourne 5.2.1941	Advisory War Council Minute (126).	Statement by Spender on his visit to Singapore.	153
122.	Sydney 14.2.1941	War Cabinet Minute (802).	Australian Chiefs of Staff's appreciation of Far Eastern situation.	154
123.	Melbourne 20.2.1941	*The Argus* [Melbourne].	Arrival of Australian troops at Singapore.	157
124.	London 11.4.1941	Reply by [British] Chiefs of Staff to Memorandum by Prime Minister of Australia. Annex IV to C.O.S.(41)230 FINAL.	Factors influencing reinforcement of Far East with capital ships if Japan enters war and US remains neutral.	157
125.	14.4.1941	Shedden to Menzies. Minute.	Comments on naval defence in Far East.	160
126.	Sydney 15.5.1941	War Cabinet Minute (1073)	Colvin's comments on reports from Singapore Conference in April 1941, and Washington Staff Conversations of March 1941.	161
127.	3.6.1941	War Cabinet Agendum.	Brooke-Popham's request for additional troops and equipment for Malaya.	164
128.	London 14.10.1941	Bruce to Curtin. Cablegram 67.	*George V* or the *Prince of Wales* will be sent to Singapore.	166

List of Documents   xxxiii

Doc.	Place & Date	Document	Content	Page
129.	8.12.1941	Curtin to Cranborne. Cablegram [778?].	As war with Japan has begun, requests an up-to-date appreciation of Far Eastern situation.	166

9. The Dutch Alliance and Portuguese Timor

Doc.	Place & Date	Document	Content	Page
130.	17.4.1940	Commonwealth govt to UK govt. Cablegram 156.	Australia concerned over status of NEI and suggests UK ascertain US attitude and possible action.	168
131.	London 11.8.1940	Caldecote to Menzies. Circular Cablegram Z214.	Britain's interest in co-operating with Dutch.	169
132.	Sydney 22.3.1941	War Cabinet Minutes (909) and (912).	Proposed co-operation with Dutch.	170
133.	3.10.1941	Fadden to Cranborne. Cablegram 649.	Requests Britain to approach Netherlands govt to approve despatch of Australian Army and Air Force units to Ambon and Koepang.	173
134.	16.10.1941	Curtin to Cranborne. Cablegram 684.	Desired that advance forces in uniform be sent to Ambon and Koepang.	173
135.	London 27.11.1941	Cranborne to Curtin. Cablegram 786.	Netherlands govt approves of some Army and Air Force personnel being despatched to Ambon and Koepang.	174
136.	Melbourne 1.12.1941	Langslow to Drakeford. Teleprinter Message M2840.	Squadrons placed in state of readiness.	174
137.	5.12.1941	Air Board to [Air Liaison Officer] Bandoeng. Radio Message.	Flights to Laha and Koepang.	175
138.	London 5.12.1941	Cranborne to Curtin. Circular Cablegram M427.	Contains text of note handed to Netherlands Minister regarding military co-operation.	175

Doc.	Place & Date	Document	Content	Page
139.	Melbourne 15.10.1941	War Cabinet. Minute (1401)	Proposed Australian co-operation in defence of Portuguese Timor.	176

10. Australia and the Higher Direction of the War — December 1941 — April 1942

Doc.	Place & Date	Document	Content	Page
140.	11.12.1941	Curtin to Churchill [via Cranborne]. Cablegram 794.	Suggests creation of a supreme authority for higher direction and co-ordinated control of Allies' activities in Pacific war.	178
141.	16.12.1941	Evatt to Casey. Cablegram 1079.	Casey to insist that Australia has separate representation from UK at conferences.	178
142.	Canberra 7.1.1942	Evatt to Casey. Cablegram 37.	Casey to press for Australian representation on body giving orders to ABDA commander.	179
143.	7.1.1942	Curtin to Churchill. Cablegram JOHCU 15.	Australia desires direct consultation in matters concerning operations in Pacific.	180
144.	Washington 13.1.1942	Casey to Evatt. Cablegram 74.	Reporting conversation with Roosevelt about Australia's inadequate representation in higher direction of Pacific campaign.	181
145.	London 19.1.1942	Cranborne to Curtin. Cablegram 72.	Proposed establishment of Far Eastern Council in London.	182
146.	21.1.1942	Curtin to Cranborne. Cablegram 68.	Does not agree with proposed establishment of Far Eastern Council in London. Desires establishment of Pacific War Council in Washington.	183

List of Documents xxxv

Doc.	Place & Date	Document	Content	Page

11. ABDA Command

Doc.	Place & Date	Document	Content	Page
147.	Washington 22.12.1941	Casey to Curtin. Cablegram 1188.	Feels that C-in-C of Pacific and Far East theatre will be MacArthur, and that it is possible for headquarters to be in Australia.	185
148.	London 29.12.1941	Churchill to Curtin. Cablegram WINCH 13.	Hopes Australia will agree to agreement reached between Roosevelt and himself. Appointment of Wavell as C-in-C.	186
149.	London 29.12.1941	Churchill to Curtin. Cablegram WINCH 14.	Text of Roosevelt/ Churchill Agreement.	187
150.	1.1.1942	Curtin to Churchill. Cablegram JOHCU 13.	Assents to Roosevelt/ Churchill Agreement.	188
151.	2.1.1942	Directive for Wavell.	Directive for Wavell by agreement among ABDA governments.	188
152.	5.1.1942	Report by Chiefs of Staff.	Concern over Australia being outside ABDA's boundaries.	192
153.	11.1.1942	Report by Chiefs of Staff.	Contains text of cable from Wavell asking if Port Darwin is in area of his responsibility.	193
154.	Batavia 15.1.1942	Wavell to British Chiefs of Staff [Washington]. Cablegram 00053.	Appreciation of situation in South-West Pacific area.	194
155.	24.1.1942	Report by Chiefs of Staff.	Australian forces to be placed at Wavell's disposal.	196
156.	7.2.1942	Curtin to Blamey [Middle East]. Cablegram 4.	ABDA's command structure.	197
157.	London 22.2.1942	Page to Curtin. Cablegram 1609.	Contains text of Wavell's cablegram to British Joint Staff Mission in Washington on situation in Java.	199

12. Malayan Fiasco

Doc.	Place & Date	Document	Content	Page
158.	Singapore 23.12.1941	Bowden to Evatt. Cablegram 73.	Urges substantial reinforcements be sent to Malaya immediately.	200
159.	London 23.12.1941	Cranborne to Curtin. Cablegram 872.	Air and land reinforcements for Malaya.	201
160.	Not Dated [c.12.1.1942]	Curtin to Churchill. Cablegram JOHCU 16.	Urges nothing be left undone to reinforce Malaya to greatest degree possible.	202
161.	14.1.1942	Churchill to Curtin. Cablegram WINCH 7.	Expects defeat in Malaya.	203
162.	Johore 19.1.1942	Bennett to Sturdee. Cablegram SP 299.	Situation of 8th Division.	204
163.	Canberra 25.1.1942	Curtin to Page [for Churchill]. Cablegram 12.	Response to situation in Malaya and in particular to suggested evacuation.	204
164.	Singapore 26.1.1942	Bowden to Evatt. Cablegram 81.	Situation in Singapore. Doubts about Percival.	206
165.	Darling Point 1.2.1942	J.I. Martin to Curtin. Letter.	Implores Curtin to get help to Singapore.	208
166.	Canberra 10.2.1942	Curtin to Page. Cablegram 17.	Contains extract of cablegram sent to Churchill, with brief review of Singapore strategy.	209
167.	Batavia 12.2.1942	Wavell to Curtin. Cablegram 01106.	Situation in Singapore is not encouraging.	209
168.	13.2.1942	Curtin to Page. Cablegram 21.	Suggests Page obtain an early appreciation on Pacific situation.	210
169.	Java 16.2.1942	Wavell to Curtin. Cablegram 1278.	Resistance at Singapore failed.	211
170.	London 16.2.1942	British War Cabinet. WM(42)21. Minute 2.	Points on discussion regarding fall of Singapore.	211
171.	Java 21.2.1942	Wavell to Curtin. Letter.	Writes of failures against Japanese, and mentions plan to use 7th Division.	212

Doc.	Place & Date	Document	Content	Page
172.	17.2.1942	Dept. of Defence. Historical note.	Percival's views on reasons for failure of Malayan campaign.	213
173.	Melbourne 2.3.1942	War Cabinet Minute (1931).	Discussion with Bennett on reasons for failure of Malayan campaign.	214

13. Rabaul, Ambon and Timor

Doc.	Place & Date	Document	Content	Page
174.	13.12.1941	Evatt to Casey. Cablegram 154.	Appreciation by Australian Chiefs of Staff on Rabaul.	216
175.	Dilli 17.12.1941	Governor of Portuguese Timor to Curtin. Cablegram [Not Numbered].	Translation of a protest over landing of Australian and Dutch troops at Dilli.	217
176.	18.12.1941	Evatt to Governor of Portuguese Timor [via Ross, British Consul]. Cablegram 3.	Reasons for Australian and Dutch troops being sent to Portuguese Timor.	218
177.	London 19.12.1941	Cranborne to Curtin. Circular Cablegram D751.	How despatch of combined force to Portuguese Timor was to be explained to Portuguese government.	218
178.	10.6.1943	Note for Forde.	Operations at Rabaul, Timor and Ambon.	219
179.	28.4.1942	Interim statement by Sturdee.	Treatment of prisoners of war by Japanese. Tol incident.	222

14. The Destination of 1 Australian Corps

Doc.	Place & Date	Document	Content	Page
180.	[Batavia] 6.2.1942	Lavarack to Sturdee. Letter.	Situation in Java and Sumatra.	224
181.	HQ. SWPA 8.2.1942	Lloyd to Rowell. Letter.	Advises against disembarking Australian troops in NEI.	225

List of Documents

Doc.	Place & Date	Document	Content	Page
182.	Batavia 14.2.1942	Wavell to Churchill and Roosevelt. Repeated to Curtin. Cablegram [Not Numbered].	Appreciation of situation in Dutch East Indies. Suggests advantages in diverting one or both Australian divisions to Burma or Australia, but not recommended.	227
183.	15.2.1942	Paper by Sturdee.	Recommends the return of AIF to Australia.	227
184.	15.2.1942	Curtin to Churchill [via Cranborne]. Repeated to Wavell. Cablegram 123.	Suggests return of AIF to Australia.	230
185.	[Batavia] 16.2.1942	Wavell to Churchill and Brooke. Cablegram 01288.	Recommends one or both Australian divisions be diverted to Burma.	231
186.	17.2.1942	Curtin to Churchill [via Cranborne]. Cablegram 127.	Requests diversion of the two Australian divisions [for the East Indies] to Australia and recall of AIF in Middle East at an early date.	231
187.	Java 18.2.1942	Wavell to Curtin. Cablegram OPXO 1529.	Wavell claims Lavarack in agreement with his view that Australian Corps be used in Burma.	231
188.	London 18.2.1942	Bruce to Curtin. Cablegram 31A.	Reasons why he feels Australian govt should agree to 7th Division going to Burma.	232
189.	London 19.2.1942	Page to Curtin. Cablegram P.47.	If an Australian division is diverted to Burma, US will send a division to Australia.	233
190.	19.2.1942	Curtin to Page. Repeated to Lavarack, Wavell and Casey. Cablegram 29.	Australian troops being diverted from NEI should come to Australia.	233
191.	London 20.2.1942	Churchill to Curtin [via Attlee]. Cablegram 233.	Argues for use of Australian troops in Burma.	234

List of Documents   xxxix

Doc.	Place & Date	Document	Content	Page
192.	22.2.1942	Curtin to Churchill [via Attlee]. Cablegram 136.	Argues that AIF be returned to Australia.	235
193.	Washington 22.2.1942	Casey to Evatt. Cablegram 342.	Roosevelt accepts Australian govt's decision.	236
194.	London 22.2.1942	Churchill to Curtin [via Attlee]. Cablegram 241.	Convoy with Australian troops temporarily diverted northward, giving Australian govt time to review decision if it wishes.	237
195.	London 23.2.1942	Bruce to Curtin. Cablegram 33A.	Appalled that convoy with Australian troops being diverted from direct route to Australia. Suggests any reaction by Curtin would be justified but urges restraint in his reply.	237
196.	23.2.1942	Curtin to Churchill [via Attlee]. Cablegram 139.	Stresses that it is impossible to reverse a decision which was made with the utmost care.	238
197.	23.2.1942	Sturdee to Shedden. Teleprinter Message M.777.	The value of any American division for defence of Australia is considerably less than an AIF division.	238
198.	London 23.2.1942	Churchill to Curtin [via Attlee]. Cablegram [Not Numbered].	Convoy with Australian troops after refuelling at Colombo will proceed to Australia.	239

15. The Fate of the *Orcades* Party

199.	12.2.1942	Curtin to Wavell. Cablegram 26.	Emphasises that concentration of AIF in one Force under its own commander is a principle of national importance.	240

Doc. Place & Date	Document	Content	Page
200. 18.2.1942	Curtin to Wavell. Cablegram 34.	Requests urgently Wavell's plans for Australian troops in Batavia.	241
201. 24.2.1942	Curtin to Page. Cablegram 32.	Page to act in London to have Wavell directed to evacuate Australian troops from Java.	241
202. London 24.2.1942	Page to Curtin. Cablegram P52.	States that, for those entitled to be evacuated from Java, mode and priority of evacuation left to commanders on the spot.	242
203. 25.2.1942	Wavell to Marshall and Dill. Repeated to Curtin. Cablegram TOR 2115.	Wavell does not feel he can remove fighting troops from Java.	243
204. Java [c.26.] 2.1942	Blackburn to Lavarack. Report.	Reporting on situation of AIF in Java.	243
205. 2.3.1942	Sturdee to Shedden. Minute.	Feels it is not practicable to get AIF out of Java.	245
206. Melbourne 2.3.1942	Sturdee to Ter Poorten. Cablegram MC.5214.	Requests that, should resistance in Java become impossible, AIF be afforded an opportunity to escape.	245
207. [Batavia] 5.3.1942	Sitwell to Sturdee. Cablegram TOR 1025.	Ordered evacuation now impossible, but should Dutch resistance cease, troops will endeavour to escape.	246

16. Two AIF Brigades to Ceylon

208. London 24.2.1942	Page to Curtin. Cablegram P.50.	Suggests Australian govt assist in defence of Ceylon by allowing 7th Division to remain temporarily.	247

List of Documents xli

Doc.	Place & Date	Document	Content	Page
209.	25.2.1942	Curtin to Page. Cablegram 33.	Doubts whether Page was speaking for Australia's interests. Not in agreement with Australian troops remaining in Ceylon.	249
210.	26.2.1942	Chiefs of Staff Report to Curtin. Teleprinter Message M.896.	Endorses views of British Chiefs of Staff on importance of holding Ceylon.	250
211.	London 27.2.1942	Page to Curtin. Cablegram P.54.	Gives a reason for Australia offering assistance in defence of Ceylon.	250
212.	London 27.2.1942	Page to Curtin. Cablegram P.55.	Method of loading the two Australian divisions would allow for diversion of a division.	251
213.	London 27.2.1942	Page to Curtin. Cablegram P.56.	Argues further for Australian assistance in Ceylon.	251
214.	28.2.1942	Report by Chiefs of Staff.	Defence of Ceylon. Effect of temporary retention in Ceylon of an Australian division on immediate security of Australia.	252
215.	28.2.1942	Sturdee to War Cabinet. Minute. [Supplement 2 to Agendum No. 106/1942.]	Believes two brigades of 6th Division are only Australian troops that could be used in Ceylon.	253
216.	2.3.1942	Curtin to Churchill [via Attlee]. Cablegram 160.	Offers two brigade groups of 6th Division to assist temporarily in defence of Ceylon.	254
217.	4.3.1942	Curtin to Page. Cablegram 38.	Notes some deficiencies in Australia's defence.	254
218.	1.7.1942	Curtin to Attlee. Cablegram 351.	Requests information on return of 16th and 17th Brigades from Ceylon.	255

17. The Defence of Mainland Australia

Doc.	Place & Date	Document	Content	Page
219.	15.12.1941	Chiefs of Staff Paper No. 1.	Appreciation of defence of Australia and adjacent areas.	256
220.	29.1.1942	Chiefs of Staff Paper No. 4	Appreciation of defence of Australia and adjacent areas.	257
221.	4.2.1942	MacKay to Forde. Memorandum.	Defence of Australia.	260
222.	17.2.1942	Forde to War Cabinet. Paper.	Defence of Australia — the govt policy recommended for adoption.	263
223.	Not Dated [c. early February 1942]	Appendix III to War Cabinet, Agendum No. 96/1942, Table.	Outline Order of Battle: AMF and AIF not including Middle East and Malaya.	263
224.	27.3.1942	Lowe to Curtin. Report.	Findings of Commission of Inquiry on bombing of Darwin by Japanese.	266
225.	Toorak 15.3.1942	E. Moore to Curtin. Letter.	Wants Curtin to make terms with Japanese.	270
226.	Kalgoorlie 24.3.1942	C. Middleton to Curtin. Letter.	Volunteering to crash a plane load of high explosives onto a Japanese aircraft-carrier.	270
227.	20–21.3.1942	Report to Australian Legation, Washington.	Present strength of Army forces and readiness of present Air Force.	271
228.	Not Dated [c.29.3.1942]	War Cabinet Agendum No. 182/1942.	Denial of resources to the enemy — directive for guidance in formulation of detailed plans.	273
229.	London 1.4.1942	Churchill to Evatt [in Washington]. Cablegram [Not Numbered].	If Australia is being heavily invaded in near future, Britain can assist with troops.	274
230.	Melbourne 23.4.1942	Prime Minister's War Conference. Minute (12)	Discussions with State Premiers on state of Australia and war.	275

Doc.	Place & Date	Document	Content	Page
231.	6.7.1943	MacKay to Curtin. Minute.	Requests steps be taken to discontinue use of term 'Brisbane Line' in connection with his memorandum of 4.2.1942.	276

18. The Arrival of the Americans

Doc.	Place & Date	Document	Content	Page
232.	Washington 22.10.1941	Casey to Evatt. Cablegram 877.	US – Australian air co-operation.	277
233.	London 5.12.1941	Cranborne to Curtin. Circular Cablegram M.424.	UK receives assurance from US of armed support.	279
234.	Washington 11.12.1941	Casey to Evatt. Cablegram 1135.	Convoy of US ships with equipment and reinforcements bound for Philippines is likely to be diverted to Brisbane.	280
235.	Melbourne 12.12.1941	Nankervis to Shedden. Note.	Contains text of message Royle received from Washington regarding arrival of US convoy.	280
236.	Washington 12.12.1941	Harries to Royle. Cablegram 1441.	Contains message for Barnes telling him he is commander of US troops in Australia, together with instructions.	281
237.	Washington 16.12.1941	Casey to Evatt. Cablegram 1160.	US war planes for Philippines may be sent via Australia.	281
238.	Washington 17.12.1941	Casey to Evatt. Cablegram 1163.	A US depot group to be established in either Brisbane or Townsville for assembly of US aircraft for Philippines.	282

xliv   List of Documents

Doc.	Place & Date	Document	Content	Page
239.	Washington 18.12.1941	Casey to Evatt. Cablegram 1173.	Hopes Australia will make available transport planes for rapid transference of stores and ammunition to Philippines. Brett appointed in command of all US military activities in Australia.	283
240.	23.12.1941	Curtin to Casey. Cablegram 1103.	Contains text of cablegram Curtin sent to Roosevelt and Churchill. Wants Singapore reinforced. Says Australia would gladly accept a US commander in Pacific area.	283
241.	15.12.1941	Chiefs of Staff Paper No. 1.	Appreciation of defence of Australia and adjacent areas, December 1941. Importance of New Caledonia.	284
242.	Washington 29.12.1941	Casey to Evatt. Cablegram 1229.	US Army determined to get as much air power to Southwest Pacific as possible.	285
243.	Washington 1.1.1942	Casey to Evatt. Cablegram 9.	Generally believed that King, as C-in-C US Fleet, will produce more forceful naval leadership.	286
244.	Washington 1.1.1942	Harries to Royle [via Casey]. Cablegram TROPIC 143.	Plans to defend islands on line of communication to the east Australian coast.	286
245.	Melbourne 4.1.1942	Brett to Shedden. Letter.	Extract from a Washington cable outlining policy Brett was to pursue.	288
246.	Canberra 8.1.1942	Curtin to Page [for Churchill]. Cablegram 3A.	Concerned over Australia's exclusion from Southwest Pacific theatre command.	289

Doc.	Place & Date	Document	Content	Page
247.	Washington 16.1.1942	Harries to Royle [via Casey]. Cablegram TROPIC 149.	Defence of New Caledonia.	289
248.	Washington 22.1.1942	Casey to Evatt. Cablegram 126.	Summary of present and prospective land and air reinforcements for Australia.	290
249.	22.1.1942	Evatt to Casey. Cablegram 101.	Comments on Australia's lack of aircraft and other equipment.	291
250.	Washington 24.1.1942	Casey to Evatt. Cablegram 148.	Roosevelt appreciated Australia's concern over aircraft shortage, but felt Australia had done pretty well.	292
251.	Washington 25.1.1942	Casey to Evatt. Cablegram 149.	Marshall pointed out the lengths to which Americans and British have gone to divert forces and equipment to Southwest Pacific.	293
252.	Washington 30.1.1942	Casey to Evatt. Cablegram 180.	Gives some insight into his work in Washington.	293
253.	Washington 22.2.1942	Harries to Royle [via Casey]. Cablegram TROPIC 181.	US forces due to leave for Australia.	294
254.	22.2.1942	Marshall to MacArthur. Radio No. 1078.	Conveys President's orders for MacArthur to leave Philippines for Australia.	295
255.	26.2.1942	War Cabinet Paper.	Future policy and strategy for conduct of war in Pacific — Australia and N.Z.	296
256.	Melbourne 21.3.1942	*The Argus* [Melbourne].	MacArthur arrives in Melbourne.	297
257.	Canberra 27.3.1942	*The Canberra Times*.	MacArthur's pledge to Australia.	298
258.	Canberra 15.4.1942	Curtin to MacArthur. Letter.	Assures MacArthur of support of Australian govt and people.	299

xlvi   List of Documents

Doc.	Place & Date	Document	Content	Page

19. The New Anglo-American Global Command Structure, March-April 1942

Doc.	Place & Date	Document	Content	Page
259.	Washington 25.3.1942	Evatt to Curtin. Cablegram P.M.5.	Recommendations of combined US and UK Chiefs of Staff as to war areas of the world.	301
260.	29.3.1942	Curtin to Evatt [in Washington]. Cablegram 10.	Opposition by Chiefs of Staff to proposed sub-division of Pacific whereby Australia is not in same area as NZ, Fiji and New Caledonia.	302
261.	Washington 31.3.1942	Evatt to Curtin. Cablegram P.M.S. 20.	Assurances given that separation of areas of command does not mean absence of joint planning and co-ordination.	303
262.	Washington 3.4.1942	Evatt to Curtin. Cablegram S.22 Part IV and Part III.	Directive to MacArthur. Definition of SWPA.	303
263.	Washington 3.4.1942	Evatt to Curtin. Cablegram S.22, Part 2.	Extract from directive to Nimitz.	305
264.	Washington 12.4.1942	Evatt to Curtin. Cablegram S.37.	Contains extract from a memorandum indicating how interests of co-operating nations are safeguarded.	306

20. The Royal Navy's Retreat from the 'Malay Barrier'

Doc.	Place & Date	Document	Content	Page
265.	25.12.1941	Royle to Shedden. Memorandum.	Considers proposed division of available Allied naval forces as strategically unsound.	307
266.	19.3.1942	Curtin to Churchill [via Attlee]. Cablegram 208.	Australia's response to naval policy advocated in a British appreciation.	308
267.	23.3.1942	Review by Shedden.	War situation from the Australian viewpoint.	309

Doc.	Place & Date	Document	Content	Page
268.	17.4.1942	Curtin to Churchill [via Attlee]. Cablegram 252.	Requests appreciation of UK, US and Japanese position regarding aircraft carriers, and a statement of UK's immediate and long range policy for combating Japanese naval forces.	310
269.	London 27.4.1942	Attlee to Curtin. Cablegram 382.	Account of Japanese fleet's foray into Bay of Bengal; and future British policy.	310

21. Making the Southwest Pacific Area Secure

Doc.	Place & Date	Document	Content	Page
270.	Canberra 26.3.1942	Advisory War Council Meeting.	Interview with MacArthur.	312
271.	19.2.1943	Review by Shedden.	Extracts from cablegram E.T. 31 of 28.5.1942 on grand strategy of war.	314
272.	Canberra 6.5.1942	Curtin to Evatt. Cablegram P.M. 57.	In view of strategy to defeat Germany first, MacArthur very sceptical about degree of assistance to be given to SWPA.	315
273.	London 8.5.1942	Evatt to Curtin. Cablegram E4.	Found both UK and US grossly underestimated Japan's strength.	315
274.	London 21.5.1942	British War Cabinet Minute. W.M. (42) 65th Conclusions, Minute 1.	Evatt puts Australia's view on 'defeat Germany first' strategy. Three Spitfire squadrons to be sent to Australia.	316
275.	London 28.5.1942	Evatt to Curtin. Cablegram E.T. 30.	Surprised finding 'beat Hitler first' strategy had been formally agreed to by Churchill and Roosevelt in December–January.	317

Doc.	Place & Date	Document	Content	Page
276.	1.6.1942	Report by General Blamey, the Chief of the Naval Staff and the Chief of the Air Staff.	Consider an offensive policy should be directed against Japan to bring about defeat of both Japan and Germany.	318
277.	Melbourne 1.5.1942	MacArthur to Blamey. Letter.	Indications of future Japanese movements.	318
278.	Melbourne 12.5.1942	MacArthur to Curtin. Letter.	Despite Japanese losses, believes they will continue offensive action in SWPA or against India.	319
279.	Canberra 13.5.1942	Curtin to Evatt [in London]. Cablegram 62.	Vital that Australia be strengthened while time and circumstances permit.	320
280.	Canberra 16.5.1942	Curtin to MacArthur. Letter.	Conveys disappointment of Advisory War Council in results of air and naval operations in Coral Sea and Northeastern Sector.	320
281.	Melbourne 18.5.1942	MacArthur to Curtin. Letter.	Believes brilliant effort at the Coral Sea saved Australia from a definite and immediate threat.	321
282.	Melbourne 11.6.1942	Notes of discussions with the Commander-in-Chief, SWPA.	Coral Sea and Midway Island actions resulted in transformation in position in SWPA.	322
283.	3.9.1942	Notes for Prime Minister's Speech.	While Australia can be confident, indications are it will be a long war.	323
284.	5.8.1942	Evatt to Dixon. Cablegram S.W. 75.	Stresses need for superior sea and airpower in Pacific theatre.	323

List of Documents   xlix

Doc.	Place & Date	Document	Content	Page
285.	Washington 15.9.1942	Roosevelt to Curtin. Letter.	Feels that Australia's present armed forces are sufficient to defeat present Japanese force in NG and provide for security of Australia.	324
286.	Brisbane 17.8.1942	Prime Minister's War Conference. Minute (40).	Operations in Solomon Islands.	325
287.	Brisbane 20–26.10.1942	[Shedden's?] Notes of discussions with C-in-C, SWPA.	Ineptitude in handling of American and Australian squadrons seen as a cause for defeat at Solomon Islands.	325
288.	Brisbane 20–26.10.1942	[Shedden's?] Notes of discussions with C-in-C, SWPA.	Amalgamation of AIF and AMF.	326
289.	Brisbane 16–20.1.1943	[Shedden's] Notes of discussions with C-in-C, SWPA.	MacArthur's observations on AIF, CMF and their prospective use; and views on amendment of Defence Act.	327
290.	Sydney 6.6.1943	Prime Minister's Speech.	Reasons for extending conscription.	328
291.	Brisbane 25–31.5.1943	[Shedden's] Notes of discussions with C-in-C, SWPA.	A homogeneous Australian army.	329
292.	30.3.1943	Curtin to Roosevelt [via Dixon]. Cablegram P.W. 25.	Quotes from his recent review to Parliament on strength of Japan.	330
293.	Brisbane 6.4.1943	MacArthur to Shedden. Teleprinter Message BXC.368.	Communique to mark first anniversary of fall of Bataan.	331
294.	Canberra 10.6.1943	Press Statement by Curtin.	Does not think enemy can now invade Australia.	331
295.	Brisbane 20–26.10.1942	[Shedden's] Notes of discussions with C-in-C, SWPA.	Political criticism of operations.	332
296.	Brisbane 16–20.1.1943	[Shedden's] Notes of discussions with C-in-C, SWPA.	General Sir Thomas Blamey.	333

List of Documents

Doc.	Place & Date	Document	Content	Page
297.	Brisbane 26.5.1943	[Shedden's] Notes of discussions with C-in-C, SWPA.	Extension of Royle's appointment as CNS.	334
298.	London 30.6.1943	Notes by Bruce on discussions with General R.H. Dewing.	Dewing claimed that on all strategical and operational questions, Curtin completely dominated by MacArthur.	335
299.	24.2.1944	Blamey to Morshead. Letter.	Condemns politicians who question his role.	336
300.	3.3.1944	Blamey to Morshead. Letter.	Refers to two of his critics, Foll and Cameron.	336
301.	16–20.1.1943	Notes by Shedden.	Impressions of MacArthur.	336
302.	Brisbane 8.6.1944	Extracts from War Historian's diaries.	Long's comments on MacArthur.	337

22. Crisis of Command: The RAAF in SWPA

Doc.	Place & Date	Document	Content	Page
303.	GHQ, SWPA 4.9.1942	MacArthur to Curtin. Letter.	Decision to create US 5th Air Force.	339
304.	HQ, AAF, SWPA 5.9.1942	General Orders No. 47 (Kenney).	Designates Bostock as AOC Coastal Command, Allied Air Forces.	340
305.	26.9.1942	Report by Chiefs of Staff.	Recommends unified operational and administrative control of RAAF under Jones.	341
306.	12.10.1942	Jones to [Shedden?]. Minute.	Urges acceptance of above recommendation.	341
307.	Melbourne, 14.10.1942	Drakeford to Curtin. Letter.	Supports Jones's recommendation.	342
308.	Port Moresby, n.d. [c. 29.11.1942]	Kenney to Bostock. Letter.	Praises Bostock.	343
309.	5.12.1942	Air Board Order AFCO 391.	Claims Jones's authority over Bostock.	343
310.	Brisbane 12.12.1942	Bostock to Mulrooney. Letter.	Refutes AFCO 391.	344

Doc.	Place & Date	Document	Content	Page
311.	Melbourne 16.12.1942	Jones to Drakeford. Minute.	Urges dismissal of Bostock because he had refuted AFCO 391.	345
312.	11.5.1943	Shedden to Curtin. Minute.	Suggests appointment of Longmore over Jones and Bostock.	347
313.	HQ, AAF, SWPA 29.5.1943.	Kenney to MacArthur. Memorandum.	Doubts whether Longmore should be put in charge of RAAF.	348
314.	Canberra 11.6.1943	Curtin to Drakeford. Letter.	Accepts MacArthur's wish that neither Longmore nor Joubert be put in charge of RAAF.	348
315.	15.4.1943	Jones to [Shedden?]. Minute.	Cites examples of Bostock not co-operating.	349
316.	Brisbane 7.11.1943	Bostock to Mulrooney. Letter.	Complains of lack of support from Air Board.	350
317.	3.12.1943	Jones to Drakeford. Minute.	Complains Bostock is exceeding his responsibilities.	350
318.	5.2.1944	MacArthur to Shedden. Teleprinter Message BXM.113.	Asks Curtin to intervene in dispute, as a matter of urgency.	351
319.	6.3.1944	Jones to Drakeford. Minute.	Complains about Bostock's insubordination.	351
320.	Brisbane 15.4.1944	Bostock to Drakeford. Letter.	Complains that Jones has broken verbal agreements.	352
321.	26.4.1944	Jones to Drakeford. Minute.	Takes grave exception to Bostock's letter of 15.4.1944.	352
322.	3.8.1944	Paper by Curtin. War Cabinet Agendum. 396/1944	Favours appointment of Park to head RAAF.	353
323.	Melbourne 4.8.1944	War Cabinet Minute. (3693)	Approves appointment of Park to head RAAF.	354
324.	Canberra 30.9.1944	Notes of discussion with C-in-C, SWPA.	MacArthur now does not want Park appointed.	355

List of Documents

Doc.	Place & Date	Document	Content	Page
325.	4.11.1944	Shedden. Personal minute.	Forecasts outcry over poor RAAF effort in SWPA.	356

23. Papua

Doc.	Place & Date	Document	Content	Page
326.	30.9.1942	Paper — 'Defence of Port Moresby'.	Australia's reinforcement of Port Moresby up to September 1942.	357
327.	HQ, NGF, n.d. [c. 31.8.1942]	Rowell to Vasey. Letter.	Doubts about AMF troops.	360
328.	HQ, NGF 1.9.1942	Rowell to Vasey. Letter.	Asks whether New Guinea should be reinforced by 16th and 17th Brigades.	360
329.	HQ, NGF 8.9.1942	Rowell to Vasey. Letter.	Despite handicaps, feels confident enemy has no hope of taking Port Moresby from north.	361
330.	Canberra 3.10.1942	Note by Shedden.	Criticism by Rowell of militia troops.	361
331.	Not Dated [c.22.9.1942]	Sir Keith Murdoch's article.	Praise for 39th Battalion in New Guinea.	362
332.	Canberra 9.10.1942	Report by Minister for the Army.	Observations made on his visit to New Guinea theatre of operations, 1–4.10.1942.	363
333.	HQ, NGF 30.8.1942	Rowell to Vasey. Letter.	Bitter over MacArthur's criticism of Clowes' handling of battle at Milne Bay.	365
334.	16.11.1942	Report on Operations — NGF, 11 August – 28 September 1942.	Report on Milne Bay Battle.	366
335.	17.9.1942	Note of conversation between the Prime Minister and the C-in-C, SWPA.	MacArthur has no confidence in Australian troops in NG. Suggests Blamey go to NG to take personal command.	366
336.	ALF, SWPA, Adv.HQ. 28.9.1942	Blamey to Rowell. Letter.	Dismisses Rowell.	368

Doc.	Place & Date	Document	Content	Page
337.	Port Moresby 28.9.1942	Blamey to Curtin. Repeated to MacArthur. Cablegram 2117.	Difficulties with Rowell.	368
338.	Canberra 3.10.1942	Note by Shedden.	Rowell's view of conflict between himself and Blamey.	369
339.	Port Moresby 8.11.1942	Blamey to Shedden. Cablegram Z 134.	Comments on possible overseas post for Rowell.	370
340.	16.11.1942	Report on Operations — NGF, 11 August–28 September 1942.	Some comments on operations in Imita Ridge area.	370
341.	HQ, NGF 30.1.1943	Operations in NG. Brief for GOC NG Force.	Brief summary of Australian advance over the Kokoda Trail.	371
342.	ALF, SWPA, Adv.HQ. 14.11.1942	Blamey to Shedden. Letter.	Looks forward to quick victory on Papuan coast.	372
343.	ALF, SWPA, Adv.HQ. 30.11.1942	Blamey to Shedden. Letter.	Japanese resisting fiercely at Gona. Expresses disappointment in 32nd US Division at Buna.	372
344.	HQ, Adv. NGF 30.11.1942	Herring to Blamey. Letter.	Weakness of 32nd US Division.	373
345.	HQ, Adv. NGF 3.12.1942	Herring to Blamey. Letter.	Eichelberger takes command of 32nd US Division.	374
346.	ALF, SWPA, Adv. HQ 4.12.1942	Blamey to Curtin. Letter.	Some problems arising from the beachhead battles.	374
347.	HQ, NGF 6.12.1942	Herring to Blamey. Letter.	Attitude of some Australian troops to killing of Japanese soldiers.	375
348.	ALF, SWPA, Adv. HQ. 9.12.1942	Blamey to Shedden. Letter.	Difficulties with operations in Papua.	376
349.	HQ, Adv. NGF. 11.12.1942	Herring to Blamey. Letter.	Features of fighting in Papua.	376
350.	HQ, Adv. NGF. 21.12.1942	Herring to Blamey. Letter.	Does not know if getting full value from air forces.	377

liv   List of Documents

Doc.	Place & Date	Document	Content	Page
351.	HQ, NGF 30.1.1943	Operations in NG. Brief for GOC NG Force.	Operations in the coastal area.	378
352.	Brisbane 16–20.1.1943	[Shedden's] Notes on discussions with C-in-C, SWPA.	MacArthur surprised by Churchill's apparent indifference to operations in NG	379
353.	Canberra 13.3.1944	Press Statement by Curtin.	Refutes Page's criticism regarding conduct of Papuan campaign.	379

24. New Guinea, January 1943-April 1944

Doc.	Place & Date	Document	Content	Page
354.	ALF, SWPA, Adv. HQ. 8.1.1943	Blamey to Herring. Letter.	Expects Japanese move against Wau.	381
355.	16.3.1944	Report on NG Operations, 23 January 1943 – 13 September 1943.	Enemy attack on Wau.	382
356.	Canberra 12.2.1943	Prime Minister's War Conference. Minute (74).	Operations in New Guinea.	383
357.	Not Dated [probably early 1944]	Report. Air Operations.	Battle of Bismarck Sea.	384
358.	Canberra 17.3.1944	Notes of [Curtin and Shedden's] discussions with C-in-C, SWPA.	MacArthur considered threat of invasion of Australia removed with defeat of Japanese in Battle of Bismarck Sea.	385
359.	HQ, NGF 9.8.1943	Herring to Blamey. Letter.	Progress report on Salamaua operation.	385
360.	16.3.1944	Report on NG Operations, 23 January 1943 – 13 September 1943.	Praise for Australian and US infantrymen.	386

List of Documents   lv

Doc.	Place & Date	Document	Content	Page
361.	Sydney 7.6.1943	Prime Minister's War Conference. Minute (80).	Future operations against Japan. MacArthur's response to Nimitz's desire for all operations in Pacific to be brought under his [Nimitz's] command.	387
362.	12.10.1944	Report on NG Operations, 4 September 1943 – 26 April 1944.	Blamey's concluding comments on NG campaign.	388

25. What Future Role for the Australian Army?

Doc.	Place & Date	Document	Content	Page
363.	Canberra 1.10.1943	War Cabinet Minute (3065).	Principles governing use of armed forces for remainder of the war.	390
364.	22.11.1943	Curtin to MacArthur. Letter.	Requests plans for use of Australian land forces.	391
365.	GHQ, SWPA 24.11.1943	MacArthur to Curtin. Letter.	Agrees to acquaint Curtin with proposed operational plans at their meeting.	392
366.	London 3.5.1944	Meeting of Prime Ministers. P.M.M. (44) 5th Meeting.	Statement of Australia's war aims.	392
367.	12.7.1944	MacArthur to Blamey. Minute.	Plans for use of Australian forces.	393
368.	Canberra 30.9.1944	Notes of discussions with the C-in-C, SWPA.	Employment of Australian forces in future operations.	394
369.	Melbourne 15.11.1944	Northcott to Shedden. Letter.	Australian forces available to C-in-C, SWPA for offensive operations.	395
370.	15.2.1945	Curtin to MacArthur. Letter.	Requests MacArthur's views on relation of strength of Australian forces to his plans in SWPA.	398
371.	GHQ, SWPA 5.3.1945	MacArthur to Curtin. Letter.	Contemplates use of all Australian forces assigned to SWPA.	399

26. The Mandate Campaigns

Doc.	Place & Date	Document	Content	Page
372.	Canberra 22.2.1945	R.G. Menzies' Speech in House of Representatives.	Critical of 'mopping-up operations' in Mandated territories.	401
373.	Canberra 26.4.1945	H.E. Holt's Speech in House of Representatives.	Critical of Mandate campaigns.	402
374.	Canberra 26.4.1945	T.W. White's Speech in House of Representatives.	Australian troops should be used in major offensive actions instead of in areas where nature would complete the victory.	402
375.	18.4.1945	Report by Fraser.	Criticism of operations in New Guinea.	403
376.	ALF, SWPA, HQ 18.5.1945	Blamey to Chifley. Letter.	Comments on Fraser's criticism.	404
377.	Canberra 17.4.1945	Curtin to MacArthur. Letter.	Contains points from a report by Blamey on Australian troops' equipment.	407
378.	19.4.1945	MacArthur to Curtin. Teleprinter Message BXC.72.	Feels equipment of Australian troops is sufficient.	409
379.	18.5.1945	Appreciation by Blamey.	Appreciation on operations of AMF in New Guinea, New Britain and Solomon Islands.	409
380.	31.7.1945	Beasley to Blamey. Letter.	War Cabinet's response to Blamey's appreciation.	411
381.	Melbourne 9.6.1945	Sinclair to Shedden. Teleprinter Message [Not Numbered].	Actions in Mandate campaigns.	412
382.	22.8.1945	*The Herald* [Melbourne].	Frederick Howard, 'Was Our War in Islands a Wasted Effort?'	414

Doc. Place & Date   *Document*   *Content*   *Page*

27. Borneo

Doc.	Place & Date	Document	Content	Page
383.	15.2.1945	Berryman to Blamey. Telegram B228.	Borneo operations to be commanded by US Eighth Army and not Allied Land Forces.	417
384.	ALF, SWPA, HQ 19.2.1945	Blamey to Shedden. Letter.	Expresses displeasure at command arrangements.	418
385.	27.2.1945	Curtin to MacArthur. Letter.	Australian forces serving outside Australia should be commanded by an Australian officer, and asks how this principle will be observed.	420
386.	5.3.1945	MacArthur to Curtin. Letter.	As assault troops include Australians, commander might be Australian.	420
387.	ALF, SWPA, HQ 5.4.1945	Blamey to Curtin. Letter.	Blamey questions MacArthur's plan for Borneo campaign.	421
388.	Melbourne 16.5.1945	Blamey to Fraser. Letter.	If Australian Military Forces' strength is to be reduced, suggests MacArthur be informed that 7th Division is not available for operations until overall plan is known.	422
389.	Canberra 18.5.1945	Chifley to MacArthur. Letter.	Conveys Blamey's advice regarding 7th Division.	424
390.	20.5.1945	MacArthur to Chifley. Teleprinter Message BXC 87.	Has committed 7th Division to Borneo campaign; requests immediate notification if Australian govt desires to withdraw Australian troops from campaign.	425

lviii   List of Documents

Doc.	Place & Date	Document	Content	Page
391.	20.5.1945	Chifley to MacArthur. Teleprinter Message CAB 213.	Australian govt agrees to employment of 7th Division as planned by MacArthur.	426
392.	Morotai 12.7.1945	Bostock to Forde. Letter.	Brief report on air operations involving Australian troops in Borneo campaign.	426

I The Distant War, 1939–1945

The struggle against Germany and Italy involved some acts of war quite close to Australia; but as the fighting, including that in which Australians participated, was overwhelmingly concentrated in theatres at the other end of the world, the 'distant war' seems an appropriate title.

We have selected seven problems for documentation in this part of the book. The first three deal with the formulation of policy guiding the use of each of Australia's three services under British command in the war against Germany and Italy. The fourth concerns various Australian worries about the deployment and equipment of its troops in the Middle East prior to their being committed to battle. There follows a sequence of documents devoted to the worst disaster suffered by Australian arms in the Middle East, the losses in Greece and Crete. The sixth incident, the invasion of Syria, was a military success. It is included because it also raised important issues concerning the role of the Australian government in determining how its forces were to be used. The seventh issue considered, the tussle between Canberra and London over the relief of the Australians besieged in Tobruk, shows an obdurate Australian leadership at work. Doubtless, this obduracy flowed in part from a belief that the Australian government had been too complaisant in previous dealings with London.

The decisions documented in this section led to a substantial Australian commitment to the war against Germany and Italy and the Vichy French in Syria. Nearly as many Australians died fighting against these enemies as in the war against Japan (about 9,300 compared with about 9,500). We have found room to include a few accounts of such fighting.

1
THE NAVY AND THE WAR AGAINST GERMANY AND ITALY, 1939–1941

The Royal Australian Navy from its inception in 1910 had been intended to operate with the Royal Navy. Detailed Admiralty advice attended its development and it had been commanded by a succession of British officers. At the outbreak of war its striking force consisted of two 8" and four 6" cruisers, seven aged destroyers and two sloops. Such ships were considered to be barely sufficient to provide protection for trade in Australian waters. Even to delay a Japanese attack in strength with them was acknowledged to be quite impossible.

On 7 November 1939, the Australian ships were formally handed over to the Admiralty and placed under its strategic control with a proviso that such action could be rescinded by Commonwealth order. Consequently, and with the exception of the 6" cruiser *Adelaide* which was considered too old to be of Admiralty use, the Australian ships were steamed hard escorting convoys and in augmenting British naval strength, principally in the Red Sea and Mediterranean. For the RAN the main Mediterranean phase of the war did not end until January 1942. By then the original destroyers had worn out and one of them, *Waterhen*, had been sunk. The sloop *Parramatta* was also lost and only twenty-four of her one hundred and sixty man crew were saved.

Even before war broke out, the Admiralty and the Australian naval staff had no doubts that RAN cruisers could be employed on Imperial duties without the formality of prior government approval. Without consulting the Menzies government, the Admiralty took control of the 6" cruiser *Perth*, which had been on transit to Australia via the Panama canal. An angry cabinet was prepared to insist that *Perth* at once be returned to Australian control. It took the Prime Minister's influence to allow the Admiralty's presumptive action to stand. But Menzies was not prepared to agree at once to the suggestion that a second cruiser should be allowed to leave Australian waters. We print the navy's reasons for its dispositions.

Document 1

Boucher [Acting Chief of Naval Staff] 29 August 1939
to Street [Minister for Defence]

Defence Department Minute Secret

I most strongly recommend that a 6" Cruiser should be despatched to the

Mediterranean in accordance with Admiralty request, for the following reasons:-

2. The world-wide disposition of all the Naval Forces of the Empire, in the event of war in Europe, includes the despatch of two cruisers from Australia, one to the West Indies and the other to the Mediterranean. These movements, together with those of all other Imperial and Dominion warships, have been worked out with great thought in peace time and are based on a co-ordinated plan. This plan is designed so that all the vital sea routes will have an adequate defence, and every Sea [sic] will have its appropriate naval protection. Ships disposed in accordance with the pre-arranged plan will, in fact, protect Australia more effectively than if retained in Australian waters, where an adequate force will still remain available.

3. If certain seas or areas are without their adequate defence, then there will be a gap in our organisation through which the enemy may thrust. Such action might cost Australia dearly. It is therefore of paramount importance to Australia that the carefully devised plans for the present situation should not be departed from.

4. Although the immediate problem is that of a European War, it has been approved for the Royal Australian Navy to make preparations for an Eastern War, in order to reach the maximum naval preparedness in shortest time. Should Eastern complications arise, a re-disposition of all Naval Forces will automatically follow, and the Australian 6" Cruisers should return forthwith to Australian waters; their pre-arranged station in an Eastern War. This stipulation should accompany the agreement, if given, to send a 6" cruiser to the War Station best suited for waging a European War (viz: the Mediterranean).

5. If threat of an Eastern War develops we should, in addition to the swift recall of our cruisers, certainly expect the British Government to strengthen the Naval Forces in Eastern and Pacific waters, in accordance with the prearranged plan. Any representations then made by Australia for the United Kingdom to accelerate the despatch of strong R.N. Forces will lose force if we are not now prepared completely to fall in with the strategic plans that have been so carefully laid.

6. Both the New Zealand Government and India have taken action to implement the pre-arranged plans by despatching H.M.S. "ACHILLES" [6" cruiser] to the America and West Indies Station and placing the Royal Indian Navy at the disposal of the Admiralty, respectively.

Minister said seen by PM and to be held for the present.
[AA: A 5954, Box 582]   FGS 31/8

On 8 September, the Dominions Office cabled suggestions as to the employment of Australian forces. We print the naval section of this cable together with Naval Board comments on the use of Australian ships.

Document 2

Shedden [Secretary, Department of Defence] to Boucher 19 September 1939

Dominions Office Cablegram 191 Most Secret
of 8th September, 1939

...

NAVY:

3."The following suggestions are based on the assumption that Japan will be neutral.

4. "H.M.A.S. Perth has already been under Admiralty orders and it would be appreciated if a second cruiser and 5 R.A.N. destroyers could also be lent for service other than on Australian station. So long as Japan remains neutral it is considered that Australian waters may be regarded as unlikely to suffer submarine attack.

5. "The most likely danger to be guarded against on Australian station under present circumstances is that of attack on shipping by armed raiders. It is considered that two cruisers and H.M.A.S. Australia (when ready) should prove adequate for this purpose. ...

7. "As regards naval personnel we should like to avail ourselves of the services of the following:-

    (a) trained naval reserves surplus to Australian requirements to be made available to the Royal Navy.

    (b) officers recruited from civil life, viz. trained civil pilots for service in the fleet air arm, and yachtsmen or ex-mercantile marine officers suitable for R.N.V.R. commissions.

    (c) telegraphists and signalmen, artificers of all kinds, scientists — electrical and w/t [wireless telegraphy] for signal school, and skilled electrical workmen, recruited from civil life.

It would be appreciated if Commonwealth Government could furnish approximate numbers of personnel likely to be immediately available under above categories, and could indicate capacity for increasing the numbers of trained personnel that will become available as the war progresses.

8. "It is presumed that Australia will take up and equip two local A.M.C.s [Armed Merchant Cruisers] in addition to three A.M.C.s now fitting out in Australia and that manning commitments for all these ships can be met locally.

9. "It is hoped that Commonwealth Government will be able to meet all requirements for D.E.M.S. [Defensively Equipped Merchant Ships] staffs at Australian posts and will assist in the provision of gun-layers (D.E.M.S.)

10."It is hoped that Australia will be able to meet requirements in mines and local defence equipment from local sources. It would be of further assistance if Australia could indicate whether she could meet any requirements of New Zealand and eastern parts of the Empire.

11. "We should be grateful if the possibility of increasing the facilities of

Cockatoo Island for building destroyers and escort vessels may be examined; and if building in private yards of whale catchers and trawlers for local defence may be considered. The extent of the requirements for trawlers is large and cannot yet be estimated."
[AA: A 5954, Box 582]

Document 3

Macandie [Secretary, Naval Board] to Shedden 26 September 1939

Minute *Most Secret*

 I am directed by the Naval Board to forward the following remarks on Dominions Office Cablegram No. 191 of 8th September, 1939:—
. . .
CRUISERS
On 29th August the Chief of the Naval Staff forwarded a minute to the Minister containing recommendations that a second cruiser should be despatched for service overseas.[1] The arguments set out in that paper (a copy of which is attached) still hold, and it is recommended that a second 6" cruiser (H.M.A.S. "HOBART" or "SYDNEY") should be made available forthwith for service where required. With two cruisers playing their part in the defence of the sea communications to and from Australia in distant waters, and the remaining cruisers employed in Australian waters, the best distribution of our available force is achieved.

DESTROYERS
The Naval Staff agree that so long as Japan remains neutral, it is unlikely that German submarines will be operating in Australian waters. Destroyers are the most effective weapon against submarines particularly when fitted with asdics, as are the Australian destroyers. It would therefore be a serious waste of effective anti-submarine facilities to retain these vessels in Australian waters when Australian trade is being attacked by submarines in distant waters.
 The "STUART" and four destroyers are in fact *on loan* from the Royal Navy. It is noted, however, that no reference to this aspect is made by the United Kingdom Government.
 In view of the foregoing, it is recommended that H.M.A.S. "STUART" and 4 destroyers should be made available for service overseas forthwith.
. . .
[AA: A 5954, Box 582]

---

1. See Document 1.

War Cabinet finally agreed to release a further 6" cruiser on 6 October. Moreover an Admiralty request was complied with to send a five destroyer flotilla to Singapore for 'intensive training'. Almost at once it was diverted to the Mediterranean. The two cruisers mentioned to Cabinet on 31 October were never to reach Australian waters, as Document 7 indicates.

Document 4

Cabinet Minute   Sydney, 31 October 1939

DESTROYERS OF THE AUSTRALIAN FLEET:
It was agreed that five destroyers be released to proceed to Europe for general purposes there and that, in return, Great Britain undertake to make available two cruisers for Australia, manned by British personnel; it was stated that such cruisers could leave for Australia next month.

In reply to enquiries whether the five destroyers could safely be released from Australian waters, Cabinet was informed by the Prime Minister and the Minister for Defence that the view of the Navy Board was that two cruisers would be of infinitely more value to Australia from the defence point of view than the five destroyers, and that the latter could more advantageously be used in countering submarine activity.
[AA: A 2697, Vol 3A]

Despite Admiralty and local Naval Board pressure, it is quite clear that Mr Menzies shared his government's early reluctance to send warships away from Australian waters even though it was necessary to escort the Second AIF to the Middle East. Not until German capital ships had been restricted to their home waters was the Australian government prepared to lift its embargo, early in 1940.

Document 5

Colvin [Chief of the Naval Staff]   15 December 1939
to Acting Minister for the Navy [Street?]

Memorandum

On the 11th December, I had an interview with the Prime Minister and explained the Naval Staff proposals for the escort to the first Australian Troop Convoy. These proposals were briefly that H.M.A.S ships "CANBERRA" and "AUSTRALIA", in addition to H.M.Ship "RAMILLIES", should escort the convoy through Australian waters and to

the limit of the Australia Station in the vicinity of the Cocos Islands.
2. The Prime Minister informed me of his objections and those of the War Cabinet to this proposal, and directed me to ask the Admiralty to provide an escort of two 8" cruisers from Fremantle onwards so that the Australian cruisers should not leave coastal waters.
3. The Admiralty have now directed two 8" cruisers (one British and one French) to escort the convoy from Fremantle. This leaves an important trade route temporarily unguarded.
4. The Prime Minister will be aware that I regretted the necessity for his decision though I recognize it was taken on political grounds which are outside my province, but since the decision has been taken the strategical situation has been altered and most agreeably improved by the successful action against the "VON SPEE".[2]
5. According to the latest intelligence, the two other pocket battleships are in Home Waters (they were sighted by a submarine on 13th December) and the possibility of raiding cruisers being at large is much reduced. In these circumstances, I would urge that the matter be now reconsidered and that my original proposal of our 8" cruisers escorting the convoy to the limits of the Australia Station be agreed to, the R.N. cruisers taking over from this point.
6. In connection with the convoy of the New Zealand troops, I have arranged for H.M.A.S. "CANBERRA", wearing the Flag of the Rear-Admiral Commanding, H.M.A. Squadron, to join the escort from New Zealand to Australia.
[AA: A 2671, 42/1939]

Britain gained the use of HMAS *Australia* in a somewhat similar fashion as she did the destroyers. The 'exchange' mentioned by Admiral Colvin never took place although *Australia* soon found herself at Scapa Flow as part of the Home Fleet. She was involved in the attempt to intercept *Gneisenau*,[3] in the Dakar operation, and in escorting Atlantic convoys. She arrived back in Fremantle on 17 December 1941.

---

2. Colvin is referring to the German pocket-battleship *Admiral Graf Spee* which, after suffering damage from hits scored by British cruisers on 13.12.1939, was scuttled in the estuary of the River Plate on 17.12.1939.

3. German battle-cruiser employed attacking merchant shipping in the Atlantic during 1941.

Document 6

War Cabinet Minute   Melbourne, 27 February 1940

(174) ... *Weekly Reports by the Chief of the Naval Staff*

. . .

(ii) *Exchange to H.M.A.S. "Australia" with Royal Navy.* The Chief of the Naval Staff pointed out that the 6-inch cruisers were obtaining war experience by service overseas and a similar course should be followed by exchanging H.M.A.S. "Australia" with an 8-inch cruiser of the Royal Navy.

The War Cabinet approved of the idea in principle and directed that the Naval Board should consult with the Admiralty and submit a recommendation to the Acting Minister for the Navy for submission to the War Cabinet. . . .

[AA: A 2673, Vol 2]

Two closely related events, Germany's successful attack upon the 'low countries' and France in May, and the Italian entry into the war on 10 June 1940, brought responses from both the Australian government and the Naval Board. One was to agree to provide more trained seamen for the Royal Navy, the other was to alter again the disposition of Australian ships along the lines of the following recommendations.

Document 7

Macandie to Cameron [Minister for the Navy]   17 May 1940

Minute

With reference to War Cabinet Minute No. 263 of 13th May, 1940, (Defence Co-ordination letter of 15th May), on the subject of the International Situation and Australia's War Effort, the Naval Board are closely examining the present Naval War Programme, with the object of ascertaining whether any acceleration is practicable, but do not anticipate that any material speeding up can be effected. The Board desire to make the following proposals designed to increase the Australian contribution to the Empire's Naval War measures:-

(i)   In view of the present situation and the more urgent need of Cruisers on Stations other than the Australia Station, that H.M. Ships "CERES" and "COLOMBO", now at Singapore, should not come to the Australia Station, but that Admiralty be informed that the Commonwealth Government are prepared for these Cruisers to be utilised elsewhere to the best advantage.

(ii) That the ten Local Defence Vessels now being constructed in Australia for the Admiralty should be manned by the R.A.N., in addition to the seven Local Defence Vessels on order for the Commonwealth Government.
(iii) That the Commonwealth Government should agree to the proposal put forward by the Admiralty that the personnel of H.M.A. Destroyers now in the Mediterranean should be made available, augmented as necessary, to man new Destroyers which are being built in the United Kingdom and will be ready towards the end of 1940.
(iv) That the Commonwealth Government should offer to continue to maintain the old Australian Destroyers, manned by R.A.N. personnel.
(v) That A/S (Anti-Submarine) officers and ratings should be entered and trained for service in the Royal Navy, in accordance with Admiralty's request, up to the maximum numbers possible having regard to the training facilities available.

2. The additional personnel made available for service overseas if the above proposals are approved, would be as under:-

(i)	R.N. complements of "CERES" and "COLOMBO" released from Australia Station	830
(ii)	Manning of ten Local Defence Vessels	600
(iii)	To augment crews of Australian Destroyers on turning over to new and larger vessels	100
(iv)	New crews for present Australian Destroyers	750
(v)	A/S officers and men — output for next twelve months	340
	Total additional personnel available overseas	2,620

3. A certain number of officers and senior ratings could not be provided from the R.A.N. immediately, but Admiralty would be asked to make up these deficiencies.
4. To give effect to the above proposals, it will be necessary immediately to provide additional temporary accommodation at Flinders Naval Depot for 200 men.
5. These proposals represent the maximum expansion in personnel which the Board consider to be practicable within the next 12 months.
[AA: A 2671, 112/1940]

Document 8

Colvin to War Cabinet   12 June 1940

Report

ITALIAN INTERVENTION — NAVAL DISPOSITIONS

1. From the Naval aspect, the new situation arising from the entry of Italy

into the war on the German side results in the addition of a large Navy to our enemies. The bulk of it is based in the Mediterranean, but destroyers, submarines and aircraft are based in the Red Sea area.

2. These forces will throw a large additional strain on the resources of the Allied Navies, particularly in the areas concerned. The threat in Australian waters is, however, affected little, if at all. Light surface forces have not the endurance to reach us, and submarines without "mother ships" could not operate effectively at such a distance from their bases. Armed raiders are possible, but this threat is not a major one.

3. On the other hand, the fight for the control of the Red Sea will be a difficult one, while areas such as the Persian Gulf and Mombasa are very liable to submarine attack. The Red Sea route must be opened as quickly as possible for the supply of reinforcements, etc. to Allied troops in the Near East.

4. It is therefore considered that we should render every possible help in our power to the Admiralty, and make available for their control and disposition to the best advantage any Naval forces available from the Australia Station. Some risks must be accepted, and those involved for Australian seaborne trade in subsequent proposals are considered to be acceptable.

PROPOSALS:
5.   *Retain on the Australia Station:*
    1 Cruiser in Eastern Australian waters — H.M.A.S. "PERTH"
    1 Cruiser in Western Australian waters — H.M.A.S. "ADELAIDE"
    1 Armed Merchant Cruiser in North Australian waters — H.M.A.S. "MANOORA"
    2 Sloops, including "WARREGO", soon to complete.
    2 Minesweepers — "DOOMBA" and "ORARA".
    Auxiliary minesweeping and anti-submarine vessels for local defence. Take up 3 further anti-submarine vessels for anti-submarine work in connection with convoys and training purposes.

    Make available to the Admiralty: (in addition to previously approved proposals)
At once:
    1 Armed Merchant Cruiser — H.M.A.S. "WESTRALIA"
    1 Sloop — "PARRAMATTA" (fitted with most up-to-date fire control arrangements)
About end July:
    1 Sloop — "YARRA" (on completion of her new fire control equipment).
[AA: A 2671, 136/1940]

On 25 November 1940, the Advisory War Council, on the suggestion of Mr Curtin, leader of the Opposition, directed the Naval Staff to reassess the deployment of Australian naval forces. It produced the following document which gave an overall account of the use made of RAN ships in the first fourteen months of war. We print most of it, because it is also a classic statement of Australia's wartime interdependence with Britain's naval strategy. Possibly one result of this reassessment was the return of *Sydney* and *Westralia* to the Australia station.

Document 9

Colvin to Hughes [Minister for the Navy]   Not Dated [c. 2 December 1940]

Memorandum   *Most Secret*

REFERENCE [ADVISORY] WAR COUNCIL
MINUTE No. 34 OF 25th NOVEMBER, 1940
REVIEW OF NAVAL DISPOSITIONS — NOVEMBER, 1940
GENERAL REVIEW.

Before any attempt is made to assess the Naval situation and problems on the Australia Station, it is essential to review the Empire's world-wide Naval responsibilities. Many factors have contributed towards making the Admiralty's problem much more difficult since the outbreak of war. The main ones are:-
(a) The defection of France and loss of French Naval forces.
(b) Occupation by Germany of coastline from Norway to Spain.
(c) Entry of Italy and consequent closing of through Mediterranean route.
(d) Big Naval liability in maintenance of men and supplies to our growing forces in the Middle East.
(e) The provision of Naval forces to guard against invasion of England.

These are some of the adverse factors which have increased the responsibilities of the Empire Naval forces almost to breaking point.

2. The first necessity in safeguarding our world-wide and Australian sea communications is that the main enemy Naval forces should be bottled up and contained by a superior force, and this requirement has to be met by allocating large sections of British naval forces to the North Sea and Mediterranean areas. Under cover of these arrangements, the remaining Empire naval forces have to be disposed so as to give the greatest degree of security possible to our far-flung sea communications against enemy raiding forces that manage to evade our main fleets. The dispositions to guard these trade routes are made on the following basis:-
(a) The most important trade routes containing the greatest amount of shipping must be given the greatest protection.
(b) Troop convoys must be given greater security than ordinary cargo vessels.
(c) Trade routes within reach of enemy submarines and shore based aircraft require provision of special protection.

(d) The distance of trade routes from enemy main bases influences the likely scale of attack on these trade routes and consequently the scale of defence required.

3. From the above it will be seen that the Atlantic trade routes, which carry a high percentage of U.K. imports and exports and which are vulnerable to heavy raiding attack and near the U.K. to large scale submarine and air attack, must be given the maximum protection possible. After the above, trade routes from U.K., India and Australia to the Middle East are the most important. After those, other ocean trade routes in the Southern Indian and Pacific Oceans have to be considered, including coastal trade in these oceans. ...

4. In spite of the utmost endeavour on the part of the Navy and the constant employment of our warships to a degree not contemplated before the war, the toll of merchant shipping lost by enemy action has increased steadily since the French defection in June and has now reached an alarming figure... The great majority of these losses have been suffered in the immediate vicinity of the U.K. from submarine and air attack. Next are losses in the Atlantic, Indian and Pacific Oceans in that order. Our dispositions and remedial measures must be based on these facts and on the overriding assumption that supplies and food to and from the United Kingdom are the most essential requirements for the waging of the war.

ENEMY NAVAL POLICY

5. The German naval policy may be summed up to date as:-
(a) Retention of a fleet in being in German waters to contain large units of the British Navy and act as a constant threat to vital U.K. communications.
(b) An intensive attack by submarine and aircraft on trade approaching and leaving the United Kingdom.
(c) Occasional break-outs of heavy ships for raiding in the Atlantic.
(d) Fitting out and despatch of merchant raiders for raiding in Atlantic, Indian and Pacific Oceans, including minelaying.

6. Regarding (c) and (d) above, this is a logical plan. Heavy ships have bigger prizes to raid in the Atlantic, and are more likely to be able to return safely from short raids in this area than further afield. Their maintenance in the Pacific or Indian Oceans, compared to that of armed and disguised merchant raiders, would be much more difficult.

7. German submarines have not operated at distances from their home bases greater than 2,000 to 3,000 miles, and the great difficulty in the maintenance of this class of vessel at considerable distances from proper bases, coupled with the wide dispersion of shipping in the Indian and Pacific Oceans, makes their use in these areas most unlikely.

8. Regarding Italian forces, our control of the eastern and western exits of the Mediterranean makes the use of their main forces outside this area very improbable. The few light forces remaining to the Italians of their Red Sea force are also unlikely to operate far from their Red Sea bases. ...

ENEMY POLICY REGARDING RAIDING AND MINELAYING IN THE INDIAN AND PACIFIC OCEANS.
Raiding.
12. In general, their policy has been to attack unescorted shipping on the trade routes well away from terminal ports and focal areas. By so doing, they avoid our naval forces guarding such areas and also air force reconnaissance and striking forces which are only able to operate for a limited distance from their aerodromes. Their policy has the grave disadvantage from the German point of view that our ships are scattered over wide expanses of ocean and difficult to find, and their victims are thus less frequent. They have endeavoured to meet this difficulty to some extent by the use of aircraft by raiding ship to locate and report our merchant ships.
Minelaying.
13. German mines have been laid in areas off the Cape of Good Hope, approaches to Auckland, and Bass Strait. These operations have probably been carried out by a German merchant vessel disguised as a neutral, although the possibility of neutral vessels, for example, Japanese, carrying out the operation cannot be entirely discounted. Mines can be laid at night, and the possibility of detection greatly decreased thereby. By a combination of disguise and laying at night, this type of attack is difficult to guard against.

AUSTRALIAN NAVAL COMMITMENTS.
14. Turning now to the Australia Station, the commitments for which the Navy, in co-operation with the other Services, is responsible are:-
   (a) The security of our territory.
   (b) The security of ports from attack by sea and air.
   (c) The security of shipping within the Station.
While the conflict is restricted to the present combatants, our territory is not threatened.
15. The naval responsibility may, therefore, be set out as follows:-
   (a) The protection of our ports from attack.
   (b) The protection of troop convoys within the Australia Station.
   (c) Protection of other shipping on the Australia Station.
16. Regarding (a) above, no such attack has been carried out to date in the Pacific or Indian Oceans. The fixed gun defences of our ports, in conjunction with air striking forces, constitute such a deterrent that attack by day can be practically ruled out and by night is considered most unlikely. The results that could be achieved by armed merchant raiders would be insignificant and the destruction of the raider very probable. With the forces at the disposal of the enemy and the opportunities for seriously damaging the British cause by attack on shipping, attack on Australian ports in the present situation is therefore considered to be a very unlikely contingency.
17. Regarding (b) above, Troop Convoys. In the next few months, these are anticipated to proceed from Australia to the Middle East at the rate of one every six weeks. In view of their great importance, a much higher measure of security has to be given them than ordinary shipping.
18. To maintain the Empire Air Training Scheme and small parties of

reinforcements for Naval and Army units abroad, it is necessary, apart from troop convoys, to send comparatively small parties of 100 to 200 in selected ships to Canada, Africa, the Middle East, and the U.K. Some additional precautions over ordinary shipping are necessary for these vessels.

19. Regarding (c) above, Other Shipping. This comprises a steady flow of overseas ships across the Indian and Pacific Oceans and coastal shipping around the Australian coast. The Australian naval responsibility is for the safety of the latter shipping and of the overseas shipping while it is on the Australia Station.

METHODS EMPLOYED IN PROTECTION OF SHIPPING.
Troop Convoys.
20. Troop convoys are escorted by cruiser forces and protection given by air forces while within flying distance of the coast. The strength of the escort varies according to intelligence, but it is emphasized that adequate escorts are always provided.

Other Shipping.
21. No ships have been lost due to raider action (not minelaying) within air striking distance of the Australian coast. Evasive routeing and dispersal of shipping across the Indian and Pacific Oceans is employed. Air and naval cover is given on the coast and within the focal areas. The problem of protection on the trade routes outside coastal and focal areas is largely outside Australian naval responsibility — the Admiralty are tackling this problem as they can make ships available for hunting, and the Naval Board propose carrying out patrols in trade routes outside air striking distance on the Australia Station, and in conjunction with New Zealand naval forces. This problem in the wide spaces of ocean is the principal trade defence one at the present time and is clearly one for co-operation between all Empire naval forces available.

22. It is stressed that the closest co-operation exists between naval and air operations, including Staffs using the same operations rooms.

PRESENT DISPOSITION OF AUSTRALIAN NAVAL FORCES.
23. ... It will be seen that we retain on the Australia Station the following forces:-
   3 Cruisers
   1 Armed Merchant Cruiser
   2 Sloops
   2 Fast Minesweepers
   7 Anti Submarine vessels
   15 Minesweepers
   1 Fleet Oiler
   3 Boom defence vessels
   Examination vessels at defended ports.
24. We have fitting out or building for the R.A.N., the following:-
   3 Tribal Class Destroyers

24 Australian minesweeping and Anti submarine vessels
4 Auxiliary Minesweepers.

25. The remaining forces are carrying out the following vital part in the Empire's naval war effort:-

H.M.A.S. "SYDNEY" and Destroyers —	Part of force holding Eastern Mediterranean and Suez Canal and co-operating with our Middle East Army.
H.M.A.S. "HOBART" and 2 Sloops —	Part of Red Sea Force keeping Red Sea route open against Italian light forces for passage of troop ships, equipment and supplies to Army in Middle East.
H.M.A.S. "WESTRALIA" (Armed Merchant Cruiser) —	Patrol in Indian Ocean on routes to Middle East.
H.M.A.S. "AUSTRALIA" —	Part of main Home Fleet containing German main forces. So stationed in view of her re-armament and modern high angle equipment, being on this account a most important unit in an area subject to attack by heavy German ships and aircraft.

25A. It should be noted that our naval forces work in close co-operation with naval forces on the adjacent stations — East Indies, China and New Zealand.

CONCLUSIONS.
26.(a) Naval dispositions must be on a world-wide plan and arranged to give heaviest protection where most required. The concentration of Empire naval forces in the North Sea and the Mediterranean has a vital bearing on the protection of Australian trade by containing the main enemy forces in these waters.
   (b) The Empire naval resources are strained to their utmost, and any reduction in strength in the main theatres may have disastrous results, not only there but on the scale of attack in Australian waters.
   (c) The mobility of naval forces makes it possible to reinforce any areas such as the Australia Station should the scale of attack increase there compared to elsewhere.
   (d) Our ability to hold and throw back the German and Italian attacks and destroy their naval forces must be a vital factor in the possibility of Japan joining issue in the Far East. As far as possible, therefore, we should throw all our resources into the present conflict.

(e) It is considered that the naval dispositions now in force adequately protect Australian trade and ports. If enemy attacks become more frequent in the Australian area, the dispositions may have to be adjusted.
(f) Fixed defences of ports and the R.A.A.F. act as a great deterrent to attacks on ports or shipping near our coasts, liberating naval forces to some extent for action on the trade routes.
(g) The building up of auxiliary units, patrol craft and the R.A.A.F., coupled with other protective measures, will have an increasing effect on our security against enemy minelaying activities.

PREPARATIONS REGARDING POSSIBLE WAR WITH JAPAN.

27. Co-ordinated plans embracing the Far East were recently discussed at the Singapore Conference.[4] Australian naval plans include the building up of bases at Darwin and Port Moresby and defences at Thursday Island. Plans were also discussed for co-operation with Dutch and American naval forces, should this be possible. The Admiralty have made plans for reinforcing naval forces in the Far East in this eventuality. Australian naval forces abroad will return to these waters in such emergency. It is not considered that our present war effort should be reduced in the main theatres by withdrawing ships at this stage to have them standing by against Japanese action, but the situation is always under close review.
[AA: A 2680, 10/1940]

The German raiders operating in the Indian Ocean and mentioned in the Naval Staff's memorandum were soon to appear in the Pacific. In December, the undefended phosphate island of Nauru was attacked. The five ships mentioned below were sunk and the shore installations were shelled.

Document 10

Memorandum for Hughes   9 December 1940

THE MINISTER FOR THE NAVY   *Secret*

Messages received from Nauru that number of vessels standing off and awaiting favourable weather to proceed alongside to load, indicate that enemy raider has shelled and destroyed some or all the vessels. One vessel at least known to have been set on fire. Vessel first seen on fire at 5 a.m. local time this morning, 8th December. Observers on shore did not then realise significance of fires. Heavy westerly weather was prevailing with low visibility. For a period nothing was visible from shore. Then at 3.30 p.m.

---

4. See Document 118.

local time visibility improved. At an estimated distance of 20 to 25 miles south of Nauru one burning vessel was sighted with another large vessel about one mile away. What was apparently shell fire was seen, and at 10 minutes past 4 burning vessel disappeared. The large vessel then made off at high speed in a south-easterly direction. The vessels which were known to be off the Island and which may have been destroyed are:
British Phosphate Commission Steamers "TRIADIC" 6,378 tons, and "TRIASTER" 6,032 tons.
Union Steamship Company steamer "KOMATA" 3,900 tons.
Norwegian Steamer "VINNI" 5,181 tons.
The British Phosphate Commission Steamer "TRIONA" 4,413 tons was due at Nauru to-day (Sunday), but no word has yet been heard of her.
Definitely known that "TRIADIC" was on fire. Fate of others uncertain.
[AA: A 5954, Box 531]

Admiral Colvin's explanation for these events is printed below. The raiders, however, returned to Nauru on 26 December, and Colvin found himself outlining his hopefully preventive action to a clearly concerned Advisory War Council.

Document 11

Colvin to Hughes   10 December 1940

Memorandum   *Secret*

IMPORTANT.
The following statement is for information, *but not for publication*.
. . .
3. Since the outbreak of war the position of shipping loading phosphates at Nauru and Ocean Islands has been a source of anxiety to the Naval Board. Situated near the equator these Islands are remote from Australia and very adjacent to the Japanese Mandated Islands. Furthermore they are undefended. A considerable volume of shipping is necessary to transport the phosphate products. There is no harbour for safe shelter in the vicinity of either Island and weather conditions frequently make loading impossible. Under these circumstances ships have to wait in the vicinity until weather improves. Depending on the length of the wait the number of ships in the vicinity increases and is liable to form a tempting target to an enemy raider. Some months ago to reduce this risk Naval Board issued instructions to the effect that movements of ships to these Islands were to be regulated so as to prevent large concentration there. Further, ships waiting in the vicinity were not to remain packed, but were to be well dispersed.
On Sunday, 8th December, there had been bad weather in the vicinity

for some time, and for this reason there were six ships in the area waiting to load. From the information available from Nauru it would appear that one of these ships has certainly been attacked and probably sunk. It is assumed that the remainder have dispersed and made for shelter as directed either to Port Moresby or Fiji. No wireless signals from them have been received and this is a hopeful sign in that they would only break wireless silence if being attacked.

4. It is probable that we shall not get reliable information on all these ships until about Friday, 13th December, when those that escaped should have reached Port Moresby or Fiji.

Proposed Action:

In view of the importance of trade to Australia and New Zealand, sufficient protection must be given to the Islands and the route to enable this trade to continue. As the trade concerns Australia and New Zealand equally, arrangements are being made between Naval Board and New Zealand Naval Board for an armed merchant cruiser to be made available in the vicinity in the immediate future. Sailings which have been temporarily suspended will be resumed as soon as detailed movements of this armed merchant cruiser can be arranged. Regarding longer range plans the Defence Committee are investigating the possibility of installing guns and possibly aircraft to assist local defence and defence of shipping against raider attack. In the event of war with Japan it might be impossible to hold these outlying Islands.

...

[AA: A 5954, Box 531]

Document 12

Macandie to Strahan, Shedden and Hodgson[5]   28 December 1940

Teleprinter Message D.1020   *Secret*

The following message timed 0900 G.M.T. 27th December, has been received from the Administrator, Nauru:-

My 2110 G.M.T. December 26th Raider named NANYO MARU arrived off Island before daylight and using morse lamp at 0550 local time signalled "NAURU" (repeated several times) do not use your wireless or I will shoot the mast down I am going to shoot the Phosphate loading jetties. This signal was complied with to save destruction human life and property. Raider opened fire at 0640 local time and shelled at close range cantilever loading jetty, all oil storage tanks, cantilever shore storage bin mooring gear store and other Phosphate buildings. Using pompoms destroyed mooring buoys.

---

5. F. Strahan, Secretary to the Prime Minister's Dept, 11.11.1935 — 24.8.1949; W.R. Hodgson, Secretary to the Dept of External Affairs, 19.11.1935 — 21.6.1945.

Various portions of shell found indicate 5.9 inch used. Oil fuel still burning. Wireless Station intact. Power Station intact except for shell splinters causing negligible damage. Private houses were not fired on. Raider had marks on sides of hull and flew Nazi flag at Gaff... .
[AA: A 5954, Box 531]

Document 13

Advisory War Council Minute   Melbourne, 9 January 1941

(83) *ENEMY RAIDERS AND DISPOSITION OF THE R.A.N.*

(The Chief of the Naval Staff [Colvin] was present for the discussion of this subject).

In view of the recent sinking of vessels in the Pacific Ocean by enemy raiders, particularly in the region of Nauru, and the bombardment of Nauru, the Chief of the Naval Staff explained the precautions taken in connection with the movements of the ships of the phosphate fleet to avoid too great a concentration at Nauru during loading, which is frequently interrupted by weather conditions. In the opinion of the Chief of the Naval Staff the recent sinkings had apparently been due to the leakage of information, and endeavours were being made to stop the possibility of leakages and to protect this trade by special measures. An armed merchantman had been sent to this area and a hunt for the raiders would be made shortly, when a cruiser became available. The Air Force was also co-operating, and on the arrival of the P.B.Y. [Catalina] flying boats the location of an additional squadron in the Islands would assist the protection of this area.

The Chief of the Naval Staff stated that information received indicated that the raiders had used an island in the Marshall Group for replenishing their supplies from a supply ship, the latter having come from Japan. In regard to the bombardment of the island, nothing could have been done to prevent it, as it occurred before it was possible to despatch a ship to this region.

Mr. Beasley[6] raised the question of better liaison between the Intelligence Sections of the Services and the civil police regarding illicit wireless stations. He also drew attention to the practice of Japanese merchant ships berthing in Australian ports at places near points of embarkation of troops. The Minister for the Navy had stated that 90% of the strength of the R.A.N. was in Australian waters, but the Minister here interpolated that, to be correct, the words "or convoying Australian troops" should be added.

The Minister for the Navy ... had no doubt of the existence of enemy agents in Australia, but pointed out that information regarding cargo being

---

6. J.A. Beasley, MHR 1928–46, at this time an ALP representative in the Advisory War Council.

loaded on to vessels and their destination is readily ascertainable through the large number of people working on wharves. This information might then be communicated to enemy sources by various means, though every endeavour to prevent it occurring in Australia was made.

The Chief of the Naval Staff stated that the Postmaster-General's Department was co-operating actively in the tracing of illicit wireless stations, and a number had been discovered. In all cases they had been amateurs, and not enemy aliens. The greatest risk was from neutral vessels which, as soon as they were outside the coastal wireless zone, could communicate information of movements of ships ascertained by them prior to departure. In answer to Mr. Beasley, the Chief of the Naval Staff stated that the routes of ships were constantly varied, and codes regularly changed. The radio stations owned by Jehovah's Witnesses had been suppressed.

Mr. Beasley emphasized the need for strengthening the Intelligence Sections of the Services, and the Minister for the Navy said that he would consider this.

[AA: A 2682, Vol I]

The government had been told by Admiral Colvin as early as February 1941 that he wanted to retire from his position as Chief of the Naval Staff and First Naval Member of the Naval Board. This retirement took effect in July and the Prime Minister expressed his appreciation of Admiral Colvin to War Cabinet. Another British officer, Admiral Sir Guy Royle, replaced Colvin in July and held the position until 1945.

Document 14

War Cabinet Minute Melbourne, 10 July 1941

(1194) *VALEDICTORY TO ADMIRAL SIR RAGNAR COLVIN, K.B.E., C.B.*

As this was the last occasion on which Admiral Sir Ragnar Colvin would be attending War Cabinet prior to relinquishing the post of First Naval Member, the Prime Minister expressed the appreciation of himself and the Government of Admiral Colvin's services to the Royal Australian Navy. He said that Admiral Colvin's rich and varied experience in Naval matters had been valued greatly by War Cabinet, particularly his wise views on strategy, which had always been expressed with the greatest frankness. He referred to Admiral Colvin's advice early in the war regarding the despatch of Australian cruisers and destroyers to the Mediterranean. This might have seemed a dispersion of our Naval strength, but the war had demonstrated the extreme mobility of Naval forces. As a result, the Royal Australian Navy had contributed to the Empire's Naval effort in a way which would not otherwise have been effected had the ships been retained in Australian waters solely for local defence.

Admiral Colvin, in reply, expressed his thanks to the Prime Minister and War Cabinet for the sentiments which had been conveyed. He said that the despatch of our ships overseas had been of the greatest benefit to the Royal Australian Navy. Australia now had a "made" Navy which had proved itself in the sternest of all tests. Every ship of size in the R.A.N. had used its guns in action. He added that "man for man and ship for ship Australia had a Navy second to none in the world."
[AA: A 2673, Vol 7]

Admiral Colvin's claim that the Australian naval contribution to the 'distant war' had *made* the RAN might, to some, appear open to question. On 19 November 1941, there occurred the strange and tragic incident of the encounter of *Sydney* with the German raider *Kormoran*. Although the mystery of *Sydney*'s final hours has not been solved, it is clear that her captain was unwise to go so close to a suspected enemy.

Document 15

Teleprinter Message D.3265   30 November 1941

Secret

FOR TRANSMISSION TO HIS EXCELLENCY THE GOVERNOR GENERAL AND THE PRIME MINISTER. FOLLOWING IS REPORT OF SATURDAYS SEARCHES
(BEGINS)
THE NAVAL BOARD REGRET THAT AFTER INTENSIVE AIR AND SURFACE SEARCH OF THE AREA NO (NO) EVIDENCE OF H.M.A.S. "SYDNEY" HAS BEEN ... SIGHTED EXCEPT TWO R.A.N. ... LIFEBELTS AND ONE CARLEY FLOAT BADLY DAMAGED BY GUNFIRE.
IT IS CONCLUDED THAT "SYDNEY" SANK AFTER THE ACTION AND FURTHER SEARCH HAS BEEN ABANDONED.
[AA: A 1608, S/51/1/6]

Document 16

War Cabinet Minute   Melbourne, 4 December 1941

(1528) ...

(iii) *H.M.A.S. "Sydney" — Action with German Raider:* (previous reference — Minute No. (1526)). The Acting Chief of the Naval Staff [Durnford] reported the results of further interrogation of German prisoners ex the "Kormoran" and read the following reconstructed account of the action:-

"The engagement took place in position 25° South 111° East on 19th November. H.M.A.S. "Sydney" on a bearing S.W. from the raider, made the first sighting at a range of 15 miles. The raider altered course from 000° to 250° and made no reply. At closer range the raider, which was flying the Dutch flag, made "Straa[t] Malakka" by light.

"At 1650H the ships were on a parallel course, speed 15 knots. "Sydney" which was abaft the raider's beam, distance less than two miles, was at action stations and made 'Make your signal letters'. "Steirmark" immediately opened fire with guns and torpedoes, her first salvo hitting "Sydney's" bridge and starting a fire forward. "Sydney" opened fire simultaneously but her first salvo was over. Early in the action the cruiser was hit by a torpedo under A turret, resulting in A and B turrets being jammed. "Sydney's" torpedo tubes were hit by a further salvo, and a bad fire was started resulting in the destruction of her aircraft.

"The action was broken off after about half an hour and "Sydney", burning fiercely and down by the bows, proceeded at 5 knots. The raider, which had received a vital hit, was now on fire amidships, with her engine room out of action. At about 1815H the raider's crew abandoned ship, and at midnight the vessel, which was scuttled, blew up.

"It is believed that "Sydney" sank at 2300H/19."

In regard to the possibility of a second German ship being present at the action, the Acting Chief of the Naval Staff stated that, in the light of investigations which had been made, the Naval authorities did not accept this view. ...
[AA: A 2673, Vol 9]

A detailed account of the movements and operations of the Australian cruisers, destroyers and sloops employed in the 'distant war' is given in the official naval histories. Suffice here to argue that they were fought hard and enjoyed some success. *Australia* had twice been hit. *Perth* had been damaged during the evacuation of Crete and had been replaced by *Hobart*. The destroyer *Waterhen* and the sloop *Parramatta* had been sunk off the North African coast. Few cruisers could have spent more time at sea than did *Canberra*. By the time she returned to Australia she had steamed 152,966 miles largely in Imperial service. *Sydney* herself, before her fateful encounter, had covered 33,020 miles mostly in the Mediterranean, sinking an Italian destroyer and the cruiser *Bartolomeo Colleoni*. By 8 December 1941, however, it was those ships which had survived the war against Germany and Italy which now had to meet the new threat presented by the superbly efficient Japanese navy. They were to do somewhat less well.

2
THE DECISION TO RAISE AND DESPATCH THE SECOND AIF

To organise the transfer of naval fighting units to Admiralty control was reasonably simple. The ships existed and were crewed by regular trained seamen. Pre-war plans for deployment had been worked out. To employ an Australian land force would, however, take time. At the beginning of 1939 the army consisted of 2,795 regular soldiers backed by 42,895 poorly equipped militiamen who had only eighteen days training a year. Yet the precedent of providing expeditionary forces to fulfill Imperial aims had been set in 1885 and reinforced in the Boer War. In the 1914–18 war Australia had supplied troops for the Middle East and five infantry divisions on the western front. Between the wars, although shy always of making a definite commitment that similar action would be followed in future, Australian governments did not discourage the expectation that it would. In 1934, Sir Maurice Hankey, Secretary of the powerful British Committee of Imperial Defence raised such a point during his visit to Australia. The Dominions Office cable of 8 September 1939 was more explicit.

Document 17

REPORT BY SIR MAURICE HANKEY,   November 1934
SECRETARY TO THE COMMITTEE OF IMPERIAL DEFENCE,
ON CERTAIN ASPECTS OF AUSTRALIAN DEFENCE.

Another reason for concentrating the expenditure available for the army on efficiency and more rapid mobilisation rather than size is that the circumstances of a major war may be such that the defence of Australia's interests may be found to lie outside of Australia altogether. For example, the communications of the Navy, which is the first line of Australia's defence, require to be safeguarded by land and air forces, not only at the bases and fuelling stations of the fleet, but also at the Suez Canal and possibly elsewhere. This is normally the responsibility of the United Kingdom, but the military and air resources of the mother country are very small in comparison with the military commitments that might arise in a major war. It is quite conceivable that an Australian Government might deem it wise and necessary, in order to defend the interests of the Commonwealth to send troops abroad... For this purpose an efficient and reasonably ready force is far more likely to be obtainable by concentrating the available expenditure over a smaller field. It is not a question of Australia's accepting any new commitment, but merely of having a force which the Government of the Commonwealth can send

overseas in an emergency if and when they decide that this is necessary to defend Australian interests. ...
[AA: A 5954, Box 582]

Document 18

Eden [Secretary of State, Dominion Affairs] to Whiskard [UK High Commissioner]   London, 8 September 1939

Cablegram 191   *Most Secret*

. . .
ARMY
12. Recommendations are based on two alternative hypotheses:-
(a) that Japan is not only neutral but adopting a friendly attitude towards the democratic countries.
(b) that Japan is neutral and reserving her attitude towards democratic countries.
13. Under hypotheses (a) while hoping that war may be of short duration we must prepare for a long war that will call for employment of all our resources. We therefore hope that Australia will exert her full national effort including preparation of her forces with a view to the despatch of an expeditionary force. It is not at present possible to make any suggestion to the Commonwealth Government as to the destination and composition of any expeditionary forces which they may see fit to provide.
14. The Commonwealth Government may like to consider whether they would prefer to relieve United Kingdom units and formations in, say, Singapore, Burma and India as and when brigades become available or whether they would prefer to delay despatch of suitable formations until complete divisions can be made available for a main theatre of war. ...
16. Under hypothesis (b), it might be thought unwise for Australia to despatch an expeditionary force oversea but the Commonwealth Government can assist by holding ready formations at short notice for reinforcement of Singapore, New Zealand, or British and French Islands in the Western Pacific. ...
[AA: A 981, Defence 59, Part I]

> Professional military advice in Australia urged a degree of caution. We print the Military Board reactions to the British suggestions, statements made by Menzies in a national broadcast on 15 September, and some careful reasoning provided by the Inspector-General and acting Chief of the General Staff, Lt-General E.K. Squires.

Document 19

Military Board[7] Report Melbourne, 13 September 1939

THE RAISING OF A SPECIAL FORCE FOR CONTINUOUS   Secret
SERVICE EITHER IN AUSTRALIA OR OVERSEAS.

1. In submitting its report the Military Board desires to re-affirm the view expressed in its memorandum of the 9th September, 1939, namely that in the present situation our military effort must primarily be directed towards meeting the requirements of home defence.

When it has been provided with its essential armament and equipment, and allowing for its expansion on mobilization, the Militia as now constituted and organized will be no stronger than is necessary for the defence of Australia against probable forms of attack.

The Board therefore recommended the adoption of those measures which it considered were best designed progressively to raise the standard of efficiency of the whole of the existing Militia Forces.

But, as the Board pointed out, those measures would in themselves contribute to the smooth and rapid raising of a special force for overseas, should the need arise.

If it be decided to raise such a force at once, the necessary steps can be put in hand. But its immediate creation simultaneously with the proposed Militia training will mean dispersion of effort and resources, at a time when concentration of both would appear essential — it will mean depriving the existing units of some of their best officers and men at a time when their services are most needed — it will mean also that the existing units will have much less equipment to train with — and, *so far as home defence is concerned*, there will be no equivalent gain to set against these disadvantages, since the new special formations and units, even when trained, will not be capable of fully effective operation as they will be without light machine guns, mortars, technical instruments and many other items of essential equipment, except in-so-far-as they might be equipped at the expense of the existing Militia.

The new special units could, of course — when trained — be sent overseas, partially equipped, the balance of their armament to be completed on arrival. The Military Board doubts however whether the possible advantage of being able to do this at a rather earlier date is sufficiently great to justify, at this juncture, the adoption of a measure which might prejudice the safety

---

7. Members of the Military Board were:- G.A. Street (Minister for Defence and the President), Maj-Gen J.D. Lavarack (Chief of the General Staff), Maj-Gen Sir C.H. Jess (Adjutant-General), Maj-Gen O.F. Phillips (Quartermaster-General and Master-General of Ordnance), J.T. Fitzgerald (Finance Member), and C.B. Laffan (Secretary).

of Australia. From the military point of view, they would advocate immediate concentration of effort and resources in personnel and material — insufficient as they are for even our most urgent needs — on the measures already recommended, and the postponement of the actual formation of the special force until the whole of the Militia have done at least one month's continuous camp training, and more equipment and other material is available.

The Board suggests, therefore, that if the Government decide to raise this force, the preliminary steps for its formation should be put in hand as quickly as is possible without delaying or hampering the proposed training of the Militia — that the selection and enlistment of the personnel (other than those drawn from the Militia)... should begin in about a month's time — that these men should be given a month's or six weeks' preliminary training — and that the force should be assembled into complete units and, where practicable, into formations, about the beginning of December, by which time all its members will have done some continuous camp training.

Should a sudden demand arise, in the meantime, for an overseas force, it could be met by volunteers from the Militia, and ex-Militiamen.

An alternative to this would be to start raising the special force at once, and to defer the proposed training of the Militia in its 50 per cent. quotas. The Board cannot advocate this, since it would not fulfil what should be our immediate object, i.e. to provide for the security of Australia as quickly as possible. ...

Conclusion

9. The Military Board considers that the creation of a special force, for continuous service in Australia or overseas, should be accepted as part of our present military policy, and as a contribution to Empire defence.

Our immediate effort, however, should be directed to ensuring the safety of Australia, and, with this end in view, the continuous training of the Militia, in 50 per cent quotas, should now be initiated.

Simultaneously, preliminary steps should be taken for raising a special force of one division and one cavalry brigade, with the object of starting its training, in units, as early as possible without prejudicing the training of the Militia.

The Military Board does not consider that a smaller force would be an appropriate initial contribution for Australia to make to the forces of the Empire overseas.

[AA: A 2671, 6/1939]

Document 20

Prime Minister Menzies   15 September 1939

National Broadcast

...

SPECIAL FORCE OF 20,000.

"Let me state right away our decisions — of which our military experts approve. *We propose to enlist forthwith an Infantry Division with its ancillary units, or a total of approximately 20,000 men. This Force will be specially enlisted for service at home or abroad, as circumstances may permit or require.* It will be enlisted for continuous service for the duration of the war and twelve months thereafter, or until its members have been lawfully discharged.

"As in the case of the A.I.F., there will be one Brigade Group raised in New South Wales, one in Victoria, and the remainder will be distributed between the other States. The Divisional Commander, the Brigade Commanders and Battalion Commanders — in fact, all commanding officers — will be provided by our Militia forces. ...

"I said just now that this Force will be enlisted for service at home or abroad. I am sure that you will at once appreciate the reason for this. We are at war as part of the British Empire. Our strategic position may very well change from time to time, according to the alignment of the combatant nations. At present the prime necessity is to ensure the defence of Australia itself. But it would be wrong to assume that throughout the duration of the war our duty would continue to be as circumscribed as that.

"The international position will have to be watched very closely from day to day; ... It may be that under some circumstances Australian forces might be used to garrison some of the Pacific Islands, to co-operate with New Zealand, to relieve British troops at Singapore, or at other posts around the Indian Ocean. Under other circumstances, it might be practicable to send Australian forces to Europe. ...

"One of the real tasks of the Government will be to do nothing which will diminish the security of Australia itself, while, at the same time, enabling Australia to play its part in the security of the Empire as a whole. In one sentence — our aim will be to make our most effective contribution at the most effective time and in the most effective place. ...

"As for the ordinary Militia — which today stands at a total of just under 80,000 — we propose to call up the whole of this Force in two drafts, each to receive a month's continuous camp training so that, in addition to the special and continuously trained army of 20,000 men, we will have this much larger force of Militia, whose training will, at the end of another two months, have reached a higher degree of efficiency than would normally be produced by two or three years of Militia work. At the end of two months, the militia position will again be reviewed, though our plans for the future have already been provisionally made for the various contingencies that might arise. ...

"Finally, may I say this to you? If you are to get the best out of your

government at a time like this, trust it. Our task is not easy: it is made no easier by carping criticism, or the assumption that we don't know our duty and the duty of Australia. There are in the present Cabinet no less than eight Ministers who served in the last war; we have the best available information and advice; our decisions on all these matters represent and have represented the deliberate view of the whole Cabinet. We will do our best, and we are confident of success because we feel that the Australian people are united on all the things that matter, and that they are prepared to see it through.["]
[AA: A 981, Defence 59, Part I]

Document 21

Squires to Shedden   Melbourne, 21 September 1939

Memorandum   *Most Secret*

With reference to the "Army" section of Dominions Office Cablegram No. 191 of 8th September, 1939; as directed by the Minister, I submit my observations on the various points raised therein.
1.- The United Kingdom recommendations are based on two hypotheses:-
(a) a benevolently neutral Japan.
(b) Japan neutral, but reserving her attitude towards the democratic countries.
A third hypothesis, namely a hostile Japan, is not mentioned.
While authoritative information about Japan's activities is so meagre, it is not possible to draw any really useful conclusions as to her future attitude towards the war in Europe or the Powers engaged therein. But in view of her known aspirations in the Pacific, it would be unsafe, for the present, to assume a more favourable situation than that outlined in hypothesis (b). And it would be unwise — in default of assurances to the contrary — to assume that Japan would not, at some future date, when the democratic Powers are deeply committed in other theatres, take advantage of their difficulties to further her own designs in the Pacific.
2.- This raises the whole question of the "scale of attack and defence" that is to be adopted as the basis of Australia's defence policy and preparations.
This question is, it is understood, to be considered by the War Cabinet in the near future, and is a matter in which all three Services are concerned. It is not proposed, therefore, to discuss it at length here, but merely to examine the specific recommendations and suggestions of the Home Government in relation to Australia's Army preparations.
Taking hypothesis (b) first.
3.- It is agreed that, while Japan's attitude is doubtful, it would be unwise to despatch oversea an expeditionary force of any great size.
As regards the suggested reinforcements for Singapore, New Zealand or the Pacific Islands, it should be possible, by the end of December, to supply battalions of the Special Force singly, or in brigades — only partially trained,

it is true, but capable of operating defensively in co-operation with better trained troops; while composite battalions or smaller units, (e.g. for the Islands) at least equally well trained, could be provided by the end of November from volunteers from the Militia, without seriously impairing the defence of Australia.

4.- While this is true of the troops themselves, it does not apply to their armament and equipment. Until the situation in regard to war material is improved, we can spare, from Australia, little more than the soldier's individual weapons, i.e. rifles and bayonets, and transport, either horsed or M.T. [Mechanical Transport]. Any armament and equipment that was needed other than this would have to be provided from elsewhere.

As regards hypothesis (a).

5.- By the 1st November, when the special division is to be assembled in brigade-groups, all its members will have done at least some preliminary training, while those drawn from the Militia or from ex-military service men, may have done a considerable amount of previous training.

It is not to be anticipated that the Division would be capable of operating effectively, as a formation, before April or May 1940; but — as suggested in para. 3 above, under hypothesis (b) — brigades could be sent overseas earlier, to relieve United Kingdom regular units in Singapore, Burma or India, (as was done with units of the United Kingdom Territorial Army in 1914), on the understanding that they were only partially trained, and would continue their training on arrival.

6.- A real objection to this proposal, from the Australian point of view, is that it might mean that the Australian troops would be relegated, for an indefinite time, to "peace" garrison duties. Were this to happen, it would be most unpopular, both with the troops themselves and throughout Australia, and would certainly be regarded as a breach of faith. While, therefore, the provision of Australian units to relieve United Kingdom units abroad, at an early stage of the war might, under this hypothesis, constitute a useful contribution to Empire defence, it is considered that a clear stipulation would be necessary that the Australian troops would not be indefinitely retained on such duties, but would be released therefrom, when fully trained, and re-assembled with the remainder of the division to participate in the war.

7.- Though the need for retaining our available armament and equipment in Australia would not be so necessary, from the point of home defence, under this hypothesis as it would be under hypothesis (b), we could still not afford to equip fully any formations sent overseas. Moreover, much of their (Australian) equipment would not be up to modern standards.

It would still be necessary, therefore, for any units or formations sent overseas to be supplied with a large proportion of their war equipment on arrival.

A hostile Japan.

8.- Under the third hypothesis mentioned in para. 1, i.e. a hostile Japan, there could be no question of sending troops out of Australia except possibly for the purpose of reinforcing the United Kingdom garrisons in the Far East, or New Zealand, or of providing garrisons for some of the Pacific Islands; and the possibility and advisabilty of doing even this would depend on the degree to which Australian territory was directly threatened. Every man and every weapon might be needed for home defence.

It is considered, therefore, that no undertaking should be given to despatch troops outside Australia in the event of Japan being hostile.
Australia's full national effort.
9.- It has been suggested that the maximum force which Australia could maintain through a long war overseas is 2 Cavalry Divisions and 5 Divisions — or their equivalent — with the appropriate non-divisional and L. of C. [Lines of Communication] units.

With the creation of the special division we shall have in Australia rather more than the equivalent of 2 Cavalry Divisions and 6 Divisions. Though this is in excess of the estimated maximum referred to above, it cannot be recommended that, under existing conditions, and in view of possible commitments under hypothesis (b), any reduction should be made in the organization of the Militia. This would become practicable only with the realization of hypothesis (a), combined with the necessity for providing and maintaining a large expeditionary force.

On the other hand, it might well be necessary, if it appeared that the situation envisaged in the third hypothesis was developing, to increase the size of the home defence forces up to the maximum that could be armed, however inadequate their armament might be by modern standards.

10.- For the present, while it is not considered necessary to mobilize the whole Militia forces (which would mean, roughly doubling their present strength), it is strongly recommended that the units of the fighting arms — light horse, artillery, engineers, signals and infantry — be brought up to, approximately, their war establishments as soon as possible. This will mean an increase of some 15,000 to 20,000 men.

Until this, and more, is done, it cannot be said that a real national effort is being made; nor is adequate preparation being made for potential requirements under hypothesis (b).

A real national effort must include also the further training of the Militia, for longer periods, after the first two months' continuous training in 50 per cent quotas.

11.- It is not proposed here to discuss in any detail the possible methods — for future adoption — of maintaining or increasing the strength of the Militia (beyond the increase advocated in para. 9 above), and/or increasing the size of the continuous service force, except to make one recommendation — which it is desired to press strongly: namely that — after the establishment of the first division — further recruitment for the Special Force should, with very few exceptions, be by way of the Militia.

This system will, it is considered, most effectively meet the requirements both of home defence and of the provision of any oversea forces which Australia may furnish. ...
[AA: A 5954, Box 582]

The 'special division' would be named the 6th Division and it was decided that the force would have the generic title '2nd AIF' largely because it was envisaged by the Military Board that more than one division would eventually be sent overseas. In November R.G. Casey, then Minister for Supply and Development, led a delegation which included Major General John Northcott [Deputy Chief of Australian General Staff] to London. High on the agenda for discussion was how and when this force might be used. Quickly, it seems, Casey was converted to the idea that two Australian divisions should be made available.

Document 22

VISIT OF MINISTERS FROM DOMINIONS AND OF A REPRESENTATIVE FROM INDIA.

London, 13 November 1939

Secret

AGREED CONCLUSIONS OF DISCUSSIONS BETWEEN OFFICIALS, HELD AT THE WAR OFFICE ON THE 3rd NOVEMBER, 1939

Subject to approval by the Australian Government of any matters of policy involved, the following conclusions were agreed upon at a meeting held at the War Office on 3rd November, 1939, and attended by Australian Military Representatives.

1. *The despatch overseas of Australian military forces.*

A force to be known as the 2nd A.I.F. was being made ready for service overseas. Its despatch would depend on a decision by the Australian Government — the foremost consideration being the Japanese situation. Further forces might subsequently be available.

2. *Composition of the Force.*

The force would consist of the 6th Division, and certain Corps troops, namely:-

Army Field Brigade
Corps Signals
Two General Hospitals
Casualty Clearing Station
Convalescent Depot
Army Field Workshop
Six Light Aid Detachments
Section of an Ordnance Field Park
The nucleus of a H.Q. of an Overseas Base
A General Base Depot.

A medium brigade of two or three batteries of 6-inch howitzers might also be raised and made ready for despatch.

3. *Organisation.*

The organisation of units would, generally speaking, be the same as in the British Army, but infantry brigades would consist of four mixed battalions each. The divisional artillery was now being organised on a regimental basis.

4. *Destination.*

The destination of the 2nd A.I.F. should, in the first place, be the Middle East, where it would complete its training.

5. *Employment.*

The force should not be used piece-meal on garrison duties, but should be kept as a definite formation for training, and subsequently in action.

6. *Dates of despatch.*

On the assumption that circumstances would permit, and that the Australian Government would give the necessary authority, the force could sail as follows:-

Divisional Headquarters and the First Brigade Group — first week in December.

Second Brigade Group at the same time, or immediately after.

Remainder of the Division — early in January.

The above dates were provisional.

7. *Equipment*

The force could be equipped in Australia with the following:-

Rifles, Lewis and Vickers guns, 18-pdrs., 4.5-inch Howitzers, mechanical transport (light trucks and 30 cwts, provided shipping is available) 6-inch Howitzers (if the medium Brigade were formed).

Anti-tank guns were not available in Australia, and information was not available as to anti-gas stores.

8. *Training*

The training of instructors should take place at courses to be held as soon as possible in Egypt.

[AA: A 5954, Box 582]

Document 23

Northcott to Squires [via Casey] London, 6 November 1939

Cablegram C.7 *Most Secret*

. . .

1. Numerical superiority of Germans on the Western Front may be approximately 2 to 1 against the Allies. Imperative that maximum effort should be made by Great Britain to ensure security of this area. A defeat of France would be a disaster of the first magnitude. Critical period estimated to be next Spring.

2. Middle East and India regarded as possible danger areas if Russian

aggression and propaganda develops. Essential to build up a reserve in the Middle East to meet possible contingencies.

3. In the Far East considered immediate danger to Australia and New Zealand is remote, and if Japan developed aggressive policy it seems most likely to be directed against allied interests in China.

4. Situation demands maximum possible co-ordinative war effort from all parts of the British Empire. Military productive programme based on 50 Divisions plus 10% reserve. Dominions' Divisions will be allotted equipment as they become available overseas.

5. Moral factor of Australian troops sent overseas at earliest date considered most important; also most effective counter to enemy propaganda regarding half-hearted Dominions co-operation. Egypt or Palestine suitable for training Sixth Division — whose arrival would enable War Office to relieve regular Divisions for France.

6. Minister agrees that our plans should be based on providing a Corps of 2 Divisions at the earliest.

7. In order to complete plans, War Office desire to know the earliest date Sixth Division could embark for Middle East, if shipping can be arranged. Owing to anticipated acute shipping position from January onwards, suggest that Headquarters and the two Brigade Groups should embark early in December, remainder beginning of January. If this is not possible, at least small portion of the Force should be sent early in December.

8. As large proportion of equipment as possible, including artillery and M.T. most desirable. New weapons, including Brens, A.T. [Anti-Tank] guns and 2" mortars etc. for training will be provided on arrival in training area and full outfit completed before movement to the war theatre.

Provision of Medium Brigade or Batteries 6" Howitzers very acceptable.

Whilst essential to maintain home defence organisation, consider we should be prepared to accept lower scale equipment for militia temporarily to provide as much as possible for the six[th] Divisions' requirements overseas. ...

[AA: A 816, 52.302.135]

Although the Defence Committee agreed with the British recommendations on 13 November, War Cabinet would not sanction the sending of any troops until they were further reassured regarding United Kingdom intentions in the event of a Japanese attack. The following cable, aided by the New Zealand decision to send troops overseas, helped to convince the full Cabinet that the 6th Division should leave the country. On 29 November Menzies told parliament that it would do so.

Document 24

Casey to Menzies — London, 23 November 1939

Cablegram C.38 — Most Secret

...Latest appreciation by the French and British General Staff now anticipates that the Germans will be able to put a total of 160 to 170 Divisions, fully equipped, into the field in all theatres by the Spring. Total allied forces likely to be available on the Western Front in France by next Spring — France 70 to 85 Divisions, depending upon the Italian situation and British 10.

Apart from any Dominions contribution do not expect to be able to train and equip more than the abovementioned 10 Divisions by the Spring.

The French Government and General Gamelin[8] are constantly pressing the British Government and the War Office to accelerate their programme, both in regard to additional troops and the production of munitions.

Have seen number of letters from both Daladier[9] and Gamelin to the British Government in which this is being most strongly urged. They represent that one Frenchman in every eight has been mobolised in the Services and in consequence of the drain on their manpower industrial and munitions output is vital and this can only be rectified by withdrawing older men and tradesmen from the army. This they dare not do from fear of jeopardising the security of France in the spring when it is anticipated that German attacks on a grand scale are likely to be launched. They point out that the British have only one in forty five called up. This latter figure is an understatement but it is nearly enough for purposes of argument, although it ignores the vast aircraft and munitions effort in Britain.

The French Government are also anxious about the effect of continued German propaganda which is concentrating upon driving a wedge between the Allies. There is a continuous stream of broadcasts now being aimed at the French people and dropping of propaganda pamphlets. These depict Britain leaving France in the lurch and being half-hearted about continuing the war. Recent German broadcasts have repeatedly stated that the Australian Government is mostly concerned with possible Japanese activities and also with selling their wool and wheat and that Australian troops will not be sent overseas.

This constantly repeated propaganda is not without its appeal and the French are beginning to be concerned.

The British and French Governments feel that the most effective reply will be to see the British Forces in France increasing and the Dominions Forces arriving from overseas. ...

---

8. Commander-in-Chief, French Ground Forces and Allied Forces in France.
9. French President and Minister for National Defence and War.

At my request naval appreciation (C.26) has been re-considered in relation to the Netherlands East Indies, and following is text of additional relevant paragraph approved by the War Cabinet. ...

"Hitherto this note has dealt only with the gravest issues of a major attack upon Singapore or a serious invasion of Australia and New Zealand. However, the question has been raised of an encroachment by Japan upon Dutch Colonies in the East Indies probably arising out of a German invasion of the Netherlands, in which event it might be assumed that we should be involved in a state of war with Japan. It seems very unlikely that the United States of America would impassively watch the acquisition by Japan of naval bases in the west and south west of the Phillipines. Such an act of Japanese aggression would certainly compromise the whole American position in the Pacific and it cannot be doubted that Japan would weigh this consideration with the utmost care before committing herself, having regard especially to the fact that she is already deeply entangled with China. The contingency must therefore be regarded as highly improbable unless, of course, Great Britain and France are getting the worst of it when many evils will descend upon us all.

However, should Japanese encroachment begin, or should Great Britain pass into a state of war with Japan, the Admiralty would make such dispositions as would enable them to offer timely resistance either to a serious attack upon Singapore or to the invasion of Australia and New Zealand. These dispositions would not necessarily take the form of stationing a fleet at Singapore, but would be of a character to enable the necessary concentrations to be made eastward in ample time to prevent a disaster.

With our present limited forces we cannot afford to have any important portions of His Majesty's fleet idle. All ships must play their part from day to day and there are always hazards of war to be faced, but the Admiralty can be trusted to make appropriate dispositions to meet events as they emerge from imagination into reality.["]

My own summing up of the position ... is as follows:

I believe the greatest menace to Australia is the possibility of Britain being beaten in Europe. As long as Britain and France are not getting the worst of it in Europe the British Government do not think there is any appreciable danger of Japan adventuring against the British or French possessions in the East. I feel the British Government's statement regarding ensuring the safety of Australia and of Singapore are satisfactory. Weighing all the factors, it appears to me that the wisest conclusion in our own and the general British interest is to send a special division abroad at the earliest.
[AA: A 816, 52.302.135]

Document 25

Cabinet Decision   Canberra, 28 November 1939

(F.C.10) *DESPATCH OF 6th DIVISION OVERSEAS.*

The following decisions were taken by the Full Cabinet:-
(i) The 6th Division, which was raised for service at home or abroad as occasion required, can be permitted to proceed overseas when it has reached a suitable stage in its training, which it is anticipated will be early in the new year.
(ii) The Government is averse to shipment of artillery or any other material needed for the maintenance of the Militia Forces unless it is capable of rapid replacement. ...
[AA: A 2673, Vol I]

In parliament, the Australian Labor Party opposed the government's decision. Outside it, others questioned its prudence as the selection of letters printed below show. In these letters the original spelling, punctuation and syntax have been retained.

Document 26

Letter

HOUSEWIVES' PROGRESSIVE ASSOCIATION

480 Cummins St,
Broken Hill
22nd Sept. 1939.

Hon W.J McKell,
  Leader State Labor Party,
  N.S.W.

Dear Mr McKell,

At the meeting of the Broken Hill Housewives Association held on the 21st September the following resolution was unanamiously carried and I have been instructed by the association to forward a copy to you as leader of the Labor Party in New South Wales. The resolution has been forwarded to the Federal Labor Leader.

"That this Association calls upon you (Mr Curtain) as leader of the Labor Party to adhere to the plank of the Labor Party which declares no service outside Australia. We appeal to you as the wives and mothers of those who are being forced through economic conscription into the Expeditionary Force to lose no time in organising the people to resist recruiting for overseas."

The following wire was sent to the Prime Minister Mr Menzies.

"This Association of wives and mothers emphatically protests against the recruiting of our men for overseas."

A copy of this wire was sent to Mr Curtain, Leader of the Opposition.

The opinion of members voiced at the meeting was that the Labor Leaders should give a lead and instruct the so-called volunteers not to sign for overseas. Australian women do not want another Anzac Day on their calander. The futility of that sacrifice is evident to us all.

       Yours faithfully
        Honora Douglas
        Hon Assistant Secretary
       HOUSEWIVES' PROGRESSIVE
       ASSOCIATION

[AA: A 1608, A 45/2/1]

Document 27

Letter

AMALGAMATED SOCIETY OF CARPENTERS AND JOINERS OF AUSTRALIA

       Queensland State Management
         Committee
         Room 16
        Trades Hall
      Brisbane 8th December, 1939

Hon. R. G. Menzies,
Prime Minister,
Parliament House,
CANBERRA. F. C. T.

Dear Sir,

I have been directed by the above Committee to enter an emphatic protest against the action of the Federal Government in sending Australian Forces overseas. We believe that such action is against the best interest of the Australian people. Why should Australia be left undefended? This will certainly be the result of this action. It is not many months ago that an appeal was made throughout Australia for volunteers for the Militia Forces.

It was stated at that time that these recruits were needed for defending Australia. You have repeatedly stated, and as late as six weeks ago, that no forces would be sent overseas and now we have your decision to send the cream of our young manhood over to the slaughter fields of France. It is indeed hard to understand such a volta face. We therefore, protest and protest strongly against this decision believing that we have the unqualified support of a majority of the people of the Commonwealth. We therefore request you to alter your decision. Yours faithfully,

Henry H. Long
STATE SECRETARY.

[AA: A 1608, A 45/2/1]

Document 28

Letter
Willimbong Shire Council
Leeton, N.S.W.
18th December, 1939.

Dear Sir,

I will be pleased if you will kindly convey to the Rt Hon. the Prime Minister of Australia the Resolutions set out hereunder, which were carried, with only one dissentient, at a Public Meeting, attended by over 600 people, held at Leeton last evening:–
Resolutions referred to:—
That this Meeting of the People of the Leeton Irrigation Area
(1) Enters its emphatic protest against the Conscription of Australian Manhood; and,
(2) Expresses its determination to resist the sending abroad of an Expeditionary Force; and
(3) Asks that the foregoing resolutions be sent to the Prime Minister.

Yours faithfully,

(SGD) R. STRUCK,

Shire President.

H.K. Nock, Esq., M.P.,
  Federal Members Rooms,
    Commonwealth Bank,
      SYDNEY, N.S.W.

[AA: A 1608, A 45/2/1]

Document 29

Letter

Fairfax St.,
Speers Point,
27/12/39.

Mr. Menzies.

Dear Sir,
 I have been instructed by my branch (Boolaroo-Speers Point branch of A.L.P.) to protest to you against sending our forces oversea.
 You seem to have all our eggs in the one basket. A win by England may be allright, but we would like an alternative. if we carry on as you are doing we would never be able to protect ourselves if we wanted to. To our way of thinking England is in no need of troops yet; & considering she has to feed them would be more of a liability. We certainly think this war will be fought different to the wars in the past, will be a battle of intelligence & we should not go into it Bull-Headed.
 We think Englands trouble will be want of boats, food, & material; & we would be aiding more if we were sending these over not troops. Any-how here's best luck.

Yours Faithfully

E.J. Williams

Sec.

[AA: A 1608, A 45/2/1]

 Such opinion understandably failed to have effect upon the government. The first troops of the 6th Division left Sydney on 9 January 1940 for the Middle East. By that time the suggestion mooted by Casey and supported by the Defence Committee, that a second division should be raised, had been seriously considered by the government. The New Zealand government declined to join in forming an ANZAC Corps, and on 28 February 1940 War Cabinet agreed that an Australian Corps should be formed by the raising of the 7th Division, the second of three AIF divisions which eventually would serve in the Middle East. Below we print the reasoning provided by the Military Board for such action.

Document 30

STATEMENT OF REASONS FOR THE   17 January 1940
MILITARY BOARD'S RECOMMENDATIONS[10]

Home Defence.
1. The security of Australia must be the primary military consideration of the Australian Government, as of the defence forces raised in Australia; and this fact has been kept in view in all the recommendations submitted by the Military Board for the organization, development and training of the military forces.
    It must be pointed out, however, that since the period immediately following the outbreak of war, the international situation has clarified considerably in certain respects. Additional data are now available on which to assess the probable action of enemy, and potential enemy, Powers, and thus to determine what action on the part of Australia will best conform with the strategical requirements of Empire defence as a whole (including the defence of Australia).
2. The situation in the Pacific indicates less likelihood of attack on Australia than was feared at the outbreak of war.
    Recent reports point to a less hostile attitude on the part of Japan towards the democratic Powers. Russian activities, economic difficulties arising from the war in China, and her relations with the U.S.A., have affected Japan in such a way as to reduce materially, if not to remove altogether, the probability of Japanese aggression against the British Pacific Dominions in the near future.
    Moreover, British battleships have been, and are being, employed East of Mediterranean.
3. At the same time, Australia's home defence is being progressively strengthened by the extended training of the Militia, by the calling up of a quota of young men (to be followed by other quotas) for a long period of compulsory training, by the increased, and increasing, production of munitions (including aircraft), and, as the Prime Minister has recently pointed out, by the training of large numbers of personnel for participation in the Empire Air Training Scheme.
Overseas requirements.
4. On the other hand, it is clear that the safety of Australia, as of the Empire as a whole, depends on the defeat of Germany.
    It is not possible at present to forecast whether the war against Germany (whether in military alliance with Russia, or not) will involve operations in more than one theatre. But it is certain that the Allies must be able effectively to oppose the enemy on land, in order that victory may eventually be achieved by the combination of effort at sea, on land, and in the air. Defeat on land must be avoided at all costs; and we know that defeat on

---

10. Presented as Appendix A to War Cabinet Agendum 22/1940, dated 25.1.1940.

land is to be feared unless the Allied land forces can be substantially increased and the increase be maintained.

The truth of this contention is proved by the recent action of the United Kingdom Government in calling up another two million men this year as well as by their appeal to Australia for an increased contribution to the Empire's armies.

First recommendation.
5. In view of these considerations, it is again recommended that approval be given for the raising of, initially, a second division, with ancillary units including Corps Troops, in order to form an Australian Corps, for service overseas, of at least two divisions.

In the opinion of the Military Board, this additional contribution to the Imperial forces overseas can be made without endangering the security of Australia, provided that the Government's present policy of training for Home Defence is maintained, and subject to the proviso that the equipment essential for Home Defence requirements is retained in this country. ...

Second recommendation.
8. The Military Board recommends that approval be given *forthwith* to the raising of a second division, and ancillary units including Corps Troops, for service overseas, and that authority be given for the essential preparations, to give effect to this, to be put in hand at once so that recruitment for the second division may begin in April. ...

[AA: A 2671, 22/1940]

3
AUSTRALIAN POLICY AND THE AIR OFFENSIVE IN EUROPE

It has been shown that there was a certain cohesive concept behind the idea of employing naval and military forces in the war against Germany and Italy. The army, eventually grouped in the Middle East, came to fight its battles under its own commanders who in turn were supported by the Australian government. Australian ships, though under the strategic direction of the Admiralty, remained part of the Royal Australian Navy and were officered and crewed by members of it. Both ships and men were liable for recall at the discretion of the Australian government. The squadrons of the regular RAAF who fought in the 'distant war' shared similar conditions. Not so favoured were those who entered the service through the Empire Air Training Scheme.

We have previously printed extracts from Dominions Office cable of 8 September 1939 with its initial proposals for the use of Australian naval and military forces. It also made three suggestions for the use of Australian air resources. The government had a brief flirtation with one of them and made a firm commitment to the other two.

Document 31

Eden to Whiskard   London, 8 September 1939

Cablegram 191   *Most Secret*

. . .
AIR FORCE:
17. At the present time the main weakness of the allies, vis-a-vis Germany, is in respect of their air strength. It is extremely important that we should do everything in our power to reduce this discrepancy as rapidly as possible and we look to the Dominions, whose resources lie outside the range of any German bombers, to ensure that this is achieved.
18. There are three possible ways by which this could be done:-
   (a) The direct despatch to Great Britain of complete units of R.A.A.F.
   (b) The substitution of Australian for U.K. squadrons oversea, e.g. Singapore, thus releasing latter for home service.
   (c) The supply of aircraft, material and trained personnel from Dominion resources.
19. Having regard to the requirements of local defence and to the fact that,

as a result of delays in the production of certain types of aircraft in England, the squadrons in Australia are still equipped with obsolescent types and cannot reinforce Singapore by air, we do not recommend either (a) or (b) in the preceding paragraph as an immediate course of action.

20. We should, however, like the proposal in (b) to be carried out as soon as appropriate Australian squadrons have completed their re-equipment. We also suggest that Australian pilots and crews now in England waiting to fly the first Sunderlands to Australia[11], should be allowed to remain, together with their aircraft, at our disposal. This assistance would be most valuable in view of our immediate requirements for trade protection.

21. With regard to proposal (c) we are aware that the Commonwealth Government have drawn up an agreed programme for the expansion of their air force. This was, however, a long term project to be developed in peace and we consider the present situation calls for a change, assuming that the immediate object is now to assist Great Britain in the European theatre.

22. What we require most is a steadily increasing supply of pilots, air observers, w/t operators and air gunners and we should be grateful if the Commonwealth Government could consider to what extent they can modify their existing programme to satisfy these requirements. We would suggest that they should make the maximum possible use of civil aviation resources for initial training.

23. We would observe that a flying training school based on our own war establishment should produce some 500 pilots per year and an air observers' school some 260 observers and 390 air gunners.

24. At the same time we appreciate that, ultimately, the Commonwealth would no doubt wish that complete Australian unit[s] come into being and should in turn be amalgamated into an Australian contingent. We do not think our suggestions are in conflict with this aim which can be achieved as and when there are adequate reserves of Australian personnel available in England to maintain contingent.

[AA: A 981, Defence 59, Part 1]

    Both the Minister for Defence, G.A. Street and the Chief of the Air Staff, Air Vice-Marshal S.J. Goble favoured the concept of an Air Expeditionary Force. Here Street sets out his reasons, and Goble his recommendations.

---

11. At the outbreak of war No. 10 Squadron RAAF had a detachment in the United Kingdom to take delivery of Sunderland flying boats intended to operate from Western Australia.

Document 32

Street to Cabinet   19–22 September 1939

Submission

DESPATCH OVERSEAS OF AN AIR EXPEDITIONARY FORCE

... Operating as an entity, an organised force would appeal to the national spirit of the country and accord with those tendencies towards independence inherent in the Australian character. It would, in regard to air action, focus patriotic effort onto a clearly defined objective, whilst, as an offshoot of the Royal Australian Air Force, it would take advantage of that esprit de corps begun in the Australian Flying Corps in the war of 1914–1918 and since developed within the Royal Australian Air Force, and which is such an important factor in air fighting. On the other hand, if individual pilots and other members of crews only are sent abroad, they would be distributed throughout the Royal Air Force and their Australian identity would be to a great extent, submerged. Action on these lines would also restrict the overseas air effort to one class of people in the community and would not allow for participation by the mechanic and artisan who comprise an important section of our people, as indeed they do of the Air Force. A further disadvantage of the latter course of action is the adverse effect it would have on the morale of the Royal Australian Air Force as now constituted, if the Service as a whole was used simply as a training ground for the Royal Air Force, and its members were not given the opportunity to take their part overseas. ...
[AA: A 2697, Vol 2]

Document 33

Goble to Shedden   22 September 1939

Minute   *Most Secret*

...
8. To sum up, my views are that we should agree in principle with the United Kingdom proposals but that, in the early stages at least, we compromise on proposals (a) and (c) by sending organised units but without aircraft and equipment — any excess pilots and crews over and above the requirements for this being sent direct to the Royal Air Force. I suggest that our policy, as regards air assistance overseas, should then be -
(a)   As the ultimate aim, to provide a complete air contingent in the main theatre or a theatre of importance, as the British Government may decide; and also, as the local defence situation allows, to send appropriate squadrons to Royal Air Force overseas commands, such as Singapore or the Middle East, to replace R.A.F. units.

(b) As an immediate and short range policy, to place an organised force at the disposal of the British Government (to be equipped overseas). (Possibly by taking over from Royal Air Force squadrons overseas, e.g., the Middle East, thus releasing R.A.F. personnel.)
(c) The maximum number of pilots, observers, air gunners and wireless operators to be trained with the resources available and which can be obtained, all such personnel over and above our own requirements being made available to the Royal Air Force.
(d) Subject to recall should the local situation deteriorate, Sunderlands with crews to be placed at the disposal of the British Government, but to operate as an Australian unit — the remainder of No. 10 (General Reconnaissance) Squadron being sent to England to make the squadron complete.
[AA: A 5954, Box 582]

The Sunderland flying-boats and crews were offered to the United Kingdom and formed 10 Squadron RAAF in Coastal Command for the rest of the war. In the meantime Stanley Bruce, Australia's High Commissioner in London, had put proposals to H.H. Balfour, the British Under-Secretary of State for Air, which were to germinate into the Empire Air Training Scheme.

Document 34

CAPTAIN BALFOUR'S NOTE   London, 22 September 1939
...
2. He [Bruce] feels that at the present time the Dominions are making various offers of help on land and sea and in the air; that these are being considered in a piecemeal manner; the result is a general "flapping round" with nothing definitely fixed, while the situation demands immediate decisions.
3. Mr. Bruce approaches the problem with the objective of having a formidable number of Dominion air squadrons operating in the Field within a maximum time of twelve months from now.
4. ...the following are his ideas:-
   While the Dominions will wish to keep the entity of their units overseas in the form of Canadian Air Contingent, Australian Air Contingent and also for New Zealand, nevertheless the pilots training problem should be approached from the point of seeing whether Dominion resources should not be pooled so far as possible, the pilots only going to their particular contingents on reporting for posting to overseas units.
   His picture is that Australia, New Zealand and Canada should each carry out their elementary training in their own territories, and so far as possible on equipment produced by the Dominions. The pilots from Australia and New Zealand, at the completion of their elementary training, should go to

Canada, where they would do their advanced training in a Dominion which can produce Service type aircraft in numbers, and which it is possible to supply from this country with such aircraft should the Dominion production be insufficient. From Canada the pilots would come to England to join the squadrons of their Dominion contingent. ...

6. Australia has agreed to send complete personnel for six squadrons, but there is a large number of young men above those required for the six squadrons who are desperately keen to have a chance of becoming pilots. They would wish themselves, however, and the Australian Government would wish, that they should be absorbed into Australian units. It is this body in excess of the six squadrons that would provide the nucleus for the immediate expansion of elementary training in Australia and the subsequent advanced training in Canada. Mr. Bruce favours fighter squadrons for the Australians, on the grounds that their temperament is peculiarly suited to this type of warfare. ...

7. ... the Australian Government has already said that the six squadrons will have to be equipped from our Home resources, quite apart from who pays. The Dominion air units would have to be supplied with equipment, either from our resources over here, or from production in Canada; or alternatively by purchase of suitable aircraft from America. ...

13. Mr. Bruce suggests that Australia and Canada should forthwith expand their production facilities for training aircraft, and the aim should be that Australia, New Zealand and Canada should be self-contained for elementary training airframes, and possibly for smaller horse-powered engines, such as the Gipsy type, or engines of the radials of power around 200 horse-power. Australia are already part-manufacturing and assembling Pratt and Whitney Wasps. ...

[AA: M100, 1]

On the understanding that the United Kingdom would supply the operational aircraft which Australia lacked, War Cabinet approved the despatch of a six squadron Air Expeditionary Force which was expected to be of use in just over five months. Events in London, however, were pulling in a different direction. Bruce cabled Menzies an outline of his thoughts on 25 September and Eden, Secretary of State for Dominion Affairs, put tentative training quotas to the Australian government on the following day. In the first week of October, War Cabinet briefly discussed how the suggested British figures might be met.

Document 35

War Cabinet Minutes Sydney, 4 October 1939

(11) *AUSTRALIAN CONTRIBUTION TO EMPIRE AIR DEFENCE*

The Chief of the Air Staff (Air Vice-Marshal Goble) and the Assistant Chief of the Air Staff (Wing Commander G. Jones) were present at a discussion ... relative to the development of the Empire's maximum strength in the air.

The Prime Minister stated that, of the estimated strength of 20,000 pilots and 30,000 air crews, Australia's quota would probably be 7,500 (3,000 pilots and 4,500 air crews).

The Chief of the Air Staff estimated the training of this number of pilots would require the following:-

70 training aircraft held at present by R.A.A.F.
130 training aircraft to be obtained from Civil Aviation.
200 — This number would train 1,000 pilots in a year.
500 — Additional would train 2,500 pilots in a year.
700   3,500

With a training course of eight months in war, as compared with ten months in peace, each flying training school taking batches of 50 would produce 250 pilots in a year, and approximately fifteen schools would be required. The Chief of the Air Staff preferred Service to Civil schools.

Further discussion was deferred until next meeting.

Melbourne, 5 October 1939

(13) ... In continuation of minute No. (11), the War Cabinet decided:-
(i) To approve in principle the scheme outlined in Dominions Office cablegram of 26th September, as it was considered that this was a very effective way in which Australia could contribute where help was most needed and at a time when it would be most required.
(ii) To send an Air Mission to Canada forthwith as desired by the United Kingdom Government.
(iii) The numbers to be raised by Australia will depend on circumstances yet to be elucidated and will be decided later.
(iv) A cablegram to be sent to the High Commissioner [Bruce] intimating approval to the scheme in principle. ...
[AA: A 2673, Vol 1]

Thus after less than six weeks of war, the Australian government was involved in designing three separate air policies. Three thousand two hundred officers and men had to be found for the Air Expeditionary Force, Bruce was calling for the Sunderland unit to be reinforced by a further twenty officers and two hundred men together with another six aircraft while at the same time it looked as if Australia would be relied on to train several thousand men for the Royal Air Force. The Air Expeditionary Force was jettisoned. Bruce spoke to the Air Ministry; Sir Geoffrey Whiskard, British High Commissioner wrote to Menzies; and then the Cabinet abandoned that particular concept.

Document 36

Note by Bruce   London, 17 October 1939

SIR ARTHUR STREET and Air Vice Marshal
C.F.A. PORTAL — Air Ministry.

I saw Street and Portal, Member of the Air Council for Personnel. ...
I said it appeared to me from the cable we had received from Australia on the 14th October asking for information as to what the provision of 6 Squadrons would mean in personnel that they were beginning to realise that their offer of 6 Squadrons immediately was rather too substantial a one.

I said that my own feeling was that they would be better advised to agree to the Sunderland Squadron at once and to throw the idea of the 6 Squadrons into the melting pot of the bigger training scheme.
Portal emphatically agreed with this and said to send 6 Squadron[s] now would be like breaking eggs instead of hatching them out.

I accordingly agreed that I would communicate with Australia down these lines.
[AA: M100, 2]

Document 37

Whiskard to Menzies   Canberra, 30 October 1939

Letter   *Secret*
                                        To be destroyed immediately

I have been requested by my Government to make the following communication to you on the subject of the Commmonwealth Government's offer to despatch an Air Expeditionary Force of six Royal Australian Air Force Squadrons.
2. The United Kingdom Government have further considered this generous offer in the light of the ready intention subsequently expressed by the Commonwealth Government to participate in the recent plan for an Empire Air Training Scheme; and the matter has been fully discussed with the Commonwealth High Commissioner in London.
3. Mr. Bruce has shown to the United Kingdom authorities his telegram to you of the 18th October, suggesting that in order to enable Australia to

make her maximum contribution to the Empire Training Scheme side by side with the development of her own Air Force, the best course would be to proceed with the creation of an Australian General Reconnaissance Squadron of nine Sunderlands and to put back into the general training scheme the balance of the personnel which would be sent overseas immediately if the six squadrons were despatched as contemplated; and they fully agree that the line which he suggests is in the circumstances the right course to follow.

4. My Government understand that the Commonwealth Government are prepared to consider the alternative proposal favourably and they have requested me to inform you that they would be very willing that in any announcement which you may wish to make you should say, if you so desire, that the change of plan is being made after the fullest consultation with His Majesty's Government in the United Kingdom.
[AA: CP 290/6, 6, Bundle 1]

Document 38

Cabinet Minute   Sydney, 31 October 1939

Present: Mr. Menzies, Mr. Hughes, Brigadier Street, Sir Henry Gullett, Senator McLeay, Senator Foll, Mr. Harrison, Mr. Lawson, Sir Frederick Stewart, Mr. Perkins, Mr. Spender, Senator Collett and Mr. Holt.

AIR EXPEDITIONARY FORCE:

The Prime Minister explained to Cabinet the position which had arisen with respect to the Air Expeditionary Force proposals, details of which he had already announced to Parliament, and he summarised the cables which had been exchanged between the United Kingdom and Commonwealth Governments. In effect, it was now proposed that, in lieu of the suggested Air Expeditionary Force, the nine ["Sunderlands"] should be manned by Australian personnel, and that the Commonwealth effort beyond that point should be concentrated upon the Empire Air Scheme.

It was agreed that a statement, the general terms of which were outlined to Cabinet, should be made by the Prime Minister on the matter.
[AA: A 2697, Vol 3A]

> The adoption of the Empire Air Training Scheme meant that there were limited opportunities for RAAF officers to gain operational command experience. The fact that it was also decided that the RAAF itself should be commanded by an imported British officer whose main task would be the training of aircrew for the United Kingdom posed the problem which emerged two years later of finding a suitably qualified successor. These documents suggest a certain lack of communication

between government members and Air Vice-Marshal Goble. It was not an edifying episode in civil-military relations.

Document 39

Menzies to Bruce   Canberra, 13 October 1939

Cablegram [Not Numbered]   *Secret and Personal*

... Our recent experience and prospective demand on air staff in connection with development of R.A.A.F. organisation of air expeditionary force and participation in Empire scheme training pilots and crews indicate imperative necessity for loaning thoroughly competent R.A.F. Officer as Chief of the Air Staff. His seniority should be higher than both Williams[12] and Goble. It is considered in view of war Williams should now return to Australia... This is a preliminary advice to enable you to submit matter to Air Ministry so that Casey may finalise selection (when he) is in London. ... [AA: M100, 2]

Document 40

War Cabinet Minute   Melbourne, 4 January 1940

PRESENT: The Rt. Hon. R.G. Menzies, K.C., M.P., Prime Minister.
           The Rt. Hon. R.G. Casey, D.S.O., M.C., M.P., Minister for Supply and Development.
           Brigadier the Hon. G.A. Street, M.C., M.P., Minister for the Army.
           The Hon. Sir Henry Gullett, K.C.M.G., M.P., Minister for External Affairs.
           Senator the Hon. H.S. Foll, Minister for the Interior.
           The Hon. Sir Frederick Stewart, M.P., Minister for the Navy.
           The Hon. J.V. Fairbairn, M.P., Minister for Air.
           The Hon. P.C. Spender, K.C., M.P., Acting Treasurer.

(112) *AGENDUM No. 8/1940 — SELECTION OF ROYAL AIR FORCE OFFICER AS CHIEF OF THE AIR STAFF, AND RESIGNATION OF AIR VICE-MARSHAL S.J. GOBLE AS CHIEF OF THE AIR STAFF.*

With reference to Minute No. (103), the Prime Minister conveyed to the War Cabinet the substance of Air Vice-Marshal Goble's letter of 22nd

---

12. Air Vice-Marshal Richard Williams, Chief of the Air Staff 1921–39 and at this time on secondment to the Royal Air Force.

December and an interview granted to him in connection with his resignation.

The Minister for Air outlined his negotiations in London for the selection of a senior Royal Air Force officer for the post of Chief of the Air Staff and the arrangements made by him for the return to Australia of Air Vice-Marshal Williams. Mr. Fairbairn explained that, under an erroneous impression that he had full authority to make an appointment to the post of Chief of the Air Staff, he had entered into a commitment with Air Chief Marshal Sir Charles Burnett, who was in his view the outstanding officer of those available for selection.

The War Cabinet confirmed the appointment of Sir Charles Burnett as Chief of the Air Staff, after the Prime Minister had emphasized that appointments to senior posts, such as Heads of Departments and Services, were the prerogative of Cabinet. Sir Charles Burnett's appointment was for a period of twelve months, but with the option of extension. His pay would be the same as the Chief of the Naval Staff, namely, salary of £3,000 per annum, three-fifths to be paid in sterling if his wife remains in England or one-fifth if she proceeds to Australia.

... Air Vice-Marshal Williams is to be granted the temporary rank of Air Marshal, while holding the position of Air Member for Personnel, or in charge of the Training Command, as may be decided after the arrival of the new Chief of the Air Staff. The War Cabinet also directed that the High Commissioner should inform Air Vice-Marshal Williams that he should clearly understand that these moves do not imply any right of reversion to the post of Chief of the Air Staff. ...

On 22nd December the War Cabinet decided to accept Air Vice-Marshal Goble's resignation from the post of Chief of the Air Staff (Minute No. (103)). Cabinet noted that, on 25th December, the Prime Minister had conveyed to the High Commissioner by cablegram advice of Air Vice-Marshal Goble's desire to obtain a Command in the Royal Air Force, and the willingness of the Commonwealth Government to second him if his services were required by the Air Ministry. The Minister for Air suggested that, as a senior officer would be required to represent the R.A.A.F. on the Board to be created in Canada to supervise the execution of the Empire Air Scheme, Air Vice-Marshal Goble might be appointed to this post... In view of the state of Air Vice-Marshal Goble's health and the strain under which he had been working, particularly since the outbreak of war, it was decided to approve of sick leave up to a period of three months. It was also approved that Air Vice-Marshal Goble should be confirmed in the rank he was temporarily holding whilst Chief of the Air Staff, the question of salary being a matter for subsequent consideration.
[AA: A 2673, Vol. I]

Document 41

Whiskard to Eden

Letter

C/o Russell Grimwade, Esq.,
FRANKSTON,
Victoria.
1st January, 1940

My dear Secretary of State,

When I received your telegram No. 341 regarding the resignation of Goble, Chief of the Air Staff here, I was staying with friends at this place — about 30 miles east of Melbourne — and the Prime Minister was spending his Christmas holidays at his country cottage at Macedon, about 40 miles west of Melbourne. I arranged to see him yesterday (Sunday) and went over by car accordingly, a pleasant drive, all along the coast, in perfect summer weather.

He told me that on receipt of Goble's resignation (both of his appointment as Chief of Air Staff and of his commission in the R.A.A.F.), he sent for him and asked the reason. Goble told him that Russell[13] was continuously intriguing behind his back, and he now found his position intolerable. Menzies said that, after all, Russell was Goble's subordinate officer, and surely it was unusual for the superior to allow his subordinate to force him to resign, to which Goble replied that he was assured that Russell had the ear of the Cabinet, so that any action by him (Goble) to check his intrigues would have been useless. Menzies then told him that the Cabinet had in fact some time ago decided to make different arrangements, necessary in view of the very large expansion of the R.A.A.F., which would involve the return of Russell to the United Kingdom, whereupon Goble at once asked to be allowed to withdraw his resignation. Menzies said he would be allowed to withdraw his resignation of his commission, which he was foolish ever to have tendered; but he could not be allowed to withdraw his resignation as Chief of Air Staff, because the new arrangements contemplated not only the return of Russell to the United Kingdom but also the supersession of Goble by someone from the United Kingdom with greater seniority and experience; whereupon Goble retired hurt.

Menzies went on to say that, while Goble's resignation was undoubtedly very convenient, as it saved them from the unpleasantness of publicly superseding him, he regarded Russell as mainly to blame for the continued friction on the Air Board. Russell not only talked a great deal too much in Clubs and other congregations of tittle-tattlers, but he was undoubtedly

---

13. Air Commodore J.C. Russell, RAF, on exchange for Air Vice-Marshal Williams.

disloyal to his colleagues. (Incidentally I met Russell for the first time at dinner at Government House, Melbourne, the other night; and both my wife, whose judgment in these matters I value, and I, took an instant dislike to him). Furthermore (as I have already reported) while he must assume that Russell had been a success in the command which he had held prior to coming to Australia, he was convinced that (apart from the disabilities of character noted above) he was not suited for any job in which he was required to advise on matters of policy. As for Goble, he had been quite adequate as Chief of Staff for a negligible Air Force such as Australia had hitherto possessed, but would be quite out of his depth in dealing with the problems arising from the creation of an Air Force which was intended to include as many as 20,000 flying personnel apart from ground personnel. He believed that Goble's service in the United Kingdom had been approved: and he was asking Bruce to arrange with the Air Ministry to send them out a really good man, of proper seniority and experience, as Chief of Air Staff, and to take Goble back into the R.A.F. and give him a command suitable for an Air Commodore (acting Vice Marshal) of his seniority.

Menzies then harked back to Russell, and said that, while he was satisfied that the Admiralty and War Office now appreciated that they must not use Australia as a waste-paper basket for their duds (Colvin, Custance and Squires, he said, had been *most* successful appointments) he was by no means sure that the Air Ministry had yet learnt this lesson. It was most important that they should. The sending out of unsuitable men here was not only bad for the Australian services (which he admitted were, in peace time at any rate, from the United Kingdom point of view unimportant) but it lowered the prestige of the United Kingdom services in Australian eyes. Machtig[14] will tell you how much importance I have, in previous letters and despatches, attached to this point. ...

Yours sincerely,
Geoffrey Whiskard

[PRO: D.O. 35/1003/1]

Document 42

Notes on A.C.M. Burnett, *while in Australia.* [Not Dated]

AIR CHIEF MARSHAL SIR CHARLES BURNETT, K.C.B., C.B.E., D.S.O. (R.A.F.).

Appointment: C.A.S. R.A.A.F. — 15/2/40 — 4/4/42
Previous Appointment: An Inspector-General of the R.A.F.
Selection: On the decision of the Australian Government, Air Minister Fairbairn interviewed several senior R.A.F. officers during his visit to

---

14. Eric G. Machtig, Permanent Under-Secretary, Dominions Office.

England in 1939, and it was considered Sir Charles Burnett would be the most acceptable to Australians, both Service and Official, though other candidates were thought equally as efficient. (Source — Mr. [R.E.] Elford, Minister's Secretary). ...

He was a broad Empire minded Scotchman; once writing to the late A.M. Drummond[15] "I am just as much a Scotchman as you are an Australian, but I am an Imperialist first and foremost." He had a keen sense of humour, and at work he was direct and forthright. He was prepared to give his staff a hearing unless they showed signs of weakness, when they were told where they got off. Preferred people to stand up and give a direct reply, and he was somewhat of a mild bully.

He had tremendous initiative and mental energy, and through knowing all the "old soldiers'" answers, it became largely a matter of "putting it over". The problems he was faced with were not a question of knowing what to do, but of how to get them done both Service and Government.

He was a born leader of men, being well illustrated when he addressed parades, particularly the talk given to Darwin men 3 days after the initial raid on 19/2/42. His health was poor, and he finally left Australia a very tired and sick man, his body would not stand up to the mental effort he made. He had a gastric ulcer, headaches and could not take corrective medicine, one affecting the other. Also his legs gave trouble, but he never lost working time. ...

He relied extensively on A.V.M. Bostock as D.C.A.S., to interpret Service and local background, and to advise him on Australian conditions. ...

Bostock loyally and energetically supported Sir Charles who worked up Bostock to follow him. He physically forced his promotion to substantive A.V.M. through Drakeford[16], also obtained C.B. for him, and he was the first to congratulate Bostock on its reception. ...

[He was e]ntirely responsible for initiating W.A.A.A.F. in spite of tremendous political opposition. Mr. McEwan [sic][17] wouldn't face it, and Secretary opposed on grounds of economy: "why put into uniform and barracks, costing money, why not use existing civil service set up and bring them [women] in as temporary civil servants?" Sir Charles knew they had to come and their value, and again it was a matter of struggling for approval.

When the E.A.T.S. [Empire Air Training Scheme] first commenced and the rush to enlist came in June '40, air crew had to wait up to 9 months and many joined the Army, there were screams from everywhere. "Put them into camps, give them a uniform and teach them their drill". He let everyone have their say, knowing full well it meant getting camps and uniforms, instructors and administrators, all of which were scarce. Also he knew how it had failed in England, as they became demoralised after a few weeks. So

---

15. Air Marshal Peter Drummond, RAF.
16. Hon. Arthur Samuel Drakeford, Minister for Air 7.10.1941 — 19.12.1949.
17. Minister for Air and Civil Aviation, 28.10.1940 — 7.10.1941.

the night classes and special swimming and shooting contests were evolved to instruct and assist, letting them feel they were not overlooked. He used to go round these night classes, perhaps 3 in a night, and address them for 10 to 15 minutes on the lines — "you all want to be fighter pilots. A fighter is purely defensive, you don't win football matches by crowding the defence of your own goal. Its Air Power, and bombers particularly, which are going to win this war." This was stated in 1940... .

Worked his staff hard, at times was very impatient, but most considerate when a genuine request was made. He was accused of being a hard task master, but worked no one harder than himself. He used to say how he hated work.

He insisted on his staff being accurate and confident. He used to make people tell the whole story. He could not abide terms "understand" or "think". Once when a question was asked and an uncertain reply commencing with, "I think, Sir...." he said, very abruptly, "Man, you don't think, either you know or you don't know, and if you don't know, go and find out."
...

He travelled widely, four times round New Guinea, including Rabaul and the Solomons, once to Malaya and another time to N.E.I. [Netherlands East Indies], apart from Mainland inspections. Usually left Melbourne on a Sunday to save time, mostly by Hudson with no special aircraft or crew; approx. 80,000 miles in two years.

[Contained in a File, Undated, RAAF Historical Branch, ACT]

> The Empire Air Training Scheme, whose chief executive officer in Australia thus became Sir Charles Burnett, had in the meantime been negotiated in Ottawa between 2 and 27 November 1939, the Australian team being led by the Minister for Air, J.V. Fairbairn. We print a War Cabinet summary of these negotiations and the scheme's provisions.

Document 43

War Cabinet Paper Not Dated [c.30 November 1939]

EMPIRE AIR TRAINING SCHEME
...
FIRST PROPOSALS:
The first proposal discussed was along the lines of the original British Government suggestion, i.e., that each Dominion should carry out its own elementary training and that all Service training be carried out in Canada. Of the total numbers to be trained eventually, the United Kingdom was to provide four-ninths whilst the remaining five-ninths was to be provided in the following ratios:

Canada .. 48
Australia .. 40
New Zealand .. 12

The preliminary estimate of the cost of the scheme on this basis was set down at $888,500,000 Canadian. Towards this the United Kingdom would contribute $140,000,000 in aircraft and equipment, the remaining $748,500,000 being contributed by the Dominions in the same ratio as their quotas, which meant that the cost to Australia would have been $274,000,000 (approximately £A85,000,000). In view of this very large expenditure outside Australia, the difficulties of dollar exchange, and the economic benefit to Australia if portion of this sum were spent locally, a proposal was made that 50% of the Service training be carried out in Australia so as to reduce the dollar exchange problem, which would reduce our payments in Canada by 50%.

AMENDED SCHEME:
Further conversations then took place in Canada and, following a telephone conversation between Mr. Fairbairn and the Prime Minister on 22nd November, the Delegation was authorised to reduce the Australian quota to a strictly population basis and to endeavour to arrange, in addition to the elementary training of the full quota of pilots and the initial training of the full quota of aircrews, that seven-ninths of the Service training of all personnel be carried out in Australia completely, leaving two-ninths only to be carried out in Canada: the total to be trained in Canada not exceeding a total of 8,000 personnel over the period of three years.

Arrangements on these lines have now been made by Mr. Fairbairn and an agreement with the United Kingdom has been initialled. A further four-party agreement has been drawn up dealing with the Canadian training and although not initialled has been assented to by Mr. Fairbairn.

The scheme as accepted now is as follows:-

PERSONNEL TO BE PROVIDED:
A total of 26,000, comprising 10,400 pilots and 15,600 observers and wireless air gunners, is to be provided by Australia by the end of March, 1943. All personnel will receive their elementary training in Australia and all will be completely trained in Australia except some 7,000 to 8,000 who will receive their Service training in Canada.

Eventually the organisations in Canada and Australia will be so developed that seven-ninths of the agreed Australian quota will be completely trained in Australia, whilst the remaining two-ninths will receive their elementary training in Australia and complete their training in Canada.

AIRCRAFT:
Elementary Trainers.-
Australia is to provide all elementary training aircraft to be used in Aus-

tralia, but Great Britain will contribute free 50% of the engines required, in kind or cash.

Intermediate Trainers.-
Australia is to provide all Wirraways for intermediate training but Great Britain will contribute the cost of the first 233 Wirraways, calculated on the price of the corresponding type in U.S.A., or provide in kind a similar aircraft to the extent necessary to supplement local production.

Advanced Training and Service Training Aircraft –
Great Britain will contribute free all aircraft required in Australia for advanced training of pilots and for the training of aircrews except for the small number of aircraft necessary for the wireless training of air gunners. The Anson aircraft will, however, be supplied less wings and if the wings are not made locally Australia must bear the cost of supply from England.

Wastage, Replacement and Spares.-
Great Britain will contribute free all aircraft to replace wastage of those originally contributed, also the appropriate maintenance spare parts.

Training Schools to be set up in Australia.
Australia will accept responsibility for the establishment and maintenance of the necessary training schools and establishments in Australia, except for the contributions in aircraft by Great Britain. The major schools to be formed are -
9 elementary flying training schools
7 Service flying training schools
4 air observers' schools
4 bombing and gunnery schools
4 wireless air gunners' schools
2 air navigation schools

INSTRUCTORS:
Great Britain offers to provide on loan, under the usual conditions, the instructors necessary to supplement those which can be provided from our own resources.

RETENTION OF AUSTRALIAN IDENTITY:
All trainees will be enlisted in the Royal Australian Air Force and attached to the Royal Canadian Air Force whilst training in Canada and to the Royal Air Force from the date of embarkation for Great Britain.
Australian personnel will be permitted to maintain the greatest degree of Australian identity practicable, by arrangement from time to time.

PAY OF PERSONNEL:
Australia will accept responsibility for all pay and allowances, etc., whilst personnel are serving in Australia.
Great Britain will pay rates of pay, allowances, pensions, etc. from date of embarkation for England.
The pay of the quota being trained in Canada will be borne pro rata by all Governments at Canadian rates of pay until completion of Service training.

The position in regard to rates of pay and general conditions of service is not yet sufficiently clear to enable a definite statement of the position to be outlined, but a full statement of the proposals with the departmental view will be submitted later after full examination.

COSTS:
Australia's share of the cost of training its quota in Canada based on proportions to be trained is estimated to be £A11,000,000 up to 31st March, 1943.
The cost of the training to be carried out in Australia has not yet been worked out in detail. As an approximate estimate, however, it may be taken that the capital expenditure involved will amount to £A20,000,000, and the maintenance expenditure for a full year at the maximum output (which will not, of course, be attained until 1943/44) will be £A15,000,000.
[AA: A 2671, 43/1939]

The German breakthrough in May, the subsequent fall of France, and Italy's entry into the war, made a greater Dominion air effort seem imperative. Already it had been decided to send an RAAF Army Co-operation squadron to the Middle East. Now No. 8 and No. 21 Squadrons were to go to Malaya so that RAF units could be released. By 1941 the quota of pilots and observers being sent to Canada had been increased by twenty-five per cent and a small number of trainees were being sent to Rhodesia. The air contribution to the 'distant war' was thus fragmented. Neither were Australian airmen adequately grouped in Britain despite provision under Article XV of the EATS agreement for some such arrangement to be made. Bruce was 'somewhat staggered' to find out in February 1940 that no one in London had given this question much thought. In fact ten months were to elapse before definite proposals were to be made. We print the comments of the Minister for Air made prior to War Cabinet's approval of such proposals on 16 January 1941.

Document 44

McEwen to War Cabinet   8 January 1941

Paper   Secret

EMPIRE AIR TRAINING SCHEME — FORMATION OF SQUADRONS MANNED BY AUSTRALIAN AIRCREWS AND INFILTRATION OF GROUND STAFFS.

Identity of Aircrews with their Respective Dominions.
1. Article 15 of the Empire Air Training Scheme Agreement reads as follows —

"The United Kingdom Government undertakes that pupils of Canada, Australia and New Zealand shall, after training is completed, be identified with their respective Dominions, either by the method of organising Dominion units and formations or in some other way, such methods to be agreed upon with the respective Dominion Governments concerned. The United Kingdom Government will initiate inter-Governmental discussions to this end."

Views of War Cabinet on Identity of Aircrew Personnel, Formation of Squadrons and Financial Responsibility.

2. Agendum No. 70/1940 which was approved, with certain modifications, by War Cabinet (vide Minute No. (206)) sets out proposals which were communicated to the High Commissioner, London, for his guidance in the inter-Governmental discussions which were to take place in London to determine these questions, those proposals being -

(a) that all Australian personnel serving with the Royal Air Force shall continue to wear Royal Australian Air Force uniform. (This was later agreed to by the United Kingdom Government.)

(b) that Royal Australian Air Force aircrew personnel be grouped into squadrons and directly 75 per cent or more aircrew personnel is Australian, those squadrons shall be called, for example, No. 701 (Australian) Squadron, Royal Air Force;

(c) that, if later it is found possible to send overseas ground personnel as well as aircrews, without endangering the capacity of the Royal Australian Air Force to carry out its commitments under the Empire Air Training Scheme, such ground personnel should be made available to the Royal Air Force on the same conditions as the aircrew personnel and should be posted to the same squadrons.

Result of Inter-Governmental Discussions of Arrangements under Article 15 of Empire Air Training Agreement.

3. A conference was to be held early in 1940 but, due to various causes, it was postponed from time to time. That conference was, however, recently held in London and I attach hereto copy of cablegram dated 23rd December ... received from the High Commissioner, embodying text of the proposals resulting from those discussions, viz.-

(a) that eighteen Royal Australian Air Force squadrons be formed for service outside Australia (in addition to the five already serving overseas) during the next eighteen months, in accordance with the following schedule -

2 by March 1941
4 between April — June 1941
3 between July — September 1941
3 between October — December 1941
3 between January — March 1942
3 by April or May 1942

(b) that the Royal Australian Air Force aircrews in excess of requirements for the above eighteen squadrons to be posted to replace wastage throughout the Royal Air Force;

(c) that all Australian pilots and aircrews, whether serving in Royal Air Force or Royal Australian Air Force formations, will wear Royal Australian Air Force uniforms, they thus retaining their Australian identity in either event;

(N.B.: The working of the abovementioned arrangements will be reviewed in September 1941 in order to determine whether the formation of the eighteen squadrons can be achieved in accordance with the programme stated, or accelerated, as well as to consider the position and organisation of our pilots and aircrews whom, under these arrangements, it may not be practicable to absorb in Royal Australian Air Force squadrons.)

(d) that Squadron Commanders, Station Commanders, and ground personnel be provided by the Royal Australian Air Force as far as possible — Royal Air Force personnel to fill vacancies pending availability of Royal Australian Air Force personnel possessing the necessary qualifications;

(e) that cost of the eighteen squadrons referred to in (a) will be borne by the United Kingdom Government, except that pay, allowances, and non-effective benefits of Royal Australian Air Force personnel to serve in those squadrons will be borne by the United Kingdom Government in accordance with Royal Air Force rates — the Commonwealth Government being responsible for any excess difference of Royal Australian Air Force rates over Royal Air Force rates. The Commonwealth Government will also continue to bear cost of the five squadrons at present serving in the United Kingdom, Middle East, and the Far East;

(f) that records and postings be the responsibility of the Air Ministry, but staff will include a proportion of Royal Australian Air Force personnel.

Infiltration of Royal Australian Air Force Personnel.

4. It will be noted in the High Commissioner's cablegram and at paragraph 3(d) above that it has been agreed as desirable that Australia should provide ground personnel required for the eighteen squadrons referred to, supplemented as necessary by a proportion of experienced Royal Air Force personnel, and that Royal Air Force personnel should be gradually exchanged for suitable Royal Australian Air Force personnel as they become available, with a view to achieving homogenous personnel in those squadrons.

5. The Air Board has advised that ground personnel (less wireless trades and armourers) in excess of requirements in Australia can be provided without adverse effect on Home Air Defence requirements as at present planned, or on existing commitments under the Empire Air Training Scheme.

Organisation.

6. There is no indication of the type of squadrons the Royal Air Force proposed to form, nor is any reference made to the organisation above that of stations. The force visualised (i.e. eighteen squadrons), together with other Royal Australian Air Force commitments which have already been developed overseas may justify a higher organisation manned by Australians,

without which it does not appear possible for senior officers of the Royal Australian Air Force to get modern war (active service) experience. In the opinion of the Air Board, it is desirable that, dependent upon the extent to which Royal Australian Air Force participation overseas grows, a higher organisation (i.e. groups and, possibly, a command) officered by our personnel may be developed.

Recommendation.

7. I recommend War Cabinet approval to -

...

(b) preparation and implementation of a plan to enlist and train all ground personnel necessary for the eighteen squadrons proposed to be manned by Royal Australian Air Force aircrews during the next eighteen months;

(c) Air Ministry to be asked to furnish advice as to types and establishments of the squadrons to be formed as above and of the proposed organisation.

[AA: A 5954, Box 236]

Administrative arrangements were improved in June 1941 when it was decided to establish a RAAF Overseas Headquarters in the United Kingdom.

Document 45

Menzies to Bruce   4 July 1941

Cablegram 3495   *Secret*

... We have considered the administrative policy which we would wish to adopt in regard to the administration and control of R.A.A.F. personnel serving overseas. Department of Air has obtained Air Ministry views and, after careful consideration, we have concluded that the following policy is best suited to meet all conditions:-

(a) Squadrons are to be called squadrons of the R.A.A.F.
(b) They are attached to R.A.F. for operations and general administration.
(c) Promotions, appointments to commands and general administration will be within the jurisdiction of the R.A.F., but consultation with the R.A.A.F. will be had on all necessary matters in general conformity with the terms of the agreement, promotions to be subject to confirmation by the Governor-General.
(d) R.A.F. have undertaken to man the 18 E.A.T.S. Squadrons with 100 per cent Australian personnel when the personnel are available, and it is assumed that they will use for the purpose of such "manning" such R.A.A.F. personnel as may be offered by the R.A.A.F. and Aus-

tralian personnel available within R.A.F. on posting, attachment, or otherwise as appropriate.

(e) R.A.F. having given this undertaking and offered to appoint a R.A.A.F. Officer to the Promotions Board, should be sufficient evidence that the undertaking given as to appointments to commands and promotions will not only be carried out but, with the R.A.A.F. representative on the Promotions Board, it will ensure that the undertaking will be satisfactorily overseen from the point of view of opportunity for R.A.A.F. personnel.

(f) Having regard to the fact that our personnel are enlisted in the R.A.A.F., their surrender to R.A.F. for general operations and control cannot relieve the R.A.A.F. of a remaining responsibility for the individual and welfare problems of R.A.A.F. personnel overseas; and for this reason it appears necessary to create an Australian organisation in close proximity to Air Ministry Headquarters.

2. To implement this policy we propose to provide a senior R.A.A.F. Officer and establish a small R.A.A.F. Overseas Headquarters in United Kingdom. That Headquarters would be responsible for the following functions:-

(a) Inspection and liaison in connection with the Empire Air Training Scheme as defined in paragraph 10 of cable dated 23rd December, 1940, from High Commissioner, London, relating to the implementation of Article XV of the Empire Air Training Scheme Agreement.

(b) Direct access to and from the R.A.A.F. personnel assigned to Air Ministry branches for duties of reception, posting, pay, accounting, records and promotion. Normally, these groups will operate in accordance with methods prescribed by the R.A.F. and suitable for use by the R.A.A.F. with the relevant R.A.F. section, and under its general disciplinary control. It is understood a section for each Dominion will be formed within each branch of the Air Ministry.

(c) Records of R.A.A.F. Personnel employed in administration duties (reception, posting, etc.) associated with the Empire Air Training Scheme, Employment, movement, promotion, discipline and leave of this staff.

(d) To be the base for receiving and dealing with enquiries from Australia on location, condition and welfare of Empire Air Training Scheme personnel; for the oversight of hospital and other exceptional leave cases; for assi[s]tance in the organisation of comforts distribution, leave, entertainment, postal arrangements, etc.; historical records, and to supervise by arrangements with Air Ministry all matters relating to reception and repatriation of personnel.

3. Your cablegram No. 305. Fully agree with your view that there should be only one organisation in United Kingdom to deal with all E.A.T.S. and Air Liaison work and that that organisation should be controlled by senior R.A.A.F. officer who it appears could continue [to] give you all assistance and advice as now tendered by Liaison Officer.

Intended that this R.A.A.F. Headquarters organisation should function subject to all the limitations referred to above and work in very closest

collaboration with High Commissioner. All matters of policy affecting appointment of R.A.A.F. personnel and squadrons abroad, as well as negotiations connected with inter-governmental agreement, would of course remain your direct responsibility as the channel between United Kingdom and Commonwealth Governments. All financial adjustments and arrangements for supply and shipping would also remain fu[n]ctions of your office. If, however, desired by you, an officer for liaison duties would still be maintained in your office. ...
[AA: A 5954, Box 236]

Japan's entry into the war posed the question of how far Australia's contribution to the distant air war should be continued. It was also clear that in some way the EATS had to be reshaped to serve more closely Australia's immediate interests. The following extracts from a document produced in April 1943 illustrate how it was hoped to accomplish both aims. The expectation that operationally experienced aircrews could be returned to Australia was not, however, easily realised as the Minister for Air's letter demonstrates.

Document 46

Statement Requested by Shedden [April 1943]

THE RELATION OF AUSTRALIAN DEFENCE TO
THE EMPIRE AIR TRAINING SCHEME

1. DECISION BY WAR CABINET TO RETAIN EMPIRE AIR TRAINING SCHEME PERSONNEL IN AUSTRALIA.
(a) On 8th December, 1941, the Chief of the Air Staff was directed by War Cabinet to submit a report as to whether aircrew trainees under the E.A.T.S. should continue to be sent abroad, having regard to -
 (i) local defence needs;
 (ii) the availability of adequate escort protection in the Pacific.
(War Cabinet Minute (1557)).
(b) On 9th December War Cabinet decided that no further trainees or aircrew personnel under the E.A.T.S. should be sent abroad for the present, in view of the difficulties of providing adequate escort protection.
(War Cabinet Minute (1558)).
(c) War Cabinet also decided that a cablegram should be prepared for despatch to the United Kingdom Government with regard to redisposition of air resources.
(War Cabinet Minute (1558)).

2. *CABLEGRAM NO. 795 of 11th DECEMBER, 1941, TO DOMINIONS OFFICE.*

Cablegram No. 795 of 11th December, 1941, to the Secretary of State for Dominion Affairs, which was despatched pursuant to the decision of War Cabinet referred to in paragraph 1(c) above, contained the following:-

"It will be recalled that in April last Mr. Menzies was categorically assured by the Secretary of State for Air that, should war occur in the Far East, there will be an immediate review of air resources with a view to their redisposition to meet the dangers on all fronts. This contingency has now arisen."...

[4.] (h) On 5th February, 1942, War Cabinet had before it Agendum No. 440/1941, Supplement 1, but consideration was deferred pending the submission of a further statement, in the light of the following observations:-

(i) The Empire Air Training Scheme was agreed to in 1939 when the only enemy was Germany. Under the strategical conditions then prevailing, it was also possible to send abroad five squadrons of the R.A.A.F.

(ii) The entry of Japan into the war has entirely transformed the strategical situation relating to the defence of Australia.

(iii) An obvious case exists for the review of the Empire Air Training Scheme insofar as Australian commitments and benefits are concerned. The monthly output for despatch overseas will reach 1,050 personnel in September, 1942.

(iv) (a) The immediate needs of the new situation are the expansion of the Home Defence Force to the strength authorised. Sixty squadrons have been approved in principle. The present plan provides for 32, of which 20 have been formed, five of these being overseas. Wastage has also to be provided for.

(b) The formation of operational squadrons from training resources required certain personnel and replacements for wastage.

(v) Reinforcements of personnel necessary to maintain existing R.A.A.F. Permanent Squadrons serving overseas, and R.A.A.F. Squadrons already formed under the Empire Air Training Scheme and serving in the Far East, have also to be provided for.

(vi) It is a question for consideration whether, in the review of the Empire Air Training Scheme, as many as possible of the number of personnel surplus to Australian requirements that may proceed overseas should not go to the Pacific theatre for ultimate concentration into infiltrated R.A.A.F. Squadrons.

As in the case of A.I.F., there are considerable advantages of an operational, psychological and maintenance nature, in the concentration of Australian personnel in this theatre.

(vii) War Cabinet particularly stressed the view that corresponding to the outward flow of personnel from Australia there should be an inward flow of personnel with overseas war experience for service in squadrons in Australia.

(viii) Finally, there is the relation of Empire Air personnel requirements to the total manpower position in Australia, particularly in respect of Army requirements for Home Defence and the A.I.F., as well as munitions production.

(War Cabinet Minute (1854)). ...

(j) ... the question was considered by War Cabinet on 24th February and the following decisions given:-

"2. It was decided that, for the present, Australia would continue to provide her agreed quota of aircrew under the Empire Air Training Scheme, subject to steps being taken to modify, where necessary, the general arrangements so as to permit of the implementation of the following measures:-

(i) Increased percentage of personnel to receive advanced training in Australia, and the quota of partially trained personnel sent abroad for advanced training to be correspondingly reduced.
(ii) Facilities for operational training in Australia to be developed to the fullest extent possible.
(iii) The acquisition of the necessary aircraft and equipment for carrying out in Australia the additional training facilities mentioned in (i) and (ii).
(iv) A regulated inward flow of Australian aircrew with war experience to be maintained in order to provide an experienced nucleus of pilots and aircrew in all R.A.A.F. units based on Australia.
(v) The retention of aircrew who have been fully trained in Australia in sufficient numbers to fill establishments of Australian squadrons serving at home and abroad.
(vi) The allotment of as many as possible other Australian aircrew not required for squadrons mentioned in (v) to fill establishments of infiltrated R.A.A.F. squadrons serving in the Pacific theatre.

"3. It was also decided that:-
(i) The despatch of trainee pilots to Rhodesia should be discontinued; and
(ii) Insofar as the implementation of the measures mentioned above will not be interfered with, aircrew who have completed their training in Australia under the Scheme may now be despatched abroad."

(War Cabinet Minute (1919)).

AIR TRAINING CONFERENCE IN CANADA, MAY, 1942:
(a) In April, 1942, the Commonwealth Government was invited to attend a conference in Canada in May to discuss air training... .
(c) On the 15th May, 1942, a memorandum embodying the views of the Department of Air on the proposed Agenda for the Conferences was approved by War Cabinet Minute (2141). It was stated that, so far as could be seen at that time, Australia would be able to continue to train air crews considerably in excess of aircrew requirements for the numbers of service type aircraft likely to be allotted for operations in Australia. Figures were given of the estimated requirements for 73 Squadrons and of the surplus then available from output for service overseas with the R.A.F. It was further stated that training capacity

could not be expanded; that the existing rate could be maintained for at least one year; and that, given priorities in respect of manpower, it was unlikely that there would be any serious shortage before March, 1945. The memorandum expressed the view that Australia should continue to participate in the Air Training Plan, and that every effort should be made to maintain the existing training capacity and standard.

(d) On the 5th June, 1942, a supplementary agreement extending the Air Training Scheme to 31st March, 1945, was signed in Ottawa, and this action was confirmed by War Cabinet on 12th June (Minute 2186), and noted by the Advisory War Council in Minute No.(994) on 9th July. The main provisions of this agreement, insofar as Australia is concerned, were:-

(1) Australia's continued participation in the E.A.T.S. until March 31st, 1945.

(2) The agreement by the Dominions to supply approximately the same quota of personnel as previously.

It also provided for the re-definition of certain provisions, the most important of which were:-

(1) Acceptance in principle -
   (i) of more satisfactory arrangements in regard to promotions of personnel overseas;
   (ii) that aircrew personnel overseas should be identified, as far as practicable, with their parent squadrons.

(2) Applications for transfer by aircrew personnel to the Air Force of their own countries will be considered subject to the circumstances concerned and the making of suitable financial arrangements.

(3) Payment by the Commonwealth of its share of training costs will be on a per capita basis according to category (i.e. pilot, observer, wireless air gunner and air gunner), such per capita cost to be paid on the numbers of trainees actually despatched to Canada for training there. ...

[AA: A 5954, Box 578]

Document 47

Drakeford to Curtin   Canberra, 11 December 1942

Letter
AVAILABILITY OF AUSTRALIAN AIRCREWS WITH WAR EXPERIENCE.

With reference to your letter of the 2nd December, on abovementioned subject, I fully concur in your view that, having regard to the war situation in the Pacific, an adequate number of Australian pilots with overseas operational experience should be available for service here, and endeavours are continuing to be made to satisfactorily achieve that objective.

You will be interested to know that substantial numbers of war operationally-experienced aircrew personnel have already been returned to Australia, the precise numbers being -

Pilots 266
Observers 57
Wireless Air Gunners
 and Air Gunners .. 130

Those numbers are considered by the Air Staff as providing an adequate and satisfactory "stiffening" for the R.A.A.F. Squadrons at present functioning, more particularly so when combined with the very large numbers of our local aircrew personnel who have had extensive operational experience against the Japanese in New Guinea and Timor, as well as on long overseas reconnaissance flights on convoy protection, antisubmarine patrol, etc. Furthermore, the full establishments of war experienced aircrew, with reserves, recently came to Australia with Nos. 452 and 457 R.A.A.F. Squadrons made available by the R.A.F. All of these categories are, of course, additional to the numbers quoted in paragraph 2.

As regards the question of receiving a regular flow in future, I might say that certain difficulties are being experienced in obtaining numbers of aircrew possessing what we regard as operational experience sufficiently adequate to justify their return to Australia, our authorities here indicating that 100 hours should be the minimum requirement in that connection.

The most recent instance was when we requested the return of 30 Hudson or Beaufort crews to reinforce the aircrew personnel of our General Reconnaissance Squadrons and Operational Training Units. Of that total, we were allotted only 12 crews and, of those, two members were unacceptable as they had had only 30 and 11 hours' operational experience respectively to their credit. The question was taken up with Overseas Headquarters, London, which advised that, from a preliminary survey of R.A.F. Commands in United Kingdom and overseas, it would appear that, in order to obtain additional numbers of pilots we may require, it would be necessary to accept pilots with a maximum of 50 hours' or less operational experience.

This advice is somewhat difficult to reconcile with the fact that many thousands of Australian-trained aircrew have proceeded overseas during the last eighteen months, large numbers of them having excellent records and a substantial number of flying hours' operational experience to their credit.

Two factors which may, however, be responsible to a degree for the advice in the penultimate paragraph are -

(a) that a great proportion of the E.A.T.S. aircrew overseas do not appear to be obtaining operational experience as rapidly as would be desirable. The Air Member for Personnel has advised that there is evidence to suggest that E.A.T.S. aircrew are "banking up" in pools overseas awaiting O.T.U. [Operational Training Unit] training, and that they have apparently to wait long periods before they are given the opportunity to go into operational work.

(b) Further, in view of the heavy wastage factor, it is quite possible that numbers of our aircrew personnel are undertaking duties of Flight Commanders and Squadron Commanders, while others, possibly, have been allotted more important posts.

These important matters are continuing as the subject of signals between these Headquarters and our London Office, as well as being covered by present discussions between Air Marshal Williams[18] and the Air Ministry authorities. I have no reason to believe that the results will not prove satisfactory.

I hope to be able to advise you more definitely within the next fortnight as to the results of those negotiations in this particular connection.
[AA: A 5954, Box 237]

One result of the changed Pacific strategic situation was the fact that only seventeen of the projected RAAF Empire Air Training Scheme squadrons were formed, five in the Middle East and twelve in the United Kingdom. They never became entirely Australian manned. The following document sets out the position regarding several of the issues previously raised following renegotiation of the agreement in March 1943.

Document 48

Notes on Advisory War Council   12 April 1943
Agendum No. 10/1943

EMPIRE AIR TRAINING SCHEME

1. *OUTLINE OF AGENDUM.*

This Agendum contains a report by the Chief of the Air Staff on the following matters relating to the Empire Air Training Scheme which were raised at a previous meeting of the Advisory War Council:-

...

(ii) the relief of Empire Air Training Scheme personnel who have served overseas for a considerable period;

(iii) the concentration of Australian personnel attached to R.A.F. Squadrons into R.A.A.F. Empire Air Training Scheme Squadrons by increasing the number of such Squadrons. ...

[2.] (ii) *Relief of Empire Air Training Scheme Personnel from Overseas Service.*

The Chief of the Air Staff refers to the following difficulties which are associated with the relief of R.A.A.F. Empire Air Training Scheme personnel from overseas service:-

---

18. Air Officer Commanding Overseas Headquarters RAAF, U.K.

(a) The R.A.A.F. training rate under the Empire Air Training Scheme agreement produces trained aircrew personnel far in excess of the number required in R.A.A.F. units in Australia. No system to provide for the return of all members can be instituted, therefore, until the numbers for whom employment is available in Australia approximate the numbers of those serving overseas.
(b) As there are many types of aircraft in use overseas which are not available in Australia, overseas personnel receive training and specialize on duties upon which, in many cases, they could not be usefully employed if returned to Australia.
(c) In addition, under the terms of the agreement personnel posted for duty overseas are placed at the disposal of the United Kingdom Government and, in return, that Government has supplied large quantities of training aircraft and facilities for the training of personnel in Australia. Any large scale withdrawal of members from overseas spheres would no doubt cause serious complications and have an appreciable effect upon R.A.F. aircrew planning.

In view of the above factors, the Chief of the Air Staff considers that it is impossible to do more at present than arrange relief upon a limited exchange basis. In his covering letter, the Minister for Air states that more than 450 operationally experienced R.A.A.F. personnel have been returned to Australia. No great difficulty is expected in arranging the necessary flow of such personnel for service in the Australian theatre of war.

(iii) *Concentration of Empire Air Training Scheme Personnel:*

The Air Ministry has agreed in principle to the concentration of R.A.A.F. personnel into Australian squadrons and will, subject to operational exigencies, take all practical steps to bring it about as rapidly as possible.

The formation of additional Australian Empire Air Training Scheme squadrons, beyond the 18 already formed, presents difficulties owing to our inability to provide the 4,000 ground crew staff required to complete establishments for the present squadrons. Certain R.A.F. squadrons are, however, being named as squadrons to receive R.A.A.F. aircrews, and this, as the Minister for Air points out, will be an added means of ensuring a greater concentration of R.A.A.F. personnel.

(Note:- On 11th January War Cabinet considered the question of providing the additional 4,000 ground staff personnel required for the above purpose. It was noted that the arrangements for the provision by Australia of full aircrews and of ground staffs as far as possible, for the manning of the 18 R.A.A.F. Empire Air Training Scheme squadrons, were made prior to the entry of Japan into the war.

War Cabinet decided that in view of the present acute shortage of manpower to meet the demands of the fighting Services, war production and essential services, no further commitments could be undertaken for the provision of personnel for service overseas.) ...

[AA: A 5954, Box 237]

From February 1944 the Empire Air Training Scheme began to wind down and in June the Air Ministry instructed that no further aircrew should be sent overseas. Thus the scheme ended nine months ahead of schedule. During its currency 27,387 aircrew were trained to an advanced stage in Australia, 10,351 were sent to Canada, and 674 to Rhodesia. The scheme's graduates served in all war theatres, and virtually every RAF squadron had at least one Australian on its strength for part of the war. We print the comments of the Chief of Air Staff on many of these aircrew.

Document 49

Jones to Drakeford   February 1946

WAR REPORT ... ROYAL AUSTRALIAN AIR FORCE
3rd September, 1939 to 31st December, 1945...

ROLL OF HONOUR

In the Royal Australian Air Force the price of victory has been high. We have received proof that 9,870 of our members gave their lives in the service of their King and Country. We can expect the final figure to be considerably higher than this for we are still endeavouring to establish the fate of 884 members known to be missing. Additional to this again are 3,290 airmen who sustained wounds or injuries while in the Service.

To the next of kin of all these members appropriate messages of sympathy have been forwarded. I wish now to record my personal sympathy and admiration for these people who gave their sons and husbands to the Service and bore with such fortitude their losses.

All Casualties to R.A.A.F. Personnel from 3rd September, 1939, to 31st December, 1945

Theatre	Killed, Died and Presumed Dead	Missing	Wounded and Injured	Total
S. & S.W. Pacific	2,835	692	1,706	5,233
Far East..	56	82	46	184
India, Burma. ..	155	92	89	336
Europe..	5,488	16	969	6,473
Middle East.. ..	1,131	1	413	1,545
Canada..	145		54	199
Other Areas.. ..	60	1	13	74
Total.. ..	9,870	884	3,290	14,044

[Printed by RAAF, Melbourne, February 1946]

4
THE MIDDLE EAST: THE 2nd AIF AND THE PRELUDE TO BATTLE

It was January 1941 before Australian troops were committed to battle at Bardia. After that they received little respite. Greece and Crete soon followed, then the defence of Tobruk and the campaign in Syria. Relations with the United Kingdom were not always cordial. Indeed, on the Australian side more often than not they were tinged with distrust. Menzies himself was more disillusioned than reassured about Britain's attitude towards Australia's needs and interests after his visit to London early in 1941. The later concern over the relief of Tobruk may therefore be interpreted as a culmination of Australian disquiet.

Before Bardia, the Australian government had two major concerns. Firstly, it was apprehensive that the troops might be made to fight without proper weapons and equipment or without suitable support from the United Kingdom. Secondly, it feared that the force might be broken up and used in a piecemeal way. This worry remained constant.

The following cable was drafted by Lt.-General E.K. Squires, Chief of the General Staff, for despatch by Menzies to Bruce on 26 January 1940. As Australian troops were reaching their camp in Palestine, Bruce cabled an appreciation from the British Chiefs of Staff.

Document 50

Squires for Bruce   Melbourne, 26 January 1940

Draft [Cablegram] [19]   *Most Secret*

"In view of forthcoming location of 2nd A.I.F. in Palestine for completion of training and equipment with modern weapons we should be glad to have earliest possible an appreciation of military situation in Near and Middle East (stop) In particular we should like information as to possible employment of Australian troops in those theatres either on active operations or temporarily on internal security duties in relief of more fully trained British troops (stop) We should be grateful also for information as to anticipated rate of provision of modern weapons and equipment for 2nd A.I.F.["]
[AA: A 2671, 55/1940]

---

19. This was despatched (unnumbered) on the same day.

Document 51

Bruce to Menzies London, 13 February 1940

Cablegram 114

. . .
Part 4: We [the British Chiefs of Staff] visualise employment of Australian troops as follows:-

If, when they are fit to take the field, the situation should require their active employment in the Middle East we should wish the Australian Government to agree to that course. If, on the other hand, the situation in the Middle East by that period was quiet we should wish to complete their equipment in France or the United Kingdom, and employ in France.

It is *NOT* our intention to employ on internal security duties in Palestine, but their very presence in the vicinity is expected to have salutary effect which will permit internal security duties to be carried out by smaller or less well-trained forces than at present.

Part 5: Cannot give at this stage any anticipated rate of provision of modern weapons and equipment. A very reasonable training scale of these has already been provided and it is the intention to increase this to war-establishment scale at least one month before the units will be considered as available for an expeditionary force.

The following are additional views of the Chiefs of the General Staff conveyed in long conversations with Ironside[20]:-

Part 2: Chiefs of the General Staff (1) do not consider German move in Danubian and Balkan countries probable in the Spring. Reasons:-

Difficulty of military operations and large number of troops necessary to employ.

(To me this is not convincing and in my view the probability of such move must be kept constantly in mind).

(2) consider the Italian intervention on the German side unlikely.

(In my view probably sound, but the whole position might be completely altered by German move attended by spectacular successes in the Danubian/Balkan countries.) ...

Part 5: Ironside stated that Australians regarded as the best troops available and when ready for utilisation will be given absolute priority in the supply of modern weapons and equipment.

[AA: A 2671, 55/1940]

---

20. General Sir Edmund Ironside, Chief of the Imperial General Staff, 4.9.1939 — 10.6.1940.

As the first troops of the 6th Division were training in the Middle East, Canberra told London of the principles which it expected would govern the employment of the 2nd AIF while under overall British command. On 25 March such conditions were accepted.

Document 52

Commonwealth Government to [Eden] Canberra, 9 March 1940

Cablegram 91 *Most Secret*

Immediate

As the 2nd Australian Imperial Force is now being despatched for co-operation with the British Army, Commonwealth Government suggest principles that are to govern the control and administration of that force while abroad should now be defined. Subject is urgent as the Commonwealth Government require to instruct the General-Officer-Commanding of the 2nd Australian Imperial Force [Blamey]. Commonwealth Government suggest the following considerations that affect the principles recommended below.

Commonwealth Government desire, as the first principle, that Australian Imperial Force should be as an Australian Force under its own commander who will have a direct responsibility to the Commonwealth Government with the right to communicate direct with that Government. Commonwealth Government also desire that no part of the force should be detached or employed apart from the main force without the consent of the General-Officer-Commanding of the 2nd Australian Imperial Force. Commonwealth Government also suggest that questions of policy regarding employment of the Force should be decided by the United Kingdom and the Commonwealth Governments in consultation, except that in an emergency the Commander of the Australian Imperial Force may at his discretion make a decision on such a question, informing the Commonwealth Government that he is so doing.

Commonwealth Government realise the necessity for a unified command over the whole forces of the Empire which are located or engaged in any one theatre, and therefore suggest as the second principle that the Australian Imperial Force should be placed under operational control of the Commander-in-Chief of the theatre in which it is serving. Commonwealth Government also realise the desirability of the Australian Force and British forces using a common line of communication thus obviating the necessity of the Australians to provide an extensive organisation for movement and maintenance additional to that established for British Army.

Commonwealth Government also realise the desirability of facilitating transfer of British forces as occasion may require and also realise the necessity for flexibility in the whole organisation.

Commonwealth Government therefore suggest as the third principle that administration of supply services and such other questions as are amenable to adoption of a common system should be controlled by the Commander-in-Chief of the force in which the Australian Imperial Force is serving subject to a financial adjustment between the respective Governments concerning the cost of such administration incurred by the United Kingdom Government. All major financial questions arising from service abroad of the 2nd Australian Imperial Force to be reserved for direct discussion between the Commonwealth and United Kingdom Governments.

Commonwealth Government also consider that it is desirable that the General-Officer-Commanding of the 2nd Australian Imperial Force should retain full control, subject to the directions of the Commonwealth Government, over such matters of internal concern as appointments[,] promotions[,] transfers and posting of personnel of the internal organisation[,] pay and finance[,] records and co-operation with the Australian Welfare organisations which can be best administered under independent control of the Australian authorities. Commonwealth Government therefore suggest as the fourth principle that administration of the 2nd Australian Imperial Force domestic matters should be a prerogative of the General-Officer-Commanding of the 2nd Australian Imperial Force subject to the general control by the Commonwealth Government.

Commonwealth Government would be glad to have agreement by the United Kingdom Government in these four principles as early as possible. Ends.
[AA: A 5954, Box 619]

Fear that the 2nd AIF might become and remain a divided force was shown when Italian entry into the war seemed imminent. The second and third convoys containing chiefly the 17th and 18th Brigades, were considered to be in danger should they attempt to pass through the Red Sea close to Italian territory. The British suggested that the convoy instead should be diverted to the United Kingdom around the Cape of Good Hope. Australia replied as follows.

Document 53

Menzies to Eden   1 May 1940

Cablegram [Not Numbered]   *Most Secret*

...
Before answering your suggestion that the second and third convoys be diverted to the United Kingdom, the Commonwealth Government would like an appreciation by your Chiefs of Staff on the likely possibilities of the prospective situation, the measures required to counter the probable plans of the enemy and to provide for the security of our interests, and the zone

in which the A.I.F. could most effectively co-operate. We can then more clearly see our part in the scheme of things. No doubt this information is readily available as the possibility of being confronted with an alliance of this nature has long been referred to in C.I.D. [Committee of Imperial Defence] documents.

<u>The Commonwealth Government is gravely concerned at the prospect of the 6th Division being split into parts located in Palestine and the United Kingdom</u>. Though this entails administrative handicaps there is also the possibility of difficulties in re-concentration from the operational point of view. In our minds the latter is imperative. Furthermore, such a wide dispersion might prejudice the fulfilment of the decision as to the theatre in which the A.I.F. should serve.

Pending the receipt of the appreciation and a decision our view is that the second convoy should be held at Colombo for a few days and in view of the urgency of the matter the Chief of the Naval Staff [Colvin] was asked to forward a signal accordingly to the Commander of escort and Admiralty.

...

[AA: A 2671, 96 and 97/1940]

> The Australian Chiefs of Staff urged War Cabinet to accept the British recommendation and provided the following appreciation of the strategic implications of Italy entering the war. It is noteworthy for its lack of information and its strong commitment to 'forward defence'.

Document 54

War Cabinet Paper   2 May 1940

STRATEGICAL APPRECIATION BY AUSTRALIAN CHIEFS OF STAFF[21]

The Chiefs of Staff are not in a position to lay before the War Cabinet an appreciation of the situation which the advent of Italy in support of the Germans would create. The necessary data as to strength and disposition of the forces concerned and the political and other intelligence needful for the purpose are not available to them.

2. The seriousness of the augmentation of enemy forces and the extension of the flanks of the areas of operation, firstly to Norway and secondly to north and east Africa, is self-evident and needs no stressing, nor is it necessary to emphasize the danger of dispersing our forces.

3. To the Empire the Suez Canal and the passage of the Red Sea have always been of immense strategical importance. Their complete safety is

---

21. General Sir Brudenell White (CGS), Admiral Sir Ragnar M. Colvin (CNS), and Air Chief Marshal Sir Charles S. Burnett (CAS).

dependent upon our control of the Mediterranean and of the Red Sea. We are not in a position to make any estimate of the length of time which would be involved in regaining control of the Mediterranean. Nor are we able to speak with any certainty of an early clearance of the Red Sea. Doubtless, effort would early be concentrated on this latter task, as it is of first importance that the Empire should be able to support the forces about Egypt and Palestine and so to isolate Abyssinia and be able to thwart any Italian action from Libya.

4. The advent of Italy into the war is unlikely seriously to affect the Naval situation in areas outside those discussed in paragraph 3 above. The main Italian Naval forces are contained in the Mediterranean, and the only small units disposed elsewhere are in the Red Sea. Apart from this area, there are no Italian forces in the Indian or Pacific Oceans. The Italians have made little preparation for arming their merchant vessels, and the menace from this source is very small.

5. Taking these factors into consideration and the other most important factor, that Germany's Naval strength has been drastically reduced in the Norwegian venture, it is considered that the prospective threat to Allied sea communications in the Pacific and Indian Oceans is very small.

6. The Cape route to the United Kingdom (which is only 10% longer than the Suez route) becomes of greater importance, and there should be no difficulty in adequately safeguarding it. Convoys proceeding via Capetown could be routed from that port through the Red Sea if and when this route was reopened.

7. Until the Red Sea route is opened, there may be difficulty in getting supplies to our Forces in the Suez Canal area, but this problem is one which the United Kingdom Government must have under review. It is clear, however, that the clearance of the Red Sea route is one of the urgent and major necessities.

8. From the Air point of view there can be no question that British shipping in the Red Sea would be open to air attack in considerable force.

9. From latest reports, which admittedly are not up to date, the Italians have in Italian East Africa ([E]ritrea and Abyssinia) some 230 bombers and some 45 fighters, including reserves. The majority of these aircraft could be transferred from one area to another without much difficulty if petrol facilities allowed. Shipping could come under Italian air attack from the entrance to the Gulf of Aden to as far north as Port Sudan. Our air forces at Aden consist of some 24 bombers and 6 fighters with reserves. We have one squadron of bombers at Nairobi, one squadron of 18 bombers at Khartoum. In the Middle East there are some five squadrons of bombers and three squadrons of fighters. The French have at Djibouti one squadron of bombers and one flight of fighters.

10. Air reinforcements could be sent from Iraq, India, Singapore and South Africa provided the situation allows.

11. Finally, we consider that if the intervention of Italy occurs, the need is emphasized of Australian assistance in the main theatre as fully and promptly as possible.

[AA: A 2671, 96 and 97/1940]

These troops in the second convoy with the 17th Brigade went to Palestine, but the Australian government remained most concerned over the prospects facing its forces in the Middle East should Italian intervention prevent Britain supplying them through the Mediterranean.

Document 55

Menzies to Eden   8 May 1940

Cablegram 208   *Most Secret*

. . .

(B) *Equipping and Reconcentration of A.I.F.*

Commonwealth Government notes with some concern the statement in your cablegram 129 of 30th April that if the war with Italy were to break out subsequent to the arrival of the contingents in Egypt, there might be considerable difficulty in equipping our troops, as necessary material has to come from United Kingdom sources.

It will be recalled that the High Commissioner, in accordance with cabled directions of 26th January, made representations on the situation in the Near and Middle East, the possibility of employment of Australian troops on active operations, and the anticipated rate of revision of modern weapons and equipment.

We would urge in view of the statement quoted that the utmost expedition be used in fully equipping our troops, the present forecast of which is given as mid-September.

Should diversion of convoys to the United Kingdom become necessary the Commonwealth Government stress the importance of reconstituting the whole Expeditionary Force at the earliest possible date, and note your assurance that this will be done.

(C) *Ultimate Theatre of Employment*

The Chiefs of Staff indicate that the most likely theatres for the employment of the A.I.F. are the Near East and France. You will no doubt raise this aspect again when the training and equipping of the Force has reached a stage to enable it to take the field. ...

[AA: CP 290/6, Bundle 3, 59]

Australian fears that the 2nd AIF would be dispersed, however, were soon realised. The third convoy was diverted to the United Kingdom, arriving with 8,000 Australian troops seven days after Italy had declared war on 10 June. These men were to become part of a garrison while Britain waited for possible invasion. Despite inadequate training, they would have been committed to fight if necessary as this Dominions Office cable gently indicated.

Document 56

Caldecote [Secretary of State, London, 12 June 1940
Dominion Affairs] to Menzies

Cablegram 202 Secret

    As the Dominion Governments will have appreciated, the success of the German attack in Northern France has produced a situation in which an attempted invasion of this country, possibly in the near future, has to be taken very seriously into account with practical effects on the disposition of all available military land forces in the United Kingdom. The policy which it had hitherto been hoped to follow in respect of Dominion troops while training in this country was to allocate them to areas primarily selected on grounds of suitability for training purposes and entirely without reference to the possibility of the troops in question having to be used as part of the available defence of the country.

    The altered situation with which we are now faced has necessitated reconsideration of the disposition of the Australian and New Zealand contingents which will very shortly be arriving in this country. It had of course been hoped to locate these contingents and to make all other arrangements connected with their arrival here with the continuation of their training solely in view... As the situation now is, it is necessary to make such arrangements for the location of contingents as will best suit the needs of the time. Every effort will of course be made to arrange for continuation of the training on the most effective lines including, so far as possible, avoidance of dispersal, but there is no alternative to locating contingents in any district in the United Kingdom where, having regard to stage of training already reached and the high quality of the troops, they will be best placed to carry out whatever defensive role it might be necessary on occurrence of an emergency to allot to them. We are confident that in the circumstances His Majesty's Government in the Commonwealth of Australia and His Majesty's Government in New Zealand will raise no objection to this. ...

[AA: CP 290/6, Bundle 3, 59]

    By the middle of June 1940, therefore, the immediate prospect of concentrating Australian troops had disappeared. So had the possibility of equipping them. The Middle East had become a potential battlezone, difficult to maintain with an Italian naval force in the Red Sea. General Sir Thomas Blamey, commander of the AIF, summed up the position from Palestine in July. In London, Bruce made many attempts to have the Middle East reinforced, particularly after Menzies realised that after ten months of war forces there 'constituted little more than peacetime garrison requirements'. We also print Bruce's version of a conversation he had with General Sir John Dill, Chief of the Imperial General Staff, on 30 August and a cable sent on Bruce's instigation to the Secretary of State for Dominion Affairs on 7 September.

Document 57

Churchill [British Prime Minister] to Menzies [via Caldecote]

London, 23 June 1940

Cablegram [Not Numbered]

Most Secret and Personal

. . .
   Although, as you will appreciate, the position at the moment is as obscure as it is grave, I should like to say how greatly we are fortified in our resolution by having with us an Australian brigade group. Their first task will be to defend the Mother Country. The more the better. I know well how anxious you are to see the early recons[ti]tution of the whole of the Australian Military Forces. Much depends on the relative importance assumed by the home and the Middle East theatres of war, and by any other specially dangerous spots. I need hardly say that the position is being watched and studied day and night, and that the earliest possible communication will be made to you. We have by no means excluded offensive action next year after the defence of this island has been made good. You may rest assured also that the needs of the Australian Imperial Force in respect of equipment, wherever they may be fighting, will be provided to our utmost ability.
[AA: CP 290/6, Bundle 3, 59]

Document 58

Blamey to White [Chief of the General Staff]

Gaza, 7 July 1940

Cipher message

   ... FRENCH CAPITULATION AFFECTS SITUATION MIDDLE EAST THREE RESPECTS(.) *FIRST* NAVY CANNOT GUARANTEE PREVENT CONSIDERABLE REINFORCEMENTS NORTH AFRICA FROM EUROPE OF GERMAN OR ITALIAN ARMOURED UNITS(.) DIFFICULTIES ENEMY ATTACK ACROSS WESTERN DESERT VERY GREAT AND WITH PROPOSED REGROUPING FORMATIONS INTO FIELD FORCE WAVELL[22] CONFIDENT HIS ABILITY MEET ANY ATTACK LIKELY FOR THE PRESENT(.) I HAVE AGREED TO ARRANGEMENTS IN PREPARATION FOR ALLOCATION TO THIS FIELD FORCE OF A BRIGADE GROUP PLUS DIV CAV REG(.) THIS AT PRESENT IS LIMIT OF AVAILABLE EQUIPMENT(.) *SECONDLY* GERMAN AIR FORCES MAY BE USED ATTACK FLEET EASTERN MEDITERRANEAN FROM ITALIAN BASES(.) UP TO PRESENT OFFENSIVE VALUE ITALIAN AIR FORCE ALMOST NEGLIGIBLE BUT IF GERMANY PREPARED DIVERT

---

22. Commander-in-Chief in the Middle East, 28.7.1939–5.7.1941.

SOME PORTION HER AIR FORCE FLEET MAY BE SUBJECTED TO MORE INTENSE SCALE OF ATTACK(.) IT WAS IN VIEW OF THIS FACTOR TOGETHER WITH DOUBTFUL ATTITUDE EGYPTIAN ARMY WHO MAN BULK AA [Anti-Aircraft] EQUIPMENT THAT I AGREED TEMPORARY CONVERSION ONE FD REGT AND ONE INF BN TO AA UNITS(.) *THIRDLY* POSSIBLE BUT NOT PROBABLE INTERNAL TROUBLE SYRIA(.) ALL WAVELL DESIRES IS PEACEFUL SYRIA AND AVOIDANCE FURTHER INTERNAL SECURITY COMMITMENTS(.) BRITISH HANDS OFF DECLARATION GENERALLY WELCOMED MIDDLE EAST BUT POSITION WILL REMAIN OBSCURE OWING PRESENCE IN SYRIA THREE FRENCH DIVISIONS PLUS SECURITY TROOPS(.) GENERAL ATTITUDE ALL THREE SERVICE CS-IN-C IS TO TAKE OFFENSIVE WHEREVER POSSIBLE BEARING IN MIND NEED FOR HUSBANDING LIMITED RESOURCES(.) THEY ARE CONFIDENT IN THEIR ABILITY TO DEAL WITH ANY ITALIAN ACTION THAT CAN BE FORESEEN AT PRESENT(.) MY OWN VIEW IS NO IMMEDIATE CAUSE FOR ANXIETY BUT SITUATION LIABLE CHANGE IN VIEW ALTERED FLEET POSITION(.) PRIME FACTOR OF SAFETY IS CONTINUANCE OF CONTROL OF EASTERN MEDITERRANEAN BY OUR FLEET(.) I WILL ENSURE THAT NO PART OF AIF IS COMMITTED ACTIVE OPERATIONS UNLESS PROPERLY EQUIPPED(.) NO REPLY YET FROM INDIA RE SUPPLY EQUIPMENT(.) MIDEAST FEEL NO RESULT LIKELY AS SIMILAR PREVIOUS REQUEST BY THEM REFUSED(.)
[AWM: 54, 243/4/6]

Document 59

Note by Bruce London, 30 August 1940

Chief of the General Imperial Staff
General Sir John DILL

Saw Dill with regard to the despatch of Wynter's[23] troops in the United Kingdom to the Middle East to join up with Blamey's. I emphasised to him the necessity for getting all the Australian troops into the one arena of war so that our maximum effort could be realised and the greatest efficiency could be achieved.

I also stressed that it was desirable to get the Australians out of England before the winter, both from a health point of view and from the disciplinary angle as I saw grave difficulties in having them in separate billets.

Dill entirely agreed and said that the War Office was most anxious to despatch our Forces to the Near East both for the reasons which I had given

---

23. Major-General H.D. Wynter, GOC 9th Division 1940–Jan. 1941.

and because of the value they would be there. He said the problem was wrapped up with that of transport but the present position was that it was anticipated half of our troops would go in the convoy on the 25th September and the other half at the beginning of November.

I asked whether it would not be possible to get them all away in October and he said present indications were that it would not, but that this point was not yet finally determined. He promised, however, to keep me in touch with the position.

I said that I assumed the troops going from here would be fully equipped and with this he agreed.

I then stressed to him the importance of the whole of our troops in the Middle East being equipped at the earliest possible moment, saying that nothing could be more disastrous than in the event of any major attack our troops being caught unequipped. I pointed out that such a happening might even strain the relations between Australia and Great Britain.

Dill assured me that he realised the importance of getting the Australian troops fully equipped at the earliest possible date, but I am inclined to think what I had said to him brought home to him more emphatically the vital necessity of doing so.

We then had a considerable conversation on the question of the position in the Middle East and I put to him my anxieties and apprehensions which it is not necessary to record here. It was clear that he was considerably disturbed at the position but I gathered he felt that the really serious danger would in great measure be removed if we could get to the end of the present month when the reinforcements now on the way would have arrived.

I told him that while I would certainly be a good deal happier if we got to the end of the present month and the reinforcements had arrived, but none the less I still felt a great deal more had to be done and I was doubtful whether the importance of the Middle East was fully realised in the War Cabinet.

We then left the matter on the understanding that I would keep up all the pressure I could to ensure the maximum support being sent to Wavell.
[AA: M100, 12]

Document 60

Menzies to Caldecote 7 September 1940

Cablegram 471 *Most Secret*

We have given consideration to position in the [M]iddle [E]ast and possible developments in the Mediterranean area.

While recognising that under no considerations should the defences of the British Isles themselves be depleted and that the first consideration must be to ensure impregnability of homeland, nevertheless we feel strongly that whole Empire position would be endangered should our forces be driven from [M]iddle East and control lost in Mediterranean.

The loss of Egypt and Palestine would destroy our prestige and imperil our diplomatic bargaining powers. It would also counteract results already achieved in defeating German thrusts at the United Kingdom.

In addition it would probably necessitate withdrawal of the fleet from the Eastern Mediterranean and would reduce the Western blockade to a point of ineffectiveness.

The door would be open for the enemy to attack Kenya and in fact the whole of Africa and they would have access to the oil fields of Iraq and Iran.

The implications of such a success would stimulate the activities of the anti-British parties in Japan and encourage them in any fresh adventure.

While we recognise the Italian advance in Somaliland has been counterbalanced by British Defence of United Kingdom and in particular of R.A.F. successes both in defence and offence, we feel that our favourable position could not be sustained if any severe blow was inflicted in [M]iddle East. We cannot stress too strongly the importance we attach to the holding of this area and urge that a maximum effort should be made there compatible with the safety of the United Kingdom.
[AA: A 1608, H41/1/3, Part 1]

Australia increased its contribution to the defence of the Middle East when it sent the 7th Division there (see Section 8). Again it was stipulated that the troops would require adequate equipment. On 13 September, Italian forces moved into Egypt. On 23 September, War Cabinet accepted the recommendation of the Chief of General Staff that the 9th Division should be formed from the nucleus of troops in the United Kingdom and sent to the Middle East also. The short cable printed below must have come as a shock to Menzies two days later. Nor could Blamey's comments sent on to Bruce have been thoroughly reassuring.

Document 61

Bruce to Menzies   London, 24 September 1940

Cablegram 836   *Most Secret*

MIDDLE EAST. Have just heard, though not yet confirmed, that air reinforcements which were being steadily sent to Middle East have been stopped. This due to the Prime Minister's [Churchill] obsession with problem of defence of these islands.

While appreciating the importance of this, do not consider that the retention of Middle Eastern air reinforcements could have marked effect here, while may be decisive in that theatre.

Am pressing strongly that flow to the Middle East should not be stopped.
[AA: CP 290/7, Bundle 2, 13]

Document 62

Menzies to Bruce	2 November 1940

Cablegram 949	*Most Secret*

The reply which I have received to a cable despatched to the G.O.C., A.I.F. [Blamey] in the Middle East, asking whether he was satisfied with the degree to which the Sixth Division was equipped, their standard of training and general preparedness, is considered by the Government to be of such importance that it is transmitted to you in full. The advices of the United Kingdom Government from time to time of the measures being taken to strengthen the equipment of the Forces in the Middle East have been noted, but you should exercise continuous pressure on the United Kingdom authorities to ensure that the A.I.F. is fully equipped as early as possible:-

G.O.C's message --

(begins) MOST SECRET. Your C.22/10. For Prime Minister from General Blamey. Part I.

I am not satisfied that the Force has been satisfactorily and fully equipped. In common with most British units in the Middle East there are considerable deficiencies yet to be made good. Sixth Australian Division is at present being concentrated in the Amariya area immediately west of Alexandria, where it is continuing its training and completing equipment. In the event of a serious enemy advance eastward it will have the role of protection of lines of communication from Maaton Bagush to Amariya. For this role I am satisfied that the portion of the Division allotted be provided adequately trained and satisfactorily equipped.

Part II. I am continually urging on G.H.Q., Middle East, the need for completion of the A.I.F. in war equipment, but the plain fact is that supplies from England are not arriving as rapidly as is desired, although considerable stocks are now coming in. The Commander in Chief [Wavell] is faced with a most difficult situation should he be compelled to accept battle before all his units are fully equipped. He cannot avoid battle since the enemy for the time being have the initiative. Under the circumstances bound to agree to the participation of Australian troops in a defensive role seeing that they are generally better equipped than the remainder of the British Forces available. There is no probability of them being employed in offensive operations at present. I am of opinion that there is no reason to anticipate a serious Italian offensive against Egypt in immediate future. The Commander in Chief has no misgivings as to the adequacy of his forces to deal with any further advance should it be made.

(G.O.C's message ends).

[AA: CP 290/9, Bundle 1]

On 9 December 1940, Wavell's army took the offensive against Italian forces. With a force of virtually two divisions which included the 6th

Division, an advance of five hundred miles was made and an Italian army of some ten divisions was routed. The Australians, first committed at Bardia, went on to take Tobruk with some 25,000 prisoners. On 6 February, they reached Benghazi. The shortage of equipment, however, remained a problem despite earlier reassurances by the British government. After Bardia, Australian soldiers used captured Italian weapons. On 12 February 1941, German troops under General Rommel arrived in Libya. Of more immediate importance to our purposes, the Australian force was once again to be scattered, this time to Greece and Crete and to one of the greatest Allied disasters of the war.

5
DISASTER IN GREECE AND CRETE

Australia's involvement in Greek affairs began when Italy invaded Greece on 28 October 1940 and troops were moved from Egypt to Crete. In February, the Greeks, fearing a German attack through Bulgaria, accepted an offer made by Anthony Eden and the CIGS, Sir John Dill, in Athens. Menzies in London had the following appreciation before him when he attended the British War Cabinet. We print his comments and his subsequent cable to Canberra. Both show him agreeing with the policy decided upon by the British War Cabinet. Frederick Shedden, Secretary, Dept of Defence Co-ordination, however, had far-seeing reservations.

Document 63

[British] War Cabinet   London, 24 February 1941

W.P. (41) 39 (Revise)   Secret

POLICY IN THE MIDDLE EAST AND EASTERN MEDITERRANEAN

REPORT BY THE CHIEFS OF STAFF COMMITTEE

...
Advantages.
3. By going to Greece:-
   (a) We take the only remaining chance of forming a Balkan front, and of getting Turkey, and possibly Yugoslavia, to enter the war on our side.
   (b) The formation of the Balkan front would have the following advantages:—
      (i) It would make Germany fight at the end of a long line of communication, and expend resources uneconomically.
      (ii) It would interfere with Germany's peaceful trade with the Balkans, and particularly with the traffic in oil from Roumania.
      (iii) It would enable us to establish a platform for the bombing of Italy and the Roumanian oilfields.
      (iv) It would keep the war going in Albania, and prevent Italy devoting her energies to re-establishing her position in North Africa.
4. If we do not assist the Greeks, the Germans will gain control of the Balkans, possibly without firing a shot. This would result in Germany:-
   (a) Acquiring naval and air bases from which to threaten our position in the Eastern Mediterranean, including Crete and the Suez Canal, and to interfere with our communications to Turkey.

(b) Being free to concentrate on Turkey; thus paving the way for a further drive to the south and east.
(c) Being able to run oil traffic from the Black Sea to the Adriatic.

Disadvantages.

5. (a) We are undertaking a commitment of which we cannot foresee the extent.
(b) If we commit all our available resources to Greece we will have nothing left to offer the Turks who are already complaining of a shortage of war material.
(c) The despatch and subsequent maintenance of a force in Greece would involve a considerable shipping commitment. As a rough estimate we might have to forego as much as one million tons of imports a year. (This figure must of course be checked).
(d) If war spreads to the Far East and it is decided to withdraw the main units of the Mediterranean Fleet, our forces in Greece would be stranded.
(e) Our forces in North Africa will have been depleted. The Germans and Italians will be able to build up forces in Tripoli, and in due course we may be faced with a considerable threat from that direction, particularly in the air. If the Greek affair went wrong, and we lost our equipment, we might be hard put to it to provide enough for Egypt, apart from the time and shipping required to get it there.
(f) Our strategic reserve in the Middle East will have been thrown in at the outset of the battle. The Germans having got our forces into Greece may turn on Turkey first.
(g) There is an acute shortage of ammunition and equipment for the Greek army. If we have to supply them to keep them in the fight, we shall have to make further inroads on the equipment required for Home Defence.

Political considerations

6. In the above balance sheet we have confined ourselves to the military aspects of the problem. Politically it seems to us that there would be serious disadvantages if we were to fail to help Greece. The effect on public opinion throughout the world, particularly in America, of our deserting a small nation which is already engaged in a magnificent fight against one aggressor and is willing to defy another, would be lamentable.

Conclusions.

7. Our considered opinion is as follows:- The possible military advantages to be derived from going to the help of Greece are considerable, though their achievement is doubtful and the risks of failure are serious[.] The disadvantages of leaving Greece to her fate will be certain and far reaching. Even the complete failure of an honourable attempt to help Greece need not be disastrous to our future ability to defeat Germany. A weighty consideration in favour of going to Greece is to make the Germans fight for what they want instead of obtaining it by default. On balance we think that the enterprise should go forward. ...

Implications

...

10. The most important implications are as follows:-
    (a) *The extent of our effort in Greece.*
    We would be definitely committed to sending three Divisions, a Polish Brigade, and an Armoured Division, together with specialist units, e.g. anti-tank and A.A.; plus 14–16 squadrons of the R.A.F.; and the Greeks have been told that what we should do in future depended on the development of the general war situation and the state of our resources. It appears to us that the following are the most important limiting factors:-
    (i) We must not endanger our ability to resist invasion.
    (ii) The shipping commitment must not be such as to jeopardise the import situation. We must not, in fact, run the risk of strangulation at home.
    (iii) we must not reduce our forces in Egypt beyond the safety line.

...

[AA: A 5954, Box 626]

Document 64

British War Cabinet   [London] 24 February 1941

Extract from W.M. (41) 20th Conclusions,   Most Secret
Minute 4

MR. MENZIES said that before an Australian force could be employed in a new theatre of war, he would have to communicate with his colleagues. The question was clearly one of balancing risks, but there were one or two points on which he would like to be reassured. How long, for instance, would it take to put our troops into Greece, in order to take up a defensive position. Could our shipping maintain the strain of the operation? He was also a little uneasy regarding the equipment of the 7th Australian Division which was to be employed in this theatre, and which was now in Palestine, and equipped on the training scale. What were the prospects of giving full equipment to this Division? If these questions could be answered favourably, it would remove certain doubts in the minds of his colleagues in Australia.

The PRIME MINISTER [Churchill] said that he did not anticipate that the German advance would take place until about the 12–15th March and our troops should arrive at their positions at about the same time.

The VICE CHIEF OF THE IMPERIAL GENERAL STAFF [Haining] said that the 7th Australian Division was fully equipped, except for divisional artillery and certain motor transport. ... It was practically certain that General Blamey would have been called into consultation on this question. He thought that Mr. Menzies could rest assured that no Australian Division would be put into line without a full establishment of the necessary weapons.

MR. MENZIES asked whether if the enterprise failed the price of failure would be confined to the loss of the equipment of an armoured division.

The PRIME MINISTER said that if we should be pressed back our troops might well have to be evacuated; but that we ought to be able to evacuate safely all but the wounded.

MR. MENZIES said that the justification for the enterprise rested on the prospect of our being able to put up a good fight. If the enterprise was only a forlorn hope, it had better not be undertaken. Could he say to his colleagues in Australia that the venture had a substantial chance of success?

The PRIME MINISTER said that in the last resort this was a question which the Australian Cabinet must assess for themselves on Mr. Menzies' advice. In his (the Prime Minister's) opinion, the enterprise was a risk which we must undertake. At the worst he thought that the bulk of the men could be got back to Egypt, where new equipment could by then be provided. ...

The War Cabinet:
(1) Authorised the Prime Minister to send a telegram to the Secretary of State for Foreign Affairs [Eden] to the effect that, subject to (2) and (4) below, the War Cabinet approved the despatch of military assistance to Greece, on the basis of the scheme outlined in the telegrams from the Secretary of State for Foreign Affairs.
(2) Took note that, before an Australian force could be employed in a new theatre of war, Mr. Menzies would have to communicate with his colleagues in Australia, and invited him to make the necessary communication.
(3) In this connection invited the Secretary of State for War [Margesson] to confirm that the equipment of the 7th Australian Division would be completed in all essentials to full scale before proceeding to Greece. ...
[AA: A 5954, Box 626]

Document 65

Menzies to Fadden [Acting Prime Minister]   London, 25 February 1941

Cablegram 153   *Most Secret and Confidential*

You are receiving from Dominions Office a cable regarding proposed military assistance to Greece. Matter is of great moment to us because the forces initially contemplated are 2 Australian divisions, 1 New Zealand division, the better part of a new British armoured division, substantial supporting artillery and air reinforcements to bring up air strength to 14 or 16 squadrons. I attended the War Cabinet when this matter was discussed and the feeling here is unanimously in favour of the enterprise. Dill and Wavell who have recommended this are both able and cautious, and after examination on the spot consider there is a reasonable prospect of successfully holding up a German advance. I have been much exercised about the action. The military arguments are fairly well balanced, though I am much impressed by the danger of abandoning Greece and so providing Germany with naval and air bases from which to threaten the whole of our position in Eastern Mediterranean. Politically the argument is, I think, strongly in favour of the undertaking. The prospect of Yugoslavia and Turkey moving is not very great though Eden is at present in Turkey making a special effort. But the prospects would entirely disappear if Greece were abandoned to a German move through Bulgaria which it is thought will happen very soon. A bold move into Greece might possibly bring Yugoslavia and Turkey in with the result that a strong Balkan front could be established. I cannot think that an abandoned Greece should therefore do anything other than weaken our position in world opinion, scare Turkey and greatly hurry the Japanese. You will of course have in mind that the enterprise is risky.

Appears that it will involve real shipping difficulties and deplete the efforts of our forces in North Africa, and that in the event of our forces in Greece being driven back an evacuation might have to occur. I have discussed all these matters fully with Churchill and subsequently with the War Cabinet. The Prime Minister has offered the view that even if the enterprise failed the loss would primarily be one of material and that the bulk of the men could be got back to Egypt where new equipment could by then be provided. If this proposal was only a forlorn hope I would not like it and I so informed the War Cabinet. But the view of Dill and Wavell is clearly that it is much more than a forlorn hope. I specifically reserved all rights of the Australian Government but you will understand that the matter is most urgent and that your view should therefore be communicated promptly. ... with some anxiety my own recommendation to my colleagues is that we should concur. ...
[AA: A 981, War 46]

Document 66

Shedden to Menzies 26 February 1941

Memorandum *Most Secret*

FUTURE EMPLOYMENT OF THE A.I.F.

...

If there had been an opportunity for discussion I would like to have submitted for your consideration the following points:-
(1) The Prime Minister of the United Kingdom has stated that in the event of Japanese aggression against Australia the necessary Naval Forces would be drawn from the Mediterranean, even to the extent of abandoning the latter. We are now committed to maintaining fairly extensive lines of communication to Greece and the commitment of ensuring the withdrawal of our Forces from the Balkans may considerably delay the period within which relief can be sent to Singapore. You will recall that the period of relief of Singapore is a vital factor in its capacity to hold out. In addition, in maintaining our lines of communication with Greece we are of course also liable to greater losses in our

Naval strength than under present conditions. It would appear therefore that the security of Singapore may hinge entirely on the question of American assistance.

(2) ... the considerations in the Chiefs of Staff Appreciation are so evenly balanced that serious consideration must be given to the reverse side of the picture. If things go against us and we have to withdraw we could not expect to carry out as successful an evacuation as Gallipoli, where there were no Air Forces, or Dunkirk, where the home strength of the R.A.F. was available to assist in the operation. ...

As the primary object of our presence in the Middle East is the defence of Egypt and the Suez canal, it is presumed that this operation will not prejudice our defence of this region.

(3) ... there are very strong reasons why the Australian Corps of three Divisions should have been kept together, provided of course that their training and equipment is on a satisfactory basis. It is rather disturbing to have the separation which will now arise. ...

(4) You will remember at our discussion with the High Commissioner [Bruce] my suggestion that the comments of the G.O.C. A.I.F. [Blamey] should be obtained on the proposed operation. A draft cablegram was prepared on this aspect for your consideration, but it was not possible to establish contact with you as to whether a cablegram on the lines proposed should be despatched and an addition to such effect made in your cablegram to the Acting Prime Minister [Fadden].

[AA: A 5954, Box 587]

War Cabinet did not seek the opinion of its own military advisers but Menzies again met the British War Cabinet and was reassured by it. Blamey, in the Middle East, offered his views on command in a letter which Menzies later claimed he never received.

Document 67

War Cabinet Minute   Sydney, 26 February 1941

PRESENT: The Hon. A.W. Fadden, M.P., Acting Prime Minister and Acting Minister for Defence Co-ordination.
The Rt. Hon. W.M. Hughes, C.H., K.C., M.P., Attorney-General and Minister for the Navy.
The Hon. P.C. Spender, K.C., M.P., Minister for the Army.
The Hon. J. McEwen, M.P., Minister for Air.
Senator the Hon. H.S. Foll, Minister for Information and Minister for the Interior.
Senator the Hon. P.A. McBride, Minister for Supply and Development.

(838) DESPATCH OF A BRITISH MILITARY FORCE TO GREECE

...
The Acting Prime Minister raised the question as to whether the views of the Chiefs of Staff should be obtained in regard to the proposed disposition of the Australian forces. After some discussion it was agreed that the decision was one for War Cabinet, particularly in view of the sentence appearing in Mr. Menzies' cablegram reading:-

"With some anxiety, my own recommendation to my colleagues is that we should concur."

It was approved that a cablegram should be despatched to Mr. Menzies stating that after full discussion and after giving full weight to the points made by him in its favour, it had been decided to concur in the proposed use of two Australian Divisions in the forces initially contemplated, but that the following points should be raised with Mr. Menzies:-

(i) Whether the full force suggested could be regarded as adequate.
(ii) Whether further forces could not be added to augment it.
(iii) Indicating that the Government's consent had been given with a full appreciation of the risky nature of the adventure.
(iv) Asking that every step should be taken to ensure that if evacuation should be forced upon us, plans for evacuation would be completed beforehand and shipping and other facilities would be available.
(v) Stressing the necessity for full and adequate modern equipment.
(vi) That further consideration of the proposal had been prevented by the necessity for an expeditious decision.
(vii) Requesting that no reference should be made in Great Britain to the presence of our troops or of British troops in Greece before we are authorised to publish it here. ...

[AA: A 2673, Vol 5]

Document 68

Menzies to Fadden   London, 1 March 1941

Cablegram 165   *Most Secret*

... With regard to reinforcements they have here in mind the despatch of a British division already in the Middle East to be followed possibly by another British division from United Kingdom if shipping is available. In addition further forces will become available as soon as the situation in Italian East Africa has been cleared up. They have given me a firm assurance that no Dominion troops will be sent to Greece unless and until they are equipped to establishment in all essentials and specific instructions on this point are being issued to the Commander in Chief Middle East [Wavell].

With regard to your point 3 I am informed that while the move is in progress shipping will always be available should a withdrawal become

necessary. After the forces are established in Greece there will be no lack of shipping to carry out a withdrawal if such a course is forced upon us. It is impossible to prepare in advance detailed plans for a withdrawal because these must finally depend on the developments in the theatre of operations. But the abundance of local shipping and the proximity of the Greek islands should facilitate the withdrawal if it became necessary.
[AA: A 5954, Box 626]

Document 69

Blamey to Menzies   Middle East, 5 March 1941

Letter   *Most Secret and Personal*

I sent a wire to you in the following terms –
'Operations Plan in preparation includes Australian Corps less one division (.) Have pointed out necessity of obtaining concurrence Australian Government (.) With New Zealand troops majority of force from dominions (.) Wavell proposes appointing Wilson[24] to command (.) As matter of principle have raised point that I should be considered for command (.) In view your presence in London Wavell is referring matter for decision (.) No personal objection whatever decision give.'

On the same day General Wavell sent a wire to the British Government stating that as a matter of policy I had raised the question contained in the wire.

I would like to make it quite clear from the outset that this is not a personal matter in any sense, and no matter what answer might be given, it will not affect me in any way or the services I, and the troops, will render.

In his cable General Wavell stated that while the force was a total of 126,000, the Australian contribution was exactly 1/3rd; 42,000. This is perfectly true of the force as set down on paper, but it is far from describing the exact position. The whole of the fighting troops, except an armoured brigade group, and a considerable body of artillery, are Australian and New Zealand. General Wavell's figures are arrived at by adding up the sum total of the force actual and potential, as set forth in an Order of Battle prepared by his Staff, and whereas the Australian and New Zealand parts are actual, a very considerable proportion of the British is only forecast, some is on its way and some of it is not even in existence.

In order to set forth the true position, I have had a brief classified numerical summary of the force ... in the proposed Order of Battle made out... From this it will be seen that while the Australian and New Zealand troops, except for hospital and one or two other essentials, are practically all fighting troops, the British troops, except for the armoured brigade and a limited number of artillery, etc. are practically all non-fighting troops.

---

24. Lt. Gen. Sir Maitland Wilson GOC, Cyrenaica 1941, Greece 1941.

It is clear that, broadly speaking, the fighting is the function of the Dominion troops while supply and Line of Communication is the main function of the British. I do not know what the ultimate force may become, but the first addition one would expect would be Morshead's division [25].

Past experience has taught me to look with misgiving on a situation where British leaders have control of considerable bodies of first class dominion troops, while dominion commanders are excluded from all responsibility in control, planning and policy.

In the circumstances I feel it was right to put forward my point of view. I had no expectation that it would have any effect beyond keeping in notice the fact that when our troops are called upon the equality of status of dominion leaders cannot be ignored.

The plan, is of course, what I feared; piecemeal despatch to Europe. I am not criticising the higher policy that has required it, but regret that it must take this dangerous form. However, we will give a very good account of ourselves.

[AA: MP 729/7, 2/421/26]

Inside two weeks, however, the Germans had moved into Bulgaria and projected Greek troop deployments to meet this threat had not been carried out. Ominously, German armoured forces were appearing in North Africa. Yet a revised agreement to help Greece was reached in Athens. Menzies heard of the worsening prospects in the British War Cabinet on 6 March. After advice received from both Menzies and Blamey, the Australian War Cabinet virtually abandoned responsibility for its policy.

Document 70

British War Cabinet   London, 6 March 1941

W.M. (41) 25th Conclusions, Minute 1
Confidential Annex   *Most Secret*

. . .

MR. MENZIES stated that the problem had been presented in a way which made it unnecessarily difficult. When the War Cabinet had arrived at their earlier decision to send military aid to Greece, our military advisers in the Middle East had stated that the operation, though hazardous, offered a reasonable chance of resisting the German advance. All the new factors brought out in recent telegrams added to the difficulties of the operation, and no reason was offered why the operation should succeed.

---

25. Australian 9th Division commanded by Major General L.J. Morshead.

The War Cabinet had not, he thought, been well informed of the facts; and the action of the Foreign Secretary [Eden] regarding the military agreement between General Dill and General Papagos [Commander-in-Chief of the Greek Army] was embarrassing. He (Mr. Menzies) had had considerable difficulty in obtaining the consent of his colleagues in Australia to the despatch of Australian troops to Greece when the operation had first been proposed; but the Commonwealth Government had finally decided in favour of the operation, on his advice. He was now in the position of having to tell his colleagues that every new factor that had arisen since their previous decision told against the operation. Although it might be true that our position *vis-a-vis* the United States would be prejudiced if we did not go to the help of Greece, it must be remembered that if we did so and were driven out the effect on our prestige might be worse.

There were two ways in which the situation might be presented to the Dominions. The first was to tell them that the proposition did not now look as good as it had before; but as the Greeks had decided to fight on in any case we could not leave them in the lurch; and that our military advisers on the spot still thought the operation had a chance of success. If the proposition was presented in this way, he was confident of the reception it would receive.

The second way was to say that the proposition was a bad one, but that it must be proceeded with because we had been committed by an agreement signed in Athens, which had not been referred home. It must be remembered that the Dominions had a vital interest in this matter, as they were providing three-fifths of the forces to be used. If they were told that they were now committed to the use of their forces in a situation which had definitely worsened, without further effective consultation, he feared that there would be a good deal of resentment. ...
[AA: A 5954, Box 626]

Document 71

Menzies to Fadden London, 8 March 1941

Cablegram M13 Most Secret

... I have had a most anxious time over this matter [aid to Greece] but think that I can say that I have fully put to the War Cabinet the points which would trouble you. Our military advisers discount the possibilities of a successful thrust by a German armour[e]d force in North Africa and there is complete confidence that the Benghazi front can be held without interfering with the new project. There is no doubt, that having regard to the facts stated in the telegrams, the proposition is not as good as it was. In my opinion two considerations affected the decisions of the War Cabinet here. The first was that Eden and Dill had made a written agreement with the Greeks and the consequences of dishonouring of such an agreement would

be disastrous. The second was that on the intrinsic merits of the matters, great weight was to be attached to the fact that notwithstanding the new and adverse circumstances, Eden, Dill and Wavell all of whom were on the spot still considered that though the adventure was hazardous there was a reasonable prospect of success. ...
[AA: A 5954, Box 528]

Document 72

Blamey to Fadden [via Spender, Minister for the Army]
Alexandria, 10 March 1941

Cablegram [Not Numbered][26]
Most Secret

...
   British Forces immediately available consist of the 6th Australian Division, 7th Australian Division, New Zealand Division, One Armoured Brigade and Ancillary Troops. 7th Australian Division and the New Zealand Division have not been trained as complete Divisions. Available later at unknown date one Armoured Division. Practically no other troops in the Middle East not fully engaged. Arrival of other formations from overseas indefinite owing to shipping difficulties. Movement now under orders will be completed probably in two months.
   The Germans have as many Divisions available as roads can carry and capacity can be greatly increased in two months. It is certain that within three or four months we must be prepared to meet overwhelming forces completely equipped and trained. Greek Forces inadequate in numbers and equipment to deal with the first irruption of the strong German Army. Air Forces available 23 Squadrons. German Air Force within close striking range of the proposed theatre of operations and large Air Force can be brought to bear early in the summer. In view of the Germans much proclaimed intention to drive us off the continent wherever we appear, landing of this small British Force would be most welcome to them as it gives good reason to attack. The factors to be weighed are for (repeat for):
   (a) The effect of failure to reinforce Greece on opinion in Turkey, Yugo-Slavia and Greece; and against (repeat against),
   (b) The effect of defeat and second evacuation if such be possible on opinion and action of the same countries and Japan.
   Military operation extremely hazardous in view of the disparity between opposing forces in numbers and training.
[AA: A 5954, Box 528]

---

26. Contained in Teleprinter Message 762, 10.3.1941.

Document 73

Fadden to Menzies   Canberra, 10 March 1941

Cablegram 123   *Most Secret*

...
We assume full consideration has been given to extremely hazardous nature of operation in view of disparity between opposing forces both in number and training. We cannot help but feel that attitude of General Papagos which at one stage of discussions was described as unaccommodating and defeatist may possibly reflect a substantial body of opinion in Greece and may indicate a lowering of morale of Greek forces. We are informed by General Blamey G.O.C. Australian Imperial Force Middle East that British forces immediately available consist of 6th Australian Division 7th Australian Division New Zealand Division one armoured brigade and ancillary troops. 7th Australian Division and New Zealand Division have not been trained as complete divisions and there are practically no other troops in Middle East not fully (engaged). Copy of his telegram was directed by Minister for Army [Spender] to be sent to you simultaneously with despatch to himself and we think it advisable that you draw attention of United Kingdom Government and its advisers to observations made by him. There can be no doubt that landing of British troops in Greece will result in every effort being made by Germany with large available forces to inflict an overwhelming defeat particularly upon British forces engaged. Aid which Empire can give is limited on available troops in Middle East and flow of reinforcements which is able to be maintained.

Difficulties with regard to maintenance of supplies of munitions and equipment are sufficiently obvious to you not to require recapitulation in this telegram. [M]ining of Suez Canal we regard as most significant and as probably not unrelated to German plans in Balkans. Ability of Germany substantially to impede traffic via Suez cannot we feel be over-estimated.

Notwithstanding these considerations War Cabinet is undivided in its view that if military advisers, having properly evaluated risks which must be run, the large fully equipped and numerically superior German forces which can be directed to these operations (gr. unde.) adequacy in numbers and equipment of Greek, to deal with first eruption of German forces advise adventure that they should agree, in the high cause to which they will be dedicated, to make troops required available for this adventure with profound conviction that they will worthily uphold glorious traditions of Australian Imperial Force fighting side by side with so gallant an ally. Commonwealth Government steadfastly stands beside United Kingdom Government in this high enterprise should it be now decided to embark upon same. ...
[AA: A 5954, Box 626]

The background to Blamey's hostility to LUSTRE is shown in his letter to Spender printed below. Given Wavell's acknowledgement that there was no formal consultation, the question arises as to why Blamey waited until 8 March before approaching Canberra with a request to present what turned out to be unfavourable views.

Document 74

Blamey to Spender   Middle East, 12 March 1941

Letter   *Most Secret*

I have to report that I was called on by the Commander-in-Chief, Middle East, to return from Cyrenaica by air on the 17th February with reference to certain plans for operations. On 18th February I saw the Commander-in-Chief, Middle East, who communicated the plans he had made for the organization of a force designated 'Lustreforce' for operations in Greece. I informed him that in my view the matter would require to be referred to Australia, and he stated that he had discussed the possibility of such an operation with the Prime Minister of Australia.

Later the Commander-in-Chief read me a telegram from London stating that the proposal had been approved at a meeting of the War Cabinet at which Mr. Menzies was present.

On 6th March I was again called in and saw the Chief of the Imperial General Staff (General Sir John Dill) with the Commander-in-Chief. I was informed that following on a visit of the Commander-in-Chief to Greece that there was some doubt as to the plans developing. Although both on this and on the previous visits my views were not asked for and I felt I was receiving instructions, I made enquiries as to what other formations would be available and when.

I was informed that one further armoured division might be looked for at an unknown date, and that beyond that there were no plans for further reinforcing formations owing to the fact that shipping could not be made available. This information was very disturbing. I had been informed in December last by the Commander-in-Chief that the intention was to send some fourteen divisions to the Middle East and that they were expected to arrive at the rate of one division per month from February onwards.

The information given me as above completely altered the whole outlook, and I ventured to remark that in my opinion the operations under consideration in Greece were 'most hazardous' in view of our limited forces. Consequently it seemed incumbent on me to submit my views to you, and I sent a cable on the 8th March as follows -

'Before AIF is committed to operations now in preparation request permission to submit my views (.) You will appreciate that as I am under operational direction of C in C Middle East I cannot do so without direction from you'.

Following upon your reply I sent the following cable to you on the 10th March and, as directed, repeated it to the Australian Prime Minister in London and informed the Commander-in-Chief, Middle East, that I had done so. [*This cable is printed as Document 72*]. ...

The Commander-in-Chief and the Chief of the Imperial General Staff, who is still here, now hold very firmly that the operation should be put in hand.

I regret that I still feel very strongly that without a definite plan for building up the strength of the force adequately within the next few months, the operation is most hazardous.

The Commander-in-Chief, Middle East, and the Chief of the Imperial General Staff are of the opinion that in view of the mountainous and difficult nature of the proposed area of operations and the limited capacity of communications in the Balkan area, the operations, although risky, have a reasonable chance of success. They do not, in my opinion, give sufficient weight to German capacity to improve this rapidly during the summer. Nor, in my opinion, is sufficient weight given to the fact that whatever we can do it is unlikely that we can prevent German air superiority in regions favourably situated for the enemy in view of relative distances. ...

As it would appear that it will be held that the operation must take place, I beg to urge most strongly that vigorous action be taken to ensure that adequate forces for the task are provided at the most rapid rate possible.
[AWM: 54, 534/2/19]

Document 75

Wavell to Churchill					Middle East, 30 March 1941

Cablegram O/52955					*Most Secret*

Private and confidential for Prime Minister from Gen. Wavell.

... I am sorry if Blamey thinks I have not kept him sufficiently in picture; I thought I had been particularly careful to give him as much consideration as possible. It is true that I did not consult him previous to our agreement with Greece[.] I do not think it would have been possible or politic to do so, but I had previously outlined to him the possibility of our intervening in Greece and took him into my confidence immediately afterwards. Please assure Menzies I do my best and while Blamey was in Palestine sent him periodically my appreciation of Middle East situation and outline of my intentions.
[PRO: Premier 3/206/3]

On 25 March a pro-Allied coup in Yugoslavia was the cause for Churchill's enthusiastic cable printed below. German response, however, was to invade Yugoslavia and Greece. Belgrade quickly succumbed and

Greece signed an armistice on 21 April. Australian forces began to fight a rearguard action towards Blamey's expected evacuation, mainly to Crete. The Australian government became rightly concerned about the future of its force. At the same time Rommel had attacked in Libya. Thus the 7th Division could not be spared for Greece while the 9th Division fell back to Tobruk. Menzies laid the blame squarely on Wavell.

Document 76

Cranborne [Secretary of State, Dominion Affairs] to Whiskard   London, 30 March 1941

Cablegram 162   *Most Secret*

... the following message from Mr. Churchill to the Acting Prime Minister...

When a month ago we decided upon Lustre it looked a rather bleak military adventure dictated by noblesse oblige. Thursday's events in Belgrade show the far-reaching effects of this and other measures we have taken on the whole Balkan situation. German plans have been upset and we may cherish renewed hope of forming a Balkan front with Turkey comprising about 70 Allied divisions from the four Powers concerned. This is of course by no means certain yet. But even now it puts Lustre in its true setting not as an isolated military act but as a prime mover in a large design. Whatever the outcome may be everything that has happened since Lustre decision was taken justifies it. ...
[AA: A 5954, Box 528]

Document 77

Menzies to Fadden   London, 15 April 1941

Cablegram M 59   *Personal and Most Secret*

...
The position in Libya undoubtedly arises from utter miscalculation on the part of Wavell. The War Cabinet was surprised as was I to learn that the whole of the British Armoured Division under Creagh [27] had been withdrawn to Cairo for repairs thus leaving Benghazi very lightly covered by one new armoured brigade. This brigade does not appear to have been well handled and has been almost eliminated.

I have protested very strongly against this chronic underestimating of

---

27. General Michael Creagh, commander of the 7th Armoured Division.

German capacity but I am sure you will agree that it is no use crying over spilt milk and that urgent salvage operations must be the order of the day.

I have queried the attempt to hold Tobruk the bulk of the forces of which consist of the 9th Australian Division plus a brigade of the 7th, but Dill considers as do the whole of the Chiefs of Staff that Tobruk is of vital importance to any counter attack, being a bridge-head on the flank of the German advance, and that so far from being abandoned it should be reinforced by sea. ...

Confidentially I may tell you that my decision to remain for another week or two arises from the fact that I appear to be the only Minister outside the Prime Minister [Churchill] who will question any of his [Wavell] views or insist upon points being examined, and as Australia has so much at stake it would be most unwise for me to leave here in the middle of a crisis. ...
[AA: A 5954, Box 626]

Document 78

Fadden to Cranborne   18 April 1941

Cablegram 237   *Most Secret*

... In the circumstances the immediate evacuation of our troops from the Mainland of Greece is essential. We note and fully concur in the decision to hold Crete in force but hope that in the redistribution of his forces the Commander in Chief in the Middle East will not find it necessary to use Australian troops for this purpose as it is the wish of my Government that, subject to any over-riding circumstances making such a course unavoidable the Australian troops in the Middle East might be reassembled together as a complete corps. ... [M]y Government places the highest importance on the maintenance of the security of our position in Egypt and the protection of the Suez Canal. We fully appreciate the difficulties with which you are faced but as a substantial body of Australian fighting troops are vitally concerned we trust that the plans for their evacuation which have been prepared in advance as requested in our earlier messages may be successfully implemented in regard to our men, and that it will be possible also to save their equipment, which will have such an important bearing on the future disposition of the troops and the manner in which they can be utilised. ...
[AA: A 981, War 46]

The threatened political repercussions following the campaign led to Blamey's appointment as Deputy Commander Middle East within a week. Although some 25,000 Australians and New Zealanders were evacuated from Greece to Crete, disaster there was just as complete. Most were armed only with rifles, and setbacks in North Africa meant that they could only be marginally reinforced. On 20 May a massive

German airborne attack was launched and the battle was over inside two weeks. We print Brigadier Vasey's dispassionate report on Crete, presented in July. In August, Blamey left no doubt as to the reasons for the overall failure in Greece.

Document 79

Dill to Wavell   London, 19 April 1941

Cablegram 62362   *Most Secret*

    Just had long talk with Menzies. He is naturally perturbed as we all are that so many Australian troops should be operating under conditions full of grave possibilities. Many people in Australia were against their Expeditionary Force leaving the country at all and many more were against the Greek venture. The possibilities of strong and dangerous political reactions in Australia exist. Menzies foresees that the cry in Australia will be that not for the first time Australian troops have been sacrificed by incompetent Imperial Generals. In your new lay-out of the higher commands which we approved no Australian figures[,] and senior and experienced Australian Generals are asked to serve under one who was recently a junior Divisional Commander — Beresford-Peirse. Australia will resent this. Two things would go a long way towards improving situation.
    (1) Appointment of General Blamey to high command such as Western Desert and
    (2) Appointment of senior Australian liaison officer to your staff.
    Please let me have your views on above.
[AA: A 5954, Box 626]

Document 80

REPORT BY BRIGADIER G.A. VASEY, C.B.E., D.S.O.,   13 July 1941
COMMANDER OF THE 19th AUSTRALIAN INFANTRY BRIGADE ...

ACCOUNT OF OPERATIONS OF AIF IN CRETE   *Secret*

    When the 19 Aust Inf Bde arrived in CRETE on 26 Apr, it was found that Maj. Gen Sir I.G. MACKAY, K.B.E., C.M.G., D.S.O., V.D. and HQ 6 Aust Div were on the island. During the next two days arrangements were made by 6 Aust Div for the accommodation of AIF troops in the area East of SUDA, and British troops in the SUDA-KANEA area. Maj. Gen MACKAY and his senior staff officers left the island on the 29 Apr, and command of the AIF Troops in CRETE passed to Comd 19 Aust Inf Bde. ...
    During the next few days an endeavour was made by CRE-FORCE [second echelon of force to Crete] to organise the various troops in the area.

Difficulties in this regard were presented not only by lack of equipment and tpt but also by the landing during this period of 1500 personnel who survived the sinking of the 'COSTA RICA' and so arrived without arms or equipment of any description. At this stage the AIF personnel in the island represented detachments from almost every unit of 6 Aust Div, as well as the majority of Corps troops, who had been in GREECE. Constant representations were made to CRE-FORCE HQ with a view to evacuating from the island all those personnel who were not required for the defence of the island. These included, amongst others, personnel of Corps HQ, 6 Aust Gen Hospital, Corps AASC [Australian Army Service Corps], 6 Aust Div HQ and many other similar units. In all some 45 different units were represented. To Co-ordinate the evacuation from the island a Liaison Officer was sent to Force HQ, and a priority list for evacuation was drawn up. Despite representations made, the evacuation from the island was very slow, and prior to the commencement of active operations on 20 May, something less than 2500 AIF personnel had been sent away, and there still remained in the island a considerable number of personnel of the services of 6 Aust Div.

The policy adopted by Maj. Gen FREYBERG [28], who had been appointed to comd the island, was to arm all the personnel on the island with rifles so that they would be available for use against parachute troops.

In the meantime, re-equipping, re-organisation and re-distribution of the tps continued. On 1 May in accordance with orders issued by CREFORCE, 1 Bn moved by MT to RETIMO. On the afternoon of 3 May I was called to Force HQ and received orders to move my HQ and two bns to GEORGIOUPOLIS, moves occasioned by this were completed by the afternoon of 4 May. ...

From this time onwards all energies were devoted to improve the defences being occupied. At RETIMO in addition to the 2/1 and 2/11 Bns there were two Greek Bns. The task of this force was the protection of the landing ground at RETIMO against air-borne attack and the beach in that vicinity against sea-borne attack. At GIORGIOPULUS [sic] where were the 7 and 8 Bns the task was to defend the eastern entrance of the defile which led from GIORGIOPULUS [sic] westwards towards SUDA and the beach east of GIORGIOUPULUS [sic]. Italian guns were made available by Force HQ and personnel of the 3 Fd Regt manned these. There were four guns at RETIMO and 6 at GIORGIOPULUS [sic]. In addition barb wire, anti-tank mines, and later anti personnel mines were provided by Force HQ, and these were all laid in the areas. One Coy plus one Pl of 2/1 MG Bn had been equipped with guns and this detachment was distributed between RETIMO and GIORGIOPULUS [sic]. About 15 May two "I" Tanks were allotted to RETIMO.

Throughout the whole period on the island intercommunication was very difficult. The only communication between 19 Bde HQ and Force HQ and RETIMO was by means of telephone lines which passed through civil

---

28. Major General B.C. Freyberg, GOC New Zealand Division.

exchanges. There was no W/T available at 19 Bde HQ, but one No.9 set was provided by Force HQ for RETIMO. In view of the difficulty of intercommunication it was fully realised that when active operations commenced it would be impossible for me to control the operations of the detachment at RETIMO, and for this reason Lt. Col CAMPBELL, CO 2/1 Bn, was informed that when operations commenced he would assume comd of all the tps in RETIMO.

Up till the 20 May when the enemy made his first air borne attacks conditions for all units were on the whole very pleasant. The weather was mild and swimming was available for the majority of the tps. Although there was a great shortage of equipment of all kinds, including cooking gear and transport, units were able to improvise cooking and feeding arrangements which worked satisfactorily. The health and morale of the tps improved greatly during this period. An organization for distributing NAAFI [Navy, Army and Air Force Institute] goods to units was set up. ...

The anticipated attack by the enemy commenced on the 20 May when he landed parachute tps in the MELMEME area and KANEA area about 1100 hrs that day, and at RETIMO and HERAKLION about 1630 hrs. ...

[Space does not permit us to print Vasey's paragraphs on the AIF's operations on Crete. We resume the extract after the battle had been lost and the evacuation begun.]

Whilst the operations described above were in progress the remaining units of the AIF as well as other British and NZ units had been withdrawn to the area at the foot of the hills near SPHAKIA [an embarkation port]. Many of these units had become disorganised owing to stragglers and the mixing of units and the result was that there was in this back area 5/7000 troops who were not in regular organised units. Force HQ, which remained on the island until the night 30/31 May, took complete control of all arrangements for embarkation. Certain AIF officers including Lt. Col. STRUTT, [Commanding Officer] 2/3 Fd Regt, were employed on embarkation duties and I understand that on each night's embarkation, the AIF received approximately one-third of the total numbers to embark. This represented a fair proportion in view of the relative strengths.

On 31 May the enemy became more active against the 7th Bn with MG [Machine Gun] and mortar fire but none of his troops approached near to the foremost localities. Some enemy were seen however moving through the hills well to the east of the position. On the afternoon of 31 May I visited General Weston, who took over command after the departure of General Freyberg, at his HQ and he informed me that the following night would be the last night of embarkation and that it would be necessary for me to hold the enemy clear of the beach until then. I submitted that I could best do this by remaining in my present position for a further 24 hours provided that he made some arrangements for the protection of the beach from the east and west. To this he agreed.

On returning to my HQ about 1700 hrs I visited the 2/7 Bn and informed the CO of the decision. He said that provided the troops could be fed he saw no reason why he should not be able to hold the present position. On my way back to my HQ I was informed that General Weston was waiting to see me. On meeting him at 1940 hrs he informed me that the embarkation plans had been altered and that that night would be the last night of embarkation but that the Navy would take 1500 troops additional to the 2000 already arranged for. He said that the additional allotment to the AIF would be 500. I allocated this to the 2/7 Bn and my own HQ. ...

Bde HQ moved at 2100 hrs and after getting to the bottom of the hill and waiting outside General Weston's HQ for some little time continued their move towards the beach. The route lay along a wadi and a very narrow track which ended by winding through the village of SPHAKIA. When some considerable distance from the beach it was found that this road was blocked with men sitting down and many officers challenged anyone approaching wanting to know what they were. Other officers represented themselves as MCOs [Movement Control Officers] and eventually one of these said that only single file was allowed through from that point and that 19 Aust Inf Bde would have to wait. With the exception of myself and two staff officers, who went forward to see what the situation was in front, 19 Aust Inf Bde remained in this position for some time. On arrival at the beach I found the embarkation proceeding smoothly and troops filling the boats brought in from the ships reasonably quickly. Not long afterwards, however, it was noticed that troops were not available on the beach when boats came in and there was considerable delay in getting the boats filled and away to the ships. I sent my two Staff Officers back to investigate the reason for this and to see if Bde HQ and 7 Bn had got through and down to the beach. They were absent some considerable time but the rate of movement of troops on to the beach had improved.

19 Aust Inf Bde arrived on the beach at about 0215 hrs and they reported that they had been continually hampered in their movement by officers and others who prevented them from moving forward. At one time my BM [Brigade Major] had a Tommy Gun pressed against him whilst he was being questioned as to what he was doing.

I had been informed by the Navy that the last boats would leave at 0230 hrs and for this last trip they had two large MLCs [Motorised Landing Craft], each capable of taking about 180 troops. Just before 0230 hrs I was informed by one of my staff that Lt. Col. Walker, CO 2/7 Bn was in fact on the beach, and as there were on the beach sufficient troops to fill the 2 MLCs they were loaded and went off to the ships. On arrival at ALEXANDRIA next day I discovered that only two officers and about 14 ORs [Other Ranks] of 2/7 Bn had in fact got off the island. It would appear therefore that the 7 Bn had been delayed longer than my own HQ and that apparently Lt. Col WALKER had arrived at the beach and gone back to push his troops forward. The fact that that night was the last night of embarkation was made known by me to only two people outside my own HQ, since it was obvious that had this fact been widely known there would have been worse congestion than in fact proved to be the case. ...

It is a most regrettable thing that a Bn which had been covering the beach and protecting the embarkation for 48 hrs and which was then ordered to embark that night should have been prevented from doing so through lack of control in the area behind the beach. Actually on this night the Navy took off 4,050 persons which was over 500 in excess of the anticipated number. ...

In all some 9000 AIF personnel were evacuated from GREECE to CRETE of which only 2500 re-embarked for EGYPT prior to the battle. The number engaged in any fighting was 3100 and this included with the 5 Inf Bns arty details and necessary services. It was a great pity that further embarkation arrangements were not made prior to 20 May. Had this been done our casualties might well have been limited to battle casualties which were comparatively light. As it was about 3500 were left behind. ...
[AA: A 2671, 374/1941]

Document 81

War Cabinet Minute   Melbourne, 4 June 1941

(1113)...

(B) WEEKLY REPORTS BY THE CHIEF OF THE GENERAL STAFF

The Army reports were noted by War Cabinet after the following subjects had been specifically mentioned:-

(i) *Casualties in Crete*. ... The Minister for the Army furnished the following information received by him from the G.O.C., A.I.F.:–

Estimated number of A.I.F. in Crete prior to attack	6,486
Total number evacuated, including 526 wounded	2,887
Number not accounted for	<u>3,599</u>

It was stated that the G.O.C. is unable to separate the categories of killed, wounded, missing and prisoners-of-war in the number unaccounted for. ...
[AA: A 2673, Vol 7]

Document 82

Blamey to [Spender?]   Cairo, 7 August 1941

Letter   *Most Secret*

...

1. The outstanding lesson of the Greek Campaign is that no reasons what-

ever should outweigh military considerations when it is proposed to embark on a campaign, otherwise failure and defeat are courted. The main principles that must be satisfied are that the objects to be secured should be fully understood, the means to achieve the objects should be adequate and the plan should be such as will ensure success.

All three essentials were lacking in the campaign in Greece, with the resultant inevitable failure. As far as my limited knowledge goes the main reason for the despatch of the force appears to have been a political one, viz., to support the Greeks to vindicate our agreed obligations.

2. In my opinion we could have been fully vindicated in this regard by other plans had a close examination been made of alternatives which were within the limits of our capacity, e.g., limiting our military commitment to the capture and retention of essential bases such as Rhodes and Crete and utilizing the air and naval arms on a considered plan to secure the best results.

I have not seen the military appreciation on which the plan was based, therefore I am not fully conversant with the exact military objects of the expedition, but understand that they were to ensure that the Greek resistance to a German invasion should be succesful. If this was so, then it does not appear that the means available were adequate to achieve this result, or even to give it a reasonable chance of success.

The plan upon which the action was based was presumably the plan upon which the defence of Greece was conducted. This was largely a political plan and never had at any time any possibility of success with the limited help we planned to give. This was obvious from an examination of the position, armament and the strength of the opposing forces and of their capacity to reinforce, and the proposed plan of operations.

3. In the examination of the proposals, I am of the opinion that what is known as 'wishful' thinking played a great part. In support I cite these facts-
(a) An order of battle was prepared showing a force of 126,000. In the event about two-fifths of this number went to Greece, but even had the plans actually laid down been adhered to, not much more than half the number could have been sent. The reasons are that primarily many of the units shown therein were not in the Middle East, and secondly because some did not even exist.
(b) Secondly, the proposals for the Force gave the number of air squadrons at twenty-three. Actually eight operated in the Campaign, and as a matter of fact it was not within the bounds of possibility to bring twenty-three into the field. This, of course was not then known to me.

4. All our later difficulties in the Middle East are the direct result of this very unfortunate adventure. These may be summed up briefly as follows:-
(i) *Naval* — Loss of sea control of the Central Mediterranean. This followed on the loss of Crete and the retention of Rhodes by the Italians. Our area of freedom of movement at sea is now considerably restricted.
(ii) *Air* — Reduction of the area of free air operation.

(iii) *Military* — Loss of Libya and consequent effect on the defence of Egypt.

Owing to loss of material and equipment, defensive action in the Western Desert has been forced on us.

Further, our capacity for offensive action in Syria was greatly reduced.

It is not within the province of this Report to go into wider issues than those given above.

5. Other lessons are -
(i) To meet the Germans successfully our training must go much farther and must include consistent training with definitely allocated air forces.
(ii) The officer in immediate command of operations must have at his disposal under his operational command, definite air force units.

Liaison with air is not an effective means. As an example, although I was in command of the operations during the retreat from Aliakmon position to the Thermopylae position, I did not see, nor have any communication of any kind from any Air Force officer during the whole period.

In regard to (i) the Germans have a more or less fixed system of advance. This is roughly on the following lines. First, motor cycles, then armoured cars, and light mechanised units with artillery, all supported by immediate air reconnaissance planes.

Our forces which were to be sent to meet these (except 6th Australian Division) had hardly even exercised as whole divisions, apart from combined training of this nature.

(iii) I have no hesitation in asserting the superiority of the Australian over the German as a fighting man. The difference, however, was more than balanced by the complete armament and training of the German army as a unified organisation.

[AA: A 2671, 373/1941]

6
THE SYRIAN CAMPAIGN

By May 1941 seven of the AIF's nine brigades in the Middle East had been in combat. The turn of the other two (21st and 25th) was to come when the 7th Division took part in the invasion of Syria, carried out between 8 June and 12 July 1941. Syria and Lebanon had been administered by France under a League of Nations mandate since the peace settlements which ended the First World War. The creation of Vichy France prompted the following initial response. Menzies' cautious reply is also printed.

Document 83

Caldecote to Menzies London, 30 June 1940

Circular Cablegram D. 299 *Secret*

SYRIA.
In view of the urgent need to avow our attitude as regards Syria, particularly for the benefit of the Turkish Government and Arab public opinion, we proposed to issue the following declaration which has in the meantime been telegraphed to Angora for the comments of His Majesty's Ambassador.
...
... His Majesty's Government declares that they could not allow Syria or Lebanon to be occupied by any hostile power or to be used as a haven for attacks upon those countries in the Middle East which they are pledged to defend, or to become the scene of such disorder as to constitute a danger to those countries. They, therefore, hold themselves free to take whatever measures they may in such circumstances consider necessary in their own interests. Any action which they may hereafter conjointly take in fulfilment of this declaration will be entirely without prejudice to the future status of the Territories now under French Mandate.
[AA: A1608, J41/1/3, Part 1]

Document 84

Menzies to Caldecote 1 July 1940

Cablegram 338 *Secret*

YOUR CIRCULAR [CABLEGRAM] D.299 AND THE PROPOSED

DECLARATION REGARDING SYRIA AND LEBANON. HAVE YOU CONSIDERED POSSIBILITY OF FRENCH TROOPS BECOMING ACTIVELY HOSTILE TO US WITH CONSEQUENT MILITARY REPERCUSSIONS OF A SERIOUS KIND TO OUR NUMERICALLY INFERIOR FORCES IN THAT ZONE? IS IT IMPOSSIBLE TO GET JOINT DECLARATION WITH TURKEY TO DEFEND SYRIA?
[AA: A 1608, J41/1/3, Part 1]

In April 1941 a pro-Axis *coup d'état* occurred in Iraq which, by terms of a 1930 treaty, was supposed to come to Britain's aid in time of war. Iraqi troops fought British forces and the revolt was not put down until 31 May, the same day as the last British troops were being evacuated from Crete. The attitude of Syria now became even more important. During the fighting in Iraq, Syrian airfields were made available to German aircraft. Consequently, the British began bombing them on 14 May. Bruce sent the following appreciation of possible further action based upon a 'general feeling' in London. In the Middle East, General Catroux, right-hand man of De Gaulle, the recognised leader of the Free French, was anxious to move into Syria. Wavell sets out his dilemma and indicates to London that the 7th Australian Division would be used in any operation while the British Ambassador in Cairo, Sir Miles Lampson, reports on 19 May.

Document 85

Bruce to Fadden   London, 16 May 1941

Cablegram 330   Most Secret

... [As] French public opinion[,] while strongly attached to North Africa as part of France's Colonial empire, is little concerned with mandated Syria, no hesitation would be felt, in view of the seriousness of the menace, in the occupation of Syria militarily. The deterrent to such action is the necessity of employing our limited forces in the most vital spots, involving a decision as to the relative importance of Cyrenaica, Crete and Syria. It is considered vital that Crete should be denied to the enemy and no forces can be spared from there. Equally Cyrenaica is of such importance that no undue risk must be run there. It is also felt that in view of the recent British patrolling success through the Mediterranean having strengthened the capacity for counter offensive and evidence that the enemy is experiencing difficulties ... present would be most unfortunate time to weaken our forces.

Nevertheless it is felt that a limited transferrence from Western desert and Egypt to Palestine is possible, but even with this reinforcement strength would not be sufficient for the move into Syria if resisted by the French. If on the other hand any French support were likely to be forthcoming,

action would be justified. Advice on this point from Wavell & Catroux who is in Palestine now awaited. Havard's[29] view is that there is a large body of French opinion in Syria to whom collaboration with Germany is anathema, and he advocates that any air action against Syrian aerodromes should be followed by military occupation.
[AA: A 1608, H41/1/3, Part 1]

Document 86

Wavell to Dill   Middle East, 17 May 1941

Cablegram 0/65182

...

3. The only British force I could make available from Palestine has gone Iraq, so Syrian commitment would involve using Free French or bringing troops from Egypt.
4. I feel strongly that Free French without strong British support would be ineffective and likely to aggravate situation and that original action must be British to be followed by Free French if successful. Similar considerations apply Polish Bde. also I am holding it as reserve for Crete.
5. If I had to make force available for Syria at present could only do it by taking 7th Aust. Div. less one Bde. out of Matruh and putting South African Bde. or remainder 4th Ind. Div. in to hold Matruh. This would mean ... taking certain risk with defence of Egypt. Risk might be acceptable if no sign further German Armoured reinforcements and Syria situation really urgent. I should have to put small tank unit with Syrian force and there would be usual difficulty in scraping together Signals, Transport and A.A.
6. I am having plans examined for force to Syria but I hope I shall not be landed with Syrian commitment unless absolutely essential. Any force I could send now would be painfully reminiscent of Jameson raid[30] and might suffer similar fate.
7. I need not remind you that Air Force is also stretched beyond limit.
8. Blamey has seen and agreed this telegram. He welcomes re-assembly of Australians in Palestine.
[PRO: CAB 105/4]

---

29. Godfrey Thomas Havard, Consul-General at Beirut from 1934.
30. Dr L. Starr Jameson (1853–1917), an administrator in the British South Africa Company, on 29 December 1895 led a force of 470 mounted men from Bechuanaland into Transvaal. Jameson's aim was to advance to Johannesburg and join the Uitlanders (non-Boer European workers) to overthrow the Kruger government. However the Uitlanders did not revolt and Jameson's force was captured a few days later. Important political consequences followed the action.

Document 87

Lampson to Eden   Cairo, 19 May 1941

Cablegram 1424

. . .

2. French Bureau at Jerusalem consider the moment is extremely favourable for action, since both our French sympathisers and Syrians have been impressed by our bombing and pamphlets. But they do not believe this favourable atmosphere will last more than 8 to 10 days unless we take further action.

3. General Catroux would like to move into Syria in about 5 days' time if he could have British troops to support the 5 Free French battalions and 300 British lorries and drivers for 5 battalions. He saw Commander-in-Chief, Middle East [Wavell], at length. This morning a meeting was held at General Headquarters, Middle East, attended by General Wavell, General Catroux, General Spears[31], Air Marshal Tedder[32] and representatives of Commander-in-Chief, Mediterranean, and Embassy. General Wavell said that it was important to obtain further confirmation of various reports of events and feelings in Syria. ... The possibilities of arrival of a German force in Syria were then discussed. The conclusion reached was that landing by sea was hardly feasible so long as the Mediterranean fleet could maintain proper reconnaissance. The despatch of troops by land could only take place if the Turks consented or were ... beaten. More probable was the despatch of airborne troops, which might arrive at the rate of 3,000 a day via Rhodes or possibly direct from Greece. For heavy material and transport they would probably have to rely on what they might be able to obtain in Syria.

4. General Wavell then summed up the position as follows:-

(1) To occupy Syria with a sufficient British-Free French Force would be the best solution. But unfortunately a sufficient force was not available;

(2) to try and occupy Syria with an insufficient force, which is all that he could muster at present, would be a dangerous operation, to which he was opposed. Even if Turkey sent forces from the North, he did not consider that we could spare enough troops for the operation;

(3) the above assumed that we could not count on the support of French army (General Catroux considered that the French High Command would allow the Germans to use aerodromes, ports and railways). If the French army resisted the Germans, the picture completely changed and he would favour going to their assistance with any forces at our disposal;

(4) we could in any case continue our air attacks against German planes

---

31. Maj-Gen Sir Edward Spears, head of British Mission to Gen de Gaulle 1940–41; First Minister to Syria and Lebanon 1942–44.
32. AOC-in-C, RAF, in the Middle East 1941–43.

in Syria and see how the position developed. He did not rule out the military occupation of Syria at a later date if he had sufficient forces and the opportunity was favourable.

5. Air Marshal Tedder said that from the Air Force point of view the occupation by Germany of Syrian aerodromes would be a most serious matter. It would add an increasing commitment which might double the strain on the Air Force in Egypt. It was most desirable to prevent this if possible. Mr. Wright, who represented me, said that we should face the possible political consequences of allowing the Germans to occupy Syria. The effect in Egypt would be most unfortunate. The effect on Turkey would be no less unfortunate and may seriously weaken Turkish will or ability to resist the German pressure. ...

[PRO: CAB 105/4]

Bruce set out his own views on 24 May and after consideration by War Cabinet, the outcome was Menzies' cable to Churchill through Bruce. In these documents there was no questioning of the assumption that Germany intended to send forces to Syria. In fact, Germany had no such intention, as her army was busily preparing to invade Russia.

Document 88

Bruce to Menzies London, 24 May 1941

Cablegram 363 *Most Secret*

Recent developments in Syria have caused me grave concern and in my view create a situation which requires the clearest and most courageous thinking.

Our major strategy in the Middle East must be to hold Egypt and to keep the fleet based on Alexandria. Side by side with this we must maintain our position in Iraq so as to deny to the enemy the oil resources of Iraq and Iran and to ensure in the event of disaster in Egypt a bridgehead in the Middle East from which, as our strength grows, we could recover our position.

To date the major threat to Egypt has come from Libya and our comparative failure to strengthen our forces concentrated on the Western Desert. A new threat is now developing from Syria which also involves our position in Iraq. This new threat to my mind cannot be taken too seriously [as,] if the Germans establish themselves in strength in Syria it is difficult to see how we could prevent them getting control of North Iraq and Iran. This would mean the complete encirclement of Turkey and cutting her off from all external sources of supply. In such circumstances in my view we are fooling ourselves if we believe she would not come under Axis control in exactly the same way as other countries have done. The establishment of this Axis control would be followed by a demand to send troops and supplies across Turkey which she would be powerless to resist. Should this happen Germany could in a few weeks place many divisions on Syrian-Palestine border and Iraq.

Faced with this pincer movement of strong German forces from Libya and Syria could we maintain our position in Egypt and if we could not, could we then in the Middle East.

In view of these possibilities it appears to me that the paramount requirement in the Middle East at the moment is to prevent the Germans from establishing themselves in Syria and that in order to do so we should be prepared to take great risks.

Today our forces are concentrated on denying Crete to the enemy and inflicting a reverse on her in Cyrenaica. While the holding of Crete and the denying of Syria to the enemy are not alternatives, it helps to clear the mind to weigh their relative significance. The possession of Crete by the enemy would facilitate his supplying of Cyrenaica, would increase his bombing capacity of the fleet base at Alexandria and would embarrass our fleet operations in the Eastern Mediterranean.

All of these are serious, but could be faced and should not make our position untenable. The presence of the enemy in force in Syria for reasons I have given earlier would certainly tend to do so.

Cyrenaica and Syria are alternatives and if by abandoning any idea of counter-offensive for the present and adopting a purely defensive strategy in Cyrenaica we could release forces which would enable us to prevent Germans establishing themselves in Syria there would seem little doubt as to what our course should be.

If, however, this is impracticable and we have to face prospect of Germans in Syria it is imperative that the whole position in the Middle East should be reviewed in the light of facts and free from wishful thinking. In this review Australia should be fully and — having so many of her troops in Middle East — specially consulted.

I have done everything in my power to press the above in all directions available to me but without I fear very much success. I suggest for your consideration the desirability, if you are in accord with my views, of your cabling Prime Minister [Churchill] direct.

[AA: A1608, J41/1/3, Part 1]

Document 89

War Cabinet Minute Canberra, 29 May 1941

PRESENT: The Rt. Hon. R.G. Menzies, K.C., M.P., Prime Minister and Minister for Defence Co-ordination.
The Rt. Hon. W.M. Hughes, C.H., K.C., M.P., Attorney-General and Minister for the Navy.
The Hon. P.C. Spender, K.C., M.P., Minister for the Army.

The Hon. J. McEwen, M.P., Minister for Air.
Senator the Hon. H.S. Foll, Minister for the Interior and Minister for Information.

(1111) *STRATEGICAL POSITION IN THE MIDDLE EAST.*

1. War Cabinet considered cablegram No. 363 of 24th May from the High Commissioner, London, relative to developments in Syria and the vital importance of preventing the Germans from establishing themselves in that region.
2. The Prime Minister reviewed the strength of British Forces in the Middle East from information received by him prior to his departure from London at the beginning of the month, and particularly referred to the supply of aircraft and armoured fighting vehicles.
3. It was decided:-
  (i) That the Prime Minister should despatch a cablegram to the Prime Minister of the United Kingdom stating that the War Cabinet had given consideration to the situation in the Middle East and observing that, whilst great importance is attached to the denial of Syria to the Germans, this should not prejudice the defence of the western frontier of Egypt. In view of the decisiveness of overwhelming air strength and, as the only manner in which the Middle East can be quickly reinforced is by Air Forces, the United Kingdom Government is to be urged to take immediate and special steps to increase the fighter strength in this region. It was considered that the good production of this type of aircraft should help to render this possible.
  (ii) That the G.O.C., A.I.F., [Blamey] should be asked to submit an appreciation of the present position in the Middle East, particular reference being made to the defence of Egypt against attack from the west, the possibility of denying the use of Syria to the Germans, and the measures which should be taken for the defence of Palestine and Iraq if the enemy establishes himself in strength in Syria. ...

[AA: A 2673, Vol 7]

Document 90

Menzies to Churchill [via Bruce]　　　　　　　　　　29 May 1941

Cablegram 2649　　　　　　　　　　　　　　　　*Most Secret*

We are much exercised by the present position in the Middle East and I would like to put one or two points quite shortly to you.

The experiences in Greece and Crete indicate that the decisive factor is overwhelming air strength. This, if developed across the Mediterranean waters between Crete and Cyrenaica, may seriously affect movements of the Mediterranean Fleet, while the establishment of German air bases in Syria would threaten not only Irak and Palestine but the Suez Canal itself.

I know enough of the tank position to believe that large and rapid reinforcements over and above those recently and boldly sent through the Mediterranean are difficult. But what of aircraft?

It is alarming to read of the enormous German preponderance. Cannot large and urgent reinforcements of fighter planes go to the Middle East, particularly in view of the good production of these types in Great Britain and the not unsatisfactory reserves?

Further, is it not possible to make some attempt at occupation of Syria by British Forces? No doubt there has been some reluctance to do this because of the possible effect upon American public opinion. But I am assured by Casey[33] on good authority in Washington that American opinion would applaud aggressive British action. Anything would appear to be better than allowing Germany to make her foothold in Syria sufficiently strong to enable a jump forward to be accomplished.

I again emphasize to you that Australia and New Zealand have a large stake of four Divisions in the Middle East, subject to deductions in Greece and Crete, in addition to their vital interest in the preservation of one of the great Empire bastions. A defeat around the Suez would be a calamity of the first magnitude, and it appears to us that the most effective counter is in the air.

I know you will have been working on this like a tiger and that you are losing sight neither of Libya nor of Syria, but you will understand the strength of the feeling of my colleagues and myself on the matter.

Any information that we could have periodically as to air strength would be invaluable and would enable us to appreciate the position clearly.

I have given some emphasis to Syria because any real establishment by Germany in that country would mean the encirclement of Turkey and by cutting her off from external sources of supply would tend to make her powerless to resist Axis demands for the passage of troops and tanks into Palestine and Irak.

Notwithstanding our anxieties, I find my people here in good heart and determined to see the struggle through to victory.

    Kind regards.
[AA: A1608, V41/1/1]

Although the 7th Division was to be a major part of the invading force, Churchill was only prepared to tell Menzies that Syria 'will be occupied at the earliest with such forces as we can find.' On 3 June, Bruce in London could get no indication of their composition and the cable we print from Menzies to Churchill shows him still in the dark. Possibly this Australian prodding could be regarded as sanction for the use of Dominion troops. As Wavell's cable to Dill shows, it was taken for granted that they would be used.

---

33. Australian Minister to Washington 5.3.1940 — March 1942.

Document 91

Menzies to Churchill [via Cranborne]   4 June 1941

Cablegram 344   *Most Secret and Personal*

. . .

4. We are concerned about the delay in the movement into Syria, though we recognise that at this distance the difficulties in allotting and marshalling troops and establishing bases are not always clearly visible.

5. There is some professional support at this end for the view, which I understand has been put forward by Smuts[34], that Syria should have priority over Cyrenaica. If it were possible to take decisive action in Syria without so weakening the Egyptian frontier as to permit of successful German attack from Libya, I would agree with this. But the impression I formed in England was that any real subtraction from the Force which you design to move into Cyrenaica might jeopardise the Canal from that side. If this is not so, an early blocking of the Syrian Inlet may well be of more immediate urgency than a Cyrenaican advance, since it is the one move which can avoid a battle on two fronts.

6. Such Army appreciations from the Middle East as we have seen still appear to us gravely to under-estimate the extent of the use which the enemy may make of airborne troops and to over-emphasise purely land operations rather than joint land and air operations. Moreover, the German speed of movement upsets all time-tables, and estimates of the possible date or period by which he may make some particular move are usually falsified. It is for these reasons that we attach such tremendous importance to air reinforcement, since it would appear that it is only by a full use of fighting planes that a dangerous German footing in Syria can be avoided. And, after all, if we hold Syria we ought to be able to command Cyprus. ...

[AA: A1608, V41/1/1]

Document 92

Wavell to Dill   Middle East, 5 June 1941

Cablegram 0/70371

Operation Exporter.

1. Force consists of 7th Australian Division, less one brigade, 5th Cavalry Brigade (1 horsed, 1 composite mechanized regiment), 5th Indian Infantry Brigade Group, Free French Group (3 battalions, 1 battery, some tanks) with

---

34. South African Prime Minister and Minister for External Affairs and Defence 1939–48; GOC Union Defence Forces in the Field 1940–49.

certain additional units (1 squadron armoured cars, who have anti-aircraft guns). S.S. [Commando] battalion co-operate by landing on coast.

2. Air Force at present available 1 bomber, 1 fighter, 1 A.C. [Army Co-operation] squadron, but hoped increase this.

3. General plan. On right, 5th Indian Infantry Brigade to occupy Deraa and line Yarmuk railway, preventing demolition of bridges, if possible. Free French then to pass through and advance on Damascus. On left, 7th Australian Divn. to advance in two columns, 1 by Merdjayun, 1 by coast road on Beirut. Calendar aim is to reach Damascus and Beirut 1st day, if possible. Next objective is Rayak. Advance will be continued to Tripoli, if possible.

5. [sic] Fighting will be avoided as far as possible, progress being at first by propaganda, leaflets and showing attitude of force. If resistance encountered, utmost force will be used.

6. I have always estimated force required for occupation Syria as two divisions and 1 armoured division or, at least, armoured brigade. Must therefore regard success of forces operation as at least problematical, dependent attitude French garrison and local population. Unless greater part of French garrison join us or ask us and attitude of population unexpectedly favourable, do not think probable we can occupy German air bases at Aleppo and Palmyra. If, however, we can secure Lebanon and control Damascus, it will at least hamper German penetration and improve air situation. Necessary warn you, however, that failure is possible if French resist firmly.

7. I have tried to obtain advantage of surprise and secrecy by representing moves north to all purely defensive and spread stories in way to reach enemy of disagreement between myself and Free French due to my refusal to enter Syria. Fear, however, that our methods and habits make secrecy most difficult. ...

[PRO: CAB 105/5]

Despite early Allied successes, the Vichy forces did fight bitterly, launching a counter-attack on 19 June. By 21 June, however, Damascus was occupied without a fight, and by 9 July the Australians had cut their way to Beirut. On 12 July, the Acre convention was signed and the fighting stopped. We print Lt-General Lavarack's[35] report to War Cabinet on the campaign.

---

35. Commander, 1 Australian Corps, June 1941-April 1942.

Document 93

Lavarack to War Cabinet   3 October 1941

Secret

REPORT ON THE OPERATIONS — 1st AUSTRALIAN CORPS — IN THE CAMPAIGN IN SYRIA, JUNE-JULY 1941[36]

...

39. The enemy offered the most determined and skilful opposition from the outset, despite the views expressed in certain quarters that he would not fight seriously, views that were at no time shared by the fighting tps or their commanders. The Vichy French, in this campaign, displayed fighting qualities in defence that make it difficult to understand the ease with which they were defeated in their own country.

40. Several factors contributed to assist them in putting up this opposition. Of these the most important were:-

(a) The nature of the country, which was perfectly adapted to defensive tactics and was intimately known to the French leaders.

(b) Their superiority in certain items of vital equipment e.g., tanks and mortars.

(c) Their superiority in numbers in the early stages of the campaign.

41. Except for the plains leading into DAMASCUS from the south and a belt of varying narrowness on the actual coast, the country consists for the most part, of high, steep, rocky ridges, fairly well spaced inland, but crowding into a tangled mass of high hills and deep gorges in the area between the LITANI River and the coast. Isolated actions by small units were therefore the rule rather than the exception. Air support was difficult, and delay action by the enemy was at a premium. Control, even by battalion and company commanders became, in some cases, impossible, and frequently the success of operations depended entirely on the leadership of platoon commanders and the fighting qualities of the individual men. These small isolated bodies of men were very subject to local counter-attack, which, as a form of delay action, was freely used by the French. Finally they made use of the difficulty of the country to delay us by the use of judiciously placed demolitions, though not to the full extent of their opportunities.

42. Although the contrary has been freely stated it must be recorded that the French were never short of weapons, ammunition, or food, except in so far as supplies were prevented from reaching their forward troops by military action. An examination of their dumps and of their various units, artillery, vehicles, tank and armoured car parks reveal the fact that in all these respects they were well provided compared with ourselves. There was in particular no shortage of ammunition, of which vast stocks still remain. The French army moreover was not short of food, whatever may have been

---

36. War Cabinet submission, 18.11.1941, F.M. Forde, Minister for Army.

the case of the civil population. In tanks, particularly, it was superior throughout. British and FF troops were without tank support with the exception of the few serviceable French tanks that they were able to capture. The British light tank is deliberately ignored in this connection since it is useless for close fighting in the presence of the lightest anti-tank defence. The French also had good mortars both light and medium, of slightly larger calibre than our own. These had long range ...and were very accurate. They were used freely, and appeared always to have plenty of ammunition, except when we were able to interrupt supply to forward areas by tactical methods. Our own 3 inch mortar, on the other hand, was practically always short of ammunition. Through the personal intervention of the C-in-C ME [Wavell] a small supply was for a time made available, but this was not sufficient to make the mortar an effective weapon. This was a considerable handicap since the nature of the country rendered a high angle weapon most effective.
43. On the other hand the 25 pdr and the Tommy gun were superior to the French equipment. The 25 pdr, in particular, was generally a trump card, since the French coloured troops could not, as a rule, be trusted to stand up to bombardment. It could not, however, always be used, since the hilly, rocky country offered few positions suitable for field artillery and made crest clearance difficult.
44. It is appropriate, when making a comparison of weapons, to refer to two factors of the highest importance which contributed to the British victory in this campaign. These were the bombardments provided in the coastal sector by the R.N., and our superiority in the air. The naval bombardments caused a great deal of destruction of enemy transport and AFVs [Armoured Fighting Vehicles] on the coast road, engaged (frequently with good effect) the enemy's gun positions, and last, but not least, caused a considerable deterioration in morale amongst troops exposed, without hope of retaliation and little of protection, to the gruelling flank fire from the sea. Air superiority, though not absolute at first, became practically so in the latter half of the campaign. In the early stages, in the coastal sector, the artillery in particular was the target of frequent bombardments and ground straffing from the air. This lasted up to the time of the attack on SIDON and was sufficiently effective to indicate what might have happened had not air superiority been well and truly established, as it was after this period. At the time of the battle of DAMOUR our strength in the air had developed sufficiently to permit of direct control of air forces by the division engaged in that action. This entailed some difficulty in providing air support on other parts of the front, e.g., at the JEBEL MAZAR and DIMAS, west of DAMASCUS, but the decisive importance of the DAMOUR battle justified the taking of risks in other sectors.
45. There is no room for doubt that these two factors, i.e., naval bombardment and air superiority, contributed decisively to the success of the campaign.
46. The French credited us with numerical strength greatly in excess of our actual numbers. At the outset of the campaign, when the available force included the 7 Aust Div (less a Brigade, but including a Pioneer Bn) the 5th

Indian Inf Bde, and the FF Division, our numbers were less than theirs. Even at the end of the campaign when reinforcements totalling 2 Bdes and 2 Bns, plus a MG [Machine Gun] Bn and various supporting units had arrived, our numbers were probably not greatly in excess of those available to the French. Despite this the French believed that we were able to relieve our Bns at will with fresh troops, and that they were defeated by a very much superior army. One French Commander, fighting north of JEZZINE, informed an Australian Brigade Commander that he had not at any time had more than 5 Bns in the sector, the Brigade Commander concerned had never had more than 3, at one time had only one.

47. All these factors, i.e., the difficulty of the country, the enemy's superiority in certain important weapons and his practical equality in numbers, go far to explain the length of time (5 weeks) taken by the Allied advance. It would not be necessary to explain this had it not been for the frequent references, official and unofficial, made to the slowness or stickiness of the operations. In the circumstances, it is probably rather remarkable that the forces available should have been able to reduce a skilful, brave, and stubborn enemy to the point of surrender in the comparatively short space of five weeks. ...

[AA: A 2671, 386/1941]

7
THE RELIEF OF TOBRUK

The importance of Tobruk lay in the fact that, apart from the minor facilities at Bengahzi, it provided the only satisfactory port along a thousand miles of desert. Its siege began in April 1941 after the unexpected German advance into Cyrenaica against an army weakened by the decision to send Australian and New Zealand troops to Greece. Tobruk's garrison became the 9th Australian Division with the 18th Brigade of the 7th Division, and some British troops. On 15 June 1941, an Allied offensive codenamed *BATTLEAXE* was launched with the aim of breaking Rommel's hold on Cyrenaica and relieving Tobruk. It was a costly failure. Soon afterwards, Australia began attempts to have her troops taken out by sea. This gave rise to a serious disagreement between successive Australian governments and that in London. The dispute echoed those Australian fears and concerns evident from the time the 2nd AIF was sent overseas. By this stage, however, such worries had been compounded by British defeats and consequent doubts over the ability of United Kingdom leadership.

We begin on a querulous note and a premonition that Australian forces would be expected to fight all the Middle East battles. Menzies' failing confidence in United Kingdom expertise and the realisation of his own insecure political position should Australian troops be needlessly lost or savaged, are evident in his cable to Blamey.

Document 94

Fadden to Menzies [in London]   12 April 1941

Cablegram 222   Most Secret

... following cable was despatched today to Blamey ...

2. We recently took up question with Bruce of greater use of Canadian troops in present conflict ... and this has been again raised in War Cabinet. We find it difficult to appreciate reason for presence of relatively small numbers of other Empire troops in Middle East and why plans were not implemented for despatch 14 divisions at rate one per month from February onwards[37] ... The importance to us of these factors is emphasized by ... the necessity to divert 7th Australian Division to Tobruk, thus materially weak-

---

37. See Document 74.

ening Lustreforce with possible dire results to our troops in Greece.

... Would appreciate early advice from you regarding possibility greater use of Canadian forces or despatch other reinforcing troops from the United Kingdom in greater numbers. ...
[AA: A2671, 123/1941]

Document 95

Menzies to Blamey   21 June 1941

Cablegram 13   *Personal and Most Secret*

I am most disturbed by the failure at and about Sollum[38]. So far as I can make out we had equality in tanks and superiority in the air, yet we failed. Your own view appears to be that training of mechanised units deficient. If this was so, please inform me whether in your opinion attack was founded upon military opinion in Egypt or on direction from London.

I am cabling you direct because I have great confidence in your judgment and would like you to let me have urgently answers to the following questions:-
1. What is your own assessment of the enemy's strength and our own on the Western Desert front and our respective capacities to increase and maintain such strength?
2. Are you satisfied that the garrison at Tobruk can hold out? Should we press for evacuation or for any other and what course?
3. What is your estimate of our real capacity to defend our bases in Egypt, with particular reference to the risks to which our Forces, particularly the Fleet, are subject?
4. What progress is being made with plans for contingencies, including the evacuation of Egypt? I understand in London that these were in hand and I would like to be assured that possible moves have been adequately provided for.

With the enemy in possession of the Dodecanese, Crete and Libya, the Middle East position appears to have new elements of doubtfulness.

A disaster at Tobruk, coming on top of those in Greece and Crete, might have far-reaching effects on public opinion in Australia, and a reverse in Egypt itself would, I think, produce incalculable difficulties in Australia.

Views which I receive from London may be unduly coloured by wishful thinking, and I still feel that they constantly under-estimate the enemy. That is why I would welcome your own full and frank view.

I do not want you to think from the foregoing that I personally have any illusions about the frequent necessity for fighting, even unsuccessfully, at

---

38. This engagement, pressed by Churchill, was regarded as an important preliminary to *BATTLEAXE*.

outposts in order to protect and strengthen our base. But at the same time I cannot allow it to be said that the attitude of the Australian Government was passive or insufficiently strong at such a critical period in the Middle East campaign. ...
[AA: A 1608, V 41/1/1]

On 18 July, Blamey received an adverse report on the physical condition of his troops at Tobruk. We print his firm minute to General Auchinleck[39] calling for their relief and Menzies' cable to Churchill making similar representations. Auchinleck was sent this cable together with a note by Churchill which we also print. But there was no response from London, as Menzies' personal telegram to Churchill indicates.

Document 96

Blamey to Auchinleck   Cairo, 18 July 1941

Minute   *Most Secret*

1. It is recommended that action be taken forthwith for the relief of the Garrison at TOBRUK. These troops have been engaged continuously in operations since March and are therefore well into their fourth month. This strain of continuous operations is showing signs of affecting the troops. ...

It may be anticipated that within the next few months a serious attack may be made on the Garrison, and by then at the present rate, its capacity for resistance would be very greatly reduced. The casualties have been considerable and cannot be replaced.

It would therefore seem wise to give consideration immediately for their relief by fresh troops and I urge that this be carried out during the present moonless period. ...

2. ... the agreed policy for the employment of Australian troops between the British and Australian Governments is that the Australian troops should operate as a single force.

Because the needs of the moment made it necessary, the Australian Government has allowed this principle to be disregarded to meet immediate conditions. But it nevertheless requires that this condition shall be observed, and I therefore desire to represent that during the present lull in active operations, action should be taken to implement this as far as possible. This is particularly desirable in view of the readiness the Australian Government has so far shown to meet special conditions as they arose. ...

[The Australian] Corps probably will be required in a month or two for

---

39. Auchinleck had succeeded Wavell as commander of the British army in the Middle East.

further operations. If it is to render full value in accordance with the wishes of the Australian Government and as agreed by the British Government, it is necessary that action be taken early for its re-assembly in order that the formations and units may be thoroughly set up as quickly as possible. ...

I can see no adequate reason why the conditions agreed between the Australian and United Kingdom Governments should not now be fulfilled. ...

[AWM: 3DRL 6643, Blamey Papers, 33.1]

Document 97

Commonwealth Government to 20 July 1941
Churchill [via Cranborne]

Cablegram 456 *Most Secret*

We regard it as of first class importance that now that the Syrian campaign has concluded, Australian troops in the Middle East should be aggregated into one force. This would not only give an opportunity for refreshment, restoration of discipline and re-equipment after the strenuous campaigns, but would also give immense satisfaction to the Australian people for whom there is great national value and significance in knowing that all Australian soldiers in any zone form one Australian unit. This principle was fully accepted by both the United Kingdom Government and ours when troops first despatched to the Middle East.

Problem has a particular bearing upon the garrison at Tobruk which has been engaged in continuous operations since March and is therefore in the position of a force with continuous front line service over a period of months, a state of affairs which must result in some decline in fighting value. If they could be relieved by fresh troops, movement of personnel only being involved, re-aggregation and equipment of Australian Imperial Force in Palestine would then present no major difficulty.

I would be glad if you could direct the British High Command in the Middle East along these lines. The comparative lull now obtaining in Libya seems to make this an ideal time for making the above move to which we attach real and indeed urgent importance. Ends.

[A copy of this cablegram was sent from the War Office to the C-in-C, Middle East and a note dated 25 July 1941 added:]

2. Full and sympathetic consideration must clearly be given to the views of the Australian Government. At the same time we realise, as no doubt does the Australian Government, that the grouping and distribution of divisions must be subject to strategical and tactical requirements, and to what is

administratively practicable. Please let us have your views as early as possible.
[PRO: Premier 3/63/2]

Document 98

Menzies to Churchill [via Cranborne]　　　　　　　　6 August 1941

Draft Cablegram[40]　　　　　　　　　　　　　　　*Most Secret*

Would appreciate early reply to my cablegram No. 456 relative to relief of Tobruk garrison and concentration of A.I.F. into one Force.
2. War Cabinet is considerably perturbed with report of G.O.C., A.I.F., to C.-in-C. Middle East regarding definite decline in health resistance of troops at Tobruk.[41] 6th Australian Division has fought continuously through Libya, Greece and Crete and a considerable proportion through Syria. 7th Division has just completed campaign in Syria. 9th Division has been continuously in operations [at Tobruk] since March. As fresher troops are available I must press for early relief of 9th Division and re-assembly of Australian Corps.
[AA: A 2671, 41/197]

> Although General Auchinleck in consultation with Churchill admitted that the Tobruk forces could be relieved without 'considerable embarrassment' this view was not revealed to the Australian government as Churchill's reply to Menzies' pressure shows.

Document 99

Churchill to Menzies [via Cross,　　　　　London, 9 August 1941
U.K. High Commissioner]

Cablegram 556　　　　　　　　　　*Most Secret and Personal*

... [Auchinleck] is as anxious as you are to relieve this garrison by United Kingdom troops, but you will agree that military factors must be the paramount consideration. It is imperative that considerable movements of shipping, etc. which would be involved in the relief of the garrison should not militate against the normal maintenance of Tobruk and thus endanger the

---

40. The file contains a letter (dated 6.8.1941) from Menzies to Spender, which confirms that the cablegram was sent that day.
41. See Document 96.

fortress. Subject to this proviso, the Commander-in-Chief Middle East will do his very best to meet your wishes.
[PRO: Premier 3/63/2]

Some progress was made towards meeting Australian wishes when on Auchinleck's instructions, the 18th Brigade of the 7th Division was brought out by sea in a moonless period. It was not enough for Blamey, nor for Arthur Fadden, who had replaced Menzies as Prime Minister. Again pressure was applied: Fadden told Churchill that he wanted to make a parliamentary statement by the middle of September to the effect that a complete withdrawal had been carried out. When Auchinleck was told, he sent the following to Churchill which we print in order to show the British viewpoint. At much the same time as Auchinleck was cabling Churchill, Fadden received a reminder from a Queensland resident with a quite decided opinion.

Document 100

Auchinleck to Churchill   Middle East, 10 September 1941

Cablegram 1558   *Most Secret*

Your 085 and 086 of 7/9.
1. The recent relief of one Australian Inf. Bde. Group and one Indian Cavalry Regt. in Tobruk by Poles showed that naval risks involved were appreciable as nearly all ships were attacked by aircraft. A continuation of relief would throw an added burden on fleet destroyers at expense of other naval operations. The burden already thrown on these destroyers by needs of maintenance is considerable. If relief is carried out it will be at expense of maintenance while it lasts but this is a risk I am prepared to accept.
2. During recent relief a minimum of 5 fighter squadrons were permanently employed in escorting ships at expense of offensive air operations on which air superiority rests and even these were inadequate. The normal allotment to cover ordinary maintenance averages 3 squadrons.
3. The relief of remainder of garrison would have to be carried out during moonless periods 17th (repeat 17th) to 27th (repeat 27th) September and 16th (repeat 16th) to 26th (repeat 26th) October because risks entailed in shipping personnel during moon periods are unwarranted.
4. Availability of troops for relief of Australians. Apart from undesirability of putting other Dominion troops into Tobruk the one (repeat one) South Africa Division is motorised and is required for mobile offensive operations, 2 (repeat 2) South Africa Div. is still untrained and New Zealand Div. is about to move into Western Desert to train for its allotted future task. 4 (repeat 4) Indian Div. which is well trained in Western warfare is already in forward area in Western Desert. 5 (repeat 5) Indian Div. is in Iraq and not

(repeat not) available. 50 (repeat 50) Div. could not (repeat not) be made available in time even if it could be spared from its important task which is only half completed. There remains 6 (repeat 6) Div. (?about to) be diluted with Indian troops which process would have to be postponed indefinitely if Division were sent to Tobruk. This is presumably not (repeat not) an insuperable difficulty so that this division could be made available though this would weaken Syria and retard for time being work on defensive positions just started.

Part 2

5. The most undesirable factor resulting from relief would be that half of it must take place during latter half of October. During this period we hope to concentrate maximum air effort in gaining air superiority in Western Desert and to complete all arrangements for a sortie from Tobruk. (?Both of)(?these) intentions (?would be) prejudiced by continuation of relief operations.

6. The health and morale of Tobruk garrison is very good but powers of endurance of the troops is noticeably reduced and this is likely to be further reduced as time goes on and I detect signs of tiredness in those in responsible positions. ...

7. It is however still just possible to relieve personnel of one more Australian Bde. by a brigade of 6 (repeat 6) Div. during latter half of September. This would leave a garrison of two Australian Bdes. one British Bde. and Polish Bde. and a mixed assortment of supporting arms. I am not (repeat not) in favour of this course as I consider that break up of 9 (repeat 9) Australian Div. with its very strong esprit de corps and high morale would definitely reduce tactical efficiency of garrison.

8. An alternative to relieving one Australian Bde. during latter half of September is to send an infantry tank battalion to Tobruk. This would have advantage of morally and materially increasing the defensive powers of garrison in addition to increasing its offensive powers in future operations. With this reinforcement I feel confident about Tobruk's power to resist attack. ...

10. I fully realise political considerations involved and great importance of meeting the wishes of Australian Government. I have placed Gen. Blamey in full possession of all facts and given him every opportunity of stating his views which are strongly in favour of effecting the relief. ... The matter has today been placed before Minister of State [Lyttelton] and other two C's in C. [Longmore and Cunningham] at a meeting of Defence Committee and they agree with my opinion that to attempt any further relief of Tobruk garrison however desirable it may be politically is not a justifiable military operation in circumstances, and would definitely prejudice chances of success of our projected offensive Western Desert.

11. Subject to your approval I propose therefore (?definitely) to abandon idea of a further large scale relief of Australian personnel in Tobruk and to reinforce garrison at once with an infantry tank battalion. ...

[PRO: Premier 3/63/2]

Document 101

Letter

L. MANSFIELD
DENTAL SURGEON

108 Bourbong Street
Bundaberg
10.9.1941

Mr. A. Fadden/
    Prime Minister
    Canberra A.C.T.

Dear Sir/
    Dont you think it about time the Tobruk garrison was relieved? People are saying that with all the alleged might of the British Empire — with millions of troops idle — the Tobruk garrison is being left. They must have relief — we want no more Cretan or Greek episodes.

                                        Yours respectfully
                                        H.L. Mansfield

[AA: A 1608, A45/2/1]

Auchinleck's arguments with Churchill's support were sent to Fadden. As demonstrated, he was not impressed with them. Now there was nothing Churchill could do except advise that the troops would at once be relieved. We print two of his cables to give the flavour of his reaction. Not that Churchill was finished. With two brigades to withdraw he renewed his request in a cable of psychological pressure. And when Curtin replaced Fadden he tried again. We print War Cabinet's consideration of his cable.

Document 102

Commonwealth Government to
Churchill [via Cranborne]

15 September 1941

Cablegram 590   *Most Secret*

3. ... following comments are made on General Auchinleck's telegram.
(1) Naval risks. These are noted but in the absence of effective naval opposition in the Mediterranean or any contemplated naval operations this does not appear to be a sufficiently weighty reason.
(2) Air protection. General Officer Commanding Australian Imperial Force [Blamey] advised early August that he had agreed to postpone relief one month to enable necessary air strength to be provided and this would also give longer hours of darkness. In view of increase in air strength and

improved situation in Syria, Iraq and Iran this reason would not appear adequate.
(3) Moonless periods. Reasons noted.
(4) Availability of troops for relief. As it was anticipated originally that we would carry out offensive operations in the Western Desert at the same time that we met a German offensive in Syria for which considerable forces would have had to be allotted it is not seen how the defence of Syria can be prejudiced in view of forces available. Frankly the reasons against relief by other Dominion troops are unconvincing.
(5) Undesirability of relief during latter half of October. It would appear possible to complete relief and instal new garrison by assumed date of proposed offensive even if anticipated date is realized which it is understood is not generally the case in large scale preparations. Reference to a sortie from Tobruk fills us with grave concern in view of advice we have had that the Ninth Division will be quite unfitted for such an operation, which will involve continuous and severe fighting.
(6) Decline in the physical powers of the troops. It is observed that the Commander-in-Chief states that although health and morale is very good, power of endurance is noticeably reduced. If the garrison cannot be relieved, it will be required to stand up to a total period of eight to nine months' continuous front-line service under conditions of great hardship, and trying climate. At the end of this time they are to carry out an offensive operation. The proposal to reinforce the garrison with one battalion of heavy tanks appears to acknowledge decreasing power to garrison and to discount the difficulties of air and naval protection previously urged against movement of personnel only.
(7) Relief will prejudice the forthcoming offensive. We do not concur in the view that further operations are likely to be compromised in view of the time factor.
4. In view of the responsibilities reposed in the General Officer Commanding Australian Imperial Force and the advice tendered by him and the General Officer Commanding the 9th Division [Maj Gen L. Morshead] which is supported by the Government's advisers here, I am bound to request that withdrawal of the 9th Division and re-concentration of the Australian Imperial Force be proceeded with. ...
[PRO: Premier 3/63/2]

Document 103

Churchill to Lyttelton [Minister for State, Middle East] London, 18 September 1941

Cablegram [Not Numbered] *Personal and Secret*

...

2. I was astounded at Australian Government's decision, being sure it would

be repudiated by Australia if the facts could be made known. Allowances must be made for a Government with a majority only of one faced by a bitter Opposition parts of which at least are isolationist in outlook.
3. It is imperative that no public dispute should arise between Great Britain and Australia. All personal feelings must therefore be subordinated to appearance of unity. ...
[PRO: Premier 3/63/2]

Document 104

Churchill to Auchinleck   London, 18 September 1941

Cablegram [Not Numbered]   *Personal and Secret*

... Whatever your and our personal feelings may be, it is our duty at all costs to prevent an open dispute with the Australian Government. All public controversy would injure foundations of Empire and be disastrous to our general position in the war. ...
[PRO: Premier 3/63/2]

Document 105

Churchill to Fadden   London, 29 September 1941

Cablegram WINCH. [Not Numbered]   *Personal and Secret*

... I think I ought to let you know for your most secret information about Tobruk that Lyttelton and I only with difficulty prevented General Auchinleck from resigning his command on the grounds that the Australian Government had no confidence in his military judgment. Had your decision been based on political grounds he would not have felt the want of confidence implied.

The September relief has been effected successfully... I still hope that you will reconsider your decision that the last [two] Australian Brigade[s] must be pulled out of Tobruk without reference to the great impending operation by which we trust all will be relieved. The exchange of [these brigades] with [others] during the October moonless period will certainly hamper the Air Force preparations for the battle by forcing them to divert their strength to providing fighter cover for the shipping involved. Every day lost [from this cause] in delivering the attack adds to the risk of being forestalled. Everything points to the first days of November, and the period during which the remaining Australian Brigade[s] would be involved is very short. Why should Australia have borne the burden of Tobruk to cut itself out of the honour?

Believe me, everyone here realizes your political embarrassments with a majority of only one. Nevertheless Australia might think this is a time to do and dare. We have been greatly pained here by the suggestion, not made by you, but implied, that we have thrown an undue burden on the Australian troops. Our debt to them is immense but the Imperial forces have suffered more casualties actually and relatively. Moreover, the British Submarine Service has lost nearly a third killed outright, and I could give you other instances.

Therefore we feel we are entitled to count upon Australia to make every sacrifice necessary for the comradeship of the Empire. But please understand that at whatever cost your orders about your own troops will be obeyed.

[Note: In square brackets are alterations made in Churchill's hand.]
[PRO: Premier 3/63/2]

Document 106

War Cabinet Minute Melbourne, 15 October 1941

(1404) *AGENDUM No. 326/1941 — RELIEF OF 9th DIVISION AT TOBRUK*

...

2. The Prime Minister [Curtin] read the following cablegram (No. 688 of 13th October) which he had received from Mr. Churchill:-
"I feel it right to ask you to reconsider once again the issue raised in my telegram Winch 1 of 30th September to your predecessor. I have heard again from General Auchinleck that he would be very greatly helped and convenienced if the remaining two Australian brigades could stay in Tobruk until the result of the approaching battle is decided.
"I will not repeat the arguments which I have already used but I will only add that if you felt able to consent, it would not expose your troops to any undue or invidious risks and would at the same time be taken very kindly as an act of comradeship in the present struggle."
3. It was decided to adhere to the decision of the previous Government that the relief of the 9th Division at Tobruk should be carried out.
[AA: A 2673, Vol 8]

In fact not all the Australian troops were relieved from Tobruk. Partly because their transport was sunk before they could be picked up, 1019 men were left in the garrison to become involved in Auchinleck's *CRUSADER* offensive and to fight their way out to link up with advancing troops. The siege of Tobruk was finally raised on 9 December. It is interesting to speculate that Blamey's firm stand against Auchinleck may have made his further employment in the Middle East difficult and might have led to a 'first class row', except that Australia's position was so parlous in February 1942 that Curtin requested Blamey be returned to command the Australian army facing the Japanese threat.

Document 107

Lyttelton to Churchill [via Lampson]   Cairo, 22 December 1941

Cablegram 4038

Blamey is becoming impossible, and I hope very much you can persuade the Australian Government to replace him.
2. Difficulty is that he will not take orders from Auchinleck and continually raises objections, generally on the pretext that orders do not concern operational matters. ...
3. He is now very little short of being insufferable. As a small instance I quote from notes of a recent conference ... Auchinleck asks "do you contest my opinion on matters of operational necessity?" to which Blamey replied "no". Auchinleck then [asked] "if I say it is an operational necessity, would you carry it out?" to which [Blamey's] retort was "that does not necessarily follow". ...
8. Lavarack would probably be an adequate substitute, but as he is a professional soldier he will possibly not find favour with the Australian Government. I am satisfied however, that if Blamey remains, it will be most prejudicial to the conduct of the war in this theatre and that Auchinleck will be hampered at every turn.
[PRO: Premier 3/63/3]

Document 108

Attlee [Lord Privy Seal]   Not Dated [c.late December 1941]
to Churchill

Minute   *Most Secret*

...
3. I suggest you should [send] a secret and personal message to Curtin. As to the line to be taken, Cranborne thinks that while any bleak demands for Blamey's dismissal would, at this juncture, create a first class row, you might be able to persuade Curtin to arrange for Blamey's employment in some other sphere, and his replacement by some other Australian Officer, on the grounds that Auchinleck and Blamey do not get on together. You may care to be reminded of the principles under which Australian force was sent to the Middle East. ...
[PRO: Premier 3/63/3]

Document 109

Churchill to Curtin   London, 7 January 1942

Draft Cablegram

[Marked 'Hold' in Churchill's hand. This cable was never sent.]
1. I have had disturbing reports that General Blamey and General Auchinleck do not see eye to eye. Time and the gravity of the situation do not permit compromise and adjustment of differences between highly placed Officers.
2. I fully recognise Blamey's qualities and services, but I have also the highest regard for, and knowledge of, Auchinleck's integrity, judgement and singleness of purpose.
3. In the circumstances, I feel that to ensure harmonious command in the Middle East it would be wise to transfer Blamey to some other sphere. It may be that in view of the turn the war has taken and the impending withdrawal of two out of three Australian Divisions to the Far Eastern theatre, you may desire the benefit of his knowledge and experience in Australia. ...
4. It is a matter of urgency for the smooth and efficient advancement of our common aims in the Middle East that Blamey should be transferred elsewhere as soon as possible.
   [On 27 February 1942 Curtin asked that Blamey be returned to Australia. Churchill noted on the bottom of the telegram:]
'Good. I am glad I did not send any telegram. He is more ardent politician than soldier.'
[PRO: Premier 3/63/3]

II The Pacific War

Part II documents crucial aspects of Australia's war strategy during the most dramatic years in her history.

The central concern of Australia's defence planners before September 1939 was how the nation might cope with a Japanese attack if Britain was heavily committed in fighting in Europe. Because Japan in 1939 was not an ally as it had been in 1914, Australia did not make as wholehearted a contribution to the 'distant war' as it had done in 1915-18 to the war in western Europe and the Mediterranean basin. The first section in this Part documents Australia's concern, from 1938 to 1941, over 'the Singapore strategy', i.e., the theory that Australia would be protected from Japan by a British fleet which, when needed, would be based at Singapore.

Nineteen other problems or incidents are documented in this Part. All, in varying degrees, involve Australia's relations with allies, or prospective allies, against Japan. These pages illustrate the switch from Britain to the United States of America as Australia's 'great and powerful friend'. The emphasis on 1942 reflects the surpassing importance of that year in Australia's history.

Section 14 deals with the sharpest disagreement ever between the Australian and British governments, Section 15 with one of the many tragedies marking Australia's fighting against Japan in the terrible weeks of early 1942. The main Australian campaigns against Japan are covered. Section 22 illustrates Australia's failure to solve the command problem in the RAAF, a failure which helped to relegate the service to a subordinate role in the fighting.

The final sections reflect America's growing role in the fighting in Australia's 'near north', and the consequent decline in the strategic significance of Australia's part in the war against Japan.

8
THE SINGAPORE STRATEGY 1938–1941

The basis of Australian inter-war defence planning against attack by the Japanese revolved around the idea of 'forward defence' from Singapore. The naval base was expected to be defended until the arrival of a British battlefleet deemed sufficiently powerful to defeat the Japanese fleet. Such policy was finally to be destroyed by the loss of *Repulse* and *Prince of Wales* on 10 December 1941 and by the fall of the Singapore base itself to the Japanese on 15 February 1942.

On 4 March 1938, Stanley Bruce, Australian High Commissioner in London, attended a meeting of the Committee of Imperial Defence. There he set out succinctly Australian views on the Singapore strategy. We print an extract of the minutes which Bruce sent to the Department of External Affairs.

Document 110

Committee of Imperial Defence *Minutes of Meeting*
London, 4 March 1938

MALAYA — PERIOD BEFORE RELIEF. *Secret*

...

Mr. Bruce said that the security of Singapore was of vital interest to the Commonwealth of Australia, and he asked for information as to the reserves which now existed in Singapore and as to the time which Singapore might be expected to last out if invested now.

Mr. Hore-Belisha[42] pointed out that it was stated in paragraph 11 of the Memorandum by the Oversea Defence Committee that 60 days' rations were now maintained in Malaya for the military and air forces, and the same amount of reserves of Army stores.

Lord Chatfield[43] said that the Chiefs of Staff ... had stated that, allowing for delays, the Fleet could be expected to arrive at latest in 70 days. Corresponding reserves of stores would therefore have to be built up. If, however, there was any delay in the initial despatch of the Main Fleet, these reserves of stores might be inadequate. It was in order to gauge whether any further allowance should be made on top of the 70 days recommended by the Chiefs of Staff, that the Committee of Imperial Defence had asked to

---

42. Secretary of State for War 28.5.1937–5.1.1940.
43. First Sea Lord and Chief of the Naval Staff 1933–38.

be informed as to the cost of reserves for periods other than 70 days. The Oversea Defence Committee, on reasoning which he felt sure his colleagues on the Chiefs of Staff Sub-Committee would accept as sound, recommended certain reserves for a 70-day "period before relief", at an estimated cost of £2,941,000. If the "period before relief" were fixed at 90 days, the cost of the corresponding reserves would probably be some figure rather more than £3,179,000, which was only the cost of reserves sufficient for 90 days' consumption. There seemed to be two alternatives, either to decide now that nothing must be allowed to stand in the way of the despatch of the Main Fleet on the outbreak of war, in which case a "period before relief" of 70 days would be correct; alternatively, if it were thought impossible to guarantee in advance the immediate despatch of the Fleet, to decide that Singapore should be stocked up with six months' supplies of all natures. The latter alternative would leave the date of sailing of the Fleet quite open, since there would be an ample margin of reserves in the Colony.

Mr. Bruce stressed the importance of ensuring that the full reserves necessary were, in fact, available at Singapore without delay. If the decision were taken now to fix the "period before relief" at 70 days, it would be realised if war came, that the immediate despatch of the fleet was essential, since, as the Chiefs of Staff had pointed out, any delay in its arrival at Singapore after the end of the "period before relief" might jeopardise the whole security of the Empire by the loss of the port. His Government would, he felt sure, like to have as large reserves as possible in Singapore, but they were hardly in a position to press too hard in this matter, since it was not they who had to face the expense. If the Committee now accepted a "period before relief" of 70 days, his Government would be keenly interested to know when action would be taken to implement this decision by the actual building up of the reserves in Singapore. ...

Sir Maurice Hankey observed that Singapore had always received a high priority in the past and would no doubt continue to do so in the future.

Mr. Bruce said that he felt in duty bound to press, on behalf of his Government, for the very highest priority to be accorded to the provision of these reserves. The whole basis of Empire defence rested on the security of Singapore. Many millions of pounds had been spent already on the base, and it would be appalling to contemplate its loss through a failure to provide it with the necessary reserves.

Mr. Hore-Belisha said he was glad to hear from Mr. Bruce of the very keen interest which the Australian Government took in the security of the Singapore base. As Mr. Bruce no doubt knew, there was a proposal to initiate conversations with the Australian Government, with a view to exploring the possibility of the provision of Australian troops to form part of the garrison of the port.

Mr. Bruce said that the provision of Australian troops for Singapore would raise political questions which might present considerable difficulty. He wished to make the position of Australia with regard to the defence of Singapore quite clear, since in answer to his strong representations for ample reserves to be provided at Singapore it was open to the United

Kingdom Government to say, with very good reason, that Australia was not bearing the cost and should not therefore try to dictate what should be done at Singapore. He recalled that when the question of the construction of the base was first raised, in about 1923, some parts of the Empire made actual contributions in cash towards its cost. Australia had made no such contribution, but she had taken on the responsibility for providing two first-class cruisers and carrying out a five-year programme of naval expansion during the years 1923-1928. She was now engaged in carrying out another defence programme, but the Australian Government would be quite prepared to discuss whether the contributions which they were now making towards Imperial Defence as a whole were sufficient.

Sir Thomas Inskip[44] said that he felt sure that the Committee fully appreciated the point of view which had been put forward by Mr. Bruce. The United Kingdom Government realised that the naval contributions of Australia were a contribution towards Imperial Defence as a whole. He welcomed the suggestion of Mr. Bruce for discussions on the present scale of Australian defence programmes. ...
[AA: A 1608, C 51/1/10]

In November 1939, R.G. Casey, then Minister for Supply and Development, was in London to discuss the despatch of Australian forces overseas. He raised the question of sending a fleet to Singapore. Here Bruce reports on one discussion while extracts from Churchill's paper, provoked by this meeting, are also printed.

Document 111

Note by Bruce   London, 20 November 1939

JOINT MEETING [BETWEEN MINISTERS OF THE UNITED KINGDOM AND OF DOMINIONS]

The Far East.
... the naval situation in the Far East in the event of Japan coming in to the war was discussed at some length. The discussion was opened by Winston [Churchill][45] ... in his remarks he very much emphasised the necessity of keeping the Fleet mobile and the determination of the United Kingdom not to move as far as the Pacific was concerned unless there was a direct threat to Singapore or to Australia on a large scale.

In the course of his remarks he dealt with the Dutch East Indies and made it clear that if Japan made any move against the Dutch East Indies we, not being at war with Japan, the United Kingdom would not be prepared to take

---

44. Minister for Co-ordination of Defence 1936-29.1.1939.
45. At this time, First Lord of the Admiralty.

any action. What could be implied from his obersation [sic] was that having one war on our hands we would not proceed to buy into a second one, but would leave the position to be straightened out after we had won the first war.

After Winston had spoken Chatfield[46] went over the story of the decisions arrived at at the 1937 Imperial Conference and the Prime Minister's[47] cables to the Prime Minister of Australia of April and June last.

After Chatfield had set out this position, I intervened saying that I did not want to deal with the broad questions involved but it was necessary that I should complete the picture of what had happened during the last 2½ years. I then pointed out the discussions which had taken place last year between myself and the First Lord [Stanhope] and the First Sea Lord [Chatfield], including the definite assurances that 7 ships would be sent to Singapore in the event of war with Japan, and I specified that the 7 ships indicated were the 5 Sovereign class and 2 more efficient and more modern. ...

Talking privately to Chatfield afterwards, two things which he said are of the very greatest interest. The first was that having advised all the Dominions not to concentrate solely on local defence, but to participate in general Empire Defence relying upon the British Navy, it was difficult for the United Kingdom to go back on this now, notwithstanding the fact that they had not got the Naval forces necessary in order effectively to deal with the situation in Home waters, in the Mediterranean and in the Pacific at the same time.

The other observation was in reply to a question of mine as to whether there was not a considerable problem in getting a reinforcing Fleet into Singapore. Chatfield admitted that there was a very real difficulty in this problem and made the significant observation that that was why it was so desirable to have the Battle Fleet in Singapore at the time when hostilities broke out with Japan[.]

In my view there are a number of gaps in the information that we have got with regard to the Naval forces in connection with Singapore and the Far East.

I have difficulty in ridding my mind of the impression that notwithstanding all that Winston says ... his own real conception of the strategy of the war is to win in the European theatre with a full concentration of our forces and not dissipate them by trying to deal with the situation in the Far East at the same time. His view would be that having won the war in the western theatre, we could then concentrate the whole of what would probably be, unless we had suffered a major naval disaster, our overwhelming forces upon restoring the situation in the Far East. ...
[AA: M100, 3]

---

46. Minister for Co-ordination of Defence 29.1.1939–10.5.1940.
47. Neville Chamberlain, Prime Minister 28.5.1937–10.5.1940.

Document 112

Churchill's *Memorandum*   London, 21 November 1939

AUSTRALIAN AND NEW ZEALAND NAVAL DEFENCE   Secret

...

SINGAPORE is a fortress armed with five 15-inch guns, and garrisoned by nearly 20,000 men. It could only be taken after a siege by an army of at least 50,000 men, who would have to be landed in the marshes and jungle of the Isthmus which connects it with the mainland. As Singapore is as far from Japan as Southampton is from New York, the operation of moving a Japanese army with all its troopships and maintaining it with men and munitions during a siege would be forlorn. Moreover, such a siege, which should last at least four or five months, would be liable to be interrupted if at any time Great Britain chose to send a superior fleet to the scene. In this case the besieging army would become prisoners of war. It is not considered possible that the Japanese, who are a prudent people and reserve their strength for the command of the Yellow Seas and China, in which they are fully occupied, would embark upon such a mad enterprise.

2. Even less likely is the invasion of Australia or New Zealand by Japan. To do this Japan would have to despatch and subsequently maintain a large army more than 3,000 miles from home, with the possibility that at any time a British fleet would arrive to cut the communications; in which case all would be lost. Such an operation in its political aspects would certainly be resented by the United States, but as long as there are well-armed Australian and New Zealand military forces and a superior British fleet in being in any part of the world, it is needless to suppose that such an enterprise would be attempted.

It is always possible that a long-range submarine or raiding cruiser might turn up and insult Australian or New Zealand shores by firing a few shells into some seaport city, or cause temporary inconvenience by disturbing the coastal trade. But Japan would hardly be likely to reap any result except resentment from such escapades.

3. The power of a predominant fleet is exercised simultaneously in all quarters of the globe in which it has bases. This is irrespective of the station it occupies at any given moment, provided that it is not permanently tied to that station. At the beginning of the present War, the Admiralty had to contemplate fighting Italy in the Mediterranean as well as Germany and the U-boats in the North Sea and the Atlantic. This was thought to be not beyond our strength. In these circumstances the first step obviously was to beat the Italians and recover the command of the Mediterranean. With the French Fleet, which is highly efficient, and as strong as the Italian, this ought to have been achieved in a few months. Meanwhile, Singapore, even if it had been attacked, could have resisted. However, if the result in the Mediterranean had been long delayed, or the German and U-boat pressure had become too severe, the Admiralty could have closed the Mediterranean

at Gibraltar and at the Suez Canal, and, sacrificing our important interests in that area, proceeded to the relief of Singapore, or, of course, a *fortiori* to the aid of Australia or New Zealand supposing either was the victim of a serious attack.

4. Now, however, that Italy is neutral and may even become a friend, the British Fleet has become again entirely mobile. Only a very few capital ships are needed in the North Sea to contain the small German Fleet and support the blockade from Scotland to Greenland. All the rest are now ranging freely about the oceans, either on convoy work, or hunting raiders. Although it is not at present within our power to place a superior battle fleet in the Home waters of Japan, it would be possible, if it were necessary, to place a squadron of battleships in the Far East sufficient to act as a major deterrent on Japanese action so far from home, or to send capital ships to Australian or New Zealand waters from the moment that the danger to either Singapore, Australia or New Zealand developed in a manner which made their protection a real and practical war need. The Admiralty accepts the full responsibility of defending Australia, New Zealand or Singapore from a Japanese attack on a large scale, and after containing the German heavy ships they have forces at their disposal for these essential purposes. The chief difficulty would arise from the stringency in destroyer strength; but this situation should improve as our building programmes develop and as the U-boat is mastered by our attack. It is, however, wise to use every vessel we possess to the highest possible advantage in the fighting area, and only to move them to other waters when the War moves thither. The Admiralty are, therefore, most grateful for the loyal and clairvoyant strategy which has to the uninstructed eye denuded Australia and New Zealand of naval force. In particular, the assistance of the Australian destroyers is of invaluable aid[48]. But we wish to make it plain that we regard the defence of Australia and New Zealand, and of Singapore as a stepping-stone to these two Dominions, as ranking next to the mastering of the principal fleet to which we are opposed, and that if the choice were presented of defending them against a serious attack, or sacrificing British interests in the Mediterranean, our duty to our kith and kin would take precedence.

It seems very unlikely, however, that this bleak choice will arise during the next year or two, which is what we have to consider at the present time.

[Paragraph 5 is printed within quotation marks in Document 24.]

6. Finally, it must be pointed out that we are now at the lowest point of our strength compared to Germany and Japan. As our new battleships now being built come into service, the relative position should steadily improve.

There are no naval grounds, therefore, always assuming that the United States is our friend, which should prevent the despatch of Australian and New Zealand armies to the decisive battlefields, where their name stands so high.

[PRO: CAB 99/1]

---

48. See Document 4.

In June 1940 the imminent collapse of France led the Dominions Office to advise Canberra that 'We see no hope of being able to despatch a fleet to Singapore'. The reasons for this were spelt out on 28 June together with a request that Australian ground and air forces be sent there.

Document 113

Caldecote to Commonwealth Government   London, 28 June 1940

Cablegram 228   *Most Secret*

2. ... Since our previous assurances ... the whole strategic situation has been radically altered by the French defeat. The result of this has been to alter the whole of the balance of naval strength in home waters. Formerly we were prepared to abandon the Eastern Mediterranean and despatch a fleet to the Far East relying on the French Fleet in the Western Mediterranean to contain the Italian Fleet. Now if we move the Mediterranean Fleet to the Far East there is nothing to contain the Italian Fleet which will be free to operate in the Atlantic or reinforce the German Fleet in home waters using bases in North West France. We must therefore retain in European waters sufficient naval forces to watch both the German and Italian Fleets and we cannot do this and send a fleet to the Far East. ...
5. ... The Chiefs of Staff consider that the urgent movement of one division and two squadrons of aircraft to Malaya is desirable as an added immediate deterrent. They ask particularly whether the equivalent of a division equipped as fully as possible could be made available, drawing if necessary on your militia pool of equipment. They realize that you could not equip these troops up to full western standards nor would this be necessary in view of the unlikelihood of the Japanese being able to bring mechanized troops with the latest form of equipment to attack them. They consider that the employment in Malaya would for the time being at any rate, be in the best interests of the Empire. ...
[AA: CP 290/6, Bundle 3, 59]

The Australian Chiefs of Staff required more information. They got it in a long appreciation provided by the British Chiefs of Staff on 11 August. We print brief extracts together with the Australian military response. Such advice was accepted by the Australian War Cabinet on 28 August. This was the background to the policy which would have seen the 7th Division go to either India or Singapore.

This decision stood for just three weeks. Churchill then decided that Singapore could still be defended by the fleet and that the 7th Division could be better used in the Middle East. This aspect of Australian war policy was obviously manufactured in London though, as Document 116 shows, with the concurrence of the Australian government.

Document 114

Caldecote to Menzies   London, 11 August 1940

Circular Cablegram Z 214   *Most Secret and Personal*

...
2. Japanese advance into Southern China and Hainan, development of communications and aerodromes in Thailand, situation in Indo China resulting from French collapse, and increased range of aircraft, would now enable Japan to develop an overland threat to Malaya, against which even the arrival of the fleet would only partially guard. At the same time, collapse of France, development of direct threat to the United Kingdom and necessity for retaining in European waters fleet of sufficient strength to match both German and Italian fleets have made it temporarily impossible for us to despatch fleet to the Far East. ...
6. ... forces in Malaya are still far short of requirements, particularly aircraft; and Japan must know that in present circumstances, we could not send adequate fleet to the Far East. ...
17. First course open to the Japanese would be direct attack on British possessions. In this event her main effort would probably be directed ultimately towards the capture of Singapore which would be necessary to secure her position permanently. ...
19. Apart from attacks on trade no serious threat to Australia or New Zealand would be likely until Japan had consolidated her position at Singapore. Even then it is unlikely the Japanese would attempt to invade Australia or New Zealand at least until they had consolidated their position in China and the Far East which would take very considerable time. ...
35. As regards defence of Malaya. Following are factors affecting this problem in the absence of the Fleet:-
(a) Necessity of preventing establishment of shore-based aircraft within close range of Singapore base.
(b) Even if Japanese had not previously established themselves in Thailand they would be more likely to attempt landing up-country in Malaya and then operate southwards, under cover of shore based aircraft, than to risk direct assault on Singapore Islands.
(c) Rice-growing country on which native population partly depends, and most government storage centres are in the North.
(d) Necessity of establishing maximum possible food reserves for garrison and for civil population. Though our sea communications with Malaya might be precarious, it would be extremely difficult for the Japanese to blockade the Malayan Peninsula completely, and we should expect to get supplies (corrupt group) to our headquarters, though not necessarily through the port of Singapore.

Above factors emphasise the necessity for holding the whole of Malaya rather than concentrating on defence of Singapore Islands. This clearly involves larger land and air forces than when the problem was merely the defence of Singapore Islands. ...

41. Our policy in the Far East until the Fleet again becomes available is to rely primarily on air power in conjunction with such naval forces as can be made available. Land forces are also essential for close defence of naval and air bases, for internal security and for dealing with such enemy land forces as might succeed in gaining footing in Malaya and British Borneo despite our air action. ...

[AA: A 1608, A 41/1/1, Part 12]

Document 115

Report by Australian Chiefs of Staff   23 August 1940

FAR EASTERN POSITION — APPRECIATION
BY UNITED KINGDOM CHIEFS OF STAFF

. . .

The Chiefs of Staff have examined the appreciation of the United Kingdom Chiefs of Staff and are in general agreement with the conclusions reached.

2. In view of the assurance given by the Prime Minister (Great Britain), as stated ... in cablegram No. 262 of 12th August :-

"If, however, contrary to prudence and self interest, Japan set about invading Australia or New Zealand on a large scale, I have explicit authority of Cabinet to assure you that we should then cut our losses in the Mediterranean and proceed to your aid, sacrificing every interest except only the defence position of this island on which all depends".

the defence of Singapore and, incidentally, the holding of Malaya remain as before of vital importance to Australia, as without Singapore, the British Fleet would have no suitable base for operations in the Far East. We consider that this assurance ... is of such importance that we should strain all our efforts and resources to co-operate in the actual defence of the area as, strategically, it now becomes, as far as Australia is concerned, of greater ultimate importance than the Middle East. ...

Summary of Conclusions:

20. The conclusions of the Chiefs of Staff are summarised hereunder:-
(a)   ... the dominant factor in regard to the defence of Australia remains the security of the Naval Base at Singapore and its availability for use by the Main Fleet.   (Paragraph 2).
(b)   Co-operation with the Dutch in the defence of the East Indies (i.e., assumption 3 of Appreciation) is of great importance ... (Paragraph 4).
(c)   Staff talks with Dutch defence authorities should be instituted as soon

as our forces are adequate — Australian Service representatives to take part. (Paragraph 5).
(d) A heavier scale of attack than that envisaged by the Appreciation is considered possible, but this in no way militates against the primary requirement of the defence of Singapore. (Paragraphs 6 and 7).
(e) No further Naval or Air contribution can be made in present circumstances. (Paragraphs 16 and 18).
(f) A force consisting of the 7th Division A.I.F. (less 26th Infantry Brigade and attached troops) and such Corps Troops and ancillary units as necessary for the maintenance of the force should be despatched to India or Malaya as soon as practicable after the end of September or mid-October respectively.
The remainder of 7th Division to be prepared to follow as soon after December, 1940, as possible. (Paragraphs 9 and 11).
(g) Further suggestions from the United Kingdom Government regarding the concealment of the despatch of troops would be appreciated.
(Paragraph 15).

[AA: A 2671, 186/1940]

Document 116

War Cabinet Minute Melbourne, 28 August 1940

(459) *AGENDUM No. 186/1940 — STRATEGICAL APPRECIATION IN RELATION TO EMPIRE CO-OPERATION AND LOCAL DEFENCE — EMPLOYMENT OF AUSTRALIAN FORCES IN MALAYA*

. . .

(ii) ... the Commonwealth Government desires to assure the United Kingdom Government of its willingness to co-operate with the despatch of the 7th Division to the theatre in which it can render the most effective support. It is realised that considerations of training and equipment preclude its despatch to the Middle East at present, although the intention ultimately to concentrate the Australian Army Corps in this region has been noted. War Cabinet would prefer that the 7th Division should go to India to complete its training and equipment, and to relieve for service in Malaya troops who are better equipped and more acclimatized. This view is supported by the Australian Service advisers, and the War Cabinet is of the opinion that the considerations of wider scope for training and greater occupation of interest, difference in climate, and a less circumscribed role than that of garrison duties at Singapore would be more compatible with the psychology of the Australian soldier.

It is realised, however, that there are other aspects of these considerations, of which transport and movement of two divisions are not the least. Therefore, should the United Kingdom Government still desire that the 7th Division should proceed to Malaya after carefully weighing the views to

which the War Cabinet attaches great importance, the latter is quite agreeable to this course. ...
[AA: A 2671, 186/1940]

Document 117

War Cabinet Minute   Melbourne, 23 September 1940

(523) *SUPPLEMENT No. 1 TO AGENDUM No. 186/1940 —
STRATEGICAL APPRECIATION IN RELATION TO EMPIRE
CO-OPERATION AND LOCAL DEFENCE – DESPATCH OF
THE 7th DIVISION TO MIDDLE EAST.*

. . .
(The Chief of the Naval Staff [Colvin] and the Chief of the General Staff [Sturdee] were present for the discussion of this Agendum).

War Cabinet considered Dominions Office cablegram No. 346 of 18th September in reply to the Australian Government's cablegram No. 457 of 29th August, relative to the original request of the United Kingdom Government for the despatch of the 7th Division to Malaya. It was noted that the United Kingdom Government now recommended the despatch of the 7th Division to the Middle East, for the following reasons:-

"After balancing the risks between the Middle East and the Far East, we now consider the needs of the situation would be best met if the 7th Australian Division, equipped from local Australian resources of a modified scale, were sent direct to the Middle East where it could complete its training more quickly than in Malaya and where its presence would meanwhile be of abstract use for internal security purposes, and would render possible the immediate release of other troops which have already completed their training. We feel that to locate the Australian Division at a half-way house, viz. India, would benefit neither the Middle East nor Malaya, to which we should propose that two Indian brigades should be sent."

The Chief of the General Staff stated that he was in agreement with the proposal for, as stated, the Division would complete its training more quickly than in Malaya, and there were advantages over training in Australia. ...
[AA: A 2673, Vol 4]

Meanwhile the Japanese had entered a ten year pact of 'mutual support' with Germany and Italy. This ominous move coupled with Japanese entry into Indo-China, led the Australian War Cabinet into agreeing with a United Kingdom proposal that a defence conference be held at Singapore. Its findings and subsequent British comments were disturbing, as the following documents indicate. Once again, Australian troops were offered for garrison duty in Singapore, a policy which was the genesis of the despatch of the 8th Division there.

Document 118

War Cabinet Minute Canberra, 26 November 1940

(632) *AGENDUM No. 254/1940 — REPORT OF SINGAPORE DEFENCE CONFERENCE, 1940 — REVIEW BY CHIEFS OF STAFF.*

(The three Chiefs of Staff were present for the discussion of this Agendum).

The conclusions and recommendations of the Singapore Defence Conference, 1940, the observations of the Australian Delegation to the Conference, and the views of the Chiefs of Staff thereon, were noted, grave concern being expressed at the most serious position revealed in regard to the defence of Malaya and Singapore, which are so vital to the security of Australia. ...

[4.] (c) *Troops for Malaya.* — The following observations of the Conference regarding Australian local defence were noted:-

"While the possibility of a major expedition against Australia or New Zealand may be ruled out initially, we must still maintain in Australia and New Zealand such Army and Air Forces as are necessary to deal with raids, and also such Naval and Air Forces as are necessary to ensure the maintenance of vital trade, protect troop and other convoys, and carry out necessary local defence duties." (Part I, paragraph 12).

It was also observed that the detailed problems concerning Australia's local defence were not considered by the Conference except insofar as these concerned the combined defences in the Far East.

In regard to the following recommendations by the Chiefs of Staff:-

"In view of the opinion of the Conference quoted above as to the possibility of invasion, and the importance of Singapore to Australian defence, the Chiefs of Staff recommend that the United Kingdom Government be informed that the Commonwealth Government would be willing to make available a Brigade Group and necessary maintenance troops with a modified scale of equipment *only*, for service in Malaya at an early date, as a contribution to the deficiencies in land forces.

"It is considered that these troops should only be located in Malaya as a temporary measure whilst completing their training and until such time as the 8th Division can be concentrated in the Middle East, when they should be relieved by Indian troops."...

[AA: A 2673, Vol 4]

Document 119

Churchill to Menzies [via Cranborne] London, 23 December 1940

Cablegram 510 Most Secret

...
1. I am most grateful for your promised help at Singapore in respect both of troops and of equipment and ammunition and hope that you will make these available as proposed. If so, we will arrange to relieve your troops in May by equivalent of a Division from India.
2. The danger of Japan going to war with British Empire is in my opinion definitely less than it was in June after the collapse of France. ...
3. The naval and military successes in the Mediterranean and our growing advantages there by land, sea and air, will not be lost upon Japan. It is quite impossible for our fleet to leave the Mediterranean at the present juncture without throwing away irretrievably all that has been gained there and all prospects for the future. ... We must try to bear our Eastern anxieties patiently and doggedly until this result is achieved, it always being understood that if Australia is seriously threatened by invasion we should not hesitate to compromise or sacrifice the Mediterranean position for the sake of our kith and kin. ...
[AA: A 1608, AA 27/1/1]

Document 120

Cranborne to Whiskard London, 28 January 1941

Cablegram 49 Most Secret and Personal

Please give the following message, which is of the highest degree of secrecy, to the Prime Minister for his most secret and personal information.
1. The following are the views of our military advisers on the report of the Singapore Defence Conference of October, 1940, and on the tactical appreciation drawn up by Commanders of the Forces at Singapore dated 16th October, 1940. ...
2. ... Although it is considered that the views of Commanders on general defence situation are unduly pessimistic, our present weaknesses in land and air forces in the Far East (particularly in air forces) are fully recognised here and everything possible is being done to remedy this situation having regard to the demands of theatres which are the scenes of war.
Air Forces.
3. It is agreed that 582 aircraft is an ideal but considered that 336 should give a very fair degree of security taking into account experience in the Middle East (where our air forces had a three to one inferiority at the start of the present campaign), in Malta and in air defence of Great Britain.

Capacity of the Japanese should not be overestimated. Target of 336 can be increased before the end of 1941 and remains subject to the general situation and supply of aircraft. ...
Land Forces — Malaya and Borneo
9. It is agreed that original recommendation contained in Chiefs of Staff appreciation for final land strength was underestimated and that 26 battalions including three for Borneo is reasonable. This figure will be reached by June 1941 after the arrival of Indian division. ...
[AA: A 1608, AA 27/1/1]

The fact that Singapore was badly defended was underlined by a short visit P.C. Spender, Minister for the Army, paid there in December 1940. We print part of his report to the Advisory War Council. Certainly the newly appointed Commander-in-Chief for the Far East, Air Chief Marshal Sir Robert Brooke-Popham may have dispelled some fears when he spoke to the War Cabinet in February 1941. Much of his statement was most optimistic and particularly the sections printed.

Document 121

Advisory War Council Minute   Melbourne, 5 February 1941

(126) *VISIT OF MINISTER FOR THE ARMY TO SINGAPORE*

At the request of Mr. Curtin [Leader of the Opposition], the Minister for the Army furnished a brief statement in regard to his visit to Singapore, during which he covered the following points:-

(i) *G.O.C. Malaya.* He was unimpressed with the capacity of Lieut.-General L.V. Bond, and thought he lacked drive and capacity.

(ii) *Singapore.*
  (a) *Military Defences.* These were inspected in company with the Chief of the General Staff (Lieut.-General Sturdee), who advised that the fixed defences appeared very good. The beach defences were not impressive and the reserve line defences not at all good.
  (b) *Air Defences.* Air defences were not strong, but he was advised they would be immediately reinforced by 100 Buffalo Brewsters [sic] from America.
  (c) *Naval Defences.* No information was available.

(iii) *Malayan Peninsula.* This was largely jungle and would be very difficult for an attacking force to penetrate. There were little or no land defences. The general picture regarding Singapore was not good, and he formed the opinion that it would be difficult to defend against a heavy major attack, which would probably come from the rear.

(iv) *Despatch of Australian Troops to Malaya.* Mr. Curtin suggested that we should reinforce Singapore instead of sending troops to the Middle

East. The Minister for the Army divulged information regarding the despatch of the Brigade Group which was then on its way to Singapore. (See War Cabinet Minute No. (632)). He outlined the action taken at Singapore to ensure adequate accommodation and assured the Council that this would be satisfactory. The force would also be adequately equipped for jungle warfare with light automatic guns. ...

[AA: A 2682, Vol 1]

Document 122

War Cabinet Minute   Sydney, 14 February 1941

PRESENT: The Hon. A.W. Fadden, M.P., Acting Prime Minister and Acting Minister for Defence Co-ordination.
The Rt. Hon. W.M. Hughes, C.H., K.C., M.P., Attorney-General and Minister for the Navy.
The Hon. P.C. Spender, K.C., M.P., Minister for the Army.
The Hon. J. McEwen, M.P., Minister for Air.
Senator the Hon. H.S. Foll, Minister for Information and Minister for the Interior.
The Rt. Hon. Sir Earle Page, G.C.M.G., M.P., Minister for Commerce.
Senator the Hon. P.A. McBride, Minister for Supply and Development and Minister for Munitions.

(802) *COMBINED FAR EASTERN APPRECIATION OF THE AUSTRALIAN CHIEFS OF STAFF — FEBRUARY, 1941 (AGENDUM No. 64/1941).*

(The three Chiefs of Staff and the Commander-in-Chief in the Far East (Sir Robert Brooke-Popham) were present during the discussion of this Agendum).

...

(ii) *Air Defence.* Sir Robert Brooke-Popham stated that the air defence at Malaya would be strengthened by the 67 Buffalo Brewster bombers [sic][49] en route from U.S.A. He understood that sixteen had left New York on 6th January and others at varying dates. The whole 67 were now on the water and the last was expected to arrive in Malaya about the middle of March.

(iii) *Hong Kong.* Sir Robert Brooke-Popham stated that he was of the opinion that Hong Kong could put up a good defence. The defences on the mainland might be overcome shortly after hostilities commenced but the island could defend itself for at least four months at

---

49. The Brewster Buffalo was, of course, a single seater fighter.

a minimum. The Chinese population in Hong Kong was a serious problem, but food stocks were held for the whole of the Garrison and civil population for up to four months' requirements. It had excellent defences although it was deficient in air defences.

(iv) *Singapore.* The plans for Singapore were based on the assumption that it could defend itself for six months until capital ships could arrive to relieve it. The food reserves were based on six months' rations for the whole of the Garrison and civil population, but the Commander-in-Chief stated that at the end of three months, if relief were not forthcoming, half rations would be issued and it would probably be possible to hold on for a total period of nine months. The plans for the defence of Singapore provided for the control of the Straits to be maintained, but if J[o]hore were taken, the facilities at the northern base would be lost, but this would not prevent the island of Singapore itself from holding out. Naturally, every effort would be made to maintain control over the whole area. No fixed defences were established at the north side of Singapore, as it was not considered, in view of the nature of the country, that they were necessary, but plans had been made to prevent landings and these provided for troops to be established as far north as possible to hold the whole of the Malayan Peninsula. The alternative to the attack on Singapore by what was termed the "front door", i.e., by sea attack, would be an attack by Japanese forces by land, but on this basis there was only one means of access and the ground, which consisted mainly of rice paddy fields, would be under water until the end of April.

It was understood that the Indian 9th Division would be despatched to Malaya, one brigade arriving in March and a further brigade at the end of April, but arrangements are at present in hand to have both the brigades available in Malaya during March which, with the present force, was regarded by Sir Robert as the minimum required to defend Malaya. If additional troops were available, the area of defence would be extended to Sarawak and British Borneo and additional reserves would be allotted to Singapore itself. The supreme need at Singapore at the moment was munitions and more aircraft.

Sir Robert expressed the opinion that if the Japanese proposed to attack Singapore they would act in the first instance by a process of infiltration from Thailand and then gradually move down the Kra Isthmus towards Singapore before declaring war. For this reason, it would be of great assistance to him in providing for the defence of Singapore if a clear policy could be defined in regard to the actions on the part of Japan that would be regarded as a casus belli, and hoped that the line could be drawn at the penetration of Southern Thailand.

(v) *Naval Assistance.* In reply to the Minister for the Navy, the Chief of the Naval Staff stated that he considered that the minimum naval strength necessary at Singapore would be a battle squadron consisting of four or five battleships and three or four cruiser squadrons consisting of between ten and twelve cruisers, but did not consider that, with the British commitments elsewhere, it would be possible to provide for this unless America joined in.

The Minister for the Army stated that it was generally accepted that Singapore was vital to the Empire and suggested that the Chiefs of Staff in the United Kingdom may not hold this view.

The Chief of the Naval Staff stated that the priority of areas for naval defence had been established by the United Kingdom Chiefs of Staff as under:-
(a) The Home Station;
(b) The Mediterranean and Suez Canal;
(c) Singapore;
and that in view of her naval commitments it was probably not possible under present circumstances for any increased strength to be allotted to Singapore.

In reply to the Minister for the Navy, Sir Robert Brooke-Popham stated that when he was leaving the United Kingdom, the directions issued to him by the Prime Minister were that he was to hold Singapore until capital ships could be sent, and had been given an assurance by Mr. Churchill that, "We will not let Singapore fall."...

(vii) *Efficiency of Aircraft.* Sir Robert Brooke-Popham stated that he regarded the Wirraway as quite a good machine for the purpose of attacking ships over short distances, but naturally they were not equal to the more up-to-date machines that were now being turned out. He was of opinion that Japanese planes were not highly efficient and that the Malayan Air Force would put up a good show against them. Some of the Japanese planes had a longer flying range than the Malayan planes. Their fighters, however, were not as good as the Buffalo Brewsters [sic] now being obtained, and our pilots were considerably superior, for the following reasons:-
(a) Training of British and Australian Air Force was more thorough and on sounder grounds;
(b) Although it would be unwise to stress it unduly, he did not look upon the Japanese as being air-minded, particularly against determined fighter opposition;
(c) The Japanese were not getting air domination in China, notwithstanding the overwhelming superiority in numbers.

He considered that his Air Force would put up a much better show against the Japanese planes than they would against the Germans, and generally he thought that the Malayan Air Force would cause such loss to the Japanese Air Force to prevent it from putting the forces out of action either in Singapore or Malaya. ...

[AA: A 2673, Vol 5]

When the decision to reinforce Singapore with elements of the 8th Division was implemented, the *Argus* introduced its front page report as follows.

Document 123

The Argus [Melbourne] 20 February 1941

WASHINGTON, Wednesday.
WORLD-WIDE INTEREST HAS BEEN CREATED IN THE ARRIVAL OF AUSTRALIAN TROOPS AT SINGAPORE. NEWS OF THEIR ARRIVAL CAME AS AN ELECTRIFYING SURPRISE TO PEOPLE IN THE U.S.A.

All American newspapers play up the story in glaring headlines, such as "Australians land at Singapore to take up defence posts."

Messages tell of the transporting of many thousands of fully equipped, "high-spirited Aussies" to the famous naval base, where they entrained for defence stations on the Malayan Peninsula.

In London, despatches from American correspondents say, the news was "chalked up all over the town" and headlines were carried right across the front pages of the papers.

The arrival of the troops once again made Australia the principal topic of interest in London.

Among the headlines one in the "Evening Standard" reads: "Singapore Hails Australians."

Those in the "Evening News" said: "Great Army of Australians Lands in Singapore. Biggest Ever Landed in Single Convoy."...

> In the meantime, Mr Menzies had gone to London to try and get some specific assurance on the despatch of a fleet to Singapore in the event of war with Japan. We print the comments of British Chiefs of Staff together with F.G. Shedden's observations.

Document 124

Reply by [British] Chiefs of Staff to London, 11 April 1941
Memorandum by the Prime Minister of Australia

Annex IV to C.O.S. (41) 230. Final. Secret

FACTORS INFLUENCING THE REINFORCEMENT OF THE FAR EAST WITH CAPITAL SHIPS IF JAPAN ENTERS THE WAR AND THE UNITED STATES REMAIN NEUTRAL.

The Need to Retain in Home Waters a Bare Minimum to Cover the Vital Approaches to the United Kingdom.

THE size of this bare minimum obviously depends on the German heavy ship strength. At present this consists of 1 Bismarck, 2 Gneisenau, 2 Scheer with 1 other Bismarck (Tirpitz) due to be ready very shortly. Assuming that

none of the above is put out of action, the bare minimum of Fleet strength in the North Atlantic area considered necessary is:—
King George V.
Prince of Wales.
Queen Elizabeth.
Hood.
Repulse.

The Mediterranean Situation.

2. In the Mediterranean to-day we are committed to land operations in the Balkans, where Australian and New Zealand Army units are deployed. The maintenance or, if need arose, the withdrawal of these forces in the absence of a capital ship force to provide cover would be extremely hazardous operations. The recent action in the Mediterranean has shown that the enemy is fully alive to the importance of this route and there is no doubt that, if he knew, as he certainly would, that the Eastern Mediterranean Fleet had left Alexandria, the Egypt/Greece route would soon become impossible to maintain. The presence of German armoured units in Libya also increases the threat to the large army in Egypt, which includes Australian troops. In these circumstances, therefore, there can be no question of an immediate withdrawal of the Eastern Mediterranean Fleet to meet an attack on Australia. Even if it were decided to abandon our Mediterranean interests, the fleet would have to remain until the end in order to cover the withdrawal of the armies.

Gibraltar.

3. Since the French went out of the war we have kept a small capital ship force at Gibraltar in order to prevent the Italian fleet entering the Atlantic, to carry out offensive operations in the Western Mediterranean and to protect trade in the North Atlantic. In the face of the extreme urgency of reinforcing the Far East and of at the same time keeping the Eastern Mediterranean fleet in being, it is considered that we might possibly take a risk at Gibraltar and rely on submarines to hold the Straits and give up offensives in the Western Mediterranean. The decision to do this can only be taken at the time; if German heavy ships are out in the North Atlantic at least one capital ship must be kept at Gibraltar to guard the convoy route to Sierra Leone.

Convoy Escorts.

4. We are at present using the old "R" Class battleships[50] as convoy escorts, in which duty they are being assisted by the capital ships of the Home Fleet. With the reduced Home Fleet shown above we should be taking very grave risks in permanently dispersing the Home Fleet on escort duties during the summer months, as the enemy might always make a change of policy and concentrate his heavy ships to cover an invasion. This was the strategy employed by Napoleon, dispersal of our main forces followed by a rapid concentration of his own to cover an invasion, and it is open to the Germans

---

50. The Royal Sovereign Class of battleships was commissioned between 1916–17.

to-day. Napoleon failed because we refused to be dispersed, but if we are not to fall into the trap to-day we must keep some of the older battleships on convoy escort work in order to free the Home Fleet from too great a dispersion. It is considered that 2 "R" Class is the minimum required, and it is [unlikely] that this commitment will be liquidated unless we can sink a proportion of the German heavy ships, since the threat of invasion is likely to remain throughout the war.

Repair and Refitting.
5. At present we have two capital ships undergoing repairs, and we must allow not less than this as an average. Urgent repairs to *Rodney* and *Renown* are still outstanding.

Forces remaining.
6. The capital ship strength remaining consists of 2 *Nelsons, Renown* and 1 R Class battleship. This is not necessarily the exact composition, since ships get damaged and need repair, and others become available. It is the intention to send *Renown* to the Indian Ocean.

7. As regards sending the remainder to the Far East it is impossible to forecast a timetable or even the actual strength. The presence of enemy heavy ships on our trade routes in the Atlantic makes most severe demands on our own heavy ship forces. We may suffer casualties, such as the *Malaya*. A situation might arise where no heavy ships other than *Renown* could be spared for the Far East.

8. On the other hand, if we had been able to put the German battlecruisers out of action before Japan intervened we might be able to despatch 2 *Nelsons* to the Far East about the same time as *Renown* and *Ark Royal* left from Gibraltar.

9. It has always been reckoned that to make certain of getting to Singapore we should have to send a force of nine capital ships, i.e., one less than the force with which the Japanese might oppose us. It is most unlikely that we shall have any such force available, in which case our fleet would have to go to Ceylon in the first instance, and then see how the situation stood. Much would depend on American action. She might be prepared to operate in the Western Pacific, as a threat to Japan, who might then refrain from sending her fleet south.

10. Conclusion.
Our ability to send capital ships to the Far East depends on:-
   (a) The strength and location of the German fleet.
   (b) The success that attends our land and sea operations in the Eastern Mediterranean theatre.
   (c) Our own capital ship strength.
   (d) The likelihood of invasion of the United Kingdom.

None of these is a factor which can be forecast with accuracy in advance. It would be misleading to attempt to lay down possible strength for the Far East, and proposed movement timetables. It is vital to avoid being weak everywhere. All we can say is that we should send a battlecruiser and a carrier to the Indian Ocean. Our ability to do more must be judged entirely on the situation at the time.

[AA: A 5954, Box 625]

Document 125

Shedden to Menzies 14 April 1941
Minute *Most Secret*

STRATEGICAL QUESTIONS AND
OBJECTIVES OF STRENGTH

...

[3. (i)] (d) ... It is now evident that, for too long, we readily accepted the general assurances about the defence of this area. It was only at the November Conference that the Australian representatives discovered the weakness of the local defence position in Malaya. It is only since we came to London that the real situation in regard to a fleet for the Far East has become apparent. ...

(ii) *Naval Defence in the Far East*

The relief of Singapore under certain contingencies does not look very reassuring[51] ...

... we must re-insure ourselves against the most unfavourable likelihood by the maximum local defence effort ...

Though the estimated scale of attack in the Indian Ocean is expected to include one or more capital ships, only capital ship "cover" is to be provided for our reinforcement convoys. With only one capital ship available in the Indian Ocean, escort by it will result in reduced frequency of sailings. A dilem[m]a may arise between risking convoys or leaving the A.I.F. inadequately supported. ...

[AA: A 5954, Box 625]

In April 1941 Admiral Colvin led an Australian delegation to the American-Dutch-British conversations (short title ADB) held at Singapore. He presented the main findings to War Cabinet on 15 May 1941.

---

51. See Document 124, paragraph 9.

Document 126

War Cabinet Minute Sydney, 15 May 1941

(1073) *SUPPLEMENT No. 1 TO AGENDUM No. 135/1941—SINGAPORE CONFERENCE — APRIL, 1941. WASHINGTON STAFF CONVERSATIONS — MARCH, 1941:*

(Previous Reference — Minute No. (972))
(The Chiefs of Staff were present for the discussion of this subject).
...
Main Features of Reports:
2. The Chief of the Naval Staff (Admiral Sir Ragnar Colvin) outlined the main features of the reports and gave his observations thereon.

The report of the American-Dutch-British Conversations embodied plans for the conduct of military operations in the Far East on the hypothesis of a war between Germany, Italy and Japan on the one hand, and the British Empire with its present allies and the United States of America on the other. The plans were based on the conclusions reached at the United States-British conversations at Washington.

Plans for a war in the Far East on the basis of American neutrality were contained in the report of the British-Dutch Conversations, which also cleared up outstanding points arising out of the Anglo-Dutch-Australian Conference of February, 1941.

The report of the United States-British Conversations set forth the general strategic principles which should guide the military collaboration of the United States and the British Commonwealth should the United States be compelled to resort to war.

3. During the discussion which took place on this subject, he expressed the following views in reply to enquiries made by the Minister for the Army [Spender]:-

(i) *Invasion of Australia.* In regard to the statement made in the report of the American-Dutch-British Conversations (paragraph 12) that attacks on Australia can be ruled out initially, the Chief of the Naval Staff stated the word "attack" was intended to be used in the sense of invasion, which conforms with the basis accepted in previous reports of recent Singapore Conferences.

Provided that Singapore and the Netherlands East Indies should hold out, he was of opinion that, at the most, Australia might be subjected to intermittent bombardment from raiding cruisers and by a sharp cruiser-borne raid on vital areas, the raid in such instances consisting of not more than a force of 100 men or thereabouts.

(ii) *Attack through New Caledonia.* Sir Ragnar Colvin suggested that it was unlikely that New Caledonia would be occupied by Japanese forces if Singapore should hold out.

(iii) *Battleship attack.* He expressed the view that an attack on Australia by battleship was unlikely in view of the distance from Japanese bases and the danger to its lines of communication. Japan would also be unlikely to sacrifice one of its older battleships for the moral advantage of an attack on Sydney. Such an attack was possible but not probable, as Japan had no convenient docks or repair establishments even in the Caroline or Marshall Islands, and with Singapore and Borneo intact would be taking a big risk for very little gain.

(iv) *Australia as source of supply to Malaya.* It was suggested to the Chief of the Naval Staff that there might be good reason for Japan to attack Australia, as she was, in effect, the main source of supply to Malaya. The Chief of the Naval Staff agreed that, for this reason, such an attack might be given consideration by Japan, but nevertheless the risk was not very great and if such an attack were contemplated, it would probably be made by an armed merchant cruiser.

(v) *Australian Land Army in initial stage of war.* In reply to the Minister for the Army, Admiral Colvin stated that a land army on the present basis contemplated by the Government would not be required in Australia in the initial stages of a war, except for training as a contingency against the fall of Singapore and the Netherlands East Indies. ...

United States Views.

4. Note was taken of the principal United States views summarised in the report of Sir Ragnar Colvin, as follows:-

(a) Europe and the North American Atlantic Seaboard were the vital areas.

(b) Singapore, while very important, was not in the United States view absolutely vital, and its loss, while undesirable, could be accepted. This view was not accepted by the British Delegation at Washington.

(c) The United States intention was, while maintaining a Naval Force at Hawaii superior to the Japanese, and thus protecting the West American Seaboard and sea communications in the Pacific, to use its Navy principally in the Atlantic, and they would, if necessary, reinforce their Atlantic Fleet from their Pacific Fleet.

(d) They intended to use the United States Pacific Fleet to operate offensively against Japanese Mandated Islands, and Japanese sea communications, and to support British Naval Forces in the South Pacific.

(e) They did not intend to reinforce their Asiatic Fleet.

(f) They expected that the Philippine Islands would not be able to hold out very long against determined Japanese attack, and were anticipating being forced to withdraw from those islands.

(g) They were prepared to provide sufficient capital ships for the Atlantic and for Gibraltar as would permit the release from these areas of British capital ships for reinforcement of the Naval Forces in the Eastern theatre. ...

Decisions of War Cabinet.

5. War Cabinet were in agreement with the plans for military co-operation outlined in the above reports. The following observations and decisions were recorded on the aspects indicated hereunder:

(a) *Unified Strategic Command — Far Eastern Theatre.* (Section V,

A.D.B.; paragraphs 22 to 28 of B.D. [British-Dutch Conversations]) The following arrangements for unified strategic command of naval and air forces operating in the Eastern Theatre were agreed to:—
  (i) The British Commander-in-Chief, China [Layton], will exercise unified strategical direction over all the Naval Forces of the Associated Powers in the Eastern Theatre (including Australia), except those employed on local defence or operating under the Commander-in-Chief, United States Asiatic Fleet. Part of the United States Asiatic Fleet will, however, come under the Commander-in-Chief, China, immediately, and the remainder under his strategic direction when Manila becomes untenable.
  (ii) The Commander-in-Chief, Far East [Brooke-Popham], is to exercise similar strategic direction of such Air Forces as the Associated Powers may make available. Insofar as Australia is concerned, the Air Forces available will not exceed two bomber squadrons, to be allotted to the Ambon-Timor area.
  (*Note*: This was approved by War Cabinet in Minute No.(909)).
  (iii) Operational control will continue to be exercised by the various authorities as at present, except at Ambon, where a Combined Headquarters is to be formed (War Cabinet Minute No. (986) and at Timor, where, as already agreed, land forces are to be under the control of an Australian Commander. It was noted that there is little possibility of strategic offensive action by land forces and a localised strategic policy is already established for land forces.
  (iv) The above arrangements are subject to the right of any Government to withdraw or withhold its forces, provided that prior information of such intention is passed to the strategic Commander concerned.

The Chief of the General Staff [Sturdee] stated that detailed arrangements in respect of command of troops at Ambon were being discussed with the Netherlands East Indies authorities as authorised by War Cabinet in Minute No. (986), and he would submit a report to War Cabinet as soon as negotiations were completed.

(b) *Initial Disposition of Naval Forces* (Appendix I, A.D.B.) In the list of initial dispositions and functions of Naval Forces, one Australian 6-inch cruiser is shown as operating in North Australian waters to escort troop convoys to Ambon, Koepang and Singapore, and is then to be at the disposition of the Commander-in-Chief, China. This is a new commitment resulting from the stationing of Australian Military and Air Forces in the Netherlands East Indies[52], thus being outside the area of Australian Naval operational control. War Cabinet approved of this arrangement.

(c) *U.S. Naval and Air Support* (Paragraphs 42 and 71(a), A.D.B.) The extent of the support to be afforded by the United States to British Naval and Air Forces south of the Equator is not defined in the report.

---

52. See Document 132 ff.

It was noted that the United States Delegation had undertaken to make enquiries in this respect and that the matter had also been taken up through the Australian Naval Attache, Washington.

(d) *Reinforcement of Singapore.* Note was taken of the view of the Commander-in-Chief, Far East ... that the reinforcement of Malaya by land and air forces since October last had so materially strengthened their position that he was most optimistic as to the ability of Singapore to hold out, and to continue to operate as a Fleet Base.

Sir Ragnar Colvin stated that he understood that developments in Iraq[53] had resulted in the diversion of forces otherwise available for Singapore.

[AA: A 2673, Vol 7]

Colvin's misgivings that Singapore would not immediately be reinforced because of 'developments in Iraq' proved well founded. In fact such developments led Brooke-Popham to ask for additional AIF units and equipment. P.C. Spender tabled the request before War Cabinet on 3 June 1941.

Document 127

War Cabinet Agendum 3 June 1941

ADDITIONAL TROOPS FOR MALAYA Secret

1. A request from the Commander-in-Chief, Far East, has been received by the Chief of the General Staff, that additional A.I.F. units should be sent to Malaya in view of the diversion of an Indian Brigade to Irak and the temporary stoppage of the reinforcement programme. He has asked for the following:-
   (a) One infantry brigade group.
   (b) One machine gun battalion and one pioneer battalion.
   (c) Additional 4.5" howitzers, anti-tank guns and light tanks.
   (d) Personnel for two anti-tank batteries.
2. With respect to the request for equipment (sub-para. (c) above), 52 field guns have already been despatched to Middle East and Malaya since war began; we are now below initial requirements and have no reserves. No additional field artillery can be permitted to leave Australia until 25-pdrs. are well into production. We cannot spare any anti-tank guns beyond the allotment to the United Kingdom of 25 per month from July production onwards. We possess only 10 light tanks and these are required for the training of the Armoured Division.
3. The personnel mentioned in (d) of para. 1 above have been despatched

---

53. See Editorial comment, page 111.

to augment the portion of 4th Anti-Tank Regiment already in Malaya.

4. The request for an infantry brigade group, a machine gun battalion and a pioneer battalion raises matters of general policy. The following are the principal A.I.F. units still in Australia and territories:-
  (a) Two infantry brigade groups.
  (b) One machine gun battalion.
  (c) Two pioneer battalions.
  (d) One army field regiment.

One infantry brigade group, less one battalion, is located in Darwin; the detached battalion is at Rabaul. The two battalions with this brigade group are earmarked for Ambon and Koepang. The infantry units are therefore disposed and not available for any other purpose. The other A.I.F. infantry brigade group is located in Eastern Command. Under present plans, the infantry brigade is held to replace the units at Darwin when the latter proceed to N.E.I. on outbreak of hostilities with Japan.

The machine gun battalion is located in Western Australia.

One pioneer battalion is at Darwin and the other in New South Wales. The former belongs to the A.I.F. in the Middle East: it has been placed in a low order of priority of despatch and owing to shortage of shipping space has been kept in Australia.

5. The defence of Darwin requires four infantry battalions as a minimum. Three battalions are therefore required in addition to the Darwin infantry battalion A.M.F. [Australian Military Forces].

The alternative means of providing these units are:-
  (a) The A.I.F. infantry brigade as at present planned.
  (b) An A.I.F. pioneer battalion and A.I.F. machine gun battalion and an A.M.F. battalion.
  (c) Three A.M.F. infantry battalions.

The first alternative is the most satisfactory. The other alternatives, whilst feasible, have features which must be borne in mind. Neither a pioneer battalion nor a machine gun battalion is the operational equivalent of an infantry battalion and each would require some reorganization before it could be so regarded.

A.M.F. battalions would have to be withdrawn from their present roles. Further, it must be appreciated that these units only approach operational efficiency in the latter part of their 90 day training period. Wastage, especially of officers, N.C.Os. [Non-Commissioned Officers] and key personnel, to A.I.F., reserved occupations and other causes, necessitates rebuilding units at the commencement of each continuous training period.

6. With respect to artillery, it has already been indicated in para. 2 above that we could not allow guns to go for the time being. An artillery regiment could not be despatched to Malaya unless it could be equipped there. As the C-in-C. Far East has asked for guns, it is clear that he could not equip it at the present juncture.

7. The despatch of further units to Malaya raises the matter of increasing our overseas commitments having in view the problem of monthly reinforcements and the formation of the Armoured Division.

With respect to Malaya, it should be borne in mind that the whole Far Eastern Area is regarded as one defence problem and from the approved conclusions of the various conferences held at Singapore, it is clear that Australian units operating there would be making a very direct contribution to the defence of Australia itself.
8. The general question of the despatch overseas of further troops and the increase in our overseas commitments of personnel are referred for consideration by War Cabinet.
[AA: A 2671, 189/1941]

In October 1941, Winston Churchill in London decided largely on his own initiative to send the new battleship *Prince of Wales* and the battlecruiser *Repulse*, which had been built in 1917, to Singapore. These ships comprised the full commitment to the 'fleet to Singapore' strategy. Bruce claims to have influenced Churchill in his decision here in a cable to John Curtin, now Prime Minister.

Document 128

Bruce to Curtin   London, 14 October 1941

Cablegram 67   *Personal Himself Only*

... original suggestion was for only older and relatively slow ships to be despatched. I have been strongly urging that Squadron should include something that could catch and kill anything that the Japanese have and stressing tremendous impression that such inclusion would create. I am now not without hope that either "George V" or "Prince of Wales" will be sent.
[AA: M100, 10]

The long-expected Japanese attack finally came on 8 December 1941 and prompted the following cablegram from John Curtin. By then perhaps it was a little late to stop the Japanese. Certainly the loss of the British capital ships led the way to a fiasco at Singapore which we document in a later section.

Document 129

Curtin to Cranborne   8 December 1941

Cablegram [778?]   *Most Secret*

THE LATEST COMPREHENSIVE APPRECIATION ON THE FAR

EASTERN POSITION WAS THAT GIVEN [T]O MR MENZIES IN REPLY TO HIS MEMORANDUM OF 29TH MARCH.

NOW THAT WAR HAS BROKEN OUT WITH JAPAN IT IS OF PARAMOUNT IMPORTANCE THAT WE SHOULD HAVE AN U[P]-TO-DATE REVIEW TO WHICH OUR PLANS FOR LOCAL DEFENCE CAN BE RELATE[D]. WE WOULD THEREFORE BE GLAD TO RECEIVE AS EARLY AS POSSIBLE THE ... APPRECIATION OF THE CHIEFS OF STAFF ON THE NEW SITUATION TOGETHER WITH THE COMMENTS OF YOUR GOVERNMENT.

[AA: A1608, V 41/1/1]

9
THE DUTCH ALLIANCE AND PORTUGUESE TIMOR

Australian security was obviously linked with that of the arc of islands to its north and east, from the East Indies to New Caledonia. European powers had sovereignty over most of these islands. When some of these powers were conquered by Germany there were major implications for Australia's near north. Australian concern is illustrated below. As it happened, it was on 17 April 1940 that the United States indicated its opposition to any forceful change in the status quo in the Netherlands East Indies.

Document 130

Commonwealth Government to United Kingdom Government 17 April 1940

Cablegram 156 Most Secret

We would infer from your recent telegrams that attack on the Netherlands by Germany is believed in many quarters to be imminent in which case any attempt to alter the status of the Netherlands East Indies becomes of vital concern to Australia.

In the course of conversation President Roosevelt and his principal advisers on several occasions in recent years have expressed the view to Australian senior Ministers that the United States could not remain indifferent to developments of this nature in the Pacific and would be forced to intervene. Recent developments and policy of neutrality may have caused reverse of opinion but it seems to us most important to ascertain at as early a stage as possible what the present view of the Administration is. To this end and if not already done we suggest that His Majesty's Ambassador [Lord Lothian] be requested to discuss the question with the United States authorities in order to ascertain their present attitude and possible action.
[AA: M100, 8]

With Holland in German hands, a Dutch government-in-exile in London, and prospects of a Japanese thrust south, it was obvious that the British Empire should seek full military co-operation with the Dutch in preparing its plans based on Singapore and the East Indies (or the 'Malay barrier', as it came to be termed in military circles). Naturally,

Australia was more anxious than Britain to arrange such co-operation. Churchill refused to give the Dutch a guarantee of British help in resisting a Japanese attack on their territory in the East Indies, because Washington would not guarantee that it would help Britain resist a Japanese attack on Dutch and British territory in the Far East. However, the Dutch took part in staff talks, for example, the conference in Singapore in the last week of February 1941; and Australia entered into specific commitments with the Dutch, commitments which were to have disastrous consequences for some two thousand Australian soldiers.

The following extract, written when the Battle of Britain was approaching its climax, indicates Britain's general interest in co-operating with the Dutch.

Document 131

Caldecote to Menzies   London, 11 August 1940

Circular Cablegram Z 214   *Most Secret and Personal*

...

38. ... Whole defence problem in the Far East would be greatly facilitated if we were certain of Dutch co-operation and could concert a plan with them. Our aim should be scheme of defence ensuring full mutual support, pooling of resources, and arrangements for rapid movement of troops to threatened points. Dutch would probably agree to prepare secret plans for defence of the Netherlands East Indies, though they might hesitate to assist us in the event of Japanese attack on British territory alone. With our present limited resources in the Far East we could not offer the Dutch any effective military support against Japanese aggression. It is not therefore recommended that staff conversations should be held with the Dutch immediately. It is most important however that plans should be concerted with the Dutch as soon as we have improved our own position in Malaya.

Meanwhile our Officers Commanding R.A.F. in the Far East should consider the problem of combined Anglo-Dutch defence plans so that conversations may take place immediately the opportunity arises. ...

39. If the Japanese attack Malaya without attacking the Netherlands East Indies, it is conceivable that Dutch co-operation would be withheld. We should then be faced with gap in our defensive system and our sea communications in the Indian Ocean would be more seriously threatened. It should, however, still be possible even without Dutch collaboration to get some supplies into Malaya intermittently but in such circumstances our difficulties in the Far East would be greatly increased. ...

[AA: A 1608, A 41/1/1, Part 12]

At the Singapore Conference of February 1941, Australian military representatives met Dutch counterparts. Subsequently their proposals for co-operation were approved by the Australian government.

Document 132

War Cabinet Minutes Sydney, 22 March 1941

(909) *AGENDUM No. 109/1941 — ANGLO-DUTCH-AUSTRALIAN CONFERENCE – SINGAPORE, FEBRUARY, 1941.*

(The Chief of the General Staff [Sturdee] and the Chief of the Air Staff [Burnett] were present for the discussion of this Agendum).

War Cabinet considered the report of the Anglo-Dutch-Australian Conference at Singapore, February, 1941, the Report of the Australian delegation to the Conference and the comments of the Australian Chiefs of Staff thereon. The following observations and decisions were recorded:-
...
Mutual Reinforcements
3. War Cabinet approved of the provision of Army units to reinforce Ambon and Koepang and also of an air striking force from Darwin to operate from advanced bases to be established in collaboration with the Netherlands East Indies authorities at Ambon and Koepang. It was noted that the provision of the above reinforcements will enable Australia to participate in the forward line and thus to operate offensively.
4. In regard to the proposal made in ... the report, that the allied forces at Ambon would be under Dutch control *at the outset*, War Cabinet was of the view that, in relation to Australian troops, this should be interpreted to mean a short transitional period after which Australian troops should come under Australian control on the arrival of our units. War Cabinet considered that there should be unified command of all troops at Ambon and that, in view of the nature and extent of the contribution being made by Australia ... it was preferable that an Australian officer should be in command.
5. War Cabinet noted that, in view of additional commitments elsewhere, two brigade groups cannot be provided in the Darwin-Ambon-Timor area, as estimated in the report, and that it is likely that one brigade group and one battalion plus a battery would be available in this area.

The Chief of the General Staff stated that he had discussed with the Netherlands East Indies Chief of the General Staff the question of the composition and strength of the Australian Forces to be made available at Ambon and Koepang, and they considered that a force of approximately 1,200 troops should be made available for reinforcement of Ambon and approximately the same number of troops for Koepang. It was proposed that the force for Ambon should be under the command of a Brigadier. War Cabinet approved of these forces being provided for the reinforcement of Ambon and Koepang.

6. It was noted that R.A.A.F. units were not to be permanently stationed at Ambon and Koepang, but that advanced bases were to be established at these localities from which Air Force units at Darwin would operate. The Air Forces available for the Darwin-Ambon-Timor area were as shown in the report, that is two bomber squadrons, and possibly an additional reinforcing squadron. One of the bomber squadrons at present consists of Wirraways, the restricted range of which will confine it to the portion of the area in the vicinity of Darwin until an intermediate landing ground is established in the Tanambar Islands, which is projected under the Dutch plans. This situation will continue until the aircraft position improves.

7. It was noted that under the arrangements agreed to at the Conference the movement of Australian troops to Ambon and Koepang is not to take place until hostilities with Japan have commenced. War Cabinet agreed that, from a military point of view, there would be every advantage in moving the troops to these localities at once, so that they might be in a position to operate effectively at short notice. In view, however, of the important political implications of such action, and the possibility that it may be regarded by Japan as provocative, it was decided that before any approach is made to the Netherlands East Indies Government, the views of the United Kingdom Government be sought as to the desirability of undertaking such action, having regard to both military and political considerations.

8. Irrespective of the arrangements finally decided upon as to the immediate despatch of troops to Ambon and Koepang, War Cabinet approved of steps being taken at once, in collaboration with the Netherlands East Indies authorities, for the despatch to Ambon and Koepang from Australia of requirements of equipment, including W/T equipment, motor vehicles, general stores, bombs, petrol, &c., for both the Australian troops to be sent to these localities and for R.A.A.F. units operating from the advanced bases at Ambon and Koepang. Financial liability for the above will be accepted by the Commonwealth Government on the understanding that the Netherlands East Indies will accept responsibility for the provision of necessary accommodation &c. for the troops and stores and ground facilities at air advanced bases. Special steps should be taken to ensure the secrecy of the above arrangements. Stores and equipment made available should conform to Dutch markings and will be ostensibly on charge to the Netherlands East Indies. ...

Co-ordinated Naval Plan for the Far East.

11. It was noted that the Conference did not formulate a co-ordinated naval plan for the Far East. War Cabinet are in complete agreement with the views of the Chiefs of Staff as to the paramount importance of the early completion of this plan. ... War Cabinet expressed great concern at the failure of the Conference to draw up such a plan, the absence of which is a serious handicap in the organisation of our Far Eastern defence measures. It was decided that the United Kingdom Government be asked to convene a conference of naval Commanders-in-Chief immediately so that a co-ordinated naval plan could be completed without further delay. ...

Naval Forces Available.
13. It was noted that the Conference recommends the return of Australian and New Zealand cruisers to their own stations when war with Japan becomes imminent, or earlier if the ships can be spared from their present dispositions. The Conference considers, however, that the return of Australian destroyers and sloops at present serving in the Mediterranean and Red Sea should be deferred until the Japanese threat becomes more of a reality in Far Eastern focal areas.
14. War Cabinet had previously expressed the view (Minute No. (790)) that in the event of war with Japan the whole of our naval forces would be required in Australian and New Zealand waters. This view is adhered to, but in view of the shortage of light surface vessels it was agreed that the return of Australian destroyers and sloops should remain in abeyance as recommended by the Conference, provided it is established that their effectiveness in the role for which they are normally employed is greater in the Mediterranean and Red Sea than in the Far Eastern area. In coming to this decision, War Cabinet are influenced by the part that such vessels have played and may be called upon to play in connection with the activities of Australian and other Empire troops in the Near and Middle East. ...

(912) *Invitation to Netherlands East Indies to send an Air Force Flight to Darwin.*
...
On the recommendation of the Minister for Air, [McEwen] it was approved that the following cable be despatched to the British Consul-General at Batavia:–
"Commonwealth Government would welcome visit to Australia of squadron or less number of Netherlands East Indies aircraft. Visit could be made only to Darwin for short period if Dutch so desire, but we would be quite agreeable to it being extended to southern States. To meet Dutch susceptibilities, we would suggest that it be regarded purely as training flight. We would concur in any alternative suggestions in this respect which Dutch may wish to make and would take steps to ensure that no publicity is given to visit if they so desire. Glad if you would sound Netherlands East Indies authorities and advise as soon as possible.
"For your private information and use at your discretion object is to pave the way for reciprocal visits by Australian Air Force to Ambon and Koepang as these are bases from which we would operate in war in collaboration with Netherlands East Indies. It is of some importance that we should be able to make reconnaissance of these bases in advance of outbreak of hostilities."
[AA: A 2673, Vol 6]

Australian stores and equipment were moved to Ambon and Timor, and work started on building the requisite military facilities. The services wanted to have some of their men, in uniform, on the islands, but the government remained wary of the possible diplomatic implications of such a step. Britain was approached to ask the Dutch government for permission for an early move; but Britain delayed, realising the Dutch might respond with a request for a British guarantee to help defend their territory if they, alone, were attacked by Japan.

The delay, though understandable, did not help Australian military preparations in the Netherlands East Indies. Three months after the first approach the Australian government sent the following message.

Document 133

Fadden to Cranborne   3 October 1941

Cablegram 649   *Most Secret*

... Commonwealth Government would be glad if approach could be made to Netherlands Government for authority for the despatch of Australian Army and Air Force Units to Ambon and Koepang ... to include the despatch of advance parties in uniform immediately. Our Service advisers attach considerable importance to despatch of latter now and we are anxious to have the permission of Netherlands Government to do this as soon as possible.
[AA: A 1608, AA 27/1/1]

Document 134

Curtin to Cranborne   16 October 1941

Cablegram 684   *Most Secret*

... It is desired that the advance forces to be sent to Ambon and Koepang referred to in telegram No. 649 of 3rd October should consist of Army personnel, 100 to each place (Ambon 13 officers and 87 other ranks: Koepang 15 officers and 85 other ranks), and Air Force personnel, 52 to Ambon and Namlea (8 officers and 44 other ranks) and 19 to Koepang (3 officers and 16 other ranks).

In view of the size of the proposed advance parties, it is considered most desirable that they should be in uniform. This would be a great aid to the maint[e]nance of discipline.
[AA: A 1608, AA 27/1/1]

It was late November, when the Japanese fleet had left the Kurile Islands on its way to attack Pearl Harbor, before the Dutch government gave its assent, in part, to Australia's request of mid-October.

Document 135

Cranborne to Curtin   London, 27 November 1941

Cablegram 786   Most Secret

...
Ambon, Koepang and Namlea.
The Netherlands reply now received points out that A.D.A. [Anglo-Dutch-Australian] conversations at Singapore in February referred to the despatch of Australian troops after outbreak of war in the Pacific. The Netherlands Government however concur in the despatch at an earlier stage, provided that the Netherlands Authorities deem this desirable having regard to the political and military situation but this is not the case at present.
2. Despatch of troops without absolute necessity might lead to undesirable incidents with the population, which in turn might have unfavourable repercussions on Netherlands-Australian relations. This applies in particular to the population of Ambon. Therefore despatch of foreign troops should in the opinion of the Netherlands Government be postponed as long as possible.
3. The Netherlands Government feel that the despatch of air force personnel would be more acceptable than army personnel, and despatch of air force personnel as indicated in paragraph 1 of your telegram ... is accordingly agreed to.
4. Besides despatch of the above air force personnel, the Netherlands Government agree to the despatch to Koepang of 30 (repeat 30) Australian infantry in addition to 14 said to be already in Dutch Timor.
5. The Netherlands Government desire that details should be arranged direct between the Netherlands East Indies and Australian Authorities.
6. They similarly desire that the Netherlands East Indies and Australian Authorities should decide when arrival of the main bodies of Australian troops is desirable and suggest that the United Kingdom Authorities in Singapore should help in co-ordination.
7. The Netherlands Government intend to inform the United States Government of the broad outline of these arrangements.
[AA: A 1608, AA 27/1/1]

Document 136

Langslow [Secretary, Department   Melbourne, 1 December 1941
of Air] to Drakeford

Teleprinter Message M 2840   Most Secret

... Chief of Air Staff [Burnett] has placed No. 2 Squadron, Laverton, No.

13 Squadron, Darwin, and No. 24 (Hudson flight) Squadron, Townsville, in a state of readiness for movement at 56 hours notice.
[AA: A5954, Box 554]

Document 137

AIR BOARD TO A.L.O. [Air   5 December 1941
Liaison Officer] BANDOENG

Radio Message

... TWO FLIGHTS R.A.A.F. HUDSONS TO MOVE LAHA AND ONE FLIGHT TO KOEPANG DAWN 7/12 (.) WAR CABINET URGENTLY REQUESTS NO PRESS PUBLICITY RE MOVE.
[AA: A5954, Box 554]

Assurances of armed support from USA led the British government to offer firm guarantees and closer military co-operation to the Dutch in the East Indies. Unfortunately, as events were soon to show, this understanding came too late to permit efficient joint military planning.

Document 138

Cranborne to Curtin   London, 5 December 1941

Circular Cablegram M.427   *Most Secret*

NETHERLANDS EAST INDIES
Following is the text of a note handed to the Netherlands Minister to-day.
In my note of 5th September I explained to Your Excellency the attitude of His Majesty's Government in the United Kingdom towards an attack on the Netherlands East Indies. The note stated that His Majesty's Government considered themselves to have already assumed the duty of safeguarding and restoring the possessions and rights of Netherlands to the best of their ability during the war and at peace. It followed therefore that an attack upon the Netherlands East Indies would leave them to do the utmost in their power to this end, though His Majesty's Government must remain the sole judge of what action or military measures on their part were practicable and likely to ach[ie]ve the common purpose.
2. His Majesty's Government have again reviewed the position in the light of recent developments and they feel that it is of urgent importance to provide the firmest basis for effective co-operation in meeting the present Japanese threat. They are accordingly for their part prepared to enter at once into a mutual understanding with the Netherlands Government

whereby each party will undertake to co-operate immediately with the other to the fullest extent of its available resources in the event of the other party being forced to take military action to repel an attack on any of its territories in the Far East.

3. His Majesty's Government have reason to believe that their views are shared by His Majesty's Government in the Commonwealth of Australia and His Majesty's Government in New Zealand and if the Netherlands Government are prepared to enter into such an understanding His Majesty's Government will at once suggest to the Governments of the two Dominions that they should also participate. ...

[AA: A 981, Japan 185 B, Part 3]

PORTUGUESE TIMOR

Australia had also been involved in lengthy but less successful diplomacy aimed at securing a privileged position in Portuguese Timor. It was much later before military co-operation was seriously considered. Nothing was arranged before the outbreak of war.

Document 139

War Cabinet Minute   Melbourne, 15 October 1941

(1401) *AGENDUM No. 270/1941 — SUPPLEMENT No. 3 — PORTUGUESE TIMOR*
...
Consideration was given to Dominions Office telegram ... regarding the defence of Portuguese Timor.

2. It was agreed that an approach should be made to the Portuguese as well as to the Netherlands authorities and that the lines of the approach should be as indicated ... i.e.:-

"We suggest that approach to the Portuguese should be on the lines of an enquiry whether they would be prepared to accept outside help if it is found necessary by the military authorities on the spot and that the approach to both the Dutch and Portuguese should seek their agreement to Australian, Dutch and Portuguese military authorities discussing locally:-

(i) The preventive action necessary;

(ii) The action which should be taken if a threat should actually eventuate.

Since, however, the local military authorities in Portuguese Timor may not be qualified for discussing strategic matters, we think that, as far as the Portuguese are concerned, it would be necessary to clear the ground possibly at this end first. If the Portuguese agree generally, the place and method of discussions could be settled later."

3. In regard to the provision of military assistance for Portuguese Timor, it was considered that, in view of the threat to Australia which would arise from a Japanese occupation of Portuguese Timor, Australia should be prepared to co-operate to the fullest practicable extent in measures for the defence of Portuguese Timor, and the following decisions were given:-
(a) The Australian Air Forces to be provided under existing plans for the reinforcement of Ambon and Koepang are also to be available for operations in Portuguese Timor.
(b) The Military Forces earmarked for Koepang are sufficient only for the defence of that place and additional troops will be required to reinforce Portuguese Timor. The additional forces necessary are estimated by the Chief of the General Staff at a Battalion and supporting troops. It was decided to accept the commitment for the despatch of Australian troops to Portuguese Timor, if the Portuguese agree to accept reinforcements from outside Portuguese Timor as a result of the approach which is now being made.

Detailed proposals as to the numbers of troops involved and equipment to be provided are to be submitted by the Department of the Army.

...

[AA: A 2673, Vol 8]

10
AUSTRALIA AND THE HIGHER DIRECTION OF THE WAR, December 1941 — April 1942

When Japan attacked at widely-separated points in the Pacific only a few Australian servicemen were immediately involved in the fighting. But the Curtin government promptly began making preparations for a long conflict. One main concern from December 1941 until April 1942, when Australia came under the protection of the United States, involved a claim for a say in the higher direction of the war. Australia, with the aim of improving Allied military efficiency, also urged the creation of a unified command in its region.

The following two documents illustrate the Curtin government's attitude.

Document 140

Curtin to Churchill [via Cranborne]   11 December 1941

Cablegram 794   *Most Secret*

War Cabinet and Advisory War Council have had under review the question of the creation of a supreme authority for the higher direction and co-ordinated control of allied activities and strategy in the war in the Pacific.
2. We feel that there is a need for a supreme authority of this nature and we think that this body should be established in the Far East, preferably at Singapore where the Commanders-in-Chief are located. It is appreciated, however, that there are difficulties in the way of setting up such an authority immediately, but it seems to us that some steps should ultimately be taken to ensure closer collaboration between the allied countries in the higher direction of the war. ...
4. We would be glad to have an expression of your views on this matter as soon as possible.
[AA: A 1608, G 33/1/2]

Document 141

Evatt [Minister for External Affairs] to Casey [Washington]   16 December 1941

Cablegram 1079   *Personal*

... I want you to press and insist that in every conference between representatives of the (Associated) Powers this Government must have opportunity of s[ep]arate representation even though it may appear unpracticable at first sight.

... danger [is] that our own point of view may be regarded as of subsidiary importance. On the contrary our point of view must be (continuously) stressed or our great needs will be over-looked. It is obvious that in some respects views of United Kingdom representative will differ from our own both in relation to supplies and forces. This Government is far from (satisfied) with results of policy of subordinating our requirements to those of others.
[AA: M100, 12]

Crucial decisions about Allied command structure were made at the 'Arcadia' conference, held in Washington from 24 December 1941 to 14 January 1942, and attended by Churchill, Roosevelt and their service chiefs. One such decision was the creation of ABDA (Australian-British-Dutch-American) Command (see Section 11). Another was the setting up of the Combined Chiefs of Staff (CCS), comprising the UK and US service chiefs. Located in Washington, the CCS was to have control, under Churchill and Roosevelt, of the war strategy of the western democracies.

Under these proposals Australia would not be represented on the body which gave orders to ABDA's commander, General Wavell. There follow extracts from Evatt's response to this.

Document 142

Evatt to Casey   Canberra, 7 January 1942

Cablegram 37   *Most Secret*

...

2. ... [W]e are much disturbed at the procedure proposed to be adopted in relation to the highest decisions affecting the South West Pacific [i.e. ABDA Command]. The method proposed not only fails to recognize our status which might be overlooked; [it ignores] our great stake and tremendous responsibilities in connection with the area. In that area our soldiers will be engaged to an increasing extent. The unanimous opinion of the Advisory War Council here which as you know includes both sides in politics is that we cannot allow the scheme to go ahead without amendments designed to give us an equal voice in final decisions. ...
4. Our general point of view is shared by the N.E.I. [Netherlands East Indies] Government whatever may be said about the Netherlands Government in London. ...
7. I need not add that you should present our views on this topic with the utmost vigor with a view to ensuring that the machinery of collaboration will

secure true and equal collaboration. Frankly we cannot afford to be sidetracked or short circuited in the way now proposed. ...
[AA: A 3300, 219]

This protest by Evatt developed into a campaign lasting several months to try to get Australian representation on a body which could give orders to theatre commanders. We print some extracts from a cable to Churchill in which Curtin stated some of Australia's wishes.

Document 143

Curtin to Churchill   7 January 1942

Cablegram JOHCU 15   *Most Secret*

Personal for Prime Minister from Prime Minister of Australia. ...
(i) *Machinery for Joint Direction.* ... [Y]ou sought approval to an agreement reached with President in which following was mentioned... in Clause (e) of agreement: (e) C. in C. would receive his orders from an appropriate joint body who would be responsible to you and to President. ... I notified Commonwealth Government's assent to agreement and stated we expected Australia would be included in the composition of the appropriate joint body to which reference was made. In our view machinery of this nature was an essential part of the plan and our assent was promptly given because (e) involved setting up such a body and our representation on it.

No further advice has been received from you regarding joint body agreement. ... [You have informed me] that U.S. Chiefs of Staff and representative in Washington of British Chiefs of Staff will constitute agencies for submitting recommendations for decisions by President and yourself. [You also inform me:] "Since London has machinery for consultations with Dominion Government and since Dutch Government is in London, British Government will be responsible for obtaining their views and agreement, and for including these in final telegram to Washington."

Though a powerful enemy has brought the conflict closer to our shores and Australian people are quite prepared to meet danger with same resolution displayed by their kinsfolk in British Isles, we hold strongly in view of large forces we will have in South Western Pacific theatre the use that will be made of Commonwealth as a base and our responsibilities for its local defence that our voice be heard in Council on Pacific strategy. We fully realize that we are not one of predominating partners in this struggle since British and American forces in South Western theatre are defending strategic centres and sources of supplies, but same military operations represent to us a vital struggle for the security of our homeland and all that we have built up in this part of the world.

My predecessor [outlined] to you at length opinions which, as leader of another party, I can state are the overwhelming views of Australian people on their right to be heard when vital decisions affecting their interests are being taken. ...

In so far as London is concerned, I stated ... that I was grateful for facilities afforded to Page[54] and suggested following principles to govern consultations on common policy:

1. It [i.e. the Australian Government] should have full knowledge of all essential facts, developments and trends of policies.
2. It should obtain this knowledge in time to express its views before decisions are taken.
3. It should have the opportunity through its accredited representative of presenting to and discussing with War Cabinet, the important committee[s] such as defence committee and Prime Minister or other senior minister any suggestions as to new policy diverse views on policy under consideration that Australia might from time to time desire to submit.

Failure to set up any joint body for operations in Pacific or to provide for more direct consultation with the Commonwealth than that contemplated ... is a situation we are quite unable to accept. ...
[AA: A 3300, 219]

A useful review of the problems of Australia's say in running the war is found in the following cable from Casey.

Document 144

Casey to Evatt   Washington, 13 January 1942

Cablegram 74   *Most Immediate*

The President returned to Washington on January 11th. I saw him today and represented to him the substance of your telegram 37 and specifically that Australia's great stake and responsibilities in the Southwest Pacific warranted our having an adequate voice in the higher direction of the campaign in the Pacific area; that Australian reaction to the present proposal for higher direction was very unfavourable and that you were extremely desirous that the organisation should be broadened so as to be truly ABDA.

His reply did not materially differ from what Churchill has said, that it had been necessary to create an organisation very hastily and that it had unfortunately not been possible to consult all Governments concerned adequately beforehand, and that the consultative machinery had to include London and Washington with the best arrangements for giving Australia and the Dutch opportunity to make their views known that could be devised. He

---

54. Special Representative of the Australian government in the United Kingdom, October 1941 — June 1942.

(the President) believed the present arrangements would undoubtedly be modified as experience was gained of their working, although his view was that it was in the common interest to ensure that speed of decision was not sacrificed. He said that he appreciated your point of view but that he was at a loss to suggest any method whereby Australian and Dutch representation could be improved on the political side. Geography created the difficulty. If we (Australia) wished to have senior military naval and air officers here in Washington, so far as he (the President) was concerned, he would have no objection at all, although he would have to consult his Chiefs of Staff as to the extent to which they could be brought into continuous consultation as apart from ad hoc discussion. He invited me to discuss this, if you so desired, with his Chiefs of Staff.

He said that he had to take the blame for having speeded up the discussions resulting in the "directive" to Wavell[55] to the extent that satisfactory prior consultation all round had not been possible. In this regard he was afraid he had offended the Dutch who, he understood, had had even less opportunity than Australia to become aware of the course of events here. His belief that speed was a vital necessity in the circumstances was the sole reason for this. ...
[AA: A 3300, 219]

Because of continued Australian complaints, Churchill tried to appease Canberra by offering a concession. It was not well received as the following documents show.

Document 145

Cranborne to Curtin   London, 19 January 1942

Cablegram 72   Most Secret and Personal

Following from the Prime Minister for the Prime Minister.

The following are proposals for machinery in London to secure full and continuous association of Australian, New Zealand and Netherlands Governments with the whole conduct of the war against Japan. A Far Eastern Council shall be established on Ministerial plane. I would preside and other members would be the Lord Privy Seal[56] (who is my deputy on the Defence

---

55. General Wavell was officially appointed Supreme Commander, SWPA, ABDA Command, on 15 January 1942.
56. Clement Attlee held this position in the British Cabinet from 11.5.1940 — 19.2.1942.

Committee) Duff Cooper[57] and representatives of Australia, New Zealand and the Netherlands.

The Australian Member would presumably be Earle Page and the New Zealand representative might be the High Commissioner to begin with. There would also be a Dutch Cabinet Minister.

The Council would be assisted by a staff group of Dominion liaison officers in consultation with the United Kingdom Joint Planners. The duties of the Council will be to focus and formulate views of the represented powers to the President, whose views will also be brought before the Council. This will not, of course, interfere with Earle Page's attending Cabinet as at present when Australian affairs are affected. Do you agree? Am also consulting Fraser[58] and the Netherlands Government.
[AA: A 5954, Box 463]

Document 146

Curtin to Cranborne   21 January 1942

Cablegram 68   *Most Secret and Personal*

Following for the Prime Minister from the Prime Minister.
1. Reference your 72. The proposal has been considered by War Cabinet and submitted to Advisory War Council, representing all political parties here.
2. The unanimous conclusion of the War Cabinet and Council is that we do not agree with the proposed Far Eastern Council in London. The Council will be purely advisory and quite out of keeping with our vital and primary interest in the Pacific sphere.
3. We desire that the accredited representative of the Australian Government shall have the right to be heard in [British] War Cabinet in the formulation and direction of policy.
4. We also desire that a Pacific War Council shall be established at Washington comprising representatives of the Governments of the United Kingdom, United States of America, Australia, China, Netherlands and New Zealand. This body would be a council of action for the higher direction of the war in the Pacific and would have associated with it the joint staff already established on which the members of the Pacific Council would also have representatives of their Services if they so desired.
[AA: A 5954, Box 463]

---

57. Duff Cooper, previously Minister for Information in the Churchill government, was in Singapore from September 1941 as Minister of State, Far East.
58. Peter Fraser, New Zealand Prime Minister, 1.4.1940–13.12.1949.

Continued pressure from Australia led to Roosevelt setting up a Pacific War Council. On 29 March Evatt told Curtin of this decision. The Council proved a disappointment to the Australians however, for it possessed no executive authority. It met weekly from 1 April 1942 to the end of the year. The frequency of meetings declined thereafter, the last being held on 11 January 1944.

We now turn to a consideration of the short history of ABDA Command.

11
ABDA COMMAND

While Australia was seeking representation in the highest Anglo-American war councils the theatre command of most immediate concern to it, ABDACOM, endured its brief, disastrous life. Our documentary account begins on the eve of the Arcadia conference (24 December 1941 to 14 January 1942), with Casey touching on some of the command issues which were to be resolved during the ensuing four months.

Document 147

Casey to Curtin Washington, 22 December 1941

Cablegram 1188 *Most Immediate*

... Certain discussions will start here on December 22nd/23rd of which you will be aware. ...

One early important matter that will undoubtedly be discussed will be that of transferred commands. Although naturally I have no direct authoritative information, I have reason to believe that the President will try very hard to have an American accepted as Commander-in-Chief in the Pacific and the Far East theatre, and that General MacArthur[59] (now in the Philippines) will probably be the individual nominated. I understand, that although not devoid of human frailities, he is a good man.

It seems clear that the President will insist that one or other of the important regional commands (European, Atlantic African combined or Pacific Far East) must go to America and Pacific Far East Command seems the obvious one.

If I am right in the above surmise (and it is no more than a surmise) then I venture to suggest that the interests of all concerned will be served by accepting the situation gracefully, even to the extent of making the suggestion ourselves, in the interest of future harmonious working together.

I would assume (this is surmise) that the countries principally concerned would have a senior staff officer or officers on the staff of each Commander-in-Chief, and that our Australian interests would be looked after in that way.

It occurs to me as not impossible that the headquarters of the Commander-in-Chief of the Pacific and the Far East might be in Australia.

---

59. General Douglas MacArthur had been seconded from the United States in 1935 to organise the defence of the Philippines. In April 1942 he was appointed Commander-in-Chief, Southwest Pacific Area.

It seems reasonably clear that the Japanese operations which will have to be coped with will be in the western and probably particularly in the south western Pacific rather than in the Pacific generally. The references by the President and others to Australia being used as a "Bridge-head or Base" would seem to indicate the desirability of the Commander-in-Chief being located there.

I would expect, however, that Honolulu or San-Francisco would be considered as possibilities (possibly in the American eye a more desirable possibility than Australia), with a deputy of the Commander-in-Chief in Australia to exercise local command.

In any event it seems to me that Singapore or Manila are too localised to be desirable headquarters. Subject to your views, I would think that there are obvious advantages in the Commander-in-Chief being located in Australia. ...
[AA: A 5954, Box 535]

From the following two documents Canberra first learnt of the proposed ABDA theatre, though that title was not yet used. Paragraph (e) of the second telegram contains the phrase 'appropriate joint body' which led to the misunderstanding between Curtin and Churchill referred to in Document 143.

Document 148

Churchill to Curtin   London, 29 December 1941

Cablegram WINCH 13   *Most Secret and Personal*

Matters have moved with great speed here and I send you the text of the sub-joined agreement which had been reached between the President and myself with the approval of his Majesty's Government. The President is sure that the Dutch will agree. I trust that I may receive the assent of your Cabinet to these arrangements designed largely for your interest and safety. The President and the American staffs regard this decision as of the utmost urgency. The initiative has come from them and the President proposes to state publicly that the appointment of General Wavell has been at his direct suggestion, endorsed by his advisers. It is desired to make public statement by 1st January at the latest.

The text of the agr[e]ement is contained in my immediately following telegram.
[AA: A 5954, Box 552]

Document 149

Churchill to Curtin　　　　　　　　London, 29 December 1941

Cablegram WINCH 14　　　　　　*Most Secret and Personal*

My immediately preceding telegram. Text of the Agreement begins:–
(a) That unity of command shall be established in the South-Western Pacific. The boundaries are not yet finally settled but presume that they would include Malay Peninsula, including Burma to the Philippine Islands and Southwards to necessary supply bases, principally Port Darwin, and ... supply line in Northern Australia.
(b) That General Wavell should be appointed C-in-C or if preferred supreme Commander of all United States, British Empire and Dutch Forces of Land, Sea and Air who may be assigned by the Governments concerned to that theatre.
(c) General Wavell, whose headquarters should in the first instance be established at Sourabaya, would have an American officer as Deputy C-in-C. It seems probable that General Brett[60] would be chosen.
(d) That the American, British and Australian and Dutch Naval Forces in the "Theatre" should be placed under the command of the American Admiral in accordance with the General principles set forth in (a) and (b).
(e) It is intended that General Wavell should have a staff in the South Pacific accessible as Foch's High Control Staff was to the Great Staffs of the British and French Armies in FRANCE[61]. He would receive his orders from an appropriate joint body who will be responsible to me as the Minister of Defence and to the President of the United States who is also C-in-C of All United States Forces.
(f) The Principal commanders comprised in General Wavell's sphere will be the C-in-C Burma, C-in-C Singapore and Malaya, C-in-C Netherlands East Indies, C-in-C Philippines and C-in-C of Southern Communications via the South Pacific and North Australia.
(g) India, for which an Acting C-in-C will have to be appointed and Australia, who will have their own C-in-C, will be outside General Wavell's sphere except as abovementioned and are the two great Nations through which men and material from Great Britain and the Middle East on the one hand, and the United States on the other, can be moved into the fighting zone.
(h) The United States Navy will remain responsible for the whole of the

---

60. Lt.-General George H. Brett of the American Army Air Force was appointed Deputy C-in-C of ABDA forces on 3 January 1942.
61. Marshal Ferdinand Foch was appointed supreme generalissimo of the allied armies on the western front following the critical German breakthrough of March 1918.

188   The Pacific War

Pacific Ocean east of the Philippine Islands, and Australasia including United States approaches to Australasia.
(i) A letter of introduction is being drafted for the Supreme Commander safeguarding necessary residuary interests of the various Governments involved and prescribing in major detail his tasks.
[AA: A 5954, Box 552]

Canberra promptly assented to the agreement.

Document 150

Curtin to Churchill   1 January 1942

Cablegram JOHCU 13   *Most Secret and Personal*

... His Majesty's Government in the Commonwealth of Australia assents to text of agreement. We expect Australia will be included in composition of appropriate joint body referred to in paragraph (e). We desire your concurrence make simultaneous announcement in Australia and desire know time and text announcement.

I wish to express our great appreciation of the cohesion now established and would like to say to you personally how appreciative we are of the great service you have rendered in your mission to U.S.A.
[AA: A 5954, Box 552]

This is the directive sent to Wavell. A copy was cabled to Curtin on 4 January 1942 and circulated to members of the Advisory War Council next day.

Document 151

Directive for Wavell   2 January 1942

U.S. Serial ABC–4/5
British Serial WW6

BY AGREEMENT AMONG THE GOVERNMENTS OF AUSTRALIA, THE NETHERLANDS, THE UNITED KINGDOM, AND THE UNITED STATES, HEREINAFTER REFERRED TO AS THE ABDA GOVERNMENTS:

1. *Area.–*
   A strategic area has been constituted, to comprise initially all land and sea areas included in the general region Burma — Malaya — Netherlands

East Indies and the Philippines; more precisely defined in Annex 1. This area will be known as the ABDA Area.

2. *Forces.-*

You have been designated as the Supreme Commander of the ABDA Area and of all armed forces, afloat, ashore, and in the air, of the ABDA Governments which are or will be:-
   a. Stationed in the Area;
   b. Located in Australian territory when such forces have been allotted by the respective governments for services in or in support of the ABDA Area.

You are not authorized to transfer from the territory of any of the ABDA Governments land forces of that government without the consent of the local commander or his government.

3. The Deputy Supreme Commander and, if required, a commander of the combined naval forces and a commander of the combined air forces will be jointly designated by the ABDA Governments.

4. No government will materially reduce its armed forces assigned to your Area nor any commitments made by it for reinforcing its forces in your Area except after giving to the other governments, and to you, timely information pertaining thereto.

5. *Strategic Concept and Policy.-*

The basic strategic concept of the ABDA Governments for the conduct of the war in your Area is not only in the immediate future to maintain as many key positions as possible, but to take the offensive at the earliest opportunity and ultimately to conduct an all-out offensive against Japan. The first essential is to gain general air superiority at the earliest possible moment, through the employment of concentrated air power. The piecemeal employment of air forces should be minimized. Your operations should be so conducted as to further preparations for the offensive.

6. The general strategic policy will therefore be:-
   a. To hold the Malay Barrier, defined as the line Malay Peninsula, Sumatra, Java, North Australia, as the basic defensive position of the ABDA Area, and to operate sea, land, and air forces in as great depth as possible forward of the Barrier in order to oppose the Japanese southward advance.
   b. To hold Burma and Australia as essential supporting positions for the Area, and Burma as essential to the support of China, and to the defense of India.
   c. To re-establish communications through the Dutch East Indies with Luzon and to support the Philippines' Garrison.
   d. To maintain essential communications within the Area.

7. *Duties, Responsibilities, and Authority of the Supreme Commander.-*

You will coordinate in the ABDA Area the strategic operations of all armed forces of the ABDA Governments; assign them strategic missions and objectives; where desirable, arrange for the formation of task forces, whether national or international, for the execution of specific operations; and appoint any officer, irrespective of seniority or nationality, to command such task forces.

8. While you will have no responsibilities in respect of the international administration of the respective forces under your command, you are authorized to direct and coordinate the creation and development of administrative facilities and the broad allocation of war materials.

9. You will dispose reinforcements which from time to time may be dispatched to the Area by the ABDA Governments.

10. You are authorized to require from the Commanders of the armed forces under your command such reports as you deem necessary in the discharge of your responsibilities as Supreme Commander.

11. You are authorized to control the issue of all communiques concerning the forces under your command.

12. Through the channels specified in Paragraph 18, you may submit recommendations to the ABDA Governments on any matters pertaining to the furtherance of your mission.

13. *Limitations.-*

Your authority and control with respect to the various portions of the ABDA Area and to the forces assigned thereto will normally be exercised through the commanders duly appointed by their respective governments. Interference is to be avoided in the administrative processes of the armed forces of any of the ABDA Governments, including free communication between them and their respective governments. No alteration or revision is to be made in the basic tactical organization of such forces, and each national component of a task force will normally operate under its own commander and will not be subdivided into small units for attachment to the other national components of the task force, except in the case of urgent necessity.

In general, your instructions and orders will be limited to those necessary for effective coordination of forces in the execution of your mission.

14. *Relations with ABDA Governments.-*

The ABDA Governments will jointly and severally support you in the execution of the duties and responsibilities as herein defined, and in the exercise of the authority herein delegated and limited. Commanders of all sea, land and air forces within your Area will be immediately informed by their respective governments that, from a date to be notified, all orders and instructions issued by you in conformity with the provisions of this directive will be considered by such commanders as emanating from their respective governments.

15. In the unlikely event that any of your immediate subordinates, after making due representations to you, still considers that obedience to your orders would jeopardize the national interests of his country to an extent unjustified by the general situation in the ABDA Area, he has the right, subject to your being immediately notified of such intention, to appeal direct to his own government before carrying out the orders. Such appeals will be made by the most expeditious method, and a copy of the appeal will be communicated simultaneously to you.

16. *Staff and Assumption of Command.-*

Your staff will include officers of each of the ABDA powers. You are empowered to communicate immediately with the national commanders in the Area with a view to obtaining staff officers essential to your earliest possible assumption of command. Your additional staff requirements will be communicated as soon as possible to the ABDA Governments through channels of communication described in Paragraph 18.

17. You will report when you are in a positition effectively to carry out the essential functions of Supreme Command, so that your assumption of command may be promulgated to all concerned.

18. *Superior Authority.-*

As Supreme Commander of the ABDA Area, you will be directly responsible to the ABDA Governments through the agency defined in Annex 2.

. . .

Annex 2

Higher Direction of War in the ABDA Area

1. On all important military matters, not within the jurisdiction of the Supreme Commander of the ABDA Area, the U.S. Chiefs of Staff and the representatives in Washington of the British Chiefs of Staff will constitute the agency for developing and submitting recommendations for decision by the President of the United States and by the British Prime Minister and Minister of Defence. Among the chief matters on which decisions will be required are:

a. The provision of reinforcements.

b. A major change in policy.

c. Departure from the Supreme Commander's directive.

2. This agency will function as follows:

a. Any proposal coming either from the Supreme Commander or from any of the ABDA governments will be transmitted to the Chiefs of Staff Committee both in Washington and in London.

b. The Chiefs of Staff Committee in London will immediately telegraph to their representatives in Washington to say whether or not they will be telegraphing any opinions.

c. On receipt of these opinions, the U.S. Chiefs of Staff and the representatives in Washington of the British Chiefs of Staff will develop and submit their recommendations to the President, and by telegraph to the Prime Minister and Minister of Defence. The Prime Minister will then inform the President whether he is in agreement with these recommendations.

3. Since London has the machinery for consulting the Dominion Governments, and since the Dutch Government is in London, the British Government will be responsible for obtaining their views and agreement, and for including these in the final telegram to Washington.

4. Agreement having been reached between the President and the Prime Minister and Minister of Defence, the orders to the Supreme Commander will be dispatched from Washington in the name of both of them.

[AA: A 3300, 219]

Australian worries at being left outside ABDA's boundaries are indicated in the following report by the three Chiefs of Staff. These complaints were transmitted to Washington and London. One result was the creation on 26 January 1942 of Anzac Area, a purely naval command covering the area from Australia's east coast to New Zealand, Fiji and north to the Equator.

Document 152

Report by Chiefs of Staff   5 January 1942

WASHINGTON CONVERSATIONS.   Most Secret
ALLIED PLANS FOR THE DEFENCE OF THE PACIFIC.

The views of the Chiefs of Staff [Burnett, Royle and Sturdee] expressed in their Report of the 1st January, on the proposals set out in telegram No. 1240 from the Australian Minister, Washington, were to the effect that the plan to exclude Australia and the adjacent islands both from the South Western Pacific area and the area for which the U.S. Pacific Fleet is responsible would isolate Australia and New Zealand, and leave them to defend a vitally important area with inadequate forces, and would be strategically unsound.

It appears to us that the map prepared by the Australian Minister, Washington, accurately depicts what would be the result of the adoption of such a plan.

To avoid this isolation from our Allies, two courses would appear to be open:-
1. Include Northern Australia and the adjacent islands in the South Western Pacific area. This appears to be the original Churchill/Roosevelt proposal which included the understanding that "the U.S. Navy will remain responsible for the whole Pacific Ocean east of the Philippines and Australasia, including the approaches to Australasia."
2. Include the Pacific area to the north east and east of Australia in the area for which the U.S. Pacific Fleet is responsible, provided that such of the forces in Australia that may be designated or allotted to or in support of the South West Pacific area should be under the general strategic control of the Supreme Commander of that area.

This latter appears to be the proposal that the Australian Minister favours, and it is a proposal with which the Chiefs of Staff agree. The effect of its adoption would be that the responsibility for the protection of the approaches to Australia from the north west would rest upon the forces in the South Western Pacific area, and from the north east and east with the U.S. Pacific Fleet. Operational bases for the U.S. Pacific Fleet could be provided in Australia.
[AA: A 5954, Box 552]

Australia's concern over ABDA's southern boundary was shared, in part, by Wavell, as the following indicates. On 24 January 1942 ABDA was extended to include a slice of northern Australia from Onslow to Normanton.

Document 153

Report by Chiefs of Staff   11 January 1942

UNIFICATION OF COMMAND   *Most Secret*
ALLIED PLANS FOR THE DEFENCE OF THE PACIFIC

1. The Chiefs of Staff report the receipt of the following cable direct from General Wavell for C.G.S.:-
    "1. It is not clear from my directive whether or not I am responsible defence PORT DARWIN. Since this defence MUST depend on CONTROL OF TIMOR SEA which is in my area it appears PORT DARWIN my responsibility but should like confirmation.
    2. Am not clear as to position in PORTUGUESE TIMOR or intentions there, please inform me further detail.
    3. Arrived Batavia today January 10th with nucleus staff and held conference with HART[62], BRETT, BURNETT and Dutch representative. Will cable result in separate telegram."
2. The following reply has been sent by C.G.S. to General Wavell:-
    "Personal for GENERAL WAVELL from STURDEE. Your 00001 of 10 Jan. First. Decision whether DARWIN is to be included in your sphere of responsibility is one for Government and has been referred to War Cabinet for advice to you direct.
    Second. Position in PORTUGUESE TIMOR is that there is at DILLI a small Dutch force and one Australian Independent Company[63]. Negotiations are at present proceeding between Australian, British, Dutch and Portuguese Governments concerning relief of Allied by Portuguese troops. Suggest you should obtain information on this from LONDON."
3. The Chiefs of Staff agree that the defence of PORT DARWIN should be included within the area of responsibility of the Supreme Commander of the A.B.D.A. Area. They note that PORT DARWIN, or in fact any part of Australia, is NOT included in the area defined in Cable No. I 459 of 4 Jan. 1942 from the Prime Minister of Great Britain and recommend:—
    (a) That the matter be taken up with the U.K. Government with a view to amendment of the area.

---

[62] Admiral T. C. Hart USN, appointed Chief of Naval Staff, ABDA Command, January 1942.

[63] An Independent Company was a commando-style unit of about 330 men, and outside the normal divisional organisation of the Australian army.

(b) That General Wavell be advised of the decision.
[AA: A 5954, Box 552]

Wavell reached Batavia on 10 January. He soon gave his superiors his assessment of the Allied position in the various territories under his command. This report made gloomy reading, but it soon became clear that Wavell had been unduly optimistic.

Document 154

Wavell to British Chiefs of Staff, Washington. [Sent by Dill to Casey]

Batavia, 15 January 1942

Cablegram 00053

Most Secret

Following is my general appreciation of the situation in South West Pacific area.

Para. 1. PHILIPPINES. With present resources see NO possibility of afford-ing General MACARTHUR support he appears to expect. Japanese occupation of TARAKAN and MENADO makes operation of air forces from Netherlands E.I. into PHILIPPINES extremely difficult even if we had sufficient air resources available. HART is sending submarines to MANILA loaded to capacity with ammunition.

Para. 2. BURMA. Position seems reasonably satisfactory at present.

Para. 3. MALAYA. Provided convoys arrive safely and up to time and that we can prevent fresh Japanese landings on East coast, hope to hold JOHORE and SINGAPORE and later stage counter offensive.

Para. 4. SUMATRA and JAVA. NO immediate threat but reinforcements of troops and A.A. equipment required as early as possible.

Para. 5. BORNEO. BALIKPAPAN, SAM[A]RINDA on East coast and possibly PONTIUNAK on West likely to be objectives of further Japanese advance to obtain oil and air bases. Small reinforcements of land forces being sent to SAM[A]RINDA otherwise can do little except ensure destruction of oil and attack with bombers (?shipping) and air targets.

Establishment of Japanese air bases in South Borneo would bring SOURABAYA and other objectives in JAVA within range of effective bomber attack.

Para. 6. Similar considerations apply to air fields in South CELEBES and AMBOINA which we can do little to defend against large scale attack.

Para. 7. TIMOR is vital connecting link in air route from Australia. Its defence constitutes difficult problem but it is NOT so immediately threatened as other points.

Para. 8. Defence of PORT DARWIN and port development there of vital importance to ABDA area but my responsibility for it NOT yet determined.

Para. 9. Immediate Japanese intention may be:-
(a) Full scale effort against SINGAPORE with fresh landing East coast.
(b) Advance South in BORNEO and CELEBES to establish air bases within range of JAVA.
(c) Measures to cut supply route between AUSTRALIA and Netherlands E. Indies by occupation of AMBOINA TIMOR and positions further East to command TORRES STRAIT.

It is possible that Japanese may att[e]mpt any two or even all above simultaneously.

Para. 10. To meet above dangers over such wide areas our resources by land, sea and air are extremely limited. We must avoid too great a dispersion of forces and our immediate objective must be confined to:-
(a) Securing SINGAPORE.
(b) Checking and hampering further Japanese advance in BORNEO and Eastwards.

Para. 11. General disposition of available forces therefore as follows:-
(a) Naval. British and Dutch surface craft mainly employed in escorting convoys into SINGAPORE. U.S.A. surface craft employed to East of BORNEO as striking force if suitable target found. Submarines employed aggressively on most likely routes of enemy shipping in area. If more cruisers and destroyers could be made available from U.S.A. to form a striking force prospect of dealing enemy effective blows and preventing him establishing himself on route between Australia and Netherlands E. Indies would be greatly enhanced.
(b) Land. Reinforcements arriving must at present be sent to SINGAPORE till that is secured. Air bases in South SUMATRA must also be strengthened with A.A. [anti-aircraft guns] and defence of JAVA must be reinforced.
(c) Air. Objectives must be:-
  (1) Recce. [reconnaissance] system to enable movements of enemy shipping to be watched and rapidly reported.
  (2) Attack on enemy shipping.
  (3) Attack on enemy air bases.
  (4) In MALAYA, co-operation with land forces and attack on enemy columns.

Distribution of air effort for immediate future between East and West threats is being worked out.
[AA: A 3300, 219]

The following document gives some indication of the forces which Australia placed at Wavell's disposal. As well, some RAN ships served in ABDA.

Document 155

Report by Chiefs of Staff   24 January 1942

DARWIN — INCLUSION IN A.B.D.A. AREA   Most Secret

The Chiefs of Staff, [Sturdee, Royle and Bostock (DCAS)] pursuant to a direction of the Advisory War Council on 20th January, considered the strength of the Army and Air Forces that should be placed at the disposal of General Wavell if and when that portion of Australia lying to the north of a line running from Onslow, Western Australia, to the south east corner of the Gulf of Carpentaria is included in the A.B.D.A. area and expressed the following conclusions:-

(1) That the Army Forces at present allocated to that portion of Australia being the minimum that is necessary for its defence should be placed at the disposal of General Wavell. These forces comprise 14,050 men and are constituted as is set out in the attachment hereto. It will be noted that, if these forces are allocated to the A.B.D.A. area, the Australian Army Forces then under the command of General Wavell will be:-

7th Military District[64]	14,050	(including 250 V.D.C. [Volunteer Defence Corps])
Sparrow Force (Timor)	1,670	
Gull Force (Ambon)	1,170	
A.I.F., Malaya	17,200	(including 2,000 2, 3 and 4 reinforcements)
V.D.C.	280	(excluding 250 at Darwin)
Total	34,370	

(2) That the R.A.A.F. Squadrons at present stationed in that portion of Australia should be placed at the disposal of General Wavell. These Squadrons are No. 2 (General Reconnaissance) and No. 12 (General Purpose). Notification of this should be accompanied by representations to the effect that these Squadrons are inadequate to defend the area and it is necessary that as soon as possible they should be reinforced with other aircraft at the disposal of General Wavell. It will be noted that, if these two Squadrons are allocated to the A.B.D.A. area, the Australian Air Forces then under the command of General Wavell will be:-
No. 1 (General Reconnaissance) Squadron)
No. 8 (General Reconnaissance) Squadron) Malaya
No. 21 (General Purpose) Squadron   )
No. 13 (General Reconnaissance) Squadron Ambon, Netherlands East Indies

---

64. Northern Territory.

No. 2 (General Reconnaissance) Squadron) Darwin, Timor
No. 12 (General Purpose) Squadron   )
It should also be represented that these Squadrons should be replaced as soon as possible with aircraft from General Wavell's resources so that they will become available for service in the sphere for which Australia remains responsible.
[AA: A 2671, 35/1942]

Australia was rightly concerned about its place in ABDA's command structure, as at the time it was assumed that three of its four AIF divisions would fight in the theatre. (See Section 14 below for details on the move of the 6th and 7th Divisions from the Middle East.) Curtin expressed his concern to London and to Blamey, Australia's senior general who was expected eventually to move to ABDA.

Document 156

Curtin to Blamey, [Middle East]   7 February 1942

Cablegram 4   *Most Secret*

1. ... I am furnishing you, in strictest confidence, the following information regarding the prospective set up in the ABDA Area commanded by Wavell:
(i) As you are no doubt aware Brett is the Deputy Supreme Commander and Intendant-General and Pownall the Chief of Staff. Ter Poorten is head of the Land Forces Branch with Playfair as Deputy. Ter Poorten is also Commander in Chief, Netherlands East Indies, and has operational control of any other Allied land forces in Netherlands East Indies territory.
(ii) You will have noted our reaction to the exclusion of Australian officers, in the cablegram to the Dominions Office quoted in my No. 2 to you.
(iii) Wavell's reply is on following lines:-
(a) On General Staff side senior Australian officer is now G.S.O.I.[-] Lavarack's H.Q. will however be within easy reach and he can be taken into consultation whenever necessary. There will thus be no lack of representation of Australian point of view.
(b) He suggests if further representation is desired that a Deputy might be appointed to Pownall or Playfair relieved by an Australian.
(iv) Darwin and hinterland has been placed under Wavell and G.O.C. of 7th Military District also controls Timor and Ambon Forces.
(v) Wavell desires to dispose one Australian Division in Java for defence of centre of island with additional role of reserve for East or West of Island. The other Division is to be used for defence of South Sumatra. He has stated that operational requirements do not at present permit concentration in Corps but actual decision will be governed by the situation at the time.
(vi) The Chief of the General Staff [Sturdee] has recommended that the most

suitable status that can be accorded to you is that you should have the right of direct access to General Wavell and senior members of his Staff and organisation on matters affecting operational, administrative and other plans and proposals insofar as they affect A.I.F.

(vii) If and when the whole of A.I.F. are transferred to ABDA Area the Chief of the General Staff visualises a probable set up to be somewhat as follows:-

(a) The G.O.C., A.I.F., ABDA Area, located in close proximity to General Wavell's H.Q. in Java and controlling the whole of A.I.F. in the ABDA Area in exactly the same manner as in the Middle East.

(b) One or two A.I.F. Divisions in Java with Corps Troops under Lieut.-General Lavarack as G.O.C., Australian Corps.

(c) 8th Division in Singapore.

(d) One A.I.F. Division in Sumatra, Darwin or some other location according to future developments.

2. I am somewhat concerned, in view of the large forces that Australia will contribute to the ABDA Area, and in view of your status as G.O.C., A.I.F., and Deputy Commander in Chief, Middle East, that some arrangement was not made to fit you into an appropriate post of operational command. The Dominions Office has stated that the organisation is not final and is subject to revision in the light of experience. It remains to be seen what that really means.

3. Would you please inform me frankly of your views on the foregoing both in respect of yourself and the A.I.F. The following differences as compared with the Middle East are noted:-

(i) You will not be Deputy Commander in Chief.

(ii) Ter Poorten will be Commander in Chief, Netherlands East Indies.

(iii) If Wavell's dispositions of the A.I.F. are agreed to, it will be distributed in Divisions, in the first stages at least. ...

[AA: A 5954, Box 552]

The points raised in the document above were of academic interest only, for Wavell's command was quickly disintegrating. Soon after the fall of Singapore on 15 February Japan completed its conquest of the East Indies. Wavell's message, printed below, gives some idea of the chaos at one stage of this final collapse. The point raised in paragraph 5(a) is covered in some detail in Section 15 below. The American Joint Chiefs of Staff felt that Wavell should move his headquarters from Java to Fremantle, but instead, after ABDA Command was closed on 25 February, Wavell went to India.

Document 157

Page to Curtin   London, 22 February 1942

Cablegram 1609   *Most Secret*

1. At the Pacific War Council Saturday night, following telegram from Wavell to British Joint Staff Mission, Washington, was considered.
Begins -
1864. February 21st CCOS 16.
1. As a result of heavy losses yesterday fighter strength in Java now reduced to less than 40. Medium and dive bombers approximately 30, heavy bombers 10. Obvious that the above force can only hope to fight for a few more days at the most. No more fighters can arrive from the East and consignments from America cannot arrive in time. Reinforcement of heavy American bombers from India has been stopped from Washington and would in any case have been insufficient.
2. There are signs that the Japanese are completing preparations for invasion of Java which obviously we can do little to prevent. Once the Japanese are landed, ground forces in the island can do little to check the advance.
3. The situation of the Imperial and American troops in the Island is as follows -

There are approximately 6,000 R.A.F. and personnel unarmed and surplus to fighting units and about 1,400 American, these I am endeavouring to evacuate forthwith. There will remain approximately 3,000 to 4,000 R.A.F., 5,500 British[.]
(Squadron 3 Hussars anti-aircraft units and miscellaneous) 3,000 Australians (including one M.G. and one pioneer battalion) belonging to 7th Australian Division about 700 Americans (mostly artillery) and A.B.D.A. Headquarters (about 250 officers and 400 other ranks).
4. I am having stock taken of shipping available in the Island should evacuation of the above be ordered by you as from the time when they can contribute nothing further effective to the defence. Doubt whether shipping for full numbers is available in the Island.
5. Immediate decisions required on the following -
   (a) Destination of Australian divisions and Corps Headquarters.
   (b) Whether arrangements should be made to hold Dutch shipping for eventual evacuation as in paragraph (3) above. The Dutch are willing to hold shipping if it is the policy to evacuate, otherwise they are anxious to sail merchant shipping to allied ports for safety.
   (c) The policy regarding these headquarters.
[AA: A 5954, Box 573]

12
MALAYAN FIASCO

Within ABDA, by far the biggest Australian contribution to the fighting was made in Malaya and Singapore, whose importance in Australian defence strategy has been made clear in Section 8 above. From its first landing at Kota Bharu around midnight on 7/8 December (local time) 1941 the Japanese invasion force made good progress. As this happened, Australia urged that substantial reinforcements be sent to Malaya. One forthright comment came from V.G. Bowden, Australian Official Representative in Singapore.

Document 158

Bowden to Evatt   Singapore, 23 December 1941

Cablegram 73   *Most Secret*

... I feel that I must emphasise that the deterioration of the air position in the Malayan defence is assuming landslide proportions and in my firm belief is likely to cause a collapse in the whole defence system. Expected arrival of modern fighter planes in boxes requiring weeks to assemble under the danger of destruction by bombing cannot save the position. The arrival of Military reinforcements expected will be absorbed in relieving the tired Front Line troops and will create little difference. British defence policy now concentrates greater companies of fighter and anti-aircraft defence on Singapore Island to protect the Naval Base; depriving the forward troops of such defence including the A.I.F.

Present measures for the reinforcement of Malayan defences can from a practical viewpoint be regarded as little more than gestures. In my belief only thing that might save Singapore would be the immediate despatch from the Middle East by air of powerful reinforcements, large numbers of the latest fighter aircraft with ample operationally trained personnel. Reinforcements of troops should be not in Brigades but in Divisions and to be of use they must arrive urgently. Anything that is not powerful, modern and immediate is futile. As things stand at present fall of Singapore is to my mind only a matter of weeks. If Singapore and the A.I.F. in Malaya are to be saved there must be very radical and effective action immediately.

Doubtful whether the visit of an Australian Minister can now have any effect as the plain fact is that without immediate air reinforcements Singapore must fall. Need for decision and action is a matter of hours not days.

[AA: A 5954, Box 571]

Britain did reinforce Singapore, but not enough to satisfy Australia, nor the commanders in Malaya. The following document indicates the scale of these reinforcements.

Document 159

Cranborne to Curtin London, 23 December 1941

Cablegram 872 *Most Secret and Personal*

...

2. ... The following air reinforcements for Malaya are in sight:-
(a) One fighter squadron with 51 Hurricanes due at Malaya about 8th January...
(b) Blenheim aircraft now in transit together with one Blenheim squadron due to leave the Middle East this week are equivalent to reinforcement by one bomber squadron with 50 per cent. reserves. The first flight of 52 Hudsons are due at Singapore in the middle of January. These Hudsons are equivalent to one squadron with 200 per cent. reserves.
(c) Escort flight cannot be provided. The transport flight must come from the Middle East and depends on operations in Libya where communications are very difficult (see paragraph 3 below).

3. We are examining the effect on the Middle East theatre of meeting the balance of immediate air requirements.

4. ... The following land reinforcements for Malaya are in sight:-
(a) One Brigade group ex the 17th Indian Division sails from Bombay 22nd December due at Malaya early in January.
(b) A second brigade of the 17th Division loads 8th January for Burma, can be directed to Malaya. One brigade of the 18th Division can arrive in Malaya on 8th January or if transhipped at Bombay 24th January. This leaves one brigade of the 17th Division and two brigades of the 18th Division for subsequent allotment. Two brigades from East Africa will probably be sent to Ceylon.
(c) One light anti-aircraft regiment (32 guns)... has been diverted to Malaya due about 8th January. Two regiments (72 guns)... could arrive at Malaya in the middle of February.
One heavy anti-aircraft regiment (16 guns)... due at Malaya about 8th January. One regiment (24 guns)... could arrive at Malaya in the middle of February.
(e) One anti-tank regiment (48 guns) ... due at Malaya at about 8th January.
(f) Reinforcements for the 9th and 11th Divisions will begin to load India about 8th January due at Malaya late in January.
(g) One light tank squadron (14 tanks) begin[s] to load Bombay 8th January due at Malaya late January. Balance of 33 tanks required for Malaya could be found from 50 light tanks which leave the Middle East for India about 3rd January.

(h) 321 anti-tank rifles are already in transit due to arrive Malaya half in January one quarter in February balance in March.
(i) 174,000 rounds of Bofors ammunition in transit due to arrive Malaya 70,000 rounds December, 61,000 rounds January, balance in March.
(j) 700 Tommy guns with 3,000,000 rounds of ammunition in transit due Malaya in January.

5. Malaya's immediate land reinforcements should therefore be completed by mid February. We are now considering what can be done to meet demands... for "further large reinforcements" both land and air.

6. We are repeating this telegram to Singapore, Canberra and Wellington. Comments end.

The vital secrecy of the foregoing information will be appreciated... .
[AA: A 5954, Box 571]

Australian airmen and seamen were in action immediately upon, or soon after, the Japanese landing, but the main body of Australians in Malaya, two brigades of the 8th Division, was stationed in Johore, in the south of the Peninsula. The soldiers' first big action, against a very confident enemy, took place on 14 January.

Document 160

Curtin to Churchill   Not Dated [c.12 January 1942]

Cablegram JOHCU 16   *Most Secret*

Wavell has repeated to us his telegram to War Office regarding plan of campaign for the operation in Malaya... . It is naturally disturbing to learn Japanese have been able to overrun, so easily the whole of Malaya except Johore and that C. in C. [Wavell] considers certain risks have to be accepted even now in carrying on his plan for the defence of this limited area.

It is observed that eighth Australian Div. is to be given task of fighting decisive battle. The Government has no doubt that it will acquit itself in accordance with the highest traditions of A.I.F. However, I urge on you that nothing be left undone to reinforce Malaya to greatest degree possible in accordance with my earlier representations and your intention. I am particularly concerned in regard to air strength as repetition of Greece and Crete campaigns would evoke a violent public reaction and such a happening should be placed outside bounds of possibility. ...
[AA: A 3300, 219]

The men of the 8th Division, just entering the battle in a desperate attempt to stop the Japanese, would not have been encouraged had they known that Churchill already thought they were doomed to defeat in Malaya.

Document 161

Churchill to Curtin   14 January 1942

Cablegram WINCH 7   *Most Secret*

...

1. I do not see how anyone could expect Malaya to be defended once the Japanese obtained the command of the sea and while we are fighting for our lives against Germany and Italy. The only vital point is Singapore Fortress and its essential hinterland. Personally my anxiety has been lest in fighting rearguard actions down the Peninsula to gain time we should dissipate the forces required for the prolonged defence of Singapore. Out of the equivalent of 4 Divisions available for that purpose, one has been lost and another mauled to gain a month or six weeks time[65]. Some may think it would have been better to have come back quicker with less loss. ...

3. I have great confidence that your troops will acquit themselves in the highest fashion in the impending battle. So far, the Japanese have only had 2 white battalions and a few gunners against them, the rest being Indian soldiers. Everything is being done to reinforce Singapore and the hinterland. Two convoys bearing the 45th Indian Brigade Group and its transport have got through, and a very critical convoy containing the leading Brigade of the British 18th Division is timed to arrive on 13th. I am naturally anxious about these 4,500 men going through the Straits of Sunda in a single ship. I hope however they will arrive in time to take their stand with their Australian brothers. I send you in immediately following telegram the full detail of what we have on the move towards this important battlefield, with the dates of arrival. There is justification in this for Wavell's hope that a counterstroke will be possible in the latter part of February.

4. You are aware no doubt that I have proposed your withdrawal of two Australian Divisions from Palestine to the new theatre of so much direct interest to Australia. The only limiting factor on their movement will be the shipping. We shall have to do our best to replace them from home. ...

[AA: A 3300, 219]

On 19 January General Gordon H. Bennett, commanding the 8th Division, described the Australians' plight as follows.

---

65. British forces in the battle for the Peninsula numbered some 80,000. From 8.12.1941 to 31.1.1942 the Japanese inflicted approximately 25,000 casualties. It could thus be argued that 3 brigades had been destroyed which otherwise would have been available for the defence of Singapore itself.

Document 162

Bennett to Sturdee Johore, 19 January 1942

Cablegram SP.299 Most Secret

... Whole situation most serious(.) MERSING GEMAS MUAR[66] fronts each held by 2 Australian Battalions with very FLIMSY support by Indian troops who have not stood firm and by new English units inexperienced in local conditions(.) Even Malaya command expressed doubt as to their reliability(.) We cannot plug up SEGAMAT[67] holes and are finding it difficult to hold present positions against overwhelming numbers(.) So far our companies have to meet attacks by whole battalions, and face all ways a situation that cannot continue for long(.) Further withdrawals contemplated ... could only be avoided if all the units here fought as our men have done(.) They have been wonderful meeting all cunning methods used by Japanese with SKILL and determination(.) Their courage is beyond words(.) It would be a pity if all their efforts have been in vain.
[AWM: 54, 553/2/3]

While the Australian government was bombarding its British counterpart with requests to send reinforcements to Malaya, Churchill briefly considered evacuating Singapore. Page, the accredited representative of the Australian government in the British War Cabinet, at once cabled this news to Australia. It prompted the sharpest rebuke Canberra had yet sent to London. Some of the harshest phrases were inserted at Evatt's insistence and may partly be explained in light of Japanese occupation of Rabaul the same day.

Document 163

Curtin to Page [for Churchill] Canberra, 25 January 1942

Cablegram 12 Most Secret

I am communicating following message as result of an emergency meeting of the War Cabinet summoned today to consider reports on situation in Malaya and New Guinea.
Part One — *Malaya.*
One. The G.O.C. Australian Imperial Forces Malaya [Bennett] reports part

---

66. Mersing is on the east coast, Gemas in inland Malaya, and Muar on the west coast.
67. Segamat is in inland Malaya.

his force has been cut off without possibility relief.⁶⁸ Now appears from information received regarding the disposition of the A.I.F. and its operations that support for it has not been forthcoming.

Two. Whilst we have no intention suggesting any criticism of the Indians who are fighting the common foe, we are getting disturbed by references made by the G.O.C. A.I.F. to their unsuitability for this type of warfare. If this is correct, we hope you are not placing too much reliance on the mere numerical strength of land forces you are sending without regard to their qualities.

Three. Page has reported the Defence Committee has been considering evacuation of Malaya and Singapore. After all the assurances we have been given, the evacuation of Singapore would be regarded here and elsewhere as an inexcusable betrayal. Singapore is a central fortress in the system of Empire and local defence. ... we understood that it was to be made impregnable and in any event it was to be capable of holding out for a prolonged period until arrival of the main fleet.

Four. Even in an emergency diversion of reinforcements should be to Netherlands East Indies and not Burma. Anything else would be deeply resented and might force N.E.I. to make a separate peace.

Five. On the faith of proposed flow of reinforcements, we have acted and carried out our part of bargain. We expect you not to frustrate the whole purpose by evacuation.

Part Two. — The Pacific Ocean.

Six. The heavy scale of the Japanese attack on Rabaul where, including other parts of the Bismarck Archipelago, there is a force of 1700, and probability of its occupation, if such has not already occurred, presage an early attack on Port Moresby. ...

Part Three. — Proposals.

Eleven. Our experiences at Ambon and Rabaul have emphasised the urgent necessity for fighter aircraft immediately. Japanese methods make it clear that without fighter protection for our aerodromes, there is every prospect of familiar enemy air attack destroying our extremely limited striking force on the ground by low attack, designed to search out individual aircraft. These tactics may be practised with impunity by the enemy against our mainland aerodromes as well as at advanced bases, owing to lack of fighter protection and almost complete absence of gun defences. A request is made for immediate allotment to the R.A.A.F. of up to 250 fighter aircraft of Tomahawk, Hurricane 2 or similar type.

Twelve. Impossible to expect us to give effective resistance with inadequate aircraft at our disposal moreover desire the allotment to R.A.A.F. of United States aircraft of suitable types which are already in Australia or are likely to arrive shortly. This course would be in substitution of aircraft long since

---

68. The 2/19th and 2/29th Battalions, cut off on the road leading southeast from Muar. Only 400 men from these two units managed to evade the Japanese and rejoin the main Allied force.

ordered for R.A.A.F. expansion programme but not yet delivered from United States.

Thirteen. Your support of above proposal with United States Authorities is requested, together with an immediate arrangement for allocation to R.A.A.F. for use at Port Moresby of Squadron of United States P.40 [Kittyhawks] fighter aircraft approaching completion at Townsville. A. Brereton[69] has communicated this request to C. in C. A.B.D.A. ...

Part Four. — General.

Fourteen. The trend of situation in Malaya and attack on Rabaul are giving rise to a public feeling of grave uneasiness at Allied impotence to do anything to stem the Japanese advance. The Government in realising its responsibility to prepare the public for the intense resisting of an aggressor, also has a duty and obligation to explain why it may not have been possible to prevent the enemy reaching our shores. It is therefore in duty bound to exhaust all the possibilities of the situation, the more so since the Australian people, having volunteered for service overseas in large numbers, find it difficult to understand why they must wait so long for an improvement in the situation when irreparable damage may have been done to their power to resist, the prestige of the Empire and the solidarity of the Allied cause. [AA: M 100]

> V.G. Bowden had been forthright in his cables to Canberra, giving his government clear warnings of the impending tragedy. With nearly all of Malaya in Japanese hands, he here sums up the series of disasters. Bowden's doubts about the capacity of General A.E. Percival GOC Malaya Command, led to Bruce making discreet enquiries in London; but Percival held his command until the surrender.

Document 164

Bowden to Evatt   Singapore, 26 January 1942

Cablegram 81   *Very Secret*

...

1. It is now over seven weeks since the Japanese campaign in Malaya was started, and although from the outset there has been a cry for immediate and powerful reinforcements and reports of promises of a maximum effort by the Imperial Government, reinforcements so far received have in practical value been little more than gestures. ... I cannot help feeling that the Imperial Government must have been fully conscious of the inadequacy of

---

69. Major-General Lewis H. Brereton, USAAF, had been MacArthur's air commander in the Philippines. In January 1942 he was given temporary command of Allied air forces, ABDA.

the land and air reinforcements they were sending and this coupled with the fact that the Singapore Garrison has now been reduced to one Regular Battalion and the Malaya Regiment and volunteers leads me seriously to the question whether from the outset of this campaign it really was the firm intention to hold Singapore.

2. In the course of an informal discussion at the close of War Council meeting today I took the opportunity of sounding views of Service Chiefs and the Governor [Sir Shenton Thomas] in this connection. A rapid collapse of British defence appearing probable, I asked Rear Admiral of Malaya[70] at what stage of developments he would demolish the Naval Base. He replied he would have to begin as soon as Japanese reached Straits of Johore. I replied "My deduction from that is that Singapore will not be held, for with the Naval Base and all natural resources of Malaya gone, Singapore will have nothing more than sentimental value." Rear Admiral of Malaya concurred, the General Officer Commanding Malaya [Percival] said nothing: only the Governor naturally maintained that Singapore would be held and said he would cable the Imperial Government for their confirmation of this intention.

3. ... if the Imperial Government has given any undertaking that the Island would be held, I venture to suggest with all due reserve that it be invited to state what plans it has prepared for achieving this.

4. From remarks of the General Officer Commanding Malaya at the War Council it appears likely that Singapore Island will be in a state of siege within a week. What I then anticipate is that the Japanese Air Force will concentrate on putting our fighter defence out of action by rendering our air-fields useless following which they would concentrate on our land defences, port facilities and essential services and ultimately make a combined attack from land and air and possibly from the sea.

5. While I believe Singapore's defences (including anti-aircraft) to be strong, I cannot see that under the circumstances described its fall could be prevented unless provision could be made for:-
(a) Substantial and effective reinforcement of fighter air-craft with all necessary ground crews for servicing.
(b) Concentrated bombing of Japanese aerodromes on the Peninsula.
(c) Some powerful form of diversion such as landing in force somewhere up the Peninsula to cut Japanese line of communication which is now highly extended (such an operation, however, would need sustained air support.)

I confess to feeling serious doubts as to the possibility of carrying such developments into effect in the time that may be available.

6. While I feel diffident in attempting to assess military qualities I confess that my experience of the present General Officer Commanding Malaya on the War Council has led me to question his suitability for such a Command. He appeared for instance to have no answer to Japanese infiltration tactics

---

70. Bowden was probably referring to Rear Admiral E.J. Spooner who was in command of the naval base.

but to retreat, and I do not remember his ever proposing any counter-offensive action. Other incidents have suggested lack of decision. If Singapore is to be held I feel that high qualities of leadership, resource and determination will be necessary and I cannot feel confident that these will be found in the present General Officer Commanding Malaya.
[AA: A 5954, Box 571]

Australians watched the debacle in Malaya with growing fear. Thousands of civilians, of course, had an even more personal interest in the fighting.

Document 165

Letter

Eastbourne
Darling Point.
1st. Feb. 1942.

Dear Mr. Curtin,

With a heart full of gratitude for what you have done & for what you are doing to save our beloved country I write to implore you while there is yet time to fight to get help to Singapore — you have had the courage to ask for the help we so urgently need. May that courage never falter till all your demands are granted.

My youngest son is in Singapore. When he enlisted all he asked was the opportunity to strike a blow for the country he loves so well. I did not demur at his going confidently believing that when the hour of trial came our lads would have the promised equipment & support. The Mothers of our soldiers will not forget what you are doing and will pray that with God's help victory will reward you & them.

That strength will be given you to bear the heavy burdens your office places on you in this sad time is the very sincere wish

of yours very sincerely,
J.I. Martin.

[AA: CP 156/1, M]

The Japanese first landed on Singapore on the night of 8 February. By the 10th a second landing had been made, the western third of the island was in Japanese hands and British defences were crumbling. There was little that Curtin could do about it except give a brief review of the Singapore strategy to stress how badly it had served Australia.

Document 166

Curtin to Page   Canberra, 10 February 1942

Cablegram 17   *Most Secret*

... It is observed that from 17th December to 27th January I have sent thirteen personal cables to Churchill on the position in the Pacific, the need for reinforcements and related question[s]. There is really nothing that can be added except every endeavour should be exerted to despatch reinforcements to retrieve the situation. You are aware ... of serious results that would follow the fall of Singapore.

I would repeat for your personal information following extract from a cable 17th January to Churchill.-

"As far back as 1937 the Commonwealth Government received [assurances] that it was the aim of the United Kingdom Government to make Singapore impregnable. When defence of Singapore was under review by the Committee of Imperial Defence in 1933, the High Commissioner pointed out grave effects that would flow from the loss of Singapore or denial of its use to main fleet. He stated that in the last resort the whole of integral defence system of Australia was based on integrity of Singapore and presence of a capital ship fleet there. He added that if this was not a reasonable possibility Australia in (balancing) a doubtful naval security against invasion would have to provide for greater land and air forces as a deterrent against such risk. I repeat these earlier facts to make quite clear the conception of Empire and local defence we have been brought to believe. It has also influenced our decisions on co-operation in other theatres from the relatively small resources we possess in relation to our commitments in a Pacific war.["]

[AA: M 100]

To the end, Wavell's method of expression remained the reverse of trenchant. With the British Empire about to sustain the most humiliating defeat in its military history, he summed up the situation as 'not encouraging'.

Document 167

Wavell to Curtin   Batavia, 12 February 1942

Cablegram 01106   *Most Secret*

Spent 10th February in Singapore and was with Gordon Bennett for about two hours. I am afraid that the situation in Singapore is not encouraging — you will have seen situation reports. So far as the 8th Division is

concerned, they have had heavy fighting in difficult country and casualties have probably been severe. Owing to aerodromes in Singapore being destroyed by artillery fire or air bombing, it has been impossible to prevent the Japanese maintaining air superiority and their infiltration tactics in very enclosed country constitute a difficult problem for defence. Troops are continuing to fight on whatever the difficulty. ...
[AWM: 54, 541/1/4]

Here, Curtin considers what should be done about Australia's defence if Singapore fell. All the territories mentioned in paragraph 2 of this cable were soon to be in Japanese hands.

Document 168

Curtin to Page   13 February 1942

Cablegram 21   *Most Secret*

...
2. The last comprehensive appreciation received from London was in Dominions Office cablegram M.476 of 23rd December. In this it was stated that to achieve our object we must hold among other vital points:-
(i) Singapore Island and Southern Malaya to give depth to defence;
(ii) Java and Southern Sumatra;
(iii) Timor.
3. As the Japanese have absorbed Malaya and are established on Singapore Island, the immediate consideration is the situation at Singapore and the prospects of holding it, including the plans for its reinforcement and relief. Please advise urgently on these aspects.
4. The next points are the effect on the general strategic plan should Singapore be lost, or should the Japanese in addition to besieging Singapore use their seapower against the Netherlands East Indies, Portuguese Timor or Australia. It is of vital importance in thinking of the ABDA Area always to associate with it... the Anzac Area as it is probable that the Japanese will continue their southward move from New Guinea to the islands to the east of Australia or to Northern Australia. You should obtain an early appreciation on the Pacific situation generally and on these points in particular. ...
[AWM: 54, 541/1/4]

British forces in Singapore surrendered on the evening of 15 February. Percival and 130,000 of his men went into captivity. Of the 15,000 Australians, about one-third were to die while prisoners.

Document 169

Wavell to Curtin   Java, 16 February 1942

Cablegram 1278

Although I have no sure information, it appears that resistance at Singapore failed last night.

I most deeply regret the loss of your fine Australian troops. I have no doubt but that to the end they acquitted themselves with their customary gallantry.

[AA: A 5954, Box 552]

Discussion in Britain's War Cabinet on the morrow of Singapore's fall included some sensible observations and the germ of a fierce argument with Australia, documented in Section 14 below.

Document 170

British War Cabinet   London, 16 February 1942

W.M. (42) 21. Minute 2.   Most Secret

THE FAR EAST
Points made in discussion on this item.

No report had yet been received giving details as to the happenings at Singapore immediately prior to the fall of the fortress. We did not know whether any troops had got away, but this seemed to be unlikely.

It was clear now that Japan was a most formidable and dangerous antagonist. The Japanese were formidable alike as fighters and as tacticians. Our military performance in Malaya had left much to be desired.

Reference was made to a report submitted by General Percival appraising Japanese strategy and fighting qualities. This report also pointed out that the Japanese relied on mechanical transport much less than we did.

In retrospect, it now seemed a pity that we had sent the 18th Division to Singapore. When we had done so, we had thought that by doing so we should enable the defence of the fortress to be continued for at least a month.

Reference was made to the fact that the Australian Prime Minister had represented that failure to attempt to defend Singapore to the utmost would be an inexcusable betrayal. But it was now clear that these troops would have been better employed elsewhere.

The same question had now to be faced as regards Sumatra and Java. The maintenance of our line of communications with China by the Burma Road was of the utmost importance. We should have to consider whether

we ought not to divert to Burma and to Australia reinforcements now on their way to the Far Eastern theatre, which might otherwise be employed to stiffen resistance in Sumatra and Java. This issue would have to be considered by the Pacific War Council at their Meeting in London on the following day.
[PRO: CAB 65/25]

After their capture of Singapore, Japanese forces quickly overran the Netherlands East Indies, gathering thousands more Australian soldiers for their prisoner of war camps. As well as the two brigades on Singapore, the Japanese captured three AIF battalions on Timor, Ambon, and Rabaul and a further 2,700 AIF troops on Java.

Wavell here writes to Curtin about these disasters, mentioning his plan for the use of the 7th Division.

Document 171

Wavell to Curtin   Java, 21 February 1942

Letter   *Personal and Secret*

I am sending this by hand of Lavarack who leaves tonight for Australia. He has attended practically all Commanders' Conferences while he has been here and is fully in touch with what has happened and can give you the picture, so I will not enter into details about what has happened here. I will only say that I am deeply sorry for the failure to hold our positions in the N.E.I. more effectively. It has been from the first a race against time and we have lost it by four or five weeks. If Malaya and Singapore could have held out for that longer and our naval and air operations in the islands north of Java had succeeded in keeping the enemy at a distance for that same period, things would have been very different, I think. We should have gained time to build up in these islands an air force which, I hope, could gradually have gained air superiority over the Japanese. The Australian Corps, once firmly installed in Sumatra and Java, would have ensured the security of our bases in these islands, and a steady flow of aircraft from both east and west and by sea route would have built up a really formidable air force. That is the situation for which I have been working ever since I took over command and, as I say, we have lost on the time factor. Whether greater foresight and skill on my part could have gained the necessary time I am unable to say; I certainly offer no excuses.

We have now got to make secure our bases in Burma and in Australia. From the military point of view it seems to me that the defence of Burma is the more dangerous and pressing problem and I therefore felt bound to recommend that the nearest available troops should be sent there, especially when they were a tried and seasoned fighting division like the 7th Australian

Division. I am naturally not in a position to judge the d[an]ger to Australia, though it seems to me that with the United States Pacific Fleet on its flank and rear the Japanese could hardly undertake any large scale invasion of Australia at present.

I need hardly say how extremely sorry I am at the losses Australia has suffered at Singapore, at Amboina, at Darwin, and now I am afraid at Koepang. It has been, I can assure you, very bitter to have watched these losses and not to have had the resources to prevent or help.

I thank you and your Government for the support you have given me since I have been in command here. I am sure that nothing that has occurred or may occur can shake the invincible determination and confidence of the Australian people. We are better men than the Japanese and can beat them and I have no doubt whatever that we shall do so. ...

[AA: A 5954, Box 552]

Bennett made a controversial escape from Singapore. He was coolly received by the army high command when he returned to Australia. However, War Cabinet, and also the British army leadership in London, were anxious to get Bennett's views on the reasons for the British Empire fiasco in Malaya.

There follow brief extracts from the assessments made by Bennett, and by Percival, who went into captivity. The latter's views were transmitted to Canberra on 17 February 1942 in Dominions Office cablegram No. 216. Bennett's comments are from the Minutes of the War Cabinet meeting of 2 March 1942, which he attended.

Document 172

MALAYAN CAMPAIGN   17 February 1942

...

16. REASONS FOR FAILURE OF MALAYAN CAMPAIGN:
(a) *Views of Lt.-General Percival:*
The Japanese success in the Malayan Campaign was due to:-
(i)   Training
(ii)   Previous war experience
(iii)   Discipline and morale.
(i) *Training:*
The Japanese are not mere imitators. They have led the world in the development of landing operations. They exploit the primary infantry virtues of marching and fighting while placing minimum reliance on mechanised transport. This, coupled with the exploitation of captured enemy mechanical transport has resulted in a battle technique peculiarly well adapted to the theatres of war in which the Japanese might have to fight. They are also quick to adapt foreign technique to their own requirements.

(ii) *Previous War Experience:* This had been gained in the war against China.

(iii) *Discipline and Morale:*

Although Japanese external discipline is apparently sloppy, a high standard of internal discipline is maintained. A strong army tradition based on loyalty to the Emperor and offensive spirit exists and is the basis of morale. [AA: A 5954, Box 578, "Malayan Campaign — December, 1941 — February, 1942, (Historical Note)"]

Document 173

War Cabinet Minute   Melbourne, 2 March 1942

(1931) *DISCUSSION WITH MAJOR-GENERAL GORDON BENNETT*

. . .

3. Major General Bennett summarised the reasons for the failure of the campaign as under:-

(1) If there had been a greater number of A.I.F. troops, Malaya might have been held. ...

(3) The Japanese won the campaign with bicycles. They had practically no artillery. The A.I.F. was well equipped and there were no shortages. The Japanese equipment was simple, with a different establishment of equipment according to the region of operations.

(4) The simple methods and organisation of the enemy were more effective than the complicated War Office system which was top-heavy with staffs and placed too great an emphasis on the clerical side.

(5) The leadership of the British troops was poor. This was due to the "old school tie" method of selection. Failures were not removed and too much attention was given to technical education rather than to development of character and personality.

(6) There was a lack of offensive spirit and troops were trained for defence. Senior officers had a retreat complex and when they reached one position they looked to the next one back. The destruction of dumps in accordance with the scorched earth policy also affected the morale of the troops.

(7) The lack of air support in the early stages was not of great moment owing to the nature of the country and the Japanese did not strafe the roads at that time, but when the Island was reached, the effect of Japanese control of the air was tremendous. It also had a considerable effect on the civilian population. Japanese planes were in the air the whole day during daylight, except for about an hour.

(8) Although they had been in Malaya over a year, the training of a great number of the troops, especially the Indians, was not designed for jungle warfare. Indian officers were not willing to undergo hardships,

nor was there the same contact between officers and men as in white units. ...

[AA: A 2673, Vol 11]

13
RABAUL, AMBON AND TIMOR

When the Pacific war began Australia promptly set about implementing its agreement with the Dutch to send troops to Ambon and Timor. As well, an AIF battalion had reached Rabaul, on New Britain, in March and April 1941. By mid-December 1941 the Australian high command had to consider what to do about the Rabaul garrison in the light of Japan's successes.

Document 174

Evatt to Casey   13 December 1941

Cablegram 154   *Most Secret*

...
FLEET BASE AT RABAUL.
The following appreciation has been submitted by the Australian Chiefs of Staff:-
Begins.
1. There are three courses of action open in respect of Rabaul:-
(a) To reinforce the existing garrison up to the strength of a Brigade Group.
(b) To withdraw the existing garrison and abandon Rabaul.
(c) To retain the existing garrison.
2. In considering these courses, we have had in mind the fact that the existing garrison was originally despatched to Rabaul to protect the Air Operational Base. In recent months a joint U.S.-Australian project has been agreed to to expand the defences of Rabaul to make it suitable for use as a fleet base for British and American naval forces. This project has, however, not been implemented by U.S.A. and we are now advised that it is most unlikely that it will be proceeded with in the near future. The function of the present garrison accordingly remains the same as that existing when the garrison was first despatched to Rabaul and on this basis we reject course (a), i.e., reinforcement. The soundness of this conclusion is supported by the very great difficulties and hazard which would be involved in transporting reinforcements from the mainland to Rabaul and in maintaining the increased force at that place.
3. Dealing with courses (b) and (c), we consider it essential to maintain an advanced observation line to give the earliest possible indication of enemy movement to the South. We must therefore rule out any question of withdrawal. This is also influenced by difficulties of sea transport as withdrawal

of our armed forces could not reasonably be made without giving the white population an opportunity of coming away. The problem of safe sea passage for the garrison and civil population is no less acute than that considered in paragraph 1 above in dealing with reinforcing the garrison. It must also be borne in mind the psychological effect which a voluntary withdrawal would have on the minds of the Dutch in N.E.I.

4. We therefore recommend that the existing garrison be retained at Rabaul. In making this recommendation we desire to emphasize the fact that the scale of attack which can be brought against Rabaul from bases in the Japanese Mandated Islands is beyond the capacity of the small garrison to meet successfully. Notwithstanding this, we consider it essential to maintain a forward air observation line as long as possible and to make the enemy fight for this line rather than abandon it at the first threat.

5. The situation will be under constant review and if U.S. cruisers and destroyers fall back on Darwin, which may be a possibility, sufficient Naval forces may become available to reinforce and supply Rabaul.

[AA: A 5954, Box 535]

An AIF battalion and an independent company reached Dutch Timor on 12 December. Within a few days, with Japanese ships allegedly nearby, it was decided to send a force to Dilli in Portuguese (east) Timor. Four hundred Australian and Dutch troops landed without fighting on 17 December, but Portuguese authorities protested.

Document 175

Governor of Portuguese Timor   Dilli, 17 December 1941
[Ferreira de Carvalho] to Curtin

Cablegram [Not Numbered]

[TRANSLATION]

The Governor of the colony of Portuguese Timor protests vigorously against the aggression, absolutely contrary to the principles of law, being carried out against this part of Portuguese territory, by Dutch and Australian forces, who claim to be acting in accordance with instructions received from the Government of the Netherlands Indies in agreement with the Government of the Commonwealth of Australia.

[AA: A981, Timor Portuguese 3, Part 1]

Document 176

Evatt to Governor of Portuguese Timor 18 December 1941
[via Ross, Australian Consul]

Cablegram 3 Secret

In reply to your communication Commonwealth Government regrets that in order defend against Japanese aggression it has been found necessary to prevent Japanese breach [of] neutrality in Timor. We assure you Portuguese sovereignty will not be impaired and in fact it is to defend that Sovereignty as well as to prevent Japanese aggression that our forces have co-operated with Netherlands Government in taking this action. Commonwealth Government desire to assist in every way possible regarding administration and economic life of colony.
[AA: A981, Timor Portuguese 3, Part 1]

Document 177

Cranborne to Curtin London, 19 December 1941

Circular Cablegram D.751 Secret

PORTUGUESE TIMOR.

1. His Majesty's Ambassador at Lisbon has been instructed to communicate to the Portuguese Government full explanation of the circumstances which:
(a) led to the despatch of the combined force to Portuguese Timor and,
(b) made it impossible for its arrival to be delayed.

While expressing the greatest regret that circumstances should have obliged the allied military authorities on the spot to act in a manner which has proved unwelcome to the Portuguese Government we are stressing the military situation of allied action necessitated by the importance of Portuguese Timor, its defenceless state, and the speed of Japanese movements since the war began. We are re-affirming our undertaking that the troops will be withdrawn as soon as the emergency is past. The Dutch have given this assurance in the communique issued on 18th December. His Majesty's Ambassador has been authorised, if he sees fit, to add further assurance that the position will be reconsidered as soon as the Portuguese Government are themselves able to make military dispositions which will ensure effective protection of Portuguese Timor against Japanese aggression. ...
[AA: A 1608, A 41/1/5, Part 4]

Japanese forces overwhelmed the small Australian contingents on Rabaul (23 January), Ambon (30 January) and Timor (20 February). The great majority of the Australians became prisoners, and suffered accordingly. Their sacrifice was useless, for they had not been able to delay Japan's advance. It had been extremely dubious strategy to put three battalions on three islands in a sea which was about to be dominated by the Japanese navy.

Nearly all the prisoners 'unaccounted for' in paragraph 1 (a)(vi) of the following document lost their lives on 1 July 1942 when the ship carrying them was sunk off Luzon by an American submarine. The editors agree with Brigadier Lind's[71] support of Lt.-Col. Roach (par. 8, below). Roach, in command of the force on Ambon, began asking for reinforcements as soon as he reached the island. He wrote privately to an officer friend of his 'disgust, and ... concern at [being] "dumped" at this outpost position'. He was relieved of his command and returned to Australia. His successor, Col. W.J.R. Scott, was captured by the Japanese and spent the rest of the war as a prisoner.

Document 178

Note for Forde [Minister for the Army]   10 June 1943

OPERATIONS AT RABAUL, TIMOR AND AMBON   Most Secret

1. After the Japanese occupation of Rabaul, Timor and Ambon, an Army Court of Inquiry was constituted to enquire into the facts and circumstances associated with the Japanese landings at those places and events subsequent thereto. Amongst the particular matters specified were the treatment of Australian prisoners of war by the Japanese and the escape of Australian troops from the above territories.

The main conclusions of the Court may be briefly summarized as follows:
(a) *Rabaul.*
(i)   The Japanese forces were far too numerous for the garrison to cope with, the garrison being forced to withdraw in order to avoid being surrounded.
(ii)   The withdrawal could only be to the South, into jungle and mountainous country. No preparations had been made for withdrawal. There were no defensive positions to fall back upon, nor any supplies of food, arms, equipment or medical stores.
(iii)   Ill-health, shortage of food, the nature of the country, ignorance of the country and of native foods, the heavy rains, the disorder which resulted from the enemy landing, the absence of any firm and positive

---

71. Commander 23 Bde, 1940–42.

leadership, and the non-existence of any plan for withdrawal and evacuation, seriously impaired the morale of the troops. The direction "Every man for himself" destroyed their existence as an organised force.

(iv) Under the influence of the factors referred to, many soldiers surrendered to the Japanese voluntarily.

(v) At Tol, on the south coast, a number of Australian soldiers who had surrendered were, after surrender, massacred by being bayonetted or shot. The number is not certain but is probably almost 150. No excuse whatever existed for this outrage. These massacres are a clear breach of the provisions of the Hague Convention of 1907, to which Japan is a party.

(vi) Approximately 343 soldiers escaped from Rabaul. There are still 710 all ranks unaccounted for, the majority of whom are almost certainly prisoners of war.

(vii) So far as can be ascertained all prisoners now in captivity have been reasonably well treated by the Japanese, but the evidence is meagre.

(b) *Timor.*

The evidence before the Court in relation to Timor was very scanty. With regard to operations at Koepang, the Court reported that it appeared that at all points the Japanese greatly outnumbered the defending force, which resisted strongly and inflicted considerable casualties, but was obliged to surrender on 23rd February, 1942. So far as operations at Dilli were concerned, the Court had no evidence which would enable it to formulate any conclusions in respect of any of the terms of reference. In respect of both Koepang and Dilli the Court was instructed to limit its investigations to the period ending on 23rd February 1942.

(c) *Ambon.*

(i) The Japanese landed forces very much superior in numbers and were assisted by aerial and naval support of which the defenders had none.

(ii) The Australian troops offered resolute and effective resistance for several days and surrendered only when further defence was not reasonably possible. Their morale was high, and they inflicted heavy losses, while their own losses were light.

(iii) A number of men escaped after all resistance had ceased, and three small parties subsequently escaped from captivity.

(iv) 803 prisoners on the Amboina side of the island have been treated with all proper consideration by the Japanese. Nothing definite is known of the prisoners on the Laha side. ...

4. *Question of Further Enquiry.*

The Minister for the Army ... referred to a number of items of evidence which in his view warranted further investigation, and proposed a wider enquiry by an independent investigator on seven points...

5. The points on which further enquiry was suggested were as follows:-

(a) The tasks allotted;

(b) Whether the forces were properly equipped for their roles and, if

proper equipment was not available, whether the forces should have been despatched;
(c) The instructions given to the Commanders to give effect to (a);
(d) The conduct of Commanders;
(e) The evacuation of the civil population from Rabaul;
(f) Whether, in view of the progress of the Japanese advance, adherence to the plans originally laid down was proper;
(g) Whether proper measures were taken to endeavour to rescue the garrisons, particularly that at Rabaul.

6. *Comment:*

The following comments may be made with regard to these matters raised by the Minister for the Army:-
(a) In the absence of the Commanders of the forces concerned and of the majority of their men, who are now in Japanese hands, it is doubtful whether any final conclusions could be drawn regarding the matters as to which further enquiry is proposed.
(b) As to the decision that there was to be no withdrawal from Rabaul, it is pointed out by General Blamey that this course was recommended by the Chiefs of Staff with full knowledge of the inadequacy of the garrison to meet a large scale Japanese attack[72] and that War Cabinet on 18th December, 1941, noted this recommendation.
(c) In regard to further investigation of the evacuation of civilians from Rabaul, it is mentioned that no specific complaint on this point is quoted by the Minister. ...
(d) With regard to the measures taken to rescue the garrisons, this has already been considered by the Court of Inquiry. ...

8. *Timor & Ambon.*

[Reference was made to] letters received from Brigadier Lind and Lieutenant-Colonel Roach, regarding the despatch of forces to Timor and Ambon. These officers referred to the following matters:-
(a) the inadequacy of the forces despatched;
(b) the failure to establish satisfactory liaison with the Netherlands East Indies, and with the Navy and Air Force;
(c) the failure to establish lines of communication and to provide proper equipment and supplies;
(d) the inadequacy of fire-power (no field artillery, no anti-aircraft artillery, and only a limited number of light automatic weapons);
(e) the failure to give adequate instructions to Commanders;
(f) the disregard of representations made by the Commanders.

Brigadier Lind further suggested that Lieutenant-Colonel Roach was relieved of his command because of the representations he addressed to Army Headquarters on certain of the above matters. Brigadier Lind con-

---

72. Blamey was C-in-C AMF and Commander Allied Land Forces Southwest Pacific Area (1942–45). See Document 174, paragraph 3.

siders those representations were fully justified by subsequent events. ...
[AA: A 5954, Box 532]

Here is a fuller description of the massacre at Tol, referred to in the preceding document. This was the worst massacre of Australian prisoners, though others occurred, for example at Parit Sulong, in southern Malaya, on 22 January and at Banka Island on 16 February 1942.

Document 179

Interim Statement by Sturdee   28 April 1942

TREATMENT OF PRISONERS OF WAR BY JAPANESE.   Most Secret

Tol Incident

On the morning of 3rd February [1942] a party of approximately 60 Australian soldiers was located at the mouth of a creek on the western shores of Henry Reid Bay near Tol Plantation. At 7 a.m. five boats were seen to come round Tol Promontory and soon after they heard small arms and mortar fire from the direction of Tol. Living in the Tol plantation houses and in those of Waitav[a]lo, which is a mile from Tol, were some 70 other troops. No lookout was being kept and these men, for the most part, were surprised while still asleep or while preparing breakfast. Twenty-two men sat on the beach with a white flag and were immediately taken prisoner. Others attempted to escape through the plantation to the bush. Many of these were captured. It is possible that some fire was directed against the enemy, one report mentioning a few shots being fired from the plantation, apparently by our troops. ...

It is evident from the stories of the survivors that, during the afternoon of the 3rd and morning of the 4th, Japanese patrols systematically combed the areas adjacent to Henry Reid Bay and that parties of prisoners were from time to time arriving at the concentration point — Tol labour quarters. Here, during the afternoon a check of names and numbers was made and identity discs were collected. Troops were fed at midday and at night, the Japanese contributing some rice for the evening meal. The prisoners were confined in a large hut for the night.

Early on the morning of 4th February, the prisoners were assembled outside the hut and, after a preliminary check, marched to Tol plantation house. Here the 22 men who had surrendered on the beach were separated and marched off. Identity discs were taken from the remainder and their names, ranks and numbers were entered in a book. At the same time all personal articles, such as paybooks, photographs, letters and papers, were collected and heaped together. The hands of individual prisoners were tied behind their backs with cord and they were made up into groups of 9 or 10, in most cases roped together. Accompanied by small escorts, these parties were then marched in various directions, through the plantation. After proceeding short distances, parties were halted, individual members were cut adrift, taken into the bush and bayonetted, cut down or shot. In the case of a party of 8 [medical] personnel, when their Red Cross Brassards were indicated, these were torn off prior to the party being slaughtered. A survivor from this party carries 10 bayonet wounds. Seventeen men captured on the morning of 4th February were taken to Waitav[a]lo House. They were questioned, their names were written down and identity discs removed. They were taken a short distance away from the house and shot with submachine guns and rifles.

Six victims, who were either shot or bayonetted, survived after being left for dead and have now returned to Australia. The Tol massacre is based on the statements of these men. ...

[AA: A 5954, Box 532]

14
THE DESTINATION OF 1 AUSTRALIAN CORPS

In February 1942, during the height of Japanese successes, there occurred probably the sharpest clash ever to have taken place between an Australian and a British government, over whether Australian troops returning from the Middle East should be disembarked in Burma or Australia. So well-known is this argument that it is generally not recognised that it was Churchill who first proposed that most of the Australian troops in the Middle East be shipped east to fight the Japanese. He raised this issue with his service chiefs in mid-December 1941. On 3 January Curtin was asked to agree to the despatch of two AIF divisions from the Middle East to the Netherlands East Indies. On 5 January the War Cabinet, acting on the advice of the Chiefs of Staff, agreed to this transfer. At that stage it was thought likely that one division would fight on Java and the other on Sumatra.

An advance party of 1 Australian Corps (6 and 7 Divisions), including its commander, General John Lavarack, reached Batavia, Java, by air on 26 January. His immediate superior was Wavell, who on 29 December had been selected as Supreme Commander of the ABDA (Australian-British-Dutch-American) theatre. Lavarack soon began to doubt whether Java and Sumatra were defensible.

Document 180

Lavarack to Sturdee [Batavia], 6 February 1942

Letter *Most Secret*

1. I reported to General Wavell at his H.Q. here on the afternoon of the 27 Jan, so have now been in the country about 10 days. ...
2. ... You will understand, I imagine, that in all decisions I may take in present circumstances there will be two guiding considerations; first the probable effect on the general war effort, and second the fact that an Australian division is cooped up in SINGAPORE, and relies largely on our efforts for its eventual relief.
3. The general situation in the South Western Pacific Command can only be described as grim. It was so before I left Middle East, and it has since deteriorated somewhat. It will not improve until the air power relationship alters considerably in our favour. The Japanese are steadily moving from aerodrome to aerodrome, apparently basing their strategy mainly on the establishment of an air net-work, which enables them to move freely at sea.

General Wavell's policy is for the present dictated practically by the enemy's. It is to retain as many air-bases and aerodromes as he can, with a view to a positive policy as soon as possible. ...

5. To all intents and purposes the N.E.I. authorities have prepared by land for a practically static defence of JAVA, with small detached forces in the other islands. The latter are being overwhelmed one by one and now hardly come into consideration. The main forces are distributed in the East and West districts of JAVA. They are dependent for their supply, signals etc., mainly on the civil arrangements in these areas, and are therefore incapable of transfer to other areas, such as SUMATRA, or even the central zone of JAVA itself. A N.E.I., division, if transferred, say, to South SUMATRA, would be unable to fight. There is however a small N.E.I. force in S. SUMATRA, around PALEMBANG, which hopes to maintain itself there until the arrival of our 7 Aust Div. In my opinion, I may say, the Japanese are most unlikely to postpone an attack on S. SUMATRA long enough to enable us to take over the area. ...

7. Therefore General Wavell's present policy is to use Aust Corps, in conjunction with the N.E.I., land forces, and such British and Allied sea and air forces as may be at his disposal, to hold the Japanese advance at SINGAPORE Island itself, in S. SUMATRA, JAVA, and the remaining unoccupied bases stretching away to Darwin. ...

8. The policy, however, may have to be changed. After all the first flight of the Australian Corps convoys can hardly arrive in less than about 3 weeks from now, though one ship, I understand, may arrive sooner. By the time the main body does arrive the Japanese may already hold S. SUMATRA. If they do it will be hopeless to try to land and eject them, under present conditions of sea and air power. Therefore I envisage the possibility that before the arrival of the first flight a decision may have to be taken to alter its destination, either to JAVA or some other vital area. I will, of course, keep in touch with the situation and ensure, as far as may be possible, that the Corps is not misused. You know that it is not always a simple matter to judge situations exactly, and that it may be necessary to take risks. I will certainly endeavour to avoid another campaign like that in Greece. ...

10. From the above you will see that I am not optimistic as regards our future in these regions. It depends on our capacity to maintain ourselves in this string of islands, and to build up our sea and air strength until we can cope with the Japanese. There is nothing so inferior, however, as inferior sea and air forces, and all the time there is a steady attrition going on which, although it may, in absolute figures, be in our favour, is relatively in the enemy's, on account of his great superiority. Even if he is, at the present, losing 1½ or 2 to 1, he can well afford it. ...

11. ... This brings me to another most important point, which is that I have had no instructions from the Government. Blamey assured me that I should find these awaiting me upon my arrival here, but there has been nothing so far. ...

[AWM: 54, 541/1/4]

Brigadier C.E.M. Lloyd, Deputy Intendant General in SWPA (ABDA Command) was the first officer to argue strongly against disembarking the Australians in the East Indies. He did so in a letter to General Rowell, Deputy Chief of the General Staff.

Document 181

Lloyd to Rowell HQ, SWPC, 8 February 1942

Letter

...
The proposed concentration ... in the NEI is in my opinion wrong for the following reasons and I personally think diversion should be ordered now to S.E. AUST PORTS.
Reasons
(1) The scale of enemy air attack over JAVA and SUMMATRA [sic] is increasing daily and by the E.T.A. [Estimated Time of Arrival] of the leading convoy will be such that disembarkation in the available ports of TANJONG PRIOK (BATAVIA) OOST HAVEN (SUMMATRA)[sic] and TJILAJAP will NOT go unchallenged and it looks on the general air situation that losses to shipping comprising the convoys are certain. ...
The A.A. defences of the relevant ports and fighter aerodromes are either non-existent or almost so and their rate of improvement cannot be steep enough to counter the hazard.
(2) The terrain of these islands — jungle and swamp with little possibility of movement off roads is most unsuitable for offensive operations. It seems to me that the Force in question is our main hitting strength and should be employed where it can hit concentrated and in country suitable to its organization and armament. Its deployment in the NEI half in one island and half in another with very doubtful sea communication between the islands will not permit the show to do justice to itself and certainly will involve it being eaten up piecemeal in defensive operations.
(3) The general naval situation is such that even the following essentials are doubtful factors
   a) The safe arrival of the Convoy
   b) The sea communications and hence the MAINTENANCE of the Force.
(4) The successful defence of the islands of JAVA and SUMMATRA [sic] will NOT prevent the JAP staging a successful invasion of Australia.
(5) The concentration is being attempted "too far forward" and without regard to "security".
(6) The successful concentration of the whole party in Australia would do more to cramp the JAP plan than the high class bush ranging which will result here. ...
[AWM: 54, 541/1/4]

Six days later, with Singapore about to fall, Lavarack again asked Sturdee and Curtin to reconsider the future role of the 6th and 7th Divisions; but his warning was not nearly as outspoken as Lloyd's. On the same day Wavell first made his fateful suggestion.

Document 182

Wavell to Churchill and Roosevelt Batavia, 14 February 1942
Appreciation repeated to Curtin

Cablegram [Not Numbered]

"... Unexpected rapid advance of enemy on Singapore and approach of escorted enemy convoy towards South Sumatra necessitates review of our plan for defence of Netherlands East Indies... ground not yet fully prepared. By naval and air action we shall do utmost to delay and defeat this new move but land defence is weak and may not long withstand attack if it lands in strength. If Singapore falls, enemy air and land forces will be available not only to attack Burma, but also to reinforce southerly action. ...

... From the purely strategic aspect there are advantages in diverting one or both divisions to Burma or Australia. But any abandonment of Dutch East Indies would obviously have most serious moral and political repercussions. We must reinforce Sumatra until it is clearly useless to do so. Subsequent reinforcement of Java would probably be unprofitable.

... We shall continue with the present plan until the situation enforces change. ...["]
[AA: A 2671, 106/1942]

It was on 15 February, the day Singapore fell, that Sturdee, as a matter of 'vital urgency', recommended to Curtin that the AIF return to Australia. We print some extracts from Sturdee's supporting document.

Document 183

PAPER BY THE CHIEF OF THE GENERAL 15 February 1942
STAFF ON FUTURE EMPLOYMENT OF A.I.F.

In view of the present situation in the S.W. Pacific Area and of information which has just come to my knowledge, I consider that the future employment of the A.I.F. requires immediate reconsideration by War Cabinet.
2. At the present moment we are in the process of transferring 64,000 troops of Aust. Corps from the Middle East to the ABDA Area. The first

flight of 17,800 is now in Bombay being restowed into smaller ships for disembarkation in N.E.I. If any change is to be made, action must be taken immediately.

3. So far in this war against Japan we have violated the principle of concentration of forces in our efforts to hold numerous small localities with totally inadequate forces which are progressively overwhelmed by vastly superior numbers. These small garrisons alone without adequate reinforcement or support never appeared to have any prospect of withstanding even a moderate scale of attack. In my opinion, the present policy of trying to hold isolated islands with inadequate resources needs review.

4. Our object at the present time should be to ensure the holding of some continental area from which we can eventually launch an offensive in the Pacific when American aid can be fully developed. This postulates the necessity for keeping open the sea and if possible the air reinforcing routes from U.S.A. This area to be held must be large enough so that, if we are pressed seriously by the Japanese, we will have room to manoeuvre our defending forces and not get them locked up in a series of small localities, e.g. islands, where the garrisons are overwhelmed piecemeal and are consequently lost as fighting resources for the duration of the war. Sacrifices of this nature can only be justified if the delay occasioned to the enemy's advance is such that the time gained enables effective measures to be organised for taking the offensive. ...

7. General Wavell's present plan is to distribute the A.I.F. and the accompanying British Armoured Brigade as follows:-

South Sumatra	.. 7 Div. and some Corps Troops.
Central Java	.. (6 Div. and balance of Corps Troops. (British Armoured Brigade.
South Central Java	.. Depots and Base Units.

The prospects of 7 Div. being able to reach South Sumatra in time seem doubtful even at the best estimate. ...

[9.] The prospects of the successful defence of Java are [also] ... far from encouraging.

10. Even assuming the successful defence of Java, this island does not provide us with a continental base from which we could build up Allied strength to take the offensive. It would be continually subject to air bombing from adjacent N.E.I. islands in Japanese hands, and the sea approaches would be open to continuous attack from Japanese naval and air forces from nearby bases.

Valuable as the holding of Java would be to impede the Japanese advance southwards, it cannot provide a strategic base upon which Allied strength can be built up, owing to its comparatively small size, the long sea route from U.S.A. and the uncertainty of keeping such route open for the enormous quantity of shipping needed to develop U.S.A. resources in manpower and fighting equipment.

An equally important factor is that, if Timor is lost, we are unable to ferry fighter and medium bomber aircraft by air to Java from their assembly bases in Australia.

11. The most suitable location for such a strategical base is Australia. It has the shortest sea route with U.S.A. of any considerable area of continuous land. Its extent is such that it cannot be completely overrun by the Japanese if we concentrate our available resources for its immediate protection whilst American strength is arriving. It has an indigenous white population which provides considerable fighting forces. It has sufficient industrial development to form a good basis for rapid expansion with American aid. Its northern shores are sufficiently close to Japanese occupied territory to make a good "jumping off" area for offensive operations, whilst its southern areas are sufficiently far from Japanese bases to ensure a reasonable degree of immunity from continuous sea and air bombardment bearing in mind the growing strength of U.S.A. Naval and Air forces.

It can therefore be accepted that Australia meets the requirements of a strategic base from which to develop our ultimate and decisive offensive.

12. The only other alternatives seem to be India and its neighbour Burma. The latter is already in the front line, more difficult of access even than Java, and possesses insufficient development to be capable of rapid expansion. ...

13. Our immediate problem is how best to assure the security of this country pending the arrival of sufficient American forces not only to safeguard this strategic base, but also to develop the offensive against Japan. ...

14. ... considerable risks are at present being taken with the security of this country, which appears to be the only practicable base from which the offensive can ultimately be launched. The return of the available A.I.F. from abroad, some 100,000 trained and war experienced troops, complete with war equipment and trained staffs, would in my opinion more than double the present security of this country.

15. To hold Java (if this is practicable) and to lose Australia would be little solace to Australia, the British Empire or the Allied cause.

Alternatively, if Australia is held and Java lost together with over three-fifths of the Australian Corps, the Australian potential for providing its quota of military forces for the eventual offensive would be very greatly reduced.

16. In view of the foregoing, I have no alternative but strongly to recommend that the Government give immediate consideration to:-

(a) The diversion to Australia of:-
   (i) that portion of the A.I.F. now at Bombay and en route to Java;
   (ii) the British Armoured Brigade in the same convoy.
(b) The diversion of the remaining two flights to Australia.
(c) The recall of 9 Aust. Div. and remaining A.I.F. in Middle East at an early date. ...

[AA: A 2671, 106/1942]

With the support of his other two Chiefs of Staff, Curtin sent to Churchill a long message embodying Sturdee's recommendations, though more in the form of a suggestion than a demand. We print some brief extracts.

Document 184

Curtin to Churchill, [via Cranborne] 15 February 1942
Repeated to Wavell

Cablegram 123 *Most Secret*

...
12. It can be argued that it is good defensive-offensive tactics to meet the enemy as far afield as possible and withdraw whilst inflicting losses on him, though suffering losses oneself. ...
13. It is however risky to hazard one's main base and largest reservoir in the theatre of operations by stringing out the resources of this reservoir along the line of the enemy's advance where, owing to superior sea power, air power and greater military strength, he can bring stronger forces to bear. This strategy invites progressive defeat along the line and ultimately imperils the capacity to defend the main base through the dispersion of forces.
14. If such is the case, the absolute security of the main base is of fundamental importance and no risk should be taken with its security. ...
15. ...
(iii) Australia, which is the main base for operations against Japan, is in jeopardy until superior sea power is regained. Even then it can be imperilled by the loss of a fleet action.
(iv) In the meantime Australia, as the main base, must be made secure.
    ...
(viii) ... it is [therefore] a matter for urgent consideration whether the A.I.F. should not proceed to the Netherlands East Indies but return to Australia. ...
(ix) The conclusions expressed above are fully co-operative. Their purpose is to ensure as far as possible the certainty of ultimate victory by defending Australia as a base, even though ground may be given to the enemy. We avoid a "penny packet" distribution of our limited forces and their defeat in detail. When we are ready for the counter-offensive, superior sea power and the accumulation of American Forces in this country will enable the A.I.F. again to join in clearing the enemy from the adjacent territories he has occupied.
[AA: A 2671, 106/1942]

Next day Wavell, though agreeing that the Netherlands East Indies could not be held, urged a different role for the Australians.

Document 185

Wavell to Churchill and Brooke [CIGS] [Batavia], 16 February 1942

Cablegram 01288 *Most Secret*

...

13. If Australian Corps is diverted I recommend that at least one division should go Burma and both if they can be administratively received and maintained. Presence of this force in Burma threatening invasion of Thailand and Indo China must have very great effect on Japanese strategy and heartening effect on China and India. It is only theatre in which offensive land operations against Japan possible in near future. It should be possible for American Troops to provide reinforcement of Australia if required. ...
[AWM: 54, 243/6/137]

The steady increase in tension between Curtin and Churchill may be traced in the following cables.

Document 186

Curtin to Churchill [via Cranborne] 17 February 1942

Cablegram 127 *Most Secret*

...

2. The Government ... requests that urgent arrangements be made for:-
(a) The diversion to Australia of that portion of the A.I.F. now at Bombay and en route to Java.
(b) The diversion of the remaining two flights to Australia.
(c) The recall of 9th Australian Division and remaining A.I.F. in Middle East at an early date. ...
[AA: A 5954, Box 573]

Document 187

Wavell to Curtin Java, 18 February 1942

Cablegram OPXO 1529

...

I have been in close touch with Lavarack throughout and you may like to know that he agrees with my view that the Australian Corps if diverted

from the Netherlands East Indies should be used to reinforce Burma.
[AWM: 54, 541/1/4]

Next day Lavarack cabled Curtin, explaining that the view attributed to him by Wavell was contingent on Australia's home defence position being satisfactory. Meanwhile on the 17th, in London, the Pacific War Council, comprising Churchill, his Chiefs of Staff and representatives of Holland, Australia and New Zealand, supported Wavell's request that at least one AIF division be landed in Burma. This request was supported by Page, Australia's representative on both the Pacific War Council and the British War Cabinet, and by Bruce, whose views on the issue follow.

Document 188

Bruce to Curtin   London, 18 February 1942

Cablegram 31A   *Most Secret. Personal. Himself.*

... in my view it is essential we should agree to the 7th Australian Division going to Burma because
(a) Its presen[ce] there offers the best hope of keeping open the Burma road.
(b) The continuance of a flow of supplies and munitions to China is of paramount importance for the fight against Japan,
(c) Even if the Division's presence did not achieve the objective of keeping the Burma Road open, the sending of it there will have a temendous [sic] effect upon China's morale and will to resist which it is imperative to maintain if we are to avoid the incalculable disaster of her throwing up the sponge[.]
(d) Added to all we have already done our action, hard pressed as we are, in sending a Division to the vital spot in Burma strengthens our position in demanding similar action to meet our necessities...
[AA: M 100]

The cable conflict now approached its climax. Page tried to persuade Curtin to change his mind in a message which mentioned some new developments.

Document 189

Page to Curtin   London, 19 February 1942

Cablegram P.47   Most Secret

...

2. You will have [just] received ... the American offer to give an additional American Division for Australia in exchange for one of our Divisions and also Wavell's further appreciation.
3. Accordingly I am holding your telegram secret until receipt of further advice. No instructions to divert its course have been sent to the convoy.
4. I have discussed the American offer with Churchill who will try to expedite arrival of this American Division in Australia if the 7th Australian Division is diverted to Burma. The 6th and 9th Divisions can still go to Australia if so determined by the Australian Government. The 6th Division is in the process of embarkation.
5. In our discussion, Churchill expressed great anxiety of the effect on China of not reinforcing Burma, especially if troops so near the battle-front and only troops that could be available are not allocated at this critical moment. Both he and Roosevelt believe that China is the ultimate key of the whole Asian situation. China has been invited to become a member of the Pacific War Council in London and their reply to that invitation is awaited. ...
[AWM: 54, 541/1/4]

Before Page's message was received Curtin had sent to London a long cable from which we print the final three paragraphs.

Document 190

Curtin to Page   19 February 1942
Repeated to Lavarack, Wavell and Casey

Cablegram 29   Most Secret

...

12. In no respect whatever have calls upon Australia for assistance elsewhere remained unanswered. When the state of the land and air defences in Malaya was revealed by the first Singapore Conference, we did not hesitate to send the bulk of an A.I.F. Division and three squadrons from the R.A.A.F. The A.I.F. formation and additional reinforcements despatched have now been lost together with garrisons in certain of the islands. We have sent Australian land and air forces to Ambon, Koepang, Portuguese Timor, New Caledonia and Solomon Islands. There are 6,250 Empire Air Scheme

Personnel abroad. Our resources are not only strained, but are desperately small. Equipment which we could not reasonably spare was furnished at the request of the British Government.

13. We feel first from the point of view of success in the War against the Axis, it is of fundamental importance to retain this base. We are also satisfied that we would be completely failing in our duty to the people of Australia if we agreed to the diversion of any Division of the A.I.F. from the N.E.I. theatre of war to which it was allocated at the suggestion of the United Kingdom Government. The object of the allocation was to stop Japan's thrust south. That object can now be achieved only by allocating the A.I.F. to Australia.

14. Therefore, because N.E.I. is now ruled out as the agreed destination of the A.I.F., it should come to Australia with the greatest possible expedition.
[AWM: 54, 541/1/4]

This message crossed one from Churchill supporting Wavell's request.

Document 191

Churchill to Curtin [via Attlee,　　　　　London, 20 February 1942
Secretary of State, Dominion Affairs]

Cablegram 233

I suppose you realise that your leading division, the head of which is sailing south of Colombo to N.E.I. at this moment in our scanty British and American shipping is the only force that can reach Rangoon in time to prevent its loss and the severance of communication with China. It can begin to disembark at Rangoon about 26th or 27th. There is nothing else in the world that can fill the gap.

2. We are all entirely in favour of all Australian troops returning home to defend their native soil and we shall help their transportation in every way. But a vital war emergency cannot be ignored and troops en route to other destinations must be ready to turn aside and take part in a battle. Every effort would be made to relieve this division at the earliest moment and send them on to Australia. I do not endorse the United States' request that you should send your other two divisions to Burma. They will return home as fast as possible but this one is needed now and is the only one that can possibly save the situation. ...

4. Your greatest support in this hour of peril must be drawn from the United States. They alone can bring into Australia the necessary troops and air forces and they appear ready to do so. As you know, the President attaches supreme importance to keeping open the connection with China without which his bombing offensive against Japan cannot be started and also most

grievous results may follow in Asia if China is cut off from all allied help.
5. I am quite sure that if you refuse to allow your troops to stop this gap ... and if in consequence of the above[, events?] affecting the whole course of the war follow[,] a very grave effect will be produced upon the President and the Washington circle on whom you are so largely dependent. See especially the inclination of the United States to move major naval forces from Hawaii into the Anzac area.
6. We must have an answer immediately as the leading ships of the convoy will soon be steaming in the opposite direction from Rangoon and every day is a day lost. I trust therefore that for the sake of all interests and above all your own interests you will give most careful consideration to the case I have set before you.
[AA: A 5954, Box 573]

Curtin replied firmly.

Document 192

Curtin to Churchill [via Attlee] 22 February 1942

Cablegram 136 *Most Secret*

... I have received your rather strongly worded request at this late stage, though our wishes in regard to the disposition of the A.I.F. in the Pacific theatre have long been known to you and carried even further by your statement in the House of Commons. Furthermore, Page was furnished with lengthy statements on our viewpoint ...
2. The proposal for additional military assistance for Burma comes from the Supreme Commander of the A.B.D.A. Area [Wavell]. Malaya, Singapore and Timor have been lost and the whole of the Netherlands East Indies will apparently be occupied shortly by the Japanese. The enemy, with superior sea and air power, has commenced raiding our territory in the north-west and also in the north-east from Rabaul. The Government made the maximum contribution of which it was capable in reinforcement of the A.B.D.A. Area. ...
4. With the situation having deteriorated to such an extent in the theatre of the A.B.D.A. Area with which we are closely associated and the Japanese also making a southward advance in the Anzac Area, the Government, in the light of the advice of its Chiefs of Staff as to the forces necessary to repel an attack on Australia, finds it most difficult to understand that it should be called upon to make a further contribution of forces to be located in the most distant part of the A.B.D.A. Area. Notwithstanding your statement that you do not agree with the request to send the other two divisions of the A.I.F. Corps to Burma, our advisers are concerned with Wavell's request for the Corps and Dill's statement that the destination of the 6th and 9th Australian Divisions should be left open, as more troops might be badly

needed in Burma. Once one division became engaged it could not be left unsupported, and the indications are that the whole of the Corps might become committed to this region or there might be a recurrence of the experiences of the Greek and Malayan campaigns. Finally, in view of superior Japanese sea power and air power, it would appear to be a matter of some doubt as to whether this division can be landed in Burma and a matter for greater doubt whether it can be brought out as promised. With the fall of Singapore, Penang and Martaban, the Bay of Bengal is now vulnerable to what must be considered the superior sea and air power of Japan in that area. The movement of our forces to this theatre therefore is not considered a reasonable hazard of war, having regard to what has gone before, and its adverse results would have the gravest consequences on the morale of the Australian people. The Government therefore must adhere to its decision. ...

6. We feel therefore, in view of the foregoing and the services the A.I.F. have rendered in the Middle East, that we have every right to expect them to be returned as soon as possible with adequate escorts to ensure their safe arrival.

7. We assure you, and desire you to so inform the President, who knows fully what we have done to help the common cause, that, if it were possible to divert our troops to Burma and India without imperilling our security in the judgment of our advisers, we should be pleased to agree to the diversion.
[AA: A 5954, Box 573]

Roosevelt accepted Curtin's decision philosophically, and said it would not affect the movement of the 41st American Division to Australia.

Document 193

Casey to Evatt   Washington, 22 February 1942

Cablegram 342   *Most Secret*

...

I delivered contents of the ... telegrams to President at once. He made very little comment, confining himself to saying "Well, if they have made their minds up, that is the way it is. I still hope, however, that they will be willing to discuss the matter in respect of last Australians to move from Middle East." ...
[AWM: 54, 541/1/4]

Churchill's response was very different.

Document 194

Churchill to Curtin [via Attlee]　　　　　London, 22 February 1942

Cablegram 241　　　　　　　　　　　　　　　*Most Immediate*

We could not contemplate that you would refuse our request and that of the President of the United States for the diversion of the leading division to save the situation in Burma. We knew that if our ships proceeded on their course to Australia while we were waiting for your formal approval they would either arrive too late at Rangoon or even be without enough fuel to go there at all. We therefore decided that the convoy should be temporarily diverted to the northward. The convoy is now too far north for some of the ships in it to reach Australia without refuelling. These physical considerations give a few days for the situation to develop and for you to review the position should you wish to do so. Otherwise the leading Australian Division will be returned to Australia as quickly as possible in accordance with your wishes.
[AA: A 5954, Box 573]

Curtin, Page and Bruce were astonished at the news contained in the above message. Bruce tried to make the best of a bad situation.

Document 195

Bruce to Curtin　　　　　　　　　　　　London, 23 February 1942

Cablegram 33A　　　　　　　　　　　　*Personal Himself Only*

Have just seen copy of telegram the Prime Minister has sent to you this afternoon. While Page is dealing with it officially and will no doubt have much to say to the Prime Minister with regard to it, I feel I must send you privately my reactions, am appalled by it and its possible repercussions. It is arrogant and offensive and contradicts the assurances given to Page that the Convoy was not being diverted from its direct route to Australia. Any reaction on your part would be justified. None the less I urge restraint in your reply. ...
[AA: M100]

Curtin's complaint to Churchill was not restrained.

Document 196

Curtin to Churchill [via Attlee]　　　　　　　　23 February 1942

Cablegram 139　　　　　　　　　　　　　　　　　Most Secret

. . .
　In your 233 it was clearly implied that the convoy was not proceeding to the northward. From 241 it appears that you have diverted the convoy towards Rangoon and had treated our approval to this v[it]al diversion as merely a matter of form. By doing so you have established a physical situation which adds to the dangers of the convoy and the responsibility of the consequences of such diversion rests upon you. ...
3. Wavell's message considered by Pacific War Council on Saturday reveals that Java faces imminent invasion. Australia's outer defences are now quickly vanishing and our vulnerability is completely exposed.
4. ... Now you contemplate using the A.I.F. to save Burma. All this has been done as in Greece without adequate air support.
5. We feel a primary obligation to save Australia not only for itself but to preserve it as a base for the development of the war against Japan. In the circumstances it is quite impossible to reverse a decision which we made with the utmost care and which we have affirmed and reaffirmed.
6. Our Chief of General Staff [Sturdee] advises although your 241 refers to the leading division only the fact is that owing to the loading of the flights it is impossible at the present time to separate the two divisions and the destination of all the flights will be governed by that of the first flight. This fact re-inforces us in our decision.
[AA: A 5954, Box 573]

　　　The suggestion that, in place of the 7th Division, Australia could be reinforced by an American division, did not impress Sturdee.

Document 197

Sturdee to Shedden [Secretary of　　　　　　23 February 1942
War Cabinet]

Teleprinter Message M.777　　　　　　　　　　Most Secret

. . .
1. From a purely military aspect, the value of any American division for the defence of Australia is considerably less than an A.I.F. division, for the following reasons:-
(a) Lack of war experience in this war;
(b) Completely different organization;

(c) Different weapons, equipment and ammunition, which complicate maintenance;
(d) No reserves of equipment or ammunition in Australia. These must be shipped here before troops can function effectively for a period. Australian resources are inadequate to re-equip with Australian pattern weapons.
(e) Temperamental difference of troops and differences in training;
(f) Probable difficulties of command inherent in Allied Forces co-operating.

...

[AA: A 5954, Box 573]

Churchill realised he had lost this battle with Curtin.

Document 198

Churchill to Curtin [via Attlee] London, 23 February 1942

Cablegram [Not Numbered]

...

1. Your convoy is now proceeding to re-fuel at Colombo. It will then proceed to Australia in accordance with your wishes.
2. My decision to move it northward during the few hours required to receive your final answer was necessary because otherwise your help, if given, might not have arrived in time.
3. As soon as the convoy was turned north, arrangements were made to increase its escort and this increased escort will be maintained during its voyage to Colombo and on leaving Colombo again for as long as practicable.
4. Of course, I take full responsibility for my action.
[AA: A 5954, Box 573]

The 7th Division began arriving in Australia in March. In this dispute Australian leaders had been intellectually superior to Wavell and Churchill. It would be difficult these days to find intelligent strategists who would endorse Churchill's and Wavell's suggested use of the Australians in February 1942. On 14 February Wavell estimated that the leading brigade of the 7th Division could not be operating in South Sumatra until 'about 8th March', and the whole Division not until 21 March. These dates could scarcely have been more than a day earlier had the Division gone to Burma. The Japanese entered Rangoon on 8 March.

15
THE FATE OF THE ORCADES PARTY

While Curtin was able to save the 7th Division from being squandered in the Burmese jungle he could not prevent its advance guard from being captured on Java. The *Orcades*, carrying 3,400 troops, mostly Australian, steamed much faster than the other troopships. It reached Batavia on 17 February.

Wavell had first intended to use 1 Australian Corps to relieve Indian troops in Malaya and carry out a counter offensive, but by 29 January, in view of the 'changed situation', he had decided that the Corps must be used in the 'first instance to secure vital areas in Sumatra and Java'. The Australian government was anxious that the Corps should not be split up into too many fragments.

Document 199

Curtin to Wavell   12 February 1942

Cablegram 26   Most Secret

General Lavarack has advised Australian Army authorities that it is proposed to dispose one Australian division for defence of centre of Java and the other division is to be located in South Sumatra.
2. You will be aware of the principles governing the control and administration of the A.I.F.... . These are of course equally applicable to the A.I.F. in the A.B.D.A. Area as in the Middle East[73]. The Government desires to emphasise that the concentration of the A.I.F. in one Force under its own commander is a principle of cardinal national importance.
3. ... The Government is ... not willing that there should be any detachments smaller than a complete division.
4. We would be glad to be kept posted with an up-to-date appreciation of the situation in the A.B.D.A. Area as our consent to the present proposal affecting the A.I.F. is necessarily dependent upon the strategical position resulting from the rapidly changing situation.
[AA: A 5954, Box 573]

Japanese began to land in south Sumatra on 14 February. Wavell promptly ordered the withdrawal of the garrison to Java. News of this

---

73. See Document 52.

caused alarm in Australia about the fate of those Australians who had just reached Java.

Document 200

Curtin to Wavell   18 February 1942

Cablegram 34   *Most Secret*

... In view of evacuation of South Sumatra, Lavarack has raised question of destination of 3,400 Australian troops now at Batavia. He considers that employment with advantage in N.E.I. no longer possible.
Would be glad to know urgently what are your own plans in regard to these men.
[AA: A 5954, Box 573]

> Three days later Australia was told that its troops in Java were being retained for the defence of aerodromes. The government, increasingly worried over their possible fate, sought to bring pressure on Wavell through London to prepare for their evacuation, if necessary.

Document 201

Curtin to Page   24 February 1942

Cablegram 32   *Most Secret*

...
In regard to paragraph 4 of Wavell's message that evacuation of Australian and other troops will be carried out if ordered by Joint Chiefs of Staff Committee, our Chief of General Staff [Sturdee] has been informed by Wavell that they cannot be evacuated in view of instructions in Combined Chiefs of Staff D.B.A. 19 [not printed here], but preparations are being made to do so if this policy is altered.
2. The Government instructed Lavarack on 19th February that if worst comes to worst some chance of withdrawal should be afforded our men. In view of present position in Java the Government insists that the necessary authority be given to Wavell to ensure that these troops be evacuated, their ultimate destination being Australia.
3. Wavell will apparently be moving headquarters 9 a.m. 25th February and it is requested that you arrange for issue of necessary orders at once.
4. This cablegram is being communicated to Casey at Washington for parallel action and also to Wavell.
[AA: A 5954, Box 573]

Page sent quite a detailed reply.

Document 202

Page to Curtin   London, 24 February 1942

Cablegram P 52   Most Secret. Himself alone.

1. Reference your telegram 32, the policy regarding evacuation of Java was carefully considered by the Pacific War Council on two occasions. As advised in my P.43 the following recommendations were made to the joint Chiefs of Staff at Washington as principles to guide Wavell:-
(1) Strenuous resistance should be maintained in Java by forces already available there in order to gain as much time as possible and delay further Japanese offensives.
(2) Non-Dutch troops already in Java should continue fighting alongside the Dutch.
2. On the second occasion, as reported in paragraph 4 of my telegram 1609, the Council recommended considerably more latitude to the Supreme Commander than on the first. It allowed him to evacuate certain classes of personnel immediately and gave an ultimate discretion to the local commanders to decide when shipping must be evacuated to prevent its destruction by air attack and who should go in them.
3. I have been informed to-day by the Chiefs of Staff that telegram No. 70 despatched to Wavell on 22nd February by the combined Chiefs of Staff, Washington, after approval by the President on behalf of America and by the Prime Minister on behalf of the Pacific Council, reads as follows:-
"All men of fighting units for whom there are arms must continue to fight without thought of evacuation, but air forces which can more usefully operate in battle from bases outside Java and all air personnel for whom there are no aircraft and such troops particularly technicians as cannot contribute to the defence of Java to be withdrawn. With respect to personnel who cannot contribute to the defence, the general policy should be to withdraw United States' and Australian personnel to Australia."
4. It seems quite impossible for the Councils at Washington or here to do more at this point of time or at this distance. Discretion as to the mode and priority of evacuation has been left to the commanders on the spot and it is assumed that Lavarack will ensure that Australian personnel receive their allocation of any ships available. ...
[AA: A 5954, Box 573]

Wavell justified his stand in a cable which went to Curtin, among other recipients.

Fate of *Orcades* party 243

Document 203

Wavell to Marshall and Dill[74] 25 February 1942
Repeated to Curtin

Cablegram TOR 2115[75] *Not For Publication*

Australian Machine Gun battalion and Pioneer Battalion with certain necessary Ancillary units were disembarked here on 18th February. They have been retained in view of explicit orders in DBA 19 and DBA 22 and will fight beside other British troops in defence of Java. Do not repeat not consider these orders give me any discretion to remove fighting troops. Their removal would have most unfortunate effect on Dutch not repeat not to mention opinion of our own troops. They will receive fully equal treatment with other troops if and when eventual evacuation is necessitated. Brigadier Sitwell[76] who remains in command has received instructions which have been repeated to COS [Chiefs of Staff] London for approval and which contain specific references to Australian troops.
[AA: A 5954, Box 573]

By this time Lavarack had left Java (he reached Melbourne on 23 February). Command of the AIF troops on Java was handed to Brigadier A.S. Blackburn.

Document 204

Blackburn to Lavarack Java, [c. 26] February 1942

Report *Most Secret*

1. As I have been informed today that mail communication with Australia is becoming increasingly difficult, I am taking this opportunity of forwarding an interim report on the subject of A.I.F. personnel in Java by the hand of Major Austin, who I am informed is tonight flying to Australia.
2. In accordance with your instructions I took over command of all A.I.F. troops in Java on 21 Feb and immediately proceeded to complete the taking over of the ground protection of the following aerodromes:- Kemajoran, Tjililitan, Semplak Tjisaoek and Tjileungsir, the two latter not being occupied until the evening of 22nd Feb. At this time all the above aerodromes were fully manned and ready for defence.

---

74. General G.C. Marshall, Chief of Staff of the U.S. Army; Field Marshal Sir John Dill, Head of the British Joint Staff Mission in Washington.
75. Contained in Teleprinter Message M.887, 26.2.1942.
76. GOC British Troops, Java.

3. Owing to the fact that a large number of stragglers were causing trouble in Batavia, I took the necessary steps to stop all leave in the city, and by putting on a strong picquet collected a further 30 odd stragglers who were at large in the city.

4. I received a number of reports that the personnel ex Singapore were in many cases unsatisfactory, their morale being bad and their training indifferent. It was further reported to me that their ability to fight if heavy pressure was put on them was very doubtful.

5. At 1630 hrs on 24 Feb Major Woods my Liaison Officer at G.H.Q., called at my H.Q. in Batavia and informed me that all British troops in Java were being placed under one central command, and that it was proposed to withdraw my force from the aerodromes and use them in another way for the defence of Java.

6. I immediately left by car for G.H.Q., arriving there at 2200 hrs on the 24 Feb and immediately contacted Major General [C.E.M.] Lloyd and discussed the whole position with him. He informed me that it had been decided to disperse Abdacom immediately. Also that all A.I.F. and other British troops in Java had been placed under the command of Major General Sitwell M.C., a former commander of an anti-aircraft brigade on the Island.

7. I interviewed Major General Sitwell at 0700 hrs 25 Feb and with him had an interview at 0800 hrs with General Ter Poorten C in C N.E.I. Army. Immediately I saw Major General Sitwell he handed me a copy of an order from Major General Playfair, Chief of General Staff S.W.P.C. [South-West Pacific Command] stating that the troops under my command would come under the orders of Major General Sitwell. ...

8. As a result of other conferences lasting most of the morning of the 25 Feb, I was ordered to take over command of what Major General Sitwell described as a "striking force" that is to say a force which would be used to counter-attack the Japanese wherever General Ter Poorten felt would be most effective. The force under my command for this purpose included the whole of the fighting units of the A.I.F. in Java and "B" Squadron of the 3rd Hussars. The American Commander in Java was also approached to place a Regiment of American Artillery, alleged to be somewhere on the Island, also under my command for use with this force.

9. On receipt of these orders I made preliminary plans for the handing over of the aerodrome defence to British troops as detailed by Major General Sitwell. When my force is relieved from aerodrome protection I propose concentrating them in some central position and putting them into strict training for the counter attack role.

10. Major General Sitwell's orders are that the British troops on the Island will fight to the end and that there will be no withdraw[a]l from the Island or surrender. I assure you that the troops under my command will fully carry out these orders so long as they remain in force.

11. I am informed that mail communications with Australia are likely to cease in the near future, but I will take every opportunity that presents itself to forward to you a full report of operations as they occur.

[AA: A 5954, Box 573]

By early March the Australian high command realised that there was little chance of saving the Australians on Java.

Document 205

Sturdee to Shedden   2 March 1942

Minute   *Most Secret*

EVACUATION OF ADVANCE PARTIES OF A.I.F. FROM JAVA.

I have discussed this question with Lt.-Gen. Sir John Lavarack. The following appears to be the present situation:-
(a) There are the following Allied Forces in Java in addition to Dutch forces ...:-
    3,000–4,000   R.A.F.
    5,500   British Army
    2,920   A.I.F. including 471 of 8 Div.
                  M.T. transferred from Singapore
                  by orders of ABDACOM.
    700   American.
(b) The bulk of the A.I.F. have been formed into a striking force combined with a squadron of British Light Tanks and probably an American Artillery Battalion. The whole to be under the command of Brigadier Blackburn A.I.F. and are placed at the disposal of General Ter Poorten.
(c) General Sitwell commanding British and Australian Forces in Java has been given orders that the British Troops on the Island will fight to the end and that there will be no withdraw[a]l from the island or surrender.
2. In view of the present situation in Java, it does not appear practicable to get the A.I.F. out of the country. ...
[AA: A 5954, Box 573]

Document 206

Sturdee to Ter Poorten   Melbourne, 2 March 1942

Cablegram MC.5214[77]   *Most Secret*

We have been informed that bulk of A.I.F. now in Java have been formed into a striking force to counter attack the Japanese wherever you feel they

---

77. Contained in Teleprinter Message M.1033, 7.3.1942.

would be most effective. These forces were merely the advanced parties of an Australian Division diverted elsewhere and my Government originally pressed for their re-embarkation. They now feel that they can no longer press for their return in view of the important role you have allotted to them. My Government, however, have asked me to convey to you their request that should resistance in due course become impossible the A.I.F. together with any other forces may be afforded an opportunity to escape so that these seasoned troops may still be available to continue the war against Japan in other theatres. I wish you every success in the arduous and noble duty of defending Java.
[AA: A 5954, Box 573]

Document 207

Sitwell to Sturdee [Batavia], 5 March 1942

Cablegram TOR 1025[78] *Most Secret*

Your MC.5214 to General Ter Poorten regarding evacuation Australian troops. Regret that any ordered evacuation now impossible owing to shipping shortage for which large number unarmed R.A.F. Technical personnel have priority and still await shipment with little prospect of getting away. Additional 2000 R.A.F. armed are now fighting as infantry in company with Australian and Englishmen. Should Dutch resistance cease troops will endeavour escape from Island in small parties in company with English troops. Am endeavouring to arrange plans for this eventuality. Australians in splendid fettle fighting magnificently and I am proud to have such men serving under my Command.
[AA: A 5954, Box 573]

The Japanese quickly disposed of the remaining Allied warships around Java, including the *Houston* and *Perth*, sunk in the Sunda Strait on the night of 28 February/1 March. At about the same time, two Japanese divisions landed, one in west and one in east Java. The Australians, in west Java under Blackburn, lost 36 men killed in combat over the next few days. Surrender was agreed upon by 8 March. Over 2,700 Australians became prisoners of war. This marked the end of seven weeks of almost unrelieved disaster for Australian servicemen fighting the Japanese, weeks without parallel in Australia's history. The nation still had to endure many months of anxiety, but as it happened, never again were the Japanese to capture such large bodies of Australian troops.

---

78. Contained in Teleprinter Message M.1029, 7.3.1942.

16
TWO AIF BRIGADES TO CEYLON

The clash between Churchill and Curtin over the destination of the 7th Division is well known in Australia. Curtin's agreement that two AIF brigades should go to Ceylon is largely forgotten, although that decision could have turned out to be a controversial one. Had the Japanese given a higher priority to Ceylon they might have been able to occupy it and round up the garrison, according to their established pattern.

As it happened, the Empire's high command reasoned that two AIF brigades might have made the difference between holding or losing Ceylon. Late in February Bruce asked his government to consider leaving the 7th Division at Ceylon for the time being. He pointed out: 'Alone we cannot protect ourselves from Japan'. In the common interest of the UK, USA and Australia, he thought Curtin should agree to the use of Australians to defend Ceylon. Shortly afterwards, Page elaborated on this principle when repeating his request.

Document 208

Page to Curtin   London, 24 February 1942

Cablegram P.50   Most Secret. Himself alone

At War Cabinet last night the rapid deterioration of the Netherlands East Indies and North Australia position caused consideration of the vital importance of Ceylon now to the Empire's war effort in general and to Australia in particular. I am sending in my following telegram the points made by the Chiefs of Staff as to its strategic value and the present state of its defences. From this you will see that the defences of this vital point are very weak, they having been accorded a lower priority to Singapore and the Netherlands East Indies.
(2) If Ceylon is attacked in force by Japanese as they can now do from Singapore by their fleet with transports, they will either capture Ceylon or they will force the retention at Ceylon of the few British battleships in the Indian Ocean to defend it and so prevent them from escorting convoys of troops and essential materials.
(3) There are still over two Australian divisions, quite apart from the 7th Division, to be transported to Australia, and all British reinforcements to the Far East to help hold Burma and India and what can be held of Netherlands East Indies.
(4) All reinforcements to the Middle East proceed through the Indian Ocean

via the Cape of Good Hope and would be in extreme jeopardy if Japan held Ceylon and her naval forces were operating from there. All of our reinforcements through Africa and the Indian Ocean of American and British aircraft would be prevented coming to Australia as ... under these circumstances we would almost certainly lose Cocos Islands and other islands by which our cable and air communications could be maintained. All Australian English shipping around the Cape would be in greater peril than under the present circumstances and need much more protection.

(5) The difficulties of British reinforcements arriving in Ceylon in time are all associated with the physical limitations of shipping and distance. Now that the convoy carrying the Australian 7th Division is to refuel in Colombo, which will take several days, I would submit for your serious consideration whether the Australian Government should offer to allow these Australian troops to remain in Ceylon until at least the 70th British Division could arrive and get into battle order, which would be a month or six weeks at the latest.

(6) The question of asking Australia for assistance in this way was not raised in War Cabinet in view of your decision regarding Burma, but as these troops are actually on the spot and their presence there may determine whether we hold Ceylon and so permit the use of battleships for protection of future convoys and lessen the danger of transport of our own troops as well as others, I think that the position from Australia's point of view alone, quite apart from its general effect on the whole strategy against Japan, should be carefully weighed.

(7) The Air Force at Ceylon is weak, but there are fighter reinforcements on the way in aircraft carriers which could reach Colombo during the first week in March. If decision is taken to offer to help in this way, America should be pressed to send by air every available bomber across the Atlantic and Africa to strengthen the position.

(8) If Ceylon is lost, the difficulties of an offensive against Japan and of using either India or Australia as a base for that offensive become very much greater than they otherwise would be.

(9) The offer of this assistance, even though on a temporary basis, from Australia, would relieve the War Cabinet in the United Kingdom of the pressing anxiety and go far towards maintaining the united effort which so far has been achieved.

[AA: A 5954, Box 573]

Curtin's initial response was most unsympathetic, as he doubted whether Page was speaking for Australia's interests. Page replied that he was convinced the statements in this cable did not represent Curtin's personal views. Probably he was right. Curtin was ill on 25 February and it appears that Evatt, the Minister for External Affairs, was responsible for drafting the cable.

Document 209

Curtin to Page   25 February 1942

Cablegram 33   *Most Secret*

I cannot fail to point out to you that your cablegrams give no impression that the Australian point of view regarding the security of the Commonwealth as the ultimate base to be held in the south-west Pacific has been advocated by you. We have certainly had no comments from you on the special information with which you have been supplied. ...

9. Your P.50 repeats for Ceylon the same request made for Burma, which has been dealt with at length. In P.51 there is a statement of views on the importance of holding Ceylon, but nothing about the importance of or capacity to hold Australia.

10. A further reply will be forwarded to you but in the meantime I would put to you the following as personal points of my own:-

(i) Whether it is the defence of Burma or Ceylon there has been no change in the fundamental need for strengthening the local defence of Australia.

(ii) With the collapse of Singapore and the Malay Barrier Australia is laid bare to attack and it is the last main base in the South-west Pacific.

(iii) As the Japanese are now in force in the Netherlands East Indies and Rabaul they are quite as likely to move against Australia as Ceylon, for you indicate in paragraph (2) that there are capital ships available in the Indian Ocean to defend Ceylon.

(iv) Do you consider, if Japan had been an enemy on the outbreak of war, that, with the loss of Singapore and the absence of a capital ship fleet, we would have agreed to send an Expeditionary Force further afield than Malaya and then only with a line of retirement to Australia?

(v) In view of our present world-wide weakness vis-a-vis the Axis there are numerous geographical centres where an A.I.F. or any other Division would be useful. From our point of view there is none east of Suez of greater importance than Australia.

(vi) I have the impression, from the cablegrams and actions such as the unauthorised diversion, the repetition of the request for the 7th Division through you and references to shipping and convoys, that we are going to have difficulty in getting the A.I.F. back to Australia. That is why I put to you at length the relation of the return of the A.I.F. to local defence and the importance of its security as a base for counter-offensive action against Japan. I want you to press this most strenuously.

11. You will no doubt recall that, owing to method of loading, the three flights of ships which include the 6th and 7th Divisions must all go to the same destination.[79]

[AA: A 5954, Box 573]

---

79. Page soon learnt that this method of loading was not so restrictive.

The Australian Chiefs of Staff agreed with Page.

Document 210

Chiefs of Staff Report to Curtin   26 February 1942

Teleprinter Message M.896   Most Secret

...

The Chiefs of Staff endorse the views of the British Chiefs of Staff on the importance of holding Ceylon. They consider Ceylon must be held at all costs. It is of even greater importance to Australian interests than Burma. If the Japanese seize Ceylon they would control the Indian Ocean, and so cut off -
(1) Communications with Australia from the West. This would make it unlikely that the A.I.F. now in the Middle East could be returned to Australia.
(2) India and China from Allied assistance.
(3) Vital oil supplies from Abadan. The Middle East is the only source of oil left, apart from America.

There is no alternative base to Colombo and Trincomalee for the Far Eastern Fleet.

The objections held to diverting an A.I.F. Division to Burma do not apply to Ceylon. In Burma there was grave doubt whether the Division could be landed in time to be effective. This can be done in Ceylon, and although the non-tactical loading of the transports constitutes a difficulty, it is one that can be overcome in a reasonable period of time.

The loss of Ceylon would involve the loss of sea-power in the Indian Ocean, and the maintenance of this sea-power is vital for the successful prosecution of the war, and for the defence of Australia.
[AA: A 5954, Box 573]

Page sent a long self-justification in reply to 'Curtin's' cable of 25 February. There follows a brief extract.

Document 211

Page to Curtin   London, 27 February 1942

Cablegram P.54   Most Secret. Himself alone

...

16. A leading reason why I have devoted so much thought and consideration

to the establishment of cordial automatically working machinery of consultation on all planes between Australia and Britain has been consciousness of the backward state of Australia's defences and the stupendous task she has to defend her continent with so few people. Even with many more people than we have at present in Australia reliance on outside help for machines of war such as special types of aeroplanes, tanks, etc., machine tools and equipment and raw materials not produced in Australia would be inevitable. In the scramble for priority in all these matters where every applicant for arms and ammunition can make a good case the maximum goodwill and feeling that there will always be the utmost co-operation are tremendous assets. Therefore in consideration of the strategic value of Ceylon to Australian and Empire communications I hope that regard will also be paid to this aspect. ...
[AA: A 5954, Box 573]

Document 212

Page to Curtin   London, 27 February 1942

Cablegram P.55   Most Secret.

Further to my telegram P.54. In regard to paragraph 11 of your telegram No. 33,[80] I am informed today on the highest authority that the two divisions have been loaded by brigade groups with the addition in each case of portions of corps and lines of communication units. Diversion of a division could therefore be achieved but would include a proportion of those units.
[AA: A 5954, Box 573]

Page reinforced his earlier arguments.

Document 213

Page to Curtin   London, 27 February 1942

Cablegram P.56   Most Secret. Himself alone.

. . .
(4) ... we have to face the facts that our Australian troops are just at the right spot and at the very moment to save a vital link in Australia's outer defences and lines of communication. While they do this important life-saving job for a month an offer is made to Australia to substitute the same number of American troops to take their place. A month later Australia

---

80. See Document 209.

would have both these Australian and American forces for Australia's defence.

(5) Everyone agrees that Australia is the main base and must be held. This point is proved beyond question in my P.54. To hold Australia and use it as a main base, we must be able to get equipment and munitions out by every available route. For that reason not numerous geographical centres but Ceylon, the only refitting and refuelling base in the Indian Ocean, is vital to Australia and Empire defence.

(6) My P.50 regarding Ceylon made it clear that in view of your decision regarding Burma the British Government was not making any formal request to you for the use temporarily of Australian troops to defend Ceylon. I may say that at 2. a.m. on Thursday morning the Prime Minister [Churchill] woke me to get my opinion of the Governor of Burma's [Dorman-Smith] cable for Australian assistance. I told the Prime Minister that you were considering the question of Ceylon. ...

[AA: A 5954, Box 573]

The Australian Chiefs of Staff reported at greater length in favour of using AIF troops to help defend Ceylon. This report was considered by War Cabinet on 2 March.

Document 214

Report by Chiefs of Staff   28 February 1942

DEFENCE OF CEYLON

...

Effect of Temporary Retention in Ceylon of an Australian Division on the immediate Security of Australia.

10. In terms of time and space, we could have expected to have had four A.I.F. Brigade Groups in Australia available for an operational role by early in April 1942. The diversion of three Brigade Groups, (i.e. one complete division,) to Ceylon means that we will have a Division less two Brigade Groups available in Australia by this date.

11. The risk of this diversion is, in our view, justified. We consider that the immediate danger to the Australian mainland is Darwin, and we do not consider an attack on the East Coast is likely until Moresby and New Caledonia have first been seized by the Japanese and the Anzac Naval Forces defeated, nor on the West coast until A.B.D.A. Naval forces have been eliminated.

Insofar as Darwin is concerned, until the port facilities are restored and air protection is available, we cannot increase the forces in that area unless the land communications are reasonably increased. We can replace the A.M.F. now there by A.I.F., but this is a long process, as it takes approximately one month to move one Brigade Group over the Central Australia L. of C. [Lines of Communication], and then only by the exclusion of a large proportion of stores now so urgently required. The diversion of a division to Ceylon would, in effect, delay the replacement of troops at Darwin a comparatively short period.

12. Turning to the reduction of the reserves in our vital Newcastle — Kembla area, it becomes necessary for us to balance this risk with all that will be implied by the loss of Ceylon. As we have stated above, Moresby and New Caledonia must fall before we are attacked in strength, in addition to which the Anzac Naval Forces must be neutralised or defeated. It must be a matter of opinion how long such operations, if attempted at all, would take the enemy, but it is our view that it is a risk that can be accepted. In the meantime, the balance of 6th Australian Division, of two Brigade Groups, would have arrived in Australia, if it is despatched in the near future.

Conclusion.

13. Should the British Government make a request for the temporary retention of an A.I.F. Division in Ceylon, we recommend that the equivalent of one Division should be retained on the following conditions:-

(a) Despatch to Australia of remaining two Brigade Groups of 6th Australian Division now awaiting embarkation;

(b) The return to Australia of the 9th Australian Division now in Syria at the earliest date;

(c) Provision of maximum possible fighter cover and bomber force in Ceylon and Southern India. ...

[AA: A 2671, 106/1942]

War Cabinet also considered a supplementary minute from Sturdee, giving details of the location of ships bringing AIF troops from the Middle East. Its last paragraph is printed.

Document 215

Sturdee to War Cabinet   28 February 1942

Minute [Supplement 2 to Agendum No. 106/1942]   Most Secret

. . .
"From the information available ... it would seem impracticable to divert anything from the first two flights now at sea, owing to the confusion of marrying up troops with equipment. Consequently it appears that if the United Kingdom Government request some A.I.F. for the garrisoning of Ceylon, it can only come from the third flight of the movement (i.e. two brigade groups of 6th Division), which has not yet embarked from Suez. H.Q. of 6th and 7th Divisions are in the first two flights and both may have already left Colombo."

[AA: A 2671, 106/1942]

Curtin's improving health allowed him again to attend War Cabinet meetings. The decision recorded below probably reflects his presence.

Document 216

Curtin to Churchill [via Attlee] 2 March 1942

Cablegram 160 Most Secret

1. We are most anxious to assist you in your anxieties over the strengthening of the garrison at Ceylon.
2. The President while fully appreciating our difficult home defence position in relation to the proposed return of the A.I.F. was good enough to suggest that he would be glad if we could see our way clear to make available some reinforcements from later detachments of the three divisions of the A.I.F. which have all been allocated from the Middle East to Australia.
3. For the purpose of temporarily adding to the garrison for Ceylon we make available to you two brigade groups of the 6th Division. These are comprised in the third flight of the A.I.F. and are embarking from Suez. We ask that adequate air support will be available in Ceylon and that if you divert the two brigade groups they will be escorted to Australia as soon as possible after their relief. We are also relying on the understanding that the 9th Division will return to Australia under proper escort as soon as possible.
4. As you know we are gravely concerned at the weakness of our defences, but we realise the significance of Ceylon in this problem and make this offer believing that in the plans you are at present making, you realise the importance of the return of the A.I.F. in defending both Australia and New Zealand. ...
[AA: A 5954, Box 573]

Two days later Curtin sent a cable which possibly was meant to emphasise the magnitude of his generosity in offering two brigades for Ceylon's defence.

Document 217

Curtin to Page 4 March 1942

Cablegram 38 Most Secret

. . .
3. We have had appreciations on the defence of A.B.D.A. and Ceylon, but no appreciation about the defence of Australia or the Anzac Area and the plans for their reinforcement, beyond our own efforts to secure the creation

of the Anzac Naval Area and the return of the A.I.F. after the decision not to reinforce Java. ... [W]e have been unable to secure an allotment of fighter aircraft for the New Guinea-Papua area from those in Australia and are suffering grievous losses in our attenuated air force because of the lack of fighters and anti-aircraft guns.
4. You ought to know that until such time as adequate naval and air forces are available, the Chiefs of Staff estimate that it would require a minimum of twenty-five Divisions to defend Australia against the scale of attack that is possible. ...
[AA: A 5954, Box 573]

The two brigades — the 16th and 17th — reached Colombo on 25 March. They were to stay there longer than Curtin expected. On 6 May he told Churchill that he was 'gratified to learn that the Australian troops in Ceylon will be relieved about the end of May'. On 19 June Curtin was told that the brigades would leave Ceylon 'as soon as possible after the 25th June'. Later, Curtin sent the following message.

Document 218

Curtin to Attlee   1 July 1942

Cablegram 351   *Most Secret*

... [T]he Naval authorities advise that the 16th and 17th Australian Infantry Brigades have not yet left Ceylon. As these units are urgently required in Australia in connection with the reorganisation and re-disposition of the Australian Land Forces and as severe acuteness of our manpower position is now being felt in respect of both Military and essential civil activities, it would be appreciated if early advice could be forwarded of the present stage of the arrangements for their return and the probable sailing date.
[AA: A 5954, Box 573]

The brigades left Ceylon on 13 July, disembarking in Australia early in August. By 20 October the 16th Brigade was in action on the Kokoda Trail. The 17th Brigade was flown to Wau in January-February 1943, checking Japanese moves to gain the village and airfield.

17
THE DEFENCE OF MAINLAND AUSTRALIA

Before the war, Australian service chiefs had not paid a great deal of attention to planning for a land campaign in Australia, for the nation's basic defence strategy was that the Royal Navy would protect Australia from invasion. Following the sinking of the *Prince of Wales* and *Repulse* on 10 December 1941, and other Japanese successes, the War Cabinet directed the Chiefs of Staff (Air Chief Marshal Sir Charles Burnett, Lt.-Gen. V.A.H. Sturdee and Vice-Admiral Sir Guy Royle) to report further on the land defence of Australia. Although Australia was not invaded, the editors feel that the planning for this possibility should be treated at some length in this section.

The War Cabinet on 12 December sought comments which the Chiefs of Staff provided on the 15th. We print extracts from this appreciation.

Document 219

Chiefs of Staff Paper No. 1 15 December 1941

CHIEFS OF STAFF APPRECIATION — DEFENCE *Most Secret*
OF AUSTRALIA AND ADJACENT AREAS —
DECEMBER, 1941

...
AREA NEWCASTLE-SYDNEY-KEMBLA-LITHGOW.
2. This is the most important industrial area in Australia, including the B.H.P. Steel works and associated companies without which Australia's munitions factories could not continue to operate. It also contains aircraft production factories and many other industrial concerns engaged in the production of munitions. Located in the area are mines producing the great bulk of Australia's coal supply.
3. SYDNEY, in addition to being the biggest centre of population in AUSTRALIA, is our main Naval base and dockyard. It is also one of the chief links in our chain of sea and air communications.
4. We consider this area of such importance that its defence, to the limit of our capacity, must not be compromised by detachments which we can not subsequently concentrate.

Having this in view, we have given the highest degree of priority to the forces allotted to the defence of the vital area and to those designated for its reinforcement.

Defence of mainland Australia   257

DARWIN.
5. DARWIN is our only main fleet operating base for the allied Naval forces at the Eastern end of the Malay Barrier and contains some 100,000 tons of Naval oil fuel. It is an important air-force station and the main centre for sea and air communication on the line N.E.I., MALAYA and MIDDLE EAST.
6. Replacement of land and air forces despatched to N.E.I. is now being effected.
   Further Army reinforcements are available in Southern Australia to be moved to DARWIN if the need arises.
7. We wish to emphasise that the anti-aircraft defences of DARWIN are relatively strong in comparison to other parts of Australia. Some increase is desirable, but can only be achieved at the expense of the vital area in New South Wales. ...
[AA: A 2671, 418/1941]

Thought was given to getting help from Canada. Although that help was not needed, the following appreciation, prepared for the information of Canadian service leaders, is an excellent summary of Australia's bleak prospects at the end of January 1942, as British Empire troops were retreating from Malaya across the Johore Causeway to Singapore Island.

Document 220

Chiefs of Staff Paper No. 4   29 January 1942

AUSTRALIAN-CANADIAN CO-OPERATION IN   Most Secret
THE PACIFIC — APPRECIATION OF DEFENCE OF
AUSTRALIA AND ADJACENT AREAS

...
RESOURCES AVAILABLE.
...
Army.
8. (a) The forces available ... total five divisions, two cavalry divisions and one armoured division, less its support group.
   (b) With the exception of units at Darwin and in the islands adjacent to Australia, troops are not completely trained or equipped. With the present rate of production, most of the major items of field army equipment can be completed by mid 1942.
   (c) The major deficiencies are as follow:-
      (i) *Tanks.*
          We have available only 10 American M.3 light tanks and a total of

70 mixed infantry and light tanks from British production have been shipped or promised for early delivery.

Local production will not commence until May 1942 and deliveries will then only be slow.

As a result, the armoured division has been equipped on a carrier basis, while the cavalry divisions, due for conversion to armoured formations, remain horsed or motorized.

(ii) *A.A. Guns.*

The rate of production of 3.7" equipments, although the maximum possible, is far short of our requirements. 3 inch 20 cwt. equipments are not yet in production. Bofors equipments are not likely to be available from local production until June 1942 at the earliest, although a few are being allotted from United Kingdom manufacture.

(iii) *R.D.F. [Radio Direction Finding (Radar)] Equipment.*

We have no stocks of G.L. [Anti-Aircraft Gun-laying] or L.C. equipment and rate of local production is very limited.

Air Force.

9. (a) *First Line Strength.*

(i) General Reconnaissance (Bomber)	Hudsons	65
(ii) General Reconnaissance (Flying Boat)	Catalinas	14
	Empire Boats	4
(iii) Light Bombers	Wirraways (Obsolete)	98
	Total:	181

NOTE: Strength above does *not* include R.A.A.F. Squadrons engaged in Malaya, but *does* include 36 Hudsons employed in N[e]therlands East Indies — Darwin Area.

(b) *Reserve Aircraft.*

The following are employed in training under the Empire Air Scheme but organised into Reserve Squadrons. They are war equipped.

(i) General Reconnaissance (Bomber)	Ansons (Obsolete)	153
	Battles ,,	36
(ii) Light Bombers	Wirraways ,,	90
	Total:	279

(c) *Personnel for Crews.*

Although partially trained crews are available in excess of immediate requirements, owing to lack of modern type aircraft crews cannot be trained to operational standard.

(d) *Potential for Training Crews.*

Except for lack of operational training facilities referred to in paragraph (c), the potential for training crews exceeds the requirements in Australia.

FACTORS LIMITING EXPANSION OF RESOURCES.
10. The principal factors limiting further expansion of our resources are:-
   (a) Man power, for which there are heavy competing demands by the Armed Forces, munitions industries, essential civil industry and agriculture;
   (b) Lack of capacity to manufacture major items of equipment such as certain types of aircraft, and engines for tanks and motor transport;
   (c) Other items of equipment, notably A.A. guns and associated stores, production of which is limited due principally to a shortage of machine tools and skilled labour.

PROBABILITY AND LIKELY SCALE OF ATTACK.
11. In order to relate our defensive problem to the resources available, it is necessary to consider the probability of attack and the likely scale thereof.

It is our view that the Japanese will concentrate on the capture of Malaya and the Netherlands East Indies and on the interruption of supplies into China and Rangoon before attempting full scale operations against the Australian mainland. At the same time we consider that they will move southward from the Mandates in order to secure bases from which further operations can be carried out. The first stage in this progressive movement, viz., the occupation of Rabaul, has already been effected.

12. So long as the Malay Barrier holds and the U.S.A. Fleet remains as a threat to the Japanese Sea Line of Communication to the South we consider it unlikely that the Australian mainland is liable to attack other than by sporadic raids by Naval Forces and ship borne aircraft, possibly accompanied by small landing parties for raiding activities. But we can not assume that Malaya and the Netherlands East Indies will hold nor that the U.S.A. Fleet will secure supremacy in the Pacific and we must therefore plan for the maximum scale of attack. The only limitation of the latter is the amount of shipping Japan has available to her. ...

THE INADEQUACY OF OUR RESOURCES TO MEET OUR LIABILITIES
14. The great extent of our vulnerable coast line, particularly on the East, renders inevitable a very large degree of dispersion of our land and air forces. The reserves available are therefore limited in number and are further limited in scope owing to the distances over which they may have to be moved to meet any serious threat.

We are, moreover, compelled to concentrate a large proportion of our land force strength on the vital area of Newcastle — Sydney — Kembla and are left dangerously weak in Queensland, Tasmania and West Australia.

15. In the Islands, the garrisons are inadequate for the scale of attack they may be called on to meet. New Caledonia, for example, requires a garrison approximating one Division with comparable air support. We have so far only been able to send one independent company trained in guerilla warfare.

16. It is clearly beyond our capacity to meet any attack of the weight that the Japanese could launch either on the mainland or in the islands. At the same time, our limitations in manpower and equipment deny us the capacity

to increase our forces to any appreciable extent. Land and air forces can only be sent to increase a garrison at one point by weakening our strength at another.

Any reinforcement, either of land or air forces, provided it is adequately trained and equipped, must increase our security and provide a greater deterrent against attack. ...
[AA: A 2671, 31/1942]

In August 1941 Major-General Sir Iven Mackay was recalled from commanding the 6th Division in the Middle East and was appointed General Officer Commanding-in-Chief, Home Forces. The following memorandum by Mackay was addressed to Forde, Minister for the Army, for consideration and direction. Readers might note that while Mackay devoted three paragraphs to the problem of defending Tasmania and Townsville, he did not mention the defence of Western Australia. Though this document did not prompt an adequate reply from the government, it shows the underlying philosophy governing the deployment of land forces defending the Australian homeland.

Document 221

Mackay to Forde   4 February 1942

Memorandum   *Most Secret*

DEFENCE OF AUSTRALIA

(Memorandum from the G.O.C. in C., Home Forces dated 4th February, 1942, to the Minister for the Army for consideration and direction).

1. Before plans for the collective use of the forces raised in the various Commands can be fully implemented, the concurrence of the Government is required in regard to the portions of Australia which it is considered vital to hold in the event of an attempted invasion by the Japanese.

2. It has already been agreed by the Government, in substance, and announced by the Prime Minister [Curtin] from time to time in broadcasts, that a state of national emergency is not for the future but is upon us now. "Is this action a military necessity for the defence of Australia?" must be the guiding question. All extraneous considerations such as cost, the comfort and convenience of the individual or of sections of the people, must be subordinated to the defence of the country and to the security of the centres and installations which are necessary to our independent existence and vital to our ability to prosecute the war successfully.

3. The above matters are associated with the military principle of concentration of the maximum forces at the vital place and time. Disobedience of this principle, i.e., dispersion of forces, leads to small detachments being

defeated piece-meal, as has already happened during this war, e.g., at Hong Kong and elsewhere. Such a policy results in the whittling away of the forces at the disposal of the C.-in-C., so that eventually he has not sufficient power of resistance left in his hands. It must be understood, therefore, that I must resist such tendency in Australia to the limit of my ability. The desire for dispersion, with its sense of false security, is common in the minds of those with little military training, and is already evident in certain sections of the public and the press.

4. I, therefore, ask for recognition of the principle of concentration of effort by the Government and the application of it in certain directions to be presently stated. Such determination of policy will strengthen the hands of G.Os.C., especially in resisting pressure from local authorities.

5. The system whereby military units in Australia are raised on a territorial basis and, in some instances, are now in training in their own territorial areas, has undoubtedly done much to create the impression that these units are for the sole purpose of local defence in those areas. This impression is particularly strong at the mo[m]ent in areas which appear most liable to attack by Japanese Land forces. In reality most of the Australian coast and many important towns must be left without troops, whilst other troops are likely to be withdrawn from dispositions in which they are now temporarily placed. It should be noted here that my remarks, though referring particularly to attacks of land forces, apply equally to defence against air attack. The main defence against air attack, however, must be provided primarily by the R.A.A.F., the Army providing defence only in the shape of anti-aircraft units.

6. It has been agreed by the Chiefs of Staff and, I understand, had the concurrence of the Government, that the area most vital to the continuance of the war effort of Australia is the Port Kembla-Sydney-Newcastle-Lithgow Area. The importance of Brisbane in the Commonwealth effort has been much enhanced by the decision to develop there an important base for U.S.A. forces, whilst the economic and military importance of Melbourne are recognised. This huge Melbourne-Brisbane region, so vital to hold and extending some 1,000 miles from North to South, has a force of scarcely 5 divisions to defend it, if we exclude the troops in Darwin, Western Australia, South Australia, Tasmania and, in Queensland, to the north of Brisbane. The retention of Melbourne-Sydney will provide security for South Australia, but all the other places mentioned must be looked upon as isolated localities.

7. Tasmania is isolated because of its separation from Australia by sea. Its garrison at present is a weak Infantry Brigade Group. Should the enemy be in a position to attempt invasion of Tasmania, it would hardly be possible, by reason of his command of the sea, and probably air also, to despatch reinforcements to its aid. Therefore, to ensure the retention of Tasmania it would be necessary to place there a sufficiently large garrison beforehand. At least a division would be required to beat off a large scale attack, but such a force could not safely be spared from the defence of the mainland.

8. The isolation of Townsville arises from its distance from Brisbane, 1,000

miles by road, and its poor communications, which are liable to be severed at any time from the sea. As in the case of Tasmania, it would be necessary, in order to hold Townsville, to place there a garrison of not less than one division, a force which could hardly be spared from the defence of the already defined vital region.

9. It would impose a very grave risk to stretch our present forces in an attempt to provide for the complete defence of Tasmania and Townsville and, from the military point of view, such a step would jeopardise the holding of the vital Melbourne-Brisbane area. I do not propose, therefore, whilst the main area remains equally threatened, to attempt to defend either Tasmania or Townsville with more troops than are in those areas now. I consider it undesirable however, for reasons of morale and psychology, to reduce the garrison in Townsville, or to withdraw troops from Tasmania to the mainland.

10. In the foregoing paragraphs I am concerned with dispositions prior to any attempted landing, so that the Army may be best disposed to protect the vital area and to meet the enemy's first thrusts. The action to be taken after any initial landing will naturally be dictated by the circumstances of such landing, but will undoubtedly involve movement and concentration of troops. It is to be anticipated that in these circumstances, both the C.-in-C. and the Government will be pressed to provide local protection by various authorities, but in such cases, only military considerations can prevail.

11. Although the arrival of U.S.A. troops in Australia in considerable numbers would undoubtedly make material changes in the situation, at the moment I cannot foresee precisely what these changes are likely to be. I am, therefore, not taking into account the presence of U.S.A. troops in Australia, but am planning only for the troops at my disposal now.

12. To sum up, I repeat that it is necessary to resist the creation of a false sense of security by dispersion of the very limited number of troops available for the defence of Australia. Any call for dispersion must be resisted if the defeat of our Army in detail is to be avoided. It may be necessary to submit to the occupation of certain areas of Australia by the enemy should local resistence be overcome, and I remind the Government that it may be necessary to accept such a possibility.

I request, lastly, that the Government will either confirm my proposal in para. 9 for the defence of Tasmania and Townsville, or give me some further direction regarding the degree of such defence.

[AA: A 2671, 96/1942]

Forde, who represented a central Queensland seat in the House of Representatives, was alarmed at Mackay's advice to concentrate military effort along a line stretching from Melbourne to Brisbane. Sturdee, the CGS, concurred generally with Mackay's view, but Forde prepared a submission for the War Cabinet which contained the following key paragraph.

Document 222

Forde to War Cabinet   17 February 1942

Paper   *Most Secret*

DEFENCE OF AUSTRALIA

. . .
The Govt. Policy That is Recommended for Adoption.
5. While admitting that in the strategical and operational field, full weight must be given to these experienced military advisers, it is the duty of the Government to define the broad lines of policy on which they should operate. I recommend, therefore, that the policy of the Government should now be defined as a determination to defend the whole of the populated areas of Australia to the utmost of our ability, and to prevent the enemy by every means within our power from obtaining a foothold on our shores. ...
[AA: A 2671, 96/1942]

The following table, which was presented to War Cabinet, shows the disposition of Australia's land forces in the homeland and adjacent islands in early February. As already noted, these forces were not fully equipped or trained. Only a small proportion of these troops were men of the AIF, as none of the four AIF divisions were then in Australia.

Document 223

APPENDIX III TO WAR CABINET   Not Dated [c. early February 1942]
AGENDUM No. 96/1942

OUTLINE ORDER OF BATTLE A.M.F.& A.I.F.   *Most Secret*
NOT INCLUDING MIDDLE EAST AND MALAYA

A. MAINLAND

Location	Outline O. of B.	Establishment
1. NORTHERN COMMAND (Queensland)	H.Q. N. Comd. 1 Cav. Bde. (of two Regts.) 7, 11 and 29 Inf. Bdes. Two Fd. Regts. each of 24 guns (18-pr. and 4.5 H) One A. Tk. Regt. One Grn. Bn. Coast and A.A. Defences	35,800

2. EASTERN COMMAND (New South Wales)	H.Q. E. Comd. 1 Cav. Div. of 2 and 4 Cav. Bdes.(each of two Regts.) 1 Div. of 9, 28 and 31 Inf. Bdes. (less one Bn.) Newcastle Covering Force of 1 and 32 Inf. Bdes. 2 Div. of 5, 8 and 14 Inf. Bdes. 1 Armd. Bde. Seven Fd. Regts. each of 24 guns (Six Regts. 25-pr., One Regt. 18-pr.) One Med. Regt., of 16 guns (6" and 60-prs.) Four A. Tk. Regts. Two Armd. Regts. Three M.G. Regts. Coast and A.A.Defences	105,200
3. SOUTHERN COMMAND (a) Victoria	H.Q. S. Comd. 2 Cav. Div. of one Cav. Bde. 3 Div. of 4, 10 and 15 Inf. Bdes. 4 Div. of 2 and 6 Inf. Bdes. 1 Armd.Div.(less 1 Armd. Bde.) Seven Fd. Regts. each of 16 guns (18-pr. & 4.5" H) One Med. Regt. of 16 guns (6" and 60-prs.) Three A. Tk. Regts. Two Armd. Regts. Two M.G. Regts. Two Grn. Bns. Coast and A.A. Defences	82,750
(b) South Australia	H.Q. 4 M.D. 6 Cav. Bde.(of two Regts) Two Inf. Bns. One Fd. Bty. of 8 guns (18-pr.) One A. Tk. Regt. One Grn. Bn. Coast and A.A. Defences	20,400

(c) Tasmania	H.Q. 6 M.D.	
	12 Inf. Bde. (of two Bns)	
	One Fd. Regt. of 16 guns	
	(18-pr. and 4.5" H)	
	One A. Tk. Regt. less two Btys.	
	One Grn. Bn.	
	Coast and A.A. Defences	12,450
4. WESTERN COMMAND	H.Q. W. Comd.	
(Western Australia)	13 Inf. Bde. (of four Bns.)	
	One Fd. Regt. of 24 guns	
	(18 pr. and 4.5" H)	
	One Fd. Tp. of 4 guns	
	(18-pr)	
	Coast and A.A. Defences	14,300

NOTES: (1) All Fd. Regts. are equipped to the extent shown.
        (2) All A. Tk. Regts., except two, are equipped with 48 guns. The balance to be equipped in March 1942.
        (3) Cav. Bdes. in all Commands are in process of conversion from horsed to motorised units.

B. ADJACENT ISLANDS

5. NEW CALEDONIA	One Independent Coy.	330
6. NEW IRELAND, NEW BRITAIN and SOLOMONS	One Independent Coy.	330
7. NEW BRITAIN	H.Q. New Guinea Area	
	One Inf. Bn.	
	One 2 pr. A. Tk.Tr.	
	Ancillary Troops	
	Coast & A.A. Defences	1,850
8. MORESBY	H.Q. 8 M.D.	
	30 Inf. Bde.	
	One Fd. Regt. of 16 guns	
	(18-pdr. and 4.5" H)	
	Coast & A.A. Defences	6,500
9. AMBON	One Bn. and Ancillary Troops	1,170
10. DUTCH TIMOR	Two Bns. and Ancillary Tps.	
	One Independent Coy.	
	Coast Defences	2,670

[AA: A 2671, 96/1942]

Although the Australian mainland was not invaded it was, of course, attacked by air and sea forces. By far the heaviest attack was the air raid on Darwin on 19 February 1942. The raid, by about 130 aircraft, was Japan's biggest single air strike since the attack on Pearl Harbor in December 1941. During the Darwin raid some of the defenders displayed great courage. Others did not, and many, including servicemen, fled south. The conduct of the Australians after the raid was so disturbing that the government appointed Mr Justice Lowe of the Supreme Court of Victoria to conduct an inquiry. Our extracts from his report to Curtin deal with the raid itself, not the aftermath.

Document 224

Lowe to Curtin   27 March 1942

Report

FINDINGS OF COMMISSION OF INQUIRY

. . .

THE RAIDS

The first raid commenced just before 10 a.m. ... A number of high altitude bombers came in from the south-east of the town, flying in a "V" formation and at a height which was variously estimated by witnesses but was probably not less than 15,000 feet. One formation consisted of 27 bombers. The bombing was that which is known as pattern bombing in which the individual machines drop their bombs at a signal from the Squadron Leader.

The first bombs fell over the harbour. Having completed their run this group of bombers after a circuit returned and dropped bombs again in pattern over the town. Much difference of opinion was expressed by witnesses as to the number of machines engaged in this attack. I am inclined to think that the view of Air Marshal Williams[81] is correct and that the number of high altitude bombers did not much (if at all) exceed 27.

After the high altitude bombers there came a number of dive bombers escorted by fighters, and these attacked the shipping in the harbour. The number of dive bombers and fighters is uncertain, but I think it probable that Air Marshal Williams is correct in his view that the total number of high altitude dive bombers and fighters did not exceed 50. The cause of confusion lies I think in the impression conveyed to witnesses that the same squadron returning for another run was an added group of enemy planes. An attack was also made about the same time by enemy machines on the R.A.A.F. aerodrome and on the civil aerodrome, and by machine-gun fire on the hospital at Berrima some 9 miles from the town, and in each case a good deal of damage was done which I shall presently particularise. The "All-clear" was sounded about 10.40 a.m.

---

81. Air Vice Marshal Williams was returning from London by air and had been delayed in Darwin by bad weather.

THE DAMAGE

(a) *On Water*: The attack upon the harbour caused great damage to installations and shipping. ... Alongside the inner limb of the pier when the raid started were berthed the "Neptuna" and the "Barossa". The "Neptuna" had among her cargo a quantity of explosives. She was set on fire by enemy bombs, as was also the "Barossa" on the opposite side of the pier. After the enemy planes had departed the "Neptuna" blew up and caused the destruction of a large section of the inner limb of the pier, and it is probable, too, that the "Barossa" was injured by this explosion. ...

Other ships lost in addition to the "Neptuna" were the "Zealandia", the "Meigs", the "Maunaloa", the "British Motorist" and the U.S.S. Destroyer "Peary". Ships damaged were the "Barossa", the "Port Mar" (U.S.), and the hospital ship "Manunda". ...

(c) *On Land*: On land the Administrator's office was hit by an enemy bomb and is a total loss. ... The Police Barracks are a total loss, together with the Police Station and the Government Offices attached. The Post Office, the Telegraph Office, the Cable Office and the Postmaster's residence all suffered either by a direct hit or blast and are a complete loss. The Civil Hospital was much damaged.... There was some damage done to two or three private residences which are probably also to be counted a complete loss. ...

A second raid occurred about 11.55 a.m. and lasted for about 20–25 minutes. This raid was by upwards of 27 heavy bombers which flew at a great height and indulged in pattern bombing, more than 200 bombs being dropped according to one observer. These bombers were unescorted by fighters. This raid caused much damage to the surface of the R.A.A.F. Station and to the Hospital thereon. No attempt was made in the second raid to bomb the town or the port.

(d) *The Aerodrome*: I have not sought to discriminate between the damage done on the R.A.A.F. Station by these two raids. The hangars and repairs shops were destroyed, the hospital damaged, and damage was also done to the hutments. The losses in aircraft were as follow:-

Australian ..	6 Hudsons destroyed on the ground,
	1 Hudson in hangar badly damaged,
	1 Wirraway badly damaged.
American ..	8 P.40's [Kittyhawks] destroyed in the air,
	2 P.40's destroyed on the ground,
	1 B.24 [Liberator] destroyed on the ground,
	1 P.40 damaged in the air. ...

LOSS OF LIFE

... It is impossible to spea[k] with certainty of the number of people who lost their lives, but I am satisfied that the number is approximately 250, and I doubt whether any further investigation will result in ascertaining a more precise figure. ...

ACCURACY OF BOMBING

All the evidence given before me concurred in the view that the bombing of the Japanese, especially the dive bombing, was extremely accurate. The high level bombing did not achieve the same degree of accuracy, but was moderately accurate and caused a great deal of damage. Air Force officers, however, expressed the view that there were no novel tactics displayed and that the performance of the Japanese aircraft was not beyond their expectations. All these officers insisted that the accuracy was due to lack of effective opposition by our own Forces, rather than to any specially high qualities displayed by the Japanese. ...

WARNING OF THE RAID

There was a general con[s]ensus of opinion that the general alarm sounded [preceded] the falling of the first bomb by a very short space of time, probably seconds. A warning that a large number of aircraft had been observed passing overhead at a great height over Bathurst Island and were proceeding southward, was received by the officer-in-charge of the Amalgamated Wireless Postal Radio Station at Darwin at 9.35 on the morning of the 19th February. That officer repeated the message to R.A.A.F. Operations at 9.37. No general alarm was given in the town until just before 10 o'clock.

Evidence was given before me that according to the routine usually observed, R.A.A.F. Operations would communicate a message to A.C.H. (Area Command Headquarters) and that A.C.H. would communicate to Navy and Army Headquarters. R.A.A.F. Operations would also, in the normal routine, communicate a message to A.R.P. [Air Raid Precautions] Headquarters.

On full consideration of the evidence, I find that the failure by R.A.A.F. Operations to communicate with A.R.P. Headquarters is inexplicable. The excuse given in evidence for the delay was based upon the fact that earlier that morning a number of U.S. planes — P.40's — had set out for Koepang and, meeting with adverse weather, had returned. Some discussion, it is said, ensued as to whether the planes referred to in the above message were the American planes returning or enemy planes, and that this discussion accounted for the greater part of the delay which ensued.

I find it difficult to accept this explanation. The evidence now shows almost conclusively that most of the American P.40's had actually landed on the R.A.A.F. station when this message was received, and that the remainder — two or possibly three machines — had remained on patrol at some height. Moreover, the direction from which the planes were reported was not that in which the P–40's would normally be returning. In any event the Station Commander, Wing Commander Griffith, stated expressly that *he* did not consider that the planes flying over Bathurst Island southward might be American planes returning. Another significant fact was the jamming by the enemy of the radio telephone from Bathurst Island after the sending of the above message.

The delay in giving the general warning was fraught with disaster. It is impossible to say with certainty what would have happened if the warning had been promptly given when received by R.A.A.F. Operations at 9.37, but it is at least probable that a number of men who lost their lives while working on ships at the pier might have escaped to a place of safety.

There is much in the evidence, too, which suggests that a warning of 20 minutes or even of 15 minutes might have enabled vessels in the harbour to get under way and move, and to have had a far better opportunity of avoiding the enemy attack than that which in fact they had. A 20 minutes warning might also have enabled the officials at the Post Office who were killed to have gone to a place of safety.

The warning received by way of Bathurst Island was not the only warning received. Military Headquarters received a separate warning through an observation post at 9.50, and there is evidence that Navy Headquarters were notified, possibly from A.C.H., at 9.45.

Much evidence was given in an attempt to fix the precise responsibility for the delay in giving the general alarm, and in tracing the actual communications which passed from R.A.A.F. Operations to other quarters. I have felt that time cannot usefully be spent in the circumstances in determining this matter, but it is plain that the Station Commander must take some responsibility for the failure of action on the part of R.A.A.F. Operations.

There is other evidence to indicate that this particular Service was conducted with some laxity. No log book was kept before 6th February, 1942 and the log book kept after that date discloses a gap in the entries between 16th and 20th February, 1942. ...
[AA: A 2670, 116/1942]

The attack upon Darwin underlined the crisis which faced the country. As press reports began to stress that invasion was imminent, many private citizens wrote to Curtin offering their views. We print letters from opposite extremes of opinion.

Document 225

Letter

40 Evelina Road,
Toorak, S.E.2
Victoria.

March 15th, 1942.
(Prayer Sunday).

Hon. John Curtin, M.H.R.
    Prime Minister for Australia,
        Canberra, A.C.T.

Dear Mr. Curtin,
    You did not start the war, and would never have done so, nor has it sprung from Australian policy. Make terms. Our drawing out will not now let anyone else down. Our being destroyed will not help to save others. There can be no dishonour in retiring from a contest so utterly unequal.
    As leader of a self-governing Dominion you have a right to take action. Act for Australia. Make terms.

Yours sympathetically,

ELEANOR M. MOORE

[AA: CP 156/1, M]

Document 226

Letter

208-A-Egan St.
Kalgoorlie.
24-3-42

To. The Hon. John Curtin.

Dear Sir,
    Having read in todays "Kalgoorlie Miner" of the offer of Mr. T.A. White of Lane Cove; Sydney, to crash a plane load of heigh explosives on to a Jap aircraft-carrier, I am writing at once in the hope that I may be the first West Australian to heartily applaud Mr. White's happy suggestion.
    To you; Sir; as the self constituted dictator of Australia. I offer my services in the same manner as Mr. White has. I am fourty-nine years old, single, with no dependants. You, Mr. Curtin, with the responsibility of the future generation, women, boys & girls, have no right to turn down any possible avenue of defensive precaution possible to take. For the enemy to know that they had to deal with certain death if they approach our shores

would do more to keep them away than any military measures yet taken. I sincerely hope, Sir, that you will give this matter the serious consideration it deserves & for the future welfare of our women & children I hope you will call for volunteers to form a death defying ring around Australia.

Yours Faithfully,

Clem Middleton

[AA: CP 156/1, M]

On 17 March General Douglas MacArthur reached Australia (see following section). This indicated the United States' commitment to Australia's defence, but for the time being the continent's land defence was the responsibility of Australian troops. The following document illustrates the state of readiness of these forces, and of the RAAF in Australia, in the latter half of March.

Document 227

Report to Australian Legation, Washington[82]   20/21 March 1942

Most Secret

. . .

ARMY

Present Strength of Army Forces:
1. ... Their state of readiness may be indicated as follows:-
Infantry Divisions: Five Divisions are reasonably well equipped in respect of artillery and automatic weapons, but are approximately 25% deficient in M.T. Their training has been directly influenced by the amount of equipment available, the flow of which has been gradual. Another three months' training would greatly increase their effectiveness for active operations.
    Training of remaining two Infantry Divisions has been retarded by shortage of equipment.
Cavalry Divisions: Two Cavalry Divisions now temporarily converted into motor divisions are deficient in a very great deal of M.T. and weapons, and their effectiveness for active operations is reduced accordingly.
Armoured Division: This Division is at present equipped as a light armoured division on a carrier basis, and is now capable of operating as such. When tank equipment arrives as promised, it is expected that one armoured brigade will be ready for operations in May and the second in June.
Anti-Aircraft Defences: Practically no light anti-aircraft for either the field

---

82. This report was sent in Cablegram S.W. 21, 25.3.1942.

army or coast defences and vital installations. Such as is available has been allocated for protection of vital air operational bases.

As regards heavy anti-aircraft defences, the field army has practically none but for protection of coast defences and vital installations some 30% of our requirements have been provided.

Expansion of Forces Proposed:
2. Present policy of expansion aims at:-
(a) Completing equipment of existing forces. This is regarded as first priority owing to the immediate Japanese threat to Australia.
(b) Providing adequate anti-aircraft defence for coast defences, aerodromes and industrial establishments.
(c) Providing additional units, particularly anti-aircraft, field and medium artillery, to ensure balanced order of battle organisation.
(d) Providing at first one, and ultimately two, additional armoured divisions by utilising existing A.M.F. armoured units and the conversion of cavalry units.
3. Equipment is the main limiting factor in giving effect to the above policy of expansion. A further expansion in the form of one or more infantry divisions may be practicable, but this will need to be considered in the light of manpower available after meeting present service needs and a gradually expanding munitions production programme. ...

Following are details regarding Air Forces:-
Readiness of Present Air Forces:
As at 15th March 1942, the operational strength of the R.A.A.F. consisted of 21 Squadrons made up as follows:- 8 Hudson Squadrons, 2 Catalina, 1 Seagull-Walrus, 8 Wirraway, 2 Kittyhawk. Nominal establishment of each squadron was Hudson 12 aircraft per squadron plus 6 in reserve, Catalina 6 plus 3, Seagull-Walrus 10 plus 9, Wirraway 12 plus 6, Kittyhawk 16 plus 8. Aircraft actually held were Hudson 71 (deficiency 73), Catalina 13 (5), Seagull-Walrus 17 (2), Wirraway 126 (18), Kittyhawk 42 (6). There is a deficiency of 84 W/T sets for Wirraways, all other operational aircraft being fully equipped with W/T. In addition to above operational squadrons, reserve units consisted of 6 Anson squadrons (establishment 18 plus 9), 6 Wirraway squadrons (12 plus 6), and 2 Battle Squadrons (12 plus 6). These squadrons are up to establishment in aircraft and crews but crews are only partly operationally trained, and W/T equipment is deficient.

Air Formations Being Raised and Estimated Date of Establishment:
2. Plans for expansion of the R.A.A.F. envisage an expansion to a total operational strength of 73 Squadrons made up as follows:- Fighter (Interceptor) 15, Fighter (Long Range) 9, Heavy Bomber 4, Dive Bomber 12, General Reconnaissance Bomber (Land) 4, General Reconnaissance Torpedo Bomber (Land) 7, General Reconnaissance Flying Boat 7, Army Co-operation (Fighter) 5, Transport (Land) 8, Transport (Sea) 1, Fleet Co-operation 1. Formation of additional squadrons will be on a mobile basis as far as possible, and will entail provision of a large number of additional aerodromes and landing grounds for their tactical employment. Subject to delivery of aircraft ammunition and equipment, it is estimated that this could

be achieved within twelve months, and that air crews can be provided from our own training organisation, leaving a balance available for service overseas. If aircraft were available, the expansion could be achieved in approximately six months. This would involve diversion of some training aerodromes to operational use and might ultimately involve provision of reinforcements from overseas to compensate for restricted training facilities in Australia. ...
[AA: A 5954, Box 571]

The government intended to apply a 'scorched earth' policy in the event of invasion. We print extracts from a document of late March which gives some details on how this policy was to be implemented.

Document 228

War Cabinet Paper   Not Dated [c. 29 March 1942]

Agendum No. 182/1942   Secret

DENIAL OF RESOURCES TO THE ENEMY

Directive for Guidance in the Formulation of Detailed Plans
Policy

Denial policy will be implemented under one of two categories, according to circumstances:-

(i) In cities, towns and localities from which the evacuation of the civil population has been ordered and from which the military forces are about to withdraw, a TOTAL denial policy will be implemented, i.e., the complete and total removal or destruction of everything likely to maintain or assist the enemy in his operations.

(ii) In cities, towns and localities in which the civil population is instructed to remain during enemy attack or occupation, a PARTIAL denial policy will be implemented, i.e., certain essential services to enable the population to live will be left intact, together with food supplies. All other services, utilities, vehicles, materials and everything likely to be of assistance to the enemy in his operations will be removed to a safe area or totally destroyed. A reasonable proportion of bulk supplies of food stuffs and clothing, blankets, etc., will be distributed to the inhabitants for concealment and future use, any remaining being removed from the area, or destroyed "in situ." ...

Appendix "A"

Installations, facilities, etc., which should be denied to the enemy:-

1. Naval, Army and Air Force installations, aerodromes, facilities and equipment.
2. Wireless, cable, telegraph stations and telephone exchanges.

3. Petrol and Oil stocks, installation and pumping equipment as well as wells and refineries.
4. Stocks of coal, raw materials, gunny bags, drums, clothing materials, boots, leather, food stocks, and alcoholic liquors. Water supplies and minimum stocks of essential foodstuffs should be left for local inhabitants but latter should, as far as possible, be distributed to the population before withdrawal to avoid bulk supplies falling into the enemy's hands.
5. Harbour facilities, especially bunkering equipment and ship repairing facilities, sources of power to work them and fresh water.
6. Transport facilities, especially road and rail bridges, locomotive repair shops, and all engines and rolling stock, sea and river vessels which cannot be removed.
7. Mine workings and machinery for getting, transporting and refining ores required by the enemy, especially wolfram, lead, zinc, nickel, cobalt, copper, manganese, bauxite, chrome, silver, gold, iron ore and engineering stores therewith.
8. Special attention should be paid to the denial of bicycles, motor vehicles, petrol, oil and producer gas units.
9. In dry areas, particularly North West Australia, Northern Territory and Central Australia, the denial of water will provide a most powerful weapon. Most complete plans are necessary to ensure demolition of pumping machinery and bores or the contamination of stocks of water before final withdrawal of local personnel.
10. Wireless installed in motor cars should be removed and when cars are parked, key and distribution point[s] should also be removed.

[AA: A 2671, 182/1942]

Although Australia was now relying primarily upon the United States for help there remained some expectation that in a dire emergency Britain would send some aid, as is shown in the following message from Churchill.

Document 229

Churchill to Evatt [in Washington][83]   London, 1 April 1942

Cablegram [Not Numbered]   *Most Strictly Secret*

... Following on a suggestion which I heard you had made I have telegraphed to Mr. Curtin telling him that the 2nd British Infantry Division will be rounding the Cape during the latter part of April and early May and that

---

83. The Australian Minister for External Affairs was attending the first meeting of the Pacific War Council in Washington.

the 8th Armoured Division will be following one month later. I have told him that if by that time Australia is being heavily invaded I should certainly divert either or both of these divisions to her aid. This would not apply in the case of localized attacks in the north or of mere raids elsewhere but that he could count on this help should invasion by say eight or ten Japanese divisions occur.

2. We must be careful not to direct our limited reserves to theatres where there will be no fighting. No one knows yet whether Japanese will strike at Australia or India or, even more likely, South China. They have enough for a considerable operation in any one of these directions but surely not in all of them at once. I am by no means convinced that Australia is the chosen target. Once the enemy shows his hand decisions can be made. ...

[AA: M 100]

All the State Premiers met with Curtin, MacArthur, Blamey, Shedden and service leaders at a Prime Minister's War Conference, in Melbourne on 23 April 1942. The following were some of the points made during a long review of the state of Australia and the war.

Document 230

Prime Minister's War Conference Minute   Melbourne, 23 April 1942

(12) *DISCUSSIONS WITH STATE PREMIERS.*

...

6. ... General MacArthur [84] said he thought a large-scale attack on Australia was possible, but not probable. There might be predatory raids, but he did not think a major attack was likely. The enemy's previous operations had been designed to achieve definite objectives — bases, oil, rubber, etc. Moreover, the inhabitants would give no assistance to an invader here. He discounted the possibility of an attack southward from Java, and a carrier-borne attack on the west coast was unlikely, at least until the base at Sourabaya had been reconstructed.

7. Reference was made to the existence of iron ore on the west coast, but it was agreed that the risks involved would not repay a Japanese attempt to exploit it. ...

9. The Commander-in-Chief of Allied Land Forces (Sir Thomas Blamey) then reviewed the position of the land forces, dealing particularly with the reorganisation of the Army and the present disposition of the forces. He pointed out that although the Army had now been given a proper command system, it was by no means ready to fight. The infantry was not much more than 50% equipped, we were very short of motor transport and had prac-

---

84. C-in-C, Southwest Pacific Area: see following section.

tically no tanks, though these were arriving. There was no non-divisional artillery, and we were deficient in engineering and similar units. ...
[AA: A 5954, Box 1]

Less than a fortnight after the remarks printed above were made, Japanese naval forces were turned back at the Battle of the Coral Sea. This was the first of four battles — the others were Midway, Papua and Guadalcanal — which ensured Australia's security from invasion.

From October 1942 E.J. Ward, a minister in Curtin's government, alleged that the Menzies and Fadden governments had approved a plan to abandon large areas of northern and Western Australia without firing a single shot. By May 1943 Ward was claiming that there had existed a 'Brisbane Line', and that the Menzies and Fadden governments had decided to defend only that part of Australia to the southeast of this 'Line'. The charges provoked a controversy which led in June to investigations by a Royal Commissioner, Charles J. Lowe, who earlier had enquired into the Darwin raid. His report lent no weight to Ward's charges; but Ward continued making them until the federal election in August 1943. Perhaps they contributed to Labor's strong polling in Queensland and Western Australia in Labor's electoral triumph.

The 'Brisbane Line' controversy was a political, not a strategic issue, and hence it is not appropriate to document it here. Readers of the documents in this section should be better placed than Australia's citizens in 1943 to judge the worth of Ward's claims.

We print only one cogent document, which is self-explanatory.

Document 231

Mackay to Curtin   6 July 1943

Minute

I request that steps be taken to discontinue use of the term Brisbane Line in connection with a memorandum submitted by me to the Minister for the Army [Forde] on 4th February 1942[85]. Although alleged to be the instigator of it, I had never heard of a Brisbane Line till the present controversy.

The use of this caption has already gained popular acceptance of something which did not exist, and I submit that the erroneous idea of a Brisbane Line should be immediately exploded.

The distorted references to my alleged plans can only be refuted by publication of the secret document in full, but this is obviously not permissible during the war. I see no reason however why this particular memorandum should not be fully discussed when the war is over and done with.
[AA: A 5954, Box 568]

---

85. See Document 221.

18
THE ARRIVAL OF THE AMERICANS

Before the Japanese attack on Pearl Harbor, the United States had shown some specific military interest in Australia and its territories. The Australians did what they could to encourage this interest. In their diplomacy, they sought to obtain from the United States some assurances of help if Japan struck south. Washington made clear that it was interested in the area to Australia's northwest when, on 17 April 1940, it warned Japan not to use force against the Netherlands East Indies. A United States decision to defend the Philippines led, in September 1941, to a pioneering flight of nine Flying Fortresses (B–17s) from Hawaii through Port Moresby and Darwin to Manila. Co-operation between Australia and the United States is illustrated in the following cable from R.G. Casey, Australia's Minister to the United States.

Document 232

Casey to Evatt   Washington, 22 October 1941

Cablegram 877   *Most Secret*

. . .
I have now seen Chief of Staff U.S. Army [Marshall] and Chief of Staff U.S. Army Air Corps [Arnold] and following is broad picture of what is in their minds.

United States is in the process of building up the air strength of the Philippines to an extent that has not been contemplated until quite recently. I have the figures which are formidable but I think safer not to refer them by telegram.

The heavy bombing aircraft in the Philippines will be predominately Boeing B 17's with smaller proportion of consolidated B 24's. The fighting aircraft at Philippines will be nearly all P40.

Air reinforcement of Philippines will not be finally completed until about April 1942, although quite formidable air strength will be there by the end of January.

Five million dollars have recently been made available for General Macarthur for new Army aerodromes in Philippines.

United States has asked Britain to provide at least without delay a new Army aerodrome in North Borneo.

Present route for flight delivery of flying fortresses is Honolulu, Midway, Wake, Moresby, Darwin, Philippines. A number of further squadrons of flying fortresses will be flying this route between now and Christmas.

I believe that consignment of 100 octane petrol in drums is about now arriving at Moresby.

Alternate air re-inforcement route (to avoid Marshall and Carolines) is being organised as quickly as possible via Honolulu Palmyra (with Canton as possible alternative) Samoa, Fiji, New Guinea, Rockhampton (or Townsville if more suitable) Darwin Philippines.

It is unlikely that the island aerodromes on this route will be ready for use before about June 1942.

It is contemplated that above-mentioned aerodromes in Australia will be used as ports of call on re-inforcement route and also for possible operational purposes. With this in view they would like to place their own U.S. supplies of high octane petrol, essential spares, bombs and maintenance mechanics at each of the abovementioned Australian aerodromes.

... General Brereton who is now arriving at Philippines to join General Macarthur is in air charge of South-West Pacific area.

United States Army Command believe that the prospective Philippine air strength will alter the whole of the strategical situation in south-west Pacific and will represent major deterrent to Japan.

It is proposed that heavy bomber squadrons from Philippines should visit from time to time Singapore, Netherlands East Indies, Australia, New Guinea return to Philippines to familiarize pilots with the area and with aerodromes.

I suggested to Chief of Staff U.S. Air Corps that some of their transient fortresses may make a stop at Dilli as silent answer to establishment of new Japanese air route which he thought good idea. Telegraph if you wish me to pursue this, giving me particulars of Dilli aerodrome.

United States Army Air authorities visualize common wireless network for air operational purposes covering Philippines, Singapore, Netherlands East Indies, North Australia. They state that United States is willing to provide any additional wireless stations necessary for the creation of the above-mentioned network which could be used in common by America, British, Dutch and Australian aircraft.

You will realise of course that there is no political commitment on the part of United States in any of the above. ...

[AA: A 981, Pacific 8]

Despite such co-operation, the Australian government was apprehensive lest Japan should strike south, avoiding American territory, and that the United States would remain neutral. So there is little doubt that the most welcome message received in Canberra from London throughout 1941 was the following one. At this time the Japanese fleet was approaching the point at which it would launch its surprise attack on Pearl Harbor.

Document 233

Cranborne to Curtin　　　　　　　　　London, 5 December 1941

Circular Cablegram M.424　　　　　　　　　　　　*Most Secret*

. . .
　The position is that we have now received an assurance of armed support from the United States.
(a) If we find it necessary either to forestall a Japanese landing in Kra Isthmus or to occupy part of the Isthmus as a counter to Japanese violation of any other part of Thailand;
(b) If the Japanese attack the Netherlands East Indies and we go at once to support the latter;
(c) If the Japanese attack us.
2. We have accordingly instructed the Commander in Chief, Far East [Brooke-Popham] that he should take action as he has suggested ... without reference to us if either
(a) He has good information that a Japanese expedition is advancing with the apparent intention of landing on Kra Isthmus, or
(b) The Japanese violate any other part of Thailand.
3. The Commander in Chief, Far East, has also been authorised in the event of a Japanese attack on the Netherlands East Indies to put into operation without further reference to us the plans already agreed with the Netherlands East Indies.
[AA: A 1608, A 41/1/1, Part 25]

　　American interest in Australia grew after the Japanese attack, for it was a vital element in Washington's plans to help the beleaguered Philippines and shore up the crumbling Allied defences in Southeast Asia. Washington's war planners assumed that Japan should not be allowed to put Australia out of the war, either by invasion or by isolating her. Japan's string of successes meant that the United States became increasingly committed to the defence of the Australasian region. On 22 February 1942 General Dwight D. Eisenhower, who on 14 December 1941 had joined the War Plans Division of the War Department as Deputy Chief for the Pacific and Far East, commented: 'Circumstances are going to pull us too strongly to the Australian area'.
　　On 7 December 1941 a US convoy of seven ships, escorted by the cruiser *Pensacola*, was on its way from Hawaii to Manila with reinforcements. It was ordered back to Hawaii, but on 12 December President Roosevelt countermanded this order and directed that the convoy proceed to Brisbane. Every effort was to be made to get the cargo to the Philippines, as the following documents illustrate.

Document 234

Casey to Evatt Washington, 11 December 1941

Cablegram 1135 Secret

As you know a convoy of American ships is likely to be diverted to Brisbane carrying American personnel, aircraft and artillery, previous destination Philippines. You also realise that American Naval Forces and Aircraft are likely to retire to Australia if forced from Philippines. It occurs to me that it would be good to suggest strongly to relevant American quarters here that a shipment of appropriate American ammunition, spare parts and bombs be sent to Australia at the earliest possible moment to enable abovementioned vessels, aircraft and weapons to be employed effectively from Australian bases if need be.
[AA: A 5954, Box 535]

Document 235

Nankervis [Secretary, Dept. of Navy] to Shedden [Secretary of Defence Co-ordination] Melbourne, 12 December 1941

Note Most Secret

I desire to forward for information the following copy of a message which has been received by the Chief of Naval Staff [Royle] from the Australian Naval Attache, Washington [Harries]. The message is dated 11th December.

"CONVOY 4002 (7 MERCHANT SHIPS) ESCORTED BY U.S. CRUISER PENSACOLA NOW IN VICINITY FIJI HAS BEEN ORDERED TO BRISBANE. CONTENTS INCLUDE 2,400 UNITED STATES ARMY AIR CORPS TROOPS[86], 2 FIELD ARTILLERY REGIMENTS, 52 A-24 FIGHTER BOMBERS, 38 TOMAHAWKS. FURTHER DETAILS EQUIPMENT AND SUBSEQUENT DISPOSAL WILL BE SIGNALLED LATER. APPROXIMATE DATE ARRIVAL 16-17 DECEMBER AUSTRALIAN TIME."
[AA: A 5954, Box 535]

---

86. There were 2,000 other troops on the convoy.

Document 236

Harries to Royle　　　　　　　　　Washington, 12 December 1941

Cablegram 1441　　　　　　　　　　　　　　　　　*Secret*

[The cable told Royle that Brigadier General Julian F. Barnes, US Army, aboard the *Pensacola* convoy, was to receive the following message:]

... YOU ARE DESIGNATED AS COMMANDER U.S. TROOPS IN AUSTRALIA WHICH INCLUDE TROOPS IN YOUR CONVOY, THOSE ALREADY THERE AND THOSE TO ARRIVE IN FUTURE. ...

... CONTACT GENERAL [MACARTHUR], U.S. FORCES ... FAR EAST AT MANILA AND PLACE YOUR FORCE UNDER HIS DIRECTION, INFORMING HIM OF UNITS, ARMAMENTS AND SUPPLIES INCLUDED. IMMEDIATELY ON ARRIVAL HAVE SENIOR AIR FORCE OFFICERS ASSEMBLE AND PREPARE FOR COMBAT ALL PLANES. MAKE EVERY EFFORT TO GET THESE PLANES TO PHILIPPINE IS. GENERAL MACARTHUR HAS BEEN REQUESTED TO SEND ADDITIONAL PILOTS TO AUSTRALIA IF PRACTICABLE. IF HE CANNOT DO THIS, CALL ... AUSTRALIAN AUTHORITIES WHO HAVE BEEN REQUESTED TO ASSIST. BEFORE UNLOADING OTHER TROOPS AND EQUIPMENT, CONSULT COMMANDING OFFICER OF YOUR NAVAL ESCORT AND C. IN C. U.S. ASIATIC FLEET TO SEE IF ANY POSSIBILITY OF MOVING TROOPS TO PHILIPPINE IS. IF THIS IS IMPRACTICABLE, UNLOAD AND USE YOUR FORCE AND SUPPLIES AS SITUATION DICTATED WITH FOLLOWING [OBJECTIVES] IN MIND: FIRST[,] AID DEFENCE OF PHILIPPINE ISLANDS. SECOND, AID OUR ALLIES. ...
[AA: A 5954, Box 535]

By mid-December the United States was doing what it could to ferry warplanes *via* Australia to the Philippines. The following three documents illustrate their growing involvement.

Document 237

Casey to Evatt　　　　　　　　　Washington, 16 December 1941

Cablegram 1160　　　　　　　　　　　　　　　　*Most Secret*

General Macarthur has telegraphed appreciation to the War Department, the gist of which is that the retention of the Philippines is the key to the Far Eastern situation. In consequence everything possible is to be done to reinforce the Philippines with fighting and heavy bombing aircraft. It is probably safer not to telegraph the proposed methods of so doing other than to say that, in the process, American fighter (P.40) and heavy bombing (B17 and possibly other) aircraft may be passing through Australia. These will be in addition to aircraft in convoy now approaching Australia of which you know. I have asked for notice of their probable arrival so that R.A.A.F. may be warned.

Above is also additional to heavy bombers which may be flown from Philippines to Australia for reconditioning and return.

United States army air corps is enquiring what air transportation (civil or otherwise) is available in Australia for transport of United States army air corps ground staff personnel, ammunition and bombs from Brisbane to Darwin ex abovementioned convoy. I have said this best discussed with Officer Commanding army air corps troops on arrival although I would relay enquiry as a warning to R.A.A.F. ...
[AA: A 5954, Box 535]

Document 238

Casey to Evatt   Washington, 17 December 1941

Cablegram 1163   *Most Secret*

...
United States is sending "in the next few days" two fast ships (President Polk and President Cooleridge) [sc. Coolidge] from the Californian coast to Australia, containing 125 P 40 fighter aircraft, 5 transport aircraft of D.C. 3 type, together with United States Army Air Corps fourth mobile depot group of about 500 officers and men. Each aircraft will be accompanied by pilot, crew, observer and armourer. Above ships will also carry some ammunition and bombs. The mobile depot group will have hand tools and such other necessary maintenance equipment and machinery as the ships can carry. This depot group is to establish itself at the most appropriate place in Australia (they presume either Brisbane or Townsville) for the assembly of the above-mentioned and subsequent arriving aircraft. Subsequently about 35 or 40 P 40 fighter aircraft with pilots, bombers and ammunition may be expected monthly as reinforcements by subsequent ships.

All of the above fighter aircraft are destined on the present plans to fly to the Philippines via Darwin and appropriate stopping places. ...
[AA: A 5954, Box 535]

Document 239

Casey to Evatt								Washington, 18 December 1941

Cablegram 1173								Most Secret

. . .

United States Army Air Corps hopeful you will be able to make available a certain number of transport planes to facilitate rapid transference of stores and ammunition to Philippines. ...

You may already have heard that General Brett who should arrive at Darwin about December 22nd has been appointed in command of all United States military activities in Australia on his arrival, with special reference to rapid transition of aircraft through Australia and thence to Philippines together with necessary stores, spare parts and ammunition. He has instructions to co-operate with United States Naval authorities and also authority to take up shipping locally with a view to opening up, if possible, a supply line by sea from Australia to Philippines for such military stores as cannot be carried by air. ...

[AA: A 5954, Box 535]

> In this appeal to Churchill and Roosevelt, Curtin raised the question of an American assuming overall command of Allied forces in the Pacific. Four days after this message was sent Curtin issued his widely-publicised press statement which included the much-quoted sentence: 'Without any inhibitions of any kind, I make it quite clear that Australia looks to America, free of any pangs as to our traditional links or kinship with the United Kingdom'.

Document 240

Curtin to Casey								23 December 1941

Cablegram 1103								Most Secret

Following is telegram ... [t]o (1) President of the United States (2) Prime Minister of Great Britain.
1. At this time of great crisis I desire to address you both while you are conferring for the purpose of advancing our common cause.
2. I have already addressed a communication to Mr. Churchill on the question of Russia which I regard as of great importance in relation to the Japanese war, and which I hope will receive the consideration of you both during the conference.
3. I refer now to a matter of more pressing importance. From all reports it is very evident that in North Malaya Japanese have assumed control of

air and of sea. The small British army there includes one Australian division, and we have sent three Air Squadrons to Malaya and two to N.E.I. The Army must be provided with air support, otherwise there will be repetition of Greece and Crete, and Singapore will be grievously threatened.

4. The fall of Singapore would mean the isolation of Philippines, the fall of N.E.I. and attempts to smother all other bases. This would also sever our communications between the Indian and Pacific Oceans in this region. The setback would be as serious to U.S.A. interests as to our own.

5. The reinforcements earmarked by United Kingdom Government for despatch seem to us to be utterly inadequate especially in relation to aircraft, particularly fighters.

6. At this time, small reinforcements are of little avail. In truth the amount of resistance to Japan in Malaya will depend directly on the amount of assistance provided by Governments of United Kingdom and United States.

7. Our men have fought and will fight valiantly. But they must be adequately supported. We have three Divisions in Middle East. Our airmen are fighting in Britain, Middle East and training in Canada. We have sent great quantities supplies to Britain, Middle East and India. Our resources here are very limited indeed.

8. It is in your power to meet the situation. Should United States desire, we would gladly accept United States Commander in Pacific area. President has said Australia will be base of increasing importance, but in order that it shall remain a base Singapore must be reinforced. ...

[AA: A 5954, Box 535]

1600 kilometres east of the central Queensland coast lay the French possession of New Caledonia. Its strategic importance is spelt out in the following extract. The American high command soon came to share this assessment, so that early in 1942 it sent a large contingent to defend the island.

Document 241

Chiefs of Staff Paper No. 1 15 December 1941

CHIEFS OF STAFF APPRECIATION — DEFENCE OF   Most Secret
AUSTRALIA AND ADJACENT AREAS —
DECEMBER 1941.

. . .

New Caledonia
17. The importance of NEW CALEDONIA is twofold:–
(a) In the hands of the enemy it would provide him with an operating base from which the scale of attack on our vital coastal shipping and shipping in the Tasman Area would be intensified. Danger from sporadic raiding

on the Australian coast would also be increased. This threat would apply equally to New Zealand.
(b) It becomes a link in the chain of joint United States — Australian air bases when aerodrome construction is completed.
(c) In the hands of the enemy, it gives him an essential source of Nickel.

Taking these considerations together, its denial to the enemy is more important than its use by us.

18. The defence of the island itself is a difficult problem. It is some 300 miles in length and landings on either coast at many places should present little trouble. While a force of the order of a brigade group could probably hold the NOUMEA area for a period, it would need a division to prevent occupation of the island by the enemy. This would require to be supported by air forces capable of dealing with strong carrier borne forces which might be brought against the defenders.

19. We have neither the land or air forces or aerodromes needed for a garrison of this magnitude, nor could we maintain such forces with our present resources.

Moreover our problem of making secure the SYDNEY, DARWIN and MORESBY areas will tax our present resources to the utmost.

20. We consider that the despatch of any large garrison to NEW CALEDONIA at present can not be contemplated. Arrangements are in hand for No. 3 Independent Company to leave SYDNEY on 16th December to enhance the morale of the Free French Forces and for demolition purposes.

At the same time, we recommend that this matter be kept under review, and that a garrison be equipped and despatched when existing priorities are completed, should the situation not have changed for the worse. ...
[AA: A 2671, 418/1941]

From the following cable, the Curtin government received indications that the United States intended to defend the 'island chain of communications' between Hawaii and Australia.

Document 242

Casey to Evatt   Washington, 29 December 1941

Cablegram 1229   *Secret*

... U.S.A. Army is determined to get as much air power (plus anti-aircraft guns and troops if necessary) as possible to the South-West Pacific. The general idea, as [Harry Hopkins][87] sketched it, was a large-scale "Air pin-

---

87. Special adviser and assistant to President Roosevelt, 1941–45.

cers" with American bombers based on India and Australia with advanced landing and fuelling grounds protected by fighters. ...

U.S. Army has plans in hand for the stationing of petrol[,] anti-aircraft defence and troops at Canton and at Palmyra and Christmas as alternatives, and is endeavouring to stimulate U.S. Navy to provide Naval protection. Latter will be difficult as U.S. Navy is hard to move after Pearl Harbour experience. ...
[AA: A 5954, Box 535]

The defensive attitude of the U.S. Navy was altered following a shake-up in its command. Admiral E.J. King was to prove to be as forceful a leader as Casey expected.

Document 243

Casey to Evatt   Washington, 1 January 1942

Cablegram 9

. . .
Admiral King was made Commander in Chief United States Fleet in all oceans on December 30th and it is generally hoped and believed here that he will produce more forceful naval leadership. As I have advised you before, United States Navy since December 7th until now has been defensive and non-belligerent, to dismay of United States Army and British. United States Army in particular has keenest interest in maintaining air reinforcement and sea transport route to Australia, and I am playing this card hard. ...
[AA: A 3300, 219]

Under the aegis of Churchill, Roosevelt and their top service advisers at the Arcadia conference, more comprehensive plans were worked out in Washington to defend the islands on the line of communication to the east Australian coast. The Australian government was informed of the latest planning in the following message.

Document 244

Harries to Royle [via Casey]   Washington, 1 January 1942

Cablegram TROPIC 143   *Most Secret*

1. *My Tropic 142*. Following is summary of points brought out at a meeting between Planning Staff of Joint Staff Mission ... and United States Officers

of same level on subject of security of bases in connection with air ferry route across Pacific:
(a) Places considered were Canton, Palmyra, Christmas, Tutuila, New Caledonia.
(b) From point of view of air ferry route, all places were now almost ready for transit of heavy bombers, except Tutuila, in late March, the use of this place was not essential providing one of first three named were held.
(c) The loss of any of three latter places would further jeopardise the security of sea communications between United States and Australia, most important to deny Japanese the nickel from New Caledonia.
(d) Canton, Palmyra, Christmas being reinforced to the limits imposed by the smallness of the island and difficulty of providing water thereon but their efficiency would be largely assisted by operations of United States Pacific Fleet based on Pearl Harbour.
(e) United States marine reinforcements were being sent to Samoa and considerable assistance is being rendered to New Zealand Garrison at Fiji, help to these two places should arrive by late January.
(f) Owing to lack of equipment and even more to lack of shipping little hope was expressed of sufficient assistance in New Caledonia from United States to be of any real value within next two months.
(g) United States Intelligence reported that they had reliable information that a deal had been arranged between Admiral Darlan[88] and Japanese Ambassador to Vichy whereby the Japanese expedition to New Caledonia would be accompanied by a Tokyo force of 200 French from Indo-China to give an air of liberation to the attempt to capture. It was further stated that Japanese had a force amounting to one division in transport now ready in Marshall Islands available to attack New Caledonia, Fiji or Samoa.
(h) Scale of attack of any of these three latter places was therefore assessed at one division assisted by naval and marine landing parties with ample naval and air support, which were as much as two carrier groups, a carrier group being described as an aircraft carrier supported by cruisers and ancillary craft. It was clear that attack could develop at any time after January 10th.
(i) Owing to unsatisfactory nature of defences of New Caledonia, Fiji and Samoa and especially those of New Caledonia the delay which must occur before these defences can be put on a satisfactory basis, again especially as regards New Caledonia and the imminent threat, it was strongly considered that the only real effective counter-measure which we could now take would be the stationing of a strong naval striking force to dispute with the Japanese the command of sea in the areas affected.

2. It is emphasised that the conclusions summarised above are those reached on a lower planning level and matter has still to be considered by directors of the plan before submission to Chief of Staff and there are

---

88. C-in-C of all Vichy French land, sea and air forces in 1942.

already strong indications that difficulty will be experienced in convincing higher United States Naval Authorities of importance of projected step outlined in paragraph 1 above.
[AA: A 5954, Box 535]

Australian-American co-operation for the defence of Australia was raised to a more formal level when senior officers of both countries held a conference in Melbourne on 3 January. General Brett read to participants at this conference extracts from messages he had received from Washington which outlined the policy he was to pursue. One of these extracts follows.

Document 245

Brett to Shedden   Melbourne, 4 January 1942

Letter

For your information I am quoting herewith paraphrased extracts from cables which I have received ...
4. Dated January 2nd -
"The following has been agreed upon by the U.S. and British Chiefs of Staff as a general strategic policy for operation in Eastern theatre (a) To hold Malay Barrier and to define as a line Malay Peninsula Sumatra Java and Northern Australia to operate from this as basic defensive position to see land and air forces disposed in as great depth as possible toward the Barrier in order to oppose any hostile southward advances. (b) To hold Burma and Australia as essential bases for the theatre and Burma to be used in addition as an essential base for the support of China Command to the defence of India. (c) To provide for the establishment of communications through the Dutch East Indies with Luzon and to support the Philippine garrison. ..."
...
[AA: A 2671, 6/1942]

It could be held that in early January America's military planners were paying a reasonable amount of attention to Australia's needs, considering all the other problems they faced. Nonetheless, the Australian government felt the continent was being neglected, as the following paragraphs indicate. When at this stage Britain and America were drawing up the boundaries for theatre commands in the Australasian region, Australia itself was excluded, as mentioned below; but the Curtin government was then assured that Washington had not lost interest in the areas outside the boundary lines.

Document 246

Curtin to Page [for Churchill]   Canberra, 8 January 1942

Cablegram 3A   Most Secret

. . .

It will be evident that with United States of America naval ships and convoys using our ports and Air Forces establishing assembly and maintenance depots and air stations in the Commonwealth, our vital centres will become obvious targets for Japanese attacks. It is observed that definition of South Western Pacific theatre now excludes whole of Australia and important (bases) such as Port Darwin and other centres being used by Americans. Presumably however this added scale of attack is to be borne by our local defence forces which have long been lacking essential supplies promised from overseas. In our opinion strategical and supply aspects are intermingled[.] We alone can present not only our particular viewpoint but needs of our capacity to ensure that support flowing through Australia can be maintained.

Same principle applies to exclusion of Australian waters from American naval zone in the Pacific. Without adequate naval protection line of communication to Australia for American supply ships cannot be maintained. As already pointed out Japanese have only to walk into New Caledonia where they would be astride this line and in a position to launch air attacks on most Northern ports being used (by) Americans for unloading aircraft and other supplies for transit to Darwin and Netherlands East Indies[89]. ...
[AA: M100]

Curtin's fears about New Caledonia should have been assuaged when reading the following cable.

Document 247

Harries to Royle [via Casey]   Washington, 16 January 1942
[Copy to Curtin and Evatt]

Cablegram TROPIC 149   Most Secret

New Caledonia. Paper now approved by British and United States Chiefs of Staff contains inter alia a recommendation as follows:
"Defence of New Caledonia should, in principle, be accepted as an Australian responsibility but that United States should, as a temporary measure, furnish forces as early as possible for defence of the Island, and after meet-

---

89. See Document 241, paragraph 17 (a).

ing the emergency in the A.B.D.A. Area, question of arming Free French troops should be taken up between United States and British Chiefs of Staff as soon as opinion has been received from Australia".

2. United States Army indicated that above decision means a force of about 22,000 men including about 16,000 Infantry, 900 Light Field Artillery, Armed with 12 — 75MM. guns, 800 Medium Field Artillery armed with 12 — 155MM. Howitzers, 2,000 Anti-Aircraft Artillery (Mobile) armed with 24 — 3" Anti-Aircraft Guns and 24 — 50 Calibre Anti-Aircraft machine guns, 520 Coast Artillery armed with 8 150MM. Guns, about 1,500 Air Corps personnel (machines//mutilated group) to come from pool being formed in Australia, miscellaneous service troops.

3. Convoy containing this force is forecast to sail from United States East Coast Port about January 21st: I understand convoy will also contain units other than those due for New Caledonia and will not be tactically stowed. Whole convoy will proceed to Australia where New Caledonian Force will be restowed tactically before proceeding to the Island.

4. Although this Force is earmarked for New Caledonia I understand final decision to send it to the Island will be taken in the light of situation (especially in A.B.D.A. Area) when convoy reaches Australia. United States War Department are particularly anxious about defence of aerodromes in Northern Australia and adjacent Dutch Island from which their Air Forces may be operating although they are fully alive to the importance of securing New Caledonia and the consequences of its occupation by the enemy. You will no doubt see instructions sent to United States Commanding General Australia [Brett] in this regard.

5. ... United States Army Authorities are most anxious for reasons of security that Free French in the Island should not know of this impending reinforcement until a short time before its actual arrival.

[AA: A 5954, Box 535]

Meanwhile, the flow of warplanes from USA continued, for despatch *via* Australia to the Netherlands East Indies. The following message (slightly edited) shows the extent of American reinforcements for Australia in early 1942.

Document 248

Casey to Evatt   Washington, 22 January 1942

Cablegram 126   Most Secret

(1) For your information following is summary of present and prospective land and air force reinforcements for Australia. ...
(2) Already in Australia -
  (a) 2,600 aircorps troops; 2,000 other troops mainly field artillery.

(b) Aircraft; 52 A24 bombers, 130 P40 fighters, 5 CA transports.
(c) 20 75 mm guns.
(3) En route and should all arrive in Australia by end of first week in February -
   (a) 7,000 troops (aircorps, engineers and miscellaneous).
   (b) 162 P40 fighters.
   (c) 10 observation (0.47.) aircraft.
(4) Contemplated (except for aircraft, dates of arrival of which cannot yet be forecast, all following should be in Australia by about end of February) -
   (a) Aircorps personnel to bring total to about 10,000; 400 aircraft warning service (radio detection) troops; about 8,300 anti-aircraft personnel.
   (b) Total of eighty heavy four-engined bombers proceeding by air via Africa or Pacific to India or [Australia]; about eighty medium two-engined bombers; additional fighter aircraft to bring total to 433 fighters but this figure subject to probability of increase.
   (c) 48 3" anti-aircraft guns; 60 60" searchlights; 192 anti-aircraft guns.
(5) Reinforcements for New Caledonia (to arrive probably by about middle of March).
   (a) about 22,000 troops (infantry, field artillery, anti-aircraft, coastal artillery and air corps personnel).
   (b) Probably 2 fighter aircraft squadrons to come from pool in Australia.
   (c) 9 150 mm. guns, 12 155 mm. Howitzers, 12 75 mm. guns, 24 3" anti-aircraft guns, 24 50 calibre anti-aircraft machine guns.
[AA: A 5954, Box 535]

While grateful for the reinforcements it was getting, Australia was constantly asking for more, and impressing the continent's importance upon Washington.

Document 249

Evatt to Casey   22 January 1942

Cablegram 101   *Most Secret*

...
Should Japan secure complete freedom of the seas, the only limit to the forces she could employ against us would be that imposed by the amount of shipping available to her.
... Any reinforcement, provided it is adequately trained and equipped, must increase our security by providing a greater deterrent to attack.
We assume that, if the proposal is implemented American troops would be subject to the Chief of the General Staff [Sturdee] in respect of training and operations.

Apart from the questions of Australian security, Australia is an admirable base for reinforcements for offensive action against the Japanese in the South West Pacific area, and it is desirable that forces available for this purpose should be located here as soon as possible.

The War Cabinet and the Advisory War Council welcome the suggestion that our land forces should be reinforced by American formations. We assume that their full equipment would be provided by the U.S.A. Government. We should like to make it clear that the provision of U.S. troops alone in the strength which you indicate is not of course the sole measurement of our needs. We have, as you are aware, serious deficiencies in aircraft and other equipment about which we have already made representations through our representatives in London and U.S.A.

[AA: A 5954, Box 554]

On 24 January Casey had one of his meetings with President Roosevelt, who responded to Australia's anxieties as indicated.

Document 250

Casey to Evatt   Washington, 24 January 1942

Cablegram 148

. . .

8. [Roosevelt] went on to speak of the convoy carrying American forces for New Caledonia and said that during the next fortnight while they were on the water if it were thought that any other area was in greater need of reinforcements than New Caledonia it would be perfectly possible to divert them to where they could most usefully be employed even to Port Moresby, the necessity to hold which he fully recognised.

9. In general he said that they were doing all they could as quickly as they could. The point was that at present there was not enough aircraft or anything else to reinforce all the threatened points. The United States was straining every nerve particularly to produce aircraft, but for a couple of months there would be substantial shortages in many theatres. He picked out opening sentence of your paragraph 11 and said that "urgent necessity for fighter aircraft immediately" was the cry from every quarter. So far as Australia and the ABDA area was concerned he thought they had done pretty well and gave figures for American aircraft there and what was on the way.

President said that he appreciated your concern but that, looking at the war picture as a whole as he was obliged to do and with knowledge of what was in preparation, he had very little anxiety for the security of Australia itself. ...

[AA: A 3300, 219]

Further evidence that Australia was not being forgotten by its 'great and powerful allies' was contained in the following message from Casey.

Document 251

Casey to Evatt   Washington, 25 January 1942

Cablegram 149

I had discussion with General Marshall (Chief of U.S. Army General Staff) on Prime Minister's telegram... .
He is completely sound on vital importance of South West Pacific war and not only acknowledges but emphasises its importance, and points out the lengths they have gone to in conjunction with British to deflect forces and equipment to South West Pacific that had been destined for other theatres. He instances the fighter aircraft that have gone to Australia that were about to be loaded for Russia; the heavy bombing aircraft (now en route to ABDA area via Africa and Pacific) that were bought and paid for by Britain and which were about to go to Britain and Middle East; the troops that are en route to Australia had been embarked (and which were disembarked, re-equipped and despatched in other ships) for Iceland and Northern Ireland. He points out that the Russians are furious, the North Africa campaign is jeopardised and British plans for the use of their troops that would have been relieved by American troops in Iceland and Northern Ireland have had to be cancelled. Marshall says that all this was planned and set in motion while Churchill was here by collaboration with British and with their ready agreement and help. ...
[AA: A 3300, 219]

The following provides a glimpse of how Casey worked in Australia's interests.

Document 252

Casey to Evatt   Washington, 30 January 1942

Cablegram 180

I think I should tell you something of the background in which I am working here.
In the American Administration everything heads up to the President who retains in his hands all major decisions, although he makes no decisions without consideration and report by his Chiefs of Staff. ...
... [T]he only people worth my while to see are the President, General

Marshall, Admiral King, and General Arnold, as regards influencing the minds of those who control the policy operations and movements of United States forces.

I make a point of seeing Harry Hopkins regularly as he is a close friend and confid[a]nt of the President and lives in the White House. I know him well personally and can talk to him frankly without risk. However, he is a sick man and can only do a few hours' work per day.

In actual fact I see a wider range of people than the above... .

As to seeing the President; he is strictly limited as to the number of people that he sees each day and it is not possible to see him very frequently owing to the many calls on his time. He keeps himself generally very well informed and in particular has a good broad grasp of the position in ABDA area and in the vicinity of Australia generally.

Up to the present I have had no difficulty in seeing Marshall, King, and Arnold whenever I want to and at short notice, although it is considered irregular for a diplomatic representative to see and do business with Chiefs of Staff. I do not think they see any other diplomatic representative other than myself. ...
[AA: A 3300, 219]

With the fall of Singapore, the United States decided that it had to make a bigger commitment to Australia's defence so as to hold the line against the Japanese. This meant a sharp break with previous policy, so that now US ground troops were to be sent to Australia.

Document 253

Harries to Royle [via Casey]   Washington, 22 February 1942

Cablegram TROPIC 181   *Most Secret*

Military reinforcements for Australia.
... Following U.S. Forces due to leave between March 1st and March 12th:
(a) From West Coast in (1) Queen Elizabeth.
(2) Fast convoy of probably three ships. Forty-first infantry division complete with engineers, quartermaster, ordnance and other services (less than two infantry regiments) — 8,350... Air Corps re-inforcements 2,500. Service troops (not of 41st Division) — 650. Probably other miscellaneous troops.
(b) From East Coast in one convoy:
   (1) Infantry regiment of 41st division — 3,450... Tank destroyer battalion — 860. Engineer service and miscellaneous troops — 7,580...
   (2) Also for despatch in convoy in 1 (b) above is a field artillery regiment

(nominal strength 1,330 ... armed with 105 MM. Howitzers) for New Caledonia.
(3) A third infantry regiment of 41st division has not yet had shipping allocated but should sail soon after remainder.
(4) U.S. orders have been definitely given for all units mentioned to move, actual details given above are necessarily tentative but probably accurate. ...
[AA: A 5954, Box 573]

The elevation of Australia's status in US defence thinking meant that a higher-ranking general had to go there. In an epochal decision, MacArthur was ordered to make the move from the Philippines. At the time, the Australian government knew nothing of this order.

Document 254

Marshall to MacArthur   22 February 1942

Radio No. 1078   Secret

From General Marshall to General MacArthur to be seen by decoding clerk only: With reference to the rapidly approaching reorganization of the ABDA area... The President directs that you make arrangements to leave Fort Mills and proceed to Mindanao. You are directed to make this change as quickly as possible.
... From Mindanao you will proceed to Australia where you will assume command of all United States troops.
It is the intention of the President to arrange with the Australian and British governments for their acceptance of you as commander of the reconstituted ABDA area. Because of the vital importance of your assuming command in Australia at an early date your delay in Mindanao will not repeat not be prolonged beyond one week and you will leave sooner if transportation becomes available earlier.
Instructions will be given from here at your request for the movement of submarine or plane or both to enable you to carry out the foregoing instructions. ...
[*The Papers of Dwight David Eisenhower. The War Years*, ed. by Chandler, A.D., Jr. (Baltimore and London, 1970), vol I, p.127, citing OPD Exec 10, item 7a]

While America was preparing to transfer MacArthur from the Philippines, the Australian and New Zealand Chiefs of Staff got together and drew up an appreciation as requested by a meeting on 23 February 1942 of the Advisory War Council, augmented by two visiting New

Zealand ministers, D.G. Sullivan and J.G. Coates. We print some extracts from that appreciation. The Anzac Area mentioned below encompassed Nauru, Fiji, New Zealand, the east Australian coast and east New Guinea. It was formed on 26 January and disbanded on 22 April.

Document 255

War Cabinet Paper 26 February 1942

FUTURE POLICY AND STRATEGY FOR CONDUCT   Most Secret
OF WAR IN THE PACIFIC — AUSTRALIA AND
NEW ZEALAND

APPRECIATION BY AUSTRALIAN AND NEW ZEALAND CHIEFS OF STAFF[90] *— 26TH FEBRUARY 1942*

Present Position:
The present position of the war in the Pacific is that, in the west, Malaya and Singapore have fallen, the Japanese have invaded Burma and are now threatening Rangoon and the Burma Road; in the south west, Borneo, Celebes, Sumatra, Ambon and Timor have been occupied and an attack on Java is impending, Darwin has been attacked by air and an attempt to occupy it is not unlikely; further to the east, New Britain, including Rabaul and New Ireland, are in Japanese hands and the enemy force in that area immediately threatens Port Moresby, New Caledonia and Fiji.
2. The Japanese have decisive air superiority and control of the seas in the areas in which they are operating and there is no present prospect of the main Japanese fleet being successfully brought to action by the fleets of the Allied Nations.
3. Australia and New Zealand are therefore in danger of attack. Their loss would mean the loss of the only bases for offensive action by the Allied Nations against the Japanese from the south east. The fall of Burma would increase their already great importance.
Basis of Planning for Australia and New Zealand:
4. In these circumstances, we think that our planning should be related from the outset to future major offensive operations and with this in view should be directed to securing Australia and New Zealand, not only to maintain the integrity of our territories and people, but also to form bases for offensive action on the part of the United Nations[91] to defeat Japan. The immediate problems that confront us are:-

---

90. W.E. Parry (CNS, NZ), and R.V. Goddard (CAS, NZ).
91. The term 'United Nations' was used during the war to describe those powers allied against the Axis. It appears to have first been publicly employed in a pledge dated 1.1.1942 not to make any separate peace with the enemy.

(1) *To secure the lines of communication from the United States to Australia and New Zealand* by holding New Caledonia and Fiji.
(2) *To prevent the further southward movement of the enemy into Australia,* either from New Britain via New Guinea, or from Timor through Darwin or down the west coast. ...
5. To achieve the necessary maximum effort requires immediate reconsideration of the organisation for allied co-operation in the Pacific in the light of the changed situation. ...
Supreme Commander:
8. We recommend that a Supreme Commander of the Anzac Area should be appointed (preferably a United States officer) and that the Supreme Commander should, *subject only to the strategic direction of the Combined Chiefs of Staff in Washington,* have the following functions:-
(1) To exercise general strategic direction over the land, sea and air forces allocated to the Area.
(2) To allocate within the area the forces and equipment that are available.
...
[AA: A 2671, 118/1942]

On 17 March Curtin was told that General MacArthur had landed in Australia. Roosevelt said he would welcome Curtin's nomination of the General to command all Allied forces in the southwest Pacific. The delighted Curtin immediately agreed. On the 18th, Australia's newspapers proclaimed the joyous news. We print a newspaper report on MacArthur's impending arrival in Melbourne.

Document 256

The Argus [Melbourne] 21 March 1942

GEN. MacARTHUR IN MELBOURNE THIS MORNING

Wants Minimum of Display

Gen. Douglas MacArthur, who has been appointed Supreme Commander of Allied Forces in SW Pacific Area, will arrive at Spencer Street station from Adelaide at 9.30am today.

He will be accompanied by Mrs. MacArthur and his 4-year-old son Arthur, and Brig.-Gen. Richard H. Marshall, who was a member of his staff in the Philippines.

Gen. MacArthur is travelling in a special car on the Adelaide express. A guard of honour of American troops will be at the station, and an Australian Army band will take part in the official welcome.

From the station the General and Mrs. MacArthur will proceed to Menzies

Hotel, where the entire sixth floor has been reserved for them. Numerous offers had been made by private citizens to place their homes at the disposal of Gen. MacArthur. ...

In the United States Army Gen. MacArthur ranks as a full General, and can be distinguished by 4 stars on each shoulder. His car will fly a 4-star flag.

"I came through and I shall return," declared General MacArthur on his arrival at an Australian country town yesterday afternoon.

"The U-S. President ordered me to break through the Jap. line and proceed to Australia for the purpose, as I understand it, of organising American offence against Japan. The primary purpose of this is relief of the Philippines."

General MacArthur was recognised by the public, and there were cheers and cries of "Welcome to Australia" as he turned and walked over towards his wife and 4-year-old son, Arthur.

Smiling and obviously pleased at this unexpected demonstration, General MacArthur walked towards his admirers, saluting them several times. There were shouts of "Goodbye and good luck" as General and Mrs. MacArthur rejoined their conveyance. They were in the town only a few minutes.

General MacArthur inspected a guard of honour of Australian soldiers, and chatted with the major in charge. Moving easily and looking lean and handsome, with the dark sallow complexion that often comes after some years in tropical islands, General MacArthur created a deep impression among those who saw him. ...

MacArthur's stature in the community was enhanced by the aura about him. He was of most impressive appearance and he found it easy to be eloquent when appropriate. Such an occasion was the reception in Parliament House, Canberra, on 26 March. We print extracts from a press report of MacArthur's speech.

Document 257

The Canberra Times   27 March 1942

LEADER'S PLEDGE TO AUSTRALIA

"We shall win or we shall die, and to this end, I pledge you the full resources of all the mighty power of my country and all the blood of my countrymen," declared the Supreme Commander in the South-Western Pacific (General MacArthur) toasting Australia and its leaders at a dinner given him by Members of Parliament last night.

"There is a link which binds our countries together which does not depend upon written protocol, upon treaties of alliance, or upon diplomatic doctrine. It goes deeper than that. It is that indescribable consanguinity of race which causes us to have the same aspirations, the same hopes and desires, and the same ideals and same dreams of future destiny," General MacArthur said.

"My presence here is tangible evidence of our unity. I have come as a soldier in a great crusade of personal liberty as opposed to perpetual slavery. My faith in our ultimate victory is invincible, and I bring to you to-night the unbreakable spirit of the free man's military code in support of our just cause. ..."

MacArthur, with the full co-operation of the local authorities, began to act as the Allied Commander-in-Chief in Australia as soon as he established himself in the country, though it was not until 18 April that he formally took command of Southwest Pacific Area (SWPA). SWPA was created as part of the overall Anglo-American rearrangement of the Allied command system, which is the subject of the following segment. Here we print a less formal document, which epitomises the spirit of the occasion.

Document 258

Curtin to MacArthur   Canberra, 15 April 1942

Letter

The Directive of the Commander-in-Chief.
1. Now that I have received advice from the Minister for External Affairs that you[r] directive has been approved by the President, I have asked the Government's advisers to submit with the utmost expedition a statement of the Australian Forces to be assigned to you and advice of the earliest date on which the new arrangement can become effective. The date is to be arranged in consultation with you.
2. This is a momentous occasion for the peoples of the United Nations. You have received a charter as Supreme Commander not from your own Government alone but also from the Governments of the United Kingdom, Australia, New Zealand and the Netherlands. You have come to Australia to lead a crusade, the result of which means everything to the future of the world and mankind. At the request of a sovereign State you are being placed in Supreme Command of its Navy, Army and Air Force, so that with those of your own great nation, they may be welded into a homogenous force and given that unified direction which is so vital for the achievement of victory.
3. Your directive, amongst other things, instructs you to prepare to take the offensive. I would assure you of every possible support that can be given you by the Government and people of Australia in making Australia secure as a base for operations, in assi[s]ting you to marshal the strength required to

wrest the initiative from the enemy and, in joining with you in the ultimate offensive, to bring about the total destruction of the common foe.
4. We hope and pray that your military efforts may be crowned with great success.
[MMBA: AUST 652, RG4 Box 1]

19
THE NEW ANGLO-AMERICAN GLOBAL COMMAND STRUCTURE, MARCH-APRIL 1942

The collapse of ABDA and continual Japanese successes necessitated a revision of the Anglo-American command structure. This was done in Washington, other capitals, such as London, suggesting changes to the American scheme. Roosevelt cabled America's considered proposals to Churchill on 9 March 1942. By 18 April agreement was reached on an arrangement which, with slight modifications, served the Allies well until victory was won.

The Curtin government heard of the American proposals from Page in London. On 13 March he told Curtin the gist of Roosevelt's suggestions. The following cable does not indicate the final American decision, as the proposals listed by Evatt were changed in several important particulars. The 'middle area' (1(A)(b)) which became a British responsibility stretched from Singapore to Libya, while the US was to share operational control with Britain over the Mediterranean as well as the Atlantic and western Europe. As well, the 'Southern Pacific Area' was not to come directly under Washington.

Document 259

Evatt to Curtin   Washington, 25 March 1942

Cablegram P.M.5   *Secret*

1. At combined United States-United Kingdom Chiefs of Staff meeting this afternoon the following recommendations were made as to war areas of the world:-
(A) The sub-division of the world (outside Russia) into three main theatres:
   (a) Pacific Theatre (United States responsibility)
   (b) Indian Ocean and Middle East Theatre (United Kingdom responsibility)
   (c) European and Atlantic Theatre (joint United States-United Kingdom responsibility)
(B) The Pacific Theatre to be divided into:-
   (a) South-west Pacific area — under General MacArthur
   (b) Southern Pacific Area — directly under Washington, i.e., in effect under Admiral King. Individual commander of this area not yet made known.
(C) The Western boundary of the Pacific theatre will not run down the

actual coast line of Western Australia, but some few hundred miles to the westward of Western Australia.
(D) The boundary between the South-west Pacific area and southern Pacific area — to be (from the south) the 160 degrees line, leaving the Solomon Islands in the south-west Pacific Area (i.e. under General MacArthur.)
(E) China to remain in the Pacific theatre and not in the Indian Ocean and Middle East theatre. ...

[AA: A 5954, Box 474]

Australia and New Zealand both objected strongly at their being in separate theatres. Washington was not persuaded by the following protest.

Document 260

Curtin to Evatt [in Washington]   29 March 1942

Cablegram 10   *Most Secret*

... Our Chiefs of Staff ... have submitted the following report:-
"The Chiefs of Staff are strongly opposed to the proposed subdivision of the Pacific area. ... It is essential to Australia that New Zealand, Fiji and New Caledonia should be in the same area as Australia, because they are all interdependent and from every point of view must be considered together. Australia's line of communications with the United States is through New Zealand, Fiji and New Caledonia, and the most effective and economic use of the forces available to defend the whole area depends upon there being unity of command so that the speedy reinforcement of any points threatened can be effected as necessary."...

[AA: A 5954, Box 474]

The Curtin government feared that the differentiation between SWPA, a US army command, and the rest of the Pacific, to come under a naval commander, could mean that Australia would lack naval protection. Evatt made enquiries in Washington and relayed the reassuring results to Canberra.

Document 261

Evatt to Curtin   Washington, 31 March 1942

Cablegram P.M.S. 20   Most Secret

...

2. It will not be possible for the moment to alter the areas of command assigned to General MacArthur on the one hand (South-West Pacific) and to the American Naval Commander (South-Pacific) on the other, but both Admiral King and General Marshall emphasise that the separation of areas does not in any way mean absence of joint planning and coordination between those concerned. ...

5. King repeatedly emphasises that in no way will he be restricted from coming into General MacArthur's area, and that as time goes on with the cooperation of Marshall and MacArthur, he will strike from island to island in a North-westerly direction with the Philippines as the ultimate objective and I therefore think that this thorny question of relative jurisdiction of commanders will gradually solve itself. ...

7. I feel confident that the appointment of MacArthur will not detract from Admiral King's desire to inflict heavy blows on the Japanese. On the contrary I feel he is determined to match MacArthur. King takes special pride in the success of the recent naval strokes which he has contrived with the main object of diverting the Japs attention from their forward bases. ...

[AA: A 3300, 233]

On 3 April Evatt cabled to Curtin, for formal approval, the draft directives to be issued to MacArthur and to the Commander-in-Chief of the Pacific Ocean Areas, Admiral Chester W. Nimitz. There follows the text of the directive to MacArthur.

Document 262

Evatt to Curtin   Washington, 3 April 1942

Cablegram S.22, Part IV   Most Secret

DIRECTIVE TO THE SUPREME COMMANDER
IN THE SOUTH-WEST PACIFIC AREA

By agreement among the Governments of Australia, New Zealand, United Kingdom, Netherlands and the United States.

1. The SOUTH-WEST PACIFIC area has been constituted as defined in Annex one[92]. Definitions of other areas of the Pacific Theatre are as shown therein.

---

92. Annex One was sent in Part III of this Cablegram. See below.

2. You are designated as the Supreme Commander of the South-West Pacific area, and of all armed forces which the governments concerned have assigned, or may assign to this area.

3. As Supreme Commander you are not eligible to command directly any national force.

4. In consonance with the basic strategic policy of the governments concerned, your operations will be designed to accomplish the following:
(a) Hold the key military regions of Australia as bases for future offensive action against Japan, and in order to check the Japanese conquest of the SOUTHWEST PACIFIC AREA.
(b) Check the enemy advance toward Australia and its essential lines of communication by the destruction of enemy combatant, troop, and supply ships, aircraft, and bases in Eastern Malaysia and the New Guinea — Bismarck — Solomon Islands Region.
(c) Exert economic pressure on the enemy by destroying vessels transporting raw materials from the recently conquered territories to Japan.
(d) Maintain our position in the Philippine Islands.
(e) Protect land, sea, and air communications within the SOUTHWEST PACIFIC Area, and its close approaches.
(f) Route shipping in the SOUTHWEST PACIFIC Area.
(G)[sic] Support the operations of friendly forces in the PACIFIC OCEAN Area and in the INDIAN Theater.
(h) Prepare to take the offensive.

5. You will not be responsible for the internal administration of the respective forces under your command, but you are authorised to direct and coordinate the creation and development of administrative facilities and the broad allocation of war materials.

6. You are authorised to control the issue of all communiques concerning the forces under your command.

7. When task forces of your command operate outside the SOUTHWEST PACIFIC area, coordination with forces assigned to the areas in which operating will be effected by the Joint Chiefs of Staff, or the Combined Chiefs of Staff, as appropriate.

8. Commanders of all armed forces within your Area will be immediately informed by their respective governments that, from a date to be notified, all orders and instructions issued by you in conformity with this directive will be considered by such commanders as emanating from their respective governments.

9. Your staff will include officers assigned by the respective governments concerned, based upon requests made directly to the national commanders of the various forces in your Area.

10. The governments concerned will exercise direction of operations in the SOUTHWEST PACIFIC area as follows :
(a) The Combined Chiefs of Staff will exercise general jurisdiction over grand strategic policy and over such related factors as are necessary for proper implementation, including the allocation of forces and war materials.

(b) The Joint U.S. Chiefs of Staff will exercise jurisdiction over all matters pertaining to operational strategy. The Chief of Staff, U.S. Army will act as the Executive Agency for the Joint U.S. Chiefs of Staff. All instructions to you will be issued by or through him.

Cablegram S.22, Part III   Washington, 3 April 1942

ANNEX ONE

. . .

DEFINITION OF SOUTHWEST PACIFIC AREA
The westerly boundary of the SOUTHWEST PACIFIC Area is the westerly boundary of the PACIFIC theatre, the area including necessary naval and air operational areas off the West Coast of AUSTRALIA. The north and east boundaries of the SOUTHWEST PACIFIC area run as follows: From CAPE KAMI (LUICHOW PENINSULA) south to Latitude 20° North; thence east to Longitude 130° East; thence south to the Equator; thence east to Longitude 165° East; south to Latitude 10° South; southwesterly to Latitude 17° South, Longitude 160° East; thence south. ...
[AA: A 3300, 233]

In the directive to Nimitz the paragraph of most immediate concern to Australia was the following.

Document 263

Evatt to Curtin   Washington, 3 April 1942

Cablegram S.22, Part 2   Most Secret

. . .
4. In consonance with the basic strategic policy of the governments concerned your operations will be designed to accomplish the following:
(a) Hold the island positions between the United States and the SOUTHWEST PACIFIC area necessary for the security of the line of communications between those regions; and for supporting naval, air and amphibious operations against Japanese forces.
(b) Support the operations of the forces in the SOUTHWEST PACIFIC area. ...
[AA: A 3300, 233]

In a cablegram to Evatt on 7 April the Curtin government made several objections to the American proposals. As they stood, MacArthur had unrestricted authority to move Australian troops out of Australian territory. As well, there was no guarantee that the Australian commander of a service could communicate with his own government. The Roosevelt administration agreed with the Australian wishes as soon as it learnt of them.

Document 264

Evatt to Curtin   Washington, 12 April 1942

Cablegram S.37   *Secret*

... I have now been furnished with an official memorandum ... This reads as follows:

QUOTE:

The following is the position of the U.S. Chiefs of Staff:
...
Proposals of the U.S. Chiefs of Staff (for operations in the Southwest Pacific Area) made to the President as U.S. Commander in Chief are subject to review by him from the standpoint of higher political considerations and to reference by him to the Pacific War Council in Washington when necessary. The interests of the nations whose forces or whose land possessions may be involved in these military operations are further safeguarded by the power each nation retains to refuse the use of its forces for any project which it considers inadvisable. Unquote

2. With regard to the right of appeal of a local commander to his own government and the freedom of communication between a local commander and his government:- It was never contemplated by the U.S. Chiefs of Staff that a local commander should be interfered with in any way in communicating directly with his own government in any manner he desired, in fact such action is a direct corollary to the principles already approved by the President and enunciated above.

This communication is explanatory of and should be read in conjunction with the directive to which it thus becomes a part.

The U.S. Chiefs of Staff would be glad to receive your formal acceptance in due course. ...

[AA: A 3300, 233]

20
THE ROYAL NAVY'S RETREAT FROM THE 'MALAY BARRIER'

Earlier sections have considered how Britain sought to maintain its position in the southeast Asian region by the use of seapower based at Singapore; and how Japanese forces ruined that strategy. During the 'time of great crisis' a recurring theme in Australian suggestions to Britain and the United States was that they combine their naval forces to confront the Japanese navy. This idea was pursued despite the loss of Singapore.

An early advocacy of this viewpoint was made by Admiral Royle in a memorandum dated 25 December 1941, in which he commented on the latest appreciation by the UK Chiefs of Staff on the Far Eastern Situation. Royle strongly opposed the British decision to divide its Far Eastern naval forces into two fleets.

Document 265

Royle to Shedden   25 December 1941

Memorandum   Most Secret

UNITED KINGDOM CHIEFS OF STAFF APPRECIATION OF
THE FAR EASTERN SITUATION FOR DISCUSSION
BETWEEN MR. WINSTON CHURCHILL AND PRESIDENT ROOSEVELT

. . .

2. Our primary objective in this Far Eastern war must be to regain control of the sea by the defeat of the Japanese Fleet, and all other objectives should be subordinated to this one.
3. In my opinion a division of our available Naval forces as proposed is strategically unsound, and I consider we should assemble in one place a combined fleet decisively superior in all types of vessel to that of the Japanese, and having done that, force an issue on the Japanese by attacking their Mandated Islands or by other operations. ...
[AA: A5954, Box 578, File — "The Importance of Sea Power in the Southwest Pacific"]

Churchill on 4 January told Curtin that there was no question for the time being 'of providing a combined fleet capable of dealing with the main Japanese Fleet'. New Zealand agreed with Australia's view, her

Prime Minister on 12 January strongly urging upon Churchill the need to concentrate Allied naval forces so as to gain naval supremacy in the Pacific.

In response to a British appreciation, a cable from Curtin to Churchill on 19 March stated the views of the Australian War Cabinet, Advisory War Council and Chiefs of Staff.

Document 266

Curtin to Churchill [via Attlee]　　　　　　　　　　　　　　19 March 1942

Cablegram 208　　　　　　　　　　　　　　　　　　　　*Most Secret*

. . .
5. We are not in entire agreement with the Naval policy advocated in the Appreciation for two main reasons:-
(1) By dividing the Allied Naval Forces into two entirely separate fleets:- one in the Indian Ocean (British) and one in the Pacific (United States), we delay the building up of a sufficiently strong force to defeat the Japanese Fleet at the earliest possible moment.
    (Note: The statement in paragraph 10 — "Allied Naval Forces in the Pacific may approach parity with the Japanese by mid-April" — is not understood.)
(2) The British Fleet is allocated a purely defensive role in the Indian Ocean whilst the United States Pacific Fleet is expected to carry out offensive roles in the Pacific.
    (Note: The same policy was advocated in the A.B.D. conversations which took place at Singapore, and was criticised by the United States Naval Staff.)
6. We therefore urge most strongly an offensive policy involving the formation of an *allied* force of British and United States naval units of sufficient strength to challenge the Japanese Fleet at any moment. ...
[AA: A 5954, Box 578]

Churchill, not surprisingly, was unmoved by the above request, while the Australians did not alter their stand.

Document 267

Review by Shedden						23 March 1942

Most Secret

THE WAR SITUATION FROM THE AUSTRALIAN VIEWPOINT
REVIEW AT 23rd MARCH, 1942
PART I — STRATEGICAL CONSIDERATIONS

1. *Strategical Position.*
    The previous review was dated 26th December, and written before the fall of Singapore. ...
    The Allied Forces have since been either captured or driven out of Malaya and Singapore, and the Japanese are in occupation of the Malay Barrier.
    Japan is now carrying out air raids on Australian territory in the Northwest and North-east and it now remains to be seen whether they move Westwards to India and Ceylon, or Southwards to Australia and the Islands to the East of Australia. It may be possible for them to move in both directions at once, or they may seek to consolidate their position and turn on Soviet Russia in the northern Spring. ...
2. *Defensive — Offensive Measures.*
    ...
    The first essential and most effective step for defence, and to enable the necessary reinforcements and supplies to be brought to Australia for offensive action, is superior naval power.
    The reactions of superior naval power on the enemy's campaign would be -
(i)   It would enable the enemy's sea lines of communication to be raided and ultimately severed.
(ii)   It would render large scale invasion a hazardous enterprise.
(iii)   It would make the maintenance of overseas forces difficult by weakening the flow of reinforcements and supplies to enemy forces in occupied Territories.
(iv)   By attacks, on Japan, it would compel the withdrawal of forces for the defence of the home bases.
    If Japan should attempt invasion by a step to step advance, naval and air power are essential for attacks on convoys and bases, and land forces should be built up to a strength sufficient to offer the maximum resistance and to inflict losses to a greater extent than the capacity of the enemy to replace them. ...
[AA: A 5954, Box 587]

In March, after having achieved its initial objectives, Japan's high command debated its next move. One possibility was to clear the British completely from the Indian Ocean. Though the idea was dropped, in

April a Japanese fleet made a foray into the northeastern Indian Ocean, bombing Colombo and Trincomalee and sinking two British cruisers and an aircraft carrier as well as the Australian destroyer *Vampire*. The Royal Navy's Eastern Fleet was forced to retreat to Kilindini, East Africa.

The Curtin government's concern is shown in the following.

Document 268

Curtin to Churchill [via Attlee]   17 April 1942

Cablegram 252   Most Secret

I wish to let you know with what uneasiness we learnt of the sinking by air attack of the DORSETSHIRE and CORNWALL, which is now followed by the sinking of the HERMES. These unfortunate happenings have been the subject of prolonged and anxious discussion by War Cabinet and Advisory War Council and they raise such vital questions that we feel constrained to ask you for full information as to the cause of them and for an appreciation of the United Kingdom, United States and Japanese position in regard to aircraft carriers types of aircraft carried and views held as to relative efficiency of the aircraft and personnel. We would also ask for a statement of the United Kingdom's immediate and long range policy for combating the Japanese Naval forces.
2. We share with you the anxiety at the repeated naval losses which have been sustained through lack of air support and I should be grateful to have information and advice on this vital matter as early as possible.
[AA: M 100]

Ten days later Curtin received an account of the Japanese fleet's foray into the Bay of Bengal. We print some extracts.

Document 269

Attlee to Curtin   London, 27 April 1942

Cablegram 382

...
I send you the following which has been prepared by the Admiralty in reply to your No. 252.
1. Narrative.
(a)   Position at 4th April. Eastern Fleet including WARSPITE, INDOMITABLE, FORMIDABLE and four 'R' class at Addu Atoll refuelling.

CORNWALL, DORSETSHIRE at Colombo, latter completing refit. HERMES and VAMPIRE at Trincomalee, training.

(b) At 1600 4th April CATALINA reported large enemy force 360 miles South East of Ceylon steering North West. Commander in Chief, Eastern Fleet appreciated enemy intentions to be a dawn raid on Colombo and Trincomalee, and that enemy would then retire to the Eastward. CORNWALL and DORSETSHIRE ordered to leave Harbour and proceed to South West to rendezvous with Commander in Chief Eastern Fleet [Somerville].

(c) In the event, after raiding Colombo, the Japanese stood on towards North West, located two cruisers and sunk them with a striking force of between 40 to 50 dive bombers. Commander in Chief was at this time about 90 miles to the South West and intended to attack with torpedo aircraft at night, but owing to corrupt signal from an aircraft no contact was made.

(d) At 1500 8th April CATALINA reported enemy force 500 miles East of Ceylon and in anticipation of a dawn raid on Trincomalee all ships were ordered to sea. HERMES and VAMPIRE sailed 0100 9th April, but were unfortunately located by an aircraft returning from a reconnaissance of Colombo and were later attacked by dive bombers and sunk. Fulmars, only fighters with necessary range, intercepted attackers but were out-classed... .

5. Near future.

Unknown factor is degree of American action in Pacific which will contain Japanese effort, but Japanese squadron recently operating in Indian Ocean was superior to our anticipated strength in next 3 months.

6. Future policy.

(a) To build up and train the Eastern Fleet with all resources that can be spared. Until then to adopt policy of weaker fleet which is to evade and remain in being while raiding whenever practicable, enemy lines of communication.

(b) To augment with American assistance shore based air strength in India and Ceylon.

(c) Next three months will be critical but when (a) and (b) have been completed, it is hoped that Eastern Fleet will be able to adopt offensive policy in Indian Ocean but action against Malaya barrier involving large scale combined operations is beyond our resources until Germany has been defeated.

[AA: A 5954, Box 571]

So, for the time being, there was to be no British naval shield covering the western and northwestern approaches to Australia. Nor, for over two-and-a-half years, would there be a combined Anglo-American fleet to face the Japanese. In the event, the Americans alone were to wrest naval supremacy from the Japanese.

21
MAKING THE SOUTHWEST PACIFIC AREA SECURE

With the Royal Navy being forced out of the eastern Indian Ocean, and with Australia almost bereft of fully-trained and equipped, battle-experienced troops, it must have seemed to many in mid-March 1942 that SWPA might disintegrate before the victorious Japanese, just as ABDA had done. Fortunately for Australia, and for MacArthur's reputation, SWPA enjoyed a reprieve while the Japanese planned and prepared for their next move. SWPA was made secure because of four Allied victories: Coral Sea (5–8 May), Midway (4–6 June), Papua (July 1942 — January 1943) and Guadalcanal (August 1942 — February 1943). Only one of these victories — Papua — was gained by MacArthur's forces, with Australians playing the main role. Section 23 is devoted to the Papuan campaign. This section deals with other features of SWPA's history during the period when it was being made secure, preparatory to its forces launching a counter-attack to regain Japanese-occupied territory from New Guinea to the Philippines.

To some Australian leaders, the task of making SWPA secure seemed to be jeopardised because London and Washington gave a higher priority to the Europe-Mediterranean-Atlantic areas of operations. Documents 271–276 illustrate differences of opinion over the 'beat Hitler first' strategy.

Some people might have thought that Australia would have a better moral basis on which to urge London and Washington to send further reinforcements to SWPA if Australian conscripts were required to serve throughout MacArthur's command. Curtin came to think that an extension of conscription was desirable, as Documents 288–291 illustrate.

The last documents, 295–302, in this section briefly illustrate the personalities and the personal inter-relationships of the men at the apex of Australia's war effort during the period when SWPA was made secure.

MacArthur and Curtin first met on 26 March 1942, when the former discussed the war in a statement to the Advisory War Council.

Document 270

Advisory War Council Meeting   Canberra, 26 March 1942

INTERVIEW WITH GENERAL DOUGLAS MACARTHUR,
SUPREME ALLIED COMMANDER IN SOUTHWEST PACIFIC

After the Prime Minister had expressed pleasure with the appointment of

General MacArthur to the position of Supreme Commander and had suitably welcomed him, General MacArthur stated :-
Attitude to Appointment.
...
There had been a lot of muddling in High Chancellories, High Commands and right along the line which had been costly to the Allies. He was in full agreement with unified command. ...
Japanese fighting qualities.
The Japanese had given an object lesson in the successful co-operation of their three Services. The Navy, Land and Air Forces had worked as one machine and he had been greatly impressed by their complete co-ordination. The Japanese were formidable fighters. Although the vast number of common soldiers were only one degree removed from savages, they were hard to beat as fighters. ...
Japanese strategy.
The Japanese are at present engaged on what he considers one of the most audacious of military adventures. They have thrown in all they have and intend to count on the weaknesses of others rather than on the strength of their strategy. There have been many vulnerable points in the Japanese communications in the last three months but General MacArthur had been unable to persuade his Government of this fact. The enemy's flanks are still vulnerable and, if pressure is applied with sufficient force, they would have to yield. ...
Importance of Pacific Zone.
There was a great clash between different schools on strategy. The two main schools could be called East and West. The eyes of a large part of the United States and of the United Kingdom are concentrated on the European conflict which they regard as all important. To others, including himself, the Pacific was the area where, fundamentally, a clash between the two groups of opposing nations should take place. The Allies should accumulate sufficient forces in the Pacific to strike a decisive blow in one place. ... To do this the Allies must take chances in other areas. The Commonwealth Government must stand up to their views on the Pacific situation against opposing views which might be held by Mr. Churchill and Mr. Roosevelt. ...
Appreciation to be submitted.
... When the full information which he had demanded, is available, he will present a general strategical conception of what he considers must be done, firstly, to make Australia secure and, secondly, to organise Australia as a base for a great counter stroke. ...
Possibility of Japanese invasion.
It would be a drastic blunder for the Japanese to undertake an invasion of Australia. He did not consider there was sufficient spoil here to warrant the risk. The Japanese, however, have a peculiar outlook. They like to create the impression in the Oriental mind that they are superior to the white man and, for this reason, they might try to overrun Australia. They are always likely to do the unexpected. Although they have treated native races badly,

especially the womenfolk, there are many "anti-white man" natives who would be impressed by a feat such as the conquest of Australia. He inclined to the opinion that our main danger is from raids. In fact, this would be the limit of sound strategy. He mentioned that our anti-aircraft defences were deplorably weak and, if raided, we must take it. ...
[AA: A 5954, Box 3]

The overall Anglo-American strategy of 'beating Germany first' influenced Washington's response to requests from Curtin and MacArthur for further reinforcements. The following extracts illustrate the reaction of MacArthur, and of the Curtin government, to this grand strategy, and its relation to the question of reinforcements.

Document 271

Review by Shedden   19 February 1943

THE OBJECTS OF GLOBAL STRATEGY   *Most Secret*
with particular relation to
THE SOUTHWEST PACIFIC AREA
. . .
Conversations in Washington — December 1941 — January 1942
   In Cablegram No. ET.30 of 28th May 1942, Dr. Evatt reported that, during Mr. Churchill's visit to Washington in December 1941 and January 1942, a written document had been prepared which embodied the agreed grand strategy of the war. The following extracts are taken from the text, which was given in Dr. Evatt's Cablegram ET.31 of 28th May 1942:-
"1. *Grand Strategy*
   (1) At American British Staff Conversations in February 1941, it was agreed that Germany was the predominant member of the Axis powers and consequently the Atlantic and European area was considered to be the decisive theatre.
   (2) Much has happened since February last, but notwithstanding the entry of Japan into the war, our view remains that Germany is still the prime enemy and her defeat is the key to victory. Once Germany is defeated, the collapse of Italy and the defeat of Japan will follow.
   (3) In our considered opinion, therefore, it should be a cardinal principle of American British strategy that only the minimum force necessary for the safeguarding of vital interests in other theatres should be diverted from operations against Germany.
"2. *Essential Features of Our Strategy*
   (4) The essential features of the above grand strategy are as follows:- ...
   (c) Closing and tightening the ring around Germany.
   (d) Wearing down and undermining German resistance by air bombardment, blockade, subversive activities and propaganda.

(e) The continuous development of offensive action against Germany.
(f) Maintaining only such positions in the Eastern theatre as will safeguard vital interests... and deny Japan access to raw materials vital to her continuous war effort while concentrating on the defeat of Germany."

...

[AA: A 5954, Box 578]

Document 272

Curtin to Evatt							Canberra, 6 May 1942

Cablegram P.M. 57						*Most Secret*

...

8. MacArthur is very sceptical about the degree of assistance that will be extended to the South West Pacific area and he expressed the opinion that it would be very difficult to get the President or Mr. Churchill to deviate from the view that all efforts have to be concentrated on knocking out Germany first. He said he could not understand the illusion that with the defeat of Germany Japan would just collapse. She would be in a very strong position either to resist attack or to bargain at any peace conference. In any event it was not the quickest way to win the war. ...
[AA: M 100]

From London, Evatt reminded Curtin as to how Churchill's government viewed the Pacific.

Document 273

Evatt to Curtin							London, 8 May 1942

Cablegram E.4							*Most Secret*

...

[9](1) The trouble here is that continual propaganda and persuasion are needed to keep the Pacific front from being regarded as a side show. So far as I know few if any public speeches have been made in London to emphasise the vital importance of the Pacific. The authorities both here and in the United States grossly under-estimated Japan's strength and the people who blundered in such a matter find it difficult to face up to the true position. ...
[AA: M 100]

While in London Evatt attended a meeting of the War Cabinet in which he and Churchill discussed Australia's position with respect to the 'beat Germany first' strategy.

Document 274

British War Cabinet Minute London, 21 May 1942

W.M. (42) 65th CONCLUSIONS, MINUTE 1. *Most Secret*

... At his Meeting with the Chiefs of Staff in the previous week he (Dr. Evatt) had been informed that the grand strategy of the war, as laid down in February, 1941, was that Germany was the dominant member of the Axis Powers whose defeat we must compass. Notwithstanding the entry of Japan into the war, the view was still held that Germany was the principal enemy, and that, once we had secured the defeat of Germany, the defeat of Japan would necessarily follow. In passing, he observed that the Australian Chiefs of Staff had not had any part in drawing up this strategy.

More recently the British Chiefs of Staff, in an *aide-memoire* on strategy, had stated that the broad strategic policy was that only after Germany's defeat would the United Nations assemble superior forces against Japan. ...

The Australian point of view was that to declare that Germany was the primary enemy and should therefore be attacked first was a thesis which was basically open to doubt. ...

... [Mr. Churchill] said that, since Japan had come into the war, Australia had made a direct appeal for help from the United States, and we had fallen in with Australia's wishes in this matter. The line of demarcation which had been drawn in the Pacific put Australia into the United States sphere. Notwithstanding this demarcation of spheres, we did not, of course, regard our obligations to do what we could to help Australia as being lessened in any way. ... Our strategy must be to use our available forces to meet the main enemy effort, whenever it might be made. At the moment it was not easy for us to forecast where Japan would strike next. ...

The Chief of the Air Staff [Sir Charles Portal] then dealt with the proposal that two Australian and one British Spitfire squadrons should be sent from this country to Australia. Since the aircraft had to be tropicalised, this would mean that they would be sent at the expense of the Middle East theatre, or of Malta. ...

DR. EVATT said that the arrival in Australia from this country of three Spitfire squadrons, including one United Kingdom Spitfire squadron, would have a tremendous effect.

This matter was then discussed by the War Cabinet, and the Ministers present agreed that these three squadrons should be sent as proposed. ... The symbolic effect of sending these squadrons from this country would be very great. Moreover, it must be borne in mind that while there were Aus-

tralian squadrons fighting in this country, and an Australian Division in the Middle East, there were at present no United Kingdom units in Australia.
...
[PRO: CAB 65/30, pp. 51-54]

Here Evatt tells Curtin of his surprise on learning that Britain and the USA had a written agreement to 'beat Hitler first'. In fact, Evatt ought not to have been surprised, as London and Washington had given several indications of their overall strategy.

Document 275

Evatt to Curtin London, 28 May 1942

Cablegram E.T. 30 Most Secret

FOR CURTIN ALONE.

It is now possible to summarize the work of our mission so far as the London end is concerned.
(A) *Grand Strategy of the War.*
(1) I have ascertained that during the visit of Churchill to Washington in December and January last the grand strategy of the war was agreed upon in accordance with Annexure A to this telegram. As I have already suggested the substance of this agreement was that notwithstanding the entrance of Japan into the war Germany would still remain the primary enemy. The strategy contemplated Germany's defeat before that of Japan. In a phrase, it was "beat Hitler first."
(2) The existence of this written arrangement came as a great surprise to myself and, I have no doubt to you. We were not consulted about the matter and neither Page nor Casey ever reported to us about it. Owing apparently to the U.S. Government's desire for secrecy it took some little insistence to get the document here. ...
[AA: A 5954, Box 474]

Blamey, Royle and Air Vice-Marshal George Jones, Chief of the Air Staff, gave their views on the 'beat Hitler first' strategy. They agreed broadly with it, but went on to make the following qualifications.

Document 276

REPORT BY GENERAL BLAMEY, THE CHIEF 1 June 1942
OF THE NAVAL STAFF AND THE CHIEF OF THE
AIR STAFF ON CABLEGRAMS E.T. 30, 31, 32 AND 33
FROM THE MINISTER FOR EXTERNAL AFFAIRS.   *Most Secret*

... We think, however, that Japanese influence upon the final outcome of the war is not yet fully realised and that, in consequence, the policy has been advocated of dealing with Japan when Germany has been defeated rather than that of striking at the Japanese as soon as possible with the strongest forces that can be made available as part of a general plan to defeat our common enemies. While Germany still remains the main enemy, Japan has become a much greater menace than the framers of the policy appear to consider.

2. We draw attention to the fact that, in paragraphs 7 and 10 of Cablegram No. E.T.32, it is recognised that the Middle East and India are strategically one theatre and that a Japanese major success against India would endanger the Middle East. Although it is not mentioned, there is also no doubt that a Japanese attack on Russia's backdoor would be of the greatest assistance to Germany and would directly and materially affect the result in the European theatre.

3. Considerations of this sort point to the conclusion that the war is one and indivisible and that it is not sufficient to adopt a merely defensive policy towards Japan which would allow the initiative to remain with her. An offensive policy against Japan is therefore advocated with a view to bringing about the defeat of Germany as well as Japan. ...

[AA: A 5954, Box 574]

By the time the previous comments had been made the Battle of the Coral Sea (5–8 May 1942) had been fought. A Japanese fleet headed for Port Moresby had turned back following losses sustained from American carrier-borne aircraft. Australian forces played a small role in the battle. The US forces involved were not under MacArthur's command, but came from the neighbouring South Pacific Command. We print no battle reports; but our next extract illustrates the worth of Allied (primarily American) intelligence.

Document 277

MacArthur to Blamey   Melbourne, 1 May 1942

Letter   *Secret*

As you know, information from many sources indicates that the Japanese will very shortly commence a drive southward from the Japanese Mandate Area and from RABAUL towards the islands and mainland in the northeastern sector of this area. Plans have been made for Naval Task Forces and our Air Force to intercept this movement.

I am hoping this will result in the destruction of a portion of the enemy force and that his plans will thereby suffer dislocation to such an extent as to afford an opportunity for our taking a limited initiative. ...
[MMBA: ALF 1]

Although the Japanese fleet was turned back MacArthur felt that Japan would try again. Possibly he exaggerated his fears so as to stress the need for further reinforcements.

Document 278

MacArthur to Curtin   Melbourne, 12 May 1942

Letter   *Secret*

... The entire history of the conduct of the war by the Japanese leads to the belief that the Japanese will continue their offensive action. By a regroupment of forces, the enemy can strike a new blow of the most dangerous potentialities against the Southwest Pacific Area or against India. ...

I cannot too strongly emphasize the need for haste in the development of this defensive bastion. The territory to be defended is vast; the means of communication are poor; the defensive forces are few in number and only partially trained. The enemy, on the other hand, if supported by major elements of his fleet, can exercise control of the sea lanes and consequently can strike with a preponderance of force on any chosen objective. We have present, therefore, in this theatre at the present time all of the elements that have produced disaster in the Western Pacific since the beginning of the war. ...
[MMBA: AUST 21]

As can be seen Curtin, like MacArthur, saw the Coral Sea battle as having provided Australia with only a temporary reprieve.

Document 279

Curtin to Evatt [in London] Canberra, 13 May 1942

Cablegram 62 *Most Secret*

. . .

(IX) If Japan should move in force against Australia and obtain a foothold as threatened to occur last week with the Coral Sea action it may be too late to send assistance. Possibly in the long run the territory might be recovered but the country may have been ravished and the peopl[e] largely decimated. History would gravely indict such a happening to a nation which sacrificed 60,000 of its men on overseas battlefield in the last war and at its peril has sent its Naval, Military and Air Forces to fight overseas in this one. In the defence of Britain after the fall of France there still remained the Navy and Air Force to repel the invad[e]r and the Air Force did so. Australia is not so favourably placed. It is a vast territory with poor communications a small Naval Squadron, a relatively small Army, neither adequately equipped nor fully trained, and a small Air Force. With superior sea power the enemy can bring to bear superior force and can sever or seriously harass the lines of communication for overseas supplies. It is imperatively and vitally urgent to strengthen this base while time and circumstances permit. ...
[AA: M 100]

The Advisory War Council was not enthusiastic about the results achieved in the Coral Sea battle, so giving rise to the following exchange.

Document 280

Curtin to MacArthur Canberra, 16 May 1942

Letter *Most Secret*

1. At the meeting of the Advisory War Council on 13th May, the recent naval and air operations against the Japanese in the Coral Sea and in the North-eastern Sector were discussed. ...
(a) It was felt that the results of the operations were rather disappointing, the more so as we had ample warning of the enemy's intentions, the prospective date of attack and the strength of his forces. With the advantage of this information we should have been able to concentrate the superior strength necessary to have ensured a complete victory. As it was, an opportunity to inflict heavy losses on the enemy was lost.
(b) The question was raised whether the maximum degree of attack by land-based aircraft had been brought to bear to counter-balance the enemy's

superiority in aircraft carriers. It was realised that limiting factors were the distance of the scene of operations from land bases and the lack of aircraft of the right type, e.g. dive bombers and torpedo bombers. ...
2. I wish to make it quite clear that, in raising with you the queries of the Council, there is no misapprehension in regard to the fact that you are accountable for operations to the United States Chiefs of Staff. ...
[AA: A 5954, Box 530]

Document 281

MacArthur to Curtin   Melbourne, 18 May 1942

Letter   *Secret*

I have read with interest your letter of May 16th conveying the analysis of the Advisory War Council with reference to the Coral Sea action. The actual tactical incidents of that battle are not yet fully known even to me and as a consequence no accurate appraisal can be made until the full facts have been reported. In this connection, it should be understood that in accordance with the directives that apply to this area the general control of the naval units was in the hands of naval commanders other than our own. ... Our land-based air forces were under this area's disposition and acted in support of the naval commander. Our Air Commander was directed to attack with all available resources in cooperation with the naval forces. I am frank to admit that I was somewhat disappointed with air operational results.

Any information that may have reached you that we knew accurately the position, strengths and intentions of the enemy is erroneous. These were largely matters of conjecture and dispositions had to be made in preparation for thrusts at several different points. The actual scene of battle was beyond the reach of any but our long-range bombers, the efficiency of which against moving targets is vitiated by the fact that they were designed for high-level bombing. Immediately after the main battle the enemy's transports and naval elements moved to the north and scattered. No opportunity presented itself for any decisive blow against them as a whole. ...

I am sorry that the Advisory War Council feels a sense of disappointment. My own feeling is to the contrary. I believe a very brilliant effort was made which undoubtedly saved Australia from a definite and immediate threat. This was only accomplished by bring[ing] in outside reinforcements which bore practically the entire brunt of the battle. Had these reinforcements not been made available a serious reverse would certainly have resulted. Port Moresby, which was the probable objective, was not even reached by the enemy and his repulse was so decisive that he has not yet been able to regroup his forces to renew the attack. Hope for the enemy's complete annihilation in view of his superior forces could hardly be expected. ...
[MMBA: AUST 26.]

A month after the Coral Sea battle Japan suffered a major defeat at Midway when she lost four aircraft carriers. This was a major turning point in the Pacific war, because with the loss of these carriers Japan no longer dominated at sea, though her armies were as yet unbeaten. We print MacArthur's assessment of Midway's significance.

Document 282

NOTES OF DISCUSSIONS WITH THE Melbourne, 11 June 1942
COMMANDER-IN-CHIEF, SOUTHWEST
PACIFIC AREA

Present: The Prime Minister
 The Commander-in-Chief, Southwest Pacific Area
 The Secretary, Department of Defence [Shedden]
 The Chief of Staff to the Commander-in-Chief
  (Major-General R.K. Sutherland)

(1) *Strategical Policy in the Southwest Pacific Area*
...
2. General MacArthur now stated that he was awaiting more definite information regarding the Japanese losses, particularly in respect of aircraft carriers, before making a new assessment of the situation, as it appeared probable that the Japanese had lost four aircraft carriers. They had consequently suffered a great reduction in their naval and air power and the Commander-in-Chief considered that the security of the Australian defensive position was assured.
3. The Commander-in-Chief then read to the Prime Minister a most secret cablegram which he had despatched to General Marshall, the Army Chief of Staff in Washington, the main points of which were as follow:-
(i) The Coral Sea and Midway Island actions having resulted in a reduction in Japanese aircraft carrier strength, an excellent opportunity was offered for offensive action against the Japanese bases in New Britain and New Ireland. This would force the Japanese back to their bases in their own Mandated Territories. ...
6. Speaking generally, General MacArthur said that the Coral Sea and Midway Island actions had resulted in a transformation of the position in the Southwest Pacific Area, and the security of Australia had been assured. It would now be merely interpreted as a timid cry for help, if we were to persist in demands for assistance for the defence of Australia. ...
[AA: A 5954, Box 3]

Curtin's notes for a speech to a secret session of Parliament on 3 September 1942 made no mention of Australia having been saved by the Battles of Coral Sea and Midway. Instead, he finished in this fashion.

Document 283

NOTES FOR PRIME MINISTER'S SPEECH   3 September 1942

Secret Session   Most Secret

. . .

VIII. *Conclusion.*
48. We can be confident about the future, but the indications are that we are in for a long war. Public morale must be strong, resolute and determined in maintaining the maximum effort and enduring the sacrifices that this will mean. The capacity to "stick it" better than the enemy may, in the last resort, be the deciding factor.
49. We have much to be thankful for. Bombs have fallen in Australia, but no part of the soil of this country has been ravaged by the enemy. The severe adjustment of the manner of our living which is called for by the figures in the Budget Statement is necessary for the maintenance of security and, however upsetting, it will not be as severe as the alternative if we are not prepared to make these sacrifices.
[AA: A 5954, Box 611]

The feeling of security, after Midway, waned a little when the Japanese advanced in Papua (see next section) and provided fierce opposition to the Americans on Guadalcanal. The question of reinforcement was raised again, one particular issue being the role of the 9th Division of the AIF. In the event, this division remained in North Africa until after it had played its part in the victory at El Alamein (October-November 1942).

Document 284

Evatt to Dixon [Australian Minister to Washington]   5 August 1942

Cablegram S.W. 75   Most Secret

. . .

2. The Government, in reviewing recently the question of the future employment of the 9th Division A.I.F., was concerned at the situation arising from the consolidation by Japan of her position in New Guinea and the Solomon Islands, and the present threat to Port Moresby. In view of the position in the Middle East, the Government has agreed to an extension of the period for the temporary retention of the 9th Division, but in doing so it has emphasized the vital importance of the Pacific theatre to Australia and the need for superior seapower and airpower in order both to wrest the initiative

from Japan and to assure the defensive position in the southwest Pacific area. The following observations were made in a cablegram to [Churchill]:-

...

The Government's willing agreement to the temporary retention of the 9th Division in the Middle East is ... conditional on an assurance being given by the United Kingdom Government that ... its representatives in Washington will be instructed to do their utmost to ensure the allotment of the aircraft required for the re-equipment of the R.A.A.F. and the provision, as personnel is trained and squadrons are organised, of the equipment required for the programme of a total of 73 squadrons by June 1943. The case for equipment is supported by the fact that 7,800 trained personnel have been sent overseas under the Empire Air Training scheme. ...
[AA: A 5954, Box 574]

Repeated requests for reinforcements led to this response from the American President.

Document 285

Roosevelt to Curtin   Washington, 15 September 1942

Letter   *Secret*

...
After considering all of the factors involved, I agree with the conclusions of the Combined Chiefs of Staff, that your present armed forces, assuming that they are fully equipped and effectively trained, are sufficient to defeat the present Japanese force in New Guinea and to provide for the security of Australia against an invasion on the scale that the Japanese are capable of launching at this time or in the immediate future. ...
[AA: A 3300, 232]

Australia had little representation in the hardfought Guadalcanal campaign. The coastwatchers played a crucial and glorious role, but the Navy's contribution was brief, and not glorious. *Canberra*, one of Australia's two heavy cruisers, was sunk in a night action in the Battle of Savo Island, in the first days of the campaign. We print some of MacArthur's comments on this loss.

Document 286

Prime Minister's War Conference Minute   Brisbane, 17 August 1942

PRESENT: The Prime Minister.
   The Commander-in-Chief, Southwest Pacific Area.
   The Secretary, Department of Defence.

(40) *Operations in Solomon Islands.*
   The Commander-in-Chief furnished a report on the operations in the Solomon Islands. He stated that 5,000 Marines had been put ashore at Tulagi and Florida, and 10,000 at Guadalcanal. The American casualties were 450 killed and wounded. ...
2. In regard to naval operations... in withdrawing the transports in two groups round Savo Island in a southward direction three Japanese cruisers and destroyers had met the two cruiser patrols, the southern one comprising the "Canberra" and "Chicago", and the northern one, consisting of the "Astoria", "Quincy" and "Vincennes". By the use of star shells the Japanese had been able to get in the first salvos. "Canberra" ultimately sank and the "Chicago" and four of the accompanying destroyers were severely damaged. The other three American cruisers, which were acting as the more northerly covering force, were sunk and certain destroyers were damaged. The losses of crews from these ships were understood to be heavy. It was estimated from intercepts that the Japanese had one and probably two cruisers sunk.[93] The remainder of their forces had proceeded northwards.
3. The Japanese had scored a definite tactical advantage in their attack on the Allied Naval Forces and had had a pronounced naval victory. ...
[AA: A 5954, Box 1]

Document 287

[SHEDDEN'S?] *NOTES OF*   Brisbane, 20–26 October 1942
DISCUSSIONS WITH
COMMANDER-IN-CHIEF, S.W.P.A.

OPERATIONS IN SOUTH PACIFIC AREA —   Most Secret
SOLOMON ISLANDS.

...

6. [MacArthur] repeated the history of the initial landing of the Americans and the loss of the four 8-inch cruisers. He said that the general view of this defeat was that the American and Australian squadrons commanded by Admirals Scott and Crutchley respectively had been handled with great ineptitude. Admiral Ghormley, the Commander of the South Pacific Area, was now being replaced by Admiral Halsey. ...
[AA: A 5954, Box 3]

---

93. In fact, Japanese losses were negligible.

Losses sustained through illness in the Papuan campaign (see Section 23) helped to persuade Curtin that some change was needed in the laws governing conscription for military service outside Australia. On the eve of the war, Parliament had passed legislation which added Australian territory (mandated or colonial) to the Australian homeland as areas within which conscripts could be compelled to serve. By November 1942 Curtin had become so mindful of the problems of 'two armies' (the AIF, which had volunteered to serve anywhere in the world, and the AMF, which could fight only in Australia and its territories), that he proposed to a Special Federal Conference of the Australian Labor Party that the militiamen (conscripts) should be sent further afield in the southwest Pacific. As it passed into law on 19 February 1943, Curtin's proposal meant that conscripts could be sent anywhere in a Southwest Pacific Zone whose northern border was the Equator, and which included all of SWPA except the Philippines, western Java and northern Borneo.

It is impossible to say how far Curtin was influenced by MacArthur in making this move, but the General's interest in the issue is amply indicated in the following extracts.

Document 288

[SHEDDEN'S?] *NOTES OF DISCUSSIONS WITH COMMANDER-IN-CHIEF, SOUTHWEST PACIFIC AREA*

Brisbane, 20–26 October 1942

Most Secret

The Amalgamation of the A.I.F. and the A.M.F.

The Commander-in-Chief said that, though it was nothing to do with him, he would, as an observer, say that there was one serious flaw in the Government's Policy — the failure to amalgamate the A.I.F. and A.M.F. by some formula which, while not giving any credit to the Opposition, would enable the Government to get out of what he felt would become an increasingly difficult position. He thought such a step by the Government to be important in view of the Australian attempts being made to influence American opinion for political reasons. General MacArthur said that the consensus of Army opinion was that a unification of the Forces was desirable. He hoped the Government would not approach him for any opinion as he could not go back on views expressed during the last war and afterwards on the necessity for power to send American troops overseas in defence of the U.S.A., and the need for the Army to be homogeneously organised for this purpose. As his views had been the subject of intense political controversy in U.S.A., they were well known.

2. I explained to General MacArthur the background regarding the Defence Act, Mr. Hughes's referenda during the last war, the policy of the Menzies Government, the pledge of Mr. Menzies at the last election, the outcome of the debate on this subject in Parliament last May, and the Labour Party's attitude towards conscription for service abroad.

3. General MacArthur said that he did not pretend to know the Australian political position, but as an observer he hoped that the Prime Minister would find a way to act and would act quickly. In his view the record of the Curtin Government was the best among the United Nations and this point was the only weakness he could detect.

4. ... He wondered whether it would be possible to produce some formula which might provide that the Government would be empowered to make available to the Commander-in-Chief for service in the Southwest Pacific Area such forces as might be asked for by the latter and approved by the Government. It is to be noted that this idea is not far removed from Mr. Curtin's statement at the 1937 elections, that Australia could not be indifferent to the defence of adjacent islands. ...
[AA: A 5954, Box 3]

As MacArthur makes clear, it was in his interests to belittle the quality of Australia's militiamen, so as to improve his chances of getting more American troops.

Document 289

[SHEDDEN'S] *NOTES ON DISCUSSIONS WITH COMMANDER-IN-CHIEF, SOUTHWEST PACIFIC AREA*   Brisbane, 16–20 January 1943

Most Secret

General MacArthur's Observations on the A.I.F., the C.M.F. and their Prospective Use.

General MacArthur said that it presented a misleading and injurious picture to Washington to talk about the total number of men in the Army in Australia, as only the two A.I.F. divisions could be considered first-class shock troops. The balance were Militia forces and a large number of these were engaged on base and line of communication duties. The result was that Washington looked at the picture of a total figure of half a million men under arms and considered that there were sufficient troops in the Southwest Pacific Area to meet Japanese threats, without further increase in the American Forces.

2. General MacArthur observed also that the number of Australian divisions was being reduced in order to keep the remainder up to strength. The total picture presented was therefore more pretentious than an examination of the facts warranted. The Commander-in-Chief added that he planned to use the 6th, 7th and 9th A.I.F. Divisions in operations in an Allied Expeditionary Force, but he did not consider that the Militia forces were fit for that type of work and would use them for garrison and defence work in the wake of the events of the expeditionary force. I said to General MacArthur that I was sure General Blamey would not agree with his assessment of the

Militia. The A.I.F. and the Militia were the same raw material, the difference, of course, being the fact that the A.I.F. had been raised early in the war on a full-time basis, whereas the Militia had been called up for part-time training only, until full-time mobilisation had been carried out following the war with Japan. There was no reason why, in due course, the Militia should not become as expert as the A.I.F., except for the battle experience of the latter. ...

Amendment of the Defence Act to Enable the C.M.F. to Serve Outside the Present Limits of the Commonwealth.

The Commander-in-Chief was asked whether he had followed in the press the efforts of the Prime Minister to obtain the authority of the Australian Labour Party to amend the Defence Act in order to enable the C.M.F. to serve outside the limits of the Commonwealth. He said that he was very glad to see that the Prime Minister's efforts had been successful and, in his own opinion, the Prime Minister had not moved a day too soon, as he was aware from reports from America that a campaign was being insidiously built up in the United States on this matter, which might have resulted in the defeat of the Australian Government by the threat of withholding American co-operation. He really did not think that any such threat would be put into effect, but such a controversy and the strained relations that would arise would give the critics of the Government a good case with which to attack it. The consequence might be that the repercussions on Australian public opinion would be very adverse to the Government.

2. General MacArthur stated in the strictest confidence that he had received an entirely reliable report that Admiral Leahy, Personal Assistant to the President, had said that if Australia did not remove the limits on the use of its forces in the Southwest Pacific Area, he would urge the President to withhold Lease-Lend assistance to the Commonwealth. ...

[AA: A 5954, Box 2]

In a speech at the New South Wales Labor Party Conference in Sydney in June 1943, Curtin reviewed his reasons for obtaining an extension of conscription.

Document 290

PRIME MINISTER'S SPEECH   Sydney, 6 June 1943

...
"The Labour party's opposition to compulsory service outside Australia had all along been based on the Menzies Government's conception that expeditionary forces to other parts of the world came first. With Labour in power and able to implement its defence policy of priority for local defence, there was a new basis for an entire transformation of Labour's attitude

towards compulsory service in those regions essential for ensuring effective defence of the Commonwealth. It was from this angle that the Government decided that the Defence Act should be amended to enable the Militia forces to serve outside Australia in the South-Western Pacific Zone. When General MacArthur unfolded his plan of operation in the South-West Pacific Area to ensure the security of Australia as a base and to push the Japanese back, it was evident that the Australian land forces must be able to be disposed in any of the islands adjacent to Australia in accordance with the Commander-in-Chief's plan. ...

"Let it be quite clear that there is no future for Australia with its white population, and no prospect of an increasingly higher standard of living, if the Japanese are to remain in possession of south-eastern Asia and the islands surrounding Australia. Australia would live under a perpetual threat of invasion and the burden of armaments would be so heavy that the Australian standard of living would be little above that of coolies. No one should be under any misapprehension that, at the Peace Conference, when the terms are dictated which will determine the future destiny of nations, the most influential voices will be those of the countries which have played their full part in defeating the enemy. The destiny of Australia and its future security may well be determined by the distance we are prepared to go in using our forces to defeat the Japanese. If the experience of this war has shown that the future security of Australia requires greater guarantees in regard to the security of islands adjacent to Australia, Australia cannot demand such guarantees if it is unwilling in war to use its forces in the ejectment of the enemy from these threatened points of attack. ..."
[AA: A 5954, Box 611 (contains printed copy of speech)]

Here, MacArthur takes a somewhat less jaundiced view of the worth of the militiamen.

Document 291

[SHEDDEN'S] *NOTES OF DISCUSSIONS* Brisbane, 25–31 May 1943
WITH COMMANDER-IN-CHIEF,
SOUTHWEST PACIFIC AREA Most Secret

A Homogeneous Australian Army
Now that the Defence Act had been amended to permit the Citizen Military Forces to serve in the Southwest Pacific Zone, the Commander-in-Chief was asked for his views, from the military angle, on the question of a homogeneous Australian Army. General MacArthur said that there was no doubt that, in fact, there should be one Army. However, the advocates of the homogeneous Army did not appear to realise that, in actual practice, it was really impossible. The A.I.F. and the Militia were comprised of the same material so far as the soldiers were concerned, but the officers and non-

commissioned officers of the A.I.F. were much superior. Most of the original officers and non-commissioned officers were specially selected and many others had gained their advancement by proof of qualities for leadership in battle. There were insufficient A.I.F. officers and non-commissioned officers to enable an adequate dilution to be spread over all the Militia Divisions.
2. General MacArthur continued that the A.I.F. had, of course, those unique fighting qualities which alone came from battle experience, but he did not contemplate using the Militia Divisions as offensive troops against the Japanese. They would, of course, prove excellent forces for defensive operations should the need arise, and their standard was constantly being improved by training.
3. Finally, the Commander-in-Chief said it was interesting to know that the A.I.F. did not want the Militia amalgamated with them as a homogeneous Army. Having volunteered for service abroad and having fought abroad and established great military reputations, they were naturally jealous of sharing them with other troops who did not have a similar record.
[AA: A 5954, Box 2]

By March, Japan had been defeated in Papua and on Guadalcanal, and had also lost heavily in the Battle of the Bismarck Sea (see Section 24). SWPA was secure, but Curtin was still anxious for reinforcements to ensure a vigorous offensive. There was a valued addition to SWPA's army in February 1943, with the return of the 9th Division.

In the following cable, Curtin quotes from his most recent review to Parliament.

Document 292

Curtin to Roosevelt [via Dixon]   30 March 1943

Cablegram P.W.25   *Most Secret*

'...
So much for the task of defeating Germany, but what about Japan? She, too, is master of vast territories with large populations and vital resources for the waging of war. Though she has suffered certain naval and air losses, her strength is still great. Like Germany, Japan prepared for this war for years and did not strike until she was ready to do so and considered the situation favourable for success. It should not be overlooked that we are fighting her at places vital to our own security and far removed from her own final ramparts of defence.' ...
[AA: A 5954, Box 579]

MacArthur put his name to many a flowery communique. The following was composed to mark the first anniversary of the fall of Bataan, on 9 April 1942.

Document 293

MacArthur to Shedden　　　　　　　　　　　　Brisbane, 6 April 1943

Teleprinter Message BXC.368　　　　　　　　　　　　　　*Secret*

On April 9 I am giving out the following statement:
"A year ago today, the dimming light of Bataan's forlorn hope fluttered and died. Its prayers by that time, and it prayed as well as fought, were reduced to a simple formula, rendered by hungry men through cracked and parching lips, 'Give us this day our daily bread.' The light failed. Bataan starved into collapse. Our flag lies crumpled, its proud pinions spat upon in the gutter; the wrecks of what were once our men and women groan and sweat in prison toil; our faithful Filipino wards, sixteen million souls, gasp in the slavery of a conquering soldiery devoid of those ideals of chivalry which have so dignified many armies. I was the leader of that LOST CAUSE and from the bottom of a seared and stricken heart, I pray that a merciful God may not delay too long their redemption, that the day of salvation be not so far removed that they perish, that it be not again too late."
[AA: A 5954, Box 579]

In June 1942 Curtin had disagreed with MacArthur in maintaining over the national radio that Australia could still be lost. Indeed, as this press release shows, twelve months were to pass before he publicly reversed such opinion and proclaimed that Australia was now secure against invasion.

Document 294

Press Statement by Curtin　　　　　　　　　　　Canberra, 10 June 1943

Meeting with General MacArthur

. . .
　The holding war imposed on us under circumstances of great difficulty has been an obligation under global strategy which has been discharged. As in the case of Britain, we had a close call at one stage. The Battle of the Coral Sea was a deliverance and the return of the A.I.F. enabled us to stop the Japanese advance in New Guinea just in time.
　I do not think the enemy can now invade this country. We have proved that, with the resources we have had, together with the command of the sea

established by the gallant United States Navy by decisive victories at Midway Island and the Solomons [sic] Islands. We are not yet immune from marauding raids which may cause much damage and loss. I believe, however, that we can hold Australia as a base from which to launch both limited and major offensives against Japan. ...
[AA: A 5954, Box 579]

At the highest level, the Australian-American alliance maintained a public image of harmony, and compared with most international alliances it was harmonious. The following extracts give glimpses of some of the most important relationships.

Here, MacArthur claims that there were unsavoury features in the political scene on his arrival in Australia.

Document 295

[SHEDDEN'S?] *NOTES OF DISCUSSIONS WITH COMMANDER-IN-CHIEF, SOUTHWEST PACIFIC AREA* Brisbane, 20–26 October 1942

Most Secret

Political Criticism of Operations.
...
3. The Commander-in-Chief said that he had no reservations in regard to the information he would furnish to the Prime Minister personally, but he refused to give to the [Advisory War] Council any particulars of plans of impending operations, as he did not trust some of the non-Government members who, in his opinion, placed political ends before the National and Allied interests. ...
5. On General MacArthur's arrival in Australia, he had found that certain people had been anxious to tell him that the Curtin Government would not last two months longer. He had probably offended people by refusing to be wined and dined by them. He had also mentioned to Mr. Menzies that it would be a good thing for the Allied cause if Mr. Curtin were in the place of Mr. Churchill or Mr. Roosevelt, and Mr. Menzies had apparently been offended by this expression of opinion. Mr. Menzies had said to Major-General Sutherland[94] that the Commander-in-Chief was working in too much with the Government, and Major-General Sutherland had replied "What do you want him to do — fight with them? He would work just as closely with any other Government."
6. General MacArthur said that he had gathered the impression that non-Government members were displeased with military successes, as failure would embarrass the Government and the High Command. Related to this

---

94. Maj.-Gen. R.K. Sutherland, MacArthur's Chief of Staff.

was the attitude of the Murdoch press[95]. He had learnt from one of his officers present at a dinner that Sir Keith Murdoch had said it was essential to shift General MacArthur to defeat the Curtin Government. The defeat of the Government was even of more importance than the defeat of the Japanese. He also understood it was the aim to move General Blamey. ...
10. The Commander-in-Chief described Sir Keith Murdoch as an Australian Quisling and thought that the full rigours of the censorship should be imposed on him. ...
[AA: A 5954, Box 3]

Here, MacArthur speaks in restrained terms of Blamey, who commanded the Australian troops who won SWPA's first victory. Later in the war the American was to make much more critical comments on his Australian subordinate.

Document 296

[SHEDDEN'S] *NOTES ON DISCUSSIONS WITH COMMANDER-IN-CHIEF, SOUTHWEST PACIFIC AREA.*

Brisbane, 16–20 January 1943

Most Secret

...

GENERAL MACARTHUR'S OPINIONS
OF CERTAIN AUSTRALIAN OFFICERS.

General Sir Thomas Blamey.
...
2. General MacArthur described General Blamey as a good, courageous Commander in the field, but not a very sound tactician. There was much criticism of him in the Australian Army, because of his past, and he certainly did not command the fullest support of all, as might be expected of a great leader. ...
8. Reverting to his separate statement regarding the organisation in the Southwest Pacific Area, General MacArthur repeated his view that General Blamey should become Commander-in-Chief of the Home Defence Forces in Australia, when responsibility for local defence was re-assigned to the Australian Government, and that Lieut.-General Morshead[96] should be the

---

95. Sir Keith Murdoch, Managing Director of *Herald* (Melb), *Sun News-Pictorial* etc. and from 1942, Chairman of Directors, Herald and Weekly Times Ltd.
96. Lt. Gen. Sir Leslie Morshead, GOC 9th Division 1941–43, 1 Corps 1944–45.

Commander of the Australian divisions associated with the Allied Expeditionary Force in the Southwest Pacific Area. ...
[AA: A 5954, Box 2]

Here, MacArthur is frank on the problem of having a Briton in command of one of the Australian armed services.

Document 297

[SHEDDEN'S] *NOTES OF DISCUSSIONS*   Brisbane, 26 May 1943
WITH COMMANDER-IN-CHIEF,
SOUTHWEST PACIFIC AREA   Most Secret

Admiral Royle — Extension of Appointment
as Chief of the Naval Staff

I informed General MacArthur that approval had been given for the extension for a period of one year of Admiral Sir Guy Royle's appointment as Chief of the Naval Staff.
2. General MacArthur said that, whilst the appointment was, of course, entirely one for the Commonwealth Government, he would not have recommended extension if the Prime Minister had asked him for his views. General MacArthur explained that he had a high opinion of Admiral Royle's professional ability and he had no complaint whatever about his co-operation with Allied Headquarters. It was, however, within General MacArthur's knowledge that Admiral Royle was one of the leading critics of the set-up in the Southwest Pacific Area, and in view of desires which existed in certain quarters both in Australia and abroad to make a change, he had no doubt that he was an influential focal point for these views. It had also been reported to him that Sir Keith Murdoch obtained information from Admiral Royle. Admiral Royle worked in close co-operation with Admiral Carpender,[97] who was also disloyal to the set-up in the Southwest Pacific Area. They were secretive in regard to Naval information, and Admiral Royle strongly opposed the disclosure of details of operations and sinkings, of which the Commander-in-Chief considered the public should be aware. General MacArthur considered this was due more to Naval reluctance than any other reason.
3. General MacArthur therefore thought it better, particularly in view of the earlier experience of the Australian Government with Sir Charles Burnett[98],

---

97. From September 1942 to November 1943 Rear Admiral Arthur S. Carpender was the commander of Allied Naval Forces, SWPA.
98. Refer to Documents 39 and 40 for the circumstances surrounding Burnett's appointment as Chief of the Air Staff.

that, if it was necessary to appoint English officers, they should not remain for longer than two years. By changing them after this period, it meant that a new officer required, during the first twelve months, to devote himself entirely to his professional duties. During the second year, he was becoming established in various circles and felt he could speak more freely. By the third year, he was a source of danger if he were critical [of] the regime or set-up.
4. General MacArthur added that, had he been asked for his opinion, he would have suggested that the time was due for the advancement of the senior R.A.N. officers to the top position. ...
[AA: A 5954, Box 2]

This brief comment on MacArthur's relations with Curtin is consistent with the latter's stated belief that it was not the politician's business to interfere with the General's strategy.

Major General R.H. Dewing, who early in 1943 had reached Australia in command of a small British Army and Air Force Liaison Staff, is here giving his comments to Bruce on his return to London.

Document 298

Notes by Bruce on Discussion   London, 30 June 1943
with GENERAL R.H. DEWING

...
We then had some conversation with regard to the position in Australia and the political aspect. Dewing paid a high tribute to the Prime Minister but said that on all strategical and operational questions he was completely under the domination of MacArthur. This view which Dewing had formed MacArthur somewhat naively confirmed in their last conversation when he said that the Prime Minister is completely in my hands on all military questions. ...
[AA: M 100]

Here Blamey condemns politicians who questioned his role in running the army. Senator H.S. Foll and A.G. Cameron were two of Blamey's most forthright critics.

Document 299

Blamey to Morshead   24 February 1944

Letter

... As you probably have seen, there has been much backchat amongst the ignorant, who divide their energies between representing their fellow country men in the august assembly of Parliament and standing in a very low place in the Military hierarchy. Their ignorance in their latter role has led them to display it in their former.

However, the press have jumped upon them unanimously, and I attended the War Advisory Council meeting last week and dealt with their babblings seriatim and in full detail, but it has tended to delay the decision as to the set up. ...
[AWM: 3DRL 6643, Blamey Papers, 170.5]

Document 300

Blamey to Morshead   3 March 1944

Letter   *Personal and Most Secret*

...
Recommendations submitted by me on 1st November last for promotions, etc., have not yet materialised, largely owing to the doings of Foll, Cameron and Company — who know exactly how an Army should be run. Luckily I think we shall prevent them from destroying it utterly.
[AWM: 3DRL 6643, Blamey Papers, 170.5]

Much was written and said about MacArthur by Australians while he was in command of SWPA. We print comments made by Shedden in January 1943 and by Gavin Long, editor of the official history of Australia in the war of 1939–1945, when he first met MacArthur, in Brisbane, on 8 June 1944.

Document 301

Notes by Shedden   16–20 January 1943

Visit to Brisbane   *Most Secret*

Impressions of General MacArthur
The conferences with General MacArthur at intervals have been interest-

ing studies of his personality and the reflection of his moods according to the general situation at the time of the interview.
2. Last April, he was very depressed. ...
7. I always find General MacArthur's personality an interesting study, and he really has to be closely studied to be properly understood. Some people, who should know better, dismiss him rather cheaply because of a certain demonstrative manner and his verbosity.
8. His demonstrative manner is due to his mercurial temperament. ...
9. Any one who has had close relations with General MacArthur cannot come away without any other impression than that he has been in the presence of a great and masterful personality. He has a broad and cultured mind and a fine command of English. He might be described as an American conservative who has faithfully maintained the standards of his British ancestors. ...
10. ... General MacArthur has a profound knowledge of military art and history, is a shrewd judge of men, and, what is essential for a successful Commander, great personal courage and leadership...
11. At 63, he has shown that his mind has not lost its resiliency and that he has not been blindly wedded to orthodoxy in the art of war, by demonstrating in the New Guinea campaign how effectively land and air forces can be used in co-operation, and how air transport can be used when movement by land and sea is impossible. ...
14. Australia is very fortunate to have such an officer responsible for operations in the Southwest Pacific Area. General MacArthur says that, should he commit a grave error in the conduct of operations, he will be the first to detect it and efface himself from the scene. ...
[AA: A 5954, Box 2]

Long's comments were made in his war diaries.

Document 302

Extracts from War Historian's Diaries Brisbane, 8 June 1944

The following note on Gen MacArthur ...
 As always with a man of whom one has only seen carefully posed photographs, he seemed a little frailler and smaller than I expected. Also I had heard so much about how impressive he can be at a conference, about his apparently inexhaustible eloquence, and his histrionic talents that it was a surprise when he put me in a deep chair away from the desk, sank into the corner of a couch a few feet away, and began to talk very quietly. Not a marked American accent (it surprised me suddenly when he said "Milnee Bay" as all Americans do). The fine, almost feminine quality of his face that is sometimes noticeable in photographs was there, with an unexpected softness, especially of the mouth. It lends itself to a sharp line for the photo-

grapher, but it is not really like that. This is a man of mind and feeling rather than a man of iron, not a Rommel or a Montgomery.

Though he spoke very quietly during most of the talk, — to which he did not want any contributions from me — he sought and needed no help and deftly and amiably disposed of efforts to lead the conversation — he would suddenly raise his voice and use a dramatic gesture to underline a telling point.

A man I would say entirely at unity with himself. Fulfilled and confident. Sensitive. Never in doubt as to his own imposing stature. Convinced that he is born to command, and enjoying this conviction sensuously, not using it as a Montgomery does.
[AWM: 54, 577/7/32]

22
CRISIS OF COMMAND: THE RAAF IN SWPA

Southwest Pacific Area's most persistent command problem, constituting one of the most remarkable episodes in Australian war policy, concerned the higher command of the Royal Australian Air Force. On 4 April 1942 Air Chief Marshal Sir Charles Burnett ceased to hold the position, Chief of the Air Staff. An attempt to secure another British officer to fill the position collapsed. Consequently, a difficult command problem was created. It was now necessary not only to administer Australia's contribution to the Empire Air Training Scheme but also to mount operations against the Japanese. A compromise decision was reached: Air Vice-Marshal W.D. Bostock was appointed Chief of Staff to Lt. General Brett, then Commander Allied Air Forces. Bostock was thus responsible for operations. Air Vice-Marshal G. Jones became Chief of the Air Staff and was given control over personnel, provision and maintenance of aircraft, supply, equipment, and training, as well as supervision of Australia's part in the Empire Air Training Scheme in general. Although such an arrangement broke the military axiom of 'unity of command' it may have functioned, given good-will between Jones and Bostock. As the following documents show, such an element was sadly lacking. We begin this segment when the aggressive General George Kenney replaced Brett in August 1942 and at once reorganised the air forces at his disposal.

Document 303

MacArthur to Curtin   GHQ, SWPA, 4 September 1942

Letter   *Secret*

In order to provide essential mobility for the United States Army Air Forces in this area, the War Department has directed the organization of a tactical unit which it has designated the "Fifth Air Force". ... In conjunction with the formation of the Fifth Air Force, it is considered advantageous to exercise operational control of [other squadrons], through appropriate Area staffs, as a single element. It is anticipated that this element be designated "Coastal Defense Command, Allied Air Forces," and that Air Vice Marshal Bostock be designated by the Commander, Allied Air Forces, to exercise operational control of the units assigned thereto. These units will be largely R.A.A.F. squadrons, but may include any number of squadrons from the Fifth Air Force. Conversely, R.A.A.F Squadrons or Groups may operate with the 5th Bomber Command or 5th Fighter Command, as, indeed, several are now operating in New Guinea.

It will be noted in this organization that no essential change is contemplated. It is not proposed to request that Air Vice Marshal Bostock be named to command R.A.A.F. units. Command will rest, as at present, with the Chief of the Air Staff. Air Vice Marshal Bostock will merely exercise operational control of certain U.S. and R.A.A.F. units assigned to the Allied Air Forces which are performing a special function. He will remain at Headquarters, Allied Air Forces, utilizing the operations, intelligence and communications facilities now existing, thus avoiding duplication and increase in overhead. Eventually, upon the withdrawal of the Fifth Air Force, the R.A.A.F. elements in the Coastal Defense Command and in Allied Air Force Headquarters will remain as an operating headquarters, thus avoiding even temporary dislocation of R.A.A.F. functions. Its disposition will, of course, then rest with the R.A.A.F.

[AA: A 5954, Box 238]

Document 304

General Orders   HQ, AAF, SWPA, 5 September 1942.

No. 47   *Secret*

1. The Coastal Command, Allied Air Forces, is hereby constituted.
2. Air Vice-Marshal W.D. BOSTOCK, C.B., O.B.E., is hereby designated Air Officer Commanding with temporary Headquarters at Brisbane, Queensland.
3. The Coastal Command, Allied Air Forces, is comprised of all R.A.A.F. operational units including operational Headquarters, and such other units of the Allied Air Forces as may be assigned or attached.
4. The Air Officer Commanding, Coastal Command, Allied Air Forces, will exercise *operational control* over all units assigned or attached.
5. The organisation of the Coastal Command, Allied Air Force, within the Allied Air Force, does not alter the functions and responsibilities of R.A.A.F. Headquarters, Melbourne, Victoria.

(Sgd.) GEORGE C. KENNEY,
Major General,
Commander.

[AWM: 3DRL 3414, Jones Papers]

The name 'Coastal Command' at once alerted Curtin to the possibility that RAAF squadrons might be relegated to a defensive, secondary role. At his instigation the name was changed to the more general, RAAF

Command. More importantly, for our purposes, Jones, backed by his fellow Chiefs of Staff and by the Minister for Air, attempted to reunify the functions of administration and operations.

Document 305

Report by Chiefs of Staff   26 September 1942

Most Secret

...
5. ... the Chiefs of Staff recommend that, while accepting the proposal that an R.A.A.F. Command, Allied Air Forces, should be established, it is desirable that this Command should be established along lines similar to the Fifth Air Force, and that there should be unified operational and administrative control. This control should be vested in the Chief of the Air Staff, but his operational responsibility should be subject to the direction of Allied Air Headquarters and would normally be exercised through the A.O.C. of the R.A.A.F. Command. This would enable day to day operational matters to be dealt with without delay by Allied Air Headquarters and the Commander, R.A.A.F. Command, and would at the same time preserve the principle of unified control of the R.A.A.F.
... the necessity is emphasised for opportunities equal to that of the Fifth Air Force being given to the R.A.A.F. for participation in operations against the enemy.
[AA: A 5954, Box 238]

Document 306

Jones to [Shedden?]   12 October 1942

Minute   *Most Secret*

... So far as the Service is concerned, the main objective sought is the acceptance of the point of view that the Headquarters of the Service should be responsible for the higher direction and control of the Service in all its activities and that the present delegation of operational control to a subordinate Headquarters is only an expedient to meet existing circumstances. The acceptance of the report by the Chiefs of Staff would not only entail acceptance of this point of view but would also establish the right of the Chief of the Air Staff to supervise the work of the operational headquarters now known as the R.A.A.F. Command and to intervene, at his discretion, should circumstances require such intervention for the greater good of the Service and this Country. It is thought that such intervention would be exceptional and that the day to day control of operations will proceed

smoothly and efficiently by direct contact between the Headquarters, Allied Air Forces and the Headquarters, R.A.A.F. Command. ...
[AWM: 3DRL 3414, Jones Papers]

Document 307

Drakeford to Curtin   Melbourne, 14 October 1942.

Letter   *Most Secret*

... I regard it as of the utmost importance that "R.A.A.F. Command" should not function independently (as was originally contemplated by Allied Air Headquarters), but should form part of the R.A.A.F. organisation, to ensure unified control of all R.A.A.F. formations, etc., subject, of course, to the maintenance of closest possible collaboration from the operational aspects with Allied Air Headquarters.
4. Actually, the main objective sought in that connection is the acceptance of the view that the Headquarters of the Service should be responsible for the administration and control of its formations and squadrons, the present delegation to Allied Air Headquarters of operational control of the squadrons in the proposed R.A.A.F. Command being due to, and should continue having regard to, the special circumstances at present obtaining.
5. Such unified control of the R.A.A.F. would also remove any possibility of dislocation in the event of the withdrawal from Australia at any time of the "Fifth Air Force".
6. For these reasons, I concur in the proposal of the Chiefs of Staff that, if a separate "R.A.A.F. Command" be established, it should be on lines similar to those of the "Fifth Air Force", and that there should be unified operational and administrative control under the Chief of Air Staff, but that operational responsibility should be subject to directions of Allied Air Headquarters. ...
[AA: A 5954, Box 238]

The battle-lines between Jones and his supporters and Bostock, largely backed by Kenney, were quickly drawn. A proposal from Jones culminated in the Air Board Order printed below.

Document 308

Kenney to Bostock
Port Moresby, Not Dated
[c. 29 November 1942]

Letter *Secret*

Am sending a letter to General Wilson asking him to call Jones and tell him that I want no action taken on his proposal re the Directorate of Operations Communications and Intelligence, until I return and discuss it with him. I expect to be back the latter part of the week and will take it up with him the first thing. It certainly sounds like a screwy idea although if he will appoint you to the job it might work. How would you feel about that as a solution?

In any event, I want to discuss the matter with you before I talk with Jones. The last thing I want to do is to relieve you of your present job and I will quarrel with you on that score. I not only sincerely believe you the best qualified officer in the R.A.A.F. to handle operations but am especially desirous of having you on my side all the way back to Tokio. ...

[AA: A 5954, Box 238]

Document 309

Air Board Order 5 December 1942

A.F.C.O.391 — ORGANISATION OF ROYAL AUSTRALIAN AIR FORCE OPERATIONAL CONTROL.
(151/2/581 — 5/12/1942).

1. Effective from 30th April, 1942, Allied Air Headquarters exercised operational control of the Royal Australian Air Force. Administrative control, however, remained unchanged. As a consequence, some re-organisation of R.A.A.F. Headquarters was necessary, and the operational staffs were attached to Allied Air Headquarters. (A.F.C.O.63/42 refers).

2. Upon transfer of Allied Air Headquarters to Brisbane, the R.A.A.F. staff attached for duty was formed into a separate unit — "Extra R.A.A.F. (Staff with Allied Air Headquarters)", under the direct command of R.A.A.F. Headquarters for administration and discipline (A.F.C.O. 180/42 refers).

3. By General Order No. 47, dated 5th September, 1942, the Commander, Allied Air Forces, constituted the Coastal Command, Allied Air Forces, to exercise operational control of certain R.A.A.F. units, and by General Order No. 53, dated 21st September, 1942, changed the name from Coastal Command to "R.A.A.F. Command, Allied Air Forces".

4. This action was taken by the Commander of Allied Air Forces as a temporary measure to facilitate his operational control of R.A.A.F. operational units assigned to him. It is intended that, on relinquishment of control by the Commander, Allied Air Forces, the staff now known as

R.A.A.F. Command, Allied Air Forces, shall revert to R.A.A.F. Headquarters as Directorates of Operations, Intelligence and Communications respectively. The staff is therefore being organised on this basis, and appropriate establishment tables are being issued.
5. This staff is to be responsible to the Commander, Allied Air Forces, for operational control only of R.A.A.F. units assigned to it by him. All matters of R.A.A.F. policy, administration, discipline, training, supply and maintenance are the responsibility of R.A.A.F. Headquarters. Nevertheless, the R.A.A.F. staff, Allied Air Forces, is to offer advice to R.A.A.F. Headquarters on all matters affecting operations, and is to give its views and relevant information on such matters as may be requested by R.A.A.F. Headquarters from time to time.
[AA: A 5954, Box 238]

Bostock was enraged at what he construed to be Jones's attempt to extend his authority, and wrote the following scathing denunciation of his rival's Air Board Order.

Document 310

Bostock to F.J. Mulrooney [Secretary Air Board]
(Copy to Commander, AAF)

Brisbane, 12 December 1942

Letter *Secret*

A.F.C.0. 391 dated 5th December, 1942, reflects a confusion of ideas, misinterprets Allied Air Forces General Order No. 47, fails to enunciate the responsibilities of the Air Officer Commanding R.A.A.F. Command and misrepresents the functions of the R.A.A.F. Command Headquarters Staff.
2. Allied Air Forces General Order No. 47 constituted the Coastal Command by the aggregation of R.A.A.F. operational units into an integral formation. The Order then designated the Air Officer Commanding and specifically charged this Officer with responsibility for the exercise of command. The name "Coastal Command" was later altered to "R.A.A.F. Command" without other change. The Commander, Allied Air Forces constituted the R.A.A.F. Command to facilitate the operational control of the Air Officer Commanding, on whom he has placed, as an individual, the responsibility of command. It is clear, therefore, that the statement in para: 3 of A.F.C.O. 391 is incomplete and inaccurate, since the Command, as such, cannot exercise operational control over itself, but must be provided with a Commander. The Commander must, in turn, set up a Headquarters and be provided with an appropriate staff.
3. The action taken by the Commander, Allied Air Forces, reflects the organisation he has decided to adopt. A change of Government Policy, or the termination of the War, are the only contingencies which he visualises

as requiring a change of organisation. The statement in para: 4 of A.F.C.O. 391 that the organisation was intended as a "temporary measure" is therefore misleading. Further, any intentions regarding future reorganisation are irrelevant and certainly should not be permitted to influence the methods to be adopted now to implement the organisation of the R.A.A.F. for war, as required by the Commander, Allied Air Forces.

4. Para: 5 of A.F.C.O. 391 is unintelligible on close examination. The staff of R.A.A.F. Command Headquarters is, of course, directly responsible to the Air Officer Commanding and not to the Commander, Allied Air Forces. R.A.A.F. units are not assigned to the staff, but to the R.A.A.F. Command as a formation. The formation is in turn commanded by the Air Officer Commanding and it is the sole function of the staff of R.A.A.F. Command Headquarters to advise the Air Officer Commanding, who, as an individual, is responsible to the Commander, Allied Air Forces. Similarly, it is ridiculous to require the staff to offer advice to R.A.A.F. Headquarters; this duty can only be carried out by the Air Officer Commanding (after taking advice of his staff) on whom the responsibility rests to obtain the administrative services necessary to carry out the orders of the Commander, Allied Air Forces.

5. The apparently deliberate omission of all mention or reference, in A.F.C.O. 391, to the Air Officer Commanding R.A.A.F. Command, has resulted in presenting a picture of a complicated and impracticable organisation for which there is no justification. The presentation of the Air Officer Commanding in the correct perspective immediately simplifies the organisation which then assumes a practical, orthodox and efficient aspect.

6. It is submitted that as A.F.C.O. 391 is badly drafted, misleading and likely to add to the already dangerous state of confusion now existing throughout the R.A.A.F., it should be withdrawn and a more suitable order published as early as possible.

[AA: A 5954, Box 238]

Jones's response to Bostock's letter was prompt and uncompromising; but, as we shall see, he failed in his attempt to have Bostock sacked.

Document 311

Jones to Drakeford   Melbourne, 16 December 1942

Minute

It is desired to draw your attention to a memorandum received from Air Vice-Marshal W.D. Bostock dated 12th December, 1942. ... You will see that this officer refers to an A.F.C.O. No. 391/1942 ... in terms which I consider cannot be overlooked. The A.F.C.O. referred to was issued after much thought, and owing to the difficulties involved had to be restricted to bare essentials. It is strictly in accordance with the terms of the agreement between the Commonwealth Government and General MacArthur by which the operational control of certain R.A.A.F. squadrons was assigned to the C-in-C.

2. The basis of Air Vice-Marshal Bostock's case is that the command of R.A.A.F. operational units was assigned to him by the Commander, Allied Air Force. This, of course, is unacceptable, because the operational control only, as apart from disciplinary control, has been assigned to General Kenney, and manifestly he is unable to assign powers which he himself does not possess. This, incidentally, is made clear in paragraphs 4 and 5 of General Kenney's General Order No. 47 of the 5th September, 1942. ...

3. The submission of a memorandum such as that under reference by a senior officer to the Headquarters of his Service can only be regarded as a very serious matter, indicating unwillingness to co-operate within the terms of the organisation laid down by competent authority.

4. Since his appointment as Chief of Staff to the Commander, Allied Air Forces, Air Vice-Marshal Bostock has consistently endeavoured to obtain control of certain aspects of administration and organisation of the R.A.A.F., and has shown great resentment when his efforts in this direction have been checked. He has allowed his attitude to be known widely throughout the Service, and the effect of this on discipline is now assuming serious proportions.

5. As you are aware, on the separation of the 5th Air Force and R.A.A.F Command staff from what was formerly Combined Staff of Allied Air Headquarters, I represented that the R.A.A.F. operations and administrative staffs should be re-united. Air Vice-Marshal Bostock bitterly opposed this, and for the sake of harmony the matter was not pressed.

6. In order to achieve the maximum degree of co-operation, a Forward Echelon of our Headquarters administrative staff was established in Brisbane, and I have no reason to believe that the Service has suffered to any great extent because of the continuance of separate control of operations and administration. This result has been achieved, however, in spite of the attitude of our operations staff in Brisbane, which has not always been co-operative.

7. In view of the position which has now arisen, I find myself forced to recommend that Air Vice-Marshal Bostock be relieved of his present appointment, and posted to some other appointment where his well known ability can be used to advantage but in which he will not be able to cause further friction between the different sections of the Service and our Allies.

[AWM: 3DRL 3414, Jones Papers]

> By March 1943, Curtin considered that it was a matter of 'vital importance' to find a way out of the divided command imbroglio. MacArthur himself felt that the situation had become 'acute and dangerous'. On 15 April, War Cabinet decided that the only solution was to acquire the services of a British officer who would outrank both Jones and Bostock and appoint him Chief of the Air Staff. Two candidates were available:

Air Chief Marshal Sir Arthur Longmore and Air Marshal Sir Philip de la Ferté Joubert. Although the Australian government came to prefer Longmore, such a move foundered on the opposition of MacArthur, as the following documents demonstrate.

Document 312

Shedden to Curtin   11 May 1943

Minute   *Most Secret*

APPOINTMENT OF AIR OFFICER COMMANDING, R.A.A.F.

. . .

4. What we want is a good experienced officer who will clear out the dead wood in the senior ranks of the R.A.A.F., sort out the best men, and establish them in the right positions with the best organisation. An R.A.F. officer can act strongly and independently and return to England when he has finished the job.
5. Either officer would be a good selection, but I incline to Air Chief Marshal Longmore for the following reasons:-
  (i) He was born in Australia. Air Marshal Joubert is of French extraction.
  (ii) I think his record is more distinguished and better suited to the needs of the Australian situation.

General Sir Thomas Blamey is well acquainted with Air Chief Marshal Longmore, but I would reserve a final opinion until I had had an opportunity to discuss this officer with him. He is also vitally concerned from the aspect of air co-operation.

> Seen by P.M.
>   F.G.S. 11/5 (initialled)
>
> Spoke to P.M. who said that he had mentioned the matter to Gen B[lamey] who had expressed the highest opinion of Sir Arthur Longmore. Ag. to be prepared for W.Cabinet recommending his appt. on same terms as Sir Chas. Burnett.
>
>   F.G.S. (initialled)
>   22/5

[AA: A 5954, Box 238]

Document 313

Kenney to MacArthur   HQ, AAF, SWPA, 29 May 1943

Memorandum:

... Both [Joubert and Longmore] appear to be second string men, decidedly not in the class of Douglas, Tedder, Harris and other top operating men in the R.A.F. Joubert has been criticised for his handling of the Coastal Command and Longmore as C-in-C of the Middle East R.A.F. Command. Joubert's personality probably suits him better for dealings with Australians and Americans. It is true that Longmore was born in Australia but he left the country at an early age and is enough of an Englishman to have stood for election to the British Parliament. He lost that contest. I do not believe it would be wise to put Longmore in charge of the R.A.A.F. when he is persona non grata with Mr. Churchill, or Joubert, who apparently has had trouble with the Air Ministry. Australia must have the goodwill of both the R.A.F. and Mr. Churchill to ensure that her needs for aircraft, equipment and personnel can be taken care of.

If one of these officers is to be selected, I recommend Joubert... .
[AA: A 5954, Box 238]

Document 314

Curtin to Drakeford   Canberra, 11 June 1943

Letter   *Most Secret*

R.A.A.F. COMMAND
PROPOSAL FOR APPOINTMENT OF AN AIR OFFICER COMMANDING. R.A.A.F.

An opportunity was recently taken to discuss the above subjects with the Commander-in-Chief, Southwest Pacific Area. ...

3. With reference to the selection of either Air Chief Marshal Longmore or Air Chief Marshal Joubert, the Commander-in-Chief expressed his disappointment that the United Kingdom Government had been unable to release one of the younger Australian born officers with suitable experience. He strongly recommended against the appointment of either Longmore or Joubert because of their age and the fact that the blemishes in their records would probably prejudice the possibility of giving inspiring leadership to the younger men of the R.A.A.F. In the circumstances, the Commander-in-Chief suggested that the present arrangement, unsatisfactory though it was, should be carried on. He proposes to arrange a conference between Lieut.-General Kenney, Major-General Sutherland and Air Vice-Marshals Bostock and Jones, with a view to exploring the possibility of improving the present arrangement to minimise the unsatisfactory features that exist.

4. Following our discussion, I have informed the Commander-in-Chief that I wish him to proceed accordingly ... [and] it is not desired to proceed with the appointment of either Air Chief Marshal Longmore or Air Chief Marshal Joubert. ...
[AA: A 5954, Box 238]

Certainly some effort was made to reconcile the Jones-Bostock conflict through conversation and conference, but to no avail. Personal vested interests were deeply involved as well as the political relationship with the Americans in the Southwest Pacific Area. The intense and continuing ill feeling which existed at the top of the air force is extensively documented in the archives. We print a selection of extracts which conveys the essence of that disgraceful contest.

Document 315

Jones to [Shedden?] 15 April 1943

Minute *Most Secret*

You asked for a brief statement of incidents in which Air Vice-Marshal BOSTOCK has been non-co-operative. A few of the main incidents are as follows:-
...
5. On occasions when I have discussed matters of organisation with General Kenney and have obtained some measure of agreement with him, Air Vice-Marshal Bostock has endeavoured to upset that agreement by representing a different point of view. This has served to confuse General Kenney's mind, and has caused considerable resentment against the R.A.A.F. in general.
6. The attitude of Air Vice-Marshal Bostock towards this Headquarters is well-known among the staffs at his own Headquarters in Brisbane and at this Headquarters in Melbourne. It is the subject of common gossip which I have endeavoured to suppress. On one occasion I had Air Vice-Marshal Bostock parade all his officers, and in his presence warned them against gossip, and informed them that the difficulties which had arisen would undoubtedly be settled by constituted authority in due course.
7. Throughout the period in which these incidents have occurred, it has been the unanimous opinion of the Air Board that Air Vice-Marshal Bostock was challenging its authority with a view to gaining control of the higher direction of the Royal Australian Air Force.
8. The situation described above is unprecedented, and is having a damaging effect on the R.A.A.F. in many ways. It can only be remedied by disciplining officers who adopt a non-co-operative and disloyal attitude to the Headquarters of their Service.
[AWM: 3DRL 3414, Jones Papers]

Document 316

Bostock to Mulrooney Brisbane, 7 November 1943
(Copy to Commander, A.A.F., for information)   HQ, RAAF Command

Letter

... The satisfactory discharge of the responsibilities laid upon me by the Commander, Allied Air Forces, is not possible without the complete support of the Air Board, since it is my view that a Commander cannot exercise efficient operational control and direction unless he is accorded a voice in the determination of policies and major matters concerning the organisation, administration, equipment supply and technical maintenance of his Command. ...
5. In the absence of a clear definition by the Air Board, I am severely handicapped because it is frequently made evident to me that the Service as a whole is confused and bewildered. Operational Commanders and Staff Officers of R.A.A.F. Headquarters as well as Staff Officers of my own Headquarters are uncertain of their responsibilities, their obligations, and the scope of their authority.
[AWM: 3DRL 3414, Jones Papers]

Document 317

Jones to Drakeford 3 December 1943

Minute *Most Secret*

...
2. Recent correspondence between R.A.A.F. Headquarters and R.A.A.F. Command on official business indicates clearly that A.V.M. Bostock is attempting to assume responsibilities which have never been allotted to him. I refer mainly to organisation and works. These are, of course, matters for which I am directly responsible to yourself.
3. It is essential that R.A.A.F. Headquarters staffs be re-integrated under one head, and I ask that the Government accept this principle which is fundamental in any organisation. It has been recommended by the Defence Committee on three separate occasions. ...
[AWM: 3DRL 3414, Jones Papers]

Document 318

MacArthur to Shedden   5 February 1944

Teleprinter Message BXM. 113   Secret

1. Bostock has made request that he be relieved of the appointment of Air Officer Commanding, R.A.A.F. Command, Allied Air Forces. His service in his present command has been superior in every respect. His efficiency, zeal and loyalty have been outstanding.
2. Grounds for request are that he considers he is unable efficiently to discharge his responsibilities to Commander, Allied Air Forces, due to present status of organisation and relationship within the R.A.A.F.
3. Owing to the increasing combat strength of R.A.A.F. and the offensive role which I plan for it in impending operations, I recommend that the Prime Minister personally review the situation as a matter of urgency. I shall take no action on Bostock's application until I know his views.
[AA: A 5954, Box 238]

Document 319

Jones to Drakeford   6 March 1944

Minute   Secret

... It is evident that Air Vice-Marshal Bostock is endeavouring to create an intolerable situation, hoping by this means to force a change. Under other circumstances, the measure of insubordination ... could only be remedied by charging the officer concerned with an offence, or by removing him from his position.
4. The point at issue relates to the organisation for the administration and operational control of Fighter Squadrons. This matter has been the subject of frequent discussions between Air Vice-Marshal Bostock, the Officer Commanding North Western Area and myself on several occasions over the last eighteen months. Twice I accepted Air Vice-Marshal Bostock's recommendations, only to find that his solution was unsatisfactory and he desired himself to change it. However, I would emphasise that the merits of my decision are not a matter which a subordinate officer has the right to challenge in this way.
5. I suggest that Air Vice-Marshal Bostock be informed that he must accept my decisions on matters which are the responsibility of the Chief of the Air Staff, and that, although his recommendations are required and will be given full consideration, he is committing a serious breach of discipline in challenging such decisions once given.
[AWM: 3DRL 3414, Jones Papers]

Document 320

Bostock to Drakeford
(Copy for Jones)

Brisbane, 15 April 1944

Letter   *Secret*

I am very disturbed to receive a copy of a report submitted by Air Vice-Marshal Jones to you, dated 11th April, 1944.

Following my discussions with Air Vice-Marshal Jones on 10th April, 1944, in Melbourne, it was clearly and definitely arranged between us, at the suggestion of Air Vice-Marshal Jones, that he should make a first draft of a joint report which he would send to me at Brisbane. In his own words, I was then to "pull it about" and return it to him for his consideration prior to submission to you. This is the second important occasion on which Air Vice-Marshal Jones has failed to observe the terms of a clearly stated verbal agreement with me.

2. Air Vice-Marshal Jones' report is misleading in that it evades vital considerations involved, while it selects minor aspects and presents them as the main issues. This is particularly true of his comments regarding the "Fighter Organisation" and the "Training of Aircrews in Reserve Pools". The whole report, by implication, offers you bad advice. ...

[AWM: 3DRL 3414, Jones Papers]

Document 321

Jones to Drakeford

26 April 1944

Minute   *Secret*

I refer to the letter dated 15th April, 1944, addressed to you by Air Vice-Marshal Bostock, a copy of which I have received, and to both the tone and contents of which I take grave exception.

2. This letter is not only unnecessarily offensive but is highly defamatory of me in my personal capacity, as well as in the way of my office and professional ability and repute.

3. In view of the circumstances, I do not intend at this stage to enter into detailed discussion concerning the matters dealt with in Air Vice-Marshal Bostock's letter, except to say that my report to you of the 11th April was intended as a preliminary advice, and as stated in my last paragraph, was forwarded to Air Vice-Marshal Bostock for checking and comment if he so desired.

4. It is an extremely grave matter when a senior officer of a Service writes of another in this strain. If statements of the kind in question are true, the officer concerning whom they are written is unworthy of his office; if they are untrue, the officer making them is guilty of a serious Service offence.

5. In these circumstances, I feel compelled to request from you as the addressee of the communication, an expression of your confidence in me as the holder of the office I occupy, and an intimation that you will advise the writer of the letter accordingly, and that any future communications are to be couched in fitting terms and submitted through the proper channels.
6. Should you not see your way clear to accede to this request, I shall feel that you do not possess that degree of confidence in me as your principal professional adviser which should exist, and I shall feel constrained to initiate such Service or other action as may be necessary to refute the imputations which have been made against my personal integrity and my professional ability and reputation.
[AWM: 3DRL 3414, Jones Papers]

A final, abortive attempt to import a British officer was made when Curtin went to London in May 1944. MacArthur simply blocked the appointment and until the end of the war the enmity between Jones and Bostock remained unchanged. What becomes clear in this episode is that no Australian leader, in face of American opposition, would willingly exercise power to prevent it.

Document 322

Paper by Curtin   3 August 1944

War Cabinet Agendum 396/1944   Top Secret

APPOINTMENT OF CHIEF OF THE AIR STAFF
...
Discussions in London — May 1944
3. During my visit to London in May, I had consultations on the matter with Mr. Churchill, the Secretary of State for Air, and the Chief of the Air Staff, as a result of which the latter submitted the names of the following officers for consideration:-
Air Marshal Sir Keith R. Park, KBE, CB, MC, DFC.
Air Vice-Marshal H.W.L. Saunders, OB, CBE, MC, DFC, MM.
...
Views of General MacArthur
5. When in Brisbane in June, I mentioned the matter to General MacArthur and said that the only practicable manner in which the administrative and operational functions of the R.A.A.F. could be integrated, appeared to be by the selection of an officer who would be in a superior position to both Air Vice-Marshal Bostock, Air Officer Commanding, R.A.A.F. Command, and Air Vice-Marshal Jones, Chief of the Air Staff.
6. General MacArthur considered that the question was entirely one for the

Australian Government, and if it wished to make an appointment as proposed, he would give the officer his fullest co-operation. In so far as the operational set-up was concerned, he thought that, apart from the southern areas, there should be an operational command of the R.A.A.F. in New Guinea and another in the Darwin area, both of which should be under the officer on the staff of the Commander of the Allied Air Forces, to whom he would be responsible for operations, whilst also being a subordinate of the new head of the R.A.A.F.

7. I informed General MacArthur that, of the two names submitted, I favoured Air Marshal Sir Keith Park, who had had distinguished operational service in the United Kingdom, Middle East and Malta.

Views of Minister for Air

8. The Minister for Air has informed me that he concurs in the selection of Air Marshal Sir Keith Park. ...

10. In the event of the proposed appointment being made to the post of Chief of Air Staff, it will be necessary to find another position for Air Vice-Marshal Jones. The Minister for Air considers that, when such development takes place, the most appropriate appointment for Air Vice-Marshal Jones would be that of Vice Chief of the Air Staff — a post in which, the Minister states, he could render most valuable services and assistance to the new R.A.F. appointee by reason of his wide knowledge of air-force administration, air staff policy, organisation, training activities etc. of the R.A.A.F.
...

12. The object of the appointment of a senior R.A.F. officer as head of the R.A.A.F. is to give effect to the principle of unified operational and administrative control of the R.A.A.F. which has already been approved by War Cabinet. General MacArthur has expressed his agreement with this principle and it is proposed that the detailed arrangements necessary to give effect to it should be made when the new appointee takes up duty. ...

[AA: A 5954, Box 238]

Document 323

War Cabinet Minute Melbourne, 4 August 1944

(3693) *AGENDUM No. 396/1944 — APPOINTMENT* Top Secret
OF CHIEF OF THE AIR STAFF

The following recommendations submitted by the Minister for Defence were approved:-
(i) The appointment of Air Marshal Sir Keith Park, R.A.F., as Chief of the Air Staff, R.A.A.F., with his present rank, pay and conditions to be arranged by the Treasurer and Minister for Air in consultation with the Prime Minister as Minister for Defence.

(ii) Re-affirmation of the principle of unified operational and administrative control of the R.A.A.F., detailed arrangements to give effect to this to be made when Air Marshal Park takes up appointment and after he has had an opportunity of examining the position.
(iii) The future appointment of Air Vice-Marshal Jones to be decided when Air Marshal Park assumes duty as Chief of the Air Staff.
[AA: A 5954, Box 238]

Document 324

NOTES OF DISCUSSIONS WITH THE COMMANDER-IN-CHIEF, SOUTHWEST PACIFIC AREA

Canberra 30 September, 1944

Top Secret

PRESENT: The Prime Minister
  The Commander-in-Chief, Southwest Pacific Area
  The Acting Secretary, Department of Defence

V. Appointment of Chief of the Air Staff

The Prime Minister referred to his previous discussions in Brisbane with General MacArthur in regard to this subject, and informed him of the aspects that had been raised in Mr. Bruce's cablegram 116 of 28th September as to the responsibilities in relation to operations of the proposed appointee — Air Marshal Park.
2. General MacArthur referred to difficulties that had existed in the past in relation to the Chief of the Air Staff and the Air Officer Commanding, R.A.A.F. Command, and the concern that the Minister for Air had felt in this regard. Nothing serious had, however, resulted, and he felt that any differences that had existed in the past were now quiet. The strategical scope of the war has gone so far forward that an entirely different situation has developed. He considered it no longer necessary to bring a senior R.A.F. Officer to Australia. General MacArthur felt that, questions having been raised, an opportunity presented itself for review, and he felt that, in replying, advice should be furnished that the tempo of the campaign had gone so fast and conditions had changed to such an extent that it was no longer necessary to proceed with the proposal.
3. General MacArthur added that, had this change taken place when it was first mooted, advantages would have accrued, but he now considered it too late to make such a change.
[AA: A 5954, Box 238]

Generally speaking, Shedden seems to have co-operated in most amicable fashion with MacArthur, but he probably was angry with the General over his opposition, at the meeting of 30 September 1944, to Park's appointment. Every historian acquainted with the facts of this shameful episode endorses Shedden's concern, expressed below in a minute meant for his record only.

Document 325

Minute by Shedden 4 November 1944
(My file only)

HIGHER ORGANISATION OF R.A.A.F. Top Secret

...[T]he whole course of this matter [had been] changed by the resubmission of the question to General MacArthur who, having blocked the appointment of either Air Chief Marshal Joubert or Longmore in May 1943, had apparently repented of his agreement to Air Marshal Park which was made with the Prime Minister in Brisbane. The objections raised by General MacArthur are not relevant to the main consideration of the Government which is its desire to have the R.A.A.F. organisation placed on a satisfactory footing for its internal administration and operational effectiveness. As stated in my note of 30th October to the Prime Minister:-

"It must not be overlooked, in connection with General MacArthur's views, that the opinion is held by senior R.A.A.F. Officers that the Americans do not wish to have a senior R.A.F. officer in the Southwest Pacific Area, and prefer the divided arrangement, because they can play one side off against the other, whereas a Senior Officer with unified control would be in a stronger position to assert the views of the R.A.A.F."

3. From the views expressed by General MacArthur, General Blamey, the Defence Committee, Air Vice-Marshal Bostock and Air Vice-Marshal Jones, the administration of the R.A.A.F. will continue to be unsatisfactory until the contemplated change is made. Some day there will be an outcry about the relatively poor R.A.A.F. effort in the Southwest Pacific Area in relation to the resources allotted to the air effort. It is not the fault of the personnel in the squadrons, who are magnificent, but is due to the set up, under which it has also been necessary to send senior officers to Europe to get operational experience which should be provided in the Southwest Pacific Area.
[AA: A 5954, Box 238}

23
PAPUA

After their seaborne assault on Port Moresby was repelled by the Americans in the Coral Sea battle the Japanese prepared to take that town by a cross-country advance after landing on the undefended north and east coasts of New Guinea. They did not succeed in taking Port Moresby; but no enemy soldiers have ever fought their way closer to the Australian homeland. The following document traces Australia's reinforcement of Port Moresby until September 1942.

Document 326

Paper[99] 30 September 1942

DEFENCE OF PORT MORESBY *Most Secret*

. . .

5. At the outbreak of war with Japan the Army strength available at Port Moresby was as follows:-

Fixed Defences)	
49th Battalion (A.M.F.))	
One Papuan (Native) Infantry)	1,589 men
Battalion (less one Company))	
One Anti-Tank Troop (A.I.F.))	
Maintenance Units)	

. . .

28. On 3rd April, 1942, the Australian Chiefs of Staff and General Brett, after consultation with Generals Sutherland and Marshall,[100] prepared an appreciation for transmission to Dr. Evatt in Washington, from which the following passage is quoted:-

"2. The area in Australia vital to the continuance of the war effort lies on the East and South East coast, generally between Brisbane and Melbourne. Port Moresby is the key to this area. An attack in force on Port Moresby could develop at any time. ..."

. . .

30. At the Advisory War Council meeting on 13th May, 1942, the Commander-in-Chief, Australian Military Forces [Blamey], stated that the

---

99. Annex No. 1 to a Statement by Shedden on the defence of Port Moresby and submitted to Curtin on 2.10.1942.
100. Maj.-Gen. Richard J. Marshall, MacArthur's Deputy Chief of Staff.

main pre-occupation of the Army was to strengthen the defences of New Guinea; the anti-aircraft defences were being increased and an additional brigade of Australian troops was to be sent there as soon as shipping and escort could be arranged. ...

Garrison at Moresby — Advisory War Council Discussions.

31. At the meeting of the Advisory War Council on 19th May, it was stated that there were 9,812 Australian troops in Port Moresby and 4,735 others were being sent there. ... Reference was made to the inclusion of 18 year old members of the A.M.F. in the forces despatched. The Chief of the General Staff [Sturdee] stated that the 7th Division, A.I.F., was required for overseas operations. ... The view was expressed that well trained and experienced troops should be sent to Port Moresby, in view of its strategic importance and the imminence of the Japanese threat to this locality... .

33. At the Advisory War Council meeting of 17th June, 1942, opposition was again expressed to the principle of despatching young soldiers to operational areas, particularly Port Moresby... .

35. On 22nd July, an enemy force landed at Gona, near Buna. There were no land forces in this area to oppose the landing. A company of Australian Infantry was at Kokoda and was reinforced between 22nd and 24th July... . Plans had been made for our forces to occupy the Buna area and the 808th U.S. Army Engineer Battalion (674 men) which had moved from Darwin to Port Moresby had been intended to take part in this operation... .

Movement of 7th Division, A.I.F.

36. On 6th August, 1942, the Commander-in-Chief, Australian Military Forces, informed the Advisory War Council:-

(a) That the movement of the 6th Division, A.I.F., from Ceylon to Australia would be completed during the coming weekend.

(b) That it had been decided, after discussion with General MacArthur, to despatch the 7th Division, A.I.F., to the Papua-New Guinea area. An Australian Corps Staff would also be sent... .

37. On 13th August the Chief of the General Staff informed the Advisory War Council that when the movement of the 7th Division, A.I.F., was completed, the Army forces available in Papua would be 4 Brigades at Moresby and 2 at Milne Bay... .

38. On 9th September the Chief of the General Staff informed the Council that there were 25,000 troops in New Guinea and Papua and another Brigade of the 7th Division, A.I.F., was arriving that day; this would bring the total to 32,000. Of these one Militia and one A.I.F. Brigade (a total of 8,000 men) were at Milne Bay... .

39. In addition to the above, the 16th Brigade, A.I.F., (6th Division), and a United States regiment of 3,500 troops are also being sent to New Guinea. This will bring the total in the area to over 40,000. ...

41. The following is a summary of the principal movements of troops to Moresby:-

April 1941 —
    49th Battalion (Militia).   ) 30th Brigade,
) A.M.F.

Jan-Feb. 1942 —
    39th and 53rd Battalions (Militia)

May 1942 —
    14th Brigade (A.M.F.)

Aug. 1942 —
    21st Brigade, A.I.F. (7th Division)

Sept. 1942 —
    25th Brigade, A.I.F. (7th Division) (arrived 9/9/42.)
    16th Brigade, A.I.F. (6th Division))
    U.S. Regiment (3,500 troops)   ) also despatched.

Note: The 7th Brigade (Militia) and the 18th Brigade,
    A.I.F. (7th Division), are at Milne Bay. ...
[AA: A 5954, Box 587]

The Japanese who landed at Gona moved inland to take Kokoda, 100 km from their beachhead, by 29 July 1942, forcing back the Australian militiamen sent to oppose them. In August reinforcements, men of the 7th Division, began to reach the fighting along the Kokoda Trail. Both AIF and militiamen were then forced back to Imita Ridge, within 50 km of Port Moresby. From 12 August until 28 September Lt.-Gen. Sydney Rowell commanded New Guinea Force, comprising all Allied troops on the island. We print some extracts from letters during this retreat.

The first letter to Vasey, Deputy CGS, who at the time was at MacArthur's Headquarters, compares the AMF troops (Australian Military Forces; militiamen) unfavourably with the AIF, whose units are distinguished by the prefix 2/. Battalions in the 2nd AIF were recruited chiefly on a territorial basis. For tradition's sake they took the numbers of their counterparts in the 1st AIF, with the prefix 2/. Militia battalions had no similiar tradition dating from the Great War, and so were designated simply as 39th Bn, 53rd Bn, and so on.

Document 327

Rowell to Vasey   HQ, NGF, Not Dated [c 31 August 1942]

Personal Letter

... Potts[1] has had to give up ISURAVA. During this action, one Coy of 53 Bn, sent to help 2/16 Bn, broke & scattered.

Although 39 Bn has done well, 53 Bn has been a dreadful commitment & I'm beginning to wonder whether any of these A.M.F. units can be relied on. We are now left here with but four A.M.F. bns & I really shudder to think what the position might be if the Wog elects to come here. ...
[AWM: 54, 225/2/5]

In the following letter Rowell suggests that New Guinea be reinforced by the two brigades of the 6th Division which in early August had reached Melbourne after some months spent in Ceylon.

'Tubby' is Maj.-Gen. A.S. Allen, commander of the 7th Division. 'Cyril' is Maj.-Gen. C.A. Clowes, Australian commander at Milne Bay.

Document 328

Rowell to Vasey   HQ, NGF, 1 September 1942

Personal Letter

...
I ... drafted a signal for the C-in-C this morning (G 3588) in which I raised again the provision of Steady troops who could be relied on to do their best, in place of A.M.F. in whom I have no confidence & neither has Tubby who, after all, is fighting the battle. ...

I do want to assure you once & for all that there is not the slightest thought of flap or panic over this business. Neither Tubby or I have ever run away from a tight position & we are not starting now. And we (including Cyril) will fight the Jap just wherever & whenever our administrative limitations permit. But it's well to have a sober realization of the fact that the instruments at hand are not too good & I really wonder whether you can leave 16 & 17 Bdes in Australia, with attack most unlikely, while we are up to our necks in it here. ...
[AWM: 54, 225/2/5]

As commander of Australian troops in the Kokoda retreat Rowell had some reason to express alarm.

---

1. Brigadier A.W. Potts, commander of the 21st Brigade (7th Division).

Document 329

Rowell to Vasey HQ, NGF, 8 September 1942

Personal Letter

...
Today has been my blackest since we came & none of the 28 days I've spent here has been free from worry. Potts said yesterday "I intend to bash him here" (ie EFOGI) yet he does nothing except get bottled up. ...

I have thought over my own position in the past few days. Nothing I've ever had in life has come easily & this task is no exception. I think I must have killed a black cat without knowing it. If I felt I'd mucked things up I would not hesitate to say so, but I feel any decisions I've made on major problems have been right & I've been knocked back by natural difficulties, by failures in leadership or fighting capacity or by a superior enemy. Perhaps a combination of all three.

I hope I'm not wrong this time in saying I'm confident the enemy has no hope of getting MORESBY from the North. His difficulties will now start & I trust we can get him on the rebound. ...
[AWM: 54, 225/2/5]

When he was no longer commander of New Guinea Force Rowell recalled several unsavoury incidents involving militia troops.

Document 330

Note by Shedden Canberra, 3 October 1942

DEFENCE OF PORT MORESBY *Most Secret*

...
He [Lt.-Gen. Rowell] was very critical of the quality of the Militia brigade despatched to Port Moresby in May. He stated that it had been selected by Major-General Lloyd, the Divisional Commander, as one of his best brigades, but prior to its departure it had made a very poor showing at a parade in a camp in New South Wales, and grave doubts were expressed as to what would be its discipline and efficiency in action. He recalled that on embarkation there had been hundreds of absentees.

Lieut.-General Rowell quoted two instances of the lack of morale, discipline and training among the Militia troops. One infantry battalion at Milne Bay refused to unload ships, and another refused to fight near Kokoda. On its retreat it encountered a large number of native porters who were carrying supplies to the front, and the troops commandeered the services of a large proportion of these porters to carry their rifles and equipment back. ...
[AA: A 5954, Box 587]

As a young journalist, Keith Murdoch had written a criticism of Sir Ian Hamilton's leadership at Gallipoli, thereby helping to bring about his recall. Now a newspaper proprietor, Sir Keith praised the 39th Battalion in an article which gives a different perspective from Rowell's letters.

Document 331

Article by Sir Keith Murdoch[2]   Not Dated [c.22 September 1942]

... The early brunt of the fighting was borne by a militia battalion. It did magnificently. ... The battalion knew a good deal about the jungle, but even it was not equipped for jungle fighting. It wore khaki uniforms and webbing equipment conspicuous against the green background. Its weapons and kit were heavier than is efficient in this fighting, its tactics were not fully adapted. These men were to be the spearhead of our advance. ... This was a Victorian battalion, not a question can be raised about its morale, its fighting spirit, its leadership. ... The 39th battalion stood in all about 37 days fighting. When relieved at Kokoda and placed in reserve at Myola it had lost heavily in numbers, it had stood the brunt of all the devices of Japanese jungle warfare but its spirit was still aggressive and strong. ...

... [T]he actions that proceeded on either side and indeed all round our force can best be described as a continuous melee in which the Japanese, avoiding stand-up fights, struck and disappeared, moved mostly in silence and darkness, waylaying patrols, even tempting them by noise tactics into snares, and striking often from the trees.

Most of our own wounded men said they had not even sighted a Japanese.
...
There was no doubt whatever about the morale of our men. Except for the few in the Signal unit which did not do well, the men went through the whole of the fight with confidence, determination and high courage. Although wearied beyond description, harassed, weakened and defeated, they were still eager to fight, and still confident of ultimate success, when relieved by others.

They made no movement of retreat that was not ordered by their leaders, and there are many instances of fighting to the death and of gravely wounded men remaining with their rifles to take toll before their own end.

But even those who worked on patrols and in small parties with resourcefulness and daring admitted somewhat ruefully that the Japanese had a high morale too and knew more about concealment, pathfinding, sniping and small force ambuscade than they had learned.

---

2. Contained in Teleprinter Message, CAB.40, of 22.9.1942, from the Chief Publicity Censor, Canberra, to Deputy Chief Publicity Censor, Brisbane.

The Japanese made no attempt to use air support. ...

We should not lose Moresby. We have great strength, great fire power and great men ready for battle in the rolling country if the Japanese dare to offer it. ...

I refuse utterly to accept any easy explanation of the Kokoda disaster. I refuse that any slur shall be cast upon the men who fought there or upon their battalion officers. Of course some failed; but they were NOT the cause of the great failure.

The nation must feel all the grief, all the distress, all the shame that belong to this grim, even terrible, episode; it must feel the anguish. It must learn and learn of this battle until these feelings are dominating it. ...
[AA: A 5954, Box 537]

Although this report by Forde was written after the Japanese had begun their retreat from Imita Ridge, most of the extracts we print relate to the Australian retreat.

Document 332

REPORT BY THE MINISTER FOR THE ARMY ON HIS VISIT TO THE NEW GUINEA THEATRE OF OPERATIONS.
1/10/1942–4/10/1942

Canberra, 9 October 1942

Most Secret

...

(ii) Superiority of Our Air Force :
The report furnished to me in regard to the superiority of our Air Force in the latter stages of the advance by the enemy over this route, is truly amazing. The heavy bombardment of the enemy's aerodromes in his base areas eventually resulted in the complete superiority of our Air force and I was informed that our bombers and fighters were attacking along the line at will, with practically no opposition from the enemy in the air. At all sections of the line which I visited, the men were loud in the praise of the air force and had implicit confidence in its capacity to beat off the enemy wherever he should appear. ...

17. *Road Construction:*
[From] the attached map ... it will be observed that at the time of Army occupation of PORT MORESBY, the made road extended for a distance of approximately 18 miles from PORT MORESBY. This road has since been extended into the jungle along a route traversing steep mountains for a distance of a further 14 miles... .

Heavy 4-wheel drive vehicles and Jeeps cars which continuously proceed along this road, bog down into its earth surface heavily which, by reason of the lack of solid or binding road-making material, presents a most difficult maintenance problem almost as great as the construction of the road itself.

... Maintenance gangs are continuously at work along the whole of this roadway splitting the trunks of the felled trees for the purpose of building corduroy surfaces on all the bad sections and even under these conditions, the roadway frequently collapses with the weight of the traffic proceeding along it. Metal or gravel surfaces are unknown as no such materials are available... .

It was indeed an inspiring sight to see these lads stripped to the waist and toiling in the tropical heat and rain to keep the roadway continuously open, thus enabling supplies and equipment to get forward to the troops in the front line. I was informed that the road was advancing at the rate of half a mile to three quarters of a mile a day, and I cannot allow the opportunity to pass without placing on record my great appreciation of the magnificent work which the Engineering Units are performing under the most difficult conditions imaginable in the construction and maintenance of this important road. ...

24. *Native Population:*

The loyalty of the native populations in the New Guinea Area and the manner in which they have thrown their efforts into our cause is one which should fill us all with a sense of great pride.

Wherever I journeyed in the New Guinea Area, I saw numbers of them employed on duties which resulted in an effective addition to our resources and manpower.

The main duties on which these people were engaged was the carrying of supplies along the jungle paths to our forward troops, the transport through almost impenetrable jungle and down the precipitous mountain sides of our wounded, the construction and maintenance of roads, the building of native bush huts for use of our troops, and on many other duties for which they were specially fitted.

Only when the complete history of the operations in this area is written will the wonderful and heroic nature of their work be fully appreciated, and the people of Australia realise what a debt of gratitude we owe to these natives of New Guinea who have displayed courage under fire which, in many instances, has not been excelled by our own troops.

Much has already been told of their work as stretcher-bearers in bringing our wounded and sick up and down precipices and mountain sides and along jungle tracks, and it is freely stated by the troops themselves that if it had not been for them, the lives of many of our wounded and seriously ill soldiers would never have been saved.

These fellows are extremely popular with our troops, and it is not exaggeration to say that they regard them with the greatest affection. We are indeed fortunate that in this jungle area where the Japanese troops have again displayed great ingenuity and cunning in their methods, the majority of the local native population is loyal to our cause and, in consequence, the enemy's infiltration tactics have not been aided and abetted by fifth column activities to anything like the same extent as was the case in other occupied countries. ...

41. *Publicity and Propaganda:*
...
It seems a great pity that we have not had an official Press Correspondent of the calibre of Dr. C.E.W. BEAN whose despatches from the theatres of war in the Middle East, Gallipoli and France were of such a meritorious nature, and portrayed so clearly the events on the operational front. The Commander-in-Chief had the greatest confidence in him, and his despatches became officially accepted as an accurate portrayal of the position and their publication was eagerly awaited thoughout the whole of Australia.

I recommend that immediate consideration should be given to the appointment of a man of similar calibre as Official War Correspondent who should confer with Dr. BEAN before taking up duty... .
[AA: A 5954, Box 532]

On the night of 25/26 August 1942 a Japanese force landed at Milne Bay, at the eastern tip of Papua, in a move aimed eventually at Port Moresby. The Japanese were out-numbered by the defenders and by 6 September had withdrawn, their first undoubted defeat on land in that war. MacArthur was sure that the Australians took too long to gain victory, and he criticised Clowes' handling of the battle. Rowell defended Clowes in a letter to Vasey.

Document 333

Rowell to Vasey   HQ, NGF, 30 August 1942

Personal Letter   *For the addressee only*

...
I am personally very bitter over this criticism from a distance and I think it damned unfair to pillory any Commander without any knowledge of the Conditions. It has now rained for 10 days at MILNE BAY & it keeps on raining. ...
[AWM: 54, 225/2/5]

Later, Rowell gave a brief report on the Milne Bay battle.

Document 334

REPORT ON OPERATIONS —   16 November 1942
NEW GUINEA FORCE

11th August to 28th Sept. 1942

...

Section 3 — Operations at Milne Bay
32. A detailed report on the operations at MILNE BAY for the period 25 August to 7 September was forwarded to Advanced LHQ. on 21 September
42. The enemy attempt to capture the air base at MILNE BAY was ... part of a plan designed eventually to capture MORESBY. It failed, first because of the obvious lack of accurate information the enemy had as to our strength and dispositions. As a result he was at no time able to gather adequate force for a move westward from his point of landing towards GILLI GILLI and his effort was exhausted in his abortive attack on No. 3 Strip on 27 August.

The second main reason for his failure was that his troops were left entirely without air support whereas MILNE force enjoyed the continuous offensive support of 75 and 76 SQNS R.A.A.F, together with such bomber co-operation as could be arranged from MORESBY.

In my view, the work of the abovementioned fighter squadrons was the decisive factor in our success and no praise can be too high for the manner in which these young pilots kept the pressure on the enemy for three days in most trying conditions. ...
[AA: A 5954, Box 532]

MacArthur was alarmed at the Japanese advance through the Owen Stanley Ranges. This was the first battle he had commanded since SWPA's creation. He was sure the Australians in New Guinea were performing badly. His concern soon led to a command crisis in New Guinea Force.

Document 335

NOTE OF CONVERSATION BETWEEN THE   *17 September 1942*
PRIME MINISTER AND THE COMMANDER-IN-CHIEF,
SOUTHWEST PACIFIC AREA   *Most Secret*

General MacArthur said he was disturbed at the situation in New Guinea and his view as to the real reason for the present unsatisfactory position is the lack of efficiency of the Australian troops in that theatre.
2. He feels quite convinced that we have superiority in numbers, but the report this morning is that once again we are withdrawing, although no casualties are reported. ...

3. ... [T]he Japanese have the same troubles as our troops, *but they are not withdrawing.*
4. General MacArthur wishes the Prime Minister to understand that the view he takes is not the view of the Australian Command. They have the utmost confidence in their ability to deal with the situation, but General MacArthur, for the reasons given, no longer has confidence. General MacArthur therefore proposes to do all he can to meet the situation, and is arranging to despatch American troops to New Guinea by air or by sea, in order to do everything possible to stem the attack. ...
6. ... General MacArthur says it is his opinion that General Blamey should proceed to New Guinea and take personal Command, not only to energise the situation, but to save himself, because, in the event of the situation in New Guinea becoming really serious, it would be difficult for General Blamey to meet his responsibility to the Australian public.
7. General MacArthur points out that he has no authority to direct General Blamey, but he will advise him that he thinks he should proceed to New Guinea. ...
9. General MacArthur went on to say that within a week he expects to have over 40,000 men in New Guinea, and, if they fight, they should have no trouble in meeting the situation. If they will not fight, 100,000 would be no good. ...
15. It is not a serious force that the Japanese have pushed across the mountains, but the fact that a small force can push us back, fills him with concern. ...
20. The Prime Minister said that, in view of the advice of General MacArthur, he would inform General Blamey that he considered he should go to New Guinea, as suggested.

Canberra, 17 September 1942

NOTE OF SECRAPHONE CONVERSATION...
The Prime Minister spoke to General Blamey... . He said that, in view of the opinion of the Commander-in-Chief, General Blamey should go to New Guinea to take command, and the latter agreed.
[AA: A 5954, Box 532]

Rowell resented Blamey's arrival at Port Moresby. Relations between the two men quickly worsened, to the point where Blamey dismissed Rowell.

Document 336

Blamey to Rowell ALF, SWPA, Adv. HQ, 28 September 1942

Letter *Personal*

Following upon our conversation this morning I regret that I feel it my duty to relieve you of the Command of the New Guinea Force.

You will please arrange to return to Australia at your early convenience and report to the Chief of the General Staff [Northcott] at Melbourne.

A copy of the message sent to the Prime Minister, and the Commander in Chief, SWPA, dealing with the matter is available for your perusal at my Office. I would be glad if you would please call there and peruse and initial it.

I have directed the Staff to ensure that all possible facilities for your departure and comfort are provided.
[AWM: 54, 33/1/4]

Here, Blamey tells Curtin and MacArthur what happened.

Document 337

Blamey to Curtin Port Moresby, 28 September 1942
Repeated to MacArthur

Cablegram 2117 *Most Secret and Personal*

...

On arrival here I informed General Rowell of my instructions from the Prime Minister and Commander in Chief, South West Pacific Area. He proved most difficult and recalcitrant, considering himself very unjustly used. I permitted him to state his case with great frankness. It was mainly a statement of grievances primarily against myself because he had received only one decoration for war services in the Middle East where certain other officers had received two.

He charged me with having failed to safeguard his interests and said that he felt that he was being made to eat dirt. All of my persuasion could not make him see the matter realistically.

On the second evening I asked General Burston[3] as an old friend of Rowell to endeavour to induce a proper frame of mind, but Burston met with no success.

---

3. Major General S.R. Burston. He and Rowell had served together in the Middle East after joining the staff of 6th Division in 1939 as colonels.

Instead of setting out full information here for me I have had to search out details and felt a definite atmosphere of obstruction. ...

I was forced to give Rowell written order defining the position. The atmosphere now completely strained. Although I have exercised great patience it is quite obvious that Rowell has taken my coming here as personally against himself that he would be seriously disruptive influence if retained here. Moreover am not satisfied that necessary energy foresight and drive is being put into certain activities. Rowell is competent but of a temperament that harbours imaginary grievances. He has had very limited experience of command. Essential to have Commander of cheerful temperament who is prepared to co-operate to the limit. ...
[AWM: 54, 33/1/4]

Back in Australia, Rowell gave Shedden his side of the story.

Document 338

Note by Shedden   Canberra, 3 October 1942

DEFENCE OF PORT MORESBY   *Most Secret*

...

3. In regard to his relations with General Blamey and his return to Australia, Lieut.-General Rowell stated that the farther they were away from each other, the better they worked. He said that he could say much about affairs in the Middle East, and if he is to be criticised for his work in New Guinea he would seek an enquiry. From what I could gather from Lieut.-General Rowell's conversation, the main ground of his resentment against General Blamey was that the latter had come to New Guinea and superimposed himself on Lieut.-General Rowell and the Corps Staff. Lieut.-General Rowell said that he had suggested to General Blamey that the latter should bring a Staff of his own, and added that Lieut.-General Lavarack and an Army Staff were available at Toowoomba and should be used. It would then appear that cross words of a personal nature followed, and from the earlier observations of Lieut.-General Rowell on the Middle East, it would seem that relations between them were not good. Lieut.-General Rowell did not consider that the cablegram sent to the Prime Minister was an accurate account of their discussions, and he thought that General Blamey had given undue prominence to certain personal aspects.
[AA: A 5954, Box 587]

After the war, when Blamey was out of the Australian army, Rowell was to become CGS; but he had nothing more to do with the Australian war effort after losing command of New Guinea Force. Here, Blamey discusses a possible overseas post for Rowell.

Document 339

Blamey to Shedden   Port Moresby, 8 November 1942

Cablegram Z.134[4]   *Most Secret*

...
Do not favour Military Mission to Russia. The position very different in scope and degree from Britain and America. ... From further information am now in better position to estimate Rowell's activities. For some years strong element has existed in the permanent staff that has been disruptive of harmony with the Militia. ... This element has been entirely self-seeking and continuously critical and intriguing. Wilmott's subversive activities related to these intrigues and good reason to believe association of Rowell and Wilmott.[5] Consider that salutary treatment of Rowell necessary both from the point of view of discipline of this coterie and his own insubordinate attitude. Am unwilling to accept him in responsible appointment under my Command. If am asked for recommendation would now recommend his retirement in the interests of the Service. If, however, the Prime Minister desired to appoint him to Russia, would raise no objection, but consider that he should revert to his substantive rank of Colonel. ...
[AA: A 5954, Box 532]

Rowell had some reason to feel unjustly treated, for he was dismissed when his troops had just begun to force the Japanese into retreat. When composing his report on New Guinea Force operations during his term as commander he would have had special satisfaction in writing the following passages.

Document 340

REPORT ON OPERATIONS —   16 November 1942
NEW GUINEA FORCE

11th August to 28th Sept. 1942

...
25. The IMITA position was occupied by 17 September and the most intensive patrolling commenced in order to gain control of the area between IMITA and IORIBAIWA which represented the final limit of the enemy

---

4. Contained in Teleprinter Message 3525, 9.11.1942.
5. Chester Wilmott, ABC representative, author of *The Struggle for Europe* (1952). On 1.11.1942 Blamey withdrew Wilmott's accreditation as a war correspondent in New Guinea.

advance. As troops new to jungle conditions became more experienced, the size of these offensive patrols was increased, and they operated up to a considerable depth in rear of the enemy's position and against his L of C. ...

An additional factor in regaining the initiative was the employment of 25 pdrs. from 14 Aust Fd. Regt from the vicinity of roadhead against the IORIBAIWA RIDGE. ...

30. By the evening of 27 Sep. 25 Inf Bde had advanced from the IMITA Ridge to the enemy's defensive position on IORIBAIWA Ridge, which was occupied early on the morning of 28 September. Information received from natives had made it clear that his supplies were in a bad way and air recess. [reconnaissances] for the few previous days had disclosed no movement of supply trains forward of MYOLA. ...

[AA: A 5954, Box 532]

On 1 October Lt.-Gen. E.F. Herring reached Port Moresby to take command of New Guinea Force. Blamey remained in New Guinea, at an Advanced Headquarters of Allied Land Forces, SWPA. The Australian advance over the Kokoda Trail is here briefly summarised.

Document 341

OPERATIONS IN NEW GUINEA.   HQ, NGF, 30 January 1943

Brief for GOC NG Force.   *Secret*

. . .

(b) *Advance through the mountains to the coast.*
During this stage the enemy was still dependent on a tenuous L of C which was subjected to constant air attack. At EORA CREEK, OIVI and GORARI frontal pressure to hold the enemy combined with encircling moves which threatened or actually cut his L of C brought about a tactical decision. In this stage our operations were based on supply by air dropping with the use of carrying parties for the collection and distribution of supplies. The conditions were exceptionally strenuous and only well trained and well led troops could have maintained the momentum of the attack. The Comd 25 Aust Inf Bde [Brig. K.W. Eather] reported that the training of his bde had been along the right lines but that the training should be made tougher, patrolling by night improved, more practice in visual training and in taking out strong [points]. This stage illustrates the great advantages conferred by air superiority, which enables air supply, in turn giving great flexibility. ...

[AWM: 54, 285/3/1]

By mid-November the campaign in the Owen Stanleys was over, and Blamey expected the Japanese beachheads at Buna, Gona and Sanananda to succumb quickly. His optimism was ill-founded.

Two United States regiments (equivalent to Australian brigades) of the 32nd Division had assembled on the right flank of the Allied advance, 'some 10 miles as the crow flies from Buna'. Blamey felt the Americans would capture Buna a day before the Australians reached Gona. In fact, the Australians took Gona on 9 December, whereas Buna did not fall until 2 January 1943.

Here, Blamey looks forward to a quick victory on the Papuan coast.

Document 342

Blamey to Shedden　　　　　ALF, SWPA, Adv. HQ, 14 November 1942

Letter　　　　　　　　　　　　　　　　　　　　　　　　　　　*Most Secret*

. . .
I think the very stiff fighting is over unless the Japanese succeed in landing forces in the next week. We expect to begin our advance on Monday morning and in a few days to sweep through to Buna and Gona. The Australian troops have defeated the bulk of the enemy forces, I believe, in the area between Kokoda and the Kumusi River. The fighting has been stiffer than any we have been called upon to carry out yet. In the jungle area near Gorari the enemy left no less than 500 dead. A pleasing feature is that in spite of the closeness of the fighting, our casualties are very much less than the enemy's and our men are definitely superior to them in jungle fighting. ...
[AA: A 5954, Box 532]

Instead of surrendering, the Japanese strongly resisted attempts to take their beachheads, and the Australians had to fight a very hard and costly campaign.

Document 343

Blamey to Shedden　　　ALF, SWPA, Adv. HQ, NG, 30 November 1942

Letter　　　　　　　　　　　　　　　　　　　　　　　　　　　*Most Secret*

As regards the position here, the Japanese is resisting fiercely in his last strong-hold. We are cracking his Gona position, and I hope that will be accomplished today as I write, and from there we will move on to Sanananda.

The Buna area has been assigned to the Americans. We have all been terribly disappointed, and I might say in confidence, that General MacArthur is equally so at the lack of force and drive shown by the 32nd American Division. They must outnumber the Japs by at least five to one on the Buna front, but to date have made no progress. We have sent fresh troops over by air to our own front where the numbers of the two brigades that went over the Kokoda track are greatly reduced. These went into action yesterday afternoon.

The country is about as vile a country as any that exists. It is low and marshy and quite a lot of scrubby jungle and numerous short tidal rivers. Such tracks as exist are mud. However, if this morning's operation to take out Gona Village is successful we will be moving on to Sanananda immediately after. ...
[AA: A 5954, Box 532]

Herring, commander of New Guinea Force, shared Blamey's views on the 32nd Division's weaknesses.

Document 344

Herring to Blamey   HQ, Adv. NGF, 30 November 1942

Letter

...
I think it fair to say that 32 U.S. Div. has still not realized that the enemy will only be beaten by hard fighting, & that whilst bombing, straffing, mortars & artillery may soften his resistance to some extent, the men who are left will fight it out & will have to be taken out & killed in hard fighting.
...
[AWM: 3DRL 6643, Blamey Papers, 170.2]

MacArthur's concern over the 32nd Division's performance at Buna caused him to send General Robert L. Eichelberger to take over command. In a celebrated meeting at Port Moresby on 30 November MacArthur told Eichelberger to 'take Buna or don't come back alive'. Eichelberger was at the divisional command post before noon on 1 December. Herring's comments testify to the speed with which he transformed the division.

Document 345

Herring to Blamey   HQ, Adv. NGF, 3 December 1942

Letter

...
   Eichelberger has turned 32 Div upside down, he personally went all round his [forward troops] in the left sector yesterday. ... There is no question that already a great improvement in organisation & control has taken place...
   There is no doubt that Eichelberger's visit to see for himself exactly what the fwd. tps are doing, has had a great effect. He practically walked into BUNA VILLAGE & no one could deter him, tho' I gather a number of windy gentlemen tried to.
   The men of both 39 & 49 Bns have arrived in good heart, marching along in the heat they are always ready to greet one with a smile, which is a very good sign. ...
[AWM: 3DRL 6643, Blamey Papers, 170.2]

   Here Blamey tells his Prime Minister of some of the problems arising from the beachhead battles.

Document 346

Blamey to Curtin   ALF, SWPA, Adv. HQ, NG, 4 December 1942

Letter   *Most Secret and Personal*

   ... The wastage in tropical warfare in undeveloped areas is immense. For example, at least one-third of our force at Milne Bay is already infected with malaria. The Buna area is an equally evil one for this disease. Our battle wastage is fairly considerable. The two together will place us in what I believe will soon be a very precarious position. I do not think for one moment that the Jap is going to take his reverses in this area without making the greatest effort to hold on and to come back later. He has shown a degree of stubbornness in the defence of Buna and Gona which makes this intention clear.
   I had hoped that our strategical plans would have been crowned with complete and rapid success in the tactical field. It was completely successful strategically in as much as we brought an American Division on to Buna and an Australian Division on to Gona simultaneously. But in the tactical field after the magnificent advance through the most difficult area, the Owen Stanley Range, it is a very sorry story.
   It has revealed the fact that the American troops cannot be classified as attack troops. They are definitely not equal to the Australian militia, and

from the moment they met opposition sat down and have hardly gone forward a yard. The action, too, has revealed a very alarming state of weakness in their staff system and in their war psychology. General MacArthur has relieved the Divisional Commander and has called up General Eichelberger the Corps Commander, and sent him over to take charge. He informs me that he proposes to relieve both the regimental commanders, the equivalent of our brigade commanders, and five out of six of the battalion commanders; and this in the face of the enemy. I am afraid now that the bulk of the fighting will fall on our troops in spite of the greatly larger numbers of the 32nd U.S. Division.

The brigades that went over the mountain track are now so depleted that they are being withdrawn and I am utilising the only remaining AIF brigade in Port Moresby and a brigade of Militia, that has been intensively trained here, and I think we will pull it off all right. ...
[AA: A 5954, Box 532]

Here, Herring tells Blamey of an incident when the 25th Bde was relieved, after it had fought its way over the Kokoda Trail and opened the assault on Gona.

Document 347

Herring to Blamey   HQ, NGF, 6 December 1942

Letter

...
Eather[6] is spending tonight with me. From what he tells me the enemy garrison or what is left of it at GONA must be having a rotten time. Our fellows on the west of the Creek pick off about 6 Japs a day & his fellows used to account for some too. As one of his Bns was moving out, one of his fellows hit a Jap & the Bn went out cheering. They look on the successful hitting of a Jap in much the same way as one might regard the bowling over of a rabbit. ...
[AWM: 3DRL 6643, Blamey Papers, 170.2]

Gona fell on 9 December, the day Blamey described his problems to Shedden.

---

6. Brigadier K.W. Eather, commander of the 25th Brigade (2/25th, 2/31st and 2/33rd Battalions), which was relieved by the 21st Brigade on 4.12.1942.

Document 348

Blamey to Shedden   ALF, SWPA, Adv. HQ, NG, 9 December 1942

Letter   Most Secret

I had hoped we would have completed the reconquest of PAPUA before this, and my hopes were largely based upon the fact of our rapid progress from the KUMUSI River towards the coast. We met no opposition at all until we got into the filthy low country of the coastal plains, and the absence even of patrols led me to expect we would meet with but little opposition. However, it appears that the Jap concentrated the whole of his energies on setting up defensive works with the object of holding the position until relief forces arrived.

We have therefore found him in very strong positions in Cape Endaiadere, along the Buna landing ground, in Buna itself, in front of Sanananda and at Gona. In some places his defences consist of strong broad embankments, built of logs and filled in with earth to a width of something like about 5' at the top, covered in some places with barbed wire and in others by jungle barricades.

We, ourselves, are in the inevitable position of any force whose advance has outstripped its capacity for maintenance at normal rates. In this roadless region we must move everything forward by air from Moresby or by tiny craft from Milne Bay. The latter is very promising and we are developing it as fast as our resources in boats permit. But one is faced with the continually acute question of relief of forward troops which must be effected by transporting them by air from Moresby to the other side. The immediate result is that our capacity to build up fire power is very limited. Artillery is essential and we have so far been able to transport a total of thirteen guns forward. This of course is hopelessly inadequate to deal with strongly prepared enemy positions in different localities. It is soley this inability to develop fire power in co-operation with infantry attack that is holding us up. ...

[AA: A 5954, Box 532]

After the fall of Gona, the Australians and Americans still had to endure six weeks of fighting before victory in Papua was complete. Here, Herring mentions some of the features of this fighting to Blamey.

Document 349

Herring to Blamey   HQ, Adv. NGF, 11 December 1942

Letter

... With regard to the fighting I think the following propositions can be made:-

1. The Jap positions in all areas are well sited, strongly built & with good fields of fire. ...
2. The Jap fights on till he is killed.
3. Attacks on Jap positions in strength have all been extremely costly, & as a rule have produced but little result. ...
4. What we want is to get the Jap to come out of his positions so that we can kill him, as he has done at BUNA beach in counter attacks [against] American posts on the beach. The Americans get a good bag here daily. ...
5. Americans at BUNA Front have really been trying since Eichelberger came... . Both here & on the Coast they are taking their casualties cheerfully & continue to be aggressive. I doubt whether any troops would do much better than they are doing at the moment. They are making a little progress each day, & are learning the tricks.
6. They are doing in fact what I have directed & that is to go quietly, take out a post here & a post there each day if possible, shoot men out of trees & generally harry the enemy, maintaining pressure everywhere & breaking down his morale. This seeemed the only proper course when we considered how little was achieved by 30 Bde's splendid effort & heavy losses, & 30 Bde is proceeding on similar lines — I believe this policy will bear fruit & is doing so, however unspectacular. ...

[AWM: 3DRL 6643, Blamey Papers, 170.2]

Although the Allies at Gona-Buna derived great benefit from air support, Herring was not always completely satisfied that his troops were getting all the help possible, as the following passage shows.

Document 350

Herring to Blamey   HQ, Adv. NGF, 21 December 1942

Letter

. . .
I don't know that we are getting full value out of the Air at the moment, I mean so far as bombing is concerned. You will have had the reports of inaccurate bombing which have disturbed our tps to some extent. The Wirraway boys all fly so low in doing their [Tactical Reconnaissance and Artillery Reconnaissance] that the tps feel the bombers could afford to come low enough to make sure of hitting what they are aiming at. It does look as if there was either bad briefing or inexperienced crews. There is no doubt that bombing in the SANANANDA area & at BUNA MISSION & GIROPA PT areas must help to demoralise the enemy. It should be possible to produce experts for these jobs who can be sure of identifying their targets

& hitting them. Perhaps you could have a talk to Kenny [sic][7] on these lines. I do feel we shd. make full use of every weapon we have got in the process of extermination. ...
[AWM: 3DRL 6643, Blamey Papers, 170.2]

Organised Japanese resistance in Papua ceased on 23 January 1943. A week later a report prepared in the Headquarters of New Guinea Force had this to say on the beachhead battles.

Document 351

OPERATIONS IN NEW GUINEA HQ, NGF, 30 January 1943

Brief for GOC NG Force Secret

...
(c) *Operations in the Coastal Area.*
Here ... the enemy was back in his base area with practically no L of C, he had artillery and a plentiful supply of ammunition and food. He was reinforced with fresh troops and had plenty of time to prepare his defences. His defences were well sited and concealed from air and ground observation. Except in the CAPE ENDAIADERE area we had either to attack along defiles between rivers and swamps or else to go through the swamps. Thick jungle, kunai grass, sago swamps and mangrove swamps covered the area. Enemy had earthwork defences of varying types and of these the "bunker" type were the most difficult to destroy. These bunkers were sited close together and often took the form of perimeter defences. Getting astride the enemy L of C in SANANANDA area did not force a withdrawal as the enemy fought it out to the last man unless he had been practically encircled and had been subjected to prolonged artillery and mortar fire. Each enemy locality or perimeter had to be crushed in turn; in most cases it was necessary to take out all the enemy bunkers together, attempts to take out one or two by themselves generally resulted in costly failure. The beach was often the best objective and it enabled us to split his forces, stop the movement of enemy barges and to make it almost impossible for the enemy commander to exercise control over his forces. In this stage we followed a deliberate methodical and progressive plan making the utmost use of our artillery and also of tanks where practicable. The prolonged and intensive fighting accentuated the strain on the administrative machine but the increased use of small craft to deliver ammunition and supplies well forward combined with the use of 5,000 native carriers enabled us to maintain heavy pressure on the enemy. Jeep tracks were developed and without the use of jeeps the scale

---

7. General George C. Kenney, Commander of Allied Air Forces, SWPA, July 1942 — August 1945.

of our artillery effort would have been greatly reduced. The enemy had no tanks and although he had much ammunition he was very inferior in artillery and made poor use of what he had. ...
[AWM: 54, 285/3/1]

The following comment on the Papuan victory is illuminating. No doubt MacArthur wished to stress that in the United States, Australia had a better friend than Britain.

Document 352

[SHEDDEN'S] NOTES ON   Brisbane, 16–20 January 1943
DISCUSSIONS WITH COMMANDER-IN-
CHIEF, SOUTHWEST PACIFIC AREA

Operations in New Guinea   *Most Secret*

...
9. General MacArthur asked if the Prime Minister had received any message from Mr. Churchill on the results of the campaign in New Guinea and, on being told that none had been received, he expressed surprise at his apparent indifference to operations so vitally affecting a part of the British Empire. ... General Marshall had been almost embarrassing in the number of his messages in the concluding phases of the campaign, but he had not heard from Field Marshal Dill.[8]
[AA: A 5954, Box 2]

More than a year later Page[9] tried to arouse controversy by criticising the conduct of the Papuan campaign, claiming that the right course was to let the Japanese 'rot to pieces from malaria, dysentery and starvation'. To refute Page, a press statement was prepared over Curtin's name.

Document 353

Press Statement by Curtin   Canberra, 13 March 1944

Sir Earle Page, M.P.

... Sir Earle Page lightly dismisses the time factor in the operations as

---

8. Churchill's personal military representative to President Roosevelt.
9. Earle Page had returned to Australia from London and the post of 'Accredited Representative' in late June 1942.

though the New Guinea campaign were unrelated to the general strategy in the Pacific... He fails to grasp the significance of what the northern coast of New Guinea meant in the way of airfields and earlier radar warnings; or that our limited air strength was greatly increased by the heavy bombers being able to operate from these airfields instead of from the mainland of Australia. Time being no object, he would apparently have surrendered the initiative to the enemy with indifference as to the length of the war and the earliest possible defeat of the enemy. His idea of d[e]pending on malaria, dysentery and hunger for results would have meant that the release of our own prisoners of war would be indefinitely postponed, and it would be they and not the Japanese who would endure the privations he mentions. ...
[AA: A 5954, Box 537]

24
NEW GUINEA, JANUARY 1943 — APRIL 1944

Although the Japanese were defeated in Papua they still held the Australian Mandated Territory of New Guinea. On 8 March 1942 they had made unopposed landings at Lae and Salamaua. They were reinforced in January 1943. As the following extracts show, Blamey was right to expect a Japanese move against Wau, an important inland centre which had an airfield.

Document 354

Blamey to Herring   ALF, SWPA, Adv. HQ, NG, 8 January 1943

Letter   *Most Secret*

...
2. At the conclusion of the present phase, the defensive phase has to be considered. It seems that the Jap convoy which came to New Guinea yesterday was aimed at Lae and Salamaua, and not at Buna. ...
  It would appear to have been about 60% successful... .
3. Whether the intention of this force is to push forward from Lae and Salamaua area towards Wau remains to be seen. This eventuality has always been present in my mind and I have kept the 17th Brigade AIF intact either to meet this threat, or as the spearhead of an advance in this area. It seems clear that the Japs on your front will be abandoned to their fate, although it is possible that efforts may be made at night to bring them some relief.
  ...
6. In the meantime the 17th Brigade AIF will be moving from Milne Bay to Port Moresby as it is replaced by the 29th Brigade. It will therefore be available in reserve unless it is felt that the situation requires its transfer to Wau at an early date. ...
[AWM: 3DRL 6643, Blamey Papers, 170.2]

The Japanese moved on Wau as Blamey had expected. By a dramatic airlift, the 17th Brigade was moved to Wau in time to forestall the enemy.
  The following extract from Blamey's official report of the battle begins with an account of the clash at Wandumi, an outpost 5 km from Wau.

Document 355

REPORT ON NEW GUINEA OPERATIONS 16 March 1944
23 JAN 43 — 13 SEP 43

Secret

...
The enemy attack on Wau:
... This attack [at Wandumi] began in the early morning of 28 Jan and developed in intensity until at dawn on 29 Jan the garrison was completely surrounded and being attacked from its front and both flanks. Repeated attacks were made by the enemy in an attempt to subdue the outpost but the garrison though forced to withdraw to the line of the [Bulolo] river, stubbornly resisted and thus succeeded in delaying the enemy advance on WAU for over 24 hours. This made possible the landing on 29 Jan of fifty seven transport aircraft containing the bulk of 2/7 Aust Inf Bn and the remainder 2/5 Aust Inf Bn. These were immediately placed in perimeter defence of WAU aerodrome and disposed in depth along the main route of approach of the enemy.

On 30 Jan the enemy launched repeated heavy attacks against our forces along the SE approaches to WAU and on the outskirts of the aerodrome but all attacks were driven off with considerable loss to the enemy. On this day 65 transport aircraft landed on the aerodrome, many being subjected to enemy small arms fire as they came in to land and whilst unloading. Carried in the aircraft were the dismantled portions of two 25 pr guns with over 600 rounds of ammunition. These were landed on the aerodrome at 0915 hrs and the guns were assembled and in action early in the afternoon.
...
Heavy fighting continued around the outskirts of WAU for several days and during this time opportunity was also taken to continually harass the enemy L of C by raids in the WANDUMI and BUIBAINING areas. ...

... [S]evere and bitter fighting ... continued each day until at dawn on 9 Feb the enemy were seen to be withdrawing across the BULOLO in the direction of WANDUMI. The withdrawal was pressed vigorously, attacks being launched against the enemy at many places along his L of C while bombing and machine gunning from the air inflicted many casualties and harassed his retreat.

WANDUMI was cleared on 12 Feb and the WAIPALI-BUIBAINING area on 26 Feb.

By 1 Mar 43 all Japanese troops were clear of the MUBO VALLEY and the immediate danger to WAU was removed.

Other Factors in the Battle for Wau

Although the enemy failed to capture WAU the position on 29 and 30 January was definitely precarious.

The cause of this lay in the difficulty of air transport in a mountainous area under exceptionally difficult conditions of climate. ...[pp.12–13]
[AWM: 54, 519/6/58]

After the narrow escape at Wau there was a lull in the land fighting in New Guinea. Here, Blamey sums up the situation for the benefit of Curtin and Shedden.

Document 356

Prime Minister's War Conference Minute   Canberra, 12 February 1943

Most Secret

Present: The Prime Minister.
        The Commander-in-Chief, Australian Military Forces.
        The Secretary, Department of Defence.

(74) *Operations in New Guinea.*
    General Blamey said that the Japanese were building themselves up very strongly in the outer screen of the defence line which covered Rabaul, the main advanced base. Lae and Salamaua were vital points in this line of defence and if the Japanese were deprived of them, a serious breach would be made in their line. Information had been received that the Japanese were bringing down three divisions for use in this area. The supply of the Australian forces at Wau by air was a more difficult proposition than that of the maintenance of the Australian forces in the Buna-Gona area. The road was being completed to Bulldog, but it would take at least four months to complete. In the meantime, Wau was a sore spot and the situation was not a very happy one.
2. General Blamey said that the Australian forces would not be ready for further offensive operations until June.
[AA: A 5954, Box 4]

A Japanese attempt to move further reinforcements to Lae was largely unsuccessful as about 80% of the convoy was destroyed in the Battle of the Bismarck Sea.

Document 357

Report   Not Dated [probably early 1944]

AIR OPERATIONS[10]   *Secret*

Indirect Air Support
The Battle of the Bismar[c]k Sea

The outstanding event in the sphere of indirect air support during the conduct of the WAU-SALAMAUA campaign was the sinking of the Japanese Convoy in what has become known as the Battle of the BISMAR[C]K SEA.

The convoy was first attacked on 2 Mar when its component parts were converging north of DAMPIER STRAITS. Aircraft of 5 US Air Force attacked the convoy and its protecting aircraft and succeeded in sinking two ships and damaging others.

On the following day the convoy, now comprising 18 ships, had arrived in the BISMAR[C]K SEA and when about 70 miles east of SALAMAUA it was attacked by a force of heavy, medium and light bombers with fighter protection. During a most intensive bombing and strafing attack, 500 lb bombs with 4-5 second delay fuses were dropped from mast height, while 1000 lb bombs were accurately dropped from medium height. Low level strafing was directed against ships and against barges in which the Japanese attempted to escape. The attack continued throughout the day and by nightfall only four ships remained afloat, two of these being badly damaged and on fire.

During the engagement enemy refuelling bases at LAE and MALAHANG were regularly and persistently bombed and this forced their aircraft to return long distances to NEW BRITAIN for refuelling. This factor together with the superiority of our fighter strength and the co-ordination, intensity and accuracy of the attack, on the ships so reduced enemy opposition that our aircraft were able to press home their attacks almost with impunity.

The ships which had survived the attack on 3 Mar were again attacked on the following day and barges carrying survivors from the convoy were strafed and sunk. ...
[AWM: 54, 519/6/58]

A year later MacArthur made the following comment on the Battle of the Bismarck Sea.

---

10. Appendix A to Blamey's Report on New Guinea Operations 23.1.1943 — 13.9.1943.

Document 358

NOTES OF [Curtin's and Shedden's]   Canberra, 17 March 1944
DISCUSSIONS WITH THE COMMANDER-IN-CHIEF,
SOUTHWEST PACIFIC AREA

. . .

(2) *The Prime Minister's Visit to Washington and London*
. . .
8. In reply to an enquiry as to when he considered the threat of invasion to Australia had been definitely removed, General MacArthur said that he finally dated this from the Bismarck Sea operation, when the Japanese had been frustrated from landing forces at Morobe which would have threatened our positions at Buna and Gona. ...
[AA: A 5954, Box 3]

> After the success at Wau, Australian troops in the region maintained pressure on Lae and Salamaua, laying some groundwork for the coming offensive. On 30 June American troops landed at Nassau Bay, 28 km south of Salamaua. Blamey's orders were to maintain pressure on Salamaua, so as to make the Japanese believe that it was the main objective, so causing them to reinforce it at the expense of Lae, which was the real target, and the key to the Ramu and Markham valleys. This 'Salamaua magnet' was to work well.
> Here, Herring gives a progress report on the Salamaua operation.

Document 359

Herring to Blamey   HQ, NGF, 9 August 1943

Letter

. . .
The SALAMAUA operation is proceeding slowly & there is little progress to report. The Japanese made a determined effort to dislodge 2/7 Bn from the Old Vickers Posn. on BOBDUBI RIDGE. It cost them very dear. At present the guns & the air are hammering away while the ground troops continue their patrolling & regrouping. ... The Americans on the Coast have still failed to capture ROOSEVELT RIDGE. The country is really terrible & reports I now have from officers who have been forward with the tps engaged in the fighting report that their morale is excellent & that they have killed quite a number of the enemy. ... Control of the American units has not I feel been altogether satisfactory; as you know their staff work is poor & they seem to be able to get everything even more muddled than would

at first sight appear possible. But I want you to know I am quite satisfied with the way their men have been fighting... .
[AWM: 3DRL 6643, Blamey Papers, 170.2]

The troops who tightened the ring around Salamaua, eventually leading to its fall, were praised by Blamey as follows.

Document 360

REPORT ON NEW GUINEA OPERATIONS 16 March 1944
23 JAN 43 — 13 SEP 43
...

TASKS OF THE ARMS OF THE ALLIED LAND FORCES Secret

Infantry
In this campaign the Australian Infantryman again proved his superiority over the Japanese. Engaged in the operation were veteran units which had seen service in the MIDDLE EAST, Militia units which were receiving their introduction into battle, and personnel of Independent Companies who had gained their knowledge of the country and the Japanese in many early audacious clashes. All troops endured the rigorous conditions of the campaign with a fortitude worthy of the highest praise and despite the long and sustained periods of contact with the enemy, their morale improved as the campaign continued. Their action in battle was magnificent. In defence, even when completely surrounded, they resisted with cool determination all attempts to dislodge them from their positions, inflicting heavy casualties on the enemy with controlled fire from their weapons. In attack, they showed their as[c]endancy over the Japanese in their studied methods and their personal initiative. Every action was carried through with an inflexible resolve to close with the enemy and destroy him.

The American soldier proved himself a tough and able fighter, quick to learn and eager to gain battle experience. ... [p.34]
[AWM: 54, 519/6/58]

The coming offensive in New Guinea would be part of numerous carefully co-ordinated moves to encircle and 'neutralise' Rabaul. The complex overall plan was code-named *CARTWHEEL*. As part of *CARTWHEEL* Australian troops would be given the task of clearing the Japanese out of the Huon Peninsula. In so doing they would help clear the way for MacArthur to move westwards along New Guinea's north coast. This would enable his advance to remain significant as a supplementary one to Nimitz's. The rivalry between MacArthur and Nimitz is indicated below.

Document 361

Prime Minister's War Conference Minute   Sydney, 7 June 1943

PRESENT: The Prime Minister.
           The Commander-in-Chief, Southwest Pacific Area.
           The Secretary, Department of Defence.

(80) *DISCUSSION WITH COMMANDER-IN-CHIEF, SOUTHWEST PACIFIC AREA.*
...

3. [General MacArthur said that] [a]part from intermediate objectives, the main aim now was to force the Japanese out of Rabaul. The nearest base to the eastern part of Australia would then be Truk and, when this progress had been achieved, a radical change would occur in the strategical position as it affected Australia.

4. The final and more prolonged stage against Japan would be the ultimate offensive action to ensure her decisive defeat and unconditional surrender.
...

6. It had come to General MacArthur's knowledge that Admiral Nimitz, Naval Commander of the Pacific Area, had submitted a memorandum to the effect that the whole of the operations in the Pacific should be brought under his command. General MacArthur had protested against this and said that if effect were given to it he would submit his resignation, in order that he might gain freedom of action and speech. ...

8. General MacArthur said that the operations contemplated would be carried out in three phases:-

(i)   The T[r]obriand Islands and Woodlark Island to the east of South Eastern New Guinea would be attacked and occupied by about 10,000 American troops in each case. ...

(ii)   An attempt would be made to take out Lae and Salamaua by transporting by air to the Markham Valley the 7th Division, and landing the 9th Division by sea to the east of Lae. It was then intended to subject both Lae and Salamaua to intense air attack, whilst at the same time exercising heavy pressure on them from ground troops. This course of action, it was hoped, would keep the casualties of ground troops down to the minimum.

      Having achieved these objectives, the intention was to press northwards to take out Finsch[h]afen and Madang and place a block against enemy action from the North from Alexishafen and Wewak. ...

(iii)   Phase (ii) will give command of the Vitiaz Strait and it is then proposed to transport, by air, forces which would occupy the Western end of New Britain as far Eastwards as Talasea and Gasmata. ...

[AA: A 5954, Box 2]

On 4 September 1943 men of the 9th Division landed about 30 km east of Lae. The 7th Division was soon in the battle, and Lae fell on 16 September, five days after Australian soldiers entered Salamaua. The 9th Division was moved to Finschhafen, where it was engaged in fierce fighting before defeating a Japanese division sent to oppose it. The 7th Division moved up the Markham-Ramu Valley, in January breaking through the Japanese defensive position at Shaggy Ridge. In April the Australian army ended its Huon Peninsula campaign when it secured Madang and Alexishafen.

We print concluding comments from Blamey's report on the campaign. Blamey writes that 'all air movement and landings occurred without incident', but does not mention that at Port Moresby on 7 September 59 soldiers about to be flown to Nadzab were killed when a Liberator (B-24) crashed into their trucks.

Document 362

REPORT ON NEW GUINEA OPERATIONS 12 October 1944
4 September 1943 — 26 April 1944

...

CONCLUSION *Secret*

General

These operations provided the Australian Military Forces with an opportunity to carry out a full-scale, coordinated offensive with an established Corps of three divisions. Two divisions only were employed in the operation, the third being retained in AUSTRALIA for use as a reserve if required.

The two Divisions became engaged in operations of a widely divergent character. 7 Aust Div became the first British Division to be transported into operations by aircraft and engage some of its personnel in an assault paratroop landing. 9 Aust Div were participant in the first amphibious operation conducted by Australian forces since the historic landing at GALLIPOLI in 1915.

Both operations were carried out as part of a larger plan embracing the removal of the Japanese forces from the strategic areas in which they constituted a threat to the safety of AUSTRALIA.

The successful conduct of the whole operation was possible only because of the efficient and ready cooperation received from Allied Naval and Allied Air Forces... .

In spite of the many difficulties associated with the conduct of warfare in undeveloped tropical countries, arising from the rugged nature of the terrain, the primitive communications and facilities, the rigid conditions of climate and the ever present ravaging diseases, the campaign was carried to a successful conclusion as a result of the skilful planning of my staff, the aggressive leadership of all Commanders, the untiring efforts of the services and the courage, determination and ability of the Australian soldier.

Tasks of the Arms of the Allied Land Forces
Infantry

Many of the infantry were required to adapt themselves to new conditions and methods of warfare during these operations.

7 Aust Div contained many veterans from battles against the Japanese at MILNE BAY, KOKODA TRAIL and BUNA — SANANANDA but it had been reinforced while in Australia with many troops without battle experience. The use of aircraft in their advance required special training to ensure speed in emplaning and deplaning and in loading and unloading their guns, vehicles and equipment. As events proved, all air movement and landings occurred without incident. The subsequent landward advance, firstly against LAE and later into the RAMU VALLEY, indicated the speed with which infantry, moved and supplied by air, can advance against enemy opposition. In the battle for KANKIRYO SADDLE the infantry closed with the Japanese after climbing the almost precipitous sides of SHAGGY RIDGE and carried the assault in bitter fighting against a well-entrenched enemy. In the later stages, 15 Aust Inf Bde, veterans of the operations at SALAMAUA, thoroughly and systematically searched the wide area between the RAMU VALLEY and the Coast, often necessitating the carrying of stores and equipment over rough mountainous country by day and by night in order to close with the retreating Japanese.

9 Aust Div met the Japanese for the first time. In the operation conducted against LAE, they exhibited their eagerness to meet the enemy by the rapidity of their advance despite the difficulties of the country and the weather. In forcing the crossing of the swollen and dangerous BUSU River against Japanese opposition and unaided by craft or bridge, they exhibited courage and determination of the highest order. In the operations at FINSCHHAFEN and SAT[T]ELBERG, the Division met the Japanese in large numbers and in every action proved their superiority as soldiers. In attempting to regain the areas captured by the Australians, the Japanese counter attacks met the devastating fire of the defenders and though attaining a measure of local success, was quickly driven back into the mountains, leaving behind many casualties. Utilising artillery and tank support to the greatest extent and ably supported from the air, the Division applied the experience gained against the German in NORTH AFRICA and illustrated to their new opponents the effect of team work on the power of a well trained and equipped force in modern war. In their close encounters with the Japanese, every individual soldier fought with a determined resolve to destroy the enemy and their ability with bayonet, rifle and automatic weapon did much to break the morale of the Japanese force as a whole. When the enemy resistance was broken, 9 Aust Div and 5 Aust Div took up the pursuit with vigour and again utilising all available supporting arms and weapons, they overcame the difficulties of movement imposed by the terrain and relentlessly exploited their success, denying the enemy any chance of reorganisation or escape. ... [pp.61–63]

[AWM: 3 DRL 6643, Blamey Papers, File No. 13]

25
WHAT FUTURE ROLE FOR THE AUSTRALIAN ARMY?

This section deals with the general political question of the army's role in the closing stages of the war, while the next two sections are devoted to the campaigns in the Mandated Territory of New Guinea, and Borneo. While the Australians were fighting in the *CARTWHEEL* battles the Curtin government was deciding on the broad principles which would govern the use of the nation's armed forces for the remainder of the war.

Document 363

War Cabinet Minute   Canberra, 1 October 1943

(3065) ...

Part II — THE WAR EFFORT OF THE SERVICES

1. *Service Commitments Overseas*

(i) *General Principles:*

War Cabinet reviewed the commitments overseas which had been entered into by Australia in respect of land, sea and air forces before the occurrence of the war in the Pacific. The following principles were affirmed:-
(a) It is of vital importance to the future of Australia and her status at the peace table in regard to the settlement in the Pacific, that her *military effort* should be concentrated as far as possible in the Pacific and that it should be on a scale to guarantee her an effective voice in the peace settlement.
(b) If necessary, the extent of this effort should be maintained at the expense of commitments in other theatres. In the interests of Australia and the British Empire in the Pacific, it is imperative that this view should be accepted by the United Kingdom and the other Dominions, especially New Zealand and Canada.
    It was decided that these views should be represented to the Prime Minister of the United Kingdom in the first instance and a picture of the whole problem placed before him.
    The A.I.F. having returned to Australia, the remaining overseas commitments relate to the Navy and Air Force. ...
[AA: A 2673, Vol 13]

Within these broad guidelines, the government had more specific intentions, as the following extract makes clear.

Document 364

Curtin to MacArthur   22 November 1943

Letter   *Most Secret*

The splendid progress of your operations has been the subject of some thought on my part and discussion by the Government in relation to your future plans and the area of employment of the Australian Forces which have been assigned to you.
2. As you are aware, the territory of Papua is part of the Commonwealth of Australia, and the Commonwealth Government holds a mandate from the League of Nations for the administration of the former German Colony of New Guinea and the former German islands situated in the Pacific Ocean and lying south of the Equator, other than the islands of Western Samoa and the island of Nauru. ... [These] "C" class mandates are in accordance with ... Article 22 of the Covenant of the League:-
"... administered under the laws of the Mandatory as integral portions of its territory..."
3. Australia therefore has a special interest in the employment of its own forces in the operations for the ejectment of the enemy from territory under its administration. Furthermore, it is essential, under the terms of your Directive, that the Government should be at least broadly aware of your ideas for the employment of the Australian Forces in any areas outside Australian and mandated territory, and of what you may contemplate in regard to operations affecting the latter areas. You will appreciate also that the Government must have regard to the legislative provisions of the Defence (Citizen Military Forces) Act 1943 which defines the limits of employment of the Citizen Forces.
4. Although, by the most complete co-operation on your part, there has never been any need to refer to the documentary basis which governs your relationship to the Australian Government...
5. ... I would greatly appreciate advice of prospective plans in regard to the use of the Australian land forces, in order that the Australian Government may consider their contemplated use.
6. It is, of course, unnecessary for me to add that this request is not prompted by any desire to interfere in any way with your conduct of operations, or to participate in the formulation of plans. The Australian Government has at all times had the utmost confidence in your handling of these matters, and is deeply appreciative of the remarkable results you have achieved with the limited resources at your disposal. ...
[AA: A 5954, Box 570]

MacArthur's reply follows.

Document 365

MacArthur to Curtin   GHQ, SWPA, 24 November 1943

Letter   Secret

I am in complete accord with the general position outlined in your letter of November 22. The desirability and necessity of your being informed of operational plans for the area are self-evident. At our meeting Tuesday I shall give you my general concept of the campaign in such detail as you may desire. In this connection, however, I call attention to the limitations with reference to operations which are imposed upon me by higher authorities. I am constantly receiving directives which modify materially my use of the forces here and at the present time am still in doubt as to master decisions with regard to the future. In addition, you of course understand that whatever plan may be made, the vicissitudes of campaign and the reaction of the enemy may result in almost instantaneous decisions by the military commander producing comprehensive changes in the projected use of the forces. Within these limitations, I shall at our conference on Tuesday acquaint you with everything that is within my scope and knowledge.
[AA: A 5954, Box 570]

A statement of Australia's war aims was made at the London meeting of Commonwealth Prime Ministers.

Document 366

Meeting of Prime Ministers   London, 3 May 1944

P.M.M. (44) 5th Meeting.   Top Secret

The War Situation — The War against Japan.

. . .

Mr. CURTIN pointed out that the Australian Government were now faced with the necessity for deciding the balance of their effort. If it were decided that more forces were to be based on Australia then more food must be sent with them or the Australian armed forces must be reduced to provide the man-power necessary to produce the additional food which would be required. ...

If the Americans wished to send more soldiers to Australia, they would have to be told that this would result in their being provided with less uniforms and less food, and that the deficiency would have to be made up

from America. In view of the distances involved and the difficulties of transportation, he felt that it was only wise to make the greatest use of the nearest sources of supply. This would only be possible if the strength of Australia's armed forces were reduced to provide the man-power which would be required. He was not suggesting that Australia should leave others to fight the war. Australians wished to have a say in how the Pacific area was to be managed, and they realised that the extent of their say would be in proportion, not to the amount of wheat, meat or clothes they produced to support the forces of other nations, but to the amount of fighting they did. There was, therefore, a minimum fighting strength below which the Australians would not go. There was also a maximum strength of Australian armed forces beyond which they could not go, and it was the balance between these limits which the Australian Government sought to fix. ...
[PRO: CAB 99/28]

On 26 June Curtin mentioned to MacArthur that he would like Australian forces represented in the operations against the Philippine Islands, in addition to their use in Australia's mandated territory. MacArthur's plans included both possibilities: Australian troops should relieve American troops in three areas which they had seized from the Japanese in various phases of the *CARTWHEEL* operations; and that two veteran Australian divisions would be employed in the Philippines' campaign. The three areas in the mandated territory were centred on Aitape on the New Guinea mainland, western New Britain, and on Bougainville and outlying smaller islands. MacArthur told Blamey officially of these plans in the following message.

Document 367

MacArthur to Blamey   12 July 1944

Minute   *Top Secret*

1. The advance to the PHILIPPINES necessitates a redistribution of forces and combat missions in the SOUTHWEST PACIFIC AREA in order to make available forces with which to continue the offensive.
2. It is desired that Australian Forces assume the responsibility for the continued neutralization of the Japanese in Australian and British territory and Mandates in the SOUTHWEST PACIFIC AREA, exclusive of the ADMIRALTIES, by the following dates:

NORTHERN SOLOMONS-GREEN ISLAND-EMIRAU ISLANDS ..
                                              1 October 1944
AUSTRALIAN NEW GUINEA .. .. 1 November 1944
NEW BRITAIN .. ..   1 November 1944

3. The forces now assigned combat missions in the above areas should be relieved of all combat responsibility not later than the dates specified in order that intensive preparations for future operations may be initiated.
4. In the advance to the PHILIPPINES it is desired to use Australian Ground Forces and it is contemplated employing initially two AIF Divisions as follows:
One Division — November 1944
One Division — January 1945
5. It is requested that this headquarters be informed of the Australian Forces available with the dates of their availability to accomplish the above plan and your general comments and suggestions.
[AA: A 5954, Box 570]

In discussions with Curtin in Canberra MacArthur discussed the future use of the Australian army.

Document 368

NOTES OF DISCUSSIONS WITH THE   Canberra, 30 September 1944
COMMANDER-IN-CHIEF, SOUTHWEST
PACIFIC AREA

PRESENT: The Prime Minister
         The Commander-in-Chief, Southwest Pacific Area
         The Acting Secretary, Department of Defence

(1) *Review of the War Situation by General MacArthur*
...
3. General MacArthur said that recent operations had been exceedingly successful, in fact, far more successful than could ever have been anticipated. He referred to the policy that he had pursued of isolating the Japanese Forces, and rendering them innocuous. To have adopted the policy of reducing the enemy occupied islands one by one would have cost many thousands of lives which he could not possibly afford, and which, in any case, would have represented so much waste. He intimated that such policy would be continued until the stage when it was necessary to endure sacrifices in the capture of the Philippines.
4. In regard to future operations, in so far as they affected the Australian Forces, they would be, firstly, the garrisoning role for neutralisation of Japanese pockets on the various islands and, secondly, the operational activities of the two A.I.F. Divisions which were to accompany the United States Forces in the advance against the Japanese. ... He stressed the policy that Briti[s]h possessions and Australian mandates should be garrisoned by British and Australian troops, and that, in the capture of British Borneo, British and Australian troops should be used. He considered it essential to

British prestige that this course should be followed. The Admiralty Islands would continue to be garrisoned by the United States Forces, as they were one of the main forward bases.

5. When asked whether the policy of neutralising Japanese pockets contemplated an effort to liquidate them, General MacArthur said that such was not his idea, and that his directive to the Commander-in-Chief, Australian Military Forces [Blamey], would be confined to neutralisation. He appreciated that Australian Local Commanders would possibly find the garrison duties irksome and might desire to undertake some active operations, but this would be a matter for direction by the Australian Authorities. Japanese pockets were of no value whatever to Japan in the war and were depreciating at the rate of ten per cent. per month. They did not present any problem. It would be sufficient for the present to garrison the islands and leave the Japanese gradually to waste away. ...

7. The arrangements for the attack against the Philippines were traversed, and the operational dates given. The Australian divisions would take part in the capture of Mindanao. They would later be employed in the capture of British Borneo, and later again in the attack on Java. ...

[AA: A 5954, Box 3]

In the following document the Chief of the General Staff, Lt. General Sir John Northcott, gave Shedden details of the deployment of the army.

Document 369

Northcott to Shedden   Melbourne, 15 November 1944

Letter   *Top Secret and Personal*

...

FORCES AVAILABLE TO C-in-C S.W.P.A. FOR OFFENSIVE OPERATIONS
1 Aust Corps
2. 1 Aust Corps is composed of the following formations:-
   (a) Corps, HQ and Corps Troops, including 4 Armd Bde.
   (b) 7 Aust Div,
   (c) 9 Aust Div
   (d) Two Beach Gps and one Base Sub-Area.
   (e) The approximate strength of the above force is about 90,000 at present, but will vary according to the final tasks and the administrative set-up arranged for the maintenance of the Corps in operations.

3. The Corps is now training in the CAIRNS-ATHERTON area for amphibious operations, and should have completed its training and be ready to move early in December. It is intended that this Corps be used by C-in-C

S.W.P.A. during the offensive operations now developing in the PHILIPPINES area. The Corps will move ex CAIRNS-TOWNSVILLE, and will be staged through to the operational area via the bases of HOLLANDIA and MOROTAI IS. ...

The Forces in New Guinea

4. Just recently HQ First Aust Army moved from AUSTRALIA to LAE in NEW GUINEA, and was given the task of relieving US Forces in the SOLOMONS, NEW BRITAIN, islands in close proximity to and on the East of NEW IRELAND, and the Northern NEW GUINEA coast line up to and including AITAPE.

5. (a) At present certain movements are in progress or contemplated, and when these are completed the field formations under command of First Aust Army in NEW GUINEA and the SOLOMONS will be distributed as under:-

Place	Forces
NEW GUINEA mainland*	HQ First Aust Army
	11 Aust Div (less 11 & 23 Inf Bdes)
SOLOMON IS (4 Bdes)	HQ 2 Aust Corps
	11 Aust Inf Bde Gp
	3 Aust Div
	HQ 4 Aust Base Sub-Area
Islands to the East of NEW BRITAIN (3 Bns)	23 Aust Inf Bde Gp
NEW BRITAIN (3 Bdes)	5 Aust Div
	HQ 5 Aust Base Sub-Area
AITAPE*	6 Aust Div
	HQ 3 Aust Base Sub-Area

[* Together totalled 4 Bdes]

(b) At present, we have to maintain a battalion group in the MERAUKE-TORRES STRAITS area to secure the straits and the airfields. It is anticipated that the Dutch will take over the MERAUKE area at a later stage, and so relieve us of this obligation but at the present time our commitment in this area where the Army maintains the Air Force is from 2-2,500 personnel.

(c) The above formations are supported by the necessary Corps, Army, and L of C Troops to enable them to operate and be maintained. Strength of First Aust Army forces in NEW GUINEA and Mandated Islands will be approximately 95,000.

6. You will note that the strength of the forces to be operating outside the mainland of Australia will shortly consist of six divisions and one armoured brigade, together with the necessary corps and force troops, amounting in all to approximately 185,000.

FORCES REMAINING IN AUSTRALIA
7. As you are aware, certain preparations were made in the NORTHERN TERRITORY to facilitate operations ex DARWIN. However, for the time being it is not intended to stage an expedition ex DARWIN, but the Naval facilities at the port of DARWIN are to be considerably expanded in making provision for the reception of British Naval Forces in the Pacific, whilst R.A.A.F. units and airfields in the area are to be maintained. In view of the favourable trend of events, the Commander-in-Chief recently decided to reduce the garrison of DARWIN from a division to one infantry brigade group, and to convert the surplus personnel to reinforcements in order to make good wastage in the overseas forces. For the reasons already stated, one brigade group must for the time being be maintained in DARWIN, and a considerable number of administrative personnel are required in order to maintain the communications to NORTHERN TERRITORY both from MT ISA and through CENTRAL AUSTRALIA and to provide the large army administrative commitments in providing and transporting the requirements of the R.A.N., R.A.A.F., C.C.C., [Civil Constructional Corps] and native population. However, the strength of DARWIN is being reduced and will probably come down to about 18,000 in the near future.
8. There has been a very large scale reduction in Coast and AA Arty on the mainland. It is intended to maintain only four defended ports on a very limited scale of coast artillery armament. These are DARWIN, FREMANTLE, SYDNEY and BRISBANE, all of which are required as Naval bases of varying degree. AA defences are being drastically reduced at present. NO defence is being provided for Australian mainland airfields. A reasonable scale of AA protection is being retained in the DARWIN port area, and to a lesser degree at FREMANTLE, whilst SYDNEY has been reduced to a very minor scale. No other city areas will have AA defences.
...
[AA: A 5954, Box 570]

While four Australian divisions were engaged in the mandates campaigns (see the following section) the 7th and 9th Divisions were waiting in Queensland for their next mission. Forde, the Minister for the Army, visited the troops and on 13 February 1945 told Curtin he was disturbed at the fall of their morale in the preceding six months, a fall 'largely due to their enforced stay on the mainland of Australia with no clearly defined indication as to when and where they may be likely to be called upon to take part in active operations'.[11] Two days later Shedden told MacArthur: 'There is a tendency in Government quarters to ask why the A.I.F. Divisions were not used earlier. Australian opinion considered it a point of honour to be associated with operations in the Philippines as an acknowledgement of American assistance to Australia'.[12] Also on 15

---

11. Forde to Curtin, 13.2.1945, AA: A 5954, Box 570.
12. Shedden to MacArthur, 15.2.1945, AA: A 5954, Box 570.

February Curtin wrote to MacArthur in unusually strong terms, mentioning the latter's directive of 12 July 1944, with its decision that two AIF divisions be allotted to the offensive against Japan. Curtin continued as follows.

Document 370

Curtin to MacArthur   15 February 1945

Letter   *Top Secret and Personal*

. . .
Elements of the 1st Australian Corps have been on the mainland for periods of up to eighteen months and have taken no part in the war since 1943. You may have gathered from press reports that there has been considerable public criticism of the inactivity of the Australian Land Forces which, in a large degree, has arisen from the members of the Forces themselves, a considerable number of whom have been under arms for four and five years. The prescription for victory laid down for the Australian people has been that they must either fight or work, and my reply to public demands for the easing of restrictions and shortages involving the release of additional men from the Forces has been that the maintenance of the strength of the fighting forces is the first priority.

In view of the great stringency of the manpower position and the heavy pressure that is being brought to bear on the Government to remedy manpower shortages and lift restrictions, I shall be confronted with a difficult situation if so many Australian troops are to be retained in an ineffective role, for it would appear that an all out effort against Japan is unlikely for a considerable period. ...

5. *Request to Commander-in-Chief, Southwest Pacific Area*

I would recall the following extract from the enclosure to my letter of 1st November:-

"The Government considers it to be a matter of vital importance to the future of Australia and her status at the peace table in regard to the settlement in the Pacific, that her military effort should be concentrated as far as possible in the Pacific and that it should be on a scale to guarantee her an effective voice in the peace settlement."

I need hardly add that these views are still the Policy of the Government whose immediate aim is to establish a better balance between the direct and indirect aspects of the War Effort. It is felt, however, that if considerations of global strategy are to retard the use of our Forces, it is illogical to keep inactive so large a part of our manpower for so long, when part of it could be making a greater contribution to the Allied War Effort in other directions where our manpower needs are so pressing.

I shall be grateful if you will furnish me with your observations on the various points I have raised in so far as they relate to your responsibilities

as Commander-in-Chief of the Southwest Pacific Area, and if you will also let me have your views on the relation of the strength of the Australian Forces to your plans in the Southwest Pacific Area. ...
[AA: A 5954, Box 570]

There follow extracts from MacArthur's reply.

Document 371

MacArthur to Curtin   GHQ, SWPA, 5 March 1945

Letter   *Top Secret*

Careful consideration has been given to your letter of 15th February 1945 with regard to the Australian War Effort and relation of the strength of the forces to the manpower conditions.

Original plans for the Philippine Campaign contemplated the employment of one Australian division in the initial assault on Leyte and one in the Lingayen landing. General Blamey, however, objected to the plan, stating that he could under no circumstances concur in the use of Australian troops unless they operated as a corps under their own corps commander. It was impossible to utilise the entire corps in the initial landing force and it was therefore necessary to amend the plan, constituting the entire force from American divisions. Plans were then prepared with a view to the employment of the Australian Corps for an operation against Aparri on the northern coast of Luzon, immediately preceding our landing at Lingayen Gulf. The developments of the campaign, however, made it possible to move directly against Lingayen, omitting the Aparri operation with consequent material and vital saving in time. It was then planned to use the Corps as the final reserve in the drive across the Central Plains north of Manila, but the enemy weakness which developed in the tactical situation obviated this necessity.

Current plans contemplate the elimination of the Japanese through a series of comparatively small operations in the Central and Southern parts of the Philippine Archipelago employing the United States Army troops that are now deployed in forward areas. Concurrently with the later phase of these operations it is proposed to attack Borneo and seize Java by overwater movement under the protection of the bases thus established. For this operation I have planned to use the Australian Corps under its own commander, operating according to the practice that has consistently been followed in the Southwest Pacific Area, under its own task force commander reporting direct to the Commander-in-Chief. It is estimated that the last phase of this operation, the assault upon Java, can be launched by the end of June. ...

My purpose in projecting this campaign is to restore the Netherlands East Indies authorities to their seat of government as has been done within

Australian and United States territory. I consider that this is an obligation that is inherent in the agreement of the five nations as expressed in the directive that established the Southwest Pacific Area. Immediately upon the re-establishment of the Netherlands East Indies government I propose to report to the Joint Chiefs of Staff that the mission of the Southwest Pacific Area has been accomplished and recommend its dissolution. It is contemplated thereafter that there will be a complete reorientation and that the British Empire and the Dutch authorities will collaborate in the complete restoration of their respective territories.

The execution of the plan as above outlined will require not only the full effort of available Australian ground forces but that of American forces as well. It is proposed to support the Australian ground forces with the R.A.A.F. Command, lending such assistance from the United States Army Air Forces as may be required. It is also hoped that the Seventh Fleet, including the Australian Squadron, will be augmented for this operation by the British Pacific Fleet.

In categorical reply to your basic question, I would state that my plans contemplate the use of all of the Australian Forces now assigned to the Southwest Pacific Area, but that upon the completion of the proposed campaign and dissolution of the Southwest Pacific Area, the question of the strength of forces to be retained, if my recommendation be followed, will be a matter for determination by the British Empire and the highest Dutch authorities. ...

[AA: A 5954, Box 570]

26
THE MANDATE CAMPAIGNS

In accordance with MacArthur's directive of 12 July 1944 four Australian divisions took over from Americans at beachheads in New Guinea. The 6th Division went to Aitape, and militia units to New Britain and Bougainville. The biggest of these three mandate campaigns was on Bougainville where an Australian offensive began on 30 December. It was 10 January 1945 before the censors allowed the press to publish news of these campaigns, which were still being fought when the war ended.

These campaigns provoked much controversy, many claiming that they had no worthwhile objective for they had no impact on the duration, let alone the outcome, of the war. We print some of the criticisms of the campaigns levelled by the Liberal Party members of Parliament.

Document 372

R.G. MENZIES'[13] SPEECH IN THE HOUSE OF REPRESENTATIVES   Canberra, 22 February 1945

... we of the British race have a profound interest in the relief of Burma, Malaya, and Singapore, and we in Australia have a particular interest in the relief of the Netherlands East Indies. ... Are we to use our major forces primarily for doing what I call "mopping-up operations" in by-passed areas, or should they be used as an integral portion of a British army to deliver those countries in the Far East which have been overrun by Japan? ...

... I should like to think ... that we were able at this time to have a division, or perhaps two divisions, of the Australian Imperial Force fighting with other British troops for the relief of Malaya, and the rescue of those men who were captured at Singapore. ...[p.58]
[*Commonwealth Parliamentary Debates*, House of Representatives, 1945, Vol 181, p.58]

---

13. Menzies had become leader of the Opposition in 1943.

Document 373

H.E. HOLT'S[14] SPEECH IN THE Canberra, 26 April 1945
HOUSE OF REPRESENTATIVES

...
The fundamental question ... is whether the campaign in the islands to the north ... is justified at all... . [p. 1107]
... The cost to the country in terms of money — and this cannot be ignored — is tremendous. It is having the effect of not only crippling Australian citizens, but also adding to our future burdens which will make the re-establishment of our fighting men all the harder to effect. ...
... No suggestion has been made by any responsible government spokesman or military leader that the Japanese to the north of Australia represent a military threat to this country to-day. No answer has been made to the claim from this side of the House that with a very much greater economy of effort we could contain the Japanese where they are, save Australian lives, and increase the Australian war effort in other directions. ...
... the terrible price we are now paying for limited gains makes an expansion of the present effort in New Guinea unjustifiable. There should be an immediate cessation of offensive operations, and we should be content to contain the enemy where he is. Only in that way will the Government restore a proper balance to the war effort of this nation, and spare the young manhood of Australia untold suffering and hardship for many months... . [pp. 1111–1112]
[*Commonwealth Parliamentary Debates*, House of Representatives, 1945, Vol 181, pp. 1107; 1111–1112]

Document 374

T.W. WHITE'S[15] SPEECH IN THE Canberra, 26 April 1945
HOUSE OF REPRESENTATIVES

...
The criticism offered by the Opposition is that valuable lives are being lost in areas where nature would complete the victory. Malaria alone would take a heavy toll of the by-passed Japanese forces, and the fact that com-

---
14. Holt had been Minister for Labour and National Service from 28.10.1940 — 7.10.1941. He was to hold that portfolio again from 19.12.1949 — 10.12.1958; be Minister for Immigration from 19.12.1949 — 24.10.1956; Treasurer from 10.12.1958 — 26.1.1966, and finally Prime Minister from 26.1.1966 — 19.12.1967.
15. White had been Minister for Trade and Customs from 14.1.1933 — 8.11.1938, and was to become Minister for Air from 19.12.1949 — 11.5.1951, and Minister for Civil Aviation from 19.12.1949 — 11.1.1951.

paratively small bodies of the enemy cannot be reinforced or supplied with equipment, and have no air cover, is sufficient reason why they should be left where they are until Japan is defeated. It is regrettable that valuable Australian lives should be lost in fighting the Japanese in well-defended island positions. It would be better if our troops were engaged in concert with their brothers in arms, the Americans, in any major actions to which they might be assigned. We have heard a great deal about ... Japanese brutality, and I trust that Australian troops will soon be used to release the dwindling 28,000 Australians in Malaya, which should be one of our main objectives. We should be pushing on through the Dutch islands towards Malaya instead of using our troops for what are admittedly minor campaigns... . [p. 1147]

[*Commonwealth Parliamentary Debates*, House of Representatives, 1945, Vol 181, p. 1147]

While F.M. Forde was with the Australian delegation at the San Francisco conference which drew up the United Nations charter, Senator James Fraser became the acting Minister for the Army. He toured the Australian battle zones and submitted a report, from which we take the following extracts. Blamey was very critical of these comments by Fraser, as the immediately succeeding document shows.

Document 375

Report by Fraser   18 April 1945

...   *Top Secret*

OPERATIONS:
36. The information supplied to me by G.Os.C. was that the Japanese have maintained their military organisation, and that the troops in all these areas are reasonably well equipped and fed, and that their discipline has been maintained, and also that a complete line of control is exercised from the higher command through formations out to the patrol areas.
37. The nature of our operations against such an enemy are arduous, exhausting and continuous. My conception of modern warfare against such an enemy is that a concerted attack should be made on his defensive positions and his bases, firstly by sea and air concurrently to blast him from these strongholds, weaken his capacity to hold these positions, and destroy his morale, so that an attack by land in force will be effective.
38. The reverse seems to be the case in the New Guinea operations. Sea attack is almost completely absent, while air attacks seem to be subsidiary to attacks by the land forces in penetrating the enemy positions. Secondly, these land forces have to fight their way, chain by chain, and mile by mile, along the coast and through impenetrable jungle, attacking the enemy at his outposts and gradually driving him back to his strongholds, which are the last to be stormed.

39. This, on the surface, appears to be wasteful of manpower, gives the enemy an opportunity to re-form his forces time and time again, and the casualty rate through sickness, more so than battle, is thus greater than would be the case if his strongholds were resolutely attacked.

40. This is a contributing cause, to my mind, of the allegations being made against the Government by the Press and others on the mainland. The feeling undoubtedly exists among the troops that the tactics they are adopting in fighting the enemy are not in accordance with the most modern ideas of warfare. ...

[AA: A 5954, Box 570]

We print some extracts from Blamey's comments on Fraser's criticisms.

Document 376

Blamey to Chifley[16]   ALF, SWPA, HQ, 18 May 1945

Letter   Top Secret

1. With reference to your letter of 7th May, 1945, I find it necessary to deal with the attachment headed 'Observations of Acting Minister for the Army on Operations in New Guinea, New Britain and the Solomon Islands' as a separate subject and at some length. ...

New Guinea

3. Firstly the Acting Minister discusses the New Guinea operations, where he says sea attack was almost absent, while air attacks seemed to be subsidiary to land attack in penetrating enemy positions.

In the operations in New Guinea referred to, the enemy held the sea board in limited strength with small detachments extending over 100 miles, the main strength being concentrated at Wewak. At the same time he had distributed a very large proportion of his force in a area beyond the Torricelli Mountains, far from the sea, where he had developed considerable self-sufficiency and maintained his forces to a considerable extent on the natives' local food supply.

The Australian forces under consideration were placed in Aitape, over 100 miles from the enemy's main base, by orders of the Supreme Commander, GHQ, to relieve American forces located there. The latter had performed an inactive role over a long period. This long period of inaction

---

16. J.B. Chifley, Minister for Post War Reconstruction and Treasurer in the Curtin Ministry, became Acting Prime Minister from April 1945 when Curtin's health began to fail. When Curtin died on 5 July, F.M. Forde temporarily became Prime Minister until 13 July when Chifley was elected Prime Minister by the ALP Caucus.

enabled the enemy to develop his self-sufficiency to a very considerable degree and allowed him to organise supply by submarine of essential military stores such as medical supplies. He was well provided with most of the other essentials for the maintenance of his forces. His equipment for operations generally was on a low scale. ...

[5.] Had it been possible to commence the operation de novo, I would naturally have preferred to have made the landing in force by a combined sea, land and air operation in the vicinity of Wewak and seize the main base, and from there pursue the campaign inland and along the coast. But in view of the position where we were forced to place our forces and, as no naval force or landing craft could be spared at that stage, it was determined, with the full knowledge and concurrence of the Supreme Commander, that the plan which was put into operation was the best. ...

[6.] I have not the least doubt, nor have any of my commanders, that this was the best plan of operations, and I think we may reasonably assert that its overwhelming success, carried out at a maximum cost of lives to the enemy and the minimum cost to ourselves, more than justifies the plan and the decision.

Bougainville

7. The second case, covered by the Acting Minister's generalisations, however, presented a completely different problem. This was Bougainville.

Here again our troops were placed at Torokina, in relief of the Americans, and I had no freedom of action to determine the base from which operations should take place. The Acting Minister's broad conceptions of war when applied to the circumstances of this case also fall down.

Except for the perimeter of Torokina, the enemy held the whole of Bougainville. Here he was able to harass, as he pleased, the garrison within the perimeter area. He was also able to develop a high degree of self-sufficiency, both in the north and the south.

8. It would have been possible, given the means, to have made landing operations either in the north or the south, but a prime function, imposed upon me, was the protection of the airfields at Torokina. I would therefore have been obliged to divide my force into two parts had the broad conception of the Minister been carried out, and a landing made either in the north or the south. This would have allowed the enemy to bring practically all his forces into one concentration and to have attacked with all his strength on my weaker position, whichever it may have been; and I would therefore have broken one of the prime rules of strategy which is to concentrate the maximum forces under command for battle, while ensuring the dispersion of the enemy. The enemy was kept dispersed and we attacked as best suited us with our whole force in hand.

9. In regard to the Acting Minister's general conception, the remarks applied to the New Guinea operation with reference to air activities, apply equally to Bougainville. Ample air forces were available but they could not be used at first to the full, because of lack of definite targets. When these were disclosed by the operations of the ground forces a very great increase and improvement took place.

10. In regard to naval forces, the Supreme Commander was not prepared to make these available, owing to his other requirements, and is not even yet prepared to do so, so that there seems still to be an indefinite period before the naval forces, essential to a landing, can be made available in this area. Moreover, no definite enemy stronghold exists on the coast, the seizure of which would give any decisive gains. The enemy's self-sufficiency has been developed inland and, no matter where a landing took place, the same conditions of having to penetrate through jungle areas would be found to exist.

11. The plan adopted to locate the enemy by patrols and find the area of his strength has been carried out steadily. The patrols are followed up by light detachments and these are of sufficient strength to deal with him as he may be met. The success of this method is already obvious. Except for a small portion in the extreme north, the whole of the north-western area has been cleared.

The advance in the south is proceeding with reasonable prudence, and in no portion so far have our forces which engaged the enemy been greater than a company of infantry, plus a few supporting tanks and supporting artillery.

Targets have been steadily uncovered for the air force and there has been the closest and happiest co-operation between the ground and air forces. In fact, the air force, both in New Guinea and Bougainville, have expressed their great satisfaction at being provided with definite tasks instead of the vague bombing of target areas which they had been carrying out previously.

12. The continued success of the operations, where only small forces are engaged on each occasion and where the bulk of the troops can be retained in hand and their morale and health steadily maintained by a limited amount of active operations, and an abundance of recreation and amenities, enable us to maintain a very low scale of sickness. The waste of manpower has been remarkably small. In action the careful control of operations has yielded an immense margin of destruction of the enemy personnel over our own losses.

...

New Britain

13. The third case is the case of New Britain.

Here effective co-operation upon land sea and air has been possible, within the small limits required, owing to the fact that the whole of the enemy installations were coastal. It was therefore possible to confine land operations to a minimum. ...

15. From the very beginning in Bougainville, the Australian equipment was immensely superior to that of the Japanese. It was completely adequate to its task. The inland positions of the enemy and the nature of the jungle covered terrain did not permit the issue to be decided by a landing at any given point by combined sea and land operations. ...

16. Had the very superior forces of the Americans, whom we relieved, been properly utilised against the inferior enemy forces, there is no question that this campaign would have been completed long before the necessity arose for the Americans to move on and be relieved by Australians. The total cost

of Australian lives, equipment and money would have been saved had this been done.

The Acting Minister appears to consider now that we should follow the same lines as the Americans, which would lead to a steady wastage of personnel and still leave, at some unknown future date, the task of eliminating the Japanese and liberating the natives for whom we are responsible. This comment also applies to operations in the Wewak area.

17. I have no hesitation in claiming that the historian of the future will say that our action was completely correct and, in the long run, by far the most economical in every way. ...

[18.] Beyond that I have no comment to make, except to say that, regarding the theories put forward by the Acting Minister dealing with the method of the conduct of the war, he [w]as attended on his visit by the Chief of the General Staff [Northcott], who is, under my direction, the Government's Chief Adviser on military affairs, and it is regretted that so competent and qualified an officer should not have been called into discussion on such purely military matters before the Minister committed himself to these very erroneous views and comments. ...

[AA: A 5954, Box 570]

There was criticism about the Australians' lack of good equipment. Blamey's comments on this public criticism are illustrated below.

Document 377

Curtin to MacArthur   Canberra, 17 April 1945

Letter   *Top Secret*

There has been some public criticism originating from Australian War Correspondents about the equipment of the Australian Military Forces for the operations on which they are engaged in New Guinea, New Britain and the Solomon Islands.

2. The essence of the criticism is that the Australian Forces are not as well equipped as the United States Forces, especially in regard to heavy engineering equipment such as bulldozers and amphibious equipment, and that the operations should not have been undertaken in the circumstances. Some statements go further and say that operations should not be carried out at all, but the Australian Forces should be employed in more offensive action elsewhere.

3. General Blamey, who has recently visited each of the operational areas, has furnished me with a report, the main points of which may be summarised as follows:-

(i)   *General Position:*
      The Australian divisions are more completely and adequately

equipped in this campaign than in any other campaign in this war. He is satisfied that adequate army equipment is available for the operations authorised, but no operations will be authorised unless both the local commander and himself are satisfied that adequate equipment is available to ensure success.

The success of operations to date, the rate of our advance, and the completely re-assuring lightness of our losses in both manpower and material are, in themselves, the best answers to the criticisms that have been made.

(ii) *Aitape Area:*
Operations necessitated, firstly, an advance south along the coast, and, secondly, the destruction of the Japanese inland beyond Torricelli Mountains and an advance southeast along inland positions. Coastal conditions, such as lack of harbour or anchorage, and seasonal heavy surf has rendered supply difficult. Nevertheless, adequate reserves, both supplies and ammunition, have been built up both on the coast and inland. Inland supply has been perforce by air, and although the position has been at times precarious owing to limited air transport and continuous adverse air weather conditions, supplies either of rations or ammunition have never failed to arrive in time. The advance along the coast has required a major engineering effort. Sixty heavy bridges have been constructed up to the maximum of approximately 300 feet lengths, requiring serviceable engineering equipment, which has been available.

(iii) *Bougainville Area:*
Over one-third of Bougainville is under our control. The advance is continuing at a satisfactory rate, but the nature of the country so far has necessitated operations by relatively small columns. Heavy equipment was in hand, but the necessity to use it so far had not arisen.

(iv) *New Britain:*
The present phase of this campaign has just been completed with outstanding success, and the enemy is bottled up in the Gazelle Peninsula. An aerodrome for the R.A.A.F. has been constructed with landing strips 6,100 ft., entirely with army labour and equipment.

4. I have published General Blamey's report with observations to the following effect:-

(i) The Service authorities are the sole judges of their equipment requirements, and at no time has the Government refused any request for fighting equipment put forward by them.

(ii) Two important factors are beyond the control of the Government — the availability of shipping and the quantity of equipment assigned from overseas sources of supply. ...

[AA: A 5954, Box 570]

General MacArthur provided Curtin with a response to the criticism just mentioned.

Document 378

MacArthur to Curtin   19 April 1945

Teleprinter Message BXC. 72   Top Secret

   Forces in Bougainville, New Britain and New Guinea have the mission of neutralising the enemy garrisons that have been isolated. These hostile forces are strategically impotent and are suffering a high rate of natural attrition. Australian Forces now engaged are continuing the missions previously assigned American elements. A local Commander in such situations has considerable freedom of action as to methods to be employed. The Australian Commanders have elected to carry out active operations in effecting neutralisation where other Commanders might decide on more passive measures. I consider that the local missions have been carried out with skill and energy and constitute an excellent accomplishment. I am of the opinion that the equipment of the troops is sufficient for the accomplishment of the assigned missions and that the provision of air transport has proven adequate. In all material ways, the enemy has been completely outclassed.
[AA: A 5954, Box 570]

   Continued criticism of the mandate campaigns prompted the government to consult Blamey. On 18 May he presented a lengthy appreciation in justification of these campaigns. Here, we print brief excerpts.

Document 379

Appreciation[17] *by* Blamey   18 May 1945

                                                  Top Secret

PART I
APPRECIATION ON OPERATIONS OF THE AMF IN NEW GUINEA, NEW BRITAIN AND THE SOLOMON ISLANDS
OBJECT
1. To conduct operations against the enemy with a view to:-
   (a) Destroying the enemy where this can be done with relatively light casualties, so as to free our territory and liberate the native population and thereby progressively reduce our commitments and free personnel from the Army;
   (b) Where conditions are not favourable for the destruction of the enemy, to contain him in a restricted area by the use of a much smaller force, thus following the principle of economy. ...

---

   17. This appreciation was presented to War Cabinet as Agendum No. 209/1945 on 22.5.1945. Blamey attended that meeting.

4. When MOROTAI had been seized, C-in-C., SWPA, stated that the enemy forces by-passed in Australian territories were strategically impotent, but at this stage the following American forces were disposed in Australian territories:-

TOROKINA Perimeter BOUGAINVILLE	— A corps of two Divisions.
OUTER SOLOMON ISLANDS	— One Division
NEW BRITAIN (GLOUCESTER)	— One Division
NEW GUINEA (AITAPE-TADJI)	— A Corps of two Divisions plus one Regimental Combat Team. ...

5. On the initiation of planning for the PHILIPPINES campaign ... the following Australian forces were used to relieve the American forces:-

BOUGAINVILLE and the OUTER SOLOMON ISLANDS	— A Corps of One Division and two Infantry Brigade Groups.
NEW BRITAIN	— One Division, since reduced to a Division of two Infantry Brigades.
NEW GUINEA (AITAPE)	— One Division.

This shows a reduction on the forces used by the Americans of the equivalent of three divisions.

6. The deployment of such substantial Australian forces, under orders of GHQ, to contain these by-passed forces refutes any claim that can be raised as to their strategic impotence. Because the offensive power of these by-passed enemy forces had not been destroyed, it was necessary to protect the American bases in the SOLOMONS and in NEW GUINEA with strong forces, as these bases were vital for the conduct of the PHILIPPINES campaign. ...

8. Just as it is necessary to destroy the JAPANESE in the PHILIPPINES, so it is necessary that we should destroy the enemy in Australian territories where the conditions are favourable for such action, and so liberate the natives from JAPANESE domination. Were we to wait until JAPAN was finally crushed, it could be said that the Americans, who had previously liberated the PHILIPPINES, were responsible for the final liberation of the natives in Australian territories, with the inevitable result that our prestige both abroad and in the eyes of the natives would suffer much harm.

PART II
POLICY OF AMF ON RELIEVING US FORCES IN
NEW GUINEA, NEW BRITAIN AND THE SOLOMON ISLANDS

Solomon Islands
1. There were three courses of action left open to me on taking over from the US Forces. These were as follows:-
Course A To take over the American defences within their perimeters as they then existed and by passive defence to protect the airfields and base installations contained within the perimeters.

Course B To go for an all out offensive against enemy strongholds with full scale air and naval support when the latter could be developed.
Course C By aggressive patrolling to gain information of enemy strengths and dispositions, about which little was known by American formations, and by systematically driving him from his garden areas and supply bases, forcing him into starvation and destroying him where found. Eventually to bring about his total destruction. ...

The only sound course of action left open was that indicated in Course C. It was therefore decided that the operations of the First Aust Army would consist of obtaining information, probing the enemy's positions and carrying out offensive operations with small forces with a view to seeking out and destroying the enemy where found. ...
[AA: A 5954, Box 570]

War Cabinet's response to Blamey's appreciation was as follows.

Document 380

Beasley [Minister for Defence] to Blamey

31 July 1945

Letter *Top Secret*

OPERATIONS IN NEW GUINEA, NEW BRITAIN AND THE SOLOMON ISLANDS

I refer to your appreciation on the operations of the Australian Military Forces in New Guinea, New Britain and the Solomon Islands, dated 18th May, 1945, and to the discussion which you had with War Cabinet on 22nd May. Following upon these discussions and subsequent consideration of the appreciation by the Advisory War Council, I wish to inform you of the following conclusions which have been reached by War Cabinet and the [Advisory War] Council:-

(i) *Objects*

The following objects stated in Part I of the appreciation were agreed to:-
"To conduct operations against the enemy with a view to:-
 (a) Destroying the enemy where this can be done with relatively light casualties, so as to free our territory and liberate the native population and thereby progressively reduce our commitments and free personnel from the Army;
 (b) Where conditions are not favourable for the destruction of the enemy, to contain him in a restricted area by the use of a much smaller force, thus following the principle of economy."

(ii) *Future Policy*

War Cabinet and the Council agreed with the future policy outlined in

Part III for operations which will lead to the reduction in the strength of the Army to the following:-

"By the end of the year it is hoped that our force can be reduced to two divisions consisting of five infantry brigade groups. If this hope is realised, the forces required will be:-
Wewak-Aitape — One Infantry Brigade Group
Bougainville — One Infantry Brigade Group
New Britain — One Division of two Infantry Brigades
Reserve — One Infantry Brigade
All Areas — Ancillary and Base Troops.
This is subject to developments in New Britain and New Ireland."

2. It is noted that the following is stated in Part III — Future Policy:-

"For the reasons given in Part II it is proposed to follow the existing policy of destroying the enemy in Bougainville and New Guinea with the object of liquidating our commitments and thereby making a progressive reduction in the strength of our forces engaged in these areas."

"In New Britain, where the reduction of Rabaul would require the use of major forces, it is proposed to continue the present economic policy of containing the enemy, but to review this policy when circumstances permit."

"The policy to be followed in regard to New Britain and New Ireland will require reconsideration later."

3. In regard to the decision as to future policy quoted in paragraph 1 (ii) above, I would inform you that it is the desire of the Government that any variation that may be proposed of the future policy for operations, as outlined in Part III of the appreciation, should be submitted to it for decision and that no new commitment is to be undertaken without its prior authority.

4. I have also forwarded a copy of this letter to the Minister for the Army [Forde].

[AA: A 5954, Box 570]

The following message gives some idea of the small-scale actions which made up the mandate campaigns.

Document 381

Sinclair [Secretary, Department of the Army] to Shedden   Melbourne, 9 June 1945

Teleprinter Message [Not Numbered]

... Armoured and Infantry thrusts into the Jap's fertile and extensive garden areas in southern Bougainville threatening him with loss of rich food storages and continued fanatical Jap resistance in hills behind Wewak in New Guinea were outstanding developments in Australian operations in S.W.P.A. [d]uring week.

For more than eighteen months Jap has systematically cultivated thousands acres of crops vegetables in southern Bougainville. ...

Australian Infantry with close tank support pushed south-east forcing two crossings of Peperu River where Japs with machine guns on eastern banks attempted a stand. However Japs evacuated these positions after leading Australians had made initial crossing and tanks and artillery in rear had covered area with fire. Our forces then poured across fords and after fierce engagement drove enemy from his bunkers on escarpments between fork of Peperu and Hari Rivers. ...

Whether Japs have prepared extensive defences on eastern banks of Hari River is being tested. A break-through across river will take our forces well into garden areas. Infantry patrols and commandos already delving deep into these areas meeting consistent and at times desperate opposition. One Australian Patrol fought half hour clash with strong enemy forces armed with machine guns and mortars. Our patrol forces withdr[e]w.

In north of Bougainville our forces have made some progress north into the Bonis Peninsula. The enemy making determined sorties — many by night — to break through our cordon but without success. In this area rifles radios ammunition stores of rice and medical equipment were found buried by Japs apparently prior to hasty evacuation.

Japs have many outer machine gun posts protecting his concentrations outside Peninsula and these have received severe battering from our Mortars.

Deep patrolling by aggressive Australian Infantry was strongly challenged in the central sector along the Numa Numa Trail. Following mortaring and shelling fighting patrols occupied a position north of Berry's Hill. A Jap attempt to infiltrate back was repulsed.

... Troops of the Sixth Australian Division are clearing Japs from high ground overlooking and dominating coastal areas in New Guinea while other forces of same division steadily driving further east from Maprik Base in inland sector. ...

... Desperate Japs being liquidated in bunkers and pillboxes... . Along rugged spurs and on slopes of ridges Jap defences being steadily reduced by artillery and mortar barrages and use of flame throwers.

Jap however as unpredictable as ever. Some of his defences been completely shattered by shellfire and remnants of his men forced withdraw but on few occasions he returned to scene of devastation to re-occupy area behind our forward infantry. His ultimate elimination entails slow and arduous fighting. ...

Mountain artillery mortars and flamethrowers were used in assault on enemy-occupied areas near Parchi River. Positions were taken after several hardpressed infantry attacks. ...

[AA: A 5954, Box 534]

At the end of the war large numbers of Japanese troops were still holding out on New Britain and Bougainville and in the Wewak hinterland. The following criticism of the mandate campaigns was published between the end of hostilities and the formal Japanese surrender.

Document 382

The Herald [Melbourne]   22 August 1945

WAS OUR WAR IN ISLANDS A WASTED EFFORT?

By Frederick Howard
Former Lieutenant-Colonel, AIF

Surrender now ends the resistance of by-passed Japanese forces in New Guinea, New Britain and the Solomons. General MacArthur wrote off those forces in April, 1944. Some months later, Australia began a series of major campaigns against them.

Were those campaigns ever really necessary?

Sixteen months ago, General MacArthur completed his strategic plan for neutralising the enemy in New Guinea.

His amphibious movement of American forces along the northern New Guinea coast captured the enemy's base of Hollandia. Between April and June, 1944, further moves virtually sealed off all the Japanese in the Solomons, New Britain and New Guinea.

It was then obvious that the war would be won on the threshold of Japan. Admiral Nimitz's Central Pacific forces were storming forward to that end. MacArthur was planning his move to the Philippines.

The unimportance of the by-passed enemy was clearly stated in the communique which MacArthur issued after the Hollandia operation.

He described the operation as having thrown "a loop of envelopment around the enemy's 18th Army, dispersed along the coast of New Guinea ... similar to the Solomons and Bismarck loops of envelopment."

"This enemy army is now completely isolated," he declared, "with its communications and supply lines severed."

BEYOND THE ENEMY POSTS

MacArthur moved his own headquarters beyond the helpless island posts of the enemy. The American holding troops left in their Torikina perimeter on Bougainville, on New Britain and in the Aitape sector of New Guinea attempted no large-scale offensives.

It was not necessary for them to do so. At least one of their own commanders has been quoted as saying that he could push forward and kill a great many Japanese if he desired, but that the result would not justify the loss of one American life.

Why was that policy changed after Australian troops had taken over the police tasks in those by-passed areas in November-December, 1944?

General MacArthur did not need the offensive. It was contrary to the whole concept of his strategy.

The Australian insistence obviously did not rest on any military necessity to destroy the Japanese in their jungle retreats. Their surrender, sooner or later, was a foregone conclusion. The argument that national prestige and our duty to the natives called for a campaign was not consistent with the facts.

If that argument had been consistently followed, we should have attacked Nauru and Ocean Islands, instead of leaving them untouched, and should have pushed the New Britain campaign forcefully, instead of accepting, as we did, the fact that it was a particularly awkward nut to crack.

As it is, Nauru is likely to come quietly into our possession without loss of one soldier's life. Could it not have been the same with Bougainville and Wewak?

There is one thing overlooked by the arguments supporting our insistence on a so-called "mopping up" campaign. It is that we had the alternative of playing a strategically and politically important role in MacArthur's invasion of the Philippines.

MacArthur's plan for that operation provided for the use of an Australian division.

The Australian authorities demurred at this. Although a force as small as a division had been made available to serve under British command in the Western Desert in 1940–41, there was a raising of objections, in 1944, to detaching a division to serve under an American Army commander in the Philippines.

Instead, we offered a corps (presumably of two divisions). Unfortunately this force could not be made ready within the time limits of the Philippines programme.

The Australian Army was therefore dropped from what was the climax of General MacArthur's campaign.

By the actions of those responsible for high policy in the Australian military effort, our troops were relegated to the "back areas" of the war at that stage.

When the Seventh and Ninth Divisions emerged from that twilight to the Borneo landings, it is significant that General MacArthur personally attended their re-entry into what his policy had consistently regarded as the strategic front.

For what happened in the meanwhile, no Australian field commander or soldier in New Guinea, New Britain or the Solomons had any reason to feel ashamed.

They fought a war which was called "mopping up" — and which demanded of them, and received, efforts as magnificent as any which the Kokoda Trail called forth.

Of the personal qualities used in the Islands War since November, 1944, not enough has been heard. Such sterling leaders and planners as Lieut.-Gen. Victor Sturdee, of First Army, and Lieut.-Gen. F.H. Berryman, chief of staff to General Blamey, are as yet too little known to the public.

Major-Gen. W. Bridgeford, field commander on Bougainville under Lieut.-Gen. Stan Savige, Major-Gen. H.C.H. Robertson with the grim assignment of New Britain, and Major-Gen. J.E.S. Stevens with the 6th Division on the Wewak front, were fine commanders worthy of a more decisive role.

ENGAGED IN EXPLORATION

Under these and other generals, our troops were committed — with the reluctant acquiescence of South-West Pacific Headquarters — to the reconquest of heartbreaking territory.

In the course of their magnificent work, some of them were engaged in virtual exploration. Their fighting patrols in New Britain and Bougainville labored through areas which no white man had previously visited. Their gallantry has not been surpassed anywhere.

If this was part of our "duty to the natives," it was strange that it had become an urgent work for the early months of 1945, after being neglected through decades of peace.

The campaigns, of course, killed Japs. They gained us such victories as Tsimba Ridge on Bougainville (after 20 days' fighting), and Smith's Knoll, into which we pumped 10,000 shells. We took Wewak in May of this year. The battle tallies showed that we were killing from 20 to 60 Japs for every Australian we lost.

PRICE PAID BY DIVISIONS

The tallies did not so readily show the price of exhaustion and sickness paid by our divisions. But at Wewak, one unit of the Sixth Division had more casualties in three months than it had incurred in nearly two years of Middle East service.

The vast strain of supply to the jungle fronts, the galley-slave effort to build roads and climb mountains, the cost in material and health, have never been estimated.

And now comes the end to our War of the Islands. It is the same end by surrender which MacArthur envisaged 16 months ago. The difference is that there are a few thousands fewer Japanese to surrender than there might have been if we had not insisted on waging active war.

There are a few hundred more dead Australians.

Maybe they would have died anyway. They might have died on the shores of Luzon. That would hardly have comforted their relatives, but their sacrifice would have achieved more direct progress on the road to Tokyo, and so increased the historic import of the gallant tragedy of their passing.

27
BORNEO

The Australian army opened its last campaign of the war on Borneo and its offshore islands. In MacArthur's headquarters the idea of an American-Australian drive through Borneo to Java was on paper by October 1944. The Borneo campaigns were conceived by MacArthur. Few others enthused over them, and there was argument over their worth. There was also argument over whether the Australians involved would come under the command of the US Eighth Army, or whether they would be commanded by an Australian directly responsible to MacArthur's headquarters. Blamey was angered by the following telegram he received from Lt. General Frank Berryman, his Chief of Staff, with its news that he was to be excluded from any role in the Borneo operations.

Document 383

Berryman to Blamey   15 February 1945

Telegram B 228   *Top Secret and Personal*

Planning basis for future operations of three AIF divisions is an advance along EAST coast BORNEO with JAVA as objective.

First objective TARAKAN by one Inf Bde Gp if land based aircraft support but, if carrier based aircraft available, BALIKPAPAN by one division task force may be first objective. After capture BALIKPAPAN it may be necessary to capture BANDJERMASIN before operations against JAVA which will be a corps operation with one assault division and one follow up division. Until shipping position is examined no definite plan can be made but it is probable that 9 and 7 divisions will move in succession through one staging area. General Chamberlin[18] states operations will be commanded by Eighth Army and NOT by Allied Landforces.

As policy questions of command, manpower and operations of First Aust Army are concerned suggest discussion with GHQ when more definite information is available.
[AA: A 5954, Box 570]

Blamey expressed his displeasure at the command arrangements in the following letter.

---

18. Maj.-Gen. Stephen J. Chamberlin, G–3 (i.e. Principal Operations Officer) on MacArthur's headquarters.

Document 384

Blamey to Shedden ALF, SWPA, HQ, 19 February 1945

Letter *Top Secret and Personal*

1. With reference to the command of the Australian Military Forces in the field, I think it is desirable that I should put the position, as I see it, for the information of the Prime Minister.

You will recall that, on the establishment of the South West Pacific Area, General MacArthur was appointed Commander-in-Chief and I was appointed Commander, Allied Land Forces. I understand my appointment was made as part of the general agreement for the acceptance of the set up of the command of the SWP Area. Except during the offensive campaign in the field in New Guinea up to the end of 1943, I have never operated as such.

My requests for American officers to establish a joint staff were met with a face saving acceptance that was completely ineffective. American troops were brought to this country and later an American army command established. At no stage was I given any information as to the proposals for their arrival or the development of the organisation. In fact, General MacArthur took upon himself the functions of Commander, Allied Land Forces and my own functions were limited to command of the Australian Military Forces.

I have never raised this question definitely before, as I was always of the opinion that the Prime Minister and General MacArthur worked in close consultation and the former was fully informed of and acquiesced in the position... . I was satisfied therefore to continue my responsibility for the control of the development in administration and operations of the Australian Military Forces.

2. With the forward advance, however, the situation has undergone a further change. It has been, throughout this war, a definitely accepted principle that our Australian national forces should be under the control of our own Australian commanders. Where, on those odd occasions, this restriction has been lifted, it has been very greatly to the detriment of the Australian Army.

In the position which has now arisen, the Australian Army has been sharply divided into two components:

(a) The First Australian Army, which is dealing with the enemy elements left behind in the New Guinea and adjacent islands area.

(b) The First Australian Corps, which has been made available for offensive operations.

GHQ, SWPA asserts its authority to exercise direct control over the First Australian Army and, in a wire received from General Berryman on 20th inst, intends to assume direct control of First Australian Corps for operations now under consideration.

3. In order to ensure an effective Australian command over its own forces, I have transferred my Advanced Headquarters from Brisbane to Hollandia and established a Forward Section, with Lieut-General Berryman as Chief of Staff, at Leyte with GHQ.

It is obvious to me that the intention of GHQ SWPA is to treat my Headquarters as a purely liaison element. You will recall that a wire received from General Berryman last week stated that the staff of GHQ SWPA intended to utilise the First Australian Corps under command of the 8th American Army. I instructed General Berryman to oppose this strongly and to put my views fully and frankly before General Chamberlin with a view to informing General MacArthur.

As a result of these conversations, General Berryman now informs me that First Australian Corps will operate directly under GHQ as already mentioned.

4. With regard to the command of New Guinea area, the position is completely unsatisfactory. GHQ claims to exercise direct command, whereas effective command of the land forces is exercised by myself. This is inevitable but, unfortunately, the means to secure fully effective control are not at my disposal.

In addition to the army command, there is an independent air force command, the control of which is exercised by General Kenney from the Philippines. The command of naval forces is also an independent command as far as New Guinea army command is concerned.

There are also seven New Zealand air squadrons operating in the area which do not operate under the Australian air force command, but under direct control from General Kenney in the Philippines. ...

The set-up of command in New Guinea is completely unsatisfactory. It is impossible to secure reasonable attention even to maintenance requirements. For example, over 4,000 personnel due for return to their units have been awaiting shipping for weeks at Townsville.

It would be a long story to give all the details of the difficulties of supply and provision resulting from the fact of distant, and I cannot help but feel not sufficiently interested, control of the First Australian Army. ...

5. It is my view that, unless the authority of the Australian command over Australian national forces is effectively asserted, an undesirable position will arise as far as the Australia[n] troops are concerned, by which they will be distributed under American control and Australian national control of its forces will be greatly weakened.

The insinuation of American control and the elimination of Australian control has been gradual, but I think the time has come when the matter should be faced quite squarely, if the Australian Government and the Australian Higher Command are not to become ciphers in the control of the Australian Military Forces.

[AA: A 5954, Box 570]

Curtin raised this issue with MacArthur in the following exchange of correspondence.

Document 385

Curtin to MacArthur   27 February 1945

Letter   *Top Secret and Personal*

...
4. I had hoped that by now it would have been possible to associate the Australian forces in greater or lesser strength with the re-conquest of the Philippines, as a reciprocal Australian gesture to the aid which the Commonwealth has received from the United States, as well as military desirability of using the Forces which have been inactive for some time. ...
5. General Blamey has also mentioned the question of the higher operational control of the Australian Forces. ...
6. It was laid down in the 1914–18 war that the Australian Forces serving outside Australia should be organised into and operate as a homogeneous formation appropriate to their strength, and that they should be commanded by an Australian Officer. This course was followed in the Middle East in the present war. ... I shall be glad, therefore, if you could inform me of the arrangement that is contemplated in regard to the operational control and command of the First Australian Corps in particular, and of the Australian Land Forces in New Guinea and adjacent islands, and of the manner in which it is proposed to ensure the observance of the basic principle I have mentioned. ...
[AA: A 5954, Box 570]

Document 386

MacArthur to Curtin   5 March 1945

Letter   *Top Secret*
...
The decision conveyed to me in your letter of 27th February 1945 to limit the Australian component of our assault forces to the 7th and 9th Divisions has been noted. I hope you will not eliminate entirely the possibility of using the 6th Division in the operation outlined above if it becomes a reality.

With reference to the command organisation, we have followed a fixed pattern since the Lae operation. The Commander-in-Chief exercises personal and direct command of Assault forces co-ordinating the action of three principal subordinates:–
- (a) Naval forces under the Commander, Allied Naval Forces.
- (b) Air Forces under the Commander, Allied Air Forces.
- (c) Ground forces under a Task Force Commander whose organisation is specifically prescribed according to the operation to be undertaken. These forces may vary from a Regimental Combat Team or Brigade Group to an Army and are commanded by an officer of appropriate

rank. In the forthcoming operation in which assault forces will include Australian troops, it is contemplated that the Commander would be an Australian officer. While General Morshead has been proposed and is entirely acceptable, I am prepared to accept another officer if designated by the Australian authorities. I consider that the assignment of the Australian Commander should be a matter for determination by the Australians. It is considered to be impossible, however, from an operational viewpoint, for the officer so designated to be concerned with command of Australian troops in New Guinea and Australia. It is essential that the Task Force Commander remain in the field with his troops and that he have no other duties of any kind. Any other course of action would unquestionably jeopardize the success of the operation and impose a risk that could not be accepted. ...

[AA: A 5954, Box 570]

Blamey questioned the wisdom of MacArthur's planning for the Borneo campaign as follows.

Document 387

Blamey to CurtinALF, SWPA, HQ, 5 April 1945

*Letter**Top Secret and Personal*

... There can be no question about the strategical correctness of the seizure of the Philippines, since this aimed straight at the heart of the Japanese ocean area. The whole of the islands comprising the Philippine group have now been seized, giving us direct command of the South China Sea from the northern point of Luzon to the southern point of Palawan.

It would be the logical and strategically correct sequence in the following operations to move down the western coast of Borneo. This would isolate all Japanese forces in Borneo, give a complete control of the South China Sea and facilitate the approach to Malaya.

Current operations do not, however, contemplate such a move. The proposal is to seize two or three points on the east coast of Borneo and to advance from there into Java.

5. (i) The present proposals envisage the complete destruction of the Japanese in the Philippines, and it is proposed in the operations against Borneo and Java, to use, in addition to 1st Australian Corps (7 and 9 Divisions), the 6th Australian Division, which is now engaged in operations on the north-east coast of New Guinea. I pointed out what I considered to be an inconsistency in this policy. It did not appear to me to be logical that the plans should contemplate the complete elimination of the Japanese in the Philippines and the withdrawal of Australian Forces from New Guinea before a similar stage had been reached there.

I raised the question with General MacArthur, who said his conception was that the Philippines would be the base for further movement against the Japanese and it was essential that no Japanese should remain in these islands. I pointed out the fact that the withdrawal of Australians from New Guinea before completion of their task in such clearing up would mean they would have to return to complete it. General MacArthur's staff have since informed me that he will make sufficient landing craft available to allow the 6th Division to seize Wewak.

In view of the intention of the American forces to destroy completely the Japanese in the Philippine Islands, it is my considered opinion that further Australian forces should not be withdrawn from New Guinea until such time as Japanese forces on Australian territory are destroyed also. It will be difficult to explain the inconsistency of policy otherwise.

(ii) I except from this Rabaul. The Japanese forces in this region have been pressed into a comparatively small area. They are well supplied and apparently strong, and I consider any attempt to capture this stronghold should be deferred for the present and we should be satisfied to contain it, since we can do so with lesser strength than the enemy force there.

6. In view of the present commitment of all six Australian Divisions in operations, it will be difficult to release additional men from the Army until the present operations are much further advanced.

The operations in Bougainville and Aitape areas are progressing, and it is hoped that by the end of June they will have arrived at a stage when the position can be reviewed further. ...

[AA: A 5954, Box 570]

A week after men of the 26th Brigade (9 Div) landed on Tarakan Island, German forces surrendered in Europe. Blamey considered the implications of that event for the scale of Australia's war effort. He still had reservations about the Borneo campaign. In particular, he questioned whether the 7th Division should be used for the proposed landing at Balikpapan, in southeastern Borneo.

Document 388

Blamey to Fraser [Acting Minister for the Army]   Melbourne, 16 May 1945

Letter   *Top Secret and Personal*

1. The termination of the war in Europe will lead to a reallocation of the whole of the Allied Military Forces. The reallocation of the Australian Military Forces must therefore now be reconsidered. ...

2. The present allocation from Australia is equivalent to approximately one division to 1.2 million population. On a similar basis this would give an

equivalent of roughly 100 American divisions and 38 British divisions (exclusive of Indian divisions). ...
... It would ... appear that there should be a very great reduction in the Australian Military Forces and this, broadly, it is suggested should be governed by the proportionate allocation of allied forces in the Pacific. On the assumption that say 50 American and 20 British divisions are likely to be involved, this should bring Australia's contribution, on a proportion to population basis, down to approximately three divisions, plus the essential base and maintenance troops. ...

[After considering the Australian army's current commitments Blamey continues:]

[3.] ... Therefore it cannot be foreseen, at present, when the forces in New Guinea can be reduced below two divisions, and this is a commitment from which we cannot withdraw.
4. If, therefore, the proposal that the Australian contribution towards the allied effort against the Japanese should be reduced to a total of approximately three divisions, it is obvious that the force for any operations other than those in New Guinea, to which Australia is committed, should be reduced to approximately one division, with necessary ancillary organisations. This division could be best organised by taking approximately one third of its organisation from each of the 6th, 7th and 9th Divisions for such commitments in the western portion of the East Indies or elsewhere as might be approved. ...
6. The area of employment of the Australian division to be specially organised for further forward operations cannot yet be determined... .
7. The Commander-in-Chief, SWPA, is very anxious to have the Australian Corps with him... .
   I also know that the Commander-in-Chief, SEAC [South-East Asia Command], [Lord Louis Mountbatten] would very eagerly welcome any contribution the Australian Government may be prepared to offer.
8. It is probable that, if the Australian contribution is allotted to SWPA, it will ultimately be included in any organisation which reaches Japan proper. This would be most popular with a great many of the troops. ...
   It is also realised that there is considerable strength of public opinion which would be anxious to participate in any operations for the recapture of Singapore. ...
9. If it is agreed that we should aim at a reduction to approximately three divisions and that one division approximately should be allocated to commitments outside of New Guinea and the mandated territory, I would suggest that the United Kingdom Government be informed accordingly and that General MacArthur be informed that the 7th Division is not available for further operations until the overall plan is known.
   I would be glad if the matter might be brought forward for the earliest consideration possible.
(a) With a view to preventing the use of the 7th Australian Division in the

capture of Balikpapan in the southern part of Dutch Borneo, so that our forces should not be committed to a role from which it would be difficult to withdraw them. ...
[AA: A 5954, Box 570]

Blamey's doubts as to whether MacArthur was wise to plan a move down the east coast of Borneo by landing the 7th Division at Balikpapan, led to J.B. Chifley, acting Prime Minister, raising the issue with MacArthur. The following exchange shows that Chifley was no less reluctant than Curtin to stand firm against MacArthur.

Document 389

Chifley to MacArthur				Canberra, 18 May 1945

Letter				*Top Secret and Personal*

I would refer to the following passages in the Prime Minister's letter of 15th February:-
"In its recent review, War Cabinet reached the conclusion that, as you had made your operational plans on the assigned strength of the Australian Forces, it would be impossible to make further reductions in the strength at this stage if your plans are being adhered to, and I was requested by War Cabinet to ascertain if such is the case.
If there has been no variation in your plans, I was asked to consult you regarding the contemplated use of the Australian Forces, with a view to determining the stage at which appropriate reductions can be made and deciding the future strengths which should be maintained. As the war effort is still in a state of disequilibrium, War Cabinet considered that the earliest opportunity should be taken to rectify it as soon as the operational situation will permit."
2. In your reply of 5th March[19], you stated:-
"In categorical reply to your basic question, I would state that my plans contemplate the use of all of the Australian forces now assigned to the Southwest Pacific Area."
3. War Cabinet [c]oncurred in the view expressed by the Prime Minister and Minister for Defence that, except for such measures as may be possible to ensure the economical use of manpower in the Forces, it would not appear, in view of your reply, that any further steps should be taken for the reduction of the present approved operational strength of six divisions and two armoured brigades, until after the completion of the next phase of operations.
4. With the end of the war in Europe and the assurance that the strength

---

19. See Document 371.

of the United Nation[s] can be concentrated against Japan, the Government has been considering the adjustments that can be made in the strength of the Australian Forces, in order to relieve the manpower stringencies and at the same time maintain a fighting effort of appropriate strength to the present stage of the war.

5. The Commander-in-Chief of the Australian Military Forces [Blamey] has pointed out that, if there is to be a substantial reduction in the strength of the Australian Military Forces, the 7th Division should not be committed to operations on the Borneo mainland, since it will form a commitment where there may be considerable fighting and where we may ultimately be committed to a very large garrison.

6. I shall be glad if you can give urgent consideration to this matter in relation to the present stage of your plans for the Borneo campaign, and furnish me with your observations. I would add that it is the desire of the Government that Australian Forces should continue to be associated with your command in the forward movement against Japan, but the Commander-in-Chief of the Australian Military Forces advises that, if a reduction in our strength is to be made, the 7th Division should not be employed for further operations until the overall plan is known.

[AA: A 5954, Box 570]

Document 390

MacArthur to Chifley   20 May 1945

Teleprinter Message BXC.87   *Top Secret*

The Borneo Campaign in all its phases has been ordered by the Joint Chiefs of Staff who are charged by the Combined Chiefs of Staff with the responsibility for strategy in the Pacific. I am responsible for execution of their directives employing such troops as have been made available to me by the Governments participating in the Allied Agreement. Pursuant to the directive of the Joint Chiefs of Staff and under authority vested in me as Supreme Commander, Southwest Pacific Area, I have ordered the 7th Division to proceed to a forward concentration area and, on a specific date, to execute one phase of the Borneo Campaign. Australian authorities have been kept fully advised of my operational plans. The concentration is in progress and it is not now possible to substitute another Division and execute the operations as scheduled. The attack will be made as projected unless the Australian Government withdraws the 7th Division from assignment to the Southwest Pacific Area. I am loath to believe that your Government contemplates such action at this time when the preliminary phases of the operation have been initiated and when withdrawal would disorganize completely not only the immediate campaign but also the strategic plan of the Joint Chiefs of Staff. If the Australian Government, however, does contemplate action along this line, I request that I be informed immediately in

order that I may be able to make the necessary representations to Washington and London. ...
[AA: A 5954, Box 570]

Document 391

Chifley to MacArthur   20 May 1945

Teleprinter Message CAB.213   *Top Secret and Personal*

1. The Government has no hesitation in agreeing to the use of the 7th Australian Division as planned by you.
2. As previously advised, it is not intended to take any steps to reduce the present approved operational strength of the Australian Army until after the completion of the next phase of operations.
3. It necessarily sought your observations, as Commander-in-Chief of the Southwest Pacific Area, on the submission of the Commander-in-Chief of the Australian Military Forces. It fully accepts your views which agree with the Government's conception of its commitments and by which it absolutely intends to abide.
[AA: A 5954, Box 570]

The landings on Tarakan, Labuan Island-Brunei Bay (10 June) and Balikpapan (1 July) achieved their immediate objectives at a cost of 568 fatal casualties in the two attacking divisions. The assault troops enjoyed massive support from ships and planes, including RAAF squadrons. Here, Bostock[20] proudly presents a brief battle report to the interim Prime Minister, F.M. Forde.

Document 392

Bostock to Forde   Morotai, 12 July 1945

Letter   *Confidential*

The late Prime Minister imposed on me (as the Operational Commander of the R.A.A.F.) the responsibility of so utilising air power that A.I.F. casualties would be reduced to a minimum.

... I now submit (from the Air Force point of view) a final report at the conclusion of the series of three operations which have established the

---

20. Air Vice-Marshal W.D. Bostock, Air Officer Commanding RAAF Command.

Australian Forces in BORNEO (at TARAKAN, BRUNEI-LABUAN ISLAND and at BALIKPAPAN).

I had placed at my disposal the three Air Forces constituting Allied Air Forces S.W.P.A. i.e. R.A.A.F. Command and the two American Air Forces (Fifth and Thirteenth). I used R.A.A.F. Command as the primary and occupying air force with the Thirteenth Air Force in support and the Fifth Air Force in reserve.

The prepared positions at BALIKPAPAN, in particular, offered the enemy an opportunity to inflict casualties on a scale comparable to those suffered by us at GALLIPOLI. Photographs revealed at least one hundred and twenty concrete gun emplacements in the ridges covering the beaches. The forty squadrons which I employed (twenty five of which were heavy bombers i.e. 300 LIBERATORS) reduced these defences to less than half a dozen effective units.

I am now able to report that the assault and occupation of these three formidable objectives in BORNEO were achieved at a cost of only 1600 casualties of a total force of over 70,000 men landed. Of these casualties the dead are 550 which is less than one per cent of the total number of personnel involved.
[AWM: 54, 81/3/9]

Appendices

APPENDIX I

Select List of Australian Office Holders 1939–1945

Prime Minister:

Robert Gordon Menzies	26.4.1939 to 29.8.1941
Arthur William Fadden	29.8.1941 to 7.10.1941
John Curtin	7.10.1941 to 5.7.1945
Francis Michael Forde	6.7.1945 to 13.7.1945
Joseph Benedict Chifley	13.7.1945 to 19.12.1949

Leader of the Opposition:

John Curtin	1.10.1935 to 7.10.1941
Arthur William Fadden	8.10.1941 to 1.7.1943
Robert Gordon Menzies	23.9.1943 to 19.12.1949

Minister for Defence:

Geoffrey Austin Street	7.11.1938 to 13.11.1939
John Curtin	14.4.1942 to 5.7.1945
John Albert Beasley	6.7.1945 to 15.8.1946

Minister for Defence Co-ordination:

Robert Gordon Menzies	13.11.1939 to 7.10.1941
John Curtin	7.10.1941 to 14.4.1942

Appendix I

Minister for the Navy:

Frederick Harold Stewart	13.11.1939 to 14.3.1940
Archie Galbraith Cameron	14.3.1940 to 28.10.1940
William Morris Hughes	28.10.1940 to 7.10.1941
Norman John Oswald Makin	7.10.1941 to 15.8.1946

Minister for the Army:

Geoffrey Austin Street	13.11.1939 to 13.8.1940
Philip Albert Martin McBride	14.8.1940 to 28.10.1940
Percy Claude Spender	28.10.1940 to 7.10.1941
Francis Michael Forde	7.10.1941 to 1.11.1946

Minister for Air:

James Valentine Fairbairn	13.11.1939 to 13.8.1940
Arthur William Fadden	14.8.1940 to 28.10.1940
John McEwen	28.10.1940 to 7.10.1941
Arthur Samuel Drakeford	7.10.1941 to 19.12.1949

Minister for Supply and Development:

Richard Gardiner Casey	26.4.1939 to 26.1.1940
Frederick Harold Stewart	26.1.1940 to 28.10.1940
Philip Albert Martin McBride	28.10.1940 to 26.6.1941
George McLeay	26.6.1941 to 7.10.1941

Minister for External Affairs:

Henry Somer Gullett	26.4.1939 to 14.3.1940

John McEwen	14.3.1940 to 28.10.1940
Frederick Harold Stewart	28.10.1940 to 7.10.1941
Herbert Vere Evatt	7.10.1941 to 19.12.1949

Chief of the Naval Staff:

Ragnar Colvin	1937 to July 1941
Guy Royle	July 1941 to 1945

Chief of the General Staff:

E.K. Squires	October 1939 to March 1940
C. Brudenell White	March 1940 to August 1940
Vernon A.H. Sturdee	August 1940 to September 1942
John Northcott	September 1942 to 1945

Chief of the Air Staff:

S.J. Goble [Acting]	February 1939 to January 1940
W.H. Anderson [Acting]	January 1940 to February 1940
C. Burnett	February 1940 to April [May] 1942*
G. Jones	May 1942 to January 1952

*There is some confusion in the records as to the date on which Burnett ceased to be Chief of the Air Staff. In the text the date is given as 4 April 1942 as in Document 42. Burnett, however, was still advising the government after this date. We have followed the date as in the Document, but this confusion should be noted.

APPENDIX II

BIOGRAPHICAL NOTES

ALANBROOKE, see BROOKE.

ALEXANDER OF TUNIS, 1st Earl (Sir Harold Alexander) (1891–1969) *British general* GOC 1 Div 1937–40; GOC Southern Cmd 1940–2; GOC Burma 1942; C-in-C ME 1942–3; Allied Supreme Cmdr in the Mediterranean 1944–5.

ALLEN, Arthur Samuel (1894–1959) *Australian army officer* C.O. 45 Bn 1918; C.O. 16 Bde 1939–41; GOC 7 Div 1941–2, 6 Div 1942–3; Cmdr N.T. Force 1943–4.

ARNOLD, Henry Harley (1886–1950) *US airman* Chief of Air Corps 1938–41; Chief of USAAF 1941–6. Member of US Joint Chiefs of Staff and of CCS.

ATTLEE, Clement Richard (1st Earl Attlee) (1883–1967) *British politician* Leader of the Labour Party 1935–55; Lord Privy Seal 11.5.40–19.2.42; S. of S. for Dominion Affairs 19.2.42–28.9.43; Deputy Prime Minister 19.2.42–1945; Lord President of the Council 28.9.43–1945; Prime Minister July 1945–1951.

AUCHINLECK, Sir Claude John Eyre (1884–1981) *British general* C-in-C India 1941, 1943–6, C-in-C ME 1941–2.

BEASLEY, John Albert (1895–1949) *Australian politician and trade union leader* MHR (NSW, Lab.) 1928–46; Minister for Supply and Shipping 1941–5, for Defence July 1945–1946; member Advisory War Council 29.10.40–31.8.45; member War Cabinet 7.10.41–1946.

BENNETT, Henry Gordon (1887–1962) *Australian soldier* C.O. 6 Bn 1915–6, 3 Inf Bde 1916–9; GOC 8 Div 1940–2, AIF Malaya 1941–2, III Corps 1942–4.

BERRYMAN, Sir Frank Horton (1894–1981) *Australian army officer* 1st AIF; GSO1 6 Div 1940–1; CRA 7 Div 1941; DCGS at LHQ 1942–4; commanded II and I Corps during 1944; COS Adv LHQ 1944–5.

BLACKBURN, Arthur Seaforth (1892–1960) *Australian soldier* 1st AIF; C.O. 2/3 MG Bn 1940–2; C.O. Blackforce in Java 1942.

BLAMEY, Sir Thomas Albert (1884–1951) *Australian soldier* GSO1 1 Div 1916–7; GOC 6 Div 1939–40, AIF in ME 1940–2; Deputy C-in-C ME 1941; GOC-in-C AMF 1942–6; Allied Land Forces Commander, SWPA, 1942–5.

BOSTOCK, William Dowling (1892–1968) *Australian air force officer* DCAS 1939–41; Air Officer Commanding RAAF Command 1942–5; MHR (Vic., non-Lab.) 1949–58.

BOUCHER, Maitland W.S. (1888–1963) *British naval officer* Second Naval Member, Australian Naval Board 1939–40 and Acting CNS at outbreak of war during Colvin's temporary absence from duty.

BOWDEN, Vivian Gordon (1884–1942) *Australian businessman and public servant* Aust. Govt. Commissioner in China 1935–41; Australian Official Representative in Singapore 1941–2; executed by Japanese 17.2.42.

BRERETON, Lewis Hyde (1890–   ) *US air force officer* Commander US Far East Air Forces in Philippines 1941–2; later held high air force commands in ME and Europe.

BRETT, George H. (1886–1963) *US air force officer* Deputy C-in-C ABDA forces Jan.-Feb. 1942; commanded US Army Forces in Australia (USAFIA) Dec. 1941-March 1942; Allied Air Forces Commander, SWPA April-Aug. 1942.

BROOKE, Alan Francis (1st Viscount Alanbrooke) (1883–1963) *British general* GOC II Corps British Expeditionary Force 1939–40; C-in-C Home Forces 1940–1; CIGS 1941–6.

BROOKE-POPHAM, Sir Robert (1878–1953) *British air force officer* C-in-C Far East 1940–1.

BRUCE, Stanley Melbourne (1st Viscount Bruce of Melbourne) (1883–1967) *Australian politician and diplomat* Prime Minister 1923–9; High Commissioner, U.K. 1933–45; Aust. Govt. Accredited Representative to U.K. War Cabinet and Pacific War Council 1942–45.

BURNETT, Sir Charles (1882–1945) *British air force officer* COS RAAF 15.2.40–4.4.42.

CALDECOTE, *see* INSKIP.

CAMERON, Archie G.S. (1895–1956) *Australian politician* Minister for Commerce and for the Navy 1940; Leader of the Country Party Sept. 1939–40.

CASEY, Richard G. (1st Baron Casey) (1890–1976) *Australian diplomat and politician* 1st AIF 1914–9; Minister for Supply & Development April 1939–1940; Leader, Aust. delegation to meeting of U.K. and Dominions Ministers, London, Oct.-Dec. 1939; member of War Cabinet 15.9.39–26.1.40; Minister, USA 1940–2; member, U.K. War Cabinet and Minister of State resident in ME 1942–3; Governor of Bengal 1944–6.

CATROUX, Georges (1877–1969) *French army officer and administrator* Served in Great War; as a supporter of de Gaulle was High Commissioner in Syria from late 1941.

CHATFIELD, Alfred Ernle M. (1st Baron of Ditchling) (1873–1967) *British naval officer* First Sea Lord and CNS 1933–8; Minister for Co-ordination of Defence with seat in War Cabinet 1939–40.

CHIFLEY, Joseph B. (1885–1951) *Australian politician* Commonwealth Treasurer 1941–9; Member of War Cabinet 7.10.41–1946; Minister for Post-War Reconstruction 1942–5; Acting Prime Minister April-July 1945; member, Advisory War Council July-Aug. 1945; Prime Minister 13.7.45-19.12.49.

CHURCHILL, Winston S. (1874–1965) *British politician* Numerous ministerial offices between 1906 and 1929; First Lord of the Admiralty 3.9.39-May 1940; Prime Minister 10.5.40–25.7.45.

CLOWES, Cyril Albert (1892–1968) *Australian army officer* 1st AIF; CRA 1 Corps 1940–1; GOC 1 Div 1942; Cmdr Milne Force 1942; GOC 11 Div 1942–3; Comd Vic L of C Area 1943–5.

COLLINS, Sir John Augustine (1899-   ) *Australian naval officer* Assistant CNS 1938–9; commanded HMAS *Sydney* 1939–41, *Shropshire* 1943–4, Aust. Squadron (and Task Force 74) 1944, 1945–6; CNS 1948–55.

COLVIN, Sir Ragnar (1882–1954) *British naval officer* CNS 1937–41. Naval adviser to High Commissioner for Aust. in London 1942–4.

COOPER, Alfred Duff (1890–1954) *British politician* Minister for Information 1940–1; British Minister of State in the Far East (based at Singapore) Aug. 1941-Jan. 1942; British ambassador in Paris Nov. 1944–1947.

CRANBORNE, Viscount (R.A.J. Cecil and 5th Marquis of Salisbury) (1893–1972) *British politician* S. of S. for Dominion Affairs 1940–2; S. of S. for the Colonies 1942; Lord Privy Seal 1942–3; Leader, House of Lords 1942–5.

CROSS, Sir Ronald Hibbert (1896–1968) *British politician and merchant banker* Minister of Shipping 1940–1; High Commissioner to Australia 16.7.1941–45.

CRUTCHLEY, Sir Victor Alexander Charles (1893–   ) *British naval officer* Commanded Aust. Squadron and Task Force 44 (later Task Force 74) 13.6.42–13.6.44.

CUNNINGHAM, Andrew Browne (later Viscount Cunningham of Hyndhope) (1883–1963) *British naval officer* Commanded British naval forces in the Mediterranean 1939–42; C-in-C Allied Naval Forces Mediterranean 1943; First Sea Lord 1943–6.

CURTIN, John (8.1.1885–5.7.1945) *Australian politician* MHR 1928–31, 1934–45. Prime Minister and Minister for Defence 7.10.41–5.7.45 (of Cottesloe, WA).

DE GAULLE, Charles (1890–1970) *French army officer and politician* Leader of the Free French movement 1940–5.

DEWING, R.H. (1891–1981) *British regular soldier* Chief of Staff, Far East 1940–1; Senior UK Army Liaison Officer in Aust. 1942; head of UK Liaison Staff in Aust. 1942–4.

DILL, Sir John Greer (1881–1944) *British army officer* GOC 1 Army Corps in France 1939–40; CIGS May 1940–Dec. 1941, then head of British Joint Staff Mission to Washington, until his death in Nov. 1944.

DIXON, Sir Owen (1886–1972) *Australian judge and diplomat* Justice of High Court, 1929–52, Chief Justice 1952–64; Minister to Washington 1942–4.

DRAKEFORD, Arthur Samuel (1878–1957) *Australian politician* Minister for Air and for Civil Aviation Oct. 1941–49; member War Cabinet 7.10.41–1946.

DRUMMOND, Sir Peter (1894–1945) *British air force officer* RFC and RAF 1916–8; Senior Air Staff Offficer HQ RAF ME 1937–41; Deputy AOC-in-C HQ RAF ME 1941–3; Air Member for Training, Air Council 1943–5.

EDEN, Sir (Robert) Anthony (1st Earl of Avon) (1897–1977) *British politician* Served in France in Great War. S. of S. for Foreign Affairs 1935–8; for Dominion Affairs 3.9.39–May 1940; for War 1940; for Foreign Affairs 1940–5; Prime Minister 1955–7.

EGGLESTON, Sir Frederic (1875–1954) *Australian politician and diplomat* 1st AIF; Aust. Minister to China 1941–4, to USA 1944–6.

EICHELBERGER, Robert Lawrence (1886–1961) *US army officer* Commanding general of US 1 Corps, arriving in Aust. in August 1942. Commanded at Buna front, Dec. 1942-Jan. 1943. Remained commander of I Corps until Sept. 1944 when he became commander of the US Eighth Army.

EISENHOWER, Dwight David (1890–1969) *US army officer and politician* Aide to MacArthur when he was military adviser to the Philippines Govt.; COS, 3rd Army 1941; head of the War Plans Division of the War Department General Staff Dec. 1941–42; commander European Theatre of Operations June 1942; Supreme Allied Commander in Europe 1944–5; President of USA 1953–60.

EVATT, Herbert Vere (1894–1965) *Australian judge and politician* Justice, High Court 1930–40; MHR 1940–60; Minister for External Affairs and Attorney-General 1941–9. President, 3rd U.N. General Assembly 1948–9.

FADDEN, Arthur William (1895–1973) *Australian politician* Minister for Air and for Civil Aviation Aug-Oct. 1940; Treasurer Oct. 1940-Oct. 1941; Prime Minister 29.8.41–7.10.41; member War Cabinet 14.8.40–7.10.41; of Advisory War Council 29.10.40–31.8.45.

FAIRBAIRN, James Valentine (1897–1940) *Australian politician* Served in Royal Flying Corps 1916–17. Minister for Civil Aviation, for Air, and Vice President of the Executive Council 26 April 1939–1940; member War Cabinet 13.11.39–13.8.40; killed in air accident, Canberra, 13.8.40.

FOLL, Hattil Spencer (1890–1977) *Australian politician* Served AIF 1915–16. Queensland Senator, non-Lab., 1917–47; Minister for the Interior 1939–40, for Information 1940–1; member War Cabinet 1939–41.

FORDE, Francis Michael (1890–1983) *Australian politician* MLA (Qld) 1917–22, 1955–7. MHR 1922–46. Minister for the Army 1941–5. Prime Minister, 6-13 July 1945; member of War Cabinet 7.10.41–1946; member of Advisory War Council 29.10.40 to 31.8.45.

FRASER, Peter (1884–1950) *New Zealand politician* M.P. (Lab.) 1918–50; Minister 1935–40; Prime Minister 1940–9; Minister for External Affairs 1943–9.

FREYBERG, Sir Bernard (1889–1963) *British and New Zealand army officer* In Great War became the youngest brigadier in the British army, and won the VC on 16 Dec. 1917. Commander 2nd N.Z. Expeditionary Force 1939–45. Commanded British forces on Crete May 1941.

GHORMLEY, Robert Lee (1883–1958) *US naval officer* Commander South Pacific Area April-Oct. 1942.

Biographical Notes   439

GLASGOW, Sir T. William (1876–1955) *Australian soldier and politician* Served South African War and in 1st AIF; GOC 1 Div 1918–9; Minister for Defence 1927–9; High Commissioner in Canada 1940–5.

GOBLE, Stanley James (1891–1948) *Australian air force officer* Served in Great War; CAS RAAF 1932–4, 1939–40 (acting); Aust. Liaison Officer to EATS, Canada, June 1940-May 1945.

GORT, 6th Viscount (John Standish Surtees Prendergast Vereker) (1886–1946) *British army officer* Served with great distinction in Great War; CIGS 1937–9; GOC British Expeditionary Force 1939-May 1940; Inspector-General to the Forces 1940–1; C-in-C Gibraltar 1941–2, Malta 1942–4.

HAINING, Sir Robert Hadden (1882–1959) *British army officer* Vice CIGS 1940–1.

HALSEY, William Frederick (1882–1959) *US admiral* Commander, South Pacific Area, 18.10.42–15.6.44; Commander, Third Fleet, 1943-Nov. 1945.

HANKEY, Lord (Sir Maurice P.A. Hankey) (1877–1963) *British civil servant and politician* Sec. War Cabinet 1916–7, Imperial War Cabinet 1917–8, Cabinet 1919–38; member of War Cabinet 3.9.39–1940; Chancellor of the Duchy of Lancaster 1940–1; Paymaster-General 1941–2.

HARRIES, David Hugh (1903–1980) *Australian naval officer* Naval Attache Washington 1941–2; Executive Officer HMAS *Shropshire* 1942–4; Deputy CNS 1944–5.

HERRING, Sir Edmund Francis (1892–1982) *Australian soldier and judge* Served in Great War; CRA 6 Div 1939–41; GOC 6 Div 1941–2, N.T. Force 1942, II Corps 1942, I Corps and NG Force 1942–3, I Corps 1943–4; Chief Justice of Victoria 1944–64.

HODGSON, W. Roy (1892–1958) *Australian public servant and diplomat* Served 1st AIF. Sec., Dept. of External Affairs 1935–45.

HUGHES, William Morris (1862–1952) *Australian politician* Prime Minister 1915–23; Attorney-General 1939–41; Minister for Industry 1939–40, Navy 1940–41; member of Advisory War Council 1940–5; member of War Cabinet 15.9.39–29.8.41.

INSKIP, Sir Thomas W.H. (Lord Caldecote) (1876–1947) *British politician* S. of S. for Dominion Affairs, 29.1.39–3.9.39, 1940; Lord Chancellor 3.9.39–1940; Leader of the House of Lords 1940; Lord Chief Justice 1940–6.

ISMAY, Hastings L. (1887–1965) *British army officer and civil servant* Chief of Staff, Minister of Defence 1940–5; Deputy Sec. (Military) War Cabinet 1940–5.

JONES, Sir George (1896-) *Australian air force officer* Served 1st AIF (AFC), 4 years; Dir. Personnel Services RAAF 1936–40, of Training 1940–2; CAS 1942–52.

JOUBERT, de la Ferté, Sir Philip (1887–1965) *British air officer* Served in France in Royal Flying Corps in Great War. AOC-in-C Coastal Command 1936–7, 1941–3.

KENNEY, George Churchill (1889–1977) *US air force officer* Commander Allied Air Forces SWPA Aug 1942–5; commanded US Fifth Air Force Sept 1942–5; commanded US Far East Air Forces June 1944–5.

KING, Ernest Joseph (1878–1956) *US naval officer* C-in-C US Fleet Dec. 1941–1945.

LAMPSON, Sir Miles (1st Baron Killearn) (1880–1964) *British diplomat* Ambassador to Egypt 1936–46.

LANGSLOW, Melville Cecil (1889–1972) *Australian public servant* Sec., Dept of Air 1939–51.

LATHAM, Sir John Greig (1877–1964) *Australian politician and judge* MHR 1922–34; Deputy Prime Minister 1931–4; Chief Justice of High Court 1935–52; Minister to Japan 1940–1.

LAVARACK, Sir John Dudley (1885–1957) *Australian army officer* GSO1 4 Div 1917–9; CGS 1935–9; GOC Southern Command 1939–40, 7 Div 1940–1, I Corps 1941–2, First Army 1942–4; Leader, Aust. Military Mission to Washington 1944–6; Governor of Qld. 1946–57.

LAYTON, Sir Geoffrey (1884–1964) *British admiral* Vice Adm Comdg 1st Battle Squadron and Second in Command Home Fleet 1939–40; C-in-C China 1940–1, Eastern Fleet 1941–2, Ceylon 1942–5.

LEAHY, William Daniel (1875–1959) *US naval officer* Chief of Naval Operations 1937–9; Ambassador to Vichy France 1940; Roosevelt's personal chief of staff, presiding over the Joint Chiefs of Staff, 1941–5.

LEWIS, Essington (1881–1961) *Australian industrialist* Managing Director Broken Hill Pty Ltd 1926–38, Chief General Manager 1938–50; Director-General of Munitions 1940–5, of Aircraft Production 1942–5.

LLOYD, Charles Edward Maurice (1899–1956) *Australian army officer* With 6 Div 1939–40, and on HQ staff I Corps 1940; GSO1 9 Div 1941; Deputy Intendant General (ABDA COM) 1942. At SWPA LHQ 1942–5, being Adjutant General AMF Feb. 1943-Feb. 1946.

LLOYD, Eric E. Longfield (1890–1957) *Australian army officer and public servant* Served in 1st AIF; Aust Govt Commissioner in Japan 1935–40; Dep. Director (1940–3) then Director (1944–53) of Commonwealth Investigation Service.

LLOYD, Herbert William (1883–1957) *Australian army officer* Served AIF 1914–9, including Gallipoli landing; MLA (NSW) 1929–30, 1932–41; Director-General, AIF Recruiting 1940–1; GOC 2nd Div. 1940–3, 1st Div. Sept. 1943–1945.

LONGMORE, Sir Arthur (1885–1970) *British air officer* A.O.C-in-C ME May 1940–41.

LOTHIAN, Lord (Philip H. Kerr) (1882–1940) *British newspaper editor and diplomat* Editor, *The Round Table* 1910–16; Ambassador, USA Aug. 1939–Dec. 1940.

LUMSDEN, Herbert (1897–1945) *British army officer* Comd 28 Armd Bde 1941–2; GOC XXX, then X Corps 1942–3; Churchill's personal representative on GHQ SWPA 1943–5. Killed on USS *New Mexico*, Lingayen Gulf 6 Jan. 1945.

LYONS, Joseph Aloysius (1879–1939) *Australian politician* Premier of Tasmania 1923–8; Prime Minister 1932–9 (died in office 7.4.39).

LYTTELTON, Oliver (1st Viscount Chandos) (1893–1972) *British politician* Minister of State in the ME June 1941–42; Minister of Production 1942–5.

MACANDIE, George Lionel (1877–1968) *Australian public servant* Sec. to Naval Board 1914–46.

MacARTHUR, Douglas (1880–1964) *US general* Commanded 42nd ('Rainbow') Div in France in 1918; COS US Army 1930–5; military adviser to Philippines Govt. 1935–42; CG US Army Forces in Far East July 1941–42; C-in-C SWPA April 1942-Aug. 1945; Supreme Commander of the Allied Powers in Japan (SCAP) 1945–50; commander of US & UN forces in Korea 1950–1.

McEWEN, Sir John (1900–1980) *Australian politician and farmer* Served 1st AIF; MHR (Vic., Country Party) 1934–71; Minister for External Affairs March-Oct. 1940, for Air and Civil Aviation 1940–1; member War Cabinet 14.3.40–7.10.41; member Advisory War Council 16.10.41–31.8.45.

MACHTIG, Eric G. (1889–1973) *British civil servant* Asst Sec for Dominion Affairs 1930–6; Asst Under-Sec D.O. 1936–9; Deputy Under-Sec, D.O. 1939; Permanent Under-Sec, D.O. 1939–40, 1940–8.

MACKAY, Sir Iven Giffard (1882–1966) *Australian army officer and teacher* Served 1st AIF, commanded 1st Inf. Bde. 1918; GOC 6 Div 1940–1, Home Forces 1941–2, 2nd Aust Army 1942–3, NG Force 1943–4; High Commissioner for Aust in India 1944–8.

MAKIN, Norman John Oswald (1889–1982) *Australian politician* MHR 1919–46, 1954–63; Minister for Navy and for Munitions 1941–6, for Aircraft Production 1945–6; member of War Cabinet 7.10.41–1946. Member of Advisory War Council 29.10.40–31.8.45.

MARSHALL, George Catlett (1880–1959) *US army officer* Served in Great War; Chief of Staff US Army 1.9.39-Nov. 1945.

MENZIES, Sir Robert Gordon (1894–1978) *Australian politician* Prime Minister 26.4.39–29.8.41; Minister for Defence Coordination 13.11.39–7.10.41; Minister for Munitions 11.6.40–28.10.40; member of War Cabinet 15.9.39–7.10.41; member of Advisory War Council 29.10.40–18.2.44. Prime Minister 19.12.49–26.1.66.

MITCHELL, Sir William (1888–1944) *Australian-born British air officer* AOC-in-C RAF ME 1939–40; IG of RAF 1940–1.

MONTGOMERY of ALAMEIN, Bernard Law Montgomery, 1st Viscount (1887–1976) *British general* Served in France in Great War; GOC 3 Div 1939–40, V Corps 1940, XII Corps 1941, Eighth Army Aug. 1942-Dec. 1943; 21st Army Group 1944–5.

MORSHEAD, Sir Leslie (1889–1959) *Australian schoolteacher and general* 1st AIF, C.O. 33 Bn; Comd 18 Bde 1939–41; GOC 9 Div 1941–3, II Corps and NG Force during 1943–4, I Corps 1944–5; fortress commander, Tobruk 14.4.41–22.10.41.

MOUNTBATTEN OF BURMA, Earl (1900–1979) *British military officer* Served in RN in 1914–18, and held various commands in RN 1939–41; Chief of Combined Operations 1942–3; Supreme Allied Commander SE Asia 1943–6.

MULROONEY, Francis Joseph (1900–) *Australian public servant* Sec. Air Board 1939–52.

MURDOCH, Sir Keith Arthur (1886–1952) *Australian journalist and newspaper proprietor* Journalist on *Age*; Dir.-General of Information June-Dec. 1940; Chairman of Directors Herald & Weekly Times Ltd. 1942–52.

NANKERVIS, Alfred Roy (1885–1956) *Australian public servant* Sec., Dept. of the Navy, Nov. 1939–1949.

NIMITZ, Chester William (1885–1966) *US naval officer* C-in-C Pacific Ocean Areas (HQ at Pearl Harbor) Dec. 1941–45.

NORTHCOTT, Sir John (1890–1966) *Australian army officer* 1st AIF; accompanied R.G. Casey to meeting of U.K. and Dominions Ministers, London, Oct.-Dec. 1939. Deputy CGS 1939–41; GOC 1 Armoured Div 1941-2, 2 Aust Corps 1942; CGS 1942–5; C-in-C British Commonwealth Occupation Force, Japan, 1945–6; Governor of NSW 1946–57.

PAGE, Sir Earle Christmas Grafton (1880–1961) *Australian politician* 1st AIF; MHR (NSW) 1919–61; Leader of the Country Party 1920–39; Prime Minister 7–26 April 1939; Minister for Commerce 1940–1; Special Envoy to British War Cabinet 1941–2; member Advisory War Council 26.8.42–29.9.43, 24.2.44–31.8.45.

PALLISER, Sir Arthur (1891–1956) *British naval officer* COS to C-in-C Eastern Fleet 1941–2; commander 1 Cruiser Squadron 1943–4; Chief of Supplies and Transport, Admiralty, 1944–6.

PAPAGOS, Alexander (1883–1955) *Greek army officer* Commanded Greek forces against Italian and German invaders Oct. 1940-April 1941.

PARKHILL, Sir Archdale (1879–1947) *Australian politician* MHR (NSW) 1927–37; Minister for Defence 1934–20.11.37; member, delegation to Imperial Conference, London, 1937.

PEIRSE, Sir Richard (1892–1970) *British air officer* Deputy CAS RAF 1937–40; AOC-in-C Bomber Command 1940–2, India 1942–3; Allied Air C-in-C SEAC.

PERCIVAL, Arthur Ernest (1887–1966) *British army officer* GOC 43 Div 1940, 44 Div 1940–1. Malaya Command May 1941–Feb 1942.

PHILLIPS, Sir Tom (1888–1941) *British naval officer* VCNS (RN) 1939–41; C-in-C Eastern Fleet May-Dec. 1941; lost with *Prince of Wales* 10.12.41.

PLAYFAIR, Ian Stanley Ord (1894–1972) *British army officer* Director of Plans, War Office 1940–1; GSO 11th Army Group SEAC 1943.

POORTEN, Hein ter (1887–1968) *Dutch army officer* C-in-C Netherlands East Indies Army Oct. 1941-March 1942; commanded Allied forces in Java which surrendered on 10.3.42.

PORTAL, Sir Charles (Viscount Portal of Hungerford) (1893–1971) *British air force officer* CAS 25.10.1940–Dec. 1945.

POWNALL, Sir Henry (1887-1961) *British army officer* Director of military operations and intelligence, War Office, 1938-41; C-in-C Far East 1941-2, Ceylon 1942-3, Persia and Iraq 1943; COS SEAC 1943-4.

PULFORD, C.W.H. (1892-1942) *British air officer* Served in Great War; AOC 20 Group 1940-1; AOC RAF Far East 1941-2; died on island near Sumatra March 1942.

RAMSAY, Sir Alan Hollick (1895-1973) *Australian teacher and army officer* Served 1st AIF; CO 2/2 Fd Regt 1939-40; CRA 9 Div 1940-3, II Corps 1943-4; GOC 5 Div 1944-5.

ROBERTSON, Sir Horace Clement Hugh (1894-1960) *Australian army officer* 1st AIF; Comd 19 Bde, Libya, 1941; GOC 1 Armoured Div 1942-3, Western Comd 1944-5, 5 Div and 6 Div 1945; C-in-C British Commonwealth Occupation Force in Japan 1946-51.

ROMMEL, Erwin (1891-1944) *German army officer* Commanded AFRIKA KORPS, Feb 1941-March 1943.

ROOSEVELT, Franklin Delano (1882-1945) *US politician* Governor (Democrat), New York State 1929-33; President, USA 1933-45.

ROSS, David (1902-) *Australian airman and public servant* Aust. Consul in Portuguese Timor from 1941 until its occupation by Japanese forces; Director of Transportation and Movement, RAAF HQ 1943-6.

ROURKE, Henry Gordon (1896-1973?) *Australian army officer* Served 1st AIF; GSO1 8 Div 1940-1; CRA 7 Div 1941-2; BGS I Corps 1942; Military Asst to Aust. Accredited Representative in the UK War Cabinet 1943-5.

ROWELL, Sir Sydney Fairburn (1894-1975) *Australian army officer* Served 1st AIF; GSO1 6 Div Oct. 1939-40; BGS 1 Aust Corps April 1940-1941; Dep. CGS Sept. 1941-42; GOC 1 Aust Corps April-Aug. 1942; GOC NG Force Aug.-Sept. 1942; Director of Tactical Investigation, War Office, 1943-6; CGS 1950-4.

ROYLE, Sir Guy Charles Cecil (1885-1954) *British naval officer* CNS 11.7.41-1945.

SAVAGE, Michael J. (7.3.1872-26.3.1940) *New Zealand politician* M.P. (Lab.) 1919-40; Leader of the Labour Party 1933-40; Prime Minister, Minister for External Affairs, and various other portfolios 1935-40.

SAVIGE, Stanley George (1890-1954) *Australian army officer and company director* Served 1st AIF; Comd 17 Bde 1939-41; GOC 3 Div 1942-4, I Corps and NG Force 1944, II Corps 1944-5.

SCOTT, Norman (1889-1942) *US naval officer* Cmdr of American naval squadron at Guadalcanal 1942; killed in action at Guadalcanal 13.11.42.

SHEDDEN, Sir Frederick Geoffrey (1893-1971) *Australian public servant* Sec. Defence Committee 1929-36; Sec. Dept. of Defence 1937-56, of War Cabinet 1939-46, Advisory War Council 1940-5; member, Council of Defence 1946-56; accompanied Prime Minister and Minister for Defence on overseas missions 1941, 1944, 1946, 1951, 1955.

SINCLAIR, Frank Roy (1892-   ) *Australian public servant* Asst Secy Dept. of Defence 1938-41; Asst Secy War Cabinet and Advisory War Council 1939-41; Sec., Army Dept. 1941-55.

SITWELL, Hervey Degge Wilmot (1896-1973) *British army officer* GOC British troops Java 1942; prisoner of war 1942-5.

SLIM, William Joseph (Viscount Slim) (1891-1970) *British army officer* GOC 10th Indian Div in Iraq, Syria and Iran from 1941 to March 1942 when he arrived in Burma, to command 1st Burma Corps. After the retreat into India, Slim commanded XV India Corps. From Oct. 1943 he was GOC Fourteenth Army. In 1945 he was appointed C-in-C Allied Land Forces in Southeast Asia. CIGS 1948-52; Gov.-Gen. Aust. 1953-60.

SMART, Edward Kenneth (1891-1961) *Australian army officer* Served 1st AIF; 3rd Military Member, Military Board Oct. 1939-1940; GOC Southern Cmd Oct. 1940-March 1942; Head of Aust. Military Mission to CCS, Washington, 1942; Aust. Military Representative, London, Oct. 1942-July 1946.

SOMERVILLE, Sir James Fownes (1882-1949) *British naval officer* Commanded Force 'H' in Mediterranean 1940-2; C-in-C Eastern Fleet March 1942-44; Head of British Admiralty Delegation to Washington 1944-5.

SPENDER, Percy Claude (1897-   ) *Australian politician and lawyer* Treasurer 1940; Minister for the Army 1940-1; member, War Cabinet 1939-40, Advisory War Council 29.10.40-31.8.45.

SQUIRES, Ernest K. (1882-1940) *British army officer* IG, AMF 1938-Oct. 1939; CGS (Aust army) Oct. 1939-3.3.40.

STANHOPE, James Richard (7th Earl) (1880-1967) *British army officer and politician* First Lord of the Admiralty 1938-9.

STRAHAN, Frank (1886-1976) *Australian public servant* Ass. Sec., Prime Minister's Dept. 1921-35; Sec., Prime Minister's Dept. 1935-49; Sec. Cabinet 1941-9.

STREET, Sir Arthur William (1892–1951) *British public servant* Under-Sec. of State for Air and Sec. of the Air Council 1939–45.

STREET, Geoffrey A. (1894–1940) *Australian army officer and politician* Served AIF 1914–19; MHR 1934–40; Minister for Defence 1938–13.11.39; Minister for the Army 13.11.39–1940, Repatriation 1940. Killed in air accident, Canberra, 13.8.40.

STURDEE, Sir Vernon Ashton Hobart (1890–1966) *Australian army officer* Served 1st AIF; GOC Eastern Command Oct. 1939-June 1940; GOC 8 Div July-Aug. 1940; CGS Aug. 1940-Sept. 1942; Head Aust. Military Mission in USA Sept. 1942-March 1944; GOC 1st Army March 1944-Dec. 1945.

SUTHERLAND, Richard Kenneth (1893–1966) *US army officer* COS to MacArthur 1939–45.

TEDDER, Arthur William (1st Baron Tedder) (1890–1967) *British air officer* Dep. AOC-in-C RAF ME 1940–1; AOC-in-C RAF ME 1941–3; Air C-in-C Mediterranean Air Command 1943; Deputy Supreme Cmdr Europe 1944–5.

THOMAS, Sir Shenton (1879–1962) *British colonial administrator* Governor and C-in-C of Straits Settlements and High Commissioner for the Malay States 1934–42.

VASEY, George Alan (1895–1945) *Australian army officer* Served 1st AIF; Assistant Adjutant and Quartermaster General 6 Div 1939–41; GSO1 6 Div 1941; Comd 19 Bde 1941; GOC 6 Div 1942, 7 Div 1942–4.

VEALE, William Charles Douglas (1895-?) *Australian army officer and civil engineer* Served 1st AIF; C.O. 2/3 Pnr Bn 1940–1; Chief Engineer N.T. 1941–2; Commander Sparrow Force 1942; Chief Engineer 2nd Army 1944–5, 1st Army 1945.

WARD, Edward John (1899–1963) *Australian politician* MHR (Lab., East Sydney) 1931, 1932–63; Minister for Labour and National Service 1941–3, for Transport and External Territories 1943–9.

WARDELL, Augustine William (1895–1967?) *Australian army officer* Served 1st AIF; Comd 25 Bde 1940; Comd AIF in UK 1940–1; Military Liaison Officer High Commissioner's Office London 1941–2; service advisor to Aust. representative on UK War Cabinet 1942–3; on staff at Land HQ, Melb. 1943–5.

WAVELL, Archibald Percival (1st Earl Wavell) (1883–1950) *British army officer* GOC-in-C British Southern Command 1938–9; C-in-C ME Jul 1939–1941; C-in-C India 1941–3; Supreme commander ABDA Jan.-Feb. 1942; Viceroy of India 1943–7.

WHISKARD, Sir Geoffrey G. (1886–1957) *British civil servant* Asst. Under-Sec., D.O. 1930–5; High Commissioner Aust. 1936–41; Permanent Sec., Ministry of Works and Buildings 1941–3; Ministry of Town and Country Planning 1943–6.

WHITE, Sir C. Brudenell (1876–1940) *Australian army officer* 1st AIF, GSO1 1 Div; Chief of Staff, Aust. Corps 1916; British Fifth Army 1918; CGS 1920–3, March-Aug. 1940; Killed in air accident 13.8.40.

WILLIAMS, Richard (1890–1980) *Australian air force officer* Served AIF (AFC), RAF, RAAF 1914–46; CAS 1921–38; Air Member for Organisation and Equipment RAAF 1940–1; AOC Overseas HQ RAAF UK 1941–2; RAAF Representative USA 1942–6.

WILSON, Henry Maitland (1st Baron Wilson) (1881–1964) *British army officer* GSO1 NZ Div 1917–8; GOC-in-C Egypt 1939–41, Cyrenaica 1941, British troops in Greece 1941, Ninth Army 1941; C-in-C Persia-Iraq Command 1942–3, ME 1943; Supreme Allied Cmdr Mediterranean Theatre 1944. Succeeded Dill as Head of British Joint Staff Mission to Washington, 1945–7.

WOODS, F.A. (1910-) *Australian livestock dealer and army officer* Capt, 21 Bde 1940–1; 9 Div 1941; Liaison Officer between HQ British troops and HQ AIF Java 1942.

WOOTTEN, Sir George Frederick (1893–1970) *Australian army officer and solicitor* Served 1st AIF 1914–9; CO 2/2 Bn 1939–40; Comd 18 Bde 1941–3; GOC 9 Div 1943–5.

WYNTER, Henry Douglas (1886–1945) *Australian army officer* Served 1st AIF; GOC Northern Command 1939–40, 9 Div 1940–1, Eastern Command 1941–2; Lt-Gen. Admin LHQ 1942–5.

SUBJECT INDEX

Admiralty Islands, 393, 395
Ambon (Amboina)
　Australian forces in, 163, 165, 170–71, 172–73, 174, 177, 196, 197, 205, 212, 213, 219–22, 233, 265
　defence, 170–73, 177
　Japanese forces in, 194, 195, 212, 219–22, 296
Anglo-Dutch-Australian Conference (February 1941), 160, 161, 166, 169, 170–72, 174, 308
Arcadia conference, Washington (1941–42), 179, 185, 286
Atlantic Ocean
　Anglo-American command over, 301
　Australian naval forces in, 9
　British naval forces in, 9, 14, 144, 157–58
　German naval forces in, 9, 14, 78, 144, 157–58
　Italian naval forces in, 146, 158
　US naval forces in, 162
Australia
　ABDACOM representation, 178–88, 191, 197–98
　NEI relations with, 168–76, 216, 217, 218, 221, 227, 243
　New Guinea defence policy, 410–12, 414–16
　SWPA representation, 306
Australia, defence, 10–18, 25–32, 42–43, 44–47, 49–51, 57–60, 65–71, 161, 162, 167, 180–81, 192, 196–97, 206, 209, 247–55, 256–76, 284–85, 296–97, 309, 316–17, 320–21, 328–30, 333, 397; *see also* ABDACOM; defence policy, Allied; SWPACOM
　ALP policy on, 328–29
　'Brisbane Line', 276
　British commitment to, 8–9, 152, 274–75, 283–84, 316–17; *see also* Singapore strategy
　Canadian co-operation on, 257
　'forward' strategy, 77–78, 140, 226; *see also* Singapore strategy
　Japanese invasion threat, 37, 89, 91, 144, 145, 147, 148, 151, 152, 161–62, 206, 209, 210, 213, 226, 229, 235, 252, 255, 256, 260, 261, 262, 263, 265, 269–71, 273–74, 275, 276, 279, 296, 297, 309, 313–14, 320, 321, 322, 323, 324, 329, 331–32, 385, 388, 402
　political attitudes to, 332–33
　public attitudes to, 38–41, 269–71, 328
　Singapore strategy, 37, 139, 140–67, 205, 208, 209, 256, 307
　US commitment to, 139, 178, 217, 229, 230, 231, 233, 234–35, 236, 238–39, 251–52, 261, 262, 268, 271, 274, 277–300, 312–13, 316, 328, 392–93, 397, 418, 420; *see also* ABDACOM; SWPA
Australia, HMAS, 6, 8–9, 10, 17, 24
Australian-British-Dutch-American Command (ABDACOM), 178–82, 185–98, 301; *see also* SWPA
　Anzac Area, 192, 193–94, 196, 210, 235, 254–55, 295, 296–97
　Australian forces under, 180–81, 195–98, 199
　Australian representation within, 178–88, 191, 197–98
　command structure, 185, 186–91, 197–98, 206n, 283, 284, 288, 295, 297, 299
　forces, 189, 194, 196–7
　headquarters, 178, 185–86, 187, 189, 198, 199, 241, 242, 244
　NEI representation within, 179, 180, 181–82, 186, 188–89, 191, 197, 198
　reorganisation of, 295, 299, 301
　US Pacific Fleet responsibility within, 187–88, 192
Australian Imperial Force (AIF), 56, 67, 145; *see also* AMF, CMF, conscription, RAN, RAAF
　AMF amalgamation with, 326–28, 329–30
　command structure, 44, 75, 76, 92, 94–95, 102, 133–35, 163, 170, 240, 260, 275, 306, 333–34, 366, 367–70, 371, 418–21
　disposition, 263–65, 271–72, 275–76
　'distant war' commitment, 25–43, 44, 390
　division and reconstitution as single force, 73, 75, 76–77, 79, 80, 81, 82–83, 84, 92, 102, 125–27, 129, 131, 149, 240

450 Subject Index

employment policy, 74, 75–77, 91–92, 390–93
political interference within, 335–36
prisoners-of-war, 210, 212, 213, 219, 220, 221, 222–23, 246, 380
Special Expeditionary Force, 25–43
training, 29, 34, 35, 38, 42, 43, 73, 74, 79, 80, 85, 89, 92, 97, 98, 109, 149, 150, 151, 165, 257, 263, 271, 312, 320, 324, 389, 395
weapons and equipment, 3, 25, 27–28, 31, 32, 34, 35, 38, 73, 74, 79, 80, 81, 82, 83, 84, 85, 86, 88, 89–90, 91, 92, 93, 98, 102, 104, 105, 109, 116, 120, 121, 126, 149, 151, 152, 154, 164, 208, 221, 239, 251, 257–58, 259, 263, 265, 271–72, 276, 312, 320, 324, 376, 389, 406, 407–9
Australian Imperial Force (AIF), 2nd
(6th Division)
formation, 25–32, 33–34, 368n
in Borneo, 420, 421
in Burma, 227, 231–32, 235–36
in Ceylon, 249, 251, 253, 254, 358, 360
in Crete, 3, 73, 86, 87, 101, 102–7, 108, 127, 284
in Egypt, 34, 35, 79, 87, 88, 89, 91, 415
in France, 40, 74, 79
in Greece, 3, 73, 86, 87–109, 127
in Java, 197, 224, 225, 226, 228, 229, 230, 231–32, 421
in Middle East, 3, 8–9, 13, 17, 34, 35, 41, 44, 73–86, 97, 98, 127, 129, 197, 415, 416
in Near East, 12, 73, 79, 82–83
in New Guinea, 255, 358, 359, 360, 381, 382, 401, 413, 416, 421, 422
in Philippines, 423
in Southwest Pacific, 197, 327
in Syria, 127, 129
in UK, 74, 76–77, 79
recall to and in Australia, 224, 226, 227–39, 253, 254, 255, 260, 263, 358, 360
(7th Division)
formation, 33, 41, 84
in Australia, 263, 395, 397, 398
in Borneo, 395, 397, 415, 417, 420, 421, 422, 423–27
in Burma, 212–13, 224, 227, 230–39, 240, 247, 248, 249, 250, 252
in Ceylon, 247–55
in Greece, 89–90, 97, 98, 101
in India, 146, 149, 150
in Java, 199, 224, 225, 226, 228, 229, 230, 231, 240–46, 395, 397, 421
in Malaya, 149–50
in Middle East, 84, 89, 97, 98, 102, 110–35, 146, 149, 150, 197, 284
in New Guinea, 327, 358, 359, 360, 361, 387, 388–89
in Philippines, 394, 395–96, 397, 415, 417, 420, 421, 422, 423–27
in Singapore, 146, 149
in Sumatra, 197, 225, 226, 228, 230, 240–41
in Syria, 110–22
at Tobruk, 123–35
recall to Australia, 224, 226, 227–39, 246, 247, 249, 254, 255
(8th Division)
in Australia, 263
in Java, 240–46
in Malaya/Singapore, 151, 152, 153–54, 156–57, 164–66, 198, 200, 202, 203, 204–5, 207, 208, 209–10, 211, 212, 214, 224, 244, 245
in Middle East, 151, 153–54, 284
(9th Division)
in Australia, 263, 395, 397, 398
in Borneo, 395, 397, 415, 417, 420, 421, 422
in Burma, 235–36
in Egypt, 323, 389
in Java, 395, 397, 421
in Middle East, 95n, 101, 102, 123–35, 229, 231, 253, 254, 284, 323–24
in New Guinea, 327, 330, 331, 387, 388–89
in Philippines, 394, 395–96, 397, 415, 417, 420, 421, 422, 423
recall to Australia, 229, 231, 233, 250, 253, 254, 255, 330
Australian Labor Party, 38–39, 276, 326, 328–29
Australian Military Forces (AMF), 25, 35, 38, 42, 165, 252, 272, 370, 391, 418; see also AIF, CMF, conscription
AIF amalgamation with, 326–28, 329–30
disposition, 263–65
in New Guinea, 357, 358, 359–60, 361, 362–63, 374, 375, 381, 386, 388, 401
in Special Expeditionary Force, 25, 27, 28, 29, 30, 32, 39–40

Balkan front, 87, 91, 101
'beat Germany first' strategy, see defence policy, Allied
Bismarck Sea, 205, 304, 414
battle, 330, 384–85
Borneo, 153, 155, 162, 194–95, 277, 417–27
Australian forces in, 394, 395, 397, 415, 417, 420, 421, 422, 423–27
counter-offensive, 394, 395, 415, 417, 421–27

Subject Index 451

Japanese forces in, 148, 194, 195, 296, 421
US forces in, 415, 417
Bougainville, 393, 401, 405–6, 408, 409, 410, 411, 412–13, 414, 415, 416, 422; *see also* Solomon Islands
Burma, 187, 188, 201, 229
   Australian forces in, 72, 212–13, 224, 227, 230–39, 240, 247, 248, 249, 250, 252
   counter-offensive, 401
   defence, 26, 31, 189, 194, 205, 212–13, 230–39, 247, 248, 249, 250, 252, 288, 296
   Indian forces in, 201
   Japanese forces in, 227, 235, 236, 239, 296

Canada, 49
   Australian defence co-operation with, 257
   EATS in, 16, 47–48, 53, 57–58, 59, 61, 68, 72, 284
   Pacific defence policy, 390
Canberra, HMAS, 8–9, 24, 324–25
Cape of Good Hope, 76, 78, 248, 274
Caroline Islands, 162, 278
Celebes, 194, 195, 296
Ceylon, 159
   Allied defence policy, 247–48, 250, 252–53
   Australian forces in, 247–55, 358, 360
   defence, 247–55, 311
   Indian forces in, 201
   Japanese air raids on, 310, 311
   Japanese threat to, 247, 248, 250, 309
China, 17, 302
   Pacific War Council representation, 183, 233
   war with Japan, 35, 37, 42, 144, 147, 156, 189, 211, 214, 231, 232, 234–35, 250, 259
Christmas Island, 286, 287
Citizen Military Forces (CMF), 326–27, 328–30; *see also* AIF, AMF
Cocos Islands, 9, 248
Combined Chiefs of Staff (CCS), creation, 179
conscription, proposed extension of, 312, 326–27, 328–30
Coral Sea, battle of, 276, 312, 318–22, 331, 357
Crete
   Australian forces in, 3, 73, 86, 87, 101, 102–7, 108, 116, 117, 127, 130, 202, 284
   casualties, 107
   defence, 87, 102–7, 108, 111, 112, 115, 116, 117

   evacuation of, 24, 101, 102, 104, 105–7, 111
   German forces in, 124
   NZ forces in, 104n, 105
   Polish forces in, 112
   strategic importance of, 108, 111, 115, 116
Cyprus, 118
Cyrenaica, 111, 115, 116, 118, 123

Darwin, 171, 225, 282, 297, 354, 358
   defence, 165, 187, 193–94, 196–97, 252–53, 257, 261, 265–69, 285, 289, 290, 397
   Japanese air raids on (1942), 56, 213, 265–69, 276, 296, 309, 323
   naval base, 18, 217, 257, 397
   NEI airforce at, 172
   RAAF in, 56, 165, 171, 196–97, 257, 266, 267, 268–69, 282, 354, 397
   US forces in, 217, 267, 268, 277, 278, 282, 289
defence policy, Allied
   air, 44–47, 49–51, 57–71, 339–41; *see also* Empire Air Training Scheme
   Australia, 10–18, 25–26, 30–32, 65–67, 161, 162, 274–75, 296–97, 316–17
   'beat Germany first' strategy, 143, 311, 312, 313, 314–15, 316, 317–18, 330
   Ceylon, 247–48, 250, 252–53
   Far East, 18, 65–67, 140–67, 168–77, 182–83, 185–91, 211–12, 247–55, 307–11
   Japan and 'neutralisation' strategy, 394–95, 409, 414
   Mediterranean, 87–91
   Middle East, 87–91, 110
   naval, 4–5, 10–18, 146, 147, 286, 307–11
   Netherlands East Indies, 168–77
   Pacific Ocean, 30–32, 192–94, 285–97, 301–11, 312–15, 322, 390, 392–93
   Singapore strategy, 37, 139, 140–67, 205, 208, 209, 256, 307

Egypt
   Australian forces in, 34, 35, 79, 87, 88, 89, 91, 102, 107, 158, 323, 415
   defence, 78, 81–82, 84, 85–86, 92, 102, 109, 111, 112, 114, 115, 116, 117, 118, 124, 158
   Italian forces in, 78, 81, 82, 84, 85–86, 87, 88
   strategic importance of, 78, 84
Empire Air Training Scheme (EATS), 15–16, 42, 47–48, 50–72, 233–34, 339; *see also* RAAF
   administration, 61–65, 68

452 Subject Index

agreements, 60–63, 67–68, 70–71
aircraft and equipment, 44–45, 46, 48, 58–59, 67, 71, 258
Canadian personnel in, 47, 59, 61
costs, 58, 60, 62, 68
NZ personnel in, 47–48, 58, 61
quotas, 57–58, 60, 67, 68
service in UK, 60, 62, 70, 284
trainees for 'home' defence, 62, 65–71
training in Australia, 47, 48, 50, 57, 58, 59, 60, 61, 67–68, 69, 71, 72, 258
training in Canada, 16, 47–48, 53, 57–58, 59, 68, 72, 284
training in Rhodesia, 60, 67, 72

Far East
Allied defence policy, 18, 65–67, 140–67, 168–77, 182–83, 185–91, 211–12, 247–55, 307–11
Allied supreme command in, 299, 301–6, 312–38, 387, 418
RAAF in, 62, 66, 69, 72, 163
US defence policy, 168, 169, 174
Far Eastern Council, 182–84
Fiji, 192, 278, 280, 287, 296, 297, 302
'forward' defence strategy, see Australia, defence
France, see also New Caledonia
attitude to Allied invasion of Syria, 111–12, 113
Australian forces in, 40, 74, 79
implications of defeat on British naval strategy, 146, 147
Vichy, 110; see also Syria

✕ Germany
invasion of Greece, 100–1, 108
invasion of Netherlands, 10, 37, 168
invasion of Russia, 114
invasion of Yugoslavia, 100, 101
naval policy, 14–15
Gibraltar, 158, 159, 162
Greece
Allied defence commitment to, 87–91, 95–97
Australian forces in, 3, 73, 86, 87–109, 116, 117, 123, 124, 127, 130, 158, 202, 225, 236, 238, 284
defence, 87–109
evacuation of, 90, 91, 92, 93–94, 101, 102, 107, 109
German forces in, 87, 88, 89, 90, 97, 98, 100–1, 102–3, 108, 113
Italian invasion of, 87, 108
'Lustreforce' offensive, failure, 103, 107–9
NZ forces in, 90, 97, 98, 123
Polish forces in, 89

Turkish attitude to Allied failure to defend, 87, 88, 91, 97
Yugoslav attitude to Allied failure to defend, 87, 91, 97
Guadalcanal, 276, 312, 323, 324, 325, 330

Hawaii, 162, 235, 277, 279, 285
Hong Kong, 154–55, 261

India, 33, 78, 82, 187, 198, 199, 229, 231, 248, 284, 291; see also Ceylon
Australian forces in, 72, 146, 149, 150, 236
defence, 5, 26, 31, 34–35, 189, 247, 250, 253, 288, 311
Japanese threat to, 275, 309, 318, 319
US forces in, 286
Indian Ocean
Anglo-American command in, 301, 302, 304
Australian naval forces in, 15, 16, 17, 23–24, 160, 248, 310, 311
British naval forces in, 14, 16, 159, 169, 247, 249, 250, 308, 309–11, 312
defence, 13–18, 29, 247–48, 250, 252, 284
German naval forces in, 14, 15, 18, 23–24, 78
Italian naval forces in, 78
Japanese naval forces in, 15, 250, 309–11
NZ naval forces in, 16
Indo-China, 147, 150, 231, 275, 287
Iran, 84, 114, 131
Iraq, 84, 111, 112, 114, 115, 116, 117, 128, 131, 164
Italy, 314
implications of entry into war, 10, 11–12, 13, 14, 17, 60, 74, 76, 77–78, 79, 87
invasion of Greece, 87, 108

Japan
Allied 'neutralisation' strategy against, 394–95, 409, 414
as hostile power, 17, 18, 20, 30–32, 33, 35, 36, 37, 42, 152, 157–59
mandated territories, 162, 217, 259, 307, 322; see also Caroline Islands; Marshall Islands
as neutral power, 6, 7, 15, 21, 26, 30–31, 42
Pacific policy, 30–32, 37, 42, 195, 259
US relations with, 37, 42, 144, 277
war with China, 35, 37, 42, 144, 147, 156, 189, 211, 214, 231, 232, 234–35, 250, 259
Java, 326
ABDACOM headquarters in, 187, 198, 199

Subject Index 453

Australian forces in, 197, 198, 199, 212, 224, 225, 226, 227, 228, 229, 230, 231–32, 240–46, 395, 417, 421
  command of Australian forces in, 417
  counter-offensive, 398, 417, 421
  defence, 189, 194, 195, 197, 199, 210, 211–12, 224, 225, 226, 227–29, 238, 240–46, 255, 288
  Japanese forces in, 199, 212, 225, 226, 242, 244, 245, 246, 275, 296

Lebanon, 110, 111
Libya, 201, 301; *see also* Tobruk
  Australian forces in, 3, 73, 86, 101–2, 126, 127
  defence, 96, 101–2, 109, 114, 123–35
  German forces in, 81, 86, 88, 95, 96, 101, 102, 114, 115, 117, 118, 124, 158
  Italian forces in, 78, 81, 84, 85–86, 87, 88

Malaya, 57, 187, 188; *see also* Singapore
  Allied command in, 206, 207–8, 212, 213, 214
  Australian forces in, 60, 140, 141, 146, 149–50, 151, 154, 156–57, 163, 164–66, 196, 200, 202, 203, 204–5, 207, 208, 214, 233, 236, 249, 258, 263, 284, 401, 403
  casualties in defence of, 203n, 210, 213
  counter-offensive, 401, 421
  defence, 140–67, 168–69, 189, 194, 195, 200–15, 233, 235, 240, 249, 257, 288, 296, 304, 309, 311
  defence campaign failure, 213–15
  evacuation of, 205
  Indian forces in, 150, 151, 152, 153, 155, 164, 201, 203, 204, 205, 214–15, 240
  Japanese forces in, 146, 147, 155, 169, 195, 200, 202, 203, 204, 205, 206, 207, 210, 211, 213–14, 259, 283–84, 307, 309
Malta, 316
Manila, 163, 186, 194, 277, 279, 281
Marshall Islands, 21, 162, 278, 287
Mediterranean Ocean
  Allied defence policy, 87–91
  Anglo-American command over, 301
  Australian naval forces in, 4–5, 7, 8, 11, 17, 22–23, 24, 172
  British naval forces in, 4, 12, 13, 14, 17, 42, 81–82, 84, 88, 91, 113, 114, 115, 116, 124, 130, 143, 144–45, 146, 147, 152, 156, 158, 159, 172
  French naval forces in, 144, 146
  German naval forces in, 81–82, 144, 147, 159

Italian naval forces in, 11–12, 14, 24, 78, 144–45, 146, 147
strategic importance of, 78, 79, 81–82, 83–84, 111
Middle East
  Allied defence policy, 87–91
  Anglo-American command in, 301, 302
  Australian forces in, 3, 8–9, 13, 15, 16, 17, 25, 34, 35, 41, 44, 46, 47, 60, 62, 70, 72, 73–86, 87, 88, 89, 91, 95n, 97, 98, 99, 100, 101–2, 107, 108, 110–35, 146, 149, 150, 151, 153–54, 158, 164, 165, 172, 187, 197, 198, 200, 201, 203, 224, 225, 227–28, 229, 231, 236, 240, 247–48, 250, 253, 254, 260, 263, 284, 317, 323–24, 368, 369, 386, 415, 416, 420
  British forces in, 152, 200, 201, 316, 348
  Canadian forces in, 123, 124
  command of Australian forces in, 92, 94–95, 102, 133–35
  defence, 34–35, 77–78, 87–89, 92, 110–35, 148, 257, 293, 318
  French forces in, 3, 111, 112, 113, 118–22
  German forces in, 81–82, 86, 101, 102, 112, 113–15, 116–17, 118, 119, 131
  Indian forces in, 118, 119, 121–22, 128–29
  Italian forces in, 78, 81–82, 84, 85–86
  NZ forces in, 9, 94–95, 117, 128
  Polish forces in, 112, 129
  reinforcements for Australian forces in, 83, 84, 112, 116–17, 118, 124, 128–29, 130–33
  South African forces in, 128
  Turkish forces in, 113
Midway Islands, 277
  battle of, 276, 312, 322, 323, 332
Milne Bay, 358, 359, 360, 381
  battle of, 276, 312, 365–66, 389

Nauru, 296, 391, 415
  German naval attack on, 18–22
Netherlands East Indies (NEI), 17, 18, 57, 195, 303, 401; *see also* Ambon, Java, Sumatra, Timor, Dutch
  ABDACOM representation, 179, 180, 181–82, 186, 189, 197, 198
  Allied defence policy, 168–77
  Australian forces in, 163, 165, 170–71, 172–76, 177, 196, 197–98, 199, 205, 212, 217, 224–35, 239, 240–46, 257, 258, 265, 284, 401, 403
  Australian relations with, 168–76, 216, 217, 218, 221, 227, 243
  defence, 148–49, 161, 162, 163, 168–76,

454 Subject Index

177, 189, 205, 210, 227, 247, 255, 257, 279, 284, 288, 289, 290–91
Dutch government restoration in, 399–400
Far East Council representation, 182, 183
Japanese forces in, 37, 142–43, 169, 175–76, 194, 195, 198, 199, 210, 212, 225, 226, 228, 235, 240, 242, 244, 245, 246, 249, 259, 279
Pacific War Council representation, 183
UK relations with, 168–76, 181–83, 400
US forces in, 278
New Britain, 265, 296, 297, 322, 384, 387, 393, 396, 401, 403, 404–12, 413, 414, 415, 416; *see also* Rabaul
New Caledonia, 168
Australian forces in, 233, 259, 265
defence, 253, 259, 284–85, 287, 289–90, 292, 297, 302
Free French forces in, 285, 290
Japanese threat to, 161, 252, 284–85, 287, 289, 290, 296
US forces in, 284, 289–90, 292, 295
New Guinea, 57, 278, 296; *see also* Milne Bay, Papua, Port Moresby
Aitape/Wewak campaign, 393, 396, 401, 404–5, 407, 408, 410, 412, 413, 414, 415, 416, 422
Australian defence policy, 410–12, 414–15
Australian forces in, 69, 255, 265, 312, 324, 326, 330, 331, 340, 354, 357–63, 364, 366–67, 370–71, 372, 374, 375, 376, 378–79, 381, 382, 383, 385, 386, 387, 388–89, 393–94, 396, 401–16, 418–19, 421–22, 423
casualties, 416
command of Australian forces in, 366, 367–70, 371, 418–21
command of US forces in, 373–74, 375
defence, 204, 205, 206, 304, 337, 357–89, 391
Dutch forces in, 396
Huon Peninsula ('Cartwheel') campaign, 386–89, 390, 393
Japanese forces in, 69, 204, 205, 206, 210, 252, 255, 296, 297, 318, 321, 323, 324, 330, 331, 357, 359, 360, 361, 362–63, 364, 365, 366, 367, 370–71, 372, 374, 375, 376, 377, 378–79, 380, 381, 382, 383, 384, 385, 386, 388, 389, 391, 402–6, 409–11, 413–14, 416, 421–22
Lae/Salamaua campaign, 385–86, 420
public criticism of 'mopping-up' campaigns, 401–16

US forces in, 292, 312, 358, 359, 367, 372, 373–75, 376, 377, 385–86, 387, 393, 395, 396, 404–7, 410–11, 414
Wau campaign, 381–82, 383, 384
New Ireland, 265, 296, 322, 396, 412
New South Wales, defence, 256, 257, 259, 261, 264, 285, 397
New Zealand, 20, 299, 307–8, 419
Anglo-American command representation, 302, 303
defence, 5, 6, 16, 17, 26, 29, 30–31, 32, 35, 37, 144, 145, 151, 192, 254, 296–97, 302
'distant war' commitment, 35, 41, 80, 390
EATS representation, 47–48, 58, 61
Far Eastern Council representation, 182, 183
Japanese threat to, 37, 144, 145, 147, 148, 151, 285, 296
Pacific defence policy, 296–97
Pacific War Council representation, 183, 232
Northern Territory, defence, 196–97, 274, 397; *see also* Darwin
North Sea
British naval forces in, 13, 17, 144, 145
German naval forces in, 144, 145

Ocean Island, 415
oil resources
in Middle East, 114, 250
in Roumania, 84, 87

Pacific Ocean
Allied defence policy, 30–32, 192–94, 285–97, 301–11, 312–15, 322, 390, 392–93
Allied supreme command in, 299, 301–6, 312–38, 387, 418
Australian naval forces in, 15, 16, 21, 163, 187, 252, 253, 318, 324, 325, 334, 400
British naval forces in, 5, 14, 16, 42, 143, 162, 216, 307–11, 334, 397, 400
German naval forces in, 14, 15, 16, 18–22, 78
Italian naval forces in, 78
Japanese naval forces in, 159, 162, 219, 224–25, 276, 303, 305, 307, 308–11, 318–22, 325, 357, 384
Japanese policy, 30–32, 37, 42, 195, 259
New Zealand naval forces in, 16, 252, 253
US naval forces in, 159, 162, 187–88, 192, 213, 216, 259, 303, 305, 307–11, 318–22, 325, 332, 384, 400, 414

Pacific War Council, 183–84, 199, 212, 232, 233, 238, 274n, 306

Subject Index 455

Palestine
  Australian forces in, 73, 77, 79, 80, 89, 112, 126, 203
  defence, 78, 84, 111, 112, 116, 117
  German forces in, 115
  strategic importance of, 78, 84
Papua, *see also* Milne Bay, New Guinea, Port Moresby
  Buna campaign, 372, 373–75, 376, 377
  defence, 357–80, 381, 391
  Gona/Sanananda campaign, 372, 373, 374–75, 376, 377–79
  Kokoda Trail campaign, 255, 358, 359–65, 370–71, 372, 373, 375, 389, 415
  Owen Stanley Ranges campaign, 366–67, 372
Pearl Harbor, 173, 265, 277, 278, 286, 287
Perth, HMAS, 4, 6, 12, 24, 246
Philippines, 187, 188, 189, 326, 421–22
  Australian forces in, 393, 394, 395–96, 397, 399, 415, 420, 423–27
  counter-offensive, 298, 303, 312, 393–94, 395, 396, 397, 399, 400, 410, 414, 415, 420, 421–22
  defence, 162, 185, 189, 194, 277–83, 284, 288, 304
  Japanese forces in, 37, 162, 279, 399, 421–22
  US defence policy, 37, 277–78
  US forces in, 185, 194, 206n, 277–83, 295, 312, 331, 399, 400, 410, 414, 415, 419, 422
Port Moresby, 18, 20, 277, 278, 367, 373, 376; *see also* New Guinea, Papua
  Australian forces in, 265, 357, 358, 359, 361–65, 375, 381, 388
  defence, 205, 206, 253, 285, 292, 357–59, 361–65, 366, 375, 381
  Japanese forces in, 205, 252, 296, 318, 321, 323, 357, 358, 361, 362–63, 365, 366
  US forces in, 292, 358, 359
Prime Minister's War Conference, Melbourne (1942), 275–76

Queensland, defence, 259, 260, 261–62, 263, 276, 397

Rabaul, 57; *see also* New Britain
  Australian forces in, 165, 212, 216, 219–20, 222–23, 412, 422
  counter-attack, 386, 387, 412, 422
  defence, 216–17, 219–22
  Japanese forces in, 204, 205, 206, 212, 217, 219, 220, 222–23, 235, 249, 259, 296, 319, 383, 386, 387, 412, 422
Red Sea, 76

Australian naval forces in, 4, 17, 172
British naval forces in, 4, 12, 14, 17, 172
Italian naval forces in, 11–12, 14, 78, 80
strategic importance of, 77–78
Rhodesia, EATS in, 60, 67, 72
Royal Australian Air Force (RAAF); *see also* WAAAF
  administration and operational control, 339, 340, 341–46, 349, 350, 351, 352, 353–54, 355, 356
  aircraft and equipment, 44–45, 46, 48, 49, 58, 59, 154, 156, 171, 196, 197, 200, 201, 205–6, 258, 259, 272, 278, 284, 292, 293, 324, 339
  Air Expeditionary Force, 25, 44–51, 52
  casualties, 72
  Coastal Command, Allied Air Forces, 339–41
  command structure, 3, 51–57, 139, 162, 334n, 339–56, 419, 420
  disposition, 272–73
  'distant war' commitment, 44–72, 390–93
  in Borneo, 426–27
  in Darwin, 56, 165, 171, 196–97, 257, 266, 267, 268–69, 282, 354, 397
  in Europe, 45, 72, 356
  in Far East, 62, 66, 69, 72, 163, 169
  in Greece, 89
  in Malaya, 60, 140, 146, 154, 155, 233, 258, 284
  in Middle East, 46, 47, 60, 62, 70, 72, 112, 284
  in NEI, 57, 170, 171, 172–73, 174–75, 177, 257, 258, 284
  in New Guinea, 69, 340, 354, 363, 366, 371, 376, 377–78, 379, 383, 388, 389, 396, 403–6, 408, 419
  in Pacific, 66, 67, 68, 72, 196–97, 339–56, 400
  in Portuguese Timor, 69, 163, 171, 177
  in UK, 60, 62, 70, 284, 317
  overseas headquarters in UK, 63, 64–65, 69, 70
  10 Squadron in Coastal Command, RAF, 45n, 47, 49–50, 51
  training, 272, 273, 324, 339, 352, 354; *see also* EATS
  US attitude to higher organisation of, 346, 347, 349, 353–54, 355–56
Royal Australian Navy (RAN)
  anti-submarine vessels, 6, 7, 8, 11, 12, 13, 16, 17
  battleships, 155
  command structure, 3, 4, 22–23, 44, 162, 334–35, 419, 420
  cruisers, 4–5, 6, 7, 8, 9, 10, 12, 13, 16, 17, 21, 22, 23–24, 155–56, 163, 172, 246, 324, 325

destroyers, 4, 6, 7, 8, 11, 16, 17, 22, 24,
    145, 172, 310
'distant war' commitment, 4-24, 390-93
escort vessels, 4, 7, 8-9, 12, 13, 15, 16,
    17, 21, 163
losses, 4, 23-24, 246, 324-25
merchant vessels, 6, 15
Royal Navy personnel in, 6, 10, 11
sloops, 4, 12, 16, 17, 24, 172

Samoa, 287, 391
Savo Island, battle of; see Canberra, HMAS
Singapore, 78, 187, 301; see also Malaya
    ABDACOM headquarters at, 178, 186
    Australian forces in, 141, 146, 149, 151,
        156-57, 163, 198, 200, 201, 207, 208,
        209-10, 211, 212, 213, 224, 225, 244,
        245, 284, 401, 423
    counter-offensive, 401, 423
    defence, 8, 26, 29, 30-31, 37, 44, 45, 46,
        91-92, 140-67, 168-69, 194, 195,
        200-15, 225, 235, 247, 257, 284, 309
    evacuation of, 204, 205
    fall of, 140, 162, 198, 200, 207, 209,
        210-12, 213, 227, 236, 249, 284, 294,
        296, 307, 309
    Japanese forces in, 155, 195, 208, 210,
        212, 214, 225, 227, 247, 307, 309
    US forces in, 278
Singapore Defence Conference
    (October 1940), 18, 150, 151, 152, 166,
        233
    (April 1941), 160, 161-64, 166
Singapore strategy, see defence policy,
    Allied
Solomon Islands, 57, 302; see also
    Bismarck Archipelago, Bougainville,
    Guadalcanal
    Australian forces in, 233, 265, 324-25,
        393, 396, 404-16, 422
    Japanese forces in, 304, 323, 325, 330,
        411
    US forces in, 323, 325, 332, 396, 410-11
South Australia, defence, 261, 264
Southwest Pacific Area (SWPA), 299,
    301-6, 312-38
    Australia as base for counter-attack in,
        180, 186, 227-30, 238, 248, 249, 252,
        284, 292, 296, 298, 299-300, 304,
        313, 332
    Australian-American security alliance in,
        312-38
    Australian representation within, 297,
        306
    command structure, 301, 302, 303-6,
        313, 333-34, 387, 418
    definition of, 301-3, 305, 312

dissolution, 400
'global' strategy and defence of, 314-18,
    398
RAAF in, 67, 72, 339-56, 400
role of Australian forces in, 326-30,
    390-400, 401-16, 422-26
Suez Canal, 17, 25, 77-78, 87, 92, 98, 102,
    117, 118, 145, 156, 249, 253, 254
Sumatra
    Australian forces in, 197, 198, 212, 224,
        225, 226, 227, 228, 230, 239, 240-41
    defence, 189, 194, 195, 197, 210,
        211-12, 224, 225, 226, 227-29, 239,
        288
    Japanese forces in, 225, 226, 240, 296
Sydney, HMAS, 7, 13, 17, 23-24
Syria
    Allied invasion of, 109, 110-22, 126, 129,
        131
    Australian forces in, 3, 73, 82, 109,
        110-22, 126, 127, 129, 253
    Free French forces in, 111, 112, 113,
        118-19, 121, 122
    French attitude to Allied invasion of,
        111-12, 113
    German forces in, 113-15, 116-17, 118,
        119, 131
    Indian forces in, 118, 119, 121-22
    Turkish forces in, 113
    Vichy French forces in, 3, 82, 119, 120,
        121-22
    US attitude to Allied occupation of, 117

Tasmania, defence, 259, 260, 261, 262, 265
Thailand, Japanese forces in, 147, 155, 231,
    279
Thursday Island, 18
Timor, Dutch
    Australian forces in, 69, 163, 165, 170,
        171, 172-73, 174, 175, 177, 196, 197,
        212, 213, 216, 217, 219, 233, 265
    defence, 170-73, 176-77, 193, 194, 197,
        210, 219-22, 228-29, 235
    Japanese forces in, 69, 177, 195, 212,
        218, 219-22, 296, 297
Timor, Portuguese
    Australian forces in, 177, 193, 217-18
    defence, 177, 193, 217-18
    Dutch forces in, 193, 217-18
    US forces in, 278
Tobruk, 3, 86, 73, 101, 102; see also Libya
    Australian forces at, 123-35
    'Battleaxe' offensive, 123, 124n
    casualties, 125, 133
    'Crusader' offensive, 129, 131, 133

government reaction to and political
  implications of siege, 129, 131–33
public reaction to siege, 124, 128, 130
relief of, 7, 123, 125–34
Turkey
  attitude to Allied failure to defend Greece,
    87, 88, 91, 97
  attitude to Allied invasion of Syria, 110,
    111, 113, 114
  Axis control of, 114–15, 117

Union of Soviet Socialist Republics (USSR),
    34–35, 42, 283, 293, 301, 309, 318
  German invasion of, 114
  US relations with, 293
United Kingdom
  Australian forces in, 60, 70, 74, 76–77,
    79, 82–83, 84, 284, 317
  defence against invasion, 13, 79, 80, 81,
    83–84, 159, 320
  NEI relations with, 168–76, 181–83, 400
  RAAF headquarters in, 63, 64–65, 69, 70
  US relations with, 88, 96, 117, 168–69
United Nations, 296, 299, 316, 327, 425
United Nations Assembly, 296, 403

United States of America (US)
  attitude to Allied invasion of Syria, 117
  attitude to RAAF high command, 346,
    347, 349, 353–54, 355–56
  Australian appeal for aid from, 283–84,
    291–94
  Far East defence policy, 168, 169, 174
  Japanese relations with, 37, 42, 144, 277
  neutrality policy, 145, 157–59, 161, 168,
    278
  Philippines defence policy, 37, 277–78
  Russian relations with, 293
  UK relations with, 88, 96, 117, 168–69

Victoria, defence, 261, 262, 264

Western Australia, defence, 259, 260, 261,
    265, 276, 302, 397
Women's Australian Auxiliary Air Force
  (WAAAF), 56; *see also* RAAF

Yugoslavia, 87
  attitude to Allied failure to defend
    Greece, 91, 97
  German invasion of, 100, 101

NAME INDEX

Alanbrooke, Viscount; *see* Brooke, Alan Francis
Alexander, Harold Rupert Leofric George, Earl Alexander of Tunis, 434
Allen, Arthur Samuel, 360, 434
Anderson, William Hopton, 433
Arnold, Henry Harley, 277, 278, 294, 434
Attlee, Clement Richard, Earl, 182n, 434
  documents by, 134, 310–11
  documents to, 234–36, 237, 238, 239, 254, 255, 308, 310
Auchinleck, Sir Claude John Eyre, 125, 127–29, 130, 131, 132, 133–34, 135, 434
  document by, 128–29
  documents to, 125–26, 132
Austin, H. McP., 243

Balfour, Harold Harington, Lord Balfour of Inchrye,
  document by, 47–48
Barnes, Julian F., 281
Bean, Charles Edwin Woodrow, 365
Beasley, John Albert, 21, 22, 431, 434
  document by, 411–12
Bennett, Henry Gordon, 203, 204–5, 209, 434
  document by, 204
  on failure of Malayan campaign, 213, 214–15
Beresford-Peirse, Sir Noel, 103
Berryman, Sir Frank Horton, 415, 417–19, 434
  document by, 417
Blackburn, Arthur Seaforth, 243, 245, 246, 435
  document by, 243–44
  report on AIF in Java, 243–44
Blamey, Sir Thomas Albert, 435
  appointment as Deputy C-in-C (ME), 102
  appreciation of mandate campaigns, 409–12
  as Allied Land Forces Commander, SWPA and C-in-C, AMF, 134–35, 197–98, 221, 225, 275–76, 317, 318–19, 327–28, 333, 334, 335, 347, 356, 357–58, 367–78, 381–86, 388–89, 393–94, 395, 399, 404–8, 409–12, 415, 417–24, 425
  as GOC, AIF (ME), 75, 76, 80, 81–82, 84, 85, 89, 92, 94–95, 97, 98, 99–100, 101, 102, 103, 107–9, 112, 116, 123–26, 127, 128, 129, 130–31, 133–35
  documents by, 81–82, 94–95, 97, 99–100, 107–9, 125–26, 318, 336, 368–69, 370, 372–73, 374–75, 376, 381–82, 384, 386, 388–89, 404–7, 409–11, 418–19, 421–24
  documents to, 124–25, 197–98, 318–19, 373, 374, 375, 376–78, 385–86, 393–94, 411–12, 417
  in New Guinea, 367–78, 381–86, 388–89, 404–8, 409–12, 418–19
  MacArthur's opinion of, 333
  on Borneo campaign, 421–24, 425
  on control of Australian forces, 417–21
  on Greek campaign, 94–95, 97, 99–100, 103, 107–9
  on political interference in army affairs, 335, 336
  on RAAF high command organisation, 347, 356
  on relief of Tobruk, 125–26, 127, 128, 129, 130–31, 133–34
  relations with General Auchinleck, 133–35
  relations with General Rowell, 367–70
Bond, Sir Lionel Vivian, 153
Bostock, William Dowling, 56, 196, 339–56, 426–27, 435
  documents by, 344–45, 350, 352, 426–27
  document to, 343
Boucher, Maitland W. S., 7, 435
  document by, 4–5
  document to, 6–7
Bowden, Vivian Gordon, 200, 206, 435
  documents by, 200, 206–8
  views on Singapore situation and General Percival's command, 206–8
Brereton, Lewis Hyde, 206, 278, 435
Brett, George Howard, 187, 193, 197, 283, 288, 290, 339, 357, 435
  document by, 288
Bridgeford, Sir William, 415
Brooke, Alan Francis, Viscount Alanbrooke, 435
  document to, 231

Name Index

Brooke-Popham, Sir (Henry) Robert (Moore), 153, 154–55, 156, 163, 164, 279, 435
Bruce, Stanley Melbourne, Viscount Bruce of Melbourne, 47–48, 49, 50–51, 55, 60, 73, 79, 80, 84, 92, 114, 116, 117, 123, 140, 141–42, 166, 206, 232, 237, 247, 355, 435
  documents by, 50, 74, 82–83, 84, 111–12, 114–15, 142–43, 166, 232, 237, 335
  documents to, 52, 63–65, 73, 85, 116–17
Burnett, Sir Charles Stuart, 77n, 170, 174–75, 192, 193, 256, 433, 435
  appointment as CAS RAAF, 52–53, 57, 334, 339, 347, 433n
  appreciation of, 55–57
Burston, Sir Samuel Roy, 368

Caldecote, Viscount, *see* Inskip, Thomas Walker Hobart
Cameron, Archie Galbraith, 335, 336, 432, 435
  document to, 10–11
Campbell, Ian Ross, 105
Carpender, Arthur Schuyler, 334
Carvalho, M. de A. Ferreira de
  document by, 217
  document to, 218
Casey, Richard Gardiner, Baron, 33, 35, 52, 117, 142, 181, 192, 277, 286, 292, 293, 299, 317, 432, 436
  documents by, 36–37, 181–82, 185–86, 236, 277–78, 280, 281–83, 285–86, 290–91, 292–94
  documents to, 34–35, 178–80, 194–95, 216–17, 233–34, 241, 283–84, 286–88, 289–90, 291–92, 294–95
Catroux, Georges, 111, 112, 113, 436
Cecil, Robert Arthur James Gascoyne-, Marquis of Salisbury, 134, 436
  documents by, 101, 152–53, 174, 175–76, 182–83, 201–2, 218, 279
  documents to, 102, 118, 126–27, 130–31, 152, 166–67, 173, 178, 183, 230, 231
Chamberlain, Arthur Neville, 143n
Chamberlin, Stephen J., 417, 419
Chatfield, Alfred Ernle Montacute, Baron, 140–41, 143, 436
Chifley, Joseph Benedict, 424, 431, 436
  documents by, 424–25, 426
  documents to, 404–7, 425–26
Churchill, Sir Winston Leonard Spencer, 84, 102, 146, 242, 332, 348, 353, 379, 390, 436
  and ABDA Command in SWPA, 178, 179, 180–81, 182, 183, 186–88, 191, 192, 193, 283, 286, 289, 301
  and AIF for defence of Burma, 224, 227, 229, 230, 231, 232, 233, 234–39, 247
  and AIF for defence of Ceylon, 247, 252, 254, 255
  and AIF for defence of Greece, 89, 90, 91, 100, 101
  and defence of Australia, 142, 144–45, 148, 152, 230, 234, 274–75
  and defence of Malaya/Singapore, 142, 144–45, 146, 152, 156, 166, 202, 203, 204, 205, 209, 227
  and Far East policy, 142–43, 169, 307–8, 310, 313, 314, 315, 316, 317
  and occupation of Syria, 114, 115, 116–18, 126
  and relief of Tobruk, 124n, 125, 126–29, 130–33
  and replacement of General Blamey, 134–35
  documents by, 81, 127–28, 131–33, 135, 144–45, 152, 186–88, 203, 234–35, 237, 239, 274–75
  documents to, 100, 116–17, 118, 126–27, 128–29, 130–31, 134, 178, 180–81, 188, 202, 204–6, 209, 227, 230, 231, 235–36, 238, 254, 283, 289, 308, 310
Clowes, Cyril Albert, 360, 365, 436
Coates, Joseph Gordon, 296
Collett, Herbert Brayley, 51
Collins, Sir John Augustine, 436
Colvin, Sir Ragnar Musgrave, 8–9, 10, 21, 55, 77, 150, 155–56, 160, 161–62, 164, 433, 436
  appreciation of on retirement as CNS, 22–23
  documents by, 8–9, 11–12, 13–18, 19–20
Cooper, Alfred Duff, 183, 436
Cranborne, Viscount; *see* Cecil, Robert Arthur James Gascoyne-
Creagh, Michael, 101
Cross, Sir Ronald Hibbert, 437
  document to, 127
Crutchley, Sir Victor Alexander Charles, 325, 437
Cunningham, Andrew Browne, Viscount Cunningham of Hyndhope, 129, 437
Curtin, John, 12, 38, 39, 130, 133, 134, 135, 153, 325, 330, 385, 387, 404n, 426, 431, 437
  advocates Australian representation in higher war councils, 178, 180–81, 182–83, 184
  advocates extension of conscription, 312, 326, 327, 328–29

and Allied command in SWPA, 185–88,
197–98, 283–84, 289, 297, 299–300,
301–6, 312–13, 315, 319–22, 331–32,
339–40, 366–67, 390–95, 397–400,
418, 419–22, 424
and Australian attitude to UK naval policy
in Far East, 307–8, 310–11
and control of Australian forces, 419–21
and defence of Australia, 166–67,
180–81, 205–6, 210, 249, 251, 260,
269–71, 274–75, 276, 279, 283–84,
289, 290, 320, 321, 322–23, 324,
331–32, 385
and defence of Burma, 224, 227, 229–30,
231–39, 240, 249
and defence of Ceylon, 247–52, 254–55
and defence of Java, 224, 227, 240–43
and defence of Malaya/Singapore, 201–3,
204–6, 208–11, 212–13, 249, 283–84
and defence of New Guinea (Papua and
mandate), 366–67, 379–80, 383, 387,
393, 407–9
and Far East policy, 166–67, 178
and future role of Australian forces,
390–93, 394–95, 397, 398–400, 420,
424
and RAAF high command organisation,
339–41, 342, 346, 347, 348–49,
353–54, 355, 356
and return of AIF to Australia, 224, 227,
229–30, 231–39, 240–42, 247–52,
254–55
and UK/US 'grand strategy', 314, 315,
317
documents by, 166–67, 173, 178,
180–81, 183, 188, 197–98, 202,
204–6, 209, 210, 230, 231, 233–34,
235–36, 238, 240, 241, 249, 254–55,
283–84, 289, 299–300, 302, 308, 310,
315, 320–21, 323, 328–29, 330,
331–32, 348–49, 353–54, 379–80,
391, 398–99, 407–8, 420
documents to, 68–70, 166, 174, 175–76,
182–83, 185–88, 199, 201–2, 203,
208, 209–10, 211, 212–13, 217, 218,
227, 231–32, 233, 234, 237, 239, 242,
243, 247–48, 250–52, 266–69,
270–71, 276, 279, 289–90, 301–2,
303–6, 310–11, 315, 317, 319, 321,
324, 339–40, 342, 347, 357–59,
368–69, 374–75, 392, 397, 399–400,
409, 420–22
looks to US for support, 283–84
Custance, G. J., 55

Daladier, Edouard, 36
Darlan, J. François, 287

de Gaulle, Charles, 111, 437
Dewing, Richard Henry, 335, 437
Dill, Sir John Greer, 80, 87, 90, 91, 96, 97,
99, 100, 102, 117, 235, 379, 437
document by, 103
documents to, 112, 118–19, 194–95, 243
on AIF in Middle East, 82–83
on General Blamey and appointments to
higher command, 103
Dixon, Sir Owen, 437
documents to, 323–24, 330
Dorman-Smith, Sir Reginald, 252
Douglas, Sir William Sholto, 348
Drakeford, Arthur Samuel, 56, 65, 71, 341,
342, 432, 437
documents by, 68–70, 342
documents to, 72, 174–75, 345–46,
348–49, 350, 351, 352–53
Drummond, Sir Peter Roy Maxwell, 56, 437
Durnford, John Walter, 23–24

Eather, Kenneth William, 371, 375
Eden, Sir (Robert) Anthony, Earl of Avon,
48, 87, 90, 91, 96, 97, 437
documents by, 26, 44–45
documents to, 54–55, 75–76, 76–77, 79,
113–14
Eggleston, Sir Frederic, 437
Eichelberger, Robert Lawrence, 373, 374,
375, 377, 438
Eisenhower, Dwight David, 279, 438
Elford, R. E., 56
Evatt, Herbert Vere, 179, 180, 184, 204,
248, 301, 302, 303, 306, 315, 316,
317, 318, 433, 438
documents by, 178–80, 216–17, 218,
291–92, 301–2, 303–6, 315, 317,
323–24
documents to, 181–82, 200, 206–8, 236,
274–75, 277–78, 280, 281–83,
285–86, 289–91, 292–94, 302, 314,
315, 320, 357

Fadden, Arthur William, 92, 93, 128, 130,
154, 180, 431, 432, 438
documents by, 98, 102, 123–24, 173
documents to, 90–91, 93–94, 96–97,
101–2, 111–12, 130, 132–33
Fairbairn, James Valentine, 52, 53, 57, 58,
432, 438
Fitzgerald, John Thomas, 27n
Foch, Ferdinand, 187
Foll, Hattil Spencer, 51, 52, 92, 116, 154,
335, 336, 438
Forde, Francis Michael, 120n, 220–21, 260,
262, 276, 397, 403, 404n, 426, 431,
432, 438

Name Index

documents by, 263, 363–65, 397
documents to, 219–21, 260–62, 411–12, 426–27
report on visit to New Guinea theatre, 363–65
Fraser, James Mackintosh
documents by, 403–4
documents to, 422–24
report on New Guinea operations, 403–7
Fraser, Peter, 183, 438
Freyberg, Bernard Cyril, Baron, 104, 105, 438

Gamelin, Maurice, 36
Ghormley, Robert Lee, 325, 438
Glasgow, Sir (Thomas) William, 439
Goble, Stanley James, 45, 49, 50, 433, 439
document by, 46–47
resignation as (Acting) CAS RAAF, 52–55
Goddard, Sir (Robert) Victor, 296n
Gort, Viscount; *see* Vereker, John Standish Surtees Prendergast
Gowrie, Alexander Gore Arkwright, Baron, 23
Griffith, Sturt De Burgh, 268, 269
Gullett, Sir Henry Somer, 51, 52, 432

Haining, Sir Robert Hadden, 89, 439
Halsey, William Frederick, 325, 439
Hamilton, Sir Ian Standish Monteith, 362
Hankey, Maurice Pascal Alers, Baron, 25–26, 141, 439
document by, 25–26
Harries, David Hugh, 280, 439
documents by, 281, 286–88, 289–90, 294–95
Harris, Sir Arthur Travers, 348
Harrison, Sir Eric John, 51
Hart, Thomas Charles, 193
Havard, Godfrey Thomas, 112
Herring, Sir Edmund Francis, 371, 373–74, 375, 376–78, 385–86, 439
documents by, 373, 374, 375, 376–78, 385–86
documents to, 381
Hodgson, William Roy, 439
document to, 20
Holt, Harold Edward, 51
speech on mandate campaigns, 402
Hopkins, Harry Lloyd, 285, 294
Hore-Belisha, (Isaac) Leslie, Baron, 140, 141
Howard, Frederick James
criticism of mandate campaigns, 414–16
Hughes, William Morris, 21, 22, 51, 92, 115, 154, 155, 156, 326, 432, 439
documents to, 13–20

Inskip, Thomas Walker Hobart, Viscount Caldecote, 142, 439
documents by, 80, 110, 146, 147–48, 169
documents to, 81, 83–84, 110–11
Ironside, William Edmund, Baron, 74
Ismay, Hastings Lionel, Baron, 439

Jameson, Dr Leander Starr, 112n
Jess, Sir Carl Herman, 27n
Jones, Sir George, 49, 70–71, 72, 317, 318, 433, 440
appointment as CAS RAAF, 339–56
documents by, 72, 341–42, 345–46, 349, 350, 351
documents to, 344–45, 350, 352
Joubert, Sir Philip de la Ferté, 347–49, 356, 440

Kenney, George Churchill, 339, 340, 342–43, 346, 348, 349, 378, 419, 440
documents by, 340, 343, 348
Kerr, Philip Henry, Marquis of Lothian, 168, 441
King, Ernest Joseph, 286, 294, 301, 303, 440

Laffan, Clarence Bernard, 27n
Lampson, Miles Wedderburn, Baron Killearn, 111, 114, 440
document by, 113–14
document to, 134
Langslow, Melville Cecil, 440
document by, 174–75
Latham, Sir John Greig, 440
Lavarack, Sir John Dudley, 27n, 134, 197, 198, 212, 227, 231–32, 240, 241, 242, 243, 245, 369, 440
documents by, 120–22, 224–25
documents to, 233–34, 243–44
report on situation in Java and Sumatra, 224–25
report on Syrian campaign, 119–22
Lawson, John Norman, 51
Layton, Sir Geoffrey, 163, 440
Leahy, William Daniel, 328, 440
Lewis, Essington, 440
Lind, Edmund Frank, 219, 221–22
Lloyd, Charles Edward Maurice, 226, 227, 244, 440
document by, 226
Lloyd, Eric Edwin Longfield, 361, 441
Lloyd, Herbert William, 441
Long, Gavin Merrick
comments on General MacArthur, 336, 337–38
Longmore, Sir Arthur Murray, 129, 347–49, 356, 441

Name Index

Lowe, Sir Charles John
  documents by, 266–69
  inquiries by, 266–69, 276
Lumsden, Herbert, 441
Lyons, Joseph Aloysius, 441
Lyttelton, Oliver, Viscount Chandos, 129, 132, 441
  document by, 134
  document to, 131–32
  on replacement of General Blamey, 134

Macandie, George Lionel, 441
  documents by, 7, 10–11, 20–21
MacArthur, Arthur, 297, 298
MacArthur, Douglas, 441
  arrival in Australia, 271, 297–99, 332–33
  as C-in-C, SWPA, 185n, 275, 297, 298, 299–300, 301, 302, 303–5, 306, 312–14, 315, 318–19, 320–22, 325, 329–38, 339–40, 346–49, 351, 353–54, 355–56, 358, 359, 360, 365–67, 368, 373, 375, 379, 384–85, 386–87, 391–400, 401, 406, 408–9, 414–16, 417, 418, 419–22, 423–26
  assessments of, 336–38
  documents by, 318–19, 321, 331, 339–40, 351, 392, 393–94, 399–400, 409, 420–21, 425–26
  documents to, 295, 299–300, 320–21, 348, 368–69, 391, 397, 398–99, 407–8, 420, 424–25, 426
  in Philippines, 185, 194, 206n, 277, 278, 281
  on Advisory War Council, 332
  on amalgamation of AIF/AMF, 326–28, 329–30
  on Bataan's fall, 331
  on Borneo campaign, 417–26
  on Coral Sea/Midway battles, 320–22
  on COS appointments, 334–35
  on RAAF high command organisation, 346–49, 353–54, 355–56
  on Solomon Islands campaign, 325
  on SWPA high command organisation (1945), 418–21
  opinion of General Blamey, 333
  relations with Curtin, 335, 418
McBride, Philip Albert Martin, 92, 154, 432
McEwen, Sir John Blackwood, 56, 92, 116, 154, 172, 432, 433, 441
  document by, 60–63
Machtig, Sir Eric Gustav, 55, 441
Mackay, Sir Iven Giffard, 103, 260, 262, 442
  documents by, 260–62, 276
McKell, Sir William John, 38
McLeay, George, 51, 432

Makin, Norman John Oswald, 432, 442
Mansfield, H. L.
  document by, 130
Margesson, (Henry) David (Reginald), Viscount, 90
Marshall, George Catlett, 277, 294, 303, 379, 442
  document by, 295
  document to, 243
Marshall, Richard J., 297, 357
Martin, J. I.
  document by, 208
Menzies, Sir Robert Gordon, 5, 8, 9, 22, 23, 35, 39, 40, 42, 48, 50, 51, 52–53, 58, 66, 73, 80, 127, 128, 152, 157, 167, 326, 332, 431, 442
  discussions with Whiskard on Goble's resignation, 54–55
  documents by, 29–30, 52, 63–65, 76–77, 79, 83–84, 85, 90–91, 93–94, 96–97, 101–2, 110–11, 116–17, 118, 124–25, 127, 401
  documents to, 36–37, 39–41, 50–51, 74, 80, 81, 84, 91–92, 94–95, 98, 110, 114–15, 123–24, 127–28, 147–48, 152, 157–59, 160, 169
  national broadcast on Special Expeditionary Force, 26, 29–30
  on establishment of RAAF overseas headquarters, 63–65
  on Greek campaign, 87, 89–91, 93–94, 95–97, 99, 100, 103, 116, 124
  on mandate campaigns, 401
  on Middle East policy, 80, 87, 92, 101–2, 115, 116–17, 123, 124–25
  on occupation of Syria, 110–11, 114, 116–17, 118
Middleton, Clem
  document by, 270–71
Mitchell, Sir William, 442
Montgomery, Bernard Law, Viscount of Alamein, 338, 442
Moore, Eleanor M.
  document by, 270
Morshead, Sir Leslie James, 95, 131, 333–34, 421, 442
  document to, 336
Mountbatten, Louis Francis Albert Victor Nicholas, Earl, 423, 442
Mulrooney, Francis Joseph, 442
  documents to, 344–45, 350
Murdoch, Sir Keith Arthur, 333, 334, 442
  praise of 39th Battalion in New Guinea, 362–63

Nankervis, Alfred Roy, 442

document by, 280
Nimitz, Chester William, 303, 305, 386, 387, 414, 443
Nock, Horace Keyworth
  document to, 40
Northcott, Sir John, 33, 368, 395, 407, 433, 443
  documents by, 34–35, 395–97

Page, Sir Earle Christmas Grafton, 154, 181, 183, 204, 205, 232, 233, 235, 237, 242, 301, 317, 443
  criticism of Papuan campaign, 379–80
  documents by, 199, 233, 242, 247–48, 250–52
  documents to, 204–6, 209, 210, 233–34, 241, 249, 254–55, 289
  views on AIF for defence of Ceylon, 247–52
Palliser, Sir Arthur, 443
Papagos, Alexander, 96, 98, 443
Park, Sir Keith Rodney, 353–56
Parkhill, Sir (Robert) Archdale, 443
Parry, William Edward, 296n
Peirse, Sir Richard, 443
Percival, Arthur Ernest, 206, 207–8, 210, 211, 443
  on failure of Malayan campaign, 213–14
Perkins, John Arthur, 51
Phillips, Owen Forbes, 27n
Phillips, Sir Tom Spencer Vaughan, 443
Playfair, Ian Stanley Ord, 197, 244, 443
Poorten, Hein ter, 170, 197, 198, 244, 245, 246, 443
  document to, 245–46
Portal, Charles, Viscount Portal of Hungerford, 50, 316, 443
Potts, Arnold William, 360, 361
Pownall, Sir Henry Royds, 197, 444
Pulford, Conway Walter Heath, 444

Ramsay, Sir Alan Hollick, 444
Roach, Leonard Nairn, 219, 221–22
Robertson, Sir Horace Clement Hugh, 415, 444
Rommel, Erwin, 86, 101, 123, 338, 444
Roosevelt, Franklin Delano, 168, 191, 192, 242, 279, 283, 285n, 293–94, 299, 301, 306, 313, 315, 324, 328, 332, 379n, 444
  and 'Arcadia' conference, 179, 185, 286, 307
  and Australia's place in Pacific war strategy, 180–82, 184, 186
  and Churchill-Curtin clash on 7th Division's destination, 233–37
  and defence of Australia, 292, 295, 297, 324
  document by, 324
  documents to, 227, 283, 330
Ross, David, 444
  document to, 218
Rourke, Henry Gordon, 444
Rowell, Sir Sydney Fairburn, 226, 359–61, 362, 365, 444
  documents by, 360–61, 365–66, 370–71
  documents to, 226, 368
  relations with General Blamey and dismissal by, 367–70
Royle, Sir Guy Charles Cecil, 22, 192, 196, 256, 280, 307, 317, 318, 334–35, 433, 444
  document by, 307
  documents to, 281, 286–88, 289–90, 294–95
Russell, John Cannan, 54–55

Saunders, Sir Hugh William Lumsden, 353–56
Savage, Michael Joseph, 444
Savige, Stanley George, 415, 444
Scott, Norman, 325, 445
Scott, William John Rendell, 219
Shedden, Sir Frederick Geoffrey, 65, 87, 157, 275, 322, 325, 355–56, 375, 383, 385, 387, 394, 395, 397, 445
  documents by, 6–7, 91–92, 160, 309, 314–15, 325, 326–28, 329–30, 332–35, 336–37, 347, 356, 357–59, 369, 379, 397
  documents to, 7, 20–21, 30–32, 46–47, 238–39, 245, 280, 288, 307, 331, 341, 349, 351, 370, 372–73, 376, 395–97, 412–13, 418–19
  impressions of General MacArthur, 336–37
Sinclair, Frank Roy, 445
  document by, 412–13
Sitwell, Hervey Degge Wilmot, 243, 244, 245, 246, 445
  document by, 246
Slim, William Joseph, Viscount, 445
Smart, Edward Kenneth, 445
Smuts, Jan Christian, 118
Somerville, Sir James Fownes, 311, 445
Spears, Sir Edward, 113
Spender, Sir Percy Claude, 51, 52, 92, 98, 99, 107, 115, 153–54, 156, 164, 432, 445
  documents to, 97, 99–100, 107–9, 127n
Spooner, E. J., 207n
Squires, Ernest Ker, 26, 55, 73, 433, 445
  documents by, 30–32, 73
  document to, 34–35

Stanhope, James Richard, Earl, 143, 445
Stevens, Sir Jack, 416
Stewart, Sir Frederick Harold, 51, 52, 432, 433
Strahan, Frank, 445
  document to, 20–21
Street, Sir Arthur William, 431, 446
  document to, 50
Street, Geoffrey Austin, 7, 8, 10, 27n, 30, 45, 50, 51, 52, 432, 446
  document by, 46
  documents to, 4–5, 8–9
Strutt, Horace William, 105
Sturdee, Sir Vernon Ashton Hobart, 84, 107, 150, 153, 163, 164, 170, 177, 192, 193, 196, 238, 241, 253, 256, 262, 291, 358, 415, 433, 446
  recommends return of AIF to Australia, 227–30
Sullivan, Daniel Giles, 296
Sutherland, Richard Kenneth, 322, 332, 348, 357, 446

Tedder, Arthur William, Baron, 113, 114, 348, 446
ter Poorten, Hein; *see* Poorten, Hein ter
Thomas, Sir (Thomas) Shenton (Whitelegge), 207, 446

Vasey, George Alan, 359, 446
  document by, 103–7
  documents to, 360–61, 365
  report of AIF operations in Crete, 103–7
Veale, William Charles Douglas, 446
Vereker, John Standish Surtees Prendergast, Viscount Gort, 439

Walker, Theodore Gordon, 106
Ward, Edward John, 276, 446
Wardell, Augustine William, 446
Wavell, Archibald Percival, Earl, 446
  appreciation of SWP situation, 194–95
  as C-in-C, ME, 81, 82, 83, 85, 90, 91, 93, 94, 97, 99, 100, 101, 102, 103, 111, 112, 113–14, 117, 118–19, 121, 125n
  as Supreme Commander ABDA, 179, 182, 186, 187–99, 202, 203, 206, 209–10, 211, 212–13, 224, 225, 227, 228, 230–32, 233, 234, 235, 238, 239, 240–43
  documents by, 100, 112, 118–19, 194–95, 209–10, 211, 212–13, 227, 231–32, 243
  documents to, 103, 188–91, 230, 233–34, 240, 241, 242
  on fall of Singapore, 209–10, 211, 212–13, 227
  on Syrian campaign, 112, 113–14, 117, 118–19
  suggests use of AIF for defence of Burma, 227, 230–32, 233, 234, 235, 238, 239
Weston, Eric Culpeper, 105–6
Whiskard, Sir Geoffrey Granville, 50, 79, 116, 447
  documents by, 50–51, 54–55
  documents to, 26, 44–45, 101, 152
  report of discussions with Menzies on Goble's resignation, 54–55
White, Sir (Cyril) Brudenell (Bingham), 77n, 433, 447
  document to, 81–82
White, T. A., 270
White, Sir Thomas Walter
  speech on mandate campaigns, 402–3
Williams, Richard, 52, 53, 70, 266, 447
Wilmott, Chester, 370
Wilson, Henry Maitland, Baron, 94, 343, 447
Woods, Frank Allan, 244, 447
Wootten, Sir George Frederick, 131, 447
Wright, Michael Robert, 114
Wynter, Henry Douglas, 82, 447